Research Design
for Social Work and
the Human Services

Research Design for Social Work and the Human Services

SECOND EDITION

JEANE W. ANASTAS

COLUMBIA UNIVERSITY PRESS

NEW YORK

Columbia University Press
Publishers Since 1893
New York   Chichester, West Sussex

Library of Congress Cataloging-in-Publication Data
Anastas, Jeane W.
    Research design for social work and the human services / by Jeane
W. Anastas. — 2nd ed.
        p.   cm.
    Rev. ed. of : Research design for social work and the human
services / Jeane W. Anastas and Marian L. MacDonald. c1994.
    Includes bibliographical references (p.) and index.
    ISBN 0–231–11890–2 (cloth : alk. paper)
    1. Social service—Research.   2. Human services—Research.
I. Title.
HV40.A7423   1999
361'.0072—dc21   99–38959

Some of the material in this volume is reprinted by permission of holders of copyright and
publication rights. See page xvi for acknowledgments.

Casebound editions of Columbia University Press books
are printed on permanent and durable acid-free paper.
Printed in the United States of America
printing number
c 10 9 8 7 6 5 4 3 2 1
p 10 9 8 7 6 5 4 3 2 1

Contents

Preface to the Second Edition

Since the publication of this book, interest in many of the issues it set out to address has grown substantially. Since it went to press in 1993, there has been an explosion of writing about the uses of qualitative research and evaluation in social work and the helping professions. This literature has indeed been advancing us in our sophistication in both doing and evaluating this kind of inquiry (see, for example, Denzin & Lincoln 1994; Drisko 1997; Gilgun, Daly, & Handel 1992; Morse & Field 1995; Padgett 1998; Reissman 1994; Sherman & Reid 1994). One major reason for the revision of the book is to incorporate this new work into an enriched discussion of flexible method research.

Even case studies, one of the oldest forms of inquiry in the helping professions, have been gaining renewed respect (Gilgun 1994). One way in which the discussion of flexible method research has been enriched in this edition is through the inclusion of an entirely new chapter on traditional case studies (chapter 4). This content parallels in some ways the existing chapter on the application of fixed methods of research to cases in chapter 8 on single-system designs. It may be that in future editions it will be possible to further differentiate among kinds and styles of flexible method, or qualitative, research in useful ways, resulting in more chapters on these design types.

Very recently, realism, the epistemological framework advanced in this book, has been explored and endorsed by other writers in social work and related fields (Kazi 1998; Pawson & Tilley 1997). Further reading of my own in the philosophy of science has only strengthened my conviction about the usefulness of this position as an inclusive yet thoroughly scientific standpoint from which to conduct practice-relevant research (Anastas 1998; Klee 1997; Orange 1995; Papineau 1996). These developments confirm the importance of continuing to strengthen and further develop our understanding of these important and emerging epistemological ideas.

Similarly, since 1993, attention to the analysis of science as it relates to groups that have traditionally been oppressed and/or excluded—in society and in social science—has continued (see, for example, Harding 1998; Hess 1995; LeVay 1996; Swigonski 1994). This edition both retains and tries to build on the inclusion and analysis of diversity issues in research.

In addition, because of the passage of time, all of the exemplars used in the 1993 edition were reviewed in the preparation of this one. Some of them were retained because they were judged to be classic enough that time has not altered their relevance. Others were replaced with more recently published works. Feedback from readers of the first edition has uniformly endorsed the inclusion of full-length studies as exemplars in the book because they bring the research design principles discussed to life so effectively. Updated exemplars should make them even more helpful and readable.

Finally, learning about research can seem like learning a new language. Users of the first edition of the book correctly observed that it could be improved by adding a glossary, which has been done as an appendix in this new edition. Readers are encouraged to make reference to it whenever they encounter a term in the text that seems unfamiliar or unclear.

The need for high-quality research in social work and the other helping professions has not diminished. The capacity of social workers and other human service professionals to generate practice-relevant research is growing. If this book can aid and inspire more people to get involved in learning about and doing research, its most important goal will have been achieved.

Preface to the First Edition

This book was originally a self-help enterprise: to produce a better text than those then available for teaching a research methods course. Three of us began the work together. We thought we already knew about doing research, and that our planned book would result mostly from a process of summary and distillation. But several years later, we find that the journey has led us into new terrain, to a new understanding, and a new way to talk about research design.

Much of what the reader knowledgeable about research will find here will seem familiar, although the way it is described and the terms that are used may be novel. Some of what such a reader will find here may seem quite unfamiliar, but we hope our approach may open up for such a reader new avenues of appreciation for a wider range of research methods and designs. For those new to research, the book endeavors to make the content accessible, to present the current controversies in the field, and to convey excitement about research as a professional enterprise.

This textbook has many goals. One of them is to present science and research from an epistemological position that can embrace a range of models of inquiry. Instead of adopting the heuristic perspective (Heineman Pieper 1985, 1989; Tyson 1992, 1995), which might best be described as a standpoint rather than as an epistemology, we embrace *fallibilistic realism* (Manicas & Secord 1983), described in chapter 1, as our epistemological framework. This perspective is one from which both what have been termed "qualitative" or naturalistic methods and traditional quantitative methods can be valued, learned, and taught. We use the terms *flexible* and *fixed* methods to differentiate these two general styles of doing research.

Our goal has been to treat both flexible and fixed methods even-handedly. But because fixed or quantitative methods have been the dominant paradigm in social science and social work research in this century, the types of research included in this tradition and the methods associated with them have been more thoroughly elaborated to date. Consequently, more space in the book is devoted to fixed methods. It is our hope and expectation that in the future this imbalance may change as flexible methods of research are more often used and more fully explicated.

Another goal of this book has been to integrate content on women and people of color into the text. This integration has been achieved both through the examples of research we have provided and through our attempt to understand how racism, sexism, heterosexism, and other forms of bias may affect the conceptualization and conduct of research. The basic perspective taken on research in this book has been shaped to some degree by the critiques of sexism and racism endemic in the traditional institutions and methods of the scientific enterprise itself. This effort at integration will no doubt be found to be incomplete, and readers may find much to criticize in this regard. Nevertheless, the book takes the position that in the context of a racist, sexist, and heterosexist society, few aspects of research methods are so completely technical that they should not be subject to such an analysis. The point is not whether or not a given method or study has been critiqued "correctly"; the point is that such analysis as an activity is the responsibility of every researcher and research consumer who claims to be concerned with social justice and professional service, just as it is in practice.

A final novel feature of this text is the inclusion of a few selected studies within the text itself as examples of the types of research being described, both flexible and fixed in method. They have been reproduced whole rather than excerpted, which is more common, to give students experience in reading complete studies—as they must learn to do as professionals—and in order that each work can be viewed in context and independently evaluated by our readers. While this makes the book seem long, these examples are referred to repeatedly throughout the text, whether the topic is research design as a whole, a sampling strategy, a specific method of data collection, or a method of data analysis. Most but not all of the studies are from social work literature. The inclusion of the studies is designed to permit teaching from what might be termed a *case study method*.

To choose examples, however, is always risky: no perfect study or report of a study is ever found. Each of these examples was chosen for a variety of reasons, but in the end the choices were to some extent arbitrary. Thus, no selected study should be seen either as an incomparable ideal or solely as an object to use in showing off a capacity to uncover flaws in others' methods or assertions. Instead, we hope that each article will serve as a springboard for learning and analysis that authors and readers will share as examples of what goes into a piece of research.

Because this book attempts to integrate discussion of a range of research methods into a single epistemological framework, the language used to discuss research design differs from what is usually encountered in books and courses about research. While different terminology always presents a challenge to readers, traditional terminology has only been altered when it seemed necessary to do so in order to represent a concept more accurately. However, as work proceeded, this necessity arose much more than anticipated.

For example, the term "flexible method research" is used in this book in preference to others: "qualitative research" confounds the form of the data with the method, while "naturalistic research" implies an epistemological position that is quite different from and more limited than the framework of realism provides. The term "flexible," in addition to being descriptive of an important feature of the method, provides a useful contrast to the generic term, "fixed," used to characterize a range of contrasting methods. The term "quantitative" is similarly rejected because it confounds the form of the data or of the analysis with the general method: narrative data can in fact be analyzed in a fixed or quantitative way or in a flexible manner. "Relational research" is used in preference to the term "correlational research," again because the term "correlational" connotes one type of statistical analysis when more than one can be used; only advanced students of statistics understand that tests of group difference and correlational measures in fact have the same derivation mathematically. The hope is that the new language adopted, once learned, may prove clarifying for the reader as it has done for the writers.

The book, then, has some lofty goals. The first and most important is to provide an overview of scientific methods as they are used in social work to advance knowledge and improve practice. It is designed for use in research methods courses, especially those taught at the master's and doctoral levels of study. There is nothing contained in this text to preclude its use at an undergraduate level; however, the experience that has shaped the work has been teaching at the graduate level in social work.

As noted earlier, the book has incorporated content both on what have traditionally been termed "qualitative" methods, which are called *flexible methods,* and on "quantitative" ones, which are called *fixed methods*. This inclusion is evident both in the series of chapters on general types of research, in which flexible methods are discussed at length in a chapter of their own, and in the series of chapters on ethics, sampling, the various data collection methods, and use of the computer, each of which contains content relevant to both fixed and flexible method research. Finally, the section on data analysis also contains a separate chapter on the analysis of narrative or unstructured data.

This book, in addition to serving as a classroom text, can also function as a handbook to guide the student or graduate professional in the conduct of research of many kinds. Most chapters, therefore, contain both conceptual material to organize the topic being discussed and quite concrete information designed to provide a "how-to" for the professional researcher. The how-to features should also prove useful to students doing group or individual research projects, including thesis and dissertation work.

The first part of the book contains an orientation to scientific inquiry and the epistemological basis for it. The standpoint adopted, fallibilistic realism (Manicas & Secord 1983), might be termed "postpositivist" (Fraser, Taylor, Jackson, & O'Jack 1991), but it provides a basis for both traditional and more naturalistic models of inquiry. The risk of embracing differing points of view is that it is possible to satisfy no one; it should be acknowledged that, in particular, those who subscribe wholeheartedly either to a constructivist framework on the one hand, or to a logical positivist one on the other, are unlikely to feel comfortable with the position we have taken. However, the framework offered will be satisfying and useful to the majority of social workers and other human service professionals who in fact have respect for a variety of methods of research. This first part also includes a chapter on problem formulation, on how research questions are framed and developed, a topic critical to the research process that is less often addressed than the other stages of the research process that derive from it. Chapter 2 also addresses the critical role that theory and knowledge, induction and deduction, and biases of several kinds may play in the shaping of a research study.

Part II covers the major types of designs used in social work research. Chapter 3 covers flexible method research in all its variety. Unlike the situation with fixed methods, which have dominated texts in the field for so long, it is not yet possible to articulate a clear typology of flexible methods of research.[1] Fixed methods, however, have been divided into descriptive, relational, and experimental designs, treated in chapters 5, 6, and 7, respectively. The category of relational research is original with us and is used to connote all of those forms of research investigating relationships among variables but in which variables are not experimentally manipulated. Some of what are usually termed quasi-experimental designs are thus discussed as relational studies and some as experiments. Chapter 8, the last chapter in part II, discusses single-subject designs as a fixed method of research.

Part II addresses general issues in the research process. Each chapter includes material on both fixed and flexible methods. Ethics in research are discussed first, in chapter 9, for they must guide each part of the research process as well as the conduct of the study as a whole. Sampling is explained in chapter 10. Principles of data collection, including the often taken-for-granted topic of the context of the research, is the topic of chapter 11.

Part IV is devoted to discussion of specific methods of data collection. Observation, interviewing, and designing questionnaires are discussed in chapters 12, 13, and 14, respectively. The chapters on observation and interviewing both incorporate material on gathering unstructured as well as structured data as these are the data collection methods most commonly used in flexible method research. These chapters and the one on questionnaires emphasize developing ways of gathering data for a study. Chapter 15, on selecting available measures, concludes part IV.

Part V, on analyzing data and disseminating the results of research, completes the review of the research process. Data analysis is divided into chapters on the content analysis of narrative data (chapter 16) and on descriptive (chapter 17) and inferential (chapter 18) statistics. A colleague, James Drisko, has contributed a chapter on using the computer for working with both qualitative and quantitative data (chapter 14). The essential step of disseminating research findings is often overlooked, so the book ends with chapter 20 on writing research reports.

When this book was begun, the idea was simply that it would improve somewhat upon the texts on research methods then available in social work and the human services. As the discussion, refinement, and articulation of ideas proceeded, however, it became evident that it was necessary to move into new intellectual territory in ways that were not originally anticipated. This journey has sometimes been a fearful but always an interesting one, and the reader, whether student, teacher, or practitioner, is invited to travel along. Readers may not always agree with the positions taken in this book, However, where we are now in the helping professions in our thinking about research will only be a way station in the rapidly evolving discourse about doing science in social work and the other human service professions.

---

1. While the revised edition in fact adds traditional case studies to the section on flexible method research, the basic situation described remains the same as of this writing.

Acknowledgments

This book began as a three-person project. The early involvement of Carolyn Jacobs of the Smith College School for Social Work as a fellow teacher, coauthor, and colleague made the task initially seem possible. Although she withdrew from the project early on, Carolyn's initial ideas helped shape the book in essential ways, and her participation in early discussions about its content was indispensable in getting the project off to a good start. In addition, Margaret H. Whalen, who contributed a chapter to the first edition, provided informal but very welcome encouragement to the project as a whole.

Marian MacDonald, my coauthor for the first edition of this book, was essential to its very existence. As teaching colleagues, we struggled together to do a better job of giving students what they needed. Marian has the courage of her intellectual convictions, which often helped propel us forward onto new ground. Unfortunately as time went on, her other professional and personal commitments did not allow her to continue to work on the book. Her essential early contributions are appropriately recognized in her coauthorship of the first edition. Also, I want to warmly thank my colleague, Jim Drisko, for his willingness to rewrite the chapter on computer uses in research for this edition. His degree of expertise in both qualitative and quantitative data analysis is quite unusual and has enriched this edition of the book immeasurably. However, despite the essential contributions of these colleagues, as the one who has sustained authorship of the book for over a decade at this point, the primary responsibility for it, including its flaws, must rest with me.

There are also several other sources of support that I have enjoyed and that deserve public acknowledgement. A Brown Foundation Award from the Smith College School for Social Work's Clinical Research Institute supported me in part in writing the first edition of this text. I also want to thank the Smith College School for Social Work and its dean at the time, Ann Hartman, for a generous sabbatical leave that enabled me to finish that work. I also want to thank the Wellesley College Center for Research on Women for the nurturing working environment provided to me as a Visiting Scholar during the 1992–93 academic year. These supports were crucial for the revision and completion of the first edition.

There were many individuals who contributed in other ways to this work at different times. Colleagues Joyce Everett, James Drisko, and Roger Miller read and commented on parts of the first manuscript, providing very helpful feedback. Other members of the permanent and adjunct faculty of the Smith College School for Social Work continue to provide generous and insightful feedback. I would also like to thank the anonymous reviewers of the original prospectus and the completed first edition for their helpful comments. I also thank Sherri Ettinger who has generously assisted in the preparation of the glossary for this revised edition.

Many students have now read various chapters in draft and have used the book in their courses over the years. As they are its most important audience, their feedback has been and continues to be extraordinarily helpful. Their responses to the material as it has evolved have been very encouraging. Only those who teach can truly appreciate how generously students in fact continuously educate their teachers. I learn from and am inspired by my students on a daily basis. In the end, of course, despite all of these generous attempts to help, responsibility for the content of this work, rests entirely with its author.

Originally Margaret Zusky, then a Senior Editor with Lexington Books, provided unwavering moral and material support to us throughout what was a very long process of completing the first edition. Her patience and her confidence in us and in this book were essential to its completion. Since then, the book has become the property of Columbia University Press. In particular, Senior Executive Editor John Michel has been an invaluable, patient, and effective supporter of this work. Thank you, John, for helping to find this book a new home and for facilitating its much-needed revision and republication.

Finally, the encouragement and forbearance of friends and family members is essential to anyone who engages in the long, absorbing, and solitary work of writing a book. To Benjamin, Rhea, and Jonathan Anastas: thank you for the support and inspiration you have all provided. Finally, for all the times during the past many years that you did without companionship, put up with preoccupation, put a much-needed meal on the table, and, most importantly, expressed unfailing encouragement and affection—thank you, Jan.

About the Author

Jeane W. Anastas is currently Professor and Associate Dean at the Shirley M. Ehren-kranz School of Social Work at New York University. She earned her baccalaureate degree in social work at the Metropolitan College, Boston University (1976), her M.S.W. with a major in research at the Boston College Graduate School of Social Work (1978), and her Ph.D. at the Heller School, Brandeis University (1982). She joined the Smith College School for Social Work faculty in 1983 as chair of the research sequence, a position she held until 1994. She then served as cochair of the school's doctoral program until 1999. From 1978 through 1982 she taught research methods and statistics on an adjunct basis at Boston University, first at the School of Social Work and later at Metropolitan College in the sociology department. She then served on the faculty of the Simmons College School of Social Work from 1980 through 1983. She also directed the Clinical Research Institute at the Smith College School for Social Work.

In addition to over 20 years' experience in teaching research to social workers, Anastas has considerable experience in conducting research in social agencies and in the community. She was the evaluator for a federally funded program serving pregnant teenagers and for a federally funded day-treatment program serving pregnant and postpartum substance-abusing women and their children in western Massachusetts. She has also consulted to national, state, and local-level research projects in the areas of eldercare, the epidemiology of child-hood emotional and behavioral problems, and mental health services for children.

Anastas has been active at state and local levels in the National Association of Social Workers, including serving for some years on its National Committee on Women's Issues. She has been appointed to the editorial board of *Affilia: The Journal of Women in Social Work* and is a consulting editor for the *Journal of Orthopsychiatry*. She has published in the areas of teaching research in social work, teen pregnancy, eldercare, substance abuse services, and gay/lesbian issues. Her most recent book, with coauthor George A. Appleby, is *Not Just a Passing Phase: Social Work with Gay, Lesbian, and Bisexual People*.

Grateful acknowledgment is made for permission to reprint the following:

The chapter 3 Exemplar, "The continuing significance of race: Antiblack discrimination in public places," by Joe R. Feagin, was first published in the *American Sociological Review* 56(1991): 101–116. Reprinted with permission from the American Sociological Association.

The chapter 4 Exemplar, "A family case study: An examination of the underclass debate," by Robin L. Jarrett, was first published in *Qualitative Methods in Family Research,* edited by Jane F. Gilgun, Kerry Daly, and Gerald Handel. Newbury Park, CA: Sage Publications, 1992. Reprinted with permission of Sage Publications.

The chapter 5 Exemplar, "The use of self-disclosure by professional social workers," by Sandra C. Anderson and Deborah L. Mandell, was first published in *Families in Society* 70(5) (1989): 259–267. Reprinted with permission from *Families in Society.*

The chapter 6 Exemplar, "Biculturalism and subjective mental health among Cuban Americans," by Manuel R. Gomez, was first published in the *Social Service Review* 64(3) (1990): 375–389. Reprinted with permission from the University of Chicago Press.

The chapter 7 Exemplar, "Preventing HIV/AIDS in drug-abusing incarcerated women through skills building and social support enchancement: Preliminary outcomes," by Nabila El-Bassel, André Ivanoff, Robert F. Schilling, Louisa Gilbert, Debra Borne, and Duan-Rung Chen, was first published in *Social Work Research* 19(3) (1995). Reprinted with permission from *Social Work Research.*

The chapter 8 Exemplar, "Empirical support for the effectiveness of respite care in reducing caregiver burden: A single-case analysis," by Cheryl A. Richey and Vanessa G. Hodges, was first published in *Research on Social Work Practice* 2(2) (1992): 143–160. Reprinted with permission from *Research on Social Work Practice.*

Figure 17.7 was first published in *Who We Are: A Second Look,* by M. Gibelman and P. H. Schervish. Washington, D.C.: NASW Press, 1997. Copyright © 1997 by the National Association of Social Workers, Inc. Reprinted by permission of the National Association of Social Workers, Inc.

Figure 9.2 copyright © 1992 by the American Psychological Association. Reprinted with permission from the American Psychological Association.

Figure 19.3 from SPSS for Windows, Rel. 8.0.0. 1997. Chicago: SPSS Inc. Used by permission of SPSS Inc. Selected passages in chapter 9 are from the National Association of Social Workers' 1997 Code of Ethics. Copyright © 1996 by the National Association of Social Workers, Inc. Reprinted by permission of the National Association of Social Workers, Inc.

Research Design
for Social Work and
the Human Services

Part I
Research Design in Context

The context of any research design is set in two fundamental ways: by its guiding assumptions about how knowledge is developed and what constitutes useful knowledge and by how its methods are joined to a specific content area through the statement of a study question. Social work, the other human service professions, and the social sciences are all in the midst of a lively debate about epistemology, about how useful knowledge is generated. The epistemological framework used in this text is explained in chapter 1, which is essential reading for use of any part of this text. Chapter 1 also provides a brief introduction to the basic types of research designs most commonly used in social work and human services research, each of which is more fully described in the chapters that make up part II. Chapter 2 describes how to develop a plan for any specific type of research by identifying a content area in need of further study and linking it to a research design through the formal statement of a research question. Ways to reduce common sources of bias in research design are also discussed.

1

The Nature of Science in the Helping Professions

> ... *scientific rationality certainly is not as monolithic or deterministic as many* *think.* .... *It has been versatile and flexible enough throughout its history to* *permit constant reinterpretation of what should count as legitimate objects and* *processes of scientific research; it is itself shaped by cultural transformations and* *must struggle within them.* ...
>
> (Harding 1991:3)

All research expresses some position about effective ways of developing knowledge. The subject of how best to advance knowledge for practice in social work and the human services has been the subject of intense, sustained argument over the past half century. This is an exciting time for research in social work and the human services because the debate has now gone on long enough to clarify the differences in points of view on the issue, to identify areas of agreement and disagreement, and to support new efforts at synthesis. In order to read and properly understand a researcher's work or to conduct research yourself, you must be able to identify the assumptions that guide it and understand the strengths and limitations of any model of research or any particular research design. A major aim of this book is to describe new ways to understand research that offer social work and the other helping professions a framework that embraces a variety of research methods previously seen as competing models.

The social work and human service professions have always had an ambivalent relationship with research. This ambivalence does not connote lukewarm but conflicted feelings, both strongly positive attitudes and quite negative ones. As a relatively young profession, social work has often sought to strengthen its knowledge base and its claims to legitimacy among competing professions through research. On the other hand, the profession has also asserted the importance of other sources of legitimacy for its methods and its goals, such as its mission of service, its sanction from the community, and its value base. In this stance, it is not unlike other clinical disciplines and helping professions. For example, medicine is a profession that flourished in some forms long before there was much scientific knowledge available on which to base its practice and in which conflicts between the injunction to serve the individual patient and the scientific imperative still frequently arise.

Unlike medicine, social work as a profession was born and has developed in an era in which science and technology have been dominant forces in Western culture. However, early in its history social work defined itself as different from sociology and the other social sciences in part because practice rather than scientific investigation was the primary interest of the profession (Zimbalist 1977). Social work deals with the whole person in context, with the interface of the person and the social environment, and with interventions designed to resolve individual, interpersonal, and social problems. It thus encompasses knowledge and fields of practice in which multiple factors and influences are routinely at work and in which the social and behavioral sciences currently offer probabilistic knowledge at best. Thus the drive to achieve a more exact science of social work has not been easily reconciled with the recognition of the primacy of practice goals on the one hand and the complexities of the problems addressed and the interventions used on the other.

One recent effect of this tension has been an intense debate within the profession about the nature of the scientific method itself and about the models of inquiry best suited for the development of knowledge for and about practice. Some have argued that if science and practice have been hard to reconcile, the profession should restrict its models of practice to methods that lend themselves to study using common and well-recognized research modes (Hudson 1978). In this paradigm, the experiment becomes the ideal model of research that other kinds of studies seek to approximate, and quantitative techniques predominate. Stemming from a logical positivist philosophy, the assumption is of a reality "out there" that can be similarly known by "objective" observers without contamination of the thing observed. The goal of investigation is to uncover the invariant regularities or "laws" of relationships among phenomena, which act on each other in repeatable, predictable ways. Much of the teaching of research in social work and in the social sciences in America today reflects this point of view (Fraser, Taylor, Jackson, & O'Jack 1991; Reamer 1993; Thyer 1993). In fact it is of interest to philosophers of science that this view has persisted as long as it has in the social sciences (Klee 1997).

In the past two decades, however, an argument has been made for constructivism as an epistemology and for the use of naturalistic and interpretive methods of inquiry in social work (Heineman 1981; Imre 1984; Riessman 1994; Ruckdeschel 1985). This argument has been based both on a critique of the failure of traditional methods to gain acceptance by practitioners and prove relevant to the practice situation and on an argument for a more relativistic view of reality and the process of knowing. What is available and relevant for study, it is argued, are the meanings, the constructions, that people, researchers and researched, place on events. According to this view, these meanings can best be uncovered and conveyed through flexible methods of inquiry, using unstructured observational or verbal data, and by acknowledging the investigator's involvement and participation in shaping the data obtained. Thus the cases for and against various models of research have largely been made on epistemological grounds, by examining the assumptions about how we know what we know that underlie the various approaches to research.

This debate in social work and other human service professions simply echoes that occurring in all of the social sciences. In social work, as in other disciplines, the discussion has tended to produce polarized positions that favor one model of research while dismissing the utility of others. However, in reality, social workers who do research and social workers who read research over a lifetime often use and value research that arises from very different methods, finding research results of many kinds to be persuasive and useful. Given this reality, this book explores how such seemingly irreconcilable epistemological positions can both be embraced.

Gradually, a third position seems to be emerging in social work: what Fraser et al. have termed a "many ways" perspective (Fraser, Taylor, Jackson, & O'Jack 1991). In various ways, the argument has been made that there are "many ways of knowing" (Hartman 1990) that may be useful to the profession at different times and in different contexts (Heineman Pieper 1989; Piele 1988; Reid 1994; Tyson 1992). The "heuristic" approach (Heineman Pieper 1985, 1989; Tyson 1992, 1995) connotes "a strategy whose goal is utility rather than certainty" (Heineman Pieper 1989:11), essentially a "pragmatic" view. There are several tenets of the heuristic approach as explicated by Heineman Pieper: facts and theories are not distinct; no facts, methods of investigation, or forms of data are privileged; causality is itself a heuristic that cannot be determined from data alone; and the researcher cannot be viewed as invisible in the conduct or results of the research. In this paradigm, objectivity is understood as "a species of report in which there is agreement among researchers," which could result from a common bias as well as from truth (Heineman Pieper 1989:17). From this perspective, "the heuristic researcher practices bias regulation through bias recognition rather than through the denial of bias" (Heineman Pieper 1989:18), just as the practitioner does. However, unlike in constructivist approaches, the heuristic approach does take the position that there is a "mind-independent reality to be known" (Tyson 1992).

This perspective is the one that best describes the scientific enterprise as many researchers understand it, although Heineman Pieper (1989) extends her definition of research beyond boundaries that most would recognize. In this text the definition of research is limited to empirical methods of knowing, including only those forms of the exercise of professional judgement that make explicit reference to some kind of observational activity addressing aspects of a mind-independent reality. It is within this emergent perspective that this text is located, but the perspective taken is identified for what it is: in the philosophical tradition of realism.

The other stream of argument that has affected the current ferment about research philosophies and methods in social work is, at bottom, political. Feminists (Davis 1986; Collins 1991; Swigonski 1994), antiracists (Akbar 1991;

Bowman 1991; Hess 1995) and other critical theorists have pointed out that the claim of legitimacy for knowledge is at least in part a political one and that the methods and products of science are not apolitical or value-free. Science as an enterprise will tend to serve the needs of some people in society more than the needs of others. Practically speaking, the tools of traditional research as they are now used demonstrably do not serve well women and people of color (McMahon & Allen-Meares 1992). The debate about research methods, then, even when not explicitly addressing political issues, often takes on the tinge of an "establishment" versus "anti-establishment" contest.

In particular, the view of research and scientific methods taken in this book owes a great deal to feminist analysis and critiques of science as a social institution. There are, of course, many "feminisms" and many feminist critiques of science. The position taken here is similar to that of Sandra Harding (1991) who states several assumptions: "science is politics by other means, and it also generates reliable information about the empirical world" (p. 10); "science contains both [politically] progressive and regressive tendencies" (p. 10), and the challenge is "how to advance the progressive and inhibit the regressive ones" (p. 11) in any research situation; "the observer and the observed are in the same causal scientific plane" (p. 11); and "it is necessary to decenter white, middle-class, heterosexual, Western" thought and experiences in scientific and professional enterprises (p. 13). This last assumption may be the most difficult to work with, both because of the identities and experiences any author may participate (and not participate) in and because these problems are currently underrecognized and underanalyzed in social work research (Hill 1980; Jacobs & Bowles 1988; McMahon & Allen-Meares 1992). The general approach the book takes to science and the generation of knowledge for social work and the human services is an inclusive one in part because it acknowledges the need for multiple and particularly for underrepresented points of view and ways of knowing to be heard and legitimated.

Why Be Scientific?

Given the difficulty that social work has had in developing a tradition of doing science within the profession, why is research still considered such an important issue in social work, social work education, and in the human services in general? With current efforts to limit health care costs and public spending for human services, the helping professions, including social work, and those who manage and control the delivery of health and mental health care rely increasingly on what is termed outcomes research in choosing the treatments and services to provide and to pay for. Similarly, Congress is demanding that the federal agencies that fund innovative demonstration programs to address social problems, such as teen pregnancy and substance abuse, also produce research results to show which kinds of programs can produce the specific outcomes desired. Public scrutiny of federal medical research in such controversial areas as HIV disease and cancer has led to questioning about what problems draw funding when and about how protocols of study do or do not serve those who have the problem and those who participate in the research. Accountability for practice and for program design are major challenges for the helping professions. In the face of these complex problems and of finite resources to fund services, research is seen as a useful tool for helping policy makers and practitioners make hard choices. This argument for research and its usefulness is essentially a pragmatic one.

In addition to these practical problems, the ferment in other fields about epistemology and how scientific knowledge is and should be generated has affected social work as well, as has already been mentioned. This debate has opened up new possibilities for research both for individual practitioners and for program evaluators. But with new and expanded boundaries has come the need for greater clarity about the nature of research and science itself. What constitutes science as opposed to other ways of generating knowledge? And just exactly what do we mean when we speak of "research"?

In this book the terms *science* and *research* mean the enterprise of learning about the natural, psychological, or social world systematically and reflexively, both by using some kind of focussed observation of that world and by applying some system of conceptualization for organizing and attributing meaning to those observations either before or after the fact. In addition, all activities called scientific are undertaken in a spirit of *skepticism,* that is, by subjecting both the ideas received in framing the research and the ideas generated from it to questioning, to a search for alternative explanations, and to scrutiny by others in the field. *Systematic* investigation means that learning and observations are undertaken according to a plan and in a focussed way, guided by a specific question or hypothesis. *Reflexiveness* means self-observation and that both the process and the results of research are studied and examined in the spirit of skepticism.

But why should society turn to research to answer tough questions? Why should a profession be able to lay a claim to legitimacy for its activities by invoking science? One answer lies in the fact that scientific investigation seems to have evolved over the years as an important corrective to common errors of thinking that human beings are prone to. The psychologist Thomas Gilovich (1991) drew on research in social and cognitive psychology to explain why the scientific method can be so helpful. As he states:

> Many of these imperfections in our cognitive and inferential tools might never surface under ideal conditions . . . but the world . . . presents us with messy data that are random, incomplete, unrepresentative, ambiguous, inconsistent, unpalatable, or secondhand. . . . [I]t is often our flawed attempts to cope with precisely these difficulties that lay bare our inferential shortcomings and produce the facts we know that just ain't so (Gilovich 1991:3).

In his book, Gilovich uses examples and findings from numerous studies of how people think and what influences thinking to develop his arguments, which will be summarized here.

First of all, Gilovich observes that people prefer to see order rather than disorder in things and will tend to impose or invent order where it does not exist, including when phenomena are really random. For example, a "clustering illusion" (p. 16) creates streaks out of random variation in numbers, and a tendency to overvalue similarities and to expect representativeness even in small samples of events contributes as well. One thing science, especially social science, can contribute, then, is a true understanding of randomness, as well as an understanding of such statistical principles as regression to the mean. This knowledge can be an important safeguard against overinterpreting observations (Paulos 1988; Bernstein 1996). However, the cost of this knowledge is that we are forced to acknowledge those areas, which are many, in which our understanding and our ability to explain or to predict are in fact minimal or nonexistent.

Gilovich (1991) also points out that humans seem to have a tendency to attend selectively to information that confirms a belief in preference to information that may disconfirm it. This tendency, of course, is the reverse of the stance demanded by the scientific method—skepticism—and may explain why skepticism is so central in research. The fact that only partial data are available may be overlooked, and data inconsistent with our preexisting ideas may be more closely scrutinized in an attempt to discount them than data consistent with them. In fact, Gilovich (1991) gives many illustrations of how confirmatory events are remembered much more clearly than nonconfirmatory ones, a tendency that is much reduced with focussed observation, as the scientific method demands.

While most of these tendencies seem to arise from how the brain itself works in processing information, there are many motivational and social contributors to erroneous beliefs that Gilovich (1991) also outlines. These factors include the "endowment effect," or the tendency to overvalue whatever is already our own, including our ideas and beliefs. They also include the "inaccuracies that are part and parcel of secondhand information" (p. 111) but that come into play whenever one relies on received information or the word of experts in preference to firsthand knowledge. They also include the exaggerated impressions of support for our own ideas as they are generated in ordinary social and even in professional interactions. Here again, the rules of the scientific method are explicitly different from those of ordinary interactions and everyday learning, emphasizing instead consideration of alternative ideas and explanations, reliance on direct observation and original investigation, and the subjecting of ideas to dissemination and critique. All of these characteristics of the scientific method in general, then, seem designed specifically to overcome the flaws that exist in ordinary human thinking.

In fact, Gilovich (1991) asserts that training in the "probabilistic" sciences, such as the social sciences, may be more effective than in the "deterministic sciences," such as physics and chemistry, for developing skills in reasoning and in the accurate weighing of evidence in everyday life. As in science, the social worker or human service professional must be a skillful observer, weighing evidence and interpreting it even while confronted with its limits and with the necessity of tolerating ambiguity and uncertainty when making decisions. Social work and the human services, in which one regularly encounters complex phenomena and incomplete or ambiguous data, are thus excellent training grounds for developing the habits of mind necessary to overcome the natural tendencies in thinking that can lead to drawing false and unwarranted conclusions. Understanding research and scientific thinking helps to develop these habits of mind.

Ways of Knowing

However valuable the scientific method may be, it is not the only valuable route to knowledge. In fact, there are many alternate routes to knowledge. The philosopher Charles Peirce (pronounced "purse") (1934), who might best be described as a pragmatist, identified five "ways of knowing," or methods commonly used to generate new information. The first is *appeal to authority*. This method involves believing that a statement is true on the grounds of its having been asserted by someone held in respect, such as an authority figure. Examples of accepting statements as true on this ground are abundant, including the great success of advertising campaigns based on endorsements by successful sports figures or other entertainers or, in the professional realm, by invoking the names of key scholars or historical figures when making an argument.

There is a reverse side to the appeal to authority method of knowing. Just as a statement can be believed because of who said it, a statement can be disbelieved on the same grounds. The familiar phrase "consider the source" refers to what is called an ad hominem (literally, "against the man") argument. In this case, an assertion may be disbelieved on the grounds of disliking or not respecting the person who made it. In the case of both types of appeal to authority, the value of a statement is determined by the source rather than the content of the statement. It is hard to imagine how the nurturance and early education of children could be accomplished in the absence of this method of knowing where the respected, unquestioned truth source for the child is the parent.

The second method of knowing Peirce termed the *method of tenacity*. As is implied by the term "tenacity," which means persistence in maintaining or adhering to an idea, statements held to be true on these grounds are ones heard believed because they are repeated by others over and over again. A person who rode on a bus and came to believe that it was going to rain the next day because he or she overheard six or seven separate conversations in which one of the parties commented that tomorrow it was supposed to rain would be accepting that weather forecast on the grounds of the method of tenacity. Much of the knowledge believed on these grounds is labeled "common sense"; it is knowledge held in common, knowledge everyone "knows" (meaning believes) and therefore asserts to be true.

Skeptical readers might find themselves asserting at this point that these first two methods of knowing have no real value. After all, everyone can recite instances where statements made to them by authority figures turned out to be wrong. And one has only to remember that at one time "everyone" except Copernicus believed that the sun revolved around the earth to realize that just because an assertion is generally believed (i.e., is a "common," or shared, view) does not mean that it is really true. While these methods of knowing are not infallible, they still have value and are commonly used, and it is important to recognize them for what they are. Even within science, at times these methods of knowing come into play as well.

Logic, or rationalism, is the third method of knowing described by Peirce. This method is fairly formal and follows standardized rules of logic. It involves beginning with an accepted statement linking a general antecedent and a general consequent, a statement conceded to be true. This initial statement is called the major premise. An example might be "All female birds lay eggs." To use logic as a method of knowing, this major premise must be followed by a minor premise. A minor premise is again a statement conceded to be true, in which a particular case is identified as an instance of the antecedent in the major premise. An example might be "Pretty is a female bird."

Logic dictates that if the major and minor premises are both true, then their pairing implies a necessarily true conclusion: If "All female birds lay eggs" and "Pretty is a female bird," then Pretty, as a female bird, must lay eggs. Reasoning to a clearly implied conclusion from a previously known major and minor premise is how new knowledge, that is, the conclusion, is rationally derived using logic.

There is a mistake that is often made by those believing they are using the method of logic. This mistake is called reasoning from the consequent, and it involves drawing an incorrect conclusion from a true major premise and a true minor premise. The error comes in pairing a major premise with a minor premise that makes an assertion about the major premise's consequent rather than its antecedent. In the preceding example, such an error would involve pairing the original major premise "All female birds lay eggs" with a different minor premise involving the major premise's consequent, for example, "Pretty lays eggs." It might seem tempting to conclude that since "all female birds lay eggs" and since "Pretty lays eggs," Pretty is a female bird. However, since there is no claim in the major premise that *only* female birds lay eggs, it is entirely possible, given the information at hand, that Pretty is an alligator.

Instances of reasoning from the consequent, as shall become clear, are not uncommon. There are many occasions when we wish to investigate effects, or consequents, in an effort to identify their putative causes. But drawing conclusions by reasoning from the consequent, however appealing, is not defensible on logical grounds. For example, if the major premise that "all adults who were sexually abused as children have eating disorders" were known to be true, it would still not be tenable to conclude that a particular adult with an eating disorder had been sexually abused as a child.

The fourth method of knowing is perhaps least understood. This method, *intuition*, is often illustrated in the history of science with the following story. The great thinker Archimedes was approached by the king of his day for help with an economic dilemma. The king had commissioned a tradesman to make him a crown of pure gold, but when the work was completed, the king suspected the tradesman of deceiving him. The king had a feeling that he was being charged for the crown as if it had been made of pure gold when, in fact, it was made of less pure (and therefore less costly) metal. The king asked Archimedes to counsel him on whether the crown was, as the tradesman claimed, pure gold so that the full debt was owed, or whether the crown was made of a gold alloy, so that punishment for the tradesman was in order.

Archimedes was at first stumped. He could not test the crown's substance using the accepted method, because that method involved melting the metal to see if it was pure. To use that method, then, would destroy the crown itself. If it did turn out to be pure gold, the king would have the satisfaction of knowing the tradesman was honest, but he would then have to pay the full bill for a crown he would no longer have.

As the story goes, Archimedes kept puzzling about the problem while performing his daily activities. And the solution occurred to him, finally, while he was beginning to take a bath. When entering the tub, he noticed that the water level rose on the side of the tub as he immersed his body; and as he got up from the tub, the water level on the side of the tub fell. He supposedly shouted in great joy "Eureka" (which means in Greek "I have it!"): He had discovered the property of the displacement of mass.

What Archimedes realized, or intuited, in that moment was that any object having a certain volume and weight would displace precisely that volume of water whatever its shape, which is the concept of specific mass. Each metal (or substance) has its own specific mass, and no two metals are exactly alike. He could therefore test whether the crown was pure gold by weighing it and then comparing the amount of water it displaced to the amount of water displaced by a block of metal having the same weight but known to be pure gold. If the crown displaced a different amount of water than the block of gold, that would prove that it was made of an alloy; if the displacement were the same, the crown would be proven to be pure gold.

The solution to the puzzle facing Archimedes, according to legend, came to him in a flash. This sudden insight, when it occurs, is known as deriving knowledge through intuition. It is perhaps the most poorly understood of Peirce's methods of knowing because it rests on feeling, and in modern Western culture, thought and feeling are not often comfortably paired. Archimedes' insight about a method to solve a problem connected what he knew about the properties of metals with the observation of the effects of his body on the bath water. The rest of the story, the exercise in demonstration, the experiment to determine the composition of the crown itself, belongs to a different method of knowing: the scientific method.

Peirce's final method of knowing is the *scientific method.* Stated most broadly, this method is *empirical* and involves conducting self-critical, systematic observation under described circumstances. *Empiricism* means that the method ultimately rests on experiential information derived through observation using the senses (sight, sound, touch, taste, or smell). Notice that much of the emphasis in this definition of the scientific method is on making explicit the nature of the observations made, the circumstances in which they were made, and the role taken by the observer in making them. Also notice that the definition does not specify anything about the nature of the observations, circumstances, or roles themselves; one kind of observation is not inherently any more "scientific" or "unscientific" than another.

The scientific method is also characterized by an attitude of skepticism or disbelief. It includes subjecting ideas, intuitions, or hunches to the possibility of disconfirmation when examined in the light of logic or of empirical evidence. It also includes subjecting the observations made and the interpretations and conclusions drawn from them first to self-scrutiny by the maker of the observations and then to scrutiny by others who are also experts on the matter under study. One of the reasons for the emphasis on describing scientific observations and methods carefully is in fact to permit such scrutiny by others. Only ideas and evidence about which there is some consensus among knowledgeable observers become part of that body of knowledge called scientific.

In the social sciences and human services, there are two major forms of inquiry, with subtypes, which qualify as instances of using the scientific method, termed in this book *fixed method* and *flexible method* research. These forms of inquiry will be introduced later in this chapter and then described in detail by subtype in the section of the book on research designs. Although each has its distinctive features, what they have in common, which is a foundation in empiricism and in skepticism, is much more important than what differentiates them.

Scientific Knowledge and Other Ways of Knowing

As Peirce's work points out, then, science is not the only route to knowledge. Alternative, equally useful methods are also available. To refuse to make use of these other methods is unnecessarily constraining. It places too great a burden on the scientific method (namely, to be the only true source of knowledge) and prohibits building and evaluating belief systems using multiple, converging methods.

It is very reassuring when two or more "ways of knowing" converge on the same truth. For example, high school students are often told by their teachers, their parents, and their peers that their futures will be brighter if they go to college. If these students read a research study reporting that 1991 college graduates earned on average $5.97 per hour more than students only finishing high school (Uchitelle 1992), they will have three reasons to believe they should if possible continue their studies: appeal to authority (statements made by their parents and teachers), the method of tenacity (repeated statements made by others), and the scientific method (the article reporting on findings about education and earnings derived through systematic observation).

It is reassuring when two or more methods of knowing converge on the same conclusion, and it is disquieting and often confusing when they don't. Divergence in conclusions, however, is not at all uncommon. Consider the rising and setting of the sun as a child might view it. The direct evidence of one's senses is that the sun travels across the sky, and for many years it was in fact believed that the earth was at the center of the universe and that the sun and stars traveled around it. When an alternate view was proposed, the one now considered scientific—that in fact the earth travels in an orbit around the sun—there was tremendous controversy, religious and civil, about it. A new theory or model of the solar system was introduced that explained the apparent motion of the sun through the sky in a different way, as a product of the motion of the earth. Only in this century with the advent of space travel have humans had direct sensory evidence of the earth as a rotating sphere that orbits around the sun. In the end, the theory of a sun-centered solar system was adopted because it provided a better explanation of a variety of things seen in the sky—even though it seemed to violate the common sense knowledge of centuries—because it was consistent with what in fact had always been seen.

There continues to be controversy over what to do when two or more ways of knowing yield conclusions that do not converge. There is no definitive answer to this dilemma. Some argue that the beauty of the scientific method is that it provides the best basis for knowledge. Those who hold to this position argue strongly that when two or more of the ways of knowing yield contradictory conclusions, if one of the ways is the scientific method, that way should hold sway. They would also argue that if one of the ways of knowing is not the scientific method (i.e., does not base its conclusion on sense-based evidence systematically gathered under described circumstances and evaluated skeptically), then the contradictory conclusions must be held as equally likely until the scientific method can arbitrate between the two.

The Scientific Debate About Science

During the first decades of this century, a particular view of the nature and methods of science was dominant in the social science and in the helping professions, including social work: *logical positivism*. This point of view has been connected to a larger set of beliefs now termed *modernism*. A brief review of the main tenets of logical positivism will help to put it and its alternative in context.

Logical positivism is based on the ideal of objectivity, or the idea that there is a reality separate from the knower and that things in the real world can be unequivocally and universally known (Fraser, Taylor, Jackson, & O'Jack 1991; Reamer 1993). It assumes that this reality is ultimately separate from the observer (Reamer 1993; Tyson 1992; Klee 1997). Operationalism, or the idea of specifying the activities or operations through which things in the real world can be apprehended by an observer, is also a key component of this perspective, leading to the often-repeated maxim: if it cannot be measured, it does not exist (Hudson 1978). Reality is thought to be ultimately knowable in some universal way through constructs that represent it and through operations that approximate those constructs, even if that knowledge is presently imperfect (Reamer 1993). Hypothetico-deductive models of inquiry are preferred in which propositions link concepts into causal statements (Klee 1997); that is, hypotheses are tested against empirical evidence and proved or disproved based on the data collected. The laboratory experiment, in which the observational context can be controlled or held constant, that is, unaffected and uncontaminated by any particular observer, and in which hypotheses about the causal relationships between measured variables can be tested, is considered the apex of scientific method in this framework (Tyson 1992; Reamer 1993).

Another major area of debate about science has to do with the role of theory in science and how data and theory relate to each other. Some science is based on the belief that data should precede theory and that in fact the role of data is to build theory in a process called *induction,* which involves inferring general theories or laws from specific, observed instances of their operation. Other science is based on the idea that theory should precede data collection and that the role of data is to "test" theory. This process is called *deduction,* which involves developing specific hypotheses, or provisional statements, about what should be observed logically given a certain theory and then testing empirically to see whether those predictions hold. Theories that hold are said to have received confirmation. When data do not confirm a theory, researchers are faced with a dilemma: They must either discard the theory as incorrect or discard the experiment as a poor test of the theory. The differences between the inductive and deductive models of the data-theory relationship are illustrated in figure 1–1. Deductive methods have predominated in the logical positivist tradition, but there have been other traditions of empirical knowledge-building in the social sciences that have depended primarily on inductive methods.

The point of view usually advanced in the social sciences in opposition to the logical positivist position has been variously described as qualitative, naturalistic, interpretive, or constructivist (Denzin & Lincoln 1994; Gergen 1985; Guba 1991; Klee 1997; Reamer 1993; Riessman 1994). Proponents of this view generally hold that individual observers construct the meanings that they assign to sensory experiences to such a degree that there is no knowledge of reality separable from the knower. Observations cannot be understood apart from the contexts in which they occur, and the meanings that affect observations thus operate on both an individual and a cultural level. Greater limitations are seen in the generalizability of any knowledge developed than in the traditional model: The emphasis is on the particular rather than the universal. However, some working in this tradition hold that theories can be generated and even "tested" (Glaser & Strauss 1967) through "thick description" of things in context and through the observer's participation in the generation of the data.

At the extreme, some positions within this general tradition, like some forms of constructionism (Gergen 1985), are not empirical, but relativistic. There is no effort to, or interest in, determining the fundamental nature of reality apart from how it is constructed and therefore perceived by whomever is observing it. Inspired by thinkers in the literary world, some have even begun to advocate deconstruction, which means accepting that any observation can be deconstructed (i.e., torn apart) to reveal multiple meanings, none of which has any claim to being more accurate or real than any of the others. According to deconstructionists, even the author of a sentence (or the originator of any created work, including a report of a scientific observation) cannot tell what that work (or observation) "really" means because he or she may not know.

Both constructivism and deconstruction state positions that delegitimate any possibility of a meaningful science. Constructivism argues that reality, while it may exist, is unknowable or at least not sharable because it is mind-dependent

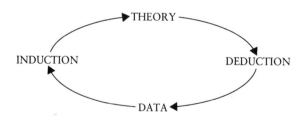

Figure 1–1 The Data-Theory Relationship

(Tyson 1992); deconstruction goes further to argue that reality as an objective (i.e., apart from perspective-determined interpretation) phenomenon does not exist. However, others within this general alternative tradition support empirical knowledge-building through such well-established methods of investigation as participant observation and ethnographic research.

One major disadvantage of the logical positivist position has to do with some internal contradictions that have been known for some time (Klee 1997). The most important of these has been called the underdetermination of theory by evidence (Anastas 1998; Klee 1997). While the model holds that theories are to be "tested" by facts, there is no research design that can eliminate all alternative explanations for what has been observed. Sometimes scientists debate what the facts (or the relevant facts) are. More often they can agree on the facts but not on what those facts "mean," or on what theory best explains them.

Another disadvantage noted in the psychological and social sciences stems from the use of operational definitions. It is very difficult to develop ways to measure psychological and social concepts that cannot be seen or touched directly. There has therefore been a tendency to reuse the measurement tools used to assess these complex concepts and then to reify specific measures, confusing them with the thing itself. The controversies surrounding the measurement of intelligence is probably the most widely known example of this problem. More importantly, there was also a tendency to conduct research on the problems or issues that lent themselves most easily to investigation using the methods available rather than letting the method of investigation follow the problem.

The disadvantage that proved ultimately most devastating, however, had to do with assumptions about data. In the logical positivist tradition, data were regarded as unequivocal. What gave science its credibility was the assumption that every scientist looking at the same bit of reality would see the same thing. This view implied that data were theory-free or at least theory-neutral, that observations could be made error-free, or that reality would always be observed or measured in the same way. What an observer saw was determined entirely by characteristics of the observed and not at all by either the perspective or the characteristics of the observer.

Thomas Kuhn, in an extremely influential book called *On the Structure of Scientific Revolutions* (1970), incisively, and to many persuasively, challenged this view. He did so by calling the very foundation of science into question, with this simple assertion: There is no such thing as theory-free observation. All observations, Kuhn argued, are theory-laden in several ways. First, it is theory (or perspective) that determines what we will observe. In any sensory situation, there are scores, even hundreds, of different phenomena that could be observed. What determines the part of the sensory field that will be attended to is some theory about what should be observed. Consider, for example, an ordinary conversation. It is a choice to attend to verbal content. One could, and in some languages one must, listen and respond to tonal intonation, to pitch, in order to communicate effectively.

Theory affects observations in another way: by dictating how observed phenomena are to be defined and therefore measured. Operational definitions had been the mechanism through which researchers had avoided confronting philosophical issues about the meaning of what they were studying. It wasn't necessary to consider the fundamental nature of a construct if it could always be identified simply, and very easily, by pointing to how it had been measured. But the solution of operational definitions had always been regarded as somewhat unsatisfactory and as side-stepping the issue of the fundamental nature of measured phenomena. Kuhn directly confronted this hidden problem by pointing out that it was in some sense ridiculous to regard an operational definition as an intellectually satisfying way to conceptualize the fundamental nature of reality. Hypothetical constructs were always at least implicitly regarded as more complex than could be reflected in any single measure of them. What Kuhn did in his argument was make explicit the fundamentally theoretical (and theory-laden) nature of scientific "reality" that is embodied in the everyday working definitions used in research.

Kuhn argued that observations were theory-laden in still a third manner. In important ways, what observers see is influenced by what they expect to see, just as it is by what is there to be observed. Expectations, based on theories, influence observations. He argued that scientific breakthroughs were not the product of the accumulation of observations, as the traditional view held, which he terms "normal science." Rather they are the product of paradigm shifts in which entire theoretical systems replaced others and changed profoundly the view of reality taken and the nature of the data that count. While normal science is essential, he argues, it is driven largely by the paradigms that shape both its interests and its methods. When paradigms shift, so do the phenomena that are considered relevant and interesting to study and so, often, do the methods for studying them.

A favorite example from the history of science illustrates how profoundly theoretical expectations may shape what is seen. As is common when a new and more powerful instrument of observation is developed, scientists look again at familiar things. For example, scientists in the time of Leeuwenhoek, who invented the microscope, saw little men, fully clothed, with tails on their heads in human semen. Conception was thus explained by these "homunculi," or little men, swimming into the womb. Were this the only example from science, it might be possible to dismiss its significance. But the fact is that science is full of examples of phenomena that were "seen" (i.e., observations that were interpreted) in accord with the theories held by those who observed them. In fact, this now-amusing observation also represented a position in what was then a long-standing paradigm war between the "ovists," who saw the origins of life as arising from within the female body, and the "spermists," who saw it as residing in the male secretion (Pinto-Correia 1997).

According to Kuhn, then, scientific knowledge cannot be regarded as theory-free or value-free. And if scientific knowledge is not theory-free, then it must be acknowledged that something in addition to, or even perhaps instead of, fundamental reality determines its observations, the data that count, its hypothetical constructs, its propositions, and its knowledge. Science can no longer be regarded as an organized set of "truths" describing and explaining "reality"; it must instead be regarded as a systematic set of interrelated belief statements, retained on the basis of their internal consistency, utility, and apparent fit with reality as perceived and as consensually agreed upon by some community of experts as constituted in a particular social context and historical moment. Science, then, is not apolitical, either: it is a social enterprise as well.

Fallibilistic Realism

Only recently has a new model of science begun to emerge. It has been called by two of its proponents for the social sciences, Manicas and Secord (1983), *fallibilistic realism*. This model seeks to incorporate the critiques of logical positivism without abandoning the concept of a knowable reality entirely (Anastas 1998; Klee 1997). It is based on realism as outlined by Harré (1972), a philosopher and historian of science, and others (Bhaskar 1989; Manicas 1987). Harré (1986) also uses the term referential realism, stating that although "*our* knowledge and *the* real world are different things" (p. 34), plausibility in the connections drawn between what we know and the way things are is a key criterion of knowledge that is scientific. In addition, the immediate and historical context in which scientific investigation takes place is considered to be an integral part of the process that must be understood in evaluating its products. The contextual complexity of research as currently understood is sketched out in figure 1–2.

Of course, the research process is even more complex in reality than is suggested in figure 1–2. The data of interest in most research in social work and

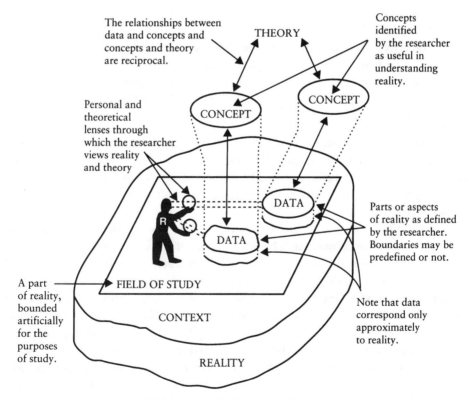

Figure 1–2 The Research Process

the human services do not reside impersonally "out there" in reality; in fact, they are embodied in people with whom the researcher interacts in some in way in order to elicit the needed information. Thus the research process is social as well as material. In addition, the context impinges in a variety of ways, historically and situationally, even determining who can occupy the role of researcher, the purpose of the research, and the audience for it. Fallibilistic realism, rooted as it is in the history of science, reflects the complexity of the research situation as it really is.

The first fundamental premise of realism is that there is an invariant reality that exists apart from any particular observer of it. For those who have taken courses in philosophy and the nature of reality, proponents of this view would hold that when a tree falls in the forest, it makes a noise whether or not there is anyone nearby to hear the sound. This premise is reflected in the term realism. This assumption implies that it is possible, in principle, to consider building a science, since there is an invariant reality to describe and explain. This position is different from constructivism on the one hand, which emphasizes the subjective and relativistic nature of empirical experience, and idealism on the other, which holds that the essence of things resides in ideal types rather than in any actual, observed instances of them. However, as Manicas and Secord (1983) put it, because theories "are constitutive of the known world, but *not* of the *world,* we may always be wrong, but *not* anything goes" (p. 401).

One of the key components of realism is the way theory and reality, or data, are understood. Harré (1972) has outlined this relationship in the following way:

1. Some theoretical terms can be used to make reference (verbal) to hypothetical entities.
2. Some hypothetical entities are candidates for existence (i.e., could be real things, qualities, and processes in the world).
3. Some candidates for existence, for reality, are demonstrable (i.e., can be indicated by some sort of gesture of pointing [operation] in the appropriate conditions) (p. 91).

Concepts may or may not have empirical referents, and even those with empirical referents may or may not be easily demonstrated. Useful concepts, then, are not reduced just to those that can be easily studied in any given way. There is a real world separate from the knower of it that can be studied empirically, at least "in the appropriate conditions."

Harré (1972) gives an example from the history of science that shows how concepts and evidence may each have independent value. The idea that microorganisms could cause disease was a theory that predated the microscope (and had its competing theories). The invention of the microscope in the seventeenth century first permitted the visual identification of bacteria, "proving" this general theory about the role of microorganisms in disease. The concept of the "virus" was then invented to indicate a residual category of microorganism, a type of microorganism that was hypothesized to exist because an infectious disease process was occurring even though no bacteria were seen. In fact, no virus was ever seen directly until the invention of the electron microscope in the twentieth century. Nevertheless, the concept of the virus was found to be useful long before the "reality" of the virus was ever demonstrated empirically, in this case visually. Thus realism both concedes a place in scientific or professional discourse for concepts for which there is no present or imaginable demonstration of an empirical referent and values the empirical processes used to demonstrate a connection between concept and reality, meaning the sensory experience of it.

The second premise of fallibilistic realism holds that while it is true that we cannot know reality either directly or perfectly, as Kuhn so powerfully pointed out, we can approach knowing this reality even though there will always be some error (i.e., theory-induced bias) in our observations and in the interpretations and conclusions based on them. Our theories and methods, then, will not be infallible. The meaning of the words "fallibilistic realism" metimes contain errors of fact or interpretation and therefore be wrong. Imperfections in the observational process will come from the observer, the reactivity of the research process itself, and the general context of any research activity, including historical and political influences.

A second implication of the term "fallibilism" refers to Popper's (1959) famous idea of falsification, that is, that theories or concepts can indeed be called into question when empirical evidence fails to support them when expected to do so. Demonstration of the existence of a concept with reference to reality also implies the possibility that such a demonstration will fail. However, as already stated, realism does *not* hold that concepts without demonstrated empirical referents are of no use or value for that reason alone, even though demonstrations of existence with reference to reality are valued. "Facts" are not dominant in this perspective; theory is.

While fallibilistic realism is thus consonant with science as ordinarily understood and as actually practiced, that is, with traditional empirical study, there are many differences between this position and logical positivism. One key concept in logical positivism that is absent in realism is causation or the primacy of causal arguments. When causation enters the discourse, the experiment becomes the pinnacle of scientific achievement, with every other method, even when acknowledged to be useful, rating only a subordinate place in the hierarchy of empirical knowledge development efforts. The purpose of scientific activity in fallibilistic realism is not to establish causal laws or even to predict; it is to describe and to improve explanation. Theory is understood to be more decisive than evidence in explaining how the world works, and the evaluation of competing theories depends on much more than empirical evidence, a point made in a different way by Kuhn (1970). In fact, realism posits the reverse of logical positivism: "Theoretical entities are not hypothetical but real; observations are not the rock bottom of science but are tenuous and always subject to interpretation" (Manicas & Secord 1983:406).

Stated another way, in realism, causal arguments and predictive statements that are infallible can *only* be made theoretically, that is, in a closed logical system. The real world as known is by definition a complex and open system. The example that Manicas and Secord (1983) give of this principle is that of salt dissolving in water, a theoretical truth. In the real world, by contrast, salt only *tends* to dissolve in water and often does so imperfectly depending on the context and on circumstance. This notion of closed and open logical systems has special relevance for understanding varieties of research design.

Manicas and Secord (1983) also note that realism is not reductionistic. Real world phenomena are understood to be complexly structured and thus can be apprehended from a variety of perspectives. Different disciplines and different investigators, then, may organize their apprehension of phenomena differently. Implicit in this statement is the idea that the perspectives that guide any scientific study must be made explicit.

Manicas and Secord (1983), in response to some of the criticisms of the received view of science, argue that social and psychological reality, as it exists in the world, exists in inherently open systems. Open systems are ones that can be entered, or exited, at any time. In laboratories, systems can be artificially closed by holding constant conditions related to the movement of phenomena. But in the real world, it is not possible to hold constant all relevant conditions. Therefore, phenomena that are studied in the real world are studied in a fluid context, that is, in an open system. Since scientific "laws" (i.e., statements of repeatedly observed regularities) vary as a function of the observational context, it is not meaningful to regard the task of science as discovering, or describing, or explaining an invariant reality, since its appearance may vary with its observational context. Moreover, in the real world, which is comprised of inherently open systems, what is content and what is context must be arbitrarily defined for each occasion of observation. Context, therefore, is inherently unpredictable before the fact.

The goal of science, then, cannot be to understand the nature of static relationships between variables. In the old, received view of science based on the logical positivist model, it was precisely this form of understanding that was the goal of science, most especially understanding the nature of the relationships between variables that would allow at least prediction and at best the production of specific effects, or causal control. In short, experimental research was considered most valuable or definitive. In fallibilistic realism, however, it makes no sense to speak of the goal of science as discovering the nature of fundamental, invariant or "causal" relationships between variables, since all relationships hold only under certain observational circumstances *and only within closed systems*. Nor is any one type of observational method, flexible or fixed, considered any more or less valuable than another.

In fallibilistic realism, the goal of science becomes something altogether different: describing or understanding the properties of specific phenomena and describing or understanding how those phenomena react or change in the presence or absence of other specific phenomena in an open system. Put more generally, the goal of science becomes to understand how phenomena are structured and how they change by describing how those phenomena look when static and how those phenomena "behave" (i.e., vary or interact) when in the presence of various constellations of other phenomena interacting with them. From this perspective, what is contributed by all forms of scientific research, whether flexible or fixed in method, is fundamentally descriptive. This statement is clear traditionally for all the models of research described in this text except for experimental research, but it is true for experiments as well.

Revisioning the Experiment

Consider the traditional view of the nature of experiments. In the received view of science, the goal of an experiment is to test causal connections, that is, to determine whether a change in one variable causes a change in another. As described in more detail in chapter 7, a tradition has developed about how these tests are to be conducted. This tradition, bases on the philosophers Hume and John Stuart Mill, addresses when it is considered scientifically acceptable to conclude that "X caused Y." Three conditions must be met. First, X must have preceded Y in time: a cause cannot come after an effect. Second, X must evidence a regular, demonstrable relationship with Y, most typically contiguity. This second condition requires demonstrating that "when X, then Y" and "when not X, then not Y" simultaneously and under any conditions. And third, arguing that X caused Y requires ruling out other explanations for why Y occurred, for example, that there is no Z that caused both X and Y to appear.

Demonstrations that meet these conditions have come to be regarded as providing the convincing evidence that X caused Y, but in reality they do not. As Hume pointed out when first considering the situation, only the argument that X *caused* Y *in the past* and *under the specific conditions observed* can be made. In fact, only the argument that X *produced* Y can be made; to argue causality requires theory to *explain* the change. An experiment can only show what happened; it cannot necessarily predict what will happen in the future or explain why things happened the way they did. Therefore experiments can only be offered as descriptions; they are not explanations of the inherent relationships between events. As Manicas and Secord (1983) state:

> On the realist view, events such as the collapse of a bridge or the cancerous growth of an organ are the conjunction of causal processes operating in open systems. . . . In general, explanation requires the resolution of the event into its components and a theoretical redescription of them: It requires causal *analysis*. Explanation thus requires knowledge of the casual properties of the configured structures *and* a historical grasp of the particular and changing configuration. Accordingly, we may often be in a position to explain some event once it has occurred, when it would have been impossible—even in principle—to predict it (p. 403).

Consider the simple example of an experiment illustrated in figure 1–3. It begins with ten corked bottles, each containing the same clear liquid (Step 1). By a flip of a coin, each bottle is designated as one that will (heads) or will not (tails) receive the experimental treatment (Step 2). The "treatment" (X) consists of removing the cork from the bottles for 15 minutes (Step 3). After the 15-minute period, each bottle is recorked and all are shaken up (Step 4). The experiment will produce the following result: the liquid in all of the uncorked bottles will turn blue, while the liquid in all of the corked bottles will remain clear.

Several points can be made about this experiment. Was there a meaningful relationship between removing the corks and having the liquid turn blue? Chance, as implemented by the flip of the coin, determined which bottles would be uncorked, not any preexisting conditions between them. Thus it is harder to argue that the bottles that were different from each other at the end differed to begin

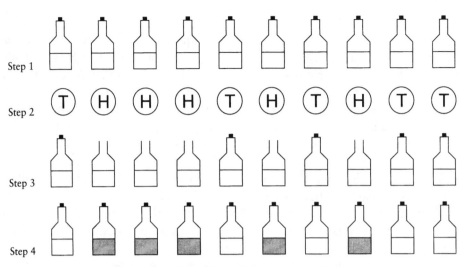

Figure 1–3 The "Blue Bottles" Experiment

with. Also, there was perfect correspondence between whether *or not* the cork was removed and the color of the liquid in the end.

Did the removal of the cork *cause* the liquid to turn blue? This classical experiment satisfies all of the conditions for making a causal agreement outlined above. However, the experiment cannot explain *why* the observed events happened. Nor does it inform us about the properties of the liquid in the bottles that caused it to behave the way it did. The experiment describes some events; it does not explain them.

Another point can be made from this example. Ask an engineer what made the liquid turn blue and she might say the removal of the cork did it. Ask a social worker and she might say it was the actions of the experimenter. Ask a chemist and she might say it was a chemical reaction between the liquid in the bottles and the oxygen allowed to enter some bottles corked when they were uncorked. Different theoretical systems and standpoints generate different ways of explaining the events observed.

As we currently understand this experiment, all of these explanations would be correct but incomplete. A complete description would include all of the elements listed above and some additional information. It would note that potassium hydroxide and methylene blue were both added to the water in each bottle. The solution in all of the bottles was in fact initially blue but then became colorless, which is when our observation of the bottles began. When some of the bottles were opened and shaken, the fluid in them became blue again because the methylene blue in them was reoxidixed by the air that entered and was brought into contact with it through shaking. In fact, if the observations had continued after Step 4, the liquid in the "blue bottles" would have become clear again, and, after a very long time, the liquid in all of the bottles would have become yellow or brown. Thus the original description of the color change, while accurate, must be recognized as holding true with a specific observation context.

In fallibilistic realism, the goal of science is not to describe causal connections between variables in static contexts but rather to understand the fundamental properties of phenomena by describing them and how they act in the presence of other phenomena in closed or open systems. The goal of science, then, is to describe properties rather than to declare propositions: It is to understand and explain phenomena well enough to know what they are like and how they will act, taking into account at least the possibility of multiple perspectives on the phenomena.

Types of Research

From the standpoint of fallibilistic realism, the various types of research methods found in the social work literature are described and discussed somewhat differently than from the traditional standpoint. In fact, one of the advantages of the new perspective offered by fallibilistic realism is that it can include and guide a variety of kinds of research without positing some as better than others. In fact, many researchers use and value a variety of kinds of research; fallibilistic realism legitimizes that stance.

Within the fallibilistic realism framework, however, two fundamentally and procedurally distinct models of empirical inquiry can be identified. Each functions to describe, but they differ in the form of questions they offer descriptive information about and in the perspective from which that information is gathered. These two modes of research are termed flexible and fixed. In fixed method research, the research methods are planned to keep the observational context fixed or relatively invariant throughout the conduct of the study. In flexible method research they are planned to allow the observational context, including the methods of observation used, to vary or to be adjusted as data are collected. Both of these methods have more in common than not in that they are planned, systematic, empirical methods of inquiry conducted from a skeptical stance. In addition, results of any study, flexible or fixed method, must be contextualized to be understood and are by definition incomplete renderings of the finite part of reality on which they focus.

Despite these similarities, flexible and fixed methods of research are quite different and are described separately in this text. In addition, because fixed methods were more highly valued in the dominant traditional framework than flexible ones were, subtypes of fixed method research have been clearly defined and described in the research literature, which is not yet true of flexible method research. All of the types and subtypes of research are descriptive, but they describe phenomena in different ways and with different purposes, incorporating different assumptions about the observational context and the reality being observed. However, while the different types and subtypes of research will be described here as if each were "pure" and always separated and separable, they are ideal types. Many good research projects in fact include elements from more than one type.

As illustrated in table 1–1, the basic types of research design differ in several key dimensions. The choice of a research design to be used depends most of all on the kind of question being asked. This dimension is covered in table 1–1 under the

Table 1–1 Overview of Major Types of Research Design

Type of Research Design	Purpose of the Research	Typical Samples	Usual Nature of Data Collected	Product of the Data Analysis	Credibility Based on:
FLEXIBLE METHOD					
Group Designs	To obtain a rich description; to define what something is more clearly.	Purposive, focal. Size may not be determined before the fact. Selection can be recursive.	Unstructured. Often interview and/or observation.[1]	Narrative organized conceptually. Production of new or enriched description.	Richness of description. Use of methods to demonstrate plausibility of interpretation.
Case Study	To describe a single instance of a phenomenon intensively and in context.	A single case embedded in context; can be typical or atypical.	Unstructured. Can combine interview and observation.[1]	Narrative. Production of new or enriched description anchored conceptually.	Richness of description. Connection between description and theory/explanation.
FIXED METHOD					
Descriptive	Determining significant facts more completely; describing facts predicted by theory.	Random, representative; large if precision of estimate to a larger population is a goal.	Structured. Interview and written self-report are the most common.	Description often rendered statistically.	Representativeness of sample; adequacy of sampling frame; adequacy of operationalization of concepts.
Relational	Matching relationships among phenomena with theory or with what is predicted by theory.	Can be focal or representative; large enough to show meaningful relationships.	Structured. Interview and written self-report are the most common.	Description often rendered statistically; use of inferential statistics common.	Suitability of sample to relationship(s) examined. Cogent explanation of relationship(s).
Experimental	To demonstrate whether the manipulation of one (or more) phenomena produces change in another (or others).	Creation of equivalent groups for comparison. Often small and atypical samples.	Structured. Quantified observation, interview, and/or written self-report are used.	Comparisons of effect(s) of intervention(s) made with inferential statistics.	Size of observed differences. Ability to eliminate the alternative explanations for results. Replication.
Single Subject	To demonstrate whether an intervention is followed by change in specific features of an individual case over time.	Case(s) with specified characteristics that can be quantitatively assessed.	Structured. Quantified observation, interview, and/or written self-report are used.	Description of change over time often rendered graphically and/or statistically.	Demonstration of change over time. Ability to eliminate alternative explanations for results. Replication.

[1]This description does not capture the fact that written case records, field notes, and researcher memos are often also treated as data and analyzed.

heading of "Purpose of the Research." There is no research method that is inherently any better or worse than any other. Better choices of design are associated with a good fit of method to the purpose of the research and to the kind of question being asked. A brief summary of each major research design type is given here; chapters 3 through 8 describe the major types and subtypes of research in the table in detail.

Flexible Method Research

The goal of flexible method research is to describe or uncover basic, often global, properties of poorly understood phenomena. These phenomena can be poorly understood either because they are newly noticed or because they are so hackneyed or problematic that they need to be examined anew. Often the purpose of the research is to discover the answer to a global question or to contribute to theory construction. This type of research has often been termed "qualitative" (as opposed to "quantitative"), but this terminology confounds the form the data usually take with the nature of the research itself. However, what this book calls flexible method research is what other works call qualitative methods.

Flexible method research is designed to provide a deep, rich, "thick" description of the phenomenon under study *in context*, often involving data that are unstructured or narrative in form. The context described is not just the context in which the data are encountered but is also the context of observation itself. Researcher and researched are both inside the frame of the picture developed. In other terms, the research is considered to take place in an open system whose boundaries include the observer as well.

In flexible method research, in principle the method follows, and is in part determined by, the nature and the content of the emerging data. By definition, the method used to collect data changes over the course of a piece of flexible method research: As the phenomenon under study becomes more completely understood, the form and content of the data that are sought to enhance that understanding changes. Fixed research methods (descriptive, relational, experimental, and single-subject) specify the method and scope of the data collection and the other research procedures at the outset, and that method of investigation remains unchanged over the course of the study. Fixed method research is thus considered to take place in a closed system.

Flexible method research most closely fits what is ordinarily known as the inductive model: The researcher intends to be guided inductively by the data to abstracted generalities. Reasoning is often from data to theory. Observations made or experiences encountered in the field early in the research process are also consciously used to adjust and further develop the data gathering and interpretive processes as the study proceeds. Thus methods as well as conclusions are data-driven and reflexive.

Within the broad category of flexible method research, however, there is a range in the degree of flexibility of method employed, the degree to which theory is used to guide the research at the outset, and the degree of focus on context as well as content. Some flexible method studies may be considered more factual, being simply designed to gather data describing a phenomenon in a new way. Other flexible method studies may be termed explanatory if theory development is their primary goal, as in the grounded theory method (Glaser & Strauss 1967). Studies traditionally termed exploratory or ethnographic, grounded theory methods, and participant observation are examples of flexible method studies.

This book divides its discussion of flexible method research into two types: studies that rely on multiple participants or informants (sample members) and those that take the form of an intensive study of a single case. These studies are often termed traditional case studies. As interest in flexible method research has been revived in social work and the human services in recent years, there has also been renewed respect for traditional case study designs (Gilgun 1994).

Fixed Method Research

Fixed method research, as the name implies, uses preplanned methods that are designed to be invariant throughout the course of the conduct of a study. This family of procedures stems from the received idea of research as "objective"; that is, through adherence to structured methods of investigation, the phenomena to be studied can best be understood, unaffected by the investigation itself. In the realist framework, this kind of research can be understood as taking place in a closed system to one degree or another. These structured methods of investigation, like flexible ones, have been applied in studies in which sample members are treated in the aggregate (as a group)—termed nomothetic designs—or studies in which one or more sample members are treated as individuals, which are termed *single-subject designs*.

Fixed method designs that are nomothetic can, in turn, be divided into three broad subtypes: descriptive, relational, and experimental research. Descriptive, relational, and experimental research can all be directed toward collecting narrative, categorical, or quantitative data. They differ greatly, however, in their purposes, goals, and in the kinds of questions they are designed to answer.

Descriptive research. The goal of descriptive research is to describe selected, predefined properties of a phenomenon on selected, predefined dimensions. Descriptive research is usually conducted to study phenomena about which there is some but insufficient understanding or to study phenomena that have been defined theoretically but not yet empirically. Researchers deduce what properties to measure on the basis of some perhaps implicit theory about the phenomenon under study but then draw inductive conclusions in detail about the properties of the phenomenon on the basis of the data obtained.

Descriptive research is guided by a series of relatively specific or narrow research questions, and the data collected are usually structured, that is, categorical or quantitative in form. Its yield is a description of some preselected properties of the phenomenon, and its results are almost always presented as quantitative descriptions that lend themselves to the use of descriptive statistics (see chapter 17), perhaps even to point or parameter estimates of a general population, as in political or opinion polling (see chapter 18). When the goal of the research is to generate precise population estimates, large samples representative of the populations of interest are required. Polls, needs assessment surveys, and other types of surveys are the classical examples of descriptive research.

Relational research. The goal of relational research is to describe relationships between selected, predefined properties of of one or more phenomena and/or selected, predefined properties of others. However, relational research is also characterized by the fact that the study is done without manipulating any of the variables in question (in contrast to the experiment). Relational research is typically conducted when there is a need to know how a phenomenon or characteristic is related to other phenomena or characteristics of a person, situation, or group, or when phenomena are well understood within themselves but not well understood in relation to their context(s). This form of research is also used when the phenomena under study cannot feasibly or ethically be manipulated at will.

Relational and experimental research are both deductive: Specific *hypotheses,* or speculations about the relationships or changes expected, are drawn logically from theory. The most crucial difference between the two is that in experimental research the phenomena of interest are manipulated to study the effects of change directly. Longitudinal and developmental studies are also considered relational research because they examine how processes of growth and maturation, or simply the passage of time itself, affect selected characteristics of the people studied.

Sample sizes in relational research are determined by the level of precision necessary in assessing any association found or the power needed to detect an association that is clinically or substantively meaningful. Data collection methods are generally highly structured, and results are generally numerical and thus handled statistically. Relational studies vary greatly in the degree of emphasis they place on the representativeness sought in the relationships described, in the degree to which the observational context can be or is controlled, and in whether they are cross-sectional or longitudinal. Many studies in epidemiology, sociology, social work, and developmental psychology are relational in nature.

Experimental research. The goal of experimental research is to describe how changes in a manipulated phenomenon or variable affect specific characteristics of those who have participated in the study. Experimental research is conducted when there is a specific question about creating change as a result of an intervention that can be manipulated at will. Experiments test hypotheses about how to alter one phenomenon so as to create change in another, hypotheses that are examined by comparing groups of study participants. Theory is essential to the design of experiments, because it is used to generate hypotheses, and because it is essential in explaining the results. Experiments may utilize *between-group designs,* when separate sample groups are compared at one point in time, *within-group designs,* when a sample is compared to itself over time, or *single-subject designs,* when a single entity is studied over time as his or her own control. Note that this description of experiments does not depend, as in the traditional view, on the idea of a causal argument; rather it is organized around creating and studying the effects of change. In the realist view, any causal statement about an experiment's findings does not depend on data as much as on the theoretical explanation that frames its results.

Data collected in experiments are generally highly structured, and data collection methods are designed to exercise a high degree of control over the observational field. The key characteristics of samples in group experimental studies is that they be *randomized* and that they be large enough so that conclusions drawn about group differences will be clinically as well as statistically meaningful. Experiments have most often been used in psychology and in clinical medicine, but there have been some experiments reported in the social work literature as well, particularly in the area of treatment and program evaluation.

Single-subject research. The final type of research design described in depth in this book are single-subject or single-system designs. These designs differ from the other fixed method designs discussed so far because they focus on studying a single client, case, or other entity over time rather than on a group of study participants. These highly structured, time-series designs have been promoted vigorously in social work in recent years as particularly well suited to research on practice. In studying the effectiveness of specific interventions using single-system design, a form of single-subject experiment has been advocated, but in fact these highly structured designs cover a spectrum of forms, as will be described. While single-subject studies have been most commonly found in behavioral psychology, some have recently made their way into the social work literature, and they are often emphasized in the teaching of research or in practice or field work in graduate and undergraduate programs in social work.

Summary: Choosing a Research Design

Fallibilistic realism provides a standpoint for doing and understanding research that considers a range of research designs and methods useful. When deciding which of these research designs to use, the decision should depend primarily on the nature of the research question to be asked. In other words, method should always follow question. Designing research often involves making a series of compromises, but one of them need, and should, not be compromising the question to fit a method. None of these methods is always superior to any of the others, and none is sufficient for knowledge development in general in and of itself. What social workers and other human service professionals are trying to understand is so complex and so multifaceted that sufficiently complete descriptions will often require bringing several of the methods available to bear on an issue. The problem formulation process, described in the next chapter, is when the focus of the research is developed and the research design selected.

The next part of this book discusses each type of research design in detail. Flexible method research is treated in two chapters, one on group designs and one on case study methods. For fixed methods, separate chapters are devoted to descriptive, relational, group experimental, and single-subject designs. These research designs were chosen for in-depth discussion because they are the ones most commonly encountered in the social work and human service literature.

Other valuable types of studies, such as meta-analytic studies, historical research, oral history methods, and studies using available data, are not included simply for lack of space and their less common use.

Fallibilistic realism as a framework requires that all kinds of studies be evaluated and discussed differently, and the chapters on research designs do this for these most common methods of inquiry in social work and the human services. Most importantly, it offers a perspective from which any kind of design choice, flexible or fixed in method, can be articulated and defended.

2

The Problem Formulation Process

Every research project must start somewhere, and this chapter is about how research projects begin. Problem formulation is the process by which a question for research is identified, developed, and joined to a method of investigation that can efficiently deliver an answer to the question. It is the part of the research process that most obviously involves creativity and artfulness. Its yield is a clearly stated researchable question and the selection of a general study strategy that has the potential to produce a useful answer to the question and to do so efficiently and ethically.

The skills involved in problem formulation include several general ones that characterize all high-quality professional activities: curiosity, openness to new ideas and ways of thinking, analytic ability, a tendency to seek out information and to want to understand things, skills in using resources efficiently, and a desire to solve problems. At best, the problem formulation process can also call upon an aesthetic sense in seeking the most elegant statement of the question and design for the research. "Elegance" in research implies a conceptual clarity combined with an efficiency of effort that together seem beautiful.

Beginning a research project can be very exciting. It can also be very frustrating because there is no clear road map for how to proceed or because there is a strong desire to "get a handle" on a problem while the way to do so is still being invented. An idea for a research project can arise in many ways but rarely appears fully formed. Rather, it usually begins as a broad area of interest, and considerable effort is needed to refine the idea or area until it can be described as a researchable question connected to a general strategy for answering that question. This chapter is about identifying ideas and formulating them for research and about how to move from general inspiration to a specific research question.

Identifying an Area of Research

Ideas for research can arise from many sources: practice experiences, personal experiences, conversations with colleagues, requests for proposals for research funding by government agencies, or from general reading. Research in social work and the human services is generally characterized by its attention to the many practical and conceptual problems that may become obvious in practice: Who is served? Who is not being served? Why? What problems are they experiencing? What is the nature and course of these problems? Which programs, services, or practice techniques are working and which are not working? This identification of research problems in the real world of professional practice has been termed the "felt need" (Wechsler, Reinherz, & Dobbin 1976). Often the best research begins with some unanswered question from practice or personal observation that sticks in one's mind or recurs stubbornly as if requiring a better answer.

The felt need driving a piece of research may initially be to find answers to practical problems or it may be largely theory-driven. Clearly some pieces of research are more purely theoretical and could be termed "basic" research while others are more clearly "applied" projects directed to short-term or practical problems. The field of social work often draws on such disciplines as psychology, sociology, and psychiatry for the theoretical research that informs its knowledge base, but there are also many examples of research in social work that have as their primary purpose the testing and development of theory, especially theory about practice. However, it may not be useful to make too much of the distinction between research with practical, descriptive, or evaluative goals and research with seemingly theoretical goals because the best research is often relevant to both theory and practice. Applied or evaluative research is always improved by making a connection with the sometimes latent but always important theory base that undergirds it, and theoretical research is useful only to the extent that its relevance for understanding individual, interpersonal, or social phenomena in the real world is made clear.

Sources of Inspiration

Whether arising directly from the field or from reading, a research question often springs from a dissatisfaction or disagreement with existing ideas or from recognizing a gap, noticing that something is missing. For example, the study of racial discrimination (Feagin 1991) included in this volume (see chapter 3) explicitly takes issue with a challenge to the "significance of race" made in sociology and the notion that class, specifically being a member of the underclass, is what produces problems for African Americans in contemporary American society (Wilson 1978, 1987). Through an in-depth study of middle-class African Americans, Feagin found that over a quarter of them had personal stories of discrimination to tell. Based on this evidence, Feagin goes on to treat as "problematic" the idea that since the 1960s "overt discrimination in the workplace and in public accommodations" have been "virtually eliminated" for middle-class black Americans (p. 101). He then analyzes the stories of his participants in depth to understand the nature of the acts of discrimination encountered and the kinds of strategies people used for dealing with them, interpreting their strategies in light of theory about how people manage face-to-face interactions in everyday life.

Gaps in knowledge that can give rise to worthwhile research can also arise as social changes proceed ahead of social provision. Much has been made in recent years of how the "ideal" American family consisting of a wage-earning father, a mother devoting herself only to rearing the children, and children under 18 living at home is now statistically in the minority. While this may be the family structure in mind when social policies are developed, this kind of family represented only 13 percent of American married-couple families in 1998, and married couples were only 54 percent of American households (U.S. Bureau of the Census, 1998). As an example of how research can grow from examining new social and familial realities, in 1985 I was involved with a colleague in a study supported by the Administration on Aging of how working women in their middle years cope with caregiving responsibilities for dependent elderly family members (Gibeau & Anastas 1989; Anastas, Gibeau, & Larson 1990). At that time, as a result of the steadily increasing numbers of women in the labor force, the need for employers to provide for child care had been articulated, if not yet realized. A parallel need to support the caregiving efforts of workers with dependent elderly family members had not yet been established despite the well-documented increase in the number of older people in society and the aging of the work force itself. This gap arose in part because of sexist assumptions about who in families is employed, who should give family care, and who should be expected to compromise labor force participation and earnings to be able to do so. For a variety of reasons, by 1993, Congress finally adopted the Family and Medical Leave Act specifically written to encompass both child care and elder or spousal care leave. Ideas about social provision had begun to catch up with social and demographic realities.

As these examples illustrate, a study area can arise because of discomfort with or even distrust in "the conventional wisdom." As Shulamit Reinharz (1985), a feminist sociologist and qualitative researcher, has observed:

> One of the hallmarks of the modern attitude and the scientific method is distrust. We moderns do not trust one another because we see that self-interest takes precedence over other considerations. Skepticism also pervades our relationship to scholarship. Science requires that we do not simply accept assertions, but rather that we seek evidence according to standardized criteria. . . . [Since] certain methodological, epistemological, and social psychological dilemmas are constraints in the production of social science knowledge . . . a social scientist learns to compound conventional distrust with academic distrust (p. 153).

In addition, she notes, a feminist is likely to distrust much of the received knowledge and the methods of any discipline or field. As illustrated in the examples above, refutations of beliefs based on sexist or racist assumptions can be very productive sources of ideas for research, for practice, and for policy.

Of course, not all research begins in controversy. There is also a rich tradition in research of collaboration and the accumulation of knowledge among cooperating researchers who build on one another's work and of research in which an investigator builds cumulatively a program of research one study at a time. This process has been termed "normal science" (Kuhn 1970). According to Kuhn (1970), normal science has one of three purposes that use empirical observation in different ways: for the determination of significant facts, the matching of facts with theory, or the extension and elaboration of theory. A social work example of the uses of normal science is found in the work of Elaine Brody, whose studies of how elderly family members are cared for in the community led her to observe that it was almost always a daughter or daughter-in-law who was providing the care. Focussing on this caregiver, Brody noted that these women were most often middle-aged and often also had care of dependent children, leading her to coin the term "sandwich generation" to describe their plight (Brody, Johnson, Fulcomer, & Lang 1983; Lang & Brody 1983). She then went on to suggest that parent care might be becoming a normative stage in family and adult development because generations are living longer (Brody 1986). Finally, her work on caregiving evolved to examine how employment does and does not impact on women's caregiving (Brody & Schoonover 1986; Brody et al. 1987) and other factors that affect caregiving, such as household composition (Brody, Kleban, Hoffman, & Schoonover 1988) and geographic distance (Schoonover, Brody, Hoffman, & Kleban 1988).

Practice experience itself can be an endless source of ideas for research studies. Selma Fraiberg's (1970) classic study of the development of children blind from birth illustrates this point well. Fraiberg, a child psychiatrist, was consulted by a child guidance agency that suddenly found itself with several blind children in its caseload. These children were all displaying signs of autistic-like behavior, such as stereotypic movements and difficulty relating to people. It was not clear why this problem was occurring since the early development of blind children had never been systematically studied; nor was it clear how to help them. Since autism was then understood as a failure in ego development arising in the mother-child relationship in the first year of life, Fraiberg decided to study the development of one blind baby intensively in those first 12 months seeking clues to the origin of this problem. It should be noted that she undertook this study while attempting treatment with the other children, not as a substitute for it.

When Fraiberg first met the baby she studied, who was then three months old, she observed almost immediately that the blind baby readily and consistently expressed attachment to the mother by smiling at the sound of her voice. This observation alone forced a modification in developmental theory, which had always said that the sight of the mother (or primary caregiver) was what induced recognition and attachment.

Fraiberg's (1970) eloquent account of this study and her discussion of the relationship between theory, research, and practice are well worth reading in the original. Aside from a "felt need" arising from practice, this study also illustrates the use of the literature: the author's first step was to try to find the answers she needed there, and her study began when she determined that a whole area of research, psychological development in blind babies, had not been empirically examined before. Theory was clearly and effectively used to focus the observations of the researchers when they visited this mother and baby in the home and to frame the significance of the events they observed. Finally, this case study was used to identify the areas in need of verification through replication and those where major questions still remained, such as the study of how blind babies used their hands as sensory organs. In the later studies that grew from the first, study questions and resources were focussed most intensively on those areas of continuing question while confirming and building on what had already been established.

In addition to practice experience, personal experience can also be a rich source of ideas for research as long as scientific skepticism can be maintained. In the example of the research on eldercare given above, one impetus for the research was the experience of one of the authors (Gibeau) as a working caregiver herself. The personal roots of research ideas are rarely described, although there are exceptions, especially in qualitative, or flexible method, research (Bloom 1986; Fine 1994; Golden 1976; Hyde 1994). This omission is in part a result of the fact that all the underlying personal motivations of researchers cannot always be known to them. It is also a product, of course, of the traditional idea that research is an "objective" activity in which personal feelings and experiences should play no part. This belief is a myth; were it true, it would render research a rather passionless activity.

In reality, without some reason to care about a topic, it is unlikely that much research would actually get done. Conversely, it is equally true that a disciplined and skeptical attitude must be maintained by the researcher when formulating ideas for a project, collecting the data, and preparing and reporting on results. "Personal theory" (Marshall & Rossman 1989) must always be examined in light of existing knowledge and tested against and tempered by the data that emerge from the study.

Immediate personal experience and convictions that are not subject to modification based on evidence can interfere with the conduct of research in several ways. The researcher can become paralyzed at some phase of the research, either because the emerging evidence does not match the preexisting experience, expectations, or convictions or because there does not seem to be a way to place any workable boundaries on the investigation. Perceptions and results can be unwittingly distorted and subsequently discredited by others for the same reasons. In short, when seeking an area in which to do research, it is important to pick a topic that elicits enough emotional involvement to inspire the needed investment of energy but that is not so emotionally laden that productive, disciplined work will be difficult to sustain. When this balance has been achieved, personal experience can be an important source of inspiration and wisdom.

From Area to Research Question

Ideas about promising areas in which to do research may come from several sources, but they are just the starting point. The next step is to refine what usually begins as a general area of investigation into the formal statement of a researchable question. The question may be quite literally that—a question or series of related questions—or it may be framed as a statement, or hypothesis, that is then subjected to efforts to demonstrate its validity. Implied by the nature and content of this research question is the type of research design to be employed and much of the detail of methodology. The formulation of the specific research question is thus a key part of the research process.

Induction Versus Deduction

One of the key features distinguishing different research questions and designs is how theory is used. Some questions are more in the nature of "what is going on here" and thus rely primarily on inductive reasoning. Others are dedicated to the testing out of propositions deriving from existing knowledge and theory in the real world or in a new portion of it. Such studies depend more on deductive reasoning in the generation of the research question.

Induction means reasoning from empirical observations or "facts" in the real world to generalizations about them, that is, to concepts or to propositions about how these concepts may relate to each other. Deduction means reasoning within theoretical systems to develop new propositions or predictions about what will be observed under certain circumstances. In reality, both deductive and inductive processes occur in the conduct of all studies as the investigator moves back and forth between theory and data in framing questions, observations, and conclusions. However, it is also true that either inductive or deductive methods often predominate in the design of any one study, and that this distinction accounts for much of the variety encountered in research designs.

Needless to say, both inductive and deductive methods can give rise to valuable research. What differs in inductive and deductive research is the ways in which theory and data work together to produce the end result. For example, the Feagin (1991) study of discrimination against middle-class blacks reprinted later in this volume illustrates research that is predominantly inductive in method. In open-ended interviews with a number of middle-class black adults, Feagin "discovered" a number of stories about unpleasant incidents in many respondents' daily lives, events that conveyed a sense of difference, distancing, or mistreatment to them based on race. He classified these reported events according to types and then used theory about how stigmatizing behavior unfolds in everyday interactions to analyze them further. Finally he framed the whole issue in terms of the ongoing debate in sociology and social policy about the relative significance of race and class for African Americans in American society today. In this instance, the reasoning was predominantly from event to concept, from data to theories that could organize and contextualize the observations made.

Gomez' (1990) study of biculturalism and subjective mental health among Cuban Americans, also included in this volume, illustrates well the deductive use of theory to guide a piece of research. Gomez used the literature to challenge the conventional view of acculturation among immigrants as a linear process proceeding from "ethnic" to "assimilated," with the latter representing the best or final outcome. He posited instead that "acculturation should be studied as an accommodation that takes place along two independent dimensions. . . . [involving] the acquisition of the host culture . . . [and] the retention of the original culture" (p. 376). Biculturalism is then defined as "a balance in this accommodation" (p. 376).

Gomez' study then derives from the general hypothesis that among Cuban Americans ". . . there would be a positive linear relationship between subjective mental health and one's level of biculturalism" (p. 377). Having selected the relevant concepts and developed careful conceptual definitions of them, he selected instruments to measure biculturalism and several aspects of subjective mental health. He then sought a representative "normal" population in which to examine his hypothesis through a survey research method. The test of his hypothesis occured in the data analysis: If biculturalism were found to correlate with his measures of subjective (or self-reported) mental health, his hypothesis would be confirmed. If not, its relevance would not be demonstrated. His finding that biculturalism was correlated with subjective mental health in the population studied can then be related both to community development, service delivery, and practice needs, and to theory about how immigrant groups may function best in modern American society.

As a research idea is being formulated, it is important to identify the style of reasoning, deductive or inductive, that will be most characteristic of the project. In reality, of course, no one can make observations completely uninfluenced by theory and by concepts. Our very language for describing things organizes them in predetermined ways. Nor is theoretical reasoning untempered by some degree of reality testing or reference to observable data. Both realms, theory and observation, are at play in any study. However, one mode of reasoning or the other ordinarily predominates in how the study question is framed and how data are generated.

Questions along the lines of "What is going on here?," especially when a new area of investigation is being defined and not much is known about it or when the conventional wisdom about an issue is being questioned, are usually ones in which inductive reasoning predominates (see chapters 3 and 4 on flexible method research). For example, Fraiberg's initial case study of the blind baby was directed to an inductive examination of the course of one child's development in pursuit of the question: What are the adaptive challenges that blindness imposes on development in infancy and how can they be successfully met?

Some social workers have recently been making a case for the use of various types of inductively driven research in social work on utilitarian grounds, that is, that the paradigm better fits the kind of thinking and evidence that practitioners most often use. As a result, it is argued, practitioners are more likely to do research of this kind, and research results of this kind will be more useful and widely used by them (Hartman 1990; Ruckdeschel 1985). Given the dominance of deductive methods and styles of research in the profession over the last decades, it is surely an important corrective to point out that inductive methods have utility. However, in reality, different questions require different kinds of information. Hence the argument made for an approach to the formulation and design of research in which the method is determined by the question at hand seems most persuasive (Heineman Pieper 1989; Outhwaite 1987; Piele 1988), always remembering that investigator preference and expertise may play some role in the choice of method as well.

Research based on deductive reasoning can have the goal of systematic, often quantitative examination of relationships among concepts or well-described phenomena, or the examination of theoretically derived expectations or practice prescriptions empirically (see, for example, chapters 6 and 7 on relational and experimental research). What such studies have in common is sufficient background theory and knowledge to specify in advance of doing the study what is to be described, examined, or tested in fairly precise terms. The existence of the phenomena or the nature of the relationships among them can be deduced from what is already known before the study begins. For example, the Gomez study (1990) drew on emergent ideas about biculturalism, on some prior but more limited empirical studies of biculturalism, and on studies that showed that assimilation did not predict mental health and well-being as it had previously been expected to do. He relied as well, of course, on methods of measurement developed in prior work. Reviewing the literature, then, is an essential step in formulating any research project, and what is found (or not found) there will have a great deal to do with the kind of study approach that is ultimately adopted.

Reviewing the Literature

A key step in refining the statement of the study question and then in determining what kind of study strategy to use is to find out what is already known about the topic that may have relevance to the study and its design. The primary resource available for this purpose is the professional literature. It has often been said that we are living in an information age, and it is certainly true that no one can expect to be entirely up-to-date in knowledge in any area at all times without special effort.

Before going into detail about how searches of the literature are conducted, it should be noted that a literature search can be an intellectual adventure. It can be fascinating to learn about what is, and is not, being written about in different fields on a given topic of interest. New lines of investigation and possibilities for distraction may seem to arise at every turn. Conversely, one may experience mingled frustration and excitement when a topic really seems to have no precedent in print. Successfully completing a good literature search can require both dogged persistence and great skills of detection. At times a literature search can become an end in itself when gathering, analyzing, and reviewing a body of published research on a specific topic results in the generation or reframing of knowledge for practice or research.

A literature search is the process of locating and retrieving all the information that is currently available on a specific issue or topic. In order to be productive and efficient, such a search must in the end be carefully focussed, although it may take some creativity and artfulness in order to define or identify the best resources for it. There are many resources available that one might draw upon in the course of a search, and the search focus might have to be stated somewhat differently for each source of information used. Sometimes, especially when the proposed study topic is a new one or when the area initially described is very broad, focussing the search itself can be a challenge. In this, as in all phases of a literature search, the services and assistance of a skilled reference librarian can be invaluable. His or her help at the beginning, however, may rest mainly in posing a series of questions in order to develop a usable and sufficiently precise set of terms for the topic that connects to the resources and data bases that will be used.

Many resources can be used in searching the literature. These include tools that give access to books, such as a library's catalogue of holdings. *Books in Print,* the standard work listing all published and forthcoming volumes, indexed by author, title, and topic, can also be consulted. Among books that may be especially useful are bibliographies and standard reference works, such as encyclopedias, handbooks, and edited collections of papers on a given topic. Such works may contain review articles that summarize the historical development in a field and provide an overview of the "state of the art" on a topic as of the date of publication. Papers reprinted in collections are often chosen because they are exemplary, are written by acknowledged leaders in the field, or have been especially widely used. Because book publishing is often a lengthy process, however, it is essential to survey the professional journal literature as well in order to obtain the most current information.

Most active scholars first get their results into print by way of the professional journals. Works appearing in scholarly periodicals are indexed and sometimes even summarized in an abstract in a number of printed and computerized sources. These include *Social Work Abstracts, Psychological Abstracts, Sociological Abstracts,* the *Social Sciences Index,* the *Index Medicus,* the *Current Index to Journals in Education,* and the *Education Index.* There are also specialized indexes, such as the *Studies on Women Abstracts*, and the *Business Periodicals Index*, which can be useful for topics in management, organizations, EAP practice, and policy. Each published index to the professional literature contains a list of the periodicals they review for content so the reader can tell which journals have been included and which have not. There are also indexes to periodical material on specific groups, such as Hispanic Americans and American blacks, but these, like the business index, include all periodicals, including newspapers and popular magazines, not just professional or scholarly sources.

Most of the indexes to the professional periodicals now exist as computerized databases. Whenever a search is planned using a computerized database, it is extremely helpful to experiment with the various terms used to see which ones are likely to be productive in locating relevant material. Databases that index their materials both by words in the titles and by terms in the abstract can retrieve materials more comprehensively than those using only titles can. A major advantage of using computerized databases for searching is that terms can be cross-referenced. For example, to find material on pregnancy among teenage Latinas, one can link the terms "pregnancy" or "teen pregnancy" on the one hand and "Latinas" on the other for articles or citations relevant to both. Otherwise, many irrelevant resources will be identified, which is both inefficient and overwhelming. This example also illustrates the importance of terminology because it is likely that the term "Hispanic" rather than "Latino" will be found. Searches of computerized databases can also be customized in other ways, such as to cover only specific years of publication, for example.

A disadvantage of using the computerized databases is that the resources contained in them only go back approximately a couple of decades since they have only recently come into wide use. Older literature, usually including any published before 1970, is often only accessible via the printed indexes. However, once recent relevant articles have been found, their reference lists are sources that can be used to identify earlier literature.

It is important to remember that there is some degree of delay in getting published materials into the indexes. This delay varies among sources. If a search of the indexes turns up repeated reference to articles in a few specific journals, it is advisable to locate those journals in print and to scan their current and most recent issues in case new materials have appeared that have not yet appeared in the databases.

For those who have computers with external communication capabilities, it is possible to use them to gain access to journal and other databases, including card catalogues at local and remote libraries, including the Library of Congress. This access may either be through the library where they reside or through the world-wide web. This affords the convenience of sifting through book and article titles from one's own desk, although the materials themselves may not be available on-line. On-line publishing, however, is likely to increase in the future.

Government documents can also be a valuable resource to use in a literature review. Among potentially useful government documents are the Congressional Record, which often contains the Congressional testimony of experts as well as the text of legislation. Reports of federally funded studies and technical reports on current social problems commissioned by various agencies of the government can be excellent sources for an overview of an issue and for recent research findings. Bureau of the Census data and reports are now available on line (www.census.gov). Most other government agencies also have web sites where data and reports are available for downloading. Printed government documents are indexed and retrieved according to a unique and complex classification system. Libraries that are repositories for government documents have staff who specialize in working with this system, and it is essential to seek their guidance in making use of these materials.

How much is enough? It is very difficult to provide concrete guidance on how much literature is "enough" when conducting a review of the literature. The feeling can be either that there is absolutely nothing "out there" or that there is so much to track down and read that the job is entirely overwhelming. While the amount of literature that must be reported on in a study or research proposal varies considerably from topic to topic, the truth is that neither feeling usually reflects reality.

When a search of the literature seems to yield nothing, it is time to consider how the topic is being defined and to consider creative alternatives. Since literature searching is so dependent on defining terms and key words in indexes, it is important to consider other words and terminology with which to describe the topic in question. Especially in other disciplines or in other time periods, issues and ideas may be named differently. In the rare instance when there really is little or nothing already in print on a specific topic, studies from closely related fields must be relied upon instead. As long as a convincing rationale for selection can be stated, it is possible and desirable simply to define the related areas that will be included (and thus delimit them as well). Theory can also be used to explain why the topic merits attention.

Sometimes, however, it seems that there is so much literature to retrieve and read that the task is impossible. Such a situation suggests that the topic of the study (and the search) has been too broadly defined. Unless the project as a whole consists of a review of the literature, as in a meta-analysis, it is advisable to begin defining what subtopic(s) the review (and the study) will address. Alternatively, it is possible to put other kinds of boundaries on the literature, such as to use certain specific theoretical approaches or literature from a specific time period. The most common remedy that is needed, however, is to define the study and search topic more narrowly, to focus the search more specifically.

A literature search is nearing an end when continuing efforts yield diminishing returns. Each hour spent in the library or at the computer yields fewer new leads. Each new reference work or article bibliography consulted yields fewer and fewer new citations. Each new article found and read yields fewer new insights. These are all signs that the search has resulted in locating enough relevant literature.

It should be noted, however, that "the literature" is dynamic. As a research project proceeds, particularly if it addresses an area of current social or professional concern, it is essential that the search be updated periodically. Updates are especially easy to do with the aid of the computerized databases when the search instructions can be made specific to recently published works.

Keeping track. A literature search is a demanding task in and of itself. Making and maintaining meticulous records of all possible sources identified and all materials used is essential. These records must be complete, including authors, exact and full titles, and all publication information, including volume, issue number, and pages for journal articles. Familiarity with the bibliographic style to be used in the final research report is invaluable at the search stage. In that way, the information needed for each type of source (newspaper, journal article, chapter in an edited volume, etc.) can be recorded immediately. Returning to the library months later to complete a citation can be extremely time-consuming and frustrating. The are a number of computer software packages on the market that will store bibliographic information and even convert citations from one bibliographic format to another on command.

The most common citation style used in social work journals is the one developed by the American Psychological Association (1994). While there is a great deal of variation in how to cite works of different kinds, there are several elements in any citation that must be included. An example of the citation of a journal article in APA style is given in figure 2–1 for illustration. The first part of the citation is the author's name, last name first, otherwise initials only (no degrees or titles). Then comes the year of publication. The title of the article is given in sentence style, that is, with the initial word capitalized and a period at the end. The journal name follows, underlined in typescript to indicate that italics will be

---

Feagin, J. R. (1991). The continuing significance of race. *American Sociological Review* 56(1):101–116.

Figure 2–1 Example the citation of a journal article in APA style.

used in printing. The volume number, underlined, must be present, along with the issue number if page numbering is not sequential across issues; finally the page numbers must be given. For a book, the city of publication and the name of the publisher follow the title, and the book title itself is in sentence style and underlined. The point of this detail is that the information is complete enough for the interested reader to be able to find the work unambiguously. Whatever the bibliographic style used, a similar amount of detail will be needed, and it is best to obtain and record it as soon as material is located.

A successful literature search will most likely yield enough information that a way to keep it organized for use will have to be developed. In fact, if it is possible, it is best to make photocopies or to print off copies of source materials. This makes it possible to refer back to information in context, and, since one's interest in a given piece of work may change over time, it ensures that all information will be available when needed. It is also essential to check that all photocopied material has complete bibliographical information with it.

A system of sorting, classifying, and storing the copied materials for retrieval must be developed. File folders indexed by topic are generally useful for this purpose. Some people file and label articles individually and then arrange the article files in topical groups. Getting to know the literature well enough to develop useful classifications for it is simply the concrete sign of developing a conceptual grasp of the subject matter itself. This conceptual organization will be useful when it is time to write up the study and to organize the content of the literature for the reader.

What can be learned. So what is the result? The first and most obvious benefit of a thorough review of the literature is information about what has already been said and done on the topic of interest. Referring to previous work demonstrates the researcher's grasp of what has gone before and helps to make the whole scholarly enterprise efficient. Gaps and inconsistencies in the published literature are often suggestive of areas where further research is needed.

In addition, the state of the previous knowledge base in a proposed area of study helps determine what kind of research approach will be necessary. If little is known or if the assumptions of previous work are questionable, the kinds of questions to be asked will most often call for a flexible study approach. On the other hand, if knowledge and measurement techniques are relatively well developed, the kinds of questions that it is reasonable to ask next will likely call for a relational or experimental study.

Information about specific study methodologies can also be gleaned from the review of the literature. What has worked in previous studies and what has not? What kinds of samples and sample recruitment methods have been used? What data collection methods and tools have been developed? What analyses have been done or are needed? This methodological information from previous studies may be useful in several ways: in assessing the published work, in designing the study to be undertaken, and in interpreting its results. Notes on the literature must therefore include methodology as well.

Most importantly, review of the literature should yield a more focussed and precise statement of the study question. The question must be stated in terms that have been given careful definition and in a manner leading toward a style of research appropriate to the state of knowledge development in the field. Questions that have already been addressed satisfactorily can be eliminated. Relevant variables that need to be taken into account can be identified and included. Critical thinking about what has been learned will move the researcher much closer to a well-formulated statement of an issue for productive study.

Study Scope: Think Small

One of the hardest parts of developing a research question is coming to terms with the limits of any single study. Since a study usually springs from caring about an issue, there is a tendency to want to do and know it all. A research study is a project undertaken to answer a specific question. If the question is well-conceptualized and the study issue has some importance, its results may have considerable meaning and even practical significance. Nevertheless, a good study may raise more questions than it answers.

In fact, the research process uses careful observation of the empirical world as a window on the larger conceptual world. For this reason, paradoxical as it seems, thinking small is in fact the way to address the big issues. The Feagin (1991) study reprinted in chapter 3 illustrates this principle well. Spontaneous remarks made in interviews on a specific theme, namely events experienced as discriminatory by people otherwise privileged in their lives, were used to reflect both on how stigmatization happens in everyday life and about the relative salience of race and class in American life, certainly large and important concepts. The study did not address all aspects of race and class or even of stigma management, and it would have been an unmanageable project had it tried to do so.

Finally, feasibility, or the resources in time, energy, and money needed to complete a study, should be considered as well in formulating a research question and deciding on the scope of a study. While methodology should follow the question and not the reverse, some consideration must be given to feasibility as the research question is taking shape. In relation to practical matters, it is probably better when resources are limited to undertake a smaller-scale study well than to undertake a more ambitious one without sufficient means for careful execution.

Types of Questions That Are Not Researchable

Are there any questions that are simply not researchable? One answer lies in the concept of questioning itself. If there is a topic or issue on which the researcher has already made up his or her mind or a proposition for which no convincing disproof can be imagined, such a topic is not suitable for research because there is really no question about it. Such a question as, "Is family therapy useful?," is likely to be one about which the practitioner has made up his or her mind long ago. Yet a question about the effectiveness of a specific theory or technique of family therapy for a particular problem or type of family, or compared to another treatment alternative, is likely to admit of different answers and could be a useful inquiry.

Many of the most interesting questions that social workers and other human service professionals ponder have to do with why people behave the way they do or with what should be done to alleviate social or personal problems. Social work practice is informed by knowledge, skills, and values; questions about competing values, for example, are not generally resolved by answers based in knowledge but rather by some process of weighing alternatives, negotiation, or choice. A question like "What is a just society" cannot be answered through research; one about how a specific income maintenance program or policy has affected a specific outcome, such as labor force participation or child poverty, can be.

The scientific method is only one way of knowing about human problems and their solutions. Therefore research cannot hope to answer all the questions posed by practice, especially those ultimate "why" ones. Research efforts can only usefully be spent on those questions that can be actually be settled by the use of empirical evidence and that admit of a variety of answers.

"So What" or "Who Cares": Defining the Significance of the Study

Research is only worth doing when the results of the study in question will matter. The first criterion of usefulness is that a study must contribute new knowledge. Research studies should yield information that may help in solving real world problems or add in some way to fundamental knowledge. Even studies that replicate others contribute information about whether the previous results were a fluke or an enduring finding.

In describing the potential practical significance of a study, it is important to define who has an interest in the results. Who wants or needs to know about the study issue(s)? How often does the problem occur? How costly is it? (see Marshall & Rossman 1989). What areas of practice and policy might be affected by the answers to the study question?

When making the argument for the practical significance of a study, it may be necessary to undertake some preliminary research in order to document the importance of the study issue. Population data, epidemiological information, service utilization data, and other similar kinds of information may help to make the case for a study. If the necessary supporting data cannot be found, perhaps a study to generate them may be worth doing.

It is also necessary to make the case for the contribution a study may make to fundamental knowledge. The review of the literature provides the information needed to make this argument. What is already known? What is not yet known or understood? How will the proposed study add to this knowledge or under-standing? How will it test or expand on existing theory or improve on previous methods of study?

Making the case for the significance of a study demonstrates the creativity of the research. The challenge is to arrange existing theory and knowledge in a new way in order to demonstrate its limitations. The description of the significance of a study creates a new view: the view of what is not now known but that could and should be.

Stating the Study Question

The end product of the problem formulation process is the formal statement of the question or hypothesis that will guide the research project. The question must be located and understood in relation to theory, existing knowledge, practice, and policy. It is also stated very specifically, indicating in its style the kind of study strategy that should be employed and in the concepts used the phenomena that will be included and assessed. The stated study question is the link between concepts on the one hand and research activities on the other.

Checking the Question and Design for Bias

While there is no substitute for continuing self-awareness in minimizing the effects of any bias on the formulation of a research project, some suggested guidelines for analyzing studies for possible racism, sexism and heterosexism are summarized here for reference (see table 2–1). This framework owes a great deal to the analysis of sexism in research developed by Eichler (1988). As these critiques are in continuous development and as understanding is rapidly advancing, it is not possible to articulate any rules that can be relied on absolutely as a formula for bias-free research. The framework is presented instead as a guide to some of the problems that have already been identified as occurring commonly in research to date. At the problem formulation stage, it is essential to think critically about the concepts being used as well as the design to be employed in order to reduce bias (National Academy of Science 1993). Consideration of both the empirical and theoretical base from which the concepts were derived and how they will be applied and defined in the research being proposed will be necessary.

Invisibility. Eichler's (1988) analysis of sexism in research goes beyond the previous enumeration of problems with specific studies or instruments to the articulation of the major errors in thinking that underlie them. The first of the problems she defines is "androcentricity," in which persons are assumed to be male rather than female. This assumption may render females as invisible or only as objects that males act upon. One often-stated goal of feminist research, therefore, is to render women's experiences visible (Davis 1986; Oleson 1994; Swigonski 1994).

There are clear parallels here to assuming that people in general or in a study are of European descent, or should have the characteristics most valued in Eurocentric traditions (Akbar 1991), or that they are heterosexual (Herek, Kimmel, Amaro, & Melton 1991). This kind of assumption renders the less powerful group invisible or, particularly in relation to gender or race, treats them primarily as objects to be acted upon by the more powerful. In the case of gay, lesbian, or

Table 2–1 A Model for Examining Sexism, Racism, and Heterosexism in Research Design

Nature of Problems[1]	Sexism	Racism	Heterosexism/ Homophobia
Invisibility	Androgentricity (Eichler 1988). Participants assumed to be male.	Participants assumed to be members of the dominant racial and ethnic group, or sample of members of nondominant groups inadequate.	Participants assumed to be heterosexual, or samples of gays or lesbians inadequate (Herek et al. 1993).
Insensitivity	Gender insensitivity (Eichler 1988); gender not included as a salient variable.	Race and ethnicity not included as salient variables, or the effects of racism are attributed to race itself.	Sexual orientation not included as a salient variable (Herek et al. 1993), or the effects of heterosexism and homophobia are attributed to sexual orientation itself.
Overgeneralization	Typically, samples are male, but results are assumed to describe females as well.	Typically, samples are not people of color, but results are assumed to describe them as well.	Typically, samples are heterosexual, but results are assumed to describe gays and lesbians as well.
Double Standards	Similar characteristics are interpreted differently in males and females.	Similar characteristics are interpreted differently in whites and people of color.	Similar characteristics are interpreted differently in heterosexuals and homosexuals.
Dichotomism	Sexual dichotomism (Eichler 1988). Gender differences exaggerated and overlapping characteristics overlooked.	Racial differences exaggerated and overlapping characteristics overlooked, sometimes because of confounding with racism (Engram 1982).	Sexual orientation differences exaggerated and overlapping characteristics overlooked.

[1]Definitions of several of the problem types as applied to sexism were described by Eichler (1988).

bisexual people or of the cultures of nondominant racial and ethnic groups, for example, this kind of thinking defines things in terms of deviance rather than simply as variation or difference. Eurocentric (Harding 1993) and assimilationist assumptions (Becerra & Zambrana 1985) or unexamined biases (Stanfield 1993) often undergird social science research on race and ethnicity, preventing people from being seen for who and what they really are.

In relation to gender, language itself may contribute to this problem, which is one reason why attention to sexism in language itself is often advocated (Miller & Swift 1980). Changing the words used to describe it may change the way a whole phenomenon is understood. Postmodern feminists also emphasize this idea because they are concerned with which voices or versions of reality are dominant and which are subjugated. Because language contains so many embedded assumptions, when beginning a study and working on the statement of a study question, it may be helpful to use the feminine pronoun, for example, to determine whether or not females have been unintentionally forgotten in the conceptualization. Similarly, imagining each study participant to be African American, Asian American, Native American, or Latino/a may help to reveal whether or not the planned research activities and anticipated results will prove relevant to those groups as well. In addition, involving group or community members in planning the research and shaping its language is essential (Becerra & Zambrana 1985; Oleson 1994; Stanfield 1993).

Overgeneralization. A related but distinct problem arising in the sample used may be overgeneralization. Overgeneralization occurs when studies of one group, ordinarily of the more powerful group, are interpreted as applying to all groups (Akbar 1991). Adult psychological and moral development is one field in which overgeneralization from men to women has been identified (Gilligan 1982). In the case of same-gender couples, it may be assumed that the type of role divisions found in heterosexual couples will be found in gay and lesbian ones as well or that the group is homogenous rather than heterogenous (Herek et al. 1991). The corrective is often to focus an investigation initially only on the group that has not been studied until it can be determined whether or not and/or under what conditions the generalizations may apply (Akbar 1991; Rogler 1999). In addition, such a strategy is often the only way to identify key characteristics, especially strengths, of the less powerful group in which the more powerful ones may be "deficient." However, probability sampling and comparative studies as design strategies should not be overlooked (Herek et al. 1991; Smith 1993).

Insensitivity. Insensitivity occurs when variation in gender, race and ethnicity, and/or sexual orientation are included in the sample or conceptualization but there is insufficient attention to the social or psychological salience of them. Stanfield has called this "the fallacy of homogeneity" (p. 19). Take the simple example of "marital status"; if legal marital status is all that is needed, the standard question format will do. However, if a sense of a person's current social and personal connection is needed, the standard question format will not adequately describe gay and lesbian respondents and perhaps some racial or ethnic groups in a study. Sometimes adequate comparison of the subgroups in the sample is not made, or insufficient attention to sampling results in a situation in which subgroups are not represented in numbers sufficient to permit comparison. There are innumerable areas in which questions about the salience of gender, race, and sexual orientation have yet to be raised, and it is essential to develop sensitivity to these issues of difference as reflected in an inclusive set of questions and response categories and in the analysis plan.

A specific widespread type of gender insensitivity cited by Eichler is "familism," described as "treating the family as the smallest unit of analysis in instances in which it is, in fact, individuals . . . who engage in certain actions, have certain experiences, and so on" (p. 8). For example, "family caregiving" for the elderly may only be an inefficient way of talking about women's family work that tends to render women's experiences and point of view invisible.

Decontextualization. Another form of insensitivity is decontextualization. This form of bias involves interpreting specific events or behaviors without reference to the historical and contemporary contexts in which they occur. Context is especially important when considering and working with groups that have experienced systematic oppression and discrimination. Confounding race with the effects of racism is a clear example of this kind of insensitivity (McMahon & Allen-Meares 1992). Similarly, early research on the psychological functioning of gay men invariably used clinical samples, that is, samples of people seeking or receiving mental health services, leading some to conclude that there was no such thing as a well-adjusted homosexual and supporting the idea that homosexuality was a form of psychopathology. This idea was first disproved by Evelyn Hooker's (1957) groundbreaking study of a nonclinical sample of gay men, since followed by many others, that found them to be no different from a comparable sample of heterosexual men in their psychological functioning (LeVay 1996).

Dichotomism. Dichotomism is in many ways the reverse problem from insensitivity. Dichotomism occurs when issues of difference are recognized but may be, in fact, exaggerated, forgetting that even though groups may differ in the aggregate, these groups overlap in that individuals in them may share characteristics. In dichotomism, in short, differences are exaggerated and similarities overlooked. For example, despite the existence of an African American middle class, individual African Americans in any study may be assumed to be less affluent than whites. Insensitivity would be to overlook the aggregate statistics that describe the relative poverty of African American households on average in America; dichotomism would overlook the fact that a given African American individual may or may not have grown up or be living in poverty or that members of different racial groups often actually share common ancestry or appearance (Stanfield 1993).

Double standards. Eichler (1988) defines the use of double standards as "evaluating, treating, or measuring identical behaviors, traits, or situations by different means" (p. 7). This problem may occur in language, conceptualization, measurement, interpretation, or the framing of policy recommendations (Herek et al. 1991). In gender studies, a problem that derives from a double standard is that of sex appropriateness, which is a problem when human traits are assigned or valued differently by gender. The Broverman, Vogel, Broverman, Clarkson, and Rosenkrantz (1972) study is a classical example of research that exposed the double standard used by mental health professionals in assessing men and women, but any study can be affected as well. Using adjective checklists, the study found that the words selected by the professionals to describe a healthy or well-adjusted male and a healthy or well-adjusted female were quite similar. However, the words used to describe a healthy or well-adjusted female were quite different from those used for the healthy male and the healthy person. The different characteristics associated with mental health for males and females suggested a "double standard" that operated to the disadvantage of women. Another often-cited example of double standards occurs when female-headed households are viewed as problematic among African Americans while being described as "alternative family structures" among Euro-American women (Stanfield 1993).

It should be noted that gender, race, class, sexual orientation, and other dimensions of difference do not occur in isolation. When dealing with any of them conjointly, the issues may not be the same as for any one of them alone. Effects of these statuses may be magnified or transformed. Even though it is important to think clearly about each dimension of difference, each individual or group will have unique combinations of characteristics that must be considered when thinking about the research question, design, or findings.

Many contemporary writers about issues of difference in research draw on standpoint theory (Collins 1991; Harding 1991, 1993; Hess 1995; Oleson 1994; Stanfield 1994; Swigonski 1994). This theory holds that members of marginalized groups—as research participants and as researchers—have valuable insights as "strangers," as "outsiders within," into the dominant social order. They must know about how things are in the dominant culture as well as how members of disempowered groups act to mitigate the problems that flow from it. Their position, or standpoint, especially when they have consciousness of it, is useful for recognizing when knowledge or research methods devalue or neglect knowledge about themselves.

These five factors—invisibility, overgeneralization, insensitivity, dichotomism, and the use of double standards—point out several ways in which studies can go wrong in dealing with gender, race, sexual orientation, and other dimensions of difference. Consideration of the standpoint of the researcher and the research participants is also essential. The analysis of these potential sources of bias should be applied as well to research in print before accepting its findings uncritically.

From Question to Design

Having defined an area for research, the next challenge is to state the research question itself and to tie it to a research design. This process is critical because the question itself to a great extent implies the design. In fact, from the statement of the study question, most methodological decisions flow directly. What results is a research design coherent in all of its parts and consonant with the research aims as embodied in the question that guides it.

Stating the Question in Researchable Terms

One of the purposes in stating the study question precisely is to specify the concepts that will be used in the study to capture reality. Each of these concepts must be defined both conceptually and operationally. This careful definition connects the study both to the broader knowledge base from which it comes and to the observable world in which it will be conducted.

Conceptual definition. Defining each important term in the study question conceptually is the first step. Major concepts in the psychological, behavioral, and social sciences often have varying definitions depending on the theoretical framework and/or research tradition from which they were derived. For example, depression may be defined as a mood or feeling state, a self-esteem problem, a thinking problem, or a diagnosis. Any study purporting to address depression, then, must indicate the specific way in which depression is being defined. Each of these ways of conceptualizing depression is different and implies markedly different techniques of measurement. A major part of the problem formulation process, then, is the selection and specification of the conceptual framework on which the study and the definition of its major concepts depends.

Operational definition. Defining each term conceptually is only the beginning. Each concept must also be defined operationally. An operational definition describes the activities, or characteristics that will serve as indicators of the phenomenon in question. In inductive research, these "operational definitions" may be developed after the fact or in an ongoing fashion (see chapters 3 and 16). They are usually called definitions of coding categories. In fixed method research, these operational definitions are generally specified in advance (see chapter 15). In either case, the original statement of the study question and the definitions of the terms in it must be conceptually clear enough to allow focus in the sampling and data gathering effort and in all other aspects of the methodology.

Types of Research Questions

Research questions are often classified according to the general kind of study strategy they suggest. Some studies are devoted to answering rather general questions about "What is going on here?" Questions like this are most often posed when little is known about the subject under study or when the area of study is being reexamined or reconceptualized. Such questions give rise to study strategies that may be quite flexible. These studies are often described in other contexts as exploratory, formulative, or qualitative. The question is structured enough to define an area of study but general enough to give rise to unexpected findings and to permit a range of options to be used in the course of the investigation as suggested by the data as they emerge. Study designs of this kind are described in depth in the chapters on flexible method research (chapters 3 and 4).

Other research questions are more specific and delimited in the areas of study they define and employ concepts that tend to permit quantitative measurement. These questions tend to give rise to study strategies that may be characterized as descriptive in design. Sometimes the study intent is stated in the form of an hypothesis, to be examined using some relational, experimental or quasi-experimental study strategy. Questions or hypotheses of these types give rise to research designs that may be characterized as fixed, that is, determined and described completely before the study itself is undertaken.

Research questions for studies using fixed designs can in turn be classified into two main groups: those that deal with questions or hypotheses of difference and those that deal with questions or hypotheses of association. A question of group difference takes the form of comparing two or more samples on selected characteristics. In this kind of design, the same variables are assessed in different groups. For example, the El-Bassel et al. (1995) study reprinted in chapter 7 compares two groups of women: those who participated in an innovative preventive intervention to enhance social support and those who participated in a standard AIDS education program prior to release from prison.

A question of association, on the other hand, asks about how two (or more) characteristics, or variables, may relate to each other in the same sample or group. The Gomez (1990) study of biculturalism and mental health among Cuban Americans proceeded in just this way. One sample was obtained and the same questions were asked of everyone in the sample. The results were obtained by examining how a measure of biculturalism did or did not correlate with the measures of subjective mental health included, such as psychological well-being, self-esteem, and job satisfaction, in the sample as a whole.

It should be clear from this discussion that the way in which a study question is stated determines the kind of study strategy or research design to be employed. All of the parts of the research process—sampling, data collection, data analysis, and the kind of conclusions that can be drawn—must, in turn, be consonant with the study question. In this way, each research design becomes a coherent whole, related ultimately to the nature of the question being asked and answered.

Developing a Coherent Design

The most important determinant of the research design is the question. However, in reality, many factors influence the design directly and indirectly, including how the question itself is put. What is the previous state of knowledge in the area in question? If little is known or if what is known needs reformulation, a relatively flexible design is suggested. If more is already known and relevant variables have already been defined for this or a closely related field, a fixed design is most often employed.

Also relevant are ethical issues. Can the proposed study be carried out ethically in relation to the use of human subjects? What procedures will be needed to ensure that ethical issues are adequately addressed? Ethical issues in research are described in detail in chapter 9; these principles and standards of practice should be reviewed whenever a study is being formulated.

Finally, issues of feasibility need to be considered. Is the time available adequate for the kind of research proposed? What other resources will be needed? What will the project cost? What can be done to reduce a project's costs in dollars or in time? For example, cross-sectional studies are often used instead of longitudinal ones usually for reasons of time and expense. Although such findings may be less definitive in addressing developmental issues or causal questions, it may be better to do a less definitive study than none at all if sufficient resources cannot be generated for the more ambitious study design.

Summary

The formulation of an idea for research and the statement of a research question is a creative process that generally proceeds in stages. First an area of general interest is identified from professional or personal experience. Most social work research springs from a "felt need" or unresolved problem with relevance for the real world of practice, program design, or policy. The best research combines utility for practice with theoretical or conceptual goals. Second, this area of interest is then systematically explored by reviewing the professional literature in order to learn what has already been done and where the gaps and unanswered questions remain. Third, this review results in a more precise articulation of the specific study aims and assumptions. Fourth, these aims and assumptions must be carefully checked for sexism, racism, and other sources of bias. Fifth, the formal statement of the study question or hypothesis is made, which provides the framework for the specification of the study strategy and methodology in detail. The following chapters describe the kinds of study designs used in social work and human services research in greater detail, including an example of each from the literature. When a study has been artfully formulated, the question and study design cohere seamlessly, whatever the type of study design used.

Part II
Types of Research Designs

This section of the book includes chapters on the most common types of research designs encountered in the literature on social work and the human services and in evaluation research. There are two chapters on flexible methods of research, one on what is usually termed qualitative research, and one on traditional case studies. The chapters on fixed methods of research include descriptive, relational, experimental, and single-subject designs. A reprinted example of each kind of research is included at the end of each chapter so that all parts of the research design can be studied and assessed.

The emphasis of each chapter is on the kinds of research questions each design is best suited for and on the relative strengths and weaknesses of each. These design types set the frameworks within which the details of method—sampling, data collection, and analysis—must fit. Studying the text of each chapter and reading the example will make the various study designs come alive.

3

Flexible Method Research

The term "flexible method research" refers to those flexible methods of systematic, empirical inquiry intended to define, explore, or map the nature of emergent, complex, or poorly understood phenomena. Because flexible method studies typically incorporate the gathering of unstructured data, they are most often termed *qualitative*, but this text defines the type by its methods as a whole, not simply by the unstructured form the data often take. These methods have typically been associated with specific social and psychological theories and epistemologies, and unfortunately they have often been dismissed or diminished by those from alternative perspectives. However, "qualitative" or flexible methods of inquiry are increasingly viewed as having great utility for research in social work and the human services across a variety of theoretical and practice perspectives (Morse & Field 1995; Padgett 1998b; Patton 1990; Riessman 1994; Ruckdeschel 1985; Sherman & Reid 1994). However, even with qualitative research, there are some tensions between research and practice activities and goals (Padgett 1998a).

The usefulness of flexible method research for social work and the social sciences has been widely debated in the social work literature in recent years (Padgett 1998a, 1998b; Reamer 1993; Riessman 1994; Sherman & Reid 1994; Social Work Research 1995; Tyson 1995). As described in chapter 1, fixed method research, including experimental, quasi-experimental, and descriptive designs, have constituted the dominant paradigm in the field at least since the 1950s (Tyson 1992, 1995; Thyer 1993), seemingly in emulation of the natural or "hard" (as opposed to "social") sciences. In an effort to establish the legitimacy of alternatives to fixed method research, the philosophical underpinnings of quantitative research, particularly logical positivism, were attacked as inherently flawed and obsolete in the natural sciences (Heineman 1981; Heineman Pieper 1985; Riessman 1994). Naturalistic, "heuristic," phenomenological, and/or ethnographic methods of research, it was argued, should supplant the dominant fixed methods because they were more concordant with the theories actually used in practice, better suited to the kinds of problems with which social workers are concerned, and better understood by practitioners (Dean & Fenby 1989; Gilgun 1994; Hartman 1990; Heineman 1981; Heineman Pieper 1985, 1989; Riessman 1994; Ruckdeschel 1985; Tyson 1992, 1995).

This debate has done a great service by reopening the profession of social work to additional and clearly valuable research methods that had indeed been undervalued and underutilized. However, opinions about the relationship of flexible to fixed methods differ. Some argue in favor of using a variety of research approaches to be fitted to the particular problems under study and to the philosophical and political worldview of the researcher (Piele 1988). Others find it useful to emphasize the epistemological differences that undergird the two methods and thus heighten the distinctions between them (Heineman Pieper 1985). However, the polarized debate sometimes seems to depend on incomplete knowledge of the paradigms at issue and on overlooking the diversity of approaches within each type, in part because the types themselves have been taken for granted and poorly or variously defined.

Within the framework of fallibilist realism (Manicas & Secord 1983), this book takes a position that may not entirely satisfy proponents of either side of the debate as currently framed: that theory and not the data or methods used to generate it is decisive in explaining reality. Therefore the method of empirical study, flexible or fixed, should be guided solely by the research question at hand and by the assumptions of the theory that underlies it. As a consequence, this point of view claims less for experimental methods than for traditional, especially in relation to the demonstration of causation, and more for flexible method research.

As a framework, fallibilist realism incorporates flexible method research well. Flexible or qualitative methods have traditionally included the researcher and the relationship of the researcher to the researched within the boundary of what is examined. Because all any study can do is approximate knowledge of phenomena as they exist in the real world (fallibilism), the process of study itself must be studied as well. Because all methods of study can produce only approximations of reality and incomplete understanding of the phenomena of interest as they exist in the real world, the findings of flexible method research can be seen as no more or less legitimate than those of any other type of study.

Although ideally the question under study should determine the research method to be used, some researchers are likely to be drawn repeatedly to philosophies, theories, and questions that tend to lead to one kind of inquiry or another. However, flexible methods of research are *not* only appropriate to questions described as "exploratory" or as preliminary to some other, more "definitive" kind of inquiry. Questions and answers deriving from flexible method research can be as conclusive (and inconclusive) as from any fixed method of study. Finally, although flexible method research has tended to be associated with and described in terms of specific theoretical or methodological paradigms (Morse & Field 1995), this book discusses them in a way that is general and applicable in a variety of theoretical contexts.

The Nature of Flexible Method Research

Flexible method research is defined primarily by the nature of the procedures used to gather data and their origins and only secondarily by the type of data gathered, which is typically unstructured. Padgett (1998b) defines it as being characterized by "recursiveness and flexibility" (p. 28). While the purposes of flexible method studies may vary considerably, the emphasis is usually on the discovery of new phenomena or on the redefinition of phenomena in a way that remains close to the experience of the research participants themselves. Sometimes this is done with little predefinition based on existing theory; at other times it is done with theory more explicitly in mind. Methods of inquiry may evolve incrementally in response to the data obtained, and sampling, data collection, and data analysis often proceed together rather than in separate stages. Because the methods are flexible, emphasis is placed on describing and understanding the researcher's participation in and development of the study as well as the participants'.

In flexible method research, unstructured data are used in order to capture the phenomena of interest in the words or actions of those who embody or live them and to capture them in context in terms that are as "experience-near" as possible. For example, Taylor and Bogdan (1984) describe such methods as being about collecting data, "people's own words and behavior," in order to understand on a personal level the meanings, "motives and beliefs behind people's actions" (p. 2). Flexible method research thus clearly depends on inductive processes.

One traditional objection to flexible methods of research has been derived from this reliance on induction. If theories are viewed as distinct from reality, then theories can be "tested" and "proved" or "disproved" when measured against this reality, which can be "objectively" known. In this model, the integrity of the scientific enterprise is protected through subjecting ideas to disproof depending on whether or not the data "fit" them. This is accomplished through a deductive process of "testing" hypotheses, which have been stated *before* data are collected, and collecting data through methods also fixed before data collection is begun. Scientific skepticism is built into the process of disproof. From this perspective, flexible methods may be good for generating ideas or new conceptions, but they are unreliable for other purposes because the conclusions arise *from* the data and are not tested *against* them.

However, this traditional logic depends on a conception of theory and ideas as separable and on an objective reality as perfectly (or perfectibly) knowable apart from the conceptions that define it and the observer(s) who experience it. Fallibilist realism (Manicas & Secord 1983) posits that theory defines and only approximates reality as we know it. It also incorporates the idea that the standpoint and experience of the observer are integral parts of the inevitable fallibility of all observation and knowledge (Manicas 1987). Scientific skepticism must be built into all parts of the research process, including an appreciation of the relative fallibility of all knowledge and all theory from historical, social, and cultural points of view.

From this perspective, flexible method research is no more inherently limited than any other form of scientific inquiry. Neither deduction nor induction has special virtue. Each is a method with potential to add to our imperfect and always evolving understanding of how and why things work the way they do.

Even though flexible and fixed methods of research may be of equal value, they proceed from quite different assumptions and in quite different ways. The "rules of method" for fixed method research are generally more clearly defined than in flexible method research. In fixed method research, all the details of the method of investigation, such as, for example, the sample size, can be specified before actually conducting the study, and any adjustments that must be made for reasons of feasibility are kept to a minimum and regarded as unfortunate deviations from plan. In flexible method research, by contrast, only the broad outlines of the plan may be specified in advance, and the study activities and methods evolve incrementally in response to the findings that emerge gradually from the data (Marshall & Rossman 1989; Morse & Field 1995; Padgett 1998b).

Part of the rationale for the fixed method approach is that adherence to an a priori method reduces the possible intrusion of the researcher's biases into the study methods and results. The rationale given for the flexibility of methods in flexible method designs is similar: that allowing the method to follow *the data* where they lead will minimize the intrusion of the researcher's own preconceptions into the study results. Also necessary, however, is building reflexivity, or self-examination, into the data-gathering process.

Another difference between much flexible and fixed method research lies in the assumptions made about the researcher. Stated in the extreme, fixed method research traditionally assumes that the researcher is an observer, separate from the phenomenon under study, who strives simply to record it in a neutral, unbiased, "objective" fashion. In flexible method research, the researcher traditionally is seen as embedded in and inseparable from the "field" in which both researcher and researched come together, connect, and negotiate purposes and understandings, "cocreating" the interaction and the data. If the researcher is defined as "part of the field," she is part of the data as well, a situation parallel to psychodynamic practice, in which the feelings of both therapist and client are under examination by the therapist (Orange 1995).

This inclusion of the researcher in the research and as a subject of scrutiny and analysis explains part of the appeal of flexible methods on political and conceptual grounds to some feminists (Davis 1986). Both the political assumptions of the research(er) and the power imbalance implicit when one is the "doer" and one is the "done to" should be examined in any research, but many forms of flexible method research seem to invite this scrutiny more explicitly or more frequently than traditional methods do. Similarly, Akbar (1991) states that heuristic and ethnographic research, which "permits the researcher . . . to observe black people where they are and to take on the responsibility of defining what's observed" (p. 720), are the most appropriate methods of empirical research to use in the African American community in the United States. However, other feminists argue that "feminists must be compelled to match modes of inquiry and analysis with the problem at hand" (Allen & Baber 1992:9), the position taken in this book.

One argument made for fixed methods of research is political in nature as well. The professions are increasingly called upon to be accountable to public and private payors, needing to document the effectiveness and efficiency of the services they provide, and the traditional way of providing such accountability has been through quantitative evaluative research on countable service costs and outcomes (Williams & Hopps 1988). There is a growing literature, however, emanating largely from the field of education, that has described the use of qualitative or flexible methods in program evaluation (Denzin & Lincoln 1994; Goetz & LeCompte 1984; Marshall & Rossman 1989; Patton 1990). In fact, the literature on evaluation research has long advocated the use of formative and/or "utilization-focussed" (Patton 1986) evaluation methods, sometimes "qualitative" in nature, used for direct feedback to program managers and personnel, especially at the early stages of program development.

An Example of Flexible Method Research

The Feagin study (1991) of discrimination against Americans of African descent in public places, reprinted at the end of this chapter, is a good example of flexible method research. It treats as problematic recent assertions in the literature that discrimination against all but underclass African Americans is of little contemporary importance.[1] It asks whether or not middle-class African Americans face discrimination in public places, what its effects are, and how they respond to it. The study method flexibly exploits data gathered in a larger study of middle-class African Americans in several cities. The sample was recruited through word of mouth, and intensive interviews were conducted by African American interviewers. There was no initial plan to focus on discrimination in public places. Rather, Feagin reports, "[T]he discussions of that discrimination were volunteered in answer to general questions about barriers to personal goals and coping strategies or in digressions in answers to specific questions on employment, education, and housing" (p. 103). Moving inductively from data to theory, then, this substudy focussed on the concern of respondents about discrimination as it emerged in the field, in the end linking the findings to discrimination as a concept and to theory about discrimination but starting from the participants' volunteered experiences. Feagin's point of view is that "these volunteered responses signal the importance of such events" (p. 103). The study sample was the 37 interviewees who happened to volunteer information about incidents of discrimination in public places.

The analysis of the data in this study illustrates the range of approaches that can be used with unstructured data. Data were analyzed in terms of incidents, not simply by informant. Some aspects of the incidents of discrimination were classified and counted so that percentages could be given of the kinds of sites where the incidents occurred (public accommodation versus street, for example) and of the types of actions and responses to them. These two dimensions could then also be examined together (see tables 1 and 2 in Feagin). Some of the analysis was thus categorical and quantitative.

---

1. Note that Feagin (1991) uses the term "black" in his article. Reflecting recent changes in standard terminology, this text uses the term "African American."

Much of the analysis, however, was concerned with coding responses to discrimination, for example, to reveal in depth the kinds of incidents that occurred and the types of responses made to them. These categories are anchored in extensive quotations from the interview transcripts to illustrate the nature and context of each type of response. The quotations serve to illustrate the concepts, and conceptual framing in the text of the article is used to draw the reader's attention to important aspects of the informants' statements as understood by the researcher. However, the quotations are extensive enough to invite the reader to consider whether or not the conclusions drawn about them are credible.

The Purposes of Flexible Method Research

Traditionally, flexible method research has been used at early or formative stages of research on a given topic, such as in pilot studies. When a phenomenon has been unstudied or poorly defined, traditional and nontraditional views alike recognize that it is impossible to frame specific hypotheses, to find or create quantified or standardized instruments with which to describe the phenomenon, or to define precisely the nature of the population and sample in which it might occur without prior "pilot," or flexible method, study. Exploring the nature of a phenomenon in context and in detail through the use of unstructured data and flexible interviewing and/or observational techniques in small samples, then, seems the only way to proceed. However, these techniques have often been used with the stated assumption that data collected in this way have little value until fed into fixed method research, a point of view that many flexible method researchers explicitly reject.

One purpose of flexible method research, then, is in initial, pilot, or formulative investigations designed to refine our understanding of new or ill-defined phenomena. Such findings may constitute an initial step in developing structured, fixed method techniques for measurement. However, there are many flexible method studies that stand alone and that describe in depth complex psychosocial phenomena in context and in ways that have never been surpassed for accuracy and verisimilitude. Examples of such studies include *All Our Kin,* concerning the "domestic survival strategies" of poor African American urban dwellers (Stack 1974); *Cloak of Competence,* describing the community adaptations of adults formerly institutionalized as mentally retarded (Edgerton 1967); *Number Our Days,* addressing the creation and maintenance of community among elderly Jewish people in Florida (Myerhoff 1978); *The Unkindest Cut,* describing how physicians, surgeons, and other hospital personnel deal with the topic of death (Millman 1977); and *Tell Them Who I Am* (Liebow 1993), which tells about homeless women and how they manage day to day.

The purposes of flexible method studies vary. Part of this variation in purpose or aim may reflect differences in the philosophical, political, and epistemological assumptions that underlie different studies even within the qualitative tradition (Guba & Lincoln 1994; Brun 1997; Drisko 1997; Olesen 1994; Morse & Field 1995). More pragmatically, using Kuhn's (1970) descriptions of the purposes of normal science, a flexible method study may be designed to describe significant facts more completely. What such studies offer are often characterized as "rich," "thick," or "experience-near" depictions of social and psychological phenomena in context. Part of what the Feagin study offers, for example, is detailed description in respondents' own words of what discrimination in public places is like and what respondents describe as the effects on them of these incidents. Such studies may ask questions like "What's going on here?"

A hallmark of flexible method research of this kind is the extent to which observations are made in context. The researcher, the people and phenomena studied, and the inferences made about them are seen as part of an open, interactive, potentially fluid situation. The credibility of the findings of flexible method studies often flows directly from this inclusion of context, of everyday social and psychological complexities, in the picture. Other flexible method studies may reflect the other purposes Kuhn (1970) describes for normal science: for matching observations with theory, describing observations predicted by a theory or paradigm, or the extension and elaboration of theory (or the extension of its application). Part of the Feagin study reflects the use of flexible method research to match observations to theory or to what theory might predict, as in his examination of variation in responses to acts of discrimination by relating them to the site (public versus private) and nature of the incidents themselves. Hence flexible method or qualitative research can serve a full range of purposes, just as fixed method research can.

One well-respected tradition in qualitative or flexible method research in the social sciences, *grounded theory methods,* are explicitly designed for "the discovery of theory from data systematically obtained and analyzed in social research" (Glaser & Strauss 1967:1). Specifically rejecting the idea that "qualitative" methods should be reserved only for "exploratory" functions, Glaser and Strauss (1967) comment on the "purposes and capacities of qualitative (flexible) and quantitative (fixed) methods" as follows: "We believe that *each form of data is useful for both verification and generation of theory*, whatever the primacy of emphasis" (emphasis theirs) (pp. 17–18). They further state: "*In many instances, both forms of data are necessary*—not quantitative used to test qualitative, but both used as supplements, as mutual verification, and, most important for us, as different forms of data on the same subject, which, when compared, will each generate different theory" (p. 18).

The grounded theory method as developed and described by Glaser and Strauss incorporates certain specific features, such as what they term analysis by "the method of constant comparison" and theoretical sampling, including seeking out the "negative case," all designed to bring rigor to the "testing" or verification of theory generated from flexible method data. The theory derived is then illustrated by "characteristic examples of the data" (p. 5). The grounded theory method, therefore, is characterized by entering the field as open as possible to new ideas, or with received ideas that have been shown to be problematical, and then conducting the investigation in such a way as to allow theory to emerge from the data and then "testing" it against additional data as the study proceeds.

It is clear, then, that flexible method research can have different purposes, from exploration and rich description to the generation, extension, and elaboration of theory. The purpose of flexible method research, as with any other type of research, must be clearly stated in the research question, and the specific methods of investigation used in the study must then suit the purpose stated.

In flexible method research, however, where methods can be more variable and where clear prescriptions about how to do things and about what can legitimately be done with data gathered are not available, there is much room for self-deception and unfounded claims. Glaser and Strauss (1967) speak of a common error that they term "exampling":

> A researcher can easily find examples for dreamed-up, speculative, or logically deduced theory after the idea has occurred. But since the idea has not been derived from the example, seldom can the example correct or change it (even if the author is willing), since the example was selectively chosen for its confirming power. Therefore, one receives the image of a proof when there is none, and the theory obtains a richness of detail that it did not earn (p. 5).

The presence of rich data alone is not enough to assert that the connection between data and theory has been convincingly demonstrated. As with fixed method research, attention to the specific methods of a flexible method study provides a safeguard against too-ready acceptance of unwarranted conclusions.

In summary, Eisner (1991) has listed several characteristics of flexible method research. The first is that it tends to be "field focused," often undertaken in the environments where the phenomena of study are found. It is usually nonmanipulative, that is, "naturalistic." The flexible method researcher uses "the self as an instrument," and the results of the research depend a great deal on the researcher's ability to identify the important issues in the setting or in the data, "to see what counts." A third feature is that flexible method studies are "interpretive" in that they try to "account for" what they give an "account of" and they do so in relation to the meanings that "the experience holds for those in the situation studied" (p. 35). As a result, flexible method studies are often characterized by "the use of expressive language and the presence of voice in text" (p. 36). Each of these qualities has its effects on the particular methods used in the elements of the research design.

Methods in Flexible Method Research

One of the hallmarks of flexible method research is that the parts of the research process—sampling, data collection, and data analysis—often do not take place in distinct and sequential steps as they do in fixed method research. The initial research plan may only specify the setting to be tried first or how the first sample member or members will be chosen. Once data collection is ongoing, further sampling and data collection activities may be defined based on what happened initially. Data are often analyzed as soon as they are collected, with the results feeding directly back into the ongoing sampling and data collection processes. In short, decisions about method evolve from the data as the study proceeds, and the parts of the research process are not as distinct from each other in time as in other kinds of research. Nevertheless, it is useful to consider the traditional elements of research design in the traditional order in relation to flexible method research. Such an examination will make clear and concrete the nature of flexible method research and how it differs from fixed methods of inquiry.

Selecting, or Sampling

Because flexible research methods differ so markedly from those used in fixed method research, methods of selecting study participants or occasions of observation and the rationales that underlie them differ as well. First of all, many flexible method studies take place in the field, in the settings in which the events in question or the people of interest are naturally found. Thus the first step in developing or evaluating a sample in flexible method research is often the choice of a study site or of the settings and occasions of observation. LeCompte and Preissle (1993) distinguish between selecting a universe of people, phenomena, or occasions to study and defining, called *sampling,* the subgroups within that universe of interest to include in a study. While sampling methods as they occur in flexible method research are covered in the chapter on sampling as well, a few points useful in evaluating flexible method research studies are discussed here.

Because the nature of the study site often determines who will be studied, it is important to consider how the locus of the research has been chosen. As in all research, convenience to the researcher always plays a role to some degree or another, but within the practical constraints that every research project must face, the point of entree to the worlds of the study participants should be carefully considered. The way the researcher is introduced into the setting, by whom, and for what purposes are all matters that will influence how the various gatekeepers and participants relate to the researcher and thus the nature of the information that will become available to the research. All of these issues—the selection of the study site, the negotiation of entree, and the selection of informants within the setting—must be explicitly set forth so that the reader may evaluate the data obtained in context (Luborsky & Rubinstein 1995).

In the process of gaining access to a study site, it is important to consider carefully the ethical and consent issues that must be negotiated with participants. Levels of assent in ehtnographic research, for example, can range from inviting a researcher into the setting to participants not even knowing or, in rare cases, being deceived about the fact that they are being studied (LeComte & Preissle 1993).

In addition, flexible method research often involves long exposure to people and settings, imposing a degree of scrutiny not often encountered in most fixed method studies. Given the volume and detail of the data obtained about both sites (specific institutions or locations) and participants (individual people) in intensive interviewing or extended observation, issues of identifiability may become quite difficult to manage. Some possible solutions to this problem, such as the alteration of characteristics to "disguise" the identity of informants, can present their own problems of distortion. Clear understandings about the ways such problems will be dealt with in the research must be negotiated with participants when the study is begun (see chapter 9 on ethics in research).

Particularly in observational studies but to some extent in interview studies as well, the role of the researcher will have an impact on the data that become available. What are informants told about the role of the researcher and the purpose of the research? As a temporary participant in the lives of informants, what roles may the researcher be asked or encouraged to take on and how will they affect the researcher's view of the situation? How intrusive will the research be on the setting through the presence of recording devices and the like? It is, of course, essential that these issues be thought through in advance and negotiated openly in the setting. If participants feel alienated, exploited, or demeaned by what the researcher does or does not do as a temporary citizen of the setting, it may not only compromise the present study but make access by future researchers more difficult as well. Eisner (1991) thus refers to the importance of "leaving the site clean" (p. 175) through sensitivity to the role issues that may arise and by addressing openly any problems that might crop up unexpectedly in the course of the research.

As has already been noted, the samples used in flexible method research are often small because of the volume of data that are generated. Because samples are small, they may be relatively homogeneous in nature in order to focus on key characteristics of interest. Thus efficiency in yielding useful data rather than statistical "representativeness" is the issue in sampling design (see chapter 10 on sampling methods). The most effective informants rather than the most typical informants may be sought (LeComte & Preissle 1993). As with all methodological decisions, it is essential that the basis for selection of study participants be carefully and explicitly spelled out in the research design and in the final research report. Only in this way will the reader be able to reach a judgment about the trustworthiness of the results bearing in mind where they came from.

Selma Fraiberg's (1970) classic study of the challenges that blindness imposes on infant development and how they can be overcome illustrates several of these points about sampling well. Her initial sample was exceedingly small— one case—and yet she was careful to seek a case with certain key characteristics and to choose it in an unbiased fashion. She resolved to study the next blind baby born in her community whom physicians had found to be free of any known neurological, medical, or sensory problems. She also chose the site carefully, the baby's home in preference to the more convenient and more controlled setting of an office or laboratory, in order to observe the mother and the child behaving "normally" with each other. Because she was interested in developmental processes, she planned her observations to occur at monthly intervals throughout the first two years of the baby's life, the period she understood theoretically to be critical for development. Theory at the time also linked early development with the emergence of autistic-like behavior, a problem she had seen in some older children blind from birth. This method of planned, partial data collection has been referred to as sampling behavior within the setting and can be a great aid in efficiency of design and data gathering. The sample Fraiberg obtained turned out to be an atypical one in that the mother and infant, while socioeconomically disadvantaged, were an unusually competent pair. However, the study provided rich data on successful adaptation and ego development in blind children and provided much information useful in designing the strategies used in the larger-scale, fixed method studies of blind infants that Fraiberg later conducted.

Flexible method designs undertaken to examine the relationship of observation to theory have samples that must be carefully planned to include variation considered to be theoretically significant. This variation may be planned from the outset or may be built in as the study unfolds and the nature of the relevant dimensions of variation becomes clear. Glaser and Strauss' (1967) concept of theoretical sampling is one well-known example of this idea. In this method, as concepts or hypotheses emerge during data collection, cases that differ in predictable ways from those already studied are deliberately sought out and included in the data collection to "test" the durability and generality of these concepts or hypotheses, which are then discarded, modified, or extended depending upon what the new data show.

Another way that sampling can be used in flexible method studies to examine relationships among variables is in terms of seeking out or studying the *negative case* (LeComte & Preissle 1993; Straus & Corbin 1990). The negative case is an example or sample member that does not seem to fit emerging concepts or theoretical ideas as observed in the majority of sample members. Intensive study of such negative cases may either result in discarding or delimiting initial ideas about the phenomena being studied or in modifying them so that the concepts are made relevant to a greater range of cases and situations. The goal is to emerge with a set of explanatory concepts or a theory that has the power to encompass and explain a range of phenomena efficiently and parsimoniously.

Because of the need to include such variation in samples, flexible method studies designed for theory-building purposes often require larger and more heterogeneous samples than those designed as descriptive. Special care must be taken to include varied, nonconforming, and unusual cases, situations, and settings—as well as more typical ones. Because data collection is usually still extensive and open-ended, such studies can therefore be quite time-consuming to undertake. Nevertheless, compromising on sample size and variation may make it difficult or impossible to distinguish individual differences from systematic ones. In short, as with fixed method designs, the sample in flexible method research must be large enough to represent small, atypical, or "negative" cases, groups, or situations adequately.

Data Collection

As already mentioned, data collection in flexible method studies most frequently involves intensive interviewing and/or observational methods, especially participant observation techniques. Each of these data collection methods is described in some detail in the chapters on interviewing and observation, respectively. This section will identify some more general data collection issues that commonly arise in flexible method research.

Flexible method research, as noted, encompasses a variety of research styles and techniques. One dimension on which data collection strategies may vary is the extent to which the data collection is planned and structured in advance or how much the data gathering itself is planned when already in the setting. Similarly, the areas to look for in the data at the analysis stage may be fairly well articulated in advance or may emerge in quite unexpected ways. Eisner (1991) refers to this as a "prefigured focus" versus an "emergent focus" (p. 176). Often a flexible method study may include both. Without some initial focus to the data gathering, the researcher can easily become overwhelmed with information from the field. However, there is little point to immersing oneself in observational or interview data if one is not prepared to be open to novel themes or perspectives as they emerge.

A major challenge in data collection for flexible method research lies in how to record, organize, and retrieve the data. In interviewing, audiotape recording is the method most often used and is extremely useful for capturing verbal data, including not just words but tone of voice, pace of speech, and the like, as well. As long as the equipment is functioning well, a useful, if cumbersome record is obtained. Now that small recorders are available, the equipment is convenient to use and unobtrusive in the setting. Needless to say, permission must be sought from research participants for all aspects of their involvement, including how any data obtained from them will be recorded. Videotaping may also be used in observational studies to great effect, especially in the study of interpersonal interactions and the nonverbal components of interactions.

Although videotapes and audiotapes provide accurate records of the events that they are focussed on, they present certain potential hazards. Researchers who use these recording techniques must be mindful of the risks they present of identification of settings and participants. If portions of videotapes are to be used in presenting research results, participants' consent to this procedure must be obtained. Precisely because they are considered such accurate recording methods, portions of audio- or videotapes may be viewed quite uncritically, and statements and events thus portrayed out of context can wittingly or unwittingly convey a quite distorted view of events as well, which may not be questioned. When in doubt, therefore, longer rather than shorter chunks of data should be recorded and displayed. Finally, if care is not taken in the accurate transcription of tapes, accuracy can be severely compromised (Poland 1995).

Ethnographic research traditions have traditionally employed field notes as the major method of recording observational and interview data. These extensive written notes, carefully labeled as to date, time, and situation of the data collection and recording process, are always prepared as close in time as possible to the observations themselves. Methods of making field notes are discussed in the ethnographic literature and learned via apprenticeship to experienced field researchers. These field notes may consist only of the data themselves when recording on site is impossible, or they may include or consist only of the researcher's reflections on the data collected. Even in this era of electronic recording methods, written field notes, diaries, or memoranda are still employed by many flexible method researchers to record the researcher's impressions, thoughts, and reactions to the data collection process and on emerging findings as the data gathering proceeds. What may seem vivid on the day of a particular encounter will fade in memory, and the thoughts, questions, and reflections of the researcher during or after the fact will otherwise find no place in the permanent record of the research. These records, if systematically kept, can be considered analyzable data in their own right or, at the very least, are a useful supplement to the data analysis process when codes are being developed and interpretations of the data sought.

It should be noted that these methods of data collection—participant observation, intensive interviewing, and the like—are extremely expensive, both costly in the amount of time they require and in the travel they often entail. Some of the methods of recording the data used—audio- and videotape recording—can be quite expensive as well. When economics are going to limit the amount or nature of the data collected, it is best to face this limitation squarely at the outset and to craft the best and most cost-effective plan possible rather than to run the risk of a truncated and compromised data collection or recording process when time or money run out in the middle of a project.

Data collection in flexible method research undertaken for the extension and elaboration of theory is really no different from other flexible method studies that concentrate most on description. However, to the extent that working hypotheses about the findings may exist at the beginning of the study or may emerge during it, special care must be taken to elicit the data needed on the one hand but not unwittingly guide the data gathering in some preconceived direction on the other.

There are two common mistakes made in gathering data in flexible method research. The first is allowing one's initial ideas to color the conversation so completely that only leading questions are asked, only confirmatory ideas are "heard" and elicited from the participants, and disconfirming ideas or behaviors are "missed," not explored or pursued, or "explained away" when they do emerge. In examining the relationship between theory and data, it is important to consider what other factors may explain an apparent relationship or may provide an alternate view of the phenomenon of interest. It is necessary to conduct all data gathering activities in such a way as to allow both hypothesized and alternative ideas to emerge. The long immersion of the researcher in the research and the shaping of later data collection by earlier observations, both characteristic of flexible method research, may make this a more common hazard.

A second common mistake, however, is in fact the reverse of the first: to fail to ask directly enough about the issues under study and about what study participants view as the relevant explanations of events or issues. Behavior may occur for reasons different from the ones people assign to it, and people genuinely may not be conscious of or willing to admit to all their reasons for behaving as they do. In short, not all "causes" of behavior are subjectively experienced as such. However, it is usually a mistake not to inquire as to what the "causes," understandings, or explanations that people assign to their behavior are. Such questions can seem intrusive or risky to ask, but the failure to do so when possible or relevant can seriously weaken the credibility of flexible method studies.

Data Analysis

As in all parts of the research process, the rules for data analysis in flexible method designs seem much less "cut and dried" than in fixed method or statistical analysis. The goal of "qualitative" or flexible method analysis has been described by Eisner (1991) as "making the case palpable," which means presenting carefully chosen excerpts from the data verbatim in order to ground concepts and results in the words of the research participants themselves. While a whole chapter of this book has been devoted to the analysis of narrative or unstructured data, this section will discuss a few key points about the process that are important to consider as a project is being designed. As with fixed method studies, it is essential that the data analysis process be anticipated and planned for from the beginning of the study. In fact, one of the hallmarks of flexible method research designs is that sampling, data collection, and data analysis processes and activities may overlap or be simultaneously ongoing. Considering data analysis as an afterthought will predictably lead to problems in any research design but especially in a flexible method study.

One of the decisions that must be faced in an analytic process is whether or not to go to the expense of preparing written transcripts of all the audio- and videotaped data. Because the most obvious challenge that any flexible method researcher will face is managing the sheer volume of data generated, transcripts have many advantages. One can scan large amounts of data rapidly by eye. One can reference transcribed data by line or by page and is not confined to sequential access as on audiotape. Finally, once transcribed, the data are in a form that allows accurate and direct use of the material in the text of the final report of the project.

However, there are also drawbacks to using transcripts. It must be remembered that a written transcript normally records only words, and, while there are conventions for recording interjections, pauses, and the like, in text, elements of sound and of nonverbal behavior are not completely captured. Context may be lost as well, which can lead to confusion or misconception about the content of what was said or meant. Certainly when transcriptions are made they must include all of what has gone on—all speakers in the situation, interviewer and interviewee—as a matter of simple accuracy and interpretability. To do less than that may give the appearance of accuracy in the data without its substance.

Because of the volume of data present, a major goal of the analytic process, in addition to extracting meaning from the data, is simply to permit efficient access to and retrieval of specific data. In the context of the analysis of quantitative data, this function is termed *data management*. Data management is essential in analyzing unstructured data as well. Each piece of data must be catalogued in such a way that it is not directly identifiable but that it can be interpreted in relation to its source and the situation from which it came. Ways to identify, store, and examine data with similar content from different sources or situations must be developed by means of a manual or electronic filing system. The use of computers to aid in this process, either with word processing programs or programs specialized for the analysis of unstructured data, is discussed in chapter 19, on working with computers.

The essence of the analysis of data in flexible method research is the extraction or assignment of meaning to the data in the record. In a verbal transcript, what unit of data will be studied—the word, the phrase, the line, or the "chunk," defined by content or theme? In a visual record, will the analysis be by frame, time segment, or some other unit? Will the verbal or visual record be sampled or used in its entirety? What concepts will be applied in the analysis? What concepts may be uncovered inductively from the materials? How can they be verified during the analytic process? This process of assigning meaning to units of data is termed *coding* and is at the heart of the process of analyzing unstructured data. Many of these techniques for coding and handling data are discussed in some detail in chapter 16, on the analysis of narrative data.

There are a few principles of data analysis that pertain in particular to flexible method studies with theory-building purposes that deserve mention here for emphasis. Because of its seemingly unstructured nature, the analysis of data from flexible method studies may present some of the same challenges to researcher skepticism that data collection does (Bunin et al. 1983). Keeping logs, writing memos, or using other forms of written self-reflection are techniques often suggested for control of researcher bias during all parts of the research process, including data analysis (Strauss & Corbin 1990; Padgett 1998b).

Preconceived or emergent ideas about relationships among variables can color an analysis of unstructured data to the extent that disconfirming data are ignored, omitted, or "explained away" as the result of invalid measurement or for some other reason. Anchoring the relationships found among variables in examples drawn from the data is, as in all analysis of unstructured data, essential, but disconfirming evidence may be omitted or competing theories and ideas never addressed. The reader, of course, may never know what data have been suppressed, but a reader will be able to discern when competing theories and ideas are left out of the description and discussion of the possible meanings of results. The effect of such omissions is that the reader loses confidence in the researcher as a reliable guide to the data and its meanings, on which the credibility of reported results rests.

How are relationships among phenomena expressed when working with unstructured data? Sometimes unstructured data are converted to quantitative form, and statistical techniques for examining group differences or correlations, often nonparametric ones for small samples (Siegel & Castellan 1988), can then be employed. In other instances, whole sets of variables seem to vary together across cases in such a way that distinct *typologies* or subsets of cases can be described. For example, Dudley's (1989) study of how residential program administrators manage relationships with neighborhood residents illustrates this approach. Using the grounded theory method of Glaser and Strauss (1967), the author sought to discern "patterns in the perspectives and approaches of the administrators" (Dudley 1989:99). Based initially on how administrators responded to complaints from neighbors, the author identified two types of approaches into which all but two of those interviews fit: those who took a "bend over backwards" approach, in which "staff and clients were expected to go out of their way" to accommodate their neighbors, and those who took a "middle of the road" approach, that didn't involve "jump[ing] through a hoop for neighbors" (Dudley 1989:102). These stances towards complaints were also reflected in such areas studied as how programs responded proactively to neighborhood norms and development and initiation of closer ties with the neighborhood.

Reliability and Validity in Flexible Method Research

Because flexible method studies employ, by definition, flexible research designs and are naturalistic in technique and philosophy, the approaches used to assess reliability and validity in fixed method designs cannot be applied in the same way to flexible method studies. In addition, the range of flexible research methods encountered in the various disciplines that use them, from anthropological ethnography to clinical case studies, may appear to have little in common. It has therefore been difficult to articulate a unitary set of methods for flexible method research that can be accepted as an ideal type or set of standards that can be applied in evaluating all flexible method studies. Sometimes, therefore, the term *trustworthiness* is used instead when the credibility of findings in flexible method research is discussed (Padgett 1998b).

Goetz and LeCompte (1984) have argued that the same terms of evaluation used in fixed method designs—*reliability* and *validity*—can be interpreted and applied to ethnographic (and other flexible method) research. Reliability refers to the consistency (or replicability) with which observations are made. Validity refers to both the consistency with which theories (or concepts) and observations are linked to each other and the value of the theory generated from the results, most especially what the results mean and to what extent and under what conditions the explanations offered for the study results will be seen as credible.

On the face of it, these issues would seem relevant to the evaluation of any study. Considerable translation must occur, however, in order to reframe any traditional discussion of reliability and validity, which has been articulated with fixed method designs, especially experiments, in mind, in a way that makes sense in relation to the aims and techniques of flexible method research (Strauss & Corbin 1990). Adding to the difficulty is the fact that the term "validity" is traditionally applied to both data collection issues (see chapter 11) and research results as a whole, especially when "cause-and-effect" arguments are made from them.

Flexible method research does not rely primarily on *manipulation* for examining changes in phenomena the way experiments do. Hence discussion of the validity of designs in flexible method research need not parallel the analysis of validity in experiments as Campbell and Stanley (1963) have classically framed it. Flexible method studies may incorporate small "experiments" or activities of the researcher in the field consciously designed to test out a reaction, like the approach of Fraiberg (1970) to the crib of the blind baby, who did not smile at the sound of her voice as she had done for her mother. These maneuvers, which are core to experimental designs, are not usually core to the purpose of a flexible method study. They are usually done only to verify a particular observation and its interpretation, not as the manipulation of the major variable under study, upon which the entire logic of the research depends.

Reliability

Like Heraclitus, for whom the river was never the same twice, the flexible method researcher may feel that it is impossible for anyone to step into the same complex social or psychological investigation and identify identical phenomena again. Flexible method research thus makes obvious what is in fact a problem for all research: that findings are a product of a particular historical moment and encounter, both empirically and theoretically. However, when designs are fluid and procedures thus not routinized, replication of observation, key to traditional notions of reliability, may seem impossible to effect.

There are several things a researcher can do, however, to make a potential replication more likely to succeed and to strengthen the veracity of the findings given. These procedures have to do with making the situation under which the results were obtained as clear as possible and checking out whether or not any other observers in the same research situation agree about what was observed. In fact, many of the methodological guidelines for flexible method research given above ultimately are designed to enhance either the reliability or validity of the results achieved.

Goetz and LeCompte (1984) name several strategies commonly used by ethnographers to reduce threats to reliability in measurement or to enhance potential interobserver agreement. These include use of "low-inference descriptors" (p. 218), multiple researchers, participant assistance in the research, and mechanically recorded data. Padgett (1998b) mentions such strategies as prolonged engagement, or the lengthy contact between researcher and participants that is often characteristic of flexible method research. This contact often affords the opportunity to make repeated observations of the same or similar phenomena. *Triangulation,* or obtaining data about a phenomenon using more than one data collection method, such as through observation and interview, also enhances reliability.

It is rare to find that all of these strategies for enhancing reliability can be used in any one flexible method study. However, each can add to the extent to which the observations made are or potentially would be considered accurate and reliable.

Validity

While the reliability of ethnographic and other forms of flexible method research is often questioned, the validity of flexible method research results is widely assumed to be strong. To the extent that the data and their interpretation are low inference, the validity of the data appears clear. Some strategies that enhance reliability also enhance validity, such as long and intimate contact with study informants often in their usual settings and in everyday situations. Direct reliance on the words and ideas of the participants themselves, and "researcher self-monitoring" in the form of a "disciplined subjectivity . . . that exposes all phases of the research activity to continual questioning and reevaluation" are also factors that enhance the credibility of the conclusions drawn (Goetz & LeCompte 1994:221).

Whether or not the results of a flexible method study are valid in the sense that they might be verified in a different or subsequent study depends on making explicit the general methods and assumptions that have informed the research (Drisko 1997; Padgett 1998b). If replications later produce different results, the basis for the difference may be understood by comparing the situations and procedures that undergirded each work. These methodological choices and assumptions include the status position from which the researcher entered the field, the role(s) assumed, and the understanding participants had of this; how informants were chosen and why; the social context in which the data were gathered; the analytic constructs and premises with which the researcher went into the field; and the methods of data collection and analysis used. Except for the explicit attention given to the researcher's role in the research endeavor, which is rarely considered anything but neutral in fixed method designs, these dimensions are not much different from what a fixed method researcher must explain to make a study replicable and its observations interpretable.

Perhaps the greatest threat to validity in flexible method research arises from what has been termed in other contexts "observer effects." Participant observation and intensive interviewing have the potential to stimulate a great deal of responsiveness in participants. Although informant accounts are what they are, they should not necessarily be accepted uncritically, although if enough time is spent in the field or enough interviews are conducted, corroboration or discrepant accounts of events can usually be obtained. It is important not to dismiss or discount contradictory or discrepant information as invalid or unreliable; rather the goal should be to develop an understanding of the situation and the informants sufficient to explain all the data obtained and all the versions given, as in studying "the negative case."

The greater threat to the validity of results, however, may rest in the observer or researcher. Participant observation and intensive interviewing have the potential to stimulate a great deal of reaction in the researcher. As Goetz and LeCompte state, "researchers must guard the instruments they use and the constructs they create from their own ethnocentrism and perceptual biases" (p. 226). Biases may arise as well from the scientific and/or disciplinary training of the researcher. For instance, the problem of "exampling" (Glaser & Strauss 1967), described earlier in the chapter, occurs when data are fitted to an observer's preconception rather than concepts being let to rise from the data themselves, giving the appearance but not the reality of validity.

Participant reaction to and confirmation of observations, concepts, and conclusions drawn, termed "member checking" (Padgett 1998b), may be the best safeguard against such distortion. But there is always the risk of the researcher uncritically adopting a particular perspective, perhaps one that is self-serving, happens to agree with the researcher's own, or which informants wish to advance (Padgett 1998b). For this problem, the review of peers and colleagues, which is part and parcel of all research endeavors, may be the best preventive measure. Thus at the center of any discussion of the validity of flexible method research is the researcher, whose subjective experience can be both the greatest asset and the greatest liability to the credibility of results. Also, the creation of an *audit trail,* or record of the research procedures used, including researcher memos and field notes, which another researcher could potentially examine, is another important safeguard in controlling researcher bias (Padgett 1998b).

Of course, a problem that affects both fixed and flexible method studies alike is that studied samples may differ from others just because of being observed. Participant observation and intensive interviewing are indeed reactive data gathering methods, although long and/or intensive involvement in the field of study may offer some opportunities to "check out" what effects of study may be occurring with the participants themselves. In the end, the credibility of the findings from flexible method studies rests on both the quality and veracity of the data obtained and the theoretical understandings and explanations offered for them. Their conclusions, of course, are ultimately judged the way any study is: by how they hold up in the eyes of the scientifically skeptical and informed reader.

Summary

Flexible method research is enjoying a revival in social work and in the social sciences as an outgrowth of critiques of traditional ways of understanding knowledge and how it is generated. Flexible method research is aimed at generating in-depth understandings of people and events in context and as they naturally develop and occur. Both the findings of such research and the methods of investigation are often described as being generated inductively, moving from observation to concept, although theory may guide flexible method studies as well. In fact, flexible method studies are quite varied in purpose and approach. The researcher is often immersed in the observational context, and the researcher and the methods of study themselves are part of what is studied and observed. As these methods of study become more widely used and appreciated, it will be possible to define a continuum of subtypes within the method, as is currently done for fixed method designs, which are discussed in chapters 5 through 8. Because of its historical and present importance, however, the traditional case study, understood as a particular form of flexible method research, is discussed in depth in the next chapter.

THE CONTINUING SIGNIFICANCE OF RACE: ANTIBLACK DISCRIMINATION IN PUBLIC PLACES[*]

JOE R. FEAGIN
University of Florida

Much literature on contemporary U.S. racial relations tends to view black middle-class life as substantially free of traditional discrimination. Drawing primarily on 37 in-depth interviews with black middle-class respondents in several cities, I analyze public accommodations and other public-place discrimination. I focus on three aspects: (1) the sites of discrimination; (2) the character of discriminatory actions; and (3) the range of coping responses by blacks to discrimination. Documenting substantial barriers facing middle-class black Americans today, I suggest the importance of the individual's and the group's accumulated discriminatory experiences for understanding the character and impact of modern racial discrimination.

Title II of the 1964 Civil Rights Act stipulates that "all persons shall be entitled to the full and equal enjoyment of the goods, services, facilities, privileges, advantages, and accommodations of any place of public accommodation . . . without discrimination or segregation on the ground of race, color, religion, or national origin." The public places emphasized in the act are restaurants, hotels, and motels, although racial discrimination occurs in many other public places. Those black Americans who would make the greatest use of these public accommodations and certain other public places would be middle-class, i.e., those with the requisite resources.

White public opinion and many scholars have accented the great progress against traditional discrimination recently made by the black middle class. A National Research Council report on black Americans noted that by the mid-1970s many Americans "believed

that . . . the Civil Rights Act of 1964 had led to broad-scale elimination of discrimination against blacks in public accommodations" (Jaynes and Williams 1989, p. 84). In interviews with whites in the late 1970s and early 1980s, Blauner (1989, p. 197) found that all but one viewed the 1970s as an era of great racial progress for American race relations. With some exceptions (see Willie 1983; Collins 1983; Landry 1987), much recent analysis of middle-class blacks by social scientists has emphasized the massive progress made since 1964 in areas where there had been substantial barriers, including public accommodations. Racial discrimination as a continuing and major problem for middle-class blacks has been downplayed as analysts have turned to the various problems of the "underclass." For example, Wilson (1978:110–11) has argued that the growth of the black middle class since the 1960s is the result of improving economic conditions and of government civil rights laws, which virtually eliminated overt discrimination in the workplace and public accommodations. According to Wilson, the major problem of the 1964 Civil Rights Act is its failure to meet the problems of the black underclass (Wilson 1987:146–47).

Here I treat these assertions as problematic. Do middle-class black Americans still face hostile treatment in public accommodations and other public places? If so, what form does this discrimination take? Who are the perpetrators of this discrimination? What is the

---

* Direct all correspondence to Joe R. Feagin, Department of Sociology, University of Florida, Gainesville, FL 32611. I am indebted to Melvin Sikes, Nijole Benokraitis, John Goering, Christine Williams, Janice Allen-Kelsey, Raphael Allen, Charles Tilly, John Butler, Nestor Rodriguez, Sharon Collins, Tony Orum, and Suzanne Harper for their insightful comments on earlier drafts of this manuscript, and to Nijole Benokraitis, Beth Anne Shelton, Bob Parker, Diane Smith, Robert Adams, Yanick Crosse, Bob Bullard, Charles Shepherd, Brenda Shepherd, Wilmer Roberts, Megan Pulliam, and Leslie Inniss for interviewing and research assistance. The Hogg Foundation for Mental Health provided partial support for this research.

impact of the discrimination on its middle-class victims? How do middle-class blacks cope with such discrimination?

ASPECTS OF DISCRIMINATION

Discrimination can be defined in social-contextual terms as "actions or practices carried out by members of dominant racial or ethnic groups that have a differential and negative impact on members of subordinate racial and ethnic groups" (Feagin and Eckberg 1980, pp. 1–2). This differential treatment ranges from the blatant to the subtle (Feagin and Feagin 1986). Here I focus primarily on blatant discrimination by white Americans targeting middle-class blacks. Historically, discrimination against blacks has been one of the most serious forms of racial/ethnic discrimination in the United States and one of the most difficult to overcome, in part because of the institutionalized character of color coding. I focus on three important aspects of discrimination: (1) the variation in sites of discrimination; (2) the range of discriminatory actions; and (3) the range of responses by blacks to discrimination.

Sites of Discrimination

There is a spatial dimension to discrimination. The probability of experiencing racial hostility varies from the most private to the most public sites. If a black person is in a relatively protected site, such as with friends at home, the probability of experiencing hostility and discrimination is low. The probability increases as one moves from friendship settings to such outside sites as the workplace, where a black person typically has contacts with both acquaintances and strangers, providing an interactive context with greater potential for discrimination.

In most workplaces, middle-class status and its organizational resources provide some protection against certain categories of discrimination. This protection probably weakens as a black person moves from those work and school settings where he or she is well-known into public accommodations such as large

stores and city restaurants where contacts are mainly with white strangers. On public streets blacks have the greatest public exposure to strangers and the least protection against overt discriminatory behavior, including violence. A key feature of these more public settings is that they often involve contacts with white strangers who react primarily on the basis of one ascribed characteristic. The study of the micro-life of interaction between strangers in public was pioneered by Goffman (1963; 1971) and his students, but few of their analyses have treated hostile discriminatory interaction in public places. A rare exception is the research by Gardner (1980; see also Gardner 1988), who documented the character and danger of passing remarks by men directed against women in unprotected public places. Gardner writes of women (and blacks) as "open persons," i.e., particularly vulnerable targets for harassment that violates the rules of public courtesy.

The Range of Discriminatory Actions

In his classic study, *The Nature of Prejudice,* Allport (1958, pp. 14–5) noted that prejudice can be expressed in a series of progressively more serious actions, ranging from antilocution to avoidance, exclusion, physical attack, and extermination. Allport's work suggests a continuum of actions from avoidance, to exclusion of rejection, to attack. In his travels in the South in the 1950s a white journalist who changed his skin color to black encountered discrimination in each of these categories (Griffin 1961). In my data, discrimination against middle-class blacks still ranges across this continuum: (1) avoidance actions, such as a while couple crossing the street when a black male approaches: (2) rejection actions, such as poor service in public accommodations; (3) verbal attacks, such as shouting racial epithets in the street; (4) physical threats and harassment by white police officers; and (5) physical threats and attacks by other whites, such as attacks by white supremacists in the street. Changing relations between blacks and whites in recent decades have expanded the repertoire of discrimination to include more subtle forms and to encompass discrimination in arenas from which blacks were formerly excluded, such as formerly all-white public accommodations.

Black Responses to Discrimination

Prior to societal desegregation in the 1960s much traditional discrimination, especially in the South, took the form of an asymmetrical "deference ritual" in which blacks were typically expected to respond to discriminating whites with great deference. According to Goffman (1956, p. 477) a deference ritual "functions as a symbolic means by which appreciation is regularly conveyed to a recipient." Such rituals can be seen in the obsequious words and gestures—the etiquette of race relations—that many blacks, including middle-class blacks, were forced to utilize to survive the rigors of segregation (Doyle 1937). However, not all responses in this period were deferential. From the late 1800s to the 1950s, numerous lynchings and other violence targeted blacks whose behavior was defined as too aggressive (Raper 1933). Blauner's (1989) respondents reported acquaintances reacting aggressively to discrimination prior to the 1960s.

Deference rituals can still be found today between some lower-income blacks and their white employers. In her northeastern study Rollins (1985, p. 157) found black maids regularly deferring to white employers. Today, most discriminatory interaction no longer involves much asymmetrical deference, at least for middle-class blacks. Even where whites expect substantial deference, most middle-class blacks do not oblige. For middle-class blacks contemporary discrimination has evolved beyond the asymmettical deference rituals and "No Negroes served" type of exclusion to patterns of black-contested discrimination. Discussing race and gender discrimination in Great Britain, Brittan and Maynard (1984) have suggested that today "the terms of oppression are not only dictated by history, culture, and the sexual and social division of labor. They are also profoundly shaped at the site of the oppression, and by the way in which oppressors and oppressed continuously have to renegotiate, reconstruct, and re-establish their relative positions in respect to benefits and power" (p. 7). Similarly, white mistreatment of black Americans today frequently encounters new coping strategies by blacks in the ongoing process of reconstructing patterns of racial interaction.

Middle-class strategies for coping with discrimination range from careful assessment to withdrawal, resigned acceptance, verbal confrontation, or physical confrontation. Later action might include a court suit. Assessing the situation is a first step. Some white observers have suggested that many middle-class blacks are paranoid about white discrimination and rush too quickly to charges of racism (Wieseltier 1989, June 5; for male views of female "paranoia" see Gardner 1988). But the daily reality may be just the opposite, as middle-class black Americans often evaluate a situation carefully before judging it discriminatory and taking additional action. This careful evaluation, based on past experiences (real or vicarious), not only prevents jumping to conclusions, but also reflects the hope that white behavior is not based on race, because an act not based on race is easier to endure. After evaluation one strategy is to leave the site of discrimination rather than to create a disturbance. Another is to ignore the discrimination and continue with the interaction, a "blocking" strategy similar to that Gardner (1980, p. 345) reported for women dealing with street remarks. In many situations resigned acceptance is the only realistic response. More confrontational responses to white actions include verbal reprimands and sarcasm, physical counterattacks, and filing lawsuits. Several strategies may be tried in any given discriminatory situation. In crafting these strategies middle-class blacks, in comparison with less privileged blacks, may draw on middle-class resources to fight discrimination.

THE RESEARCH STUDY

To examine discrimination, I draw primarily on 37 in-depth interviews from a larger study of 135 middle-class black Americans in

Boston, Buffalo, Baltimore, Washington, D.C., Detroit, Houston, Dallas, Austin, San Antonio, Marshall, Las Vegas, and Los Angeles. The interviewing was done in 1988–1990; black interviewers were used. I began with respondents known as members of the black middle class to knowledgeable consultants in key cities. Snowball sampling from these multiple starting points was used to maximize diversity.

The questions in the research instrument were primarily designed to elicit detailed information on the general situations of the respondents and on the barriers encountered and managed in employment, education, and housing. There were no specific questions in the interview schedule on public accommodations or other public-place discrimination; the discussions of that discrimination were volunteered in answer to general questions about barriers to personal goals and coping strategies or in digressions in answers to specific questions on employment, education, and housing. These volunteered responses signal the importance of such events. While I report below mainly on the responses of the 37 respondents who detailed specific incidents of public discrimination, in interpreting the character and meaning of modern discrimination I also draw on some discussions in the larger sample of 135 interviews and in five supplementary and follow-up interviews of middle-class blacks conducted by the author and two black consultants.

"Middle class" was defined broadly as those holding a white-collar job (including those in professional, managerial, and clerical jobs), college students preparing for white-collar jobs, and owners of successful businesses. This definition is consistent with recent analyses of the black middle class (Landry 1987). The subsample of 37 middle-class blacks reporting public discrimination is fairly representative of the demographic character of the larger sample. The subsample's occupational distribution is broadly similar to the larger sample and includes nine corporate managers and executives, nine health care or other professionals, eight government officials, four college students, three journalists or broadcasters, two clerical or sales workers, one entre-

preneur, and one retired person. The subsample is somewhat younger than the overall sample, with 35 percent under age 35 vs. 25 percent in the larger sample, 52 percent in the 35–50 bracket vs. 57 percent, and 11 percent over 50 years of age vs. 18 percent. The subsample is broadly comparable to the larger sample in income: 14 had incomes under $36,000, seven in the $36,000–55,000 range, and 16 in the $56,000 or more range. All respondents had at least a high school degree, and more than 90 percent had some college work. The subsample has a somewhat lower percentage of people with graduate work: 39 percent vs. 50 percent for the larger sample. Both samples have roughly equal proportions of men and women, and more than sixty percent of both samples reported residing in cities in the South or Southwest—37 percent of the overall sample and 34 percent of the subsample resided in the North or West.

DESCRIPTIVE PATTERNS

Among the 37 people in the subsample reporting specific instances of public-place discrimination, 24 reported 25 incidents involving public accommodations discrimination, and 15 reported 27 incidents involving street discrimination. Some incidents included more than one important discriminatory action; the 52 incidents consisted of 62 distinguishable actions. The distribution of these 62 actions by broad type is shown in Table 1.

Although all types of mistreatment are reported, there is a strong relationship between type of discrimination and site, with rejection/poor-service discrimination being most common in public accommodations and verbal or physical threat discrimination by white citizens or police officers most likely in the street.

The reactions of these middle-class blacks reflect the site and type of discrimination. The important steps taken beyond careful assessments of the situation are shown in Table 2. (A dual response is recorded for one accommodations incident.)

The most common black responses to racial hostility in the street are withdrawal or a verbal reply. In many avoidance situations

Table 1. Percentage Distribution of Discriminatory Actions By Type and Site: Middle-class Blacks in Selected Cities, 1988–1990

Type of Discriminatory Action	Site of Discriminatory Action	
	Public Accommodations	Street
Avoidance	3	7
Rejection/poor service	79	4
Verbal epithets	12	25
Police threats/harassment	3	46
Other threats/harassment	3	18
Total	100	100
Number of actions	34	28

Table 2. Percentage Distribution of Primary Responses to Discriminatory Incidents by Type and Site: Middle-Class Blacks in Selected Cities, 1988–1990

Response to Discriminatory Incident	Site of Discriminatory Incident	
	Public Accommodations	Street
Withdrawal/exit	4	22
Resigned acceptance	23	7
Verbal response	69	59
Physical counterattack	4	7
Response unclear	—	4
Total	100	99
Number of responses	26	27

(e.g., a white couple crossing a street to avoid walking past a black college student) or attack situations (e.g., whites throwing beer cans from a passing car), a verbal response is difficult because of the danger or the fleeting character of the hostility. A black victim often withdraws, endures this treatment with resigned acceptance, or replies with a quick verbal retort. In the case of police harassment, the response is limited by the danger, and resigned acceptance or mild verbal protests are likely responses. Rejection (poor service) in public accommodations provides an opportunity to fight back verbally—the most common responses to public accommodations discrimination are verbal counterattacks or resigned acceptance. Some black victims correct whites quietly, while others respond aggressively and lecture the assailant about the discrimination or threaten court action. A few retaliate physically. Examining materials in these 37 interviews and those in the larger sample, we will see that the depth and complexity of contemporary black middle-class responses to white discrimination accents the changing character of white-black interaction and the necessity of continual negotiation of the terms of that interaction.

RESPONSES TO DISCRIMINATION: PUBLIC ACCOMMODATIONS

Two Fundamental Strategies: Verbal Confrontation and Withdrawal

In the following account, a black news director at a major television station shows the interwoven character of discriminatory action and black response. The discrimination took the form of poor restaurant service, and the responses included both suggested withdrawal and verbal counterattack.

> He [her boyfriend] was waiting to be seated. . . .He said, "You go to the bathroom and I'll get the table. . . . " He was standing there when I came back: he continued to stand there. The restaurant was almost empty. There were waiters, waitresses, and no one seated. And when I got back to him, he was ready to leave, and said, "Let's go." I said, "What happened to our table?" He wasn't seated. So I said. "No. we're not leaving, please." And he said. "No, I'm leaving." So we went outside, and we talked about it. And what I said to him was, you have to be aware of the possibilities that this is not the first time that this has happened at this restaurant or at other restaurants. but this is the first time it has happened to a black news director here or someone who could make an issue of it, or someone who is prepared to make an issue of it.
>
> So we went back inside after I talked him into it and, to make a long story short, I had the manager come. I made most of the people who were there (while conducting myself professionally the whole time) aware that I was incensed at being treated this way. . . .I said, "Why do you think we weren't seated?" And the manager said, "Well, I don't really know." And I said, "Guess." He said, "Well I don't know, because you're black?" I said. "Bingo. Now isn't it funny that you didn't guess that I didn't have any money" (and I opened up my purse) and I said, "because I certainly have money. And isn't it odd that you didn't guess that it's because I couldn't pay for it because I've got two American Express cards and a Master Card right here. I think it's just funny that you would have assumed that it's because I'm black." . . .And then I took out my card and gave it to him and said, "If this happens again, or if I hear of this happening again, I will bring the full wrath of an entire news department down on this restaurant." And he just kind of looked at me. "Not [just] because I am personally offended. I am. But because you have no right to do what you did, and as a people we have lived a long time with having our rights abridged. . . ." There were probably three or four sets of diners in the restaurant and maybe five waiters/waitresses. They watched him standing there waiting to be seated. His reaction

to it was that he wanted to leave. I understood why he would have reacted that way, because he felt that he was in no condition to be civil. He was ready to take the place apart and . . . sometimes it's appropriate to behave that way. We hadn't gone the first step before going on to the next step. He didn't feel that he could comfortably and calmly take the first step, and I did. So I just asked him to please get back in the restaurant with me, and then you don't have to say a word, and let me handle it from there. It took some convincing, but I had to appeal to his sense of, this is not just you, this is not just for you. We are finally in a position as black people where there are some of us who can genuinely get their attention. And if they don't want to do this because it's right for them to do it, then they'd better do it because they're afraid to do otherwise. If it's fear, then fine, instill the fear.

This example provides insight into the character of modern discrimination. The discrimination was not the "No Negroes" exclusion of the recent past, but rejection in the form of poor service by restaurant personnel. The black response indicates the change in black-white interaction since the 1950s and 1960s, for discrimination is handled with vigorous confrontation rather than deference. The aggressive black response and the white backtracking underscore Brittan and Maynard's (1984, p. 7) point that black-white interaction today is being renegotiated. It is possible that the white personnel defined the couple as "poor blacks" because of their jeans, although the jeans were fashionable and white patrons wear jeans. In comments not quoted here the news director rejects such an explanation. She forcefully articulates a theory of rights—a response that signals the critical impact of civil rights laws on the thinking of middle-class blacks. The news director articulates the American dream: she has worked hard, earned the money and credit cards, developed the appropriate middle-class behavior, and thus has under the law a *right* to be served. There is defensiveness in her actions too, for she feels a need to legitimate her status by showing her purse and credit cards. One important factor that enabled her to take such assertive action was her power to bring a TV news team to the restaurant. This power marks a change from a few decades ago when very few black Americans had the social or economic resources to fight back successfully.

This example underscores the complexity of the interaction in such situations, with two levels of negotiation evident. The negotiation between the respondent and her boyfriend on withdrawal vs. confrontation highlights the process of negotiating responses to discrimination and the difficulty in crafting such responses. Not only is there a process of dickering with whites within the discriminatory scene but also a negotiation between the blacks involved.

The confrontation strategy can be taken beyond immediate verbal confrontation to a more public confrontation. The president of a financial institution in a Middle Atlantic city brought unfavorable publicity to a restaurant with a pattern of poor service to blacks:

> I took the staff here to a restaurant that had recently opened in the prestigious section of the city, and we waited while other people got waited on. And decided that after about a half hour that these people don't want to wait on us. I happened to have been in the same restaurant a couple of evenings earlier, and it took them about forty-five minutes before they came to wait on me and my guest. So, on the second incident, I said, this is not an isolated incident, this is a pattern, because I had spoken with some other people who had not been warmly received in the restaurant. So, I wrote a letter to the owners. I researched and found out who the owners were, wrote a letter to the owners and sent copies to the city papers. That's my way of expressing myself, and letting the world know. You have to let people, other than you and the owner, know. You have to let others know you're expressing your dismay at the discrimination, or the barrier that's presented to you. I met with the owners. Of course, they wanted to meet with their attorneys with me, because they wanted to sue me. I told them they're welcome to do so, I don't have a thing, but fine they can do it. It just happens that I knew their white attorney. And he more or less vouched that if I had some concern that it must have been legitimate in some form. When the principals came in—one of the people who didn't wait on me

> was one of the owners, who happened to be waiting on everybody else—we resolved the issue by them inviting me to come again. And if I was fairly treated, or if I would come on several occasions and if I was fairly treated I would write a statement of retraction. I told them I would not write a retraction, I would write a statement with regard to how I was treated. Which I ultimately did. And I still go there today, and they speak to me, and I think the pattern is changed to a great degree.

This example also demonstrates the resources available to many middle-class black Americans. As a bank executive with connections in the white community, including the legal community, this respondent used his resources not only to bring discrimination to public attention but also to pressure a major change in behavior. He had the means to proceed beyond the local management to both the restaurant owners and the local newspapers. The detailed account provides additional insight into the black-white bargaining process. At first the white managers and owners, probably accustomed to acquiescence or withdrawal, vigorously resisted ending the blatant discrimination. But the verbal and other resources available to the respondent forced them to capitualte and participate in a negotiation process. The cost to the victor was substantial. As in the first incident, we see the time-consuming and energy-consuming nature of grappling with poor-service discrimination. Compared to whites entering the same places, black Americans face an extra burden when going into public accommodations putatively made hospitable by three decades of civil rights law protection.

The confrontation response is generally so costly in terms of time and energy that acquiescence or withdrawal are common options. An example of the exit response was provided by a utility company executive in an east coast city:

> I can remember one time my husband had picked up our son . . . from camp; and he'd stopped at a little store in the neighborhood near the camp. It was hot, and he was going to buy him a snowball. And the proprietor of the

store—this was a very old, white neighborhood, and it was just a little sundry store. But the proprietor said he had the little window where people could come up and order things. Well, my husband and son had gone into the store. And he told them, "Well, I can't give it to you here. but if you go outside to the window, I'll give it to you." And there were other [white] people in the store who'd been served [inside]. So, they just left and didn't buy anything.

Here the act seems a throwback to the South of the 1950s, where blacks were required to use the back or side of a store. This differential treatment in an older white neighborhood is also suggestive of the territorial character of racial relations in many cities. The black response to degradation here was not to confront the white person or to acquiesce abjectly, but rather to reject the poor service and leave. Unlike the previous examples, the impact on the white proprietor was negligible because there was no forced negotiation. This site differed from the two previous examples in that the service was probably not of long-term importance to the black family passing through the area. In the previous sites the possibility of returning to the restaurants, for business or pleasure, may have contributed to the choice of a confrontational response. The importance of the service is a likely variable affecting black responses to discrimination in public accommodations.

Discrimination in public accommodations can occur in many different settings. A school board member in a northern city commented on her experiences in retail stores:

[I have faced] harassment in stores, being followed around, being questioned about what are you going to purchase here. . . . I was in an elite department store just this past Sunday and felt that I was being observed while I was window shopping. I in fact actually ended up purchasing something, but felt the entire time I was there—I was in blue jeans and sneakers, that's how I dress on a Saturday—I felt that I was being watched in the store as I was walking through the store, what business did I have there, what was I going to purchase, that kind of thing. . . . There are a few of those white people that won't put change in your

hand, touch your skin—that doesn't need to go on. [Do you tell them that?] Oh. I do, I do. That is just so obvious. I usually [speak to them] if they're rude in the manner in which they deal with people. [What do they say about that?] Oh, stuff like, "Oh, excuse me." And some are really unconscious about it, say "Excuse me," and put the change in your hand, that's happened. But I've watched other people be rude, and I've been told to mind my own business . . . . [But you still do it?] Oh, sure, because for the most part I think that people do have to learn to think for themselves, and demand respect for themselves . . . . I find my best weapon of defense is to educate them, whether it's in the store, in a line at the bank, any situation, I teach them. And you take them by surprise because you tell them and show them what they should be doing, and what they should be saying and how they should be thinking. And they look at you because they don't know how to process you. They can't process it because you've just shown them how they should be living, and the fact that they are cheating themselves, really, because the racism is from fear. The racism is from lack of education.

This excessive surveillance of blacks' shopping was reported by several respondents in our study and in recent newspaper accounts (see Jaynes and Williams 1989, p. 140). Several white stereotypes seem to underlie the rejection discrimination in this instance—blacks are seen as shoplifters, as unclean, as disreputable poor. The excessive policing of black shoppers and the discourtesy of clerks illustrate the extra burden of being black in public places. No matter how affluent and influential, a black person cannot escape the stigma of being black, even while relaxing or shopping. There is the recurring strain of having to craft strategies for a broad range of discriminatory situations. Tailoring her confrontation to fit the particular discrimination, this respondent interrupted the normal flow of the interaction to call the whites to intersubjective account and make a one-way experience into a two-way experience. Forced into new situations, offending whites frequently do not know how "to process" such an aggressive response. Again we see how middle-class blacks can force a reconstruction of traditional responses by whites to blacks. The intensity of her discussion suggests that the attempt to "educate" whites comes with a heavy personal cost, for it is stressful to "psych" oneself up for such incidents.

The problem of burdensome visibility and the inescapable racial stereotyping by whites was underscored in the reply of a physician in an east coast city to a question about whether she had encountered barriers:

> Yes. All the time. I hate it when you go places and [white] people . . . think that we work in housekeeping. Or they naturally assume that we came from a very poor background. . . .A lot of white people think that blacks are just here to serve them, and [that] we have not risen above the servant position.

Here the discriminatory treatment comes from the white traveller staying in a hotel. This incident exemplifies the omnipresence of the stigma of being black—a welldressed physician staying in an expensive hotel cannot escape. Here and elsewhere in the interview her anger suggests a confrontational response to such situations.

Middle-class black parents often attempt to protect their children from racial hostility in public places, but they cannot always be successful. A manager at an electronics firm in the Southwest gave an account of his daughter's first encounter with a racial epithet. After describing racist graffiti on a neighborhood fence in the elite white suburb where he lives, he described an incident at a swimming pool:

> I'm talking over two hundred kids in this pool; not one black. I don't think you can go anywhere in the world during the summertime and not find some black kids in the swimming pool. . . . Now what's the worst thing that can happen to a ten-year-old girl in a swimming pool with all white kids? What's the worst thing that could happen? It happened. This little white guy called her a "nigger." Then called her a "motherfucker" and told her to "get out of the goddamn pool." . . . And what initiated that, they had these little inner tubes, they had about fifteen of them, and the pool owns them. So you just use them if they are vacant. So there was a tube setting up on the bank, she got it, jumped

in and started playing in it. . . . And this little white guy decided he wanted it. But, he's supposed to get it, right? And he meant to get it, and she wouldn't give it to him, so out came all these racial slurs. So my action was first with the little boy. "You know you're not supposed to do that. Apologize right now. Okay, good. Now, Mr. Lifeguard, I want him out of this pool, and you're going to have to do better. You're going to have to do better, but he has to leave out of this pool and let his parents know, okay?"

Taking his daughter back the next day, he observed from behind a fence to make certain the lifeguard protected her. For many decades black adults and children were excluded from public pools in the South and Southwest, and many pools were closed during the early desegregation period. These accommodations have special significance for middle-class black Americans, and this may be one reason the father's reaction was so decisive. Perhaps the major reason for his swift action was because this was the first time that his daughter had been the victim of racial slurs. She was the victim of cutting racist epithers that for this black father, as doubtless for most black Americans, connote segregated institutions and violence against blacks. Children also face hostility in public accommodations and may never shake this kind of experience. At a rather early point, many black parents find it necessary to teach their children how to handle discriminatory incidents.

The verbal responses of middle-class blacks to stigmatization can take more subtle forms. An 80-year-old retired schoolteacher in a southern city recounted her response to a recent experience at a drapery shop:

> The last time I had some draperies done and asked about them at the drapery shop, a young man at that shop—when they called [to him], he asked, and I heard him—he said, "The job for that nigger woman." And I said to the person who was serving me, "Oh my goodness. I feel so sorry for that young man. I didn't know people were still using that sort of language and saying those sorts of things." And that's the way I deal with it. I don't know what you call that. Is that sarcasm? Sarcasm is pretty good. . . .Well I've done that several times. This being 1989 . . . I'm surprised that I find it in this day and time.

One white clerk translated the schoolteacher's color in a hostile way while the other apparently listened. Suggested here is the way many whites are content to watch overt racist behavior without intervening. The retired teacher's response contrasts with the more confrontational reactions of the previous examples, for she used what might be called "strategic indirection." With composure she directed a pointedly sarcastic remark to the clerk serving her. Mockery is a more subtle tactic blacks can use to contend with antilocution, and this tactic may be more common among older blacks. Later in her interview this angry woman characterizes such recurring racial incidents as the "little murders" that daily have made her life difficult.

Careful Situation Assessments

We have seen in the previous incidents some tendency for blacks to assess discriminatory incidents before they act. Among several respondents who discussed discrimination at retail stores, the manager of a career development organization in the Southwest indicated that a clear assessment of a situation usually precedes confrontations and is part of a repertoire of concatenated responses:

If you're in a store—and let's say the person behind the counter is white—and you walk up to the counter, and a white person walks up to the counter, and you know you were there before the white customer, the person behind the counter knows you were there first, and it never fails, they always go, "Who's next." Ok. And what I've done, if they go ahead and serve the white person first, then I will immediately say, "Excuse me, I was here first, and we both know I was here first." . . . If they get away with it once, they're going to get away with it more than once, and then it's going to become something else. And you have to, you want to make sure that folks know that you're not being naive, that you really see through what's happening. Or if it's a job opportunity or something like that, too, [we should do the] same thing. You first try to get a clear assessment of what's really going on and sift through that information, and then . . . go from there.

The executive's coping process typically begins with a sifting of information before deciding on further action. She usually opts for immediate action so that whites face the reality of their actions in a decisive way. Like the account of the school board member who noted that whites would sometimes not put money directly in her hand, this account illustrates another aspect of discrimination in public accommodations: For many whites racial hostility is imbedded in everyday actions, and there is a deep, perhaps subconscious, recoil response to black color and persona.

The complex process of evaluation and response is described by a college dean, who commented generally on hotel and restaurant discrimination encountered as he travels across the United States:

When you're in a restaurant and . . . you notice that blacks get seated near the kitchen. You notice that if it's a hotel, your room is near the elevator, or your room is always way down in a corner somewhere. You find that you are getting the undesirable rooms. And you come there early in the day and you don't see very many cars on the lot and they'll tell you that this is all we've got. Or you get the room that's got a bad television set. You know that you're being discriminated against. And of course you have to act accordingly. You have to tell them. "Okay, the room is fine, [but] this television set has got to go. Bring me another television set." So in my personal experience, I simply cannot sit and let them get away with it [discrimination] and not let them know that I know that that's what they are doing. . . .

When I face discrimination, first I take a long look at myself and try to determine whether or not I am seeing what I think I'm seeing in 1989, and if it's something that I have an option [about]. In other words, if I'm at a store making a purchase. I'll simply walk away from it. If it's at a restaurant where I'm not getting good service, I first of all let the people know that I'm not getting good service, then I [may] walk away from it. But the thing that I have to do is to let people know that I know that I'm being singled out for a separate treatment. And then I might react in any number of ways—depending on where I am and how badly I want whatever it is that I'm there for.

This commentary adds another dimension to our understanding of public discrimination, its cumulative aspect. Blacks confront not just isolated incidents—such as a bad room in a luxury hotel once every few years—but a life-long series of such incidents. Here again the omnipresence of careful assessments is under-scored. The dean's interview highlights a major difficulty in being black—one must be constantly prepared to assess accurately and then decide on the appropriate response. This long-look approach may indicate that some middle-class blacks are so sensitive to white charges of hypersensitivity and paranoia that they err in the opposite direction and fail to see discrimination when it occurs. In addition, as one black graduate student at a leading white university in the Southeast put it: "I think that sometimes timely and appropriate responses to racially motivated acts and comments are lost due to the processing of the input." The "long look" can result in missed opportunities to respond to discrimination.

Using Middle-Class Resources for Protection

One advantage that middle-class blacks have over poorer blacks is the use of the resources of middle-class occupations. A professor at a major white university commented on the varying protection her middle-class status give her at certain sites:

> If I'm in those areas that are fairly protected, within gatherings of my own group, other African Americans, or if I'm in the university where my status as a professor mediates against the way I might be perceived, mediates against the hostile perception, then it's fairly comfortable.... When I divide my life into encounters with the outside world, and of course that's ninety percent of my life, it's fairly consistently unpleasant at those sites where there's nothing that mediates between my race and what I have to do. For example, if I'm in a grocery store, if I'm in my car, which is a 1970 Chevrolet, a real old ugly car, all those things—being in a grocery store, in casual clothes, or being in the car—sort of advertises something that doesn't have anything to do with my status as far as people I run into are concerned.

> Because I'm a large black woman, and I don't wear whatever class status I have, or whatever professional status [I have] in my appearance when I'm in the grocery store, I'm part of the mass of large black women shop-ping. For most whites, and even for some blacks, that translates into negative status. That means that they are free to treat me the way they treat most poor black people, because they can't tell by looking at me that I differ from that.

This professor notes the variation in discrimi-nation in the sites through which she travels, from the most private to the most public. At home with friends she faces no problems, and at the university her professorial status gives her some protection from discrimination. The increase in unpleasant encounters as she moves into public accommodations sites such as grocery stores is attributed to the absence of mediating factors such as clear symbols of middle-class status—displaying the middle-class symbols may provide some protection against discrimination in public places.

An east coast news anchorperson reported a common middle-class experience of good service from retailers over the phone:

> And if I was seeking out a service, like renting a car, or buying something, I could get a wonder-ful, enthusiastic reaction to what I was doing. I would work that up to such a point that this per-son would probably shower me with roses once they got to see me. And then when I would show up, and they're surprised to see that I'm black, I sort of remind them in conversation how welcome my service was, to put the embar-rassment on them, and I go through with my dealings. In fact, once my sister criticized me for putting [what] she calls my "white-on-white voice" on to get a rental car. But I needed a rental car and I knew that I could get it. I knew if I could get this guy to think that he was talk-ing to some blonde, rather than, you know, so, but that's what he has to deal with. I don't have to deal with that, I want to get the car.

Being middle-class often means that you, as many blacks say, "sound white" over the phone. Over the phone middle-class blacks and they get fair treatment because the white person assumes the caller is white, while they receive poorer (or no) service in person. Race is the only added variable in such interpersonal contact situations. Moreover, some middle-class blacks intentionally use this phone-voice resource to secure their needs.

RESPONSES TO DISCRIMINATION: THE STREET

Reacting to White Strangers

As we move away from public accommodations settings to the usually less protected street sites, racial hostility can become more fleeting and severer, and thus black responses are often restricted. The most serious form of street discrimination is violence. Often the reasonable black response to street discrimination is withdrawal, resigned acceptance, or a quick verbal retort. The difficulty of responding to violence is seen in this report by a man working for a media surveying firm in a southern industrial city:

> I was parked in front of this guy's house. . . . This guy puts his hands on the window and says, "Get out of the car, nigger." . . . So, I got out, and I thought, "Oh, this is what's going to happen here." And I'm talking fast. And they're, "What are you doing here?" And I'm, "This is who I am. I work with these people. This is the man we want to put in the survey." And I pointed to the house. And the guy said, "Well you have an out-of-state license tag, right?" "Yea." And he said, "If something happened to you, your people at home wouldn't know for a long time, would they?" . . . I said, "Look, I deal with a company that deals with television. [If] something happens to me, it's going to be a national thing" . . . . So, they grab me by the lapel of my coat, and put me in front of my car. They put the blade on my zipper. And now I'm thinking about this guy that's in the truck [behind me], because now I'm thinking that I'm going to have to run somewhere. Where am I going to run? Go to the police? [laughs] So, after a while they bash up my headlight. And I drove [away].

Stigmatized and physically attacked solely because of his color, this man faced verbal hostility and threats of death with courage.

Cautiously drawing on his middle-class resources, he told the attackers his death would bring television crews to the town. This resource utilization is similar to that of the news director in the restaurant incident. Beyond this verbal threat his response had to be one of caution. For most whites threatened on the street, the police are a sought-after source of protection, but for black men this is often not the case.

At the other end of the street continuum is nonverbal harassment such as the "hate stare" that so traumatized Griffin (1961). In her research on street remarks, Gardner (1980) considered women and blacks particularly vulnerable targets for harassment. For the segregation years Henley (1978) has documented the ways in which many blacks regularly deferred to whites in public-place communications. Today obsequious deference is no longer a common response to harassment. A middle-class student with dark skin reported that on her way to university classes she had stopped at a bakery in a white residential area where very few blacks live or shop. A white couple in front of the store stared intently and hatefully at her as she crossed the sidewalk and entered and left the bakery. She reported that she had experienced this hate stare many times. The incident angered her for some days thereafter, in part because she had been unable to respond more actively to it.

In between the hate stare and violence are many other hostile actions. Most happen so fast that withdrawal, resigned acceptance, or an immediate verbal retort are the reasonable responses. The female professor quoted earlier described the fleeting character of harassment:

> I was driving. This has [happened] so many times, but one night it was especially repugnant. I think it had to, with my son being in the car. It was about 9:30 at night, and as I've said, my car is old and very ugly, and I have been told by people shouting at intersections that it's the kind of car that people think of as a low-rider car, so they associate it with Mexican Americans, especially poor Mexican Americans. Well, we were sitting at an intersection waiting to make a turn, and a group of middle-class looking white boys drives up in a nice car. And they start shouting

things at us in a real fake-sounding Mexican American accent, and I realized that they thought we were Mexican Americans. And I turned to look at them, and they started making obscene gestures and laughing at the car. And then one of them realized that I was black, and said, "Oh, it's just a nigger." And [they] drove away.

This incident illustrates the seldom-noted problem of "cross discrimination"—a black person may suffer from discrimination aimed at other people of color by whites unable to distinguish. The white hostility was guided by certain signals—an old car and dark skin—of minority-group status. The nighttime setting, by assuring anonymity, facilitated the hurling of racist epithets and heightened the negative impact on this woman, who found the harassment especially dangerous and repulsive because she was with her son. She drove away without replying. Later in the interview she notes angrily that in such incidents her ascribed characteristic of "blackness" takes precedence over her achieved middle-class characteristics and that the grouped thinking of racism obscures anything about her that is individual and unique.

For young middle-class blacks street harassment can generate shock and disbelief, as in the case of this college student who recounted a street encounter near her university in the Southwest:

I don't remember in high school being called a "nigger" before, and I can remember here being called a "nigger." [When was this?] In my freshman year, at a university student parade. There was a group of us, standing there, not knowing that this was not an event that a lot of black people went to! [laughs] You know, our dorm was going, and this was something we were going to go to because we were students too! And we were standing out there and [there were] a group of white fraternity boys—I remember the southern flag—and a group of us, five or six of us, and they went past by us, before the parade had actually gotten underway. And one of them pointed and said, "Look at that bunch of niggers!" I remember thinking, "Surely he's not talking to us!" We didn't even use the word "nigger" in my house. . . . [How did you feel?] I

think I wanted to cry. And my friends—they were from a southwestern city—they were ready to curse them, and I was just standing there with my mouth open. I think I wanted to cry. I could not believe it, because you get here and you think you're in an educated environment and you're dealing with educated people. And all of this backward country stuff . . . you think that kind of stuff is not going on, but it is.

The respondent's first coping response was to think the assailants were not speaking to her and her friends. Again we see the tendency for middle-class blacks to assess situations carefully and to give whites the benefit of the doubt. Her subsequent response was tearful acquiescence, but her friends were ready to react in a more aggressive way. The discriminators may have moved on before a considered response was possible. This episode points up the impact of destructive racial coding on young people and hints at the difficulty black parents face in socializing children for coping with white hostility. When I discussed these street incidents involving younger blacks with two other black respondents, one a southern civil rights activist and the other an Ivy League professor, both noted the problem created for some middle-class black children by their well-intentioned parents trying to shelter them from racism.

It seems likely that for middle-class blacks the street is the site of recurring encounters with various types of white malevolence. A vivid example of the cumulative character and impact of this discrimination was given by another black student at a white university, who recounted his experiences walking home at night from a campus job to his apartment in a predominantly white residential area:

So, even if you wanted to, it's difficult just to live a life where you don't come into conflict with others. Because every day you walk the streets, it's not even like once a week, once a month. It's every day you walk the streets. Every day that you live as a black person you're reminded how you're perceived in society. You walk the streets at night: white people cross the streets. I've seen white couples and individuals dart in front of cars to not be on the same side of the street. Just the other day, I was walking down the street, and this white female with a child, I saw her pass a young white male about 20 yards ahead. When she saw me, she quickly dragged the child and herself across the busy street. What is so funny is that this area has had an unknown white rapist in the area for about four years. [When I pass] white men tighten their grip on their women. I've seen people turn around and seem like they're going to take blows from me. The police constantly make circles around me as a I walk home, you know, for blocks. I'll walk, and they'll turn a block. And they'll come around me just to make sure, to find out where I'm going. So, every day you realize [you're black]. Even though you're not doing anything wrong; you're just existing. You're just a person. But you're a black person perceived in an unblack world. (This quote includes a clarification sentence from a follow-up interview.)

In a subsequent comment this respondent mentioned that he also endured white men hurling beer cans and epithets at him as he walked home. Again the cumulation of incidents is evident. Everyday street travel for young black middle-class males does not mean one isolated incident every few years.

Unable to "see" his middle-class symbols of college dress and books, white couples (as well as individuals) have crossed the street in front of cars to avoid walking near this modest-build black student, in a predominantly white neighborhood. Couples moving into defensive postures are doubtless reacting to the stigma of "black maleness." The student perceives such avoidance as racist, however, not because he is paranoid, but because he has previously encountered numerous examples of whites taking such defensive measures. Many whites view typical "street" criminals as black or minority males and probably see young black males as potentially dangerous (Graber 1980, p. 55). This would seem to be the motivation for some hostile treatment black males experience in public places. Some scholars have discussed white perceptions of black males as threatening and the justifiability of that perception (Warr forthcoming), but to my knowledge there has been no discussion in the

literature of the negative impact of such perceptions on black males. This student reports that being treated as a pariah (in his words, a "criminal and a rapist") has caused him severe psychological problems. When I discussed this student's experiences with a prominent black journalist in a northeastern city, he reported that whites sometimes stop talking—and white women grab their purses—on downtown office-building elevators when he enters. These two men had somewhat different responses to such discrimination, one relatively passive and the other aggressive. In a follow-up interview the student reported that he rarely responded aggressively to the street encounters, apart from the occasional quick curse, because they happened too quickly. Echoing the black graduate student's comments about processing input and missed opportunities, he added: "I was basically analyzing and thinking too much about the incident." However, the journalist reacts more assertively; he described how he turns to whites in elevators and informs them, often with a smile, that they can continue talking or that he is not interested in their purses.

On occasion, black middle-class responses to street hostility from white strangers are even more aggressive. A woman who now runs her own successful business in a southwestern city described a car incident in front of a grocery store:

We had a new car . . .and we stopped at 7–11 [store]. We were going to go out that night, and we were taking my son to a babysitter. . . . And we pulled up, and my husband was inside at the time. And this person, this Anglo couple, drove up, and they hit our car. It was a brand new car. So my husband came out. And the first thing they told us was that we got our car on *welfare*. Here we are ablebodied. He was a corporate executive. I had a decent job, it was a professional job, but it wasn't paying anything. But they looked at the car we were driving, and they made the assumption that we got it from welfare. I completely snapped; I physically abused that lady. I did. And I was trying to keep my husband from arguing with her husband until the police could come. . . . And when the police came they interrogated them: they didn't arrest us, because there was an off-duty cop who had seen the whole incident and said she provoked it.

Here we see how some whites perceive blacks, including middle-class blacks, in interracial situations. The verbal attack by the whites was laced with the stereotype about blacks as welfare chiselers. This brought forth an angry response from the black couple, which probably came as a surprise to the whites. This is another example of Brittan and Maynard's (1984, p. 7) point that discriminatory interaction is shaped today by the way in which oppressors and oppressed mediate their relative positions. Note too the role of the off-duty police officer. The respondent does not say whether the officer was white or black, but this detail suggests that certain contexts of discrimination have changed—in the past a (white) police officer would have sided with the whites. This respondent also underscores her and her husband's occupational achievements, highlighting her view that she has attained the American middle-class ideal. She is incensed that her obvious middle-class symbols did not protect her from verbal abuse.

The importance of middle-class resources in street encounters was dramatized in the comments of a parole officer in a major West Coast city. He recounted how he dealt with a racial epithet:

> I've been called "nigger" before, out in the streets when I was doing my job, and the individual went to jail. . . . [OK, if he didn't call you a "nigger," would he have still gone to jail?] Probably not. [Was the person white?] Yes, he was. And he had a partner with him, and his partner didn't say anything, and his partner jaywalked with him. However, since he uttered the racial slur, I stopped him and quizzed him about the laws. And jaywalking's against the law, so he went to jail.

On occasion, middle-class blacks have the ability to respond not only aggressively but authoritatively to street discrimination. This unusual response to an epithet was possible because the black man, unknown to his assailant, had police authority. This incident also illustrates a point made in the policing litera-

ture about the street-level discretion of police officers (Perry and Sornoff 1973). Jaywalking is normally a winked-at violation, as in the case of the assailant's companion. Yet this respondent was able to exercise his discretionary authority to punish a racial epithet.

Responses to Discrimination by White Police Officers

Most middle-class blacks do not have such governmental authority as their personal protection. In fact, white police officers are a major problem. Encounters with the police can be life-threatening and thus limit the range of responses. A television commentator recounted two cases of police harassment when he was working for a survey firm in the mid-1980s. In one of the incidents, which took place in a southern metropolis, he was stopped by several white officers:

> "What are you doing here?" I tell them what I'm doing here. . . . And so me spread on top of my car. [What had you done?] Because I was in the neighborhood. I left this note on these peoples' house: "Here's who I am. You weren't here, and I will come back in thirty minutes." [Why were they searching you?] They don't know. To me, they're searching, I remember at that particular moment when this all was going down, there was a lot of reports about police crime on civilians. . . . It took four cops to shake me down, two police cars, so they had me up there spread out. I had a friend of mine with me who was making the call with me, because we were going to have dinner together, and he was black, and they had me up, and they had him outside. . . . They said, "Well, let's check you out." . . .And I'm talking to myself, and I'm not thinking about being at attention, with my arms spread on my Ford [a company car], and I'm sitting there talking to myself. "Man, this is crazy, this is crazy."
>
> [How are you feeling inside?] Scared, I mean real scared. [What did you think was going to happen to you?] I was going to go to jail. . . . Just because they picked me. Why would they stop me? It's like, if they can stop me, why wouldn't I go to jail, and I could sit in there for ten days before the judge sees me. I'm thinking all this crazy stuff. . . . Again, I'm talking to myself. And the guy takes his stick. And he doesn't

whack me hard, but he does it with enough authority to let me know they mean business. "I told you stand still; now put your arms back out." And I've got this suit on, and the car's wet. And my friend's hysterical. He's outside the car. And they're checking him out. And he's like, "Man, just be cool, man." And he had tears in his eyes. And I'm like, oh, man, this is a nightmare. This is not supposed to happen to me. This is not my style! And so finally, this other cop comes up and says, "What have we got here Charlie?" "Oh, we've got a guy here. He's running through the neighborhood, and he doesn't want to do what we tell him. We might have to run him in." [You're "running through" the neighborhood?] Yeah, exactly, in a suit in the rain?! After they got through doing their thing and harassing me, I just said. "Man this has been a hell of a week."

And I had tears in my eyes, but it wasn't tears of upset. It was tears of anger; it was tears of wanting to lash back. . . . What I thought to myself was, man, blacks have it real hard down here. I don't care if they're a broadcaster; I don't care if they're a businessman or a banker. . . . They don't have it any easier than the persons on skid row who get harassed by the police on a Friday or Saturday night.

It seems likely that most black men—including middle-class black men—see white police officers as a major source of danger and death (See "Mood of Ghetto America" 1980, June 2, pp. 32–34; Louis Harris and Associates 1989; Roddy 1990, August 26). Scattered evidence suggests that by the time they are in their twenties, most black males, regardless of socioeconomic status, have been stopped by the police because "blackness" is considered a sign of possible criminality by police officers (Moss 1990; Roddy 1990, August 26). This treatment probably marks a dramatic contrast with the experiences of young white middle-class males. In the incident above the respondent and a friend experienced severe police maltreatment—detention for a lengthy period, threat of arrest, and the reality of physical violence. The coping response of the respondent was resigned acceptance somewhat similar to the deference rituals highlighted by Goffman. The middle-class suits and obvious corporate credentials (for example, survey question-naires and company car) did not protect the

two black men. The final comment suggests a disappointment that middle-class status brought no reprieve from police stigmatization and harassment.

Black women can also be the targets of police harassment. A professor at a major white university in the Southwest describes her encounters with the police:

When the cops pull me over because my car is old and ugly, they assume I've just robbed a convenience store. Or that's the excuse they give: "This car looks like a car used to rob a 7–11 [store]." And I've been pulled over six or seven times since I've been in this city—and I've been here two years now. Then I do what most black folks do. I try not to make any sudden moves so I'm not accidentally shot. Then I give them my identification. And I show them my university I.D. so they won't think that I'm someone that constitutes a threat, however they define it, so that I don't get arrested.

She adds:

[One problem with] being black in America is that you have to spend so much time thinking about stuff that most white people just don't even have to think about. I worry when I get pulled over by a cop. I worry because the person that I live with is a black male, and I have a teen-aged son. I worry what some white cop is going to think when he walks over to our car, because he's holding on to a gun. And I'm very aware of how many black folks accidentally get shot by cops. I worry when I walk into a store, that someone's going to think I'm in there shop-lifting. And I have to worry about that because I'm not free to ignore it. And so, that thing that's supposed to be guaranteed to all Americans, the freedom to just be yourself is a fallacious idea. And I get resentful that I have to think about things that a lot of people, even my very close white friends whose politics are similar to mine, simply don't have to worry about.

This commentary about a number of encounters underscores the pyramiding character of discrimination. This prominent scholar has faced excessive surveillance by white police officers, who presumably view blacks as likely criminals. As in the previous example, there is great fear of white officers, but her response is somewhat different: She draws on her middle-class resources for protection; she cautiously interposes her middle-class status by pulling our a university I.D. card. In the verbal exchange her articulateness as a professor probably helps protect her. This assertive use of middle-class credentials in dealing with police marks a difference from the old asymmetrical deference rituals, in which highlighting middle-class status would be considered arrogant by white officers and increase the danger. Note, too, the explicit theory of rights that she, like many other middle-class blacks, holds as part of her American dream.

CONCLUSION

I have examined the sites of discrimination, the types of discriminatory acts, and the responses of the victims and have found the color stigma still to be very important in the public lives of affluent black Americans. The sites of racial discrimination range from relatively protected home sites, to less protected workplace and educational sites, to the even less protected public places. The 1964 Civil Rights Act guarantees that black Americans are "entitled to the full and equal enjoyment of the goods, services, facilities, privileges, advantages, and accommodations" in public accommodations. Yet the interviews indicate that deprivation of full enjoyment of public facilities is not a relic of the past; deprivation and discrimination in public accommodations persist. Middle-class black Americans remain vulnerable targets in public places. Prejudice-generated aggression in public places is, of course, not limited to black men and women—gay men and white women are also targets of street harassment (Benokraitis and Feagin 1986). Nonetheless, black women and men face an unusually broad range of discrimination on the street and in public accommodations.

The interviews highlight two significant aspects of the additive discrimination faced by black Americans in public places and elsewhere: (1) the cumulative character of an *individual's* experiences with discrimination; and

(2) the *group's* accumulated historical experiences as perceived by the individual. A retired psychology professor who has worked in the Midwest and Southwest commented on the pyramiding of incidents:

> I don't think white people, generally, understand the full meaning of racist discriminatory behaviors directed toward Americans of African descent. They seem to see each act of discrimination or any act of violence as an "isolated" event. As a result, most white Americans cannot understand the strong reaction manifested by blacks when such events occur. They feel that blacks tend to "over-react." They forget that in most cases, we live lives of quiet desperation generated by a litany of *daily* large and small events that whether or not by design, remind us of our "place" in American society.

Particular instances of discrimination may seem minor to outside white observers when considered in isolation. But when blatant acts of avoidance, verbal harassment, and physical attack combine with subtle and covert slights, and these accumulate over months, years, and lifetimes, the impact on a black person is far more than the sum of the individual instances.

The historical context of contemporary discrimination was described by the retired psychologist, who argued that average white Americans

> . . . ignore the personal context of the stimulus. That is, they deny the historical impact that a negative act may have on an individual. "Nigger" to a white may simply be an epithet that should be ignored. To most blacks, the term brings into sharp and current focus all kinds of acts of racism—murder, rape, torture, denial of constitutional rights, insults, limited opportunity structure, economic problems, unequal justice under the law and a myriad of . . . other racist and discriminatory acts that occur daily in the lives of *most* Americans of African descent—including professional blacks.

Particular acts, even antilocution that might seem minor to white observers, are freighted not only with one's past experience of discrimination but also with centuries of racial discrimination directed at the entire group, vicarious oppression that still includes racially translated violence and denial of access to the American dream. Antiblack discrimination is a matter of racial-power inequality institutionalized in a variety of economic and social institutions over a long period of time. The microlevel events of public accommodations and public streets are not just rare and isolated encounters by individuals; they are recurring events reflecting an invasion of the microworld by the macroworld of historical racial subordination.

The cumulative impact of racial discrimination accounts for the special way that blacks have of looking at and evaluating interracial incidents. One respondent, a clerical employee at an adoption agency, described the "second eye" she uses:

> I think that it causes you to have to look at things from two different perspectives. You have to decide whether things that are done or slights that are made are made because you are black or they are made because the person is just rude, or unconcerned and uncaring. So it's kind of a situation where you're always kind of looking to see with a second eye or a second antenna just what's going on.

The language of "second eye" suggests that blacks look at white-black interaction through a lens colored by personal and group experience with cross-institutional and cross-generational discrimination. This sensitivity is not new, but is a current adaptation transcending, yet reminiscent of, the black sensitivity to the etiquette of racial relations in the old South (Doyle 1937). What many whites see as black "paranoia" (e.g., Wieseltier 1989, June 5) is simply a realistic sensitivity to white-black interaction created and constantly reinforced by the two types of cumulative discrimination cited above.

Blacks must be constantly aware of the repertoire of possible responses to chronic and burdensome discrimination. One older respondent spoke of having to put on her "shield" just before she leaves the house each morning. When quizzed, she said that for more than six decades, as she leaves her home, she has tried

to be prepared for insults and discrimination in public places, even if nothing happens that day. This extraordinary burden of discrimination, evident in most of the 135 interviews in the larger sample, was eloquently described by the female professor who resented having to worry about lifethreatening incidents that her "very close white friends . . . simply don't have to worry about." Another respondent was articulate on this point:

> . . . if you can think of the mind as having one hundred ergs of energy, and the average man uses fifty percent of his energy dealing with the everyday problems of the world—just general kinds of things—then he has fifty percent more to do creative kinds of things that he wants to do. Now that's a white person. Now a black person also has one hundred ergs: he uses fifty percent the same way a white man does, dealing with what the white man has [to deal with], so he has fifty percent left. But he uses twenty-five percent fighting being black, [with] all the problems being black and what it means. Which means he really only has twenty-five percent to do what the white man has fifty percent to do, and he's expected to do just as much as the white man with that twenty-five percent. . . . So, that's kind of what happens. You just don't have as much energy left to do as much as you know you really could if you were free, [if] your mind were free.

The individual cost of coping with racial discrimination is great, and, as he says, you cannot accomplish as much as you could if you retained the energy wasted on discrimination. This is perhaps the most tragic cost of persisting discrimination in the United States. In spite of decades of civil rights legislation, black Americans have yet to attain the full promise of the American dream.

Joe R. Feagin *holds the Graduate Research Professorship in sociology at the University of Florida. His research is primarily in the areas of racial/ethnic relations and city development. He is the author of* Discrimination American Style *(Prentice Hall, 1978) and* Racial and Ethnic Relations *(third edition: Prentice Hall, 1989).*

REFERENCES

Allport, Gordon. 1958. The *Nature of Prejudice*. Abridged. New York: Doubleday Anchor Books.

Benokraitis, Nijole and Joe R. Feagin. 1986. *Modern Sexism: Blatant, Subtle and Covert Discrimination*. Englewood Cliffs: Prentice-Hall.

Blauner, Bob. 1989. *Black Lives, White Lives*. Berkeley: University of California Press.

Brittan, Arthur and Mary Maynard. 1984. *Sexism, Racism and Oppression*. Oxford: Basil Blackwell.

Collins, Sheila M. 1983. "The Making of the Black Middle Class." *Social Problems* 30: 369–81.

Doyle, Betram W. 1937. *The Etiquette of Race Relations in the South*. Port Washington, NY: Kennikat Press.

Feagin, Joe R. and Douglas Eckberg. 1980. "Prejudice and Discrimination." *Annual Review of Sociology* 6:1–20.

Feagin, Joe R. and Clairece Booher Feagin. 1986. *Discrimination American Style* (rev. ed). Melbourne, FL: Krieger Publishing Co.

Gardner, Carol Brooks. 1980. "Passing By: Street Remarks, Address Rights, and the Urban Female." *Sociological Inquiry* 50: 328–56.

____. 1988. "Access Information:Public Lies and Private Peril." *Social Problems* 35:384–97.

Goffman. Erving. 1956. "The Nature of Deference and Demeanor." *American Anthropologist* 58:473–502.

____. 1963. *Behavior in Public Places*. New York: Free Press.

____. 1971. *Relations in Public*. New York: Basic Books.

Graber, Doris A. 1980. *Crime News and the Public*. New York: Praeger.

Griffin, John Howard. 1961. *Black Like Me*. Boston: Houghton Mifflin.

Henley, Nancy M. 1978. *Body Politics*. Englewood Cliffs, N.J.: Prentice-Hall.

Jaynes, Gerald D. and Robin Williams, Jr. (eds.). 1989. *A Common Destiny: Blacks and American Society*. Washington, D.C.: National Academy Press.

Landry. Batt. 1987. *The New Black Middle Class*. Berkeley: University of California Press.

Louis Harris and Associates. 1989. *The Unfinished Agenda on Race in America*. New York: NAACP Legal Defense and Educational Fund.

"The Mood of Ghetto America." 1980, June 2. *Newsweek*, pp. 32–4.

Moss, E. Yvonne. 1990. "African Americans and the Administration of Justice." Pp. 79–86 in *Assessment of the Status of African-Americans,* edited by Wornie L. Reed. Boston: University of Massachusetts, William Monroe Trotter Institute.

Perry, David C. and Paula A. Sornoff. 1973. *Politics at the Street Level*. Beverly Hills: Sage.

Raper, Arthur F. 1933. *The Tragedy of Lynching*. Chapel Hill: University of North Carolina Press.

Roddy, Dennis B. 1990, August 26. "Perceptions Still Segregate Police, Black Community." *The Pittsburgh Press*. p. Bl.

Rollins, Judith. 1985. *Between Women*. Philadelphia: Temple University Press.

Warr, Mark. Forthcoming. "Dangerous Situations: Social Context and Fear of Victimization." *Social Forces*.

Wieseltier, Leon. 1989, June 5. "Scar Tissue." *New Republic*, pp. 19–20.

Willie, Charles. 1983. *Race, Ethnicity, and Socioeconomic Status*. Bayside: General Hall.

Wilson, William J. 1978. *The Declining Significance of Race*. Chicago: University of Chicago Press.

____. 1987. *The Truly Disadvantaged: The Inner City, the Underclass, and Public Policy*. Chicago: University of Chicago Press.

Reprinted with permission from the *American Sociological Review* 56 (1991):101–116.

4

Flexible Methods:
Case Study Design

O ne of the most time-honored forms of research in the helping professions is the traditional case study. Psychodynamic theorists still refer to Freud's (and other) case studies. Case studies of specific organizations or corporations abound in the management literature, and they are also common in the family therapy, medical, and education fields. Life history research often employs case study design (Martin 1995), and case study research has continued in use despite disparagement of it in the research literature (Gilgun 1994; Yin 1994).

Case studies are used for many purposes—in journalism, in legal and policy decision-making, and in teaching, as well as in research. When does a case study constitute research? What uses does the case study have as a research design? How is a good research case study designed? This chapter will answer these questions for traditional case studies, that is, those forms of case study that use narrative data and flexible methods of investigation; chapter 8 discusses the quantitative or fixed method form of case study research.

Defining Case Study Research

The defining characteristic of case study research, of course, is that it focuses on a single unit that is studied (Gilgun 1994; Patton 1990; Ruckdeschel, Earnshaw, & Firrek 1994). That single unit may be and most commonly is a person, but it may also be a couple, a family, an organization, a community, an event, or any other type of single entity. Similarly, Stake (1994) calls it the "study [of] a specific, unique, bounded system" (p. 237).

In fact, case study research sometimes includes more than one case. However, when multiple cases are used, each is treated and described as an individual unit rather than aggregating the information about the cases as is done in group designs (Yin 1994; Stake 1994). Case study research is thus idiographic, which is the technical term for research that is case—rather than group—based in its design.

The well-designed traditional case study has several defining characteristics. Yin (1994) argues that the case study strategy should be considered a research method when "a 'how' or 'why' question is being asked about a contemporary set of events over which the investigator has little or no control" (p. 9). By "control," he means that the researcher is not in a position to manipulate or experiment with the phenomenon of interest. However, this kind of manipulation or planned intervention is made in the case study format when single-subject designs, or fixed method case studies of the effects of specific interventions are undertaken, as discussed in chapter 8. Traditional case studies, however, take the events of interest as "given" and gather information about and analyze them after the fact. Thus case studies of the traditional kind may be either *prospective* or *retrospective;* that is, they may be planned ahead of time or after the fact, gathering data as the events of interest unfold or through documents and recall afterwards. Single-system designs, on the other hand, are always prospective.

Yin (1994) defines the case study as "an empirical inquiry that investigates a contemporary phenomenon within its real-life context, especially when the boundaries between phenomenon and context are not clearly evident" (p. 13). Extensive description of the context in which the case is found is thus characteristic of case studies (Gilgun 1994; Patton 1990; Ruckdeschel et al. 1994). This description includes both the context in which the case itself was embedded and the observational context in which the data about the case were gathered.

Case studies can also be especially useful for examining the process of change, whether developmental or induced by intervention efforts (Fonagy & Moran 1993; Gilgun 1994). Case studies can therefore be quite useful in evaluation research (Patton 1990; Ruckdeschel et al. 1994). Case studies of this kind focus on "what happened, that is, on how the intervention worked and what the major actors in the implementation process did" (Gilgun 1994:377). This use of the case study is common in medicine, psychiatry, education, and social work. The case study has thus been an essential tool in examining what helps and how in the human services for a long time.

In Kuhn's (1970) terms, intensive examination of a case in context could be used for discovery, "for recognizing both that something IS and WHAT it is" (p. 85), including what its context is and what the thing itself is. The case study can also be used for matching facts with theory or describing those facts directly predicted by a theory or paradigm (Kuhn 1970), including describing the nature of the context in which a phenomenon occurs. The Jarrett (1992) case study of how a female-headed African American family copes with poverty (reprinted in this chapter) is of the second type. It uses intensive study of a single family to examine how well ideas about inner-city life derived from statistical studies of groups fit (and do not fit) with what life may actually be like for individual members of that group.

Case studies have many more variables of interest than sources of data (Yin 1994), especially when they rely on multiple sources of evidence. One reason for limiting the number of cases used in a study is to enable the researcher to gather very extensive data about that individual instance of a phenomenon. Typically, multiple sources of data are used (Gilgun 1994; Yin 1994). The Jarrett (1992) study, for example, uses both interviews and repeated observations of the family for its data.

Case studies are most productive when they use theory and prior conceptualizations to guide data collection and analysis (Fonagy & Moran 1993; Yin 1994). For this reason, case studies share with experiments and other forms of flexible method research the fact that they rely on the conceptual soundness of the conclusions drawn for their generalizability, not on having a statistically representative sample. Gilgun (1994) calls this "analytic generalization" (p. 372), noting that its logic can be either inductive or deductive. This point of view is fully compatible with fallibilistic realism (Manicas & Secord 1983) which emphasizes the role of conceptual understanding, that is, the role of the theoretical lens through which observed phenomena are understood, in all research. As Gilgun (1994) puts it, "generalizabilty depends on how well case studies are conceptualized [and] whether they are represented in sufficient detail so that they are interpretable . . ." (p. 372).

In sum, traditional case study research, sometimes termed "qualitative case study" research (Fonagy & Moran 1993; Gilgun 1994; Ruckdeschel et al. 1994), uses single units as the focus of study. It is typically a data-rich form of study that can be used for theory generation, theory elaboration, and/or examining the goodness of fit between theory and data describing the case. The case is usually studied in context. In the traditional case study, there is usually not a deliberate manipulation introduced as part of the research, as there is in single-system designs (see chapter 8). However, traditional case studies can be used to study change processes, whether related to maturation and development, historical change, or how treatment processes unfold. These areas are often of interest to human service professionals. In addition, because human service professionals practice and commonly think in case-based ways, this form of research is often very appealing to them.

Hallmarks of Quality in Case Study Research

The first criterion of a well-designed case study is that the *guiding question or conceptualization be made clear at the outset* (Fonagy & Moran 1993; Stake 1994; Yin 1994). Case study findings are most persuasive when they are linked to theory, and it is in the formulation of the research question itself that this link should be made. This standard of quality is no different than for other forms of research, of course. It is repeated here because of the fact that case studies rely on what Gilgun (1994) calls analytic rather than statistical generalization. The foundation for the generalizability of case study findings is thus laid in how the question is stated, that is, the set of theoretical ideas in which it is embedded. It is also repeated because those who defend the traditional case study as a valuable research method all make the same point about the importance of the question and its relation to theory, whether related to the examination of existing theory or the generation of new theoretical ideas. Stake (1994) terms this the "instrumental case study" in which "a case is examined to provide insight into an issue or refinement of a theory" (p. 237).

One criterion of a well-designed case study is that the questions, concepts, and data collection methods are designed in such a way that disconfirming ideas and evidence can be and are identified (Fonagy & Moran 1993). Unfortunately, published accounts of case study research do not often address this issue. However, it is part of the obligation of the case study researcher, as in other forms of research, to gather and analyze data in such a way as to honestly elicit and report unexpected findings, including those that tend to contradict the ideas that guided the study at the outset.

Case studies always emphasize the uniqueness and "particularity" of what is being studied even when the relevance to more general concepts, theories, or issues is being examined (Stake 1994). This uniqueness often extends to the historical background, physical setting, economic and political context, and the nature of the researcher's access to it. Hence high-quality case studies provide detailed information about the case in context. This detail about the nature and circumstances of the case study often makes it intrinsically interesting, both to researcher and reader, simply as descriptive information.

Although no one case can ever be considered statistically representative of any phenomenon, *care must be taken in how the case or cases are selected for study.* Whether the case study is prospective or retrospective, the characteristics of the case that make it a useful instance for making observations about the specific study question being pursued must be clear. Similarly, the things that proved to be atypical in ways that influence the theoretical ideas that can be generated from it must also be spelled out. Unfortunately, this aspect of case study design is often overlooked or inadequately discussed.

Another standard of quality in the case study method that is often invoked is that *data ideally should be drawn from multiple sources or even through different data collection methods*, that is, using interview, observation, and/or written documents whenever possible (Fonagy & Moran 1994; Gilgun 1994; Yin 1994). Having multiple occasions of observation, multiple informants, and even multiple methods of data gathering all tend to lend credibility to the information on which conclusions in case study research are based. This strategy of gathering many forms and instances of data describing the same phenomenon is termed *triangulation* in the literature on case study research and in the literature on flexible method, or qualitative, research in general (Padgett 1998; Patton 1990). For this reason, a well-designed case study, even though limited to the examination of a single unit, can involve as much data collection and data analysis as a group-based flexible method study.

Another hallmark of quality in traditional case studies is that *the data on which conclusions are based exist in a form that is "intersubjectively available" in some form of "durable record"* (Fonagy & Moran 1993:67). That typically means, for example, that when interview or clinical data are used audiotapes are made to record them, and, in turn, transcripts of the verbatim recordings are generated from them for analysis. Some systematic method of recording observational and other forms of data is also needed (see chapter 12 on observation). Accurate records of the data permit another researcher to view the data that supports the conclusions drawn. Even though this is rarely done, the fact that it might be done helps keep the researcher true to the data in drawing conclusions from them.

As in other forms of flexible method research, *some description and analysis of the relationship of the researcher to the researched* is also characteristic of high-quality case studies. Is the researcher also the person providing the treatment being studied? Initially, how familiar or unfamiliar is the researcher with the people and/or setting being studied? What were the understandings conveyed to the person or people being studied about the nature of the research, the uses to which the data would be put, and who the researcher is or was in the setting during the conduct of the research? These questions go beyond informed consent and the other ethical considerations common to all kinds of research studies. They refer to the flexible method tradition, also found in the traditional case study, of including the person and subjective experiences of the researcher within the boundaries of what is studied (see chapter 1). This is especially necessary in case study research because of the prolonged exposure of the researcher to the individual case studied that is often characteristic of the intensive and extensive data collection involved. As Stake (1994) puts it, "Qualitative case study is characterized by the main researcher spending substantial time, on site, personally in contact with activities and operations of the case, reflecting, revising meanings of what is going on" (p. 242). This prolonged immersion in the research situation makes a reflexive process essential.

A somewhat different example of the use of theory in case study research is Fraiberg's (1970) classic study of the process of psychological development in a blind infant. Having been asked in the 1960s to treat a number of blind children who seemed autistic, Fraiberg needed to develop an understanding of how blindness at birth may compromise personality development and adaptation in such infants. She and a colleague decided to make monthly home visits to observe a particular blind baby interact with her mother. When they first met this infant at the age of three months, the baby, named Toni, immediately "tossed one hypothesis out of the crib" by smiling with recognition and delight when her mother approached her crib and spoke to her. Theory at the time said that infants bonded with their caregivers by sight; this baby had done so by sound. The researchers "experimented" in the field by approaching the infant and speaking to her themselves, but the baby reserved her expressions of pleasure and delight for the sound of her mother's voice. While the study goes on to describe the points in early development that did prove challenging to the infant because of her blindness, this first portion of the study demonstrated how a study based on unstructured observation of one case can indeed examine theory and suggest how it might be modified.

Fraiberg's continuing observations of this baby over time revealed that autistic-like behaviors did emerge when the lack of vision threatened to cause an impasse in motor development in the second half of the first year. Just when the baby might have been expected to creep, she began instead to lie prone and use repetitive movements for self-stimulation. The mother's spontaneous intervention, the introduction of a walker, constituted a natural experiment in therapy that solved the problem for her child; the pleasures of motion through space, once experienced in the walker, were enough to set this baby back on course in motor development. However, prior to this observation, the critical role of vision in motor development, specifically in stimulating creeping by moving toward an object seen, had not been understood.

This initial case study also identified other developmental issues needing study, such as the importance of the use of hands for blind infants and the relationship of cognitive development to sensory development in the substitution of sound for sight as a stimulus for grasping activity. Thus the first case study, arising directly out of practice, gave rise not only to theoretical insights and therapeutic techniques but also to a later, much larger program of structured, observational research into those areas of early development in blind children that still needed to be better understood.

The Fraiberg study of Toni incorporates all of the hallmarks of quality in case study research outlined above. She begins with a clearly stated question that guides the research: What adaptive challenges does blindness impose on infant development and how can they be overcome? This question grew out of clinical experience that showed that some but not all children blind from birth developed autistic-like behaviors, that is, developmental problems. Fraiberg also used her theoretical knowledge of early childhood development as a lens through which to observe and interpret her observations of Toni. However, she is also quite ready to observe and report disconfirming evidence, as when she notes that Toni recognized and demonstrated attachment to her mother based on the sound of her voice when the theory of the time said it was the sight of the mother that produced attachment in the child. In addition, the case to be studied was very carefully chosen both on theoretical grounds—so that the phenomenon of interest could most clearly be observed—and in an unbiased manner.

The case study of Toni also involved the gathering of large amounts of data through both observation and informal interviews over a long period of time. These data were quite deliberately gathered in context, in the naturalistic setting of the home, which is also typical of a well-designed case study. Behaviors could be seen repeatedly (verified) and changes in them noted. Because of the expense at the time of making a filmed record of what she saw, Fraiberg brought with her a second observer with whom she could verify and discuss the interpretation of the observations she made. Nowadays, it is likely that an intersubjectively available record of the data could be more easily and cheaply produced with a video camera than with a second professional observer. She also considered and commented very thoughtfully on her own subjective reactions to events that she observed, the professional role she assumed in the setting, and the ethical and professional dilemmas she experienced in the participant-observer role.

Fraiberg (1970) goes on to speak of how this first case study generated a later, larger-scale inquiry. The second study was designed both to verify observations made in the study of Toni and to generate new findings about the questions that the study of Toni either left unanswered or raised as new ones. This is a common use of the case study—as a pilot inquiry that will guide later larger-scale research. However, this does not mean that the pilot or preliminary study is the only legitimate use of the method. Had Fraiberg done no further research on blindness in babies, her study of Toni would still have made a contribution in itself. However, the well-designed clinical case study is one way in which human service professionals can contribute to the development of new research traditions addressing previously unstudied problems encountered on the front lines of client and community service.

An Example of Case Study Research

Jarrett's (1992) case study of "the complexity of low-income African-American family life (p. 172)," like the Feagin study reprinted in the previous chapter, takes as its conceptual starting point Wilson's (1987) analysis of the urban "underclass." Using both focus group (Jarrett 1994) and case study research, Jarrett seeks to learn more about how some ". . . well-functioning families continue to reside in impoverished areas despite the tremendous odds that Wilson articulates so well" (p. 173). She uses a case study approach, in her words, to "generate a comprehensive and holistic understanding of social events within a single setting" (p. 176), in this instance a single household in an urban neighborhood with high rates of poverty. She uses this study method to obtain "firsthand knowledge of real-life situations and processes within naturalistic settings . . ." and "an understanding of the subjective meanings that actors give to the behaviors and events being observed and discussed" (p. 176). These are typical goals for case studies that use flexible methods of inquiry.

The methods used in conducting this study are typical of flexible method case study research. Jarrett describes a "key informant," using a pseudonym, who allowed her household and family to be studied as an individual case. The term "key informant" comes from the anthropological literature and refers to a group member who steps forward to volunteer to give the research "stranger" access to the culture or group she wants to study. The researcher's access is therefore both facilitated and limited by the social and personal networks of the informant. In this instance, for example, other members of "Diane's" household and family— her mother, sisters, and others—also became sample members through their relationships with Diane.

As is typical of traditional case studies, the data collection in this study was both intensive and extensive. Data were gathered in context, that is, during weekly or biweekly visits to Diane's home over a period of four months. This method of data collection in context gave access to both planned and unplanned data collection opportunities. Both interviewing and observation were used, methods described as "participant observation," "informal group discussions," which were sometimes tape-recorded, and "topically-guided formal interviews," also tape-recorded, especially with Diane and her mother, that were sometimes private and sometimes not (Jarrett 1992:177–178). Historical data on how the composition of the household had changed over time were also collected and displayed in the study report. Thus extensive data were gathered, although limited to one household and the individuals who were or had been living there. This design, involving large amounts of data on a single unit or case and collected in context through more than one method over an extended period of time, is typical of a well-designed case study. Some key findings—about the flexibility and extensiveness of the mutual aid and household arrangements, for example—might not have emerged as clearly without the opportunity to observe the typical comings-and-goings within the household over time.

Data analysis was done using transcriptions of the tape-recorded interviews, coding for content themes. The published report does not explain how observational data were recorded or specifically how they were used in the data analysis. Thus these case study data were handled in the analysis in the same way that similar data from a flexible method study of a group of respondents would have been. The amount of data available for analysis was no less rich and the approach to the analysis was no less thorough and rigorous even though only one "case" was studied.

The way that Jarrett weaves data and interpretation together in her presentation of the findings from her case study is typical. The three major sections of the findings section have theory-derived titles: "Household Composition and Female Headship," "Geographic Concentration and Social Isolation of Poor Families," and "Neighborhoods' Effects on Family Life-Styles." Within each section she restates the conventional understanding of the issue and then presents case-based data, often verbatim, that she interprets as calling into question or refining these conventional understandings.

The key findings that emerged from this case study indeed illustrated how statistical aggregates, while accurate in cross-section, may mask adaptive patterns that exist in some families to support the "single mothers" (and others) among them. For example, Jarrett observed that the exchange of tangible and intangible resources within the family she studied extended well beyond the boundaries of the residence. Diane, the welfare mother who was the key informant for the study, was both a recipient and a provider of this mutual aid. Both interview data and repeated observations made in the household over time supported this interpretation of events. As Yin (1994) notes, intensive data collection and rigorous data analysis are needed in case studies to support the validity of the conclusions drawn from them.

As prior ethnographic studies had done, the Jarrett case study also documents the coping strategies that at least some families employ to insulate themselves from or at least mitigate the negative effects of "street culture" on the family. For example, specific efforts to protect the home from vandalism and make sure the young children in the household have adequate adult supervision are described in detail. Diane's family is depicted as "home-centered" and focussed on child-rearing despite the presence of crime and drugs in the neighborhood.

Thus in some ways the author presents this case as a "negative case" (Strauss & Corbin 1990) illustrating that neighborhood culture need not always be household culture and raising questions about some of the generalizations made about poor families headed by African American women. The case study is not used to suggest that all such families function the way that this one does, and no one who does research describing how groups function in the aggregate, or on average, believes that all families function according to the statistical norm. Conversely, the meaning and credibility of this case study do not come from any assertion that this case represents the total group statistically. Rather it comes from the connections drawn between the observations made of the case and the concepts used in the literature to describe these families in general. It is designed to show *how* families manage to do better than might be predicted from their household composition and place of residence and *in what ways* they manage to cope with the economic and social difficulties they face. It is more a study of family coping processes than specific outcomes, a goal that is well suited to the case study design.

Methods in Case Study Research

One common misconception about the traditional case study is that it is an easy form of research to conduct (Gilgun 1994; Yin 1994). In fact, like all research designs, traditional case studies should be employed only when there is a good fit between the research question being posed and what the case study method can deliver. In addition, an effective case study must be carefully designed and executed if its findings are to be credible.

Selection of the Case

Because only a single unit is used in case study research, careful thought must be given to how a case or cases are chosen for inclusion in the study. In fact, as Stake (1994) puts it, "understanding the critical phenomena may depend on choosing the right case" (p. 243). Unfortunately, however, this aspect of case study research is not often adequately addressed either in the methodological literature or in published reports of case study research.

Yin (1994) provides by far the best description of the logic that can and should inform the selection of cases for study. He mentions three approaches to case selection that can be productive. The first is the use of the "critical case" (p. 38), chosen because it has all of the innate and situational characteristics necessary for examining a well-developed theory. The analogy Yin makes is to a well-designed experiment (see chapter 7). The cases and conditions of study are in no way statistically representative or "ordinary." In contrast they are selected and designed because of the opportunity they afford for the examination of theory.

The Jarrett (1992) study can be seen as using the "critical case" technique although the author does not defend the choice in those terms. Yet, she chooses to study the household of an African American never-married mother receiving AFDC and rearing children apparently without a father present in a poor or economically transitional urban neighborhood. These are the theoretical conditions under which family dysfunctions of certain kinds are predicted to be present. Jarrett's goal is to demonstrate that some families are able to function differently in these same conditions.

Yin's (1994) second type of case selection is the "extreme or unique" (p. 39). This kind of case study is quite common in the clinical literature of many fields, including psychology and medicine. The choice of case is based on how a rare or

extreme form of disorder or functioning can shed light on more general mechanisms. Case presentations selected in this way, although not research, are also
commonly used in journalism and policy advocacy to draw attention to unmet
needs and the negative consequences of political decisions.

The third rationale for case selection discussed by Yin (1994) is called the
"revelatory" case (p. 40). Yin defines this situation as existing "when an investigator has an opportunity to observe and analyze a phenomenon previously inaccessible to scientific investigation" (p. 40). This situation best describes the
Fraiberg (1970) case study of Toni, the baby blind from birth. Fraiberg recounts
her surprise when reviewing the literature to find that no one had ever previously
actually studied the early phases of development in blind children.

In Fraiberg's case, however, the revelatory case did not simply present itself
fortuitously to her. Once she realized that no such study had previously been done,
she set out do the study in the most productive situation possible. Fraiberg (1970)
was careful to seek a case with certain key characteristics and to choose it in an
unbiased fashion. For example, she decided to exclude from study any blind baby
who had any other known medical, neurological, or sensory difficulties in order to
assess the effects of blindness per se on development. The sample, or case,
Fraiberg obtained for study turned out, in fact, to be an atypical one in that the
mother and infant, while socioeconomically disadvantaged, were an unusually
competent pair. In part for this reason, the case study provided rich data on
successful adaptation and ego development in blind children.

One issue Yin (1994) does not explicitly address is that often more than one
case of a given kind, especially the "critical" or "exemplary" types, are potentially
available for study. In such a case, the researcher, like Jarrett (1992), must find a
way to choose among them, both for study and for report. As in other forms of
sample selection, inclusion and exclusion criteria may need to be developed (see
chapter 10 on sampling). Skillful use of sample selection criteria can aid immeasurably in making the findings theoretically interpretable and meaningful.

When the researcher is in the position of selecting among cases for study,
some unbiased way of making the selection should be used. This strategy is not
important in case study design to enhance generalizability. Instead it is important
because of potential investigator influences on the findings, or what are termed in
experimental design, *selection effects.* If the subjectivity of the researcher influences the case chosen for study, it may also be influencing the findings. Fraiberg
(1970) deals explicitly with this issue by stating that she chose the next blind baby
born in her community that met her selection criteria as the one she would study.
Jarrett (1992), however, does not explain fully how she chose the nine women
from among those who volunteered to have their families individually studied in
depth or how and why she chose from among the nine cases studied the specific
case to present in her article.

Multiple case study approaches. Yin (1994) discusses very cogently the use of
multiple cases as a strategy. He points out that the use of more than one case is
often seen as automatically lending credibility to case study findings. This conclusion is based, however, on a misplaced use of what he terms "sampling logic

(p. 45)," or the rationale that guides descriptive research using group designs (see chapter 5). Instead the use of multiple-case designs, like experiments, is based on *replication logic* (p. 45), that is, credibility that rests on being able to reproduce a result on a separate, repeated occasion of study of the same phenomenon. Stake (1994) terms this "the collective case study" (p. 237), where theory-based case research is extended to a number of cases rather than to just one.

When describing the selection of multiple cases in this type of design, Yin (1994) states, "Every case should serve a specific purpose within the overall scope of inquiry" (p. 45). Therefore one might choose to study an additional case or cases to demonstrate that it is possible to predict similar findings in more than one instance. By contrast, one might choose to study one or more additional cases that will show contrasting results but for predictable reasons based in the theory generated from or guiding the first case study. Note that either way, the findings of multiple-case study designs do not rest on aggregating or averaging findings across cases. Instead each of the multiple cases constitutes a replication of the other *if* the predicted findings of similarity or difference in fact occur (Stake 1994). This kind of study, while too rarely done or done correctly, in fact has great potential to contribute to knowledge development in the helping professions.

Data Collection

Many of the hallmarks of quality in case study research have to do with data collection. Large amounts of data are usually collected, often using more than one data collection method. It is also characteristic of case study research that phenomena are studied in context, meaning that data are derived from naturalistic, or everyday, settings—the home, the community, the day-to-day world of professional practice. Often there is also an effort to verify the data gathered, either by using more than one observer or by recording observations and interview data in such a way that another professional could have access to it for checking out the interpretations made of it. Like other forms of flexible method research, the case study therefore often results in prolonged engagement of the researcher with the case being studied and the generation of large amounts of data, often as much as in a group-based flexible method study (Padgett 1998).

Fraiberg's (1970) study of Toni illustrates these principles well. First of all, Fraiberg chose the data collection context carefully, choosing to observe Toni and her mother in their everyday context, at home, rather than in the office or laboratory. Had she not done so, she likely would have missed certain key events, like the mother's introduction of a walker that resolved the development impasse that occurred when the baby did not begin to creep when predicted. The impasse revealed that sight is important in the development of locomotion in that babies seem to creep toward some object that they want to touch. A blind baby sees nothing to creep toward, but the walker, which is easily moved "by accident," afforded Toni the proprioceptive pleasure of motion that she then sought to provide for herself through walking. In the office, the researchers would have seen that the baby had begun to move about, but the mother may or may not have thought to mention the fact that she had given the child a walker. In the home, the walker was there to be seen. Similarly, by being in the home where the family's adaptations to poverty were in fact enacted, Jarrett (1992) saw events, such as Diane's care of her sister's children, that she might not have asked about or Diane might not have thought to mention in an interview because it was a taken-for-granted part of her life. Both the Jarrett and Fraiberg studies used observation and conversation (interviews) together for data collection. Data in one form could be used to corroborate, or elaborate on, the other in a process that is termed triangulation (see chapter 11). As Stake (1994) defines it:

> Triangulation has been generally considered a process of using multiple perceptions to clarify meaning, verifying the repeatability of an observation or interpretation. But, acknowledging that no observations or interpretations are perfectly repeatable, triangulation serves also to clarify meaning by identifying different ways the phenomenon is being seen (p. 241).

As in any form of research, triangulation thus adds credibility to the findings of case study research.

Fraiberg (1970) and Jarrett (1992) both "sampled" the observational context, or the behaviors they were interested in. They did so by observing the case of interest at intervals over time. Because she was interested in infant development, for example, Fraiberg (1970) was quite explicit about stating that she needed the study period to extend for some time. She planned her observations to occur at monthly intervals over the first two years of the baby's life, the period she understood theoretically to be critical for the development and emergence of autistic behavior were it to occur. One way Jarrett (1992) addressed the family's adaptive processes was to ask about the history of the composition of the household retrospectively. Changes in residence do not occur at any predictable or very frequent interval. Thus retrospective data were easier to obtain than prospective data on this issue, and recall of concrete events, such as who lived in the home in a given year, is reasonably reliable. Infants, on the other hand, develop and change at a rapid and somewhat predictable rate, making the prospective data collection plan a reasonable one.

Fraiberg (1970) also brought a second observer with her on her visits to Toni's home, an example of making data "intersubjectively available." Except for making audiotaped records of the interviews and some of the unplanned group conversation with the family that she conducted, Jarrett (1994) does not really address this aspect of her data collection in the case study. However, she does note that her focus group interviews with a number of women similar to Diane (Jarrett 1994) did provide some indirect corroboration of what she observed in this one family. Jarrett (1992) also used a multiple case study approach. Although these data are not presented in the reprinted study of the Moore family, the other eight families she studied in depth as cases could in fact be treated as replications, or opportunities to see whether or not similar patterns of successful adaptation to life in low-income neighborhoods were observed, that is, as in multiple case design.

Jarrett (1992) unfortunately says little about her subjective reactions and relationship to the family she came to know so well. Fraiberg (1970), on the other hand, comments at length about the benefits and drawbacks that the relationship she developed with Toni's mother posed for the research. In fact, the entire account she gives of the research can be said to focus on the ethical dilemmas that commonly arise in the researcher-researched relationship. When the case being studied is a vulnerable one and need becomes evident, the helping professional has to decide how much to intervene as a helper or "stand by" as an observer (see chapter 9).

Data Analysis

Data analysis in case study design basically involves "the organization and communication of findings" (Gilgun 1994:376). Case study data, as in other forms of research, are organized according to the conceptual or theoretical categories or issues that are most salient in making the results interpretable. A good case study report discusses what the categories are and how they were derived. Both Fraiberg (1970), who depended on the infant developmental theory of the time, and Jarrett (1992), who discusses differing theoretical views about how poverty in the urban African American community affects family values and family life, do this. They then describe their observations of the case they studied in terms of the major concepts derived from these theories. This involves an analytic strategy known as pattern matching, or comparing patterns in the data with what theory might predict (Stake 1994; Yin 1994). Pattern matching can be used either to confirm theoretical ideas or to show where theory might be questioned because the data do not "fit," as when the blind infant Toni demonstrated with her selective smiling that sight is not needed for bonding with the mother (Fraiberg 1970). While some case studies may be simply descriptive, having a theoretical or conceptual framework within which to present case study findings is generally regarded as preferable (Gilgun 1994; Yin 1994).

One of the hallmarks of case study research, as in other flexible method designs, is the richness of the data that result. As Gilgun (1994) notes, the findings of case studies generally present "the multiple patterns of phenomena . . . by describing the context and conditions under which the patterns appear . . . using multiple sources of evidence [for] thick description" (p. 376). This necessary style of presentation results in the readability and common appeal of case study research reports even to nonresearch oriented readers. In short, a good case study report often tells one or more stories in an accessible and interesting way.

Yin (1994) presents several precepts that are useful as guidelines in the process of analyzing case study data. First the analysis "should show that it relied on all the relevant evidence" (p. 123). While no case study report can or should recount every observation made or every instance of a phenomenon encountered, there must be some basis on which to trust that findings presented were based on a process of analysis that took all of the available data into account. As in other forms of flexible method research, some account of how this was done must be given. In addition, enough descriptive data must be presented so that the reader of the case study report has an idea of the kind of evidence on which a given conclusion was based (Gilgun 1994) and can form some idea of whether or not the data seem to support the interpretation given to it.

One way to ensure that the most relevant data are included, as Yin (1994) notes, is to present an analysis that addresses "the most significant aspect of [the] case study" (p. 123). The very richness of the data obtained may make it difficult to keep the main questions that initially gave rise to the case study central to the analysis and presentation of results. Opportunities to explore new or unexpected findings should not be overlooked. However, the process of analysis and presentation of results must be organized around the most important questions and findings from the study. This process yields the "analytic generalization" (p. 372) that Gilgun (1994) sees as key to case study research.

It is essential that the analysis and discussion of results in case study research be critical and skeptical in spirit. For this reason, data analysis in case studies:

> . . . should include *all major rival interpretations* [emphasis in the original]. If someone else has an alternative interpretation for one or more of your findings, make this alternative into a rival. Is there evidence to address this rival? If so, what are the results? If not, how can the rival be restated as a loose end to be investigated on future studies? (Yin 1994:123).

Stake (1994) also emphasizes considering alternative explanations or interpretations of case study data. This advice, of course, is relevant to all forms of research. However, because case studies depend so centrally on theory for generalizability (Gilgun 1994), exploration of all possible explanations for the findings is very important to them. On the other hand, those who have minimized the usefulness of case studies often note in their criticisms that this vital analytic step has been overlooked.

Yin's (1994) final piece of advice is necessary for all forms of research: "bring your own *prior, expert knowledge* [emphasis in the original] to your case study" (p. 124). Professional knowledge and critical thinking skills are indispensable to an effective data analysis in any form of research. However, they can be especially vital in flexible method research, whether group- or case-based, that generates large amounts of narrative data that must be reduced to its essentials.

Summary

Traditional case studies are currently being rediscovered as a worthwhile research strategy for social work and the human services (Gilgun 1994; Yin 1994). The hallmark of these studies is that they focus on a single unit—person, family, organization, community—and then study that unit in depth and in context. Case studies rely for their credibility on an intensive data gathering effort, which allows for patterns of observation to emerge, and on the soundness of the conceptual or theoretical explanations of the data. The case study method can be a useful tool for examining assessment and intervention issues as they arise in professional practice (Gilgun 1994).

Flexible method research, whether case- or group-based, is often intuitively appealing to practitioners. This appeal rests in part on the nature of the data presented, which is often rich, detailed, and narrative in form. However, this appeal is often based on an underestimation of the effort and skill required to conduct high-quality flexible method research. Like all research designs flexible method studies are useful for some kinds of questions and not for others. The next chapters in this section describe the various forms of fixed method research commonly used in social work and the human services—the kinds of questions they can answer and the methods typical of each.

A FAMILY CASE STUDY
An Examination of the Underclass Debate

ROBIN L. JARRETT
Loyola University of Chicago

In this chapter, I argue that qualitative methods constitute an important approach for capturing the complexity of low-income African-American family life. I base my argument on a two-step qualitative study that began with focus group interviews and moved to in-depth case studies based on participant observation and in-depth interviews of multiple family members. I used this two-step approach to explore hypotheses from William J. Wilson's (1987) *The Truly Disadvantaged*. Wilson and others currently involved in the "underclass" debate, though citing different causes (e.g., Auletta, 1982; Lemann, 1986; Murray, 1984), derive many of their insights on African-American family life from aggregate data and statistical analyses of family structure and dynamics. What often emerges from such approaches is a generalized profile of dysfunctional families. In a few instances, my qualitatively derived findings overlapped with Wilson's analysis, but in general I found inner-city African-American family life to be far more complex and heterogeneous than the more quantitatively based research suggests (Burton & Jarrett, 1991; Jarrett, 1991). This chapter is based upon data

from the Moore family (not their real name), a multigeneration African-American family. My detailed research with the Moores sheds light on three components of Wilson's discussion: the economic vulnerability of households headed by women, geographic concentration and social isolation of impoverished families, and negative neighborhood effects on individual and family life-styles.

My findings in the present study are consistent with findings on family life from existing ethnographies, many done 20 or more years ago. These studies move beyond one-dimensional profiles and provide descriptions of well-functioning families within impoverished neighborhoods (Aschenbrenner, 1975; Clark, 1983; Hannerz, 1969; Jeffers, 1967; Ladner, 1971; Stack, 1974; Sullivan, 1985; Valentine, 1978; Williams & Kornblum, 1985). My research suggests that well-functioning families continue to reside in impoverished areas despite the tremendous odds that Wilson articulates so well.

To make my argument, I first outline key issues from the current "underclass" debate on family life and poverty and describe the quantitative data used. Next, I discuss the general use of the qualitative case study and its applications to low-income, African-American families. Then, I examine hypotheses from the underclass debate using in-depth data from the case study of the Moore family. Finally, I summarize the strengths and limitations of the qualitative case study and its value in portraying low-income family life.

AUTHOR'S NOTE: This research was funded by grants from the Spencer Foundation and a Rockefeller Foundation Minority-Group Post-Doctoral award. Support from Professor Richard P. Taub and the Chicago Department of Human Services staff also made the research possible. Margaret Breslau and Carol Gagliano skillfully transcribed and coded the intensive interviews. Saadia Adell, Deanne Orput, Chris Schiller, and Pat Summers did similar work with the focus group interviews. Jane Gilgun, Kirsten Gronbjerg, Helena Z. Lopata, and Rebecca Blank offered helpful comments on an earlier draft of this paper. Any inaccuracies are those of the author. Ann Barret provided useful editorial comments. The participation of the Moore family is sincerely appreciated.

THE UNDERCLASS DEBATE

The rise in female-headed households and nonmarital childbearing among low-income

African-Americans has spurred researchers to reexamine the relationship between family life and poverty. Not since the 1970s has this issue been so intensely argued (Katz, 1989). Under the rubric "the underclass debate," a number of hypotheses have been advanced to explain changes in household and family formation patterns (Auletta, 1982; Bane & Ellwood, 1984a, 1984b; Lemann, 1986; McLanahan, Garfinkel, & Watson, 1988; Murray, 1984; Vinovski, 1988; Wilson, 1987). For a broader overview, see Cook and Curtin (1987), Jencks (1988); Jencks and Mayer (1989), Jencks and Peterson (1991), McGeary and Lynn (1988), Massey and Eggers (1990), and Ricketts and Sawhill (1988).

Wilson's book *The Truly Disadvantaged* (1987) offers an important scholarly statement on the plight of African-American poor and provides the conceptual framework for the present discussion. Using a comprehensive approach based on macro- and micro-levels of analysis, Wilson examines the impact of economic change on inner-city neighborhoods, families, individuals, and social mobility.

Wilson (1987) depicts inner-city communities, particularly those with rates of concentrated poverty at or above 40%, as chaotic and disorganized. According to Wilson, such neighborhoods lack functional social institutions and house the most socially and economically disadvantaged individuals and groups. Due to the loss of middle- and working-class families, present-day residents have few positive examples to emulate. Socially isolated from mainstream institutions and economically secure relatives and neighbors, inner-city dwellers are exposed to role models whose ghetto-specific behaviors limit social mobility.

Defining the underclass as a heterogeneous collection of extremely disadvantaged groups and individuals who live outside of mainstream society, Wilson (1987) includes households headed by women in this category. He characterizes them as examples of the most economically insecure families and, in the absence of a stable male provider, at risk for long-term poverty and welfare dependency. Moreover, he sees children in such families as especially at risk. On the basis of their living arrangements, Wilson implies that children who spend a significant portion of time in mother-only households are not only economically vulnerable but susceptible to the negative effects of neighborhood impoverishment.

Wilson (1987) bases his arguments on national and local data, including statistics on community poverty levels, female headship, family dissolution, family poverty rates, out-of-wedlock births, welfare dependency, unemployment, crime, and school dropout, as well as secondary references to other quantitative studies. He relies on aggregate statistical data to make inferences about individual behaviors and neighborhood processes. While explicitly noting the heterogeneity of individuals within the group he labels underclass, Wilson pays little attention to the issue of heterogeneity between families within the larger neighborhood. Clearly, quantitative data are important in documenting broad demographic changes in family and neighborhood patterns and establishing relationships between variables. Such data, however, often do not extensively explore the processes associated with these changes, nor their meaning.

Ethnographic Research Challenges Generalized Findings

A review of the existing ethnographic literature (Jarrett, 1990) indicates that family processes and dynamics, such as strong parental supervision of youth, isolation from street-oriented life-styles, network coalitions with conventionally oriented families, pooled family resources, household interdependence, and flexible living arrangements, are critical in ameliorating the detrimental effects of neighborhood impoverishment. Despite limited neighborhood resources for family maintenance, youth in families with these characteristics are more likely to exhibit mainstream social mobility outcomes, such as school completion, economic independence, and postponement of early parenthood. In contrast, youth in families lacking these vital dimensions are less likely to exhibit conventional social mobility outcomes.

QUALITATIVE APPROACHES TO AFRICAN-AMERICAN FAMILY LIFE AND POVERTY

This project began with exploratory focus group interviews, followed by in-depth interviews and participant observation. The project's goal was to gain a broader view of poor families than is available in contemporary discussions. Key themes were first explored in group interviews and later examined in more detail in intensive interviews.

Focus Group Interviews

A method for gathering qualitative data through group interaction, focus group interviews are primarily concerned with subjective perceptions, opinions, attitudes, values, and feelings. An interviewer or moderator convenes a homogeneous group of respondents to discuss a particular topic or issue. Focus group interviews are particularly useful for exploring the range and patterns of subjective perspectives in a relatively short period of time (Bellenger, Bernhardt, & Goldstucker, 1976; Calder, 1977; Downs, Smeyak, & Martin, 1980; Hedges, 1985; Merton, Fiske, & Kendall, 1956; Morgan, 1988; Morgan & Spanish, 1984; Smith, 1972).

Ten focus groups were conducted between January and July 1988 with a total of 82 low-income African-American women. The sample was purposive and drawn from Chicago-wide Head Start programs. Based on profiles of women hypothesized to be at risk for long-term poverty, I established criteria for selection to include: (a) never-married mothers; (b) recipients of AFDC at the time of the interviews; and (c) residents of low-income or economically transitional neighborhoods in the city of Chicago. Most of the women began their childbearing careers as adolescents. The focus group sample differed from the usual research emphasis on adolescents in concentrating instead on older, never-married mothers in their early to middle twenties. In choosing research respondents past adolescence, the study traced young women in the early stages of the family life cycle when decisions concerning household formation, family maintenance, and active parenting are most salient.

Interviewing and Observations

In-depth interviewing and limited participant observation began in the fall of 1988 and continued for 9 months. Although many of the women who participated in the focus group interviews also agreed to participate in this phase of the study, due to time constraints only nine families were targeted. A key consideration in the selection process was the willingness of other family members to participate.

The Case Study

The case study is a detailed and in-depth investigation of a single unit (Becker, 1970; Yin, 1989). Units of analysis include individuals, families, organizations, and communities. Frequently used in medical and psychological investigations, the case study in social science research generates a comprehensive and holistic understanding of social events within a single setting (Aschenbrenner, 1975; Bulmer, 1986; Cohler & Grunebaum, 1981; Gilgun, 1991; Handel, 1991). Case studies that rely upon qualitative methods are desirable when researchers seek firsthand knowledge of real-life situations and processes within naturalistic settings (Burgess, 1982, 1984; Bulmer, 1986; Emerson, 1981, 1983) and an understanding of the subjective meanings that actors give to the behaviors and events being observed and discussed (Burgess, 1984; Emerson, 1981; Jorgensen, 1989).

The Moore Family

Diane Moore, who participated in the focus group interviews, became a key informant for this case study. (All names, including names of neighborhoods, are pseudonyms.) She provided access to the family. She and her sisters generally fit the current demographic profiles of unmarried mothers discussed in the underclass debate. Diane relies on AFDC income and bore a child outside of marriage when she was 20 years old, slightly older than women typified in current discussions. Three of her siblings, Belinda, Marlene, and Sandra, all bore children when they were adolescents. Although the key informants were Diane and later her mother, Ella, informal conversations with Diane's three sisters provided additional data. Weekly or biweekly for 4 months, I visited the home Diane and her two children shared with her parents and other family members. I tape-recorded interviews, usually 1-1/2 hours in length. I supplemented the interviews with half-day observational periods and informal discussion.

Topically Guided, Informal Interviews

Guided by issues in the underclass debate, particularly those concerning household and family formation patterns and their dynamics, I chose topics for exploration in the focus groups and more detailed examination in the intensive interviews. Topics included individual life histories and genealogies, residence life histories, child care and socialization, intergenerational relations, female-male relationships, and welfare, work, and social opportunities.

I set up the interviews to be topically guided, yet informal in tone and style, and in some respects, conversational and free flowing. I encouraged informants to discuss what they perceived as the important dimensions of these issues and to do so in the language and categories they deemed meaningful. I wanted to approximate as much as possible a chat between friends (Burgess, 1984; di Leonardo, 1984; Spradley, 1979; Yancey & Rainwater, 1970). Due to the instrumental task at hand, however, most visible through the embeddedness of questions (Fetterman, 1989), the interviews were different from pure conversations; they were "conversations with a purpose" (Burgess, 1984, p. 102). The flexibility of the interviews facilitated the emergence of new and unanticipated data (Fetterman, 1989; Taylor & Bogdan 1984). Overall, a diverse range of information was collected.

I conducted most of the taped interviews with Ella and Diane separately. Some privacy was assured by interviewing mother and daughter on separate days, when one or the other was absent, or in separate parts of the house. Sometimes, however, this was impossible. Children were almost always present and some interviews were interrupted by resident or visiting kin. On such occasions, we ended our taped individual interviews, but I became involved in informal group discussions. Some-times I taped the group sessions. Together, the collective interviews furnished multiple perspectives on issues. On other occasions, informal discussions and participant observation were the primary activities. These periods provided an opportunity to observe family dynamics and to compare the relationship between verbal accounts and actual behavior.

Data Analysis

The interviews were transcribed, and the transcriptions were coded using The Ethnograph (Seidel, Kjolseth, and Seymour, 1988), a computer program for managing qualitative data. Although the categories of the research provided broad topics for initial coding, the interview data elaborated on the general codes, adding greater specificity to them. New codes were developed as unanticipated topics emerged from the interview data. Once the data were coded, comparisons were made between interviews. Because Diane Moore alone participated in the focus group discussions, comparisons between the individual and group interviews were done only in her case. I gave attention to similarities and differences among key topics, as well as interpretations of particular events. Observations from the field notes provided a contextual background for interpreting the interview data.

FINDINGS

As discussed earlier, I used the data from the Moore family to examine three components of Wilson's (1987) discussion: the economic vulnerability of households headed by women, the geographic concentration and social isolation of impoverished families, and neighborhood effects on family life-styles.

Household Composition and Female Headship

The economic vulnerability of households headed by women figures prominently in Wilson's (1987) discussion of the underclass. As he explicitly documents numerical increases in female headship among poor African-American women, he implicitly suggests that such families are handicapped because of the absence of a male provider. By concentrating on the living arrangements of single mothers and their children, it is easy to conclude that female-headed households receive little or no support for day-to-day functioning. When female-headed households are viewed independently, their connection to larger familial units and, perhaps most important, access to domestic support are obscured (Stack, 1974). Although one-shot surveys may be correct in documenting who lives within a particular household at a given time and longitudinal panel surveys may document change over time, most have not focused on between-household interactions nor interactions within larger family units. Intensive interviews and observations, in contrast, can more effectively discern the nature and content of familial relationships as well as the organizational principles undergirding them.

Flexible Household Arrangements

In this section, I illustrate how flexible household arrangements provide support to single mothers and children, irrespective of marital status or living arrangements. The Moore family fits Martin and Martin's (1978) definition of an extended family. It is

a multigenerational, interdependent kinship system which is welded together by a sense of obligation to relatives; is organized around a "family base" household; is generally guided by a "dominant family figure"; extends across geographical boundaries to connect family units to an extended family network; and has a built-in mutual aid system for the welfare of its members and the maintenance of the family as a whole. (p. 1)

The base household consists of Pervis and Ella Moore, members of the grandparent generation. Ella is the instrumental and affective core around which family life revolves. Ella and Pervis have 5 children and 14 grand-children. Figure 10.1 identifies key members of this extended family.

Sub Extended Households

Family members, though bound together by a sense of communal responsibility, may or may not live coresidentially. Several separate but interdependent, sub extended households cluster around the base household of Pervis and Ella. When the Moore family living arrangements are examined over time, the significance of the distinction between family membership and household composition is highlighted. Precipitated by domestic, economic, and personal crises, households expand and contract to accommodate family members. Although living arrangements are extremely fluid, the core of interdependent kin remains stable. Figure 10.2, constructed from interview data, shows the changes in

The Moore Family

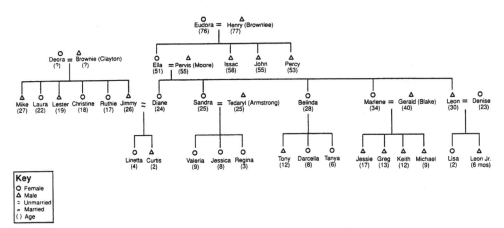

Figure 10–1 The Moore Family

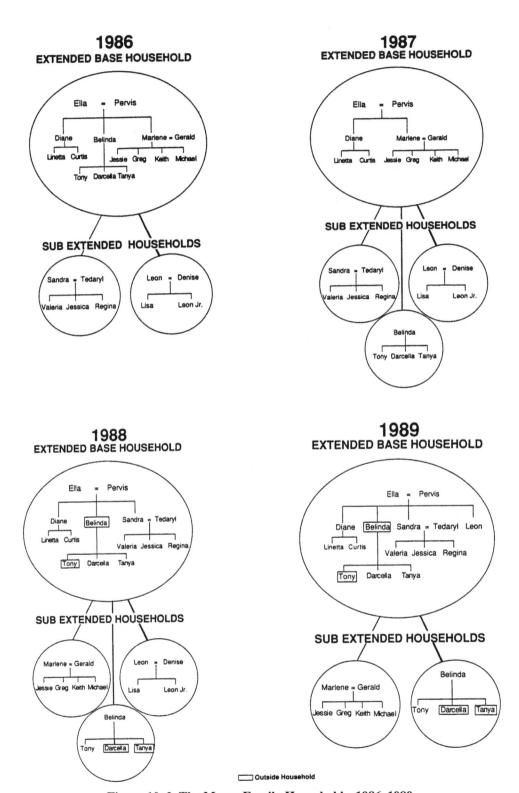

Figure 10–2 The Moore Family Households, 1986–1989

living arrangements for a 4-year period, 1986–1989.

In 1986, the base household of Pervis and Ella consisted of the grandparent couple, three daughters (Diane and her sisters Belinda and Marlene), Marlene's husband (Gerald), and the nine children of the three daughters. Diane and her two children resided consistently in the base household. A single, unemployed parent, Diane never lived independently. Economic and medical crises led to the incorporation of the families of the other two daughters. Gerald, for example, was ill, and Belinda was unemployed. The families of the other two Moore adult children (Sandra and Leon) were economically secure and lived in separate, but related, households.

In 1987, the base household consisted of Pervis and Ella, Diane and her two children, and Marlene, her husband Gerald, and their four children. Belinda had secured a job and moved to an independent household with her three children. The other two Moore adult children and their families continued to live independently.

In 1988, the household composition shifted once again. Although Pervis and Ella, along with Diane and her children, formed the consistent household core, the life circumstances of other family members changed. Gerald's health improved and he, Marlene (a Moore daughter), and their children moved out of the base household. Sandra, her husband Tedaryl, and their three children moved into the household. Belinda's two daughters moved back into the household of Pervis and Ella although Belinda kept her oldest child with her in her separate residence. Tedaryl's loss of his job and Belinda's child care problems motivated these household realignments. Sub extended units not living in the base household then included the families of three of the Moore adult children (two-parent households of Marlene and Gerald and Leon and Denise and the female-headed household of Belinda and her son Tony). In 1989, the composition of the base household remained unchanged except for one addition: Leon, then separated from his wife, moved in.

Internal Dynamics of Households

A closer look at the internal dynamics of households illustrates the nature of family relationships and the types of support various members receive. For the Moores, domestic tasks and kinship roles extend beyond the residential boundaries of individual households. Belinda (who at that time lived in a separate residence) and Sandra, describing the family's daily and weekly routine, underscore household interdependence:

Sandra: I got up, washed clothes. . . . I washed all day. . . . 12 o'clock came, I was still washing. . . . I kept getting interrupted. Marlene came over to wash in between mine. I went on and let her do it . . . helped her washing over a little bit, so she helped mine over a little bit. I let her go and wash 'cause I knew she had to go back home.

Belinda: I'm getting ready to help Mama with her bathroom. I told Diane if you go half with me we can get the bathroom a vanity set.

The distinction between family membership and household composition points out the limitations some surveys and census data have in helping us to understand the degrees of support independent heads of households may receive from kin and close family friends. Consider the case of Belinda. A standardized survey asking for household composition in 1987 would elicit the response that Belinda and her three children were the sole occupants of their household. Based on official census codes, Belinda would be considered a female head of household. Consequently, some quantitative researchers might assume that Belinda, an unmarried single mother living alone with her children, had little or no social or economic support.

Participant observation and interviewing would reveal otherwise. Even when Belinda lived independently, as she did at the time of the interviews, she remained interactionally linked to the base household. Belinda's daily routine typically included visits to the parental household of Pervis and Ella, where in 1988 two of her three children were being fostered by Diane. Tony, Belinda's oldest child, remained in the household with her. She felt that the younger girls, Tanya and Darcella, unlike their older brother, required more supervision. As an example of household linkages, Diane and Belinda discuss their child care arrangements:

Diane: I was at home any way. I had to run by and pick up Tanya and Darcella anyway because Belinda was at work. Anyway, I don't have nobody to keep Linetta and Curtis, so I started keeping Tanya and Darcella. . . . After they got out of school . . . I told Belinda they gonna go to school over here. It save us gas money running back to your house and missing them sometimes and they be sitting out there . . . trying to wait.

Belinda: I tell Tanya and Darcella, when I'm not here, Diane's in charge. She's responsible for them. They go to her for everything. And she will come to me to know what's going on, or if they bring something to me, I will let her know. That's the way we do it. Whatever she say is just fine 'cause I know she's not going to mistreat them. I couldn't work like I'm doing [without Diane's help]. . . . I just don't have a choice. I have to work in order to keep a roof over my head. It's hard trying to do it on your own and raise kids. You got to run a whole household and all the bills that's on you. If you don't get out here and work, where you going to live? Can't live off of aid. You get tired of aid.

Fosterage, or the practice of maintaining children in a household in which the parent does not reside (Stack, 1974), further solidifies personal and household interdependence. But most important, it provides support to single mothers and their children.

Diane, who lives coresidentially with her parents, as discussed earlier, has strong support from Jimmy Clayton, the father of her children, and his family, and when Jimmy is not able to help, Diane's mother does:

I got help from my mother and the kids' father. . . . Jimmy helped. He buy Pampers. . . . If I didn't have the money, he didn't have the

money right then, [my mother] would loan it to us. . . . Sometime she would say: "Naw, you don't have to pay this back." Or she would just go out and buy [it]. So, I got help [in] different situations. So, I never really was in a bind.

Genealogical information further documents strong kinship links to Jimmy and his family. When I asked Diane to list people she considered relatives, she included Jimmy and gave a detailed account of his maternal kin:

[My kids'] grandmother, Deora, [lives] on Hale. And [the kids] have auntie[s], Christine and Laura . . . and [they] got two uncles, Lester and Mike . . . and another aunt, Ruthie. . . . Curtis and Linetta got some cousins. . . . That's Mike's son and daughter. . . . And Laura has . . . what's her name?. . . I got her picture upstairs. . . . Maybe I'll run upstairs and get [her] picture. [Diane goes upstairs and returns.] Angie is the girl's name.

The genealogical information suggests extensive knowledge and contact with Jimmy's family. In our conversations, she also showed a working knowledge of paternal and more distant kin.

Data from a short questionnaire I administered after the focus group interview provided additional information on the bonds between Diane and Jimmy's family. In response to the question, "When you have a problem, or when you are feeling sad or depressed, who do you go to talk over that problem?" Diane listed her mother, sisters, and Deora Clayton, her children's paternal grandmother. Also as part of the locating information, when asked to "Give the name, address, and telephone number of people with whom you keep in touch," Diane again listed Deora Clayton.

Recent census surveys can potentially identify mother-child subunits within individual households, but they are often unable to link accurately these subunits to other interdependent households (see Bane & Ellwood, 1984a). Consequently, a survey researcher might conclude that Diane, an unmarried mother, is rearing her children, Curtis and Linetta, without a father and possibly in isolation from the father's family. This inference would be incorrect. The interdependence of Belinda and Marlene and their families with the base household also would not be apparent.

Distinctions Between Family Membership and Household Composition

The in-depth data illustrate a major point. *Family membership* refers to a set of socially defined kinship relationships, but *household composition* refers to residence or living arrangements. Depending on the time frame, the two may or may not overlap (Yanagisako, 1979). As illustrated by the Moores, family members who are in daily and weekly interaction with one another do not always live coresidentially. When family and associated domestic functions are largely defined by coresidence—an implicit assumption in the Wilson thesis and one drawn from an idealized model of the nuclear family (Reed, 1988)— extraresidential relationships are overlooked. Among the Moores, when a broader definition of family is used, one that transcends narrowly defined coresidential arrangements, household composition becomes less significant as an indicator of family dynamics. Thus, single mothers and children may live independently but receive social, economic, and child care support from other households. Similarly, parental roles can be fulfilled in the absence of a legal, coresidential marital union.

Geographic Concentration and Social Isolation of Impoverished Families

The second dimension of Wilson's (1987) argument I address in this chapter is his view, based on demographic data, that contemporary, inner-city neighborhoods are increasingly made up of the most impoverished families. Wilson argues that these families, geographically concentrated in decaying neighborhoods, lack sustained interaction with more economically secure relatives.

Previous ethnographic literature on low-income neighborhoods and families, however, indicates that, depending on the composition of kinship networks, family and individual interactions may transcend local geographic

boundaries (Aschenbrenner, 1975; Clark, 1983; Hannerz, 1969; Jeffers, 1967; Martin & Martin, 1978; Zollar, 1985). Within heterogeneous family networks including a variety of persons at differing socioeconomic levels, poor family members were found to be in contact with working- and middle-class relatives. Recent in-depth data from the Moores allow us to track neighborhood locations and interaction patterns of key family members and explore Wilson's thesis.

At the time of the intensive interviews, the base household and three of the sub extended households were located primarily within the almost exclusively African-American Thorndale community. Data from 1980 census indicated that although it was not among the most impoverished communities in Chicago (less than 20% of the population was below the poverty level), Thorndale nevertheless experienced social and economic problems. Unemployment, business failures, mortgage defaults, and gang-related problems increased between 1970 and 1980 (Chicago Fact Book Consortium, 1984). Indeed these are strong indicators that the 1990 census data will reveal worsening conditions that more accurately describe the conditions under which the Moore family currently live. For example, during this 10-year period, unemployment rates rose from 4.2 to 8.3%, and in a community of approximately 64,500, single-parent families increased from 2,700 to 5,600 (City of Chicago, Department of Human Services, 1990). Moreover, many of Thorndale's impoverished families were concentrated on particular blocks or within "pockets of poverty," thereby approximating the ecology of neighborhoods with higher overall rates of poverty.

When the adult children of Pervis and Ella lived outside of Thorndale, a largely working-class neighborhood, they all resided in economically comparable or economically improved neighborhoods. Leon, who returned to the parental household in 1989, lived in Avon Park, a working-class neighborhood. Prior to Sandra's return in 1988, she and her family lived in Gulf Stream, a middle-class suburb. In 1985, preceding Marlene's return to Thorndale, she and her family lived in Eastern

Ridge, a neighborhood with a combined working- and middle-class population.

Although none of Pervis and Ella's adult offspring live in deteriorated, impoverished neighborhoods, the Moore family has links to two households located in such areas: the Brownlees and the Claytons. The household of Ella's parents, Deora and Henry Brownlee, is located some 20 miles away in Highpoint, an extreme poverty area. According to census data, at least 40% of the households were below the poverty line in 1980. The household of Jimmy Clayton, the father of Diane's children, is located in the even more impoverished neighborhood of Chesterfield, nearly 10 miles away from the Moore base household. Census data documented that at least 50% of the households in Chesterfield were below the poverty line in 1980. Both neighborhoods are expected to show greater impoverishment in the 1990 census.

To some extent, the geographic location of households in Thorndale parallels the socioeconomic status of different family members. Mirroring the working-class status of Thorndale, the grandparent generation is stably employed in working-class occupations: Ella works as a lunchroom manager in a high school, and Pervis is employed at Vistar, a plastic casing factory. Some of the adult offspring duplicate their parent's socioeconomic status: Marlene works for the telephone company; Leon works for a local bus company; and Belinda, assisted by her mother, recently became employed as a teacher's aide. They, too, live in working-class neighborhoods.

A Refinement of the Geographic Concentration and Social Isolation Thesis

The case study materials underscore why some poor individuals do not live in neighborhoods with high concentrations of poverty and why some economically secure individuals do. Moreover, they highlight the nature of the interactions between family members in neighborhoods with varying socioeconomic statuses. Diane currently receives welfare, as other family members have on occasion. Recently, San-

dra made the transition from work to welfare, and Belinda made the transition from welfare to work. Yet none of the Moore siblings have ever lived in neighborhoods of high poverty concentration as adults. Now retired, Ella's parents, Henry and Eudora, had consistent employment histories: Henry worked most of his adult life at Vistar (along with his son-in-law, Pervis), and Eudora worked at several factory jobs. Yet they continue to live in a neighborhood of high poverty concentration.

As single parents and potentially economically vulnerable, Diane and Belinda are unlikely to reside in impoverished neighborhoods as long as they are buffered by the larger extended family. Due to age and existing social ties, it is equally unlikely that Eudora and Henry will move to a more economically secure neighborhood. As Ella points out: "My mother [Eudora] never, never lived anywhere else, and I think it is her favorite part of town."

Despite the geographic dispersal of households in neighborhoods of differing socioeconomic levels, family members continue to interact with one another. Ella describes contact with her parents' household:

> I spend time with my mother. . . . My father and three of my brothers live there. I'm the only one out of the house. . . . I like to go over there at least once a week, or if I'm over there in that area, I just drop in to see how they doing. . . . When I first started working, I was more or less sleeping and eating over there and dressing out of a suitcase, because I couldn't really come all the way home, get some rest, and then go back to work. . . . I spend quite a bit of time with [my mother]. Sometimes I have to take her to different appointments. . . . We be talking about some of the relatives, . . . how they doing, . . . or what they did at church. . . . My father [sits] in the living room and he'll look at TV and let the women have the kitchen.

Similarly, Diane provided a great deal of information on the extent of the contact her children have with their father and his family, who live in an impoverished area in a household largely reliant on income from ADFC; the children have daily contact with their father and frequently visit him in his home.

The data offer an addendum to Wilson's hypotheses concerning geographic concentration and social isolation.

Although it is true that some poor, as exemplified by members of the Clayton household (Jimmy's family), live in impoverished neighborhoods, working-class individuals, as exemplified by members of the Brownlee household, may also live there. Conversely, poor individuals, as represented by Diane and, depending on the availability of work, Belinda Moore, may live in working-class neighborhoods. These data highlight—a point that remains implicit in the concentration thesis—that residence in a particular neighborhood is not in all cases directly related to individual socioeconomic status, but influenced by the presence or absence of external sources of support as well as stages in the family life cycle.

When family is defined largely as a nuclear, coresidential arrangement and neighborhood is conceived exclusively as a geographic entity, as they are in the Wilson (1987) book, social relations that transcend household and neighborhood boundaries are obscured. Examples from the Moore family indicate that some families more accurately function as a network of interacting individuals. Linked by affective and instrumental ties, these relationships exist across household and neighborhood boundaries (Olson, 1984; Wireman, 1984).

Neighborhoods' Effects on Family Life-Styles

Based on profiles derived from census data, Wilson (1987) focuses almost exclusively on families overwhelmed by negative neighborhood forces. He provides little information on functional families within poor neighborhoods. Yet, ethnographic research documents heterogeneous family life-styles and coping strategies within low-income neighborhoods (Aschenbrenner, 1975; Clark, 1983; Hannerz, 1969; Ladner, 1971; Valentine, 1978; Williams, 1981; Williams & Kornblum, 1985). Moreover, Wilson fails to address the strategies that some families employ to ameliorate the potentially debilitating effects of poverty. Firsthand accounts from the Moore family illustrate the issue of life-style heterogeneity and provide examples of family dynamics that obviate the adverse consequences of neighborhood impoverishment.

Members of the Moore family recognize and cope with the neighborhood conditions Wilson outlines. Ella notes:

> The jobs are folding up. . . . We wouldn't have so much crime as when they was with jobs. . . . Now you got gang banging, you got stealing automobiles, and dope and stuff like this. You got a lot of people now that's out of jobs. So you got a lot of people on relief.

Ella corroborates that some of the problematic social conditions Wilson (1987) ascribes to the most impoverished neighborhoods also exist in Thorndale. However, in contrast to the universally negative neighborhood effects Wilson depicts, her description indicates positive coping strategies:

> The neighbors across the street, they watch out for us. And if any of us go on vacation, we'll tell them to keep an eye on the house. . . . So we're pretty close. This block itself is pretty nice so far. We don't have too many gang bangers. . . . I always pull my car up in the drive and I always come through the back. So they actually don't know whether I'm in here. . . . They don't know when somebody's here or not.

Far from being victims of their environment, Ella further discusses how as parents she and Pervis coped with the environmental risks of the housing projects, where they lived before they moved to their present single-family home:

> I usually kept them restricted until I came home or until their daddy came home. Then, if he let them go out and play, fine. Or if I came home, I would let them play on the ramp until I got ready to feed them. It worked out real nice 'cause that way my husband was home at night and I was home during the day. So they always had an adult at home or someone there with them while they was young. . . . I didn't bother about youngsters running in and out of the house and all that stuff or them staying out, not going to school and running the streets some-

where. I kept a hand on them. I didn't have to run up to the school with them, because both of us would always tell them that more than us was watching them. . . . Our children was pretty good. . . . I was fortunate enough that they wasn't having babies at 10 and 11, 13 years old. They did try to finish high school. . . . Diane is doing pretty much like I did. She participate quite a bit with her kids' activities. She spend a lot of time with them.

Similar socialization and management strategies are currently employed with the grandchildren within the Thorndale neighborhod.

Although less stable individual and family patterns exist in the Thorndale neighborhood—the result of economic factors—the Moores lead a stable, home-centered life, in which they perform routine, domestic tasks. An excerpt from Diane's description of a typical day, much of which was confirmed through observation, illustrates this point:

> On a Monday I do all my house chores for the whole week. . . . Like now, I'm washing. . . . [After the children are in school] I may be washing my clothes and cleaning up the house. . . . Then I pick the kids up. I may still be washing. Then, when they come in from school, I make them change their clothes. . . . I clean up go out and mop, iron. . . . I iron every day. I don't iron all my clothes up 'cause they'd be right back wrinkled. . . . I clean up the living room, dining room, . . . clean the fish bowl out. . . . I set the garbage out for the garbage man to come. . . . Tuesday, until three o'clock, it's the same as Monday. . . . Sometimes I do volunteer work at the school. . . . The only day I tell them "no" is on the day I wash and that's mostly on Monday. But any other day of the week, I volunteer anytime. . . . Wednesday's the day that I have free where all day I can come home. . . . Thursday from three to six I'm across the street [baby-sitting]. . . . Fridays, I do anything that I have to do that I ain't done in the beginning of the week. Sundays, I get up, get the kids ready for church. . . . We get out of bed, get washed up, get our clothes on, get ready for church. . . . I'm in the choir, the kids in the choir. . . . We at church, singing in the choir, praising the Lord.

Sandra describes a similar routine, which includes daily cooking, going to church, watching television, and visiting relatives.

A Variety of Life-Styles

Thequalitative data document the presence of various individual and family life-styles within African-American neighborhoods. In response to neighborhood conditions, home-oriented patterns coexist with street-oriented life-styles in the working-class and low-income neighborhoods where the Moores have lived. (See, for example, Gans, 1982; Hannerz, 1969; Howell, 1973.) Although family members are exposed to street-oriented patterns—stealing, drug dealing, gang banging—such exposure does not encourage them to adapt this alternative life-style.

In the home, much of the family routine, quite mundane in nature, centers around the fulfillment of domestic and child care responsibilities. Despite early childbearing, nonmarital childbearing, or both, and in some cases, reliance on AFDC income, women in the Moore family are considered competent, if not exemplary, mothers. The children of the mothers' generation (Ella and Pervis's grandchildren) are performing well in school and have been sheltered from the potential pitfalls of the neighborhood. To a large extent, the stability of the Moores derives from their sense of communal obligation to one another. By pooling resources, various households are stabilized during crises. Overall, they represent a well-functioning family.

DISCUSSION

Critics maintain that methodological biases limit the reliability and validity of qualitative data (Denzin, 1970; Emerson, 1981). Their concerns have some basis. Retrospective life history interviews may be compromised by memory lapses, informants' need to present a coherent narrative, or their developmentally changing interpretive schemes (Becker, 1970; Denzin, 1970; Plummer, 1983). In general, interviews can elicit idealized accounts that depart from actual behavior (Becker & Geer, 1969). Participant observation may be hampered by over-rapport and biased reports (Miller, 1969; Schwartz & Schwartz, 1969). Further, focus group dynamics potentially inhibit individual disclosures (Hedges, 1985; Morgan, 1988). More fundamentally, researcher characteristics—race, social class, age, and gender—can have an impact on each of these methodological strategies (di Leonardo, 1984; Sawyer, 1973; Warren, 1988; Warren & Rasmussen, 1977; Wax, 1979; Yancey & Rainwater, 1970).

All research methods, both qualitative and quantitative, are inherently limited, but researchers employ a variety of strategies to reduce sources of bias. This study's use of multiple methods, including focus group interviews, individual interviews, and limited participant observation, as well as multiple sources of information and multiple interviews, provided checks on potential threats to reliability and validity.

Often viewed as exclusively descriptive, case studies are assumed to be of little or no value for theory development. Further, the ability to provide generalizable propositions from a single example is questioned. In both instances the criticisms are ill-founded (Becker, 1970; Bulmer, 1986; Gilgun, 1991; Yin, 1989). Although true experiments focusing on individual behavior are powerful tests of theory, qualitative data have theory-generating capabilities. (See Gilgun, Chapter 3, this volume.) Qualitative data can inductively generate new theories or inform existing theories. Embedded in the experiences of real people and situations, such theories more closely approximate social reality (Bulmer, 1986; Emerson, 1983). Observations from the Moore family provide an example of how the qualitative case study can offer theoretical direction to the underclass debate.

Although focusing on one family, the case study materials here are interpreted within a larger body of research findings. As discussed earlier, in-depth data from the Moore family are consistent with past ethnographies with respect to family life-styles, family-neighborhood interactions, and family composition and dynamics. Thus, when the single case study is examined in light of existing research, it approximates a comparative research design. It does not stand alone. Moreover, as part of a larger research focus, the single case study

adds to the larger cumulative knowledge base (Suttles, 1986).

Some poor African-American families are adversely effected by the conditions of poverty. Others manage to cope, despite economic obstacles. In light of the interconnectedness of their lives, often within the same neighborhoods, a well-rounded research agenda seeks to explain both outcomes. As illustrated by the case study materials, family process dimensions that explain these differences can be fully explored using qualitative approaches.

Research does not exist in a vacuum, but is effected by the larger social and political content in which it is conducted (Rainwater & Pittman, 1967; Suttles, 1976). The types of information sought on some poor African-American families contradict idealized norms and values, encouraging stereotypical depictions of their lives and neighborhoods. Yet if the goals of research are to provide accurate portrayals of the poor and to generate effective and humane public policies, then these efforts must be informed by the firsthand accounts of those whose lives are directly touched by poverty. Qualitative methods provide an avenue for their voices.

REFERENCES

Aschenbrenner, J. (1975). *Lifelines: Black families in Chicago.* New York: Holt, Rinehart & Winston.

Auletta, K. (1982). *The underclass.* New York: Random House.

Bane, M. J., & Ellwood, D. T. (1984a). *The dynamics of children's living arrangements* (Working Paper Contract No. HHS-100–82–0038). Washington, DC: U. S. Department of Health and Human Services.

Bane, M. J., & Ellwood, D. T. (1984b). *Single mothers and their living arrangements* (Working Paper Contract No. HHS-100–82–0038). Washington, DC: U. S. Department of Health and Human Services.

Becker, H. S. (1970). *Sociological work: Method and substance.* Chicago: Aldine.

Becker, H. S., & Geer, B. (1969). Participant observation and interviewing: A comparison. In G. J. McCall & J. L. Simmons (Eds.), *Issues in participant observation: A text and reader* (pp. 322–331). Reading, MA: Addison-Wesley.

Bellenger, D., Bernhardt, K. L., & Goldstucker, J. L. (1976). *Qualitative research in marketing.* Chicago: American Marketing Association.

Bulmer, M. (1986). The value of qualitative methods. In M. Bulmer, with K. G. Banting, S. S. Blume, M. Carley, & C. Weiss (Eds.), *Social science and social policy* (pp. 180–204). Boston: Allen & Unwin.

Burgess, R. G. (1982). *Field research: A sourcebook and field manual.* London: Allen & Unwin.

Burgess, R. G. (1984). *In the field: An introduction to field research.* Boston: Allen & Unwin.

Burton, L. M., & Jarrett, R. L. (1991). *Studying African-American family structure and process in underclass neighborhoods: Conceptual considerations.* Paper presented at the annual meeting of the American Sociological Association, Cincinnati, OH.

Calder, B. J. (1977, August). Focus groups and the nature of qualitative marketing research. *Journal of Marketing Research, 14,* 353–364.

Chicago Fact Book Consortium. (1984). *Local community fact book of Chicago metropolitan area: Based on the 1970–1980 census.* Chicago: Chicago Review.

City of Chicago, Department of Human Services. (1990). *1990 Community needs assessment: Head Start.* Chicago: Department of Planning, Research and Development.

Clark, R. M. (1983). *Family life and school achievement: Why poor Black children succeed or fail.* Chicago: University of Chicago Press.

Cohler, B. J., & Grunebaum, H. U. (1981). *Mothers, grandmothers, and daughters: Personality and child care in three-generational families.* New York: John Wiley.

Cook, T., & Curtin, T. (1987). The mainstream and the underclass: Why are the differences so salient and the similarities so unobtrusive? In J. C., Masters & W. P. Smith (Eds.), *Social comparison, social justice, and relative deprivation: Theoretical, empirical, and policy perspectives* (pp. 218–264). Hillsdale, NJ: Lawrence Erlbaum.

Denzin, N. K. (1970). *The research act: A theoretical introduction to sociological methods.* Chicago: Aldine.

Downs, C., Smeyak, G. P., & Martin, E. (1980). *Professional interviewing.* New York: Harper & Row.

Emerson, R. M. (1981). Observational field work. *Annual Review of Sociology, 7,* 351–378.

Emerson, R. M. (1983). *Contemporary field research: A collection of readings.* Prospect Heights, IL: Waveland.

Fetterman, D. M. (1989). *Ethnography: Step by step.* Newbury Park, CA: Sage.

Gans, H. J. (1982). *The urban villagers: Group and class in the life of Italian-Americans* (expd. and upd. ed.). New York: Free Press.

Gilgun, J. F. (1991). *A case for case studies in social work research.* Manuscript submitted for publication.

Handel, G. (1991). Case study in family research. In J. R. Feagin, A. M. Orum, & G. Sjoberg (Eds.), *A case for the case study* (pp. 244–268). Chapel Hill: University of North Carolina Press.

Hannerz, U. (1969). *Soulside: Inquiries into ghetto culture and community.* New York: Columbia University Press.

Hedges, S. (1985). Group interviewing. In R. Walker (Ed.), *Applied qualitative research* (pp. 239–269). Brookfield, VT: Gower.

Howell, J. (1973). *Hard living on Clay Street: Portraits of blue collar families.* New York: Anchor.

Jarrett, R. L. (1990). *A comparative examination of socialization patterns among low-income African-Americans, Chicanos, Puerto Ricans, and Whites: A review of the ethnographic literature.* New York: Social Science Research Council.

Jarrett, R. L. (1991). *Ethnographic contributions to the study of African-American families and children: Past and future directions.* Paper presented at preconference meeting of the Society for Research on Child Development, Seattle, August 16–17.

Jeffers, C. (1967). *Living poor: A participant observer study of priorities and choices.* Ann Arbor, MI: Ann Arbor Press.

Jencks, C. (1988). Deadly neighborhoods. *The New Republic, 198,* 23–32.

Jencks, C., & Mayer, S. E. (1989). *The social consequences of growing up in a poor neighborhood: A review.* Evanston, IL: Northwestern University, Center for Urban Affairs and Policy Research.

Jencks, C., & Peterson, P. E. (Eds.). (1991). *The urban underclass.* Washington, DC: Brookings Institution.

Jorgensen, D. L. (1989). *Participant observation: A methodology for human studies.* Newbury Park, CA: Sage.

Katz, M. B. (1989). *The undeserving poor: From the war on poverty to the war on welfare.* New York: Pantheon.

Ladner, J. A. (1971). *Tomorrow's tomorrow: The black woman.* New York: Anchor.

Lemann, N. (1986, June). The origins of the underclass. *Atlantic Monthly, 258,* 31–55.

di Leonardo, M. (1984). *The varieties of ethnic experience: Kinship. class, and gender among California Italian-Americans.* Ithaca, NY: Cornell University Press.

McGeary, M. G., & Lynn, L. E. (Eds.). (1988). *Urban change and poverty.* Washington, DC: National Academy Press.

McLanahan, S., Garfinkel, I., & Watson, D. (1988). Family structure, poverty, and the underclass. In M. G. McGeary & L. E. Lynn (Eds.), *Urban change and poverty* (pp. 102–147). Washington, DC: National Academy Press.

Martin, E., & Martin, J. M. (1978). *The black extended family.* Chicago: University of Chicago Press.

Massey, D., & Eggers, M. (1990). The ecology of inequality: Minorities and the concentration of poverty, 1970–1980. *American Journal of Sociology, 95,* 1153–1188.

Merton, R. K., Fiske, M., & Kendall, P. (1956). *The focused interview: A manual of problems and procedures.* Glencoe, IL: Free Press.

Miller, S. M. (1969). The participant observer and "overrapport." In G. J. McCall & J. L. Simmons (Eds.), *Issues in participant observation: A text and reader* (pp. 87–89). Reading, MA: Addison-Wesley.

Morgan, D. L., (1988). *Focus groups as qualitative research.* Beverly Hills, CA: Sage.

Morgan, D. L., & Spanish, M. T. (1984). Focus groups: A new tool for qualitative research. *Qualitative Sociology, 7,* 253–270.

Murray, C. (1984). *Loosing Ground: American social policy, 1950–1980.* New York: Basic Books.

Olson, P. (1982). Urban neighborhood research: Its development and current focus. *Urban Affairs Quarterly, 17,* 491–518.

Plummer, K. (1983). *Documents of life: An introduction to the problems and literature of a humanistic method.* Boston: Allen & Unwin.

Rainwater, L, & Pittman, D. J. (1967). Ethical problems in studying a politically sensitive and deviant community. *Social Problems, 14,* 357–366.

Reed, A., Jr. (1988, February 6). The liberal technocrat. *The Nation, 246,* 167–170.

Ricketts, E. R., & Sawhill, I. V. (1988). Defining and measuring the underclass. *Journal of Policy Analysis and Management, 7,* 316–25.

Sawyer, E. (1973). Methodological problems in studying so-called "deviant" communities. In J. Ladner (Ed.), *The death of white sociology* (pp. 361–379). New York: Random House.

Schwartz, M. S., & Schwartz, C. G. (1969). Problems in participant observation. In G. J. McCall & J. L. Simmons (Eds.), *Issues in participant observations: A text and a reader* (pp. 89–105). Reading, MA: Addison-Wesley.

Seidel, J. V., Kjolseth, R., & Seymour, E. (1988). The Ethnograph. Qualis Research Associates, PO Box 3219, Littleton, CO 80161.

Smith, J. M. (1972). *Interviewing in market and social research.* Boston: Routledge & Kegan Paul.

Spradley, J. P. (1979). *The ethnographic interview.* New York: Holt, Rinehart & Winston.

Stack, C. B. (1974). *All our kin: Strategies for survival in a Black community.* New York: Harper & Row.

Sullivan, M. (1985). *Teen fathers in the inner city.* New York: Ford Foundation.

Suttles, G. D. (1986). School desegregation and the "national community." In J. Praeger, D. Longshore, & M. Seeman (Eds.), *School desegregation research: New directions in situational analysis* (pp. 47–78). New York: Plenum.

Taylor, S. J., & Bogdan, R. (1984). *Introduction to qualitative methods: The search for meanings* (2nd ed.). New York: John Wiley.

Valentine, B. L. (1978). *Hustling and other hard work: Life styles in the ghetto.* New York: Free Press.

Vinovski, M. (1988). Teenage pregancy and the underclass. *Public Interest, 93,* 87–96.

Warren, C.A.B. (1988). *Gender issues in field research.* Beverly Hills, CA: Sage.

Warren, C.A.B., & Rasmussen, P. K. (1977). Sex and gender in field research. *Urban Life, 6,* 349–369.

Wax, R. H. (1979). Gender and age in fieldwork and fieldwork education: No good thing is done by any man alone. *Social Problems, 26,* 509–522.

Williams, M. (1981). *On the street where I lived.* New York: Holt, Rinehart & Winston.

Williams, T., & Kornblum, W. (1985). *Growing up poor.* Lexington, MA: Lexington.

Wilson, W.J. (1987). *The truly disadvantaged: The inner city, the underclass, and public policy.* Chicago: University of Chicago Press.

Wireman, P. (1984). *Urban neighborhoods, networks, and families: New forms for old values.* Lexington, MA: Lexington.

Yanagisako, S. J. (1979). Family and household: The analysis of domestic groups. *Annual Review of Anthropology, 8,* 161–205.

Yancey, W. L., & Rainwater, L. (1970). Problems in the ethnography of the urban underclass. In R. Habenstein (Ed.), *Pathways to data: Field methods for studying ongoing social organizations* (pp. 245–269). Chicago: Aldine.

Yin, R. K. (1989). *Case study research: Designs and methods* (rev. ed.). Newbury Park, CA: Sage.

Zollar, A. C. (1985). *A member of the family: Strategies for Black family continuity.* Chicago: Nelson-Hall.

Qualitative Methods in Family Research. Jane F. Gilgun, Kerry Daly, & Gerald Handel (Eds.). Newbury Park, CA: Sage Publications, 1992.

5

Fixed Methods: Descriptive Research

Because science is empirical, all research is in some sense descriptive. The empirical nature of research means that statements are made only after evidence has been seen (or heard, or smelled, or tasted, or touched) to substantiate them. When a report of any scientific investigation is presented, a description of the evidence put forward to substantiate the conclusions is always offered. It is in this sense, then, that all scientific research can be considered descriptive. However, some fixed method studies are called descriptive as a distinct type.

What then makes a fixed method study descriptive as opposed to relational or experimental? Descriptive research has as its purpose developing a better understanding of a phenomenon in detail. Descriptive studies usually have as their purpose the first two aims of normal science as described by Kuhn (1970): ". . . attempts to increase the accuracy and scope with which . . . facts . . . are known" (p. 25) or "determination . . . [of] those facts that . . . can be compared directly with the predictions from . . . theory" (p. 26). The Anderson and Mandell study of social workers' use of self-disclosure reprinted in this chapter illustrates the first purpose well: to describe in more detail social workers' use of self-disclosure in their practice.

From the standpoint of fallibilistic realism (Manicas & Secord 1983), the aim of descriptive research is to clarify the nature of a phenomenon in a specified, static context while viewed from a specific, fixed perspective. Descriptive research methodology can be thought of as defining a closed system in which the boundaries of what is to be studied, the procedures used to study it, and the relationship of the observer to the observed are fixed or held constant throughout the conduct of the study. Although there is no single "right" perspective or point of view from which such a study can be conducted, a particular perspective is chosen and used.

Descriptive research, then, is directed toward clarifying a phenomenon's appearance or nature. Descriptive research is analogous to taking and developing still photographs. The scene depicted may be shown in great detail, but what is depicted is entirely dependent on where the photographer was standing, what the photographer decided to focus on, and how much of the context the photographer decided to leave in or out when the picture was taken and the print prepared. The greatest strength of this form of research is that its results can be perhaps among the most unambiguous. Its greatest limitation is that its picture is static, limited to a specific point in time and to a particular observational context as seen from one particular point of view.

Descriptive research addresses what a phenomenon looks like rather than how it works or functions. The study of function, of the phenomenon in its relationship to other phenomena, is the province of relational and experimental research. Describing the nature of a phenomenon when static and in a static context, typically using data collection tools in standardized ways, is the purpose of descriptive research.

In the traditional view of research in which the experiment is viewed as the apex of method, descriptive research can be seen as lacking rigor and even as being "nonscientific" because it is not addressed to making causal arguments. In fallibilistic realism (Manicas & Secord 1983), data and theory are never wholly separable and, if anything, theory and concepts are primary. Therefore both describing things empirically and understanding what they are from a given theoretical perspective are equally important.

There is one arena where descriptive research, even traditionally, has always been seen as legitimate: when researchers and policy analysts have an interest in determining what is usual, that is, "normal," for a given characteristic, population, or setting. This sort of question is answered by collecting what are known as normative data, which is information gathered to provide a straightforward description of what is seen to exist in the population or setting under study. A description of the average number of children in United States households collected by the Census Bureau is one example of normative data. One of the most common uses of normative data is in psychological testing in providing a context for understanding any individual case seen, and another form, survey data, is becoming ubiquitous in political life as polling organizations track public opinion about political issues and politicians seemingly on a daily basis.

Descriptive research is often misconstrued as a description of a phenomenon in some essential, absolute sense. Such a conception is inappropriate. Whenever a phenomenon is described, it is described in some context. That context is not exhaustive of all the circumstances within which the phenomenon exists. Since the properties of a phenomenon may differ in different contexts, it is essential to recall that in descriptive research, phenomena are described in a static state in a specific and also static context. It follows, then, that the characteristics of the context must be described as a backdrop for whatever description of the phenomenon is derived.

Descriptive research differs in its essential nature from flexible method research. As was discussed in the preceding chapter, flexible method research involves data collection procedures that may shift over the course of the work. The nature of the change in them is not predictable at the start of the study, and in fact it should not be, for it is the nature of the data unfolding as the study progresses that directs it.

described a complex "structure of intellect" model that first posited 120 separate factors, theoretically derived (Guilford 1967), and later 150 (Guilford 1977). Notice that the strategy was theory driven: Guilford's complex conceptual model of intelligence, for example, largely based on logically derived theory, provided a basis for designating the specific tasks he then used to measure each specific dimension of intelligence as described in his model.

The field of intelligence testing, however, has been full of controversy, controversies that illustrate the strengths and weaknesses of descriptive research. It is important to keep in mind that in descriptive research, in which theory drives the methods of data collection themselves, one can only see what one is looking for. Put differently, the conceptual and operational definitions used in the research place constraints on the nature of the description that can be derived from it. The data themselves are meant to be a corrective. However, there are at least three ways that data can fail to provide a corrective to theory, all illustrated in some of the controversies about intelligence testing that have arisen.

First of all, the very conceptions of a phenomenon that guide the research initially will color what is found. In intelligence research, for example, Thurstone and Guilford held a conception of intelligence that was diametrically opposed to that of Spearman. Spearman believed that there was one underlying, pervasive factor in intelligence that he called general intelligence, or "*g*." As a consequence of his theoretical position, Spearman developed tests that he believed allowed him to describe general intelligence. The findings from the use of his tests affirmed his conceptual definition, and theoretical position, about what the underlying nature of intelligence would be. Spearman, Thurstone, and Guilford all used essentially the same method to study the structure of intelligence: administer a specific intelligence test to a large number of people and describe the dimensions of intelligence demonstrated using factor analysis. In the case of Spearman's work, however, unlike Thurstone's or Guilford's, there appeared to be much more overlap in how people responded to different tasks. In other words, what Spearman observed and described was to no small extent constrained by what he was looking for. His original definition of intelligence, which was theoretically derived, had given rise to observational procedures that resulted in his seeing features of the phenomenon that tended to conform to what he expected them to look like. Gould (1981) even makes the point that the specific mathematical methods of factor analysis used by Spearman, on the one hand, and Thurstone, on the other, just like item selection for tests, tended in each case to confirm the theory that each researcher held. Therefore it is essential in descriptive and, in fact, in any form of fixed method research, that the theory or conceptual framework that guides it and all the details of method be made explicit at the outset.

Nonquantitative studies can be subject to this same dilemma. In any descriptive research, one observes only the features of the phenomenon that one has decided before the fact to examine. The features one selects to examine, as well as the ways in which one observes or recognizes them, will be largely a function of the expectations one carries into the original research. In this way, descriptive research is like all the other designs: it cannot provide definitive answers all by itself. Like other forms of research, it substantiates certain kinds of statements, in this case quantitative or qualitative descriptions, that then inform the further development of theory. In the final analysis, the value of specific descriptive statements rises and falls with the theory (or set of conceptual definitions) within which each is embedded. In Kuhn's (1970) terms, descriptive research is part of "normal science," and its findings may identify anomalies that raise important questions about existing theory or suggest features of a phenomenon that will have to be considered in any new conceptualization of it.

The second way of overlooking the corrective that data can provide to theory in descriptive research is, fortunately, rare: making up data to support a position or overlooking information that does not conform to what was expected or desired in the results. One of the major debates about the concept of intelligence has always been about whether or not (or to what extent) it is an inherited trait. The classical way to study the heritability of various human characteristics has been to study identical twins—who have the same genetic endowment—who have been separated at birth and reared in different homes—as in adoption—that is, in different environments. The degree to which such pairs of twins turn out to resemble each other in some trait in adulthood is then taken to show the degree of heritability of the characteristic in question. This technique has been used to study a variety of human characteristics in addition to intelligence, including serious mental illness, such as schizophrenia, alcoholism, and recently, even sexual orientation.

Identical twins reared apart are difficult to find, but Cyril Burt, an eminent British psychologist, late in his career published studies of a number of them showing a high degree of heritability of intelligence. In the 1970s, however, several scholars began reviewing his work and proved to the satisfaction of most observers that Burt had most likely fabricated the bulk of the data on which his published twin studies of intelligence were based (Gould 1981). Resorting to the fabrication or falsification of data when findings do not support a theory is very rare, and the sanctions against such behavior in the scholarly and professional worlds are severe. The fact that such incidents do occur from time to time, however, is an important reminder of how essential the ethics of scholarship are in preserving the integrity of all research. When the theories guiding a piece of research are firmly held, the temptation to alter or dismiss findings that do not confirm them can be intense.

Finally, while resorting to fabrication or falsification of data is clearly a deliberate act, unexamined attitudes may operate in descriptive research in ways that can also have a profound effect on the findings of research. In particular, attitudes of white supremacy or male superiority, for example, can affect what theories are held and how research is done (see table 2–1 on racism, sexism, and heterosexism in research). In the field of intelligence testing, for example, there has been enormous controversy about the study of supposed "racial differences" in intelligence or, specifically, in measured IQ. For example, a famous article published in 1969 (Jensen 1969) took the position that there were "inherited and ineradicable differences" between African Americans and "whites" (Gould 1981:235), an article that continues to generate controversy to this day. In fact, Gould (1981) makes the case that there is a subtext to the whole history of research on human intelligence, especially in the United States: the drive to establish the supremacy of the male of northern European descent to all others, those of other racial and ethnic groups and, to a lesser degree, to women. One of the reasons for asserting a high degree of heritability of IQ was to support the idea of innate and immutable differences between racial and ethnic groups; Jensen (1969), for example, cited and relied heavily (but not exclusively) on the then-accepted twin studies by Burt that turned out to be based on fabricated data.

Gould (1981), a biologist and paleontologist, points out how the idea of the heritability of intelligence has been logically misused in suggesting that racial (or other population groups) may differ in IQ:

> The common fallacy consists in assuming that if heredity explains a certain percentage of variation within a group, it must also explain a similar percentage of the variation in average IQ between groups—whites and blacks, for example. But variation among individuals within a group and differences in mean values between groups are separate phenomena. . . . Human height has a higher heritability than any value ever proposed for IQ. Take two separate groups of males. The first, with an average height of 5 feet 10 inches, live in a prosperous American town. The second, with an average height of 5 feet 6 inches, are starving in a third-world village. Heritability is about 95 percent or so in each place—meaning that only relatively tall fathers tend to have relatively tall sons and that relatively short fathers short sons. This high within-group heritability argues neither for nor against the possibility that better nutrition in the next generation might raise the average height of third-world villagers above that of prosperous Americans. Likewise, IQ could be highly heritable within groups, and the average difference between whites and blacks in America might still only record the environmental disadvantages of blacks (Gould 1981:157).

Whatever the data show, then, must still be interpreted through the lens of theoretical understanding of the various concepts involved.

A Social Work Example of Descriptive Research

The Anderson and Mandell (1989) study of the use of self-disclosure by social workers illustrates a simpler form of descriptive research common in social work: the survey. Although not at the level of asserting a general theory of practice analogous to a theory of the structure of intelligence, concepts guide this work as well. The report of the study begins with a discussion of the concept of self-disclosure; drawing on prior theoretical and empirical studies, it defines self-disclosure and differentiates it from similar concepts, such as "self-involving responses." It also summarizes the guidelines for the use of self-disclosure as represented in the literature.

Among the defining characteristics of the Anderson and Mandell (1989) study are these two essential features: (1) the same method applied in the same context was used to study the phenomenon as reported by every person surveyed, and (2) the study produced empirically grounded descriptive statements about the concept in question. The research questions guiding the study were clearly designed to produce a detailed picture of a conceptually defined phenomenon in a specific context: What is the extent of the use of self-disclosure among professional social workers in Oregon and to what extent do these social workers report adhering to guidelines governing the use of this technique? The phenomenon to be described, self-disclosure as used by social workers in clinical practice, was clearly identified. The specific features of it and of the context of its use that the researchers were interested in were identified as well, both in the questions asked in the survey and in the people who were chosen to provide the answers.

As the report of this study makes clear, theory guided this descriptive research in at least three of the ways outlined earlier: in the specification of (a) selection criteria for the sample, (b) the properties of the phenomenon to be measured, and (c) the context in which the observations took place and in which the phenomenon occurred. As to the sample, while it was limited to the state in which the study was done as matter of convenience, an effort was made to identify a population for study within that state that was representative of the group of interest: social workers in clinical practice. Thus this study was not actually based on a sample, or segment of a larger population; rather it was a study of an entire population, or, at least, the segment of it that responded to the survey.

In fact, a major purpose of this research was to describe the use of self-disclosure in a population or context, among social workers, where it had not been described before. Note, for example, that social workers on the list obtained who were identified as not in clinical practice were eliminated from the study at the outset. Also note that the list used, that of registered social workers, was thought to represent professional social workers, that is, those in the profession with a high degree of training and experience.

The data for this study were collected by means of a mailed survey and thus consisted of self-reports by respondents rather than direct observation. This choice of method was most likely due to the desire to find a way to collect data from a large and representative, rather than a small, group of participants and to do so in a way that would most likely not affect the conduct of practice itself. As is typical of descriptive and other fixed method forms of research, the questions asked of each respondent were standardized, that is, invariant from one person to the next. In fact, in addition to developing questions about self-disclosure based on the review of the literature, an existing tool, the Jourard Self-Disclosure Questionnaire (p. 264), was employed. Use of such a standardized instrument can confer the benefit of making results directly comparable with those of other studies employing the same questionnaire (see chapter 15 on the use of existing data collection instruments).

The specific practice context of each worker was allowed to vary by location and theoretical orientation, but these contexts were described and reported as part of the findings of the study. In fact, the data were analyzed to examine whether practice context, such as the nature of the employment setting or the self-reported theoretical orientation of the respondent, were associated with any variation in the reported use of self-disclosure in practice. Thus while the observational context was held constant, some other aspects of the context of the phenomenon that could not be held constant but that could theoretically be expected to affect the phenomenon under study, namely the use of self-disclosure, were assessed and the contextual variation systematically described. Some additional contextual variables potentially affecting self-disclosure were also assessed, such as the demographic characteristics of the worker. Other contextual variables identified in the literature, like characteristics of the client, could not be efficiently examined in a study in which respondents were asked about their practices in general, since they had individual clients of varying kinds.

There was one way in which theory guides descriptive research, however, that was not discussed by the authors of this study: point of view. In this respect, this study is no different from most other descriptive studies undertaken from the traditional standpoint on research. It assumes disinterested, "objective," observers who do not affect what is observed except through the explicit methodological decisions made and already discussed. Yet it is possible that respondents to the survey made some assumptions about the point of view of the authors of the survey, seeking, perhaps unconsciously, clues in the wording of the questions or in the auspices of the study and maybe adjusting their responses as a result. The point of view of researchers is least often discussed in a study when it is a traditional one and most often discussed when it is not. Whether or not it is discussed, however, point of view does exist and may affect what respondents report and/or how findings are interpreted and used. Perhaps because one study author is an educator, for example, Anderson and Mandell emphasize the finding that few respondents reported having formal training in the use of self-disclosure and recommend that more content on the issue be provided in graduate training programs.

The findings section of the article proceeds from the data to draw logical conclusions for theory. Based on the data collected, Anderson and Mandell conclude that self-disclosure is quite widely used by social workers but less often by those with a psychodynamic orientation to practice than by others. They also conclude that the responding workers were "quite conversant with the principles of self-disclosure" (p. 266) based on the fact that a higher percentage of respondents endorsed reasons for using self-disclosure that were endorsed in the literature, such as for increasing client self-disclosure, than reasons that were not, such as decreasing therapist anxiety (see table 1 in the article). Thus the meaning of the quantitative results, in this case percentages, were interpretable only with reference to the theory that guided the research from the start. However, it should be noted that any social workers' reasons for using self-disclosure that had not been predicted or anticipated and thus included among the response choices on the questionnaire went unrecorded and were thus "invisible" to this study.

The limitations of this study as described by the authors in the final few paragraphs of the article, that is, the questions that remained unanswered about the phenomenon of self-disclosure, speak to three of the issues identified earlier as key to descriptive research: who is in the sample, what was observed, and what are the contextual issues affecting the phenomenon seen. Are these findings different from previous ones because the sample is different or because the phenomenon studied, the self-reported use of self-disclosure in practice, has changed, that is, has become more common? Would changing the context of observation to an in vivo, or observational, method reveal something different about self-disclosure than a self-reporting method of study showed? Would contextual therapist factors like marital status be found to have an effect on self-disclosure, as found in previous studies, if gender could be controlled or if the sample were larger? These questions are empirical ones that can be answered only by further descriptive or relational research.

Methods in Descriptive Research

Because the methodology of a descriptive study is theory driven, it can be planned in its entirety in advance of the conduct of the study itself. Because of their deductive and invariant nature, the methods used in descriptive research resemble most closely those described traditionally as "objective" methods of research, except that control over and manipulation of variables is not included. First the research questions are developed and stated, and then the parts of the research process—sampling, data collection, and data analysis—are planned and conducted in the order stated. Although the parts of the research process are separate in time and in conception, each has a vital and interlocking role to play in producing findings that are credible.

Sampling

Because of the inductive nature of the conclusions drawn, the development of a sample is key in all descriptive research. While all of these points are made in greater depth in the chapter on sampling, issues affecting samples for descriptive research in particular are reviewed briefly here.

One important feature of descriptive research that drives the development of samples for it involves the development of selection criteria. As will be recalled, the fundamental purpose of descriptive research is to provide a description of a phenomenon when static and in a static context. That description will necessarily be derived by examining the phenomenon as it appears in specific cases. That is, selected cases of the phenomenon of interest will be examined and described in selected contexts and on selected variables. The selection criteria for the sample specify exactly the characteristics and contexts of each sample member that qualify him or her for inclusion in the study. When, as is common, compromises must be made in how these characteristics are defined for practical reasons, this fact must be acknowledged when conclusions are drawn.

Statements made on the basis of descriptive research can be expected to have generality, that is, to be also "true" of unobserved cases in unobserved circumstances, to the extent that the observed cases and circumstances provide a "good" representation of unobserved ones. Whenever possible, then, it is desirable to have the cases that are studied selected in a fashion that maximizes the probability that they will provide a good representation of the larger body of instances they are designed to reflect.

As will be discussed in the chapters on sampling and on inferential statistics, the most reliable method of guaranteeing representativeness is to make selections on the basis of pure chance, that is, with some technique involving a random method of selection. If the research interest is in describing a phenomenon on selected variables when the phenomenon is static and in a specific static context, then the sampling method should include a way to identify, and in fact catalogue, the entire population or universe of persons in which the phenomenon exists. Then, using some credibly random process, the subset of that population that will comprise the study sample can be identified and selected from that list. Provided that the random sample is also large, chances then are very good that sample statistics will provide an acceptably accurate and stable basis for drawing inferences about how the phenomenon would be likely to look in other cases also from the population, were it to be described on the same selected variables and in the same static context.

Stated differently, descriptions of study samples can be taken as also true of unobserved larger groups to the extent that those study samples are representative of the larger population. And the two determinants of whether they can be expected in fact to be representative are: (1) the manner in which the sample was chosen (with a random procedure being essential), and (2) the size of the sample. The acceptable definition for largeness is in part a function of how much variability there is on the described dimensions; the more variability there is, the larger the sample will have to be to produce an acceptably narrow range for estimating population values (see chapter 18 on inferential statistics, specifically parameter estimation).

Data Collection

The first set of decisions that must be made about data collection in descriptive research is to specify the characteristics of the phenomenon and its context that will be the focus of study. Whatever the topic of the research may be, there may seem to be an infinite number of things about the topic that would be nice to know. However, for reasons of efficiency and effectiveness, only some aspects of a phenomenon and its context can be included in any one study. The point of view, theoretically and heuristically, of the researcher will determine some of these choices. Prior knowledge and conceptual work will also guide them. For example, in the Anderson and Mandell (1989) study, self-disclosure was carefully distinguished from what was termed "self-involving responses," and the questions and instructions on the survey itself then had to make the distinction clear to the respondent. Deciding what to study or focus on can be very challenging.

Descriptive research can use any one of the major data collection methods: observation, interviews, and self-report or written measures. Observation can capture visible behaviors and other nonverbal kinds of information and can do so in a structured, repeatable way. Survey interviewing is usually highly structured (see the Gomez [1990] study included as an example in chapter 6); it may be done in person or over the telephone. All of us with telephones have most likely been participants in telephone interviews conducted for market or opinion research. Interviewers and observers conducting descriptive research are usually trained in how to present themselves and to gather data in ways that are as nonintrusive and as standardized as possible. Sometimes, as in the assessment of intelligence and other forms of psychological testing, the data gathering context as well as the questions asked are also carefully standardized and controlled.

Self-report measures, which may be the kind of data collection most commonly associated with descriptive research, may be administered in person or mailed out or distributed for anonymous return. For the purposes of descriptive research, self-report measures are usually highly structured both in how the questions are developed and presented and in the response options that are offered to respondents.

Whatever mode of data collection is used, because of the need to keep the observational context constant throughout the study, data gathering methods in descriptive research are generally standardized. Most often response categories are fixed or structured as well. Because of the difficulty inherent in developing efficient and effective standardized tools for data collection, available instruments are often sought out for use (see chapter 15 on selecting available measures). When the description is made using instruments that are themselves well understood, the information those tools generate can be interpreted clearly with reference to what the information means about the parameters of the phenomenon under study. However, the danger in this practice is that the phenomenon of interest will be defined or delimited to what the tool can capture rather than being determined by theory, making examination of the goodness of fit of the conceptions embedded in each tool with the study it will be used in essential.

Data Analysis

As stated earlier, quantification is typical of the results of descriptive research. When samples are large, it can be extremely difficult to handle, analyze, and summarize the volume of narrative data that can result. Descriptive statistics are powerful tools for just that task: the efficient summarization of large amounts of data that describe a group. When the goal of the research is to make factual estimates about a phenomenon as it exists in a population based on a sample of that population, inferential statistics exist that can do so with a specific degree of confidence in the results. When the goal is to uncover the structure of a phenomenon by examining the relationship among its various properties, statistical techniques like correlation and factor analysis exist that can do so mathematically. There are many reasons, then, why descriptive research depends so often on quantitative results for its findings.

Of course, descriptive research need not be quantitative. To be informative, descriptive research need only generate unambiguous statements about predefined phenomenon features and the interrelationships among them. When those statements are expressed in quantitative form, the basis for understanding the numerical data is clear: Everyone familiar with statistics knows the exact meaning of the mean, the standard deviation, the range, and correlation coefficients (or component or factor loadings in more complex cases). But when statements are expressed in verbal form (e.g., "Most people completed the task with ease"), specific meanings are not necessarily clear. Moreover, standardized ways of assessing the reliability of data commonly used in quantitative research have not yet been developed for narrative data. Nevertheless, information need not be expressed in numerical form to be useful, as the following excerpt from the Fraiberg (1970) study of 10 blind infants illustrates. Her topic here is how blind babies learn to reach for an object that makes a noise:

> At five months Robbie enjoys holding a bell in his hands and ringing it. If we withdraw the bell from his hands and ring it within easy reach of his hands, there is no gesture of reach, the hands remain motionless. At eight months of age we bring Robbie's oldest and most treasured toy within easy reach of his hands. It is playing its familiar music. Robbie looks alert, attentive, shows recognition on his face. He makes no gesture of reach. We finally give him his musical dog and he hugs it and mouths it. After awhile we withdraw the dog from his hands. He is angry at the loss. He can still hear the music. It is within easy reach. He does not even make a gesture toward the toy. . . . At ten months of age, if we sound the bell which Robbie is very fond of, there is still no gesture of reach. But now we see an interesting behavior of the hands. At the sound of the bell Robbie's hands go through the motion of grasping and ungrasping and once we see the hands executing the motion of ringing the bell. Still no reach, but now for the first time we can read the message in the hands that the sound of the bell connotes graspability and evokes a memory of bell ringing. . . . At eleven months and three days of age, Robbie hears the bell and for the first time makes a direct reach for the bell and attains it (Fraiberg 1970:129–30).

These data are presented to demonstrate that a blind baby does not reach for the sound of something in the same way that a sighted baby reaches for the sight of an object. Reaching for the sound of something seems to have to await the conceptual development of the idea that an object is permanent and has an existence separate from the experience of it, the object concept, that occurs in all babies in the last quarter of the first year. Her description, though narrative and also supported by aggregate, numerical data, conveys the meaning of her findings clearly.

Of course it is always possible to quantify narrative data. The point to remember, however, is that it is the product of the study, that is, descriptive statements about a specific phenomenon, and the nature of the method, that is, fixed or held invariant throughout, which determines whether it is or is not a piece of descriptive research. The nature of the data, quantitative or narrative, is irrelevant.

There is a way in which quantitative data are much easier to analyze than are narrative data, and this point should be openly acknowledged. There is a long tradition of accepted rules governing how to summarize (i.e., communicate, capture for others) quantitative data and generalize from them. These rules are made explicit in the rules for statistics that will be discussed in chapters 17 and 18 on descriptive and inferential statistics. There are not yet, however, uniformly accepted rules for how to organize and summarize (i.e., describe) narrative material, much less how to go about generalizing from them.

Summary

The basic logic of descriptive research is fairly straightforward. It rests on the belief that part of what is fundamental to understanding a phenomenon is documenting that phenomenon's properties in detail as they exist in specific contexts. One way of understanding this form of research is to view it as directed toward depicting a defined phenomenon's structure. Descriptive research cannot document a phenomenon's function—that task is left to relational and experimental research. It is directed instead toward developing a clear understanding of how a phenomenon looks rather than how it operates. And it is this discovery of structure that allows one to develop theoretical models explaining (at least structurally) how, and even why, phenomena might function as they do.

Descriptive designs, then, are aimed at taking and developing pictures. Well done, descriptive research shows literally what a phenomenon of interest looks like. The greatest strength of this research is that it is perhaps among the most unambiguous in its results. The greatest limitation of this research is that it can be considered superficial: It speaks only to what is, not necessarily how it is and certainly not why it is. As long as there remain basic questions about the nature of the phenomena that comprise social and psychological life, however, descriptive research will remain an important part of science in the helping professions.

THE USE OF SELF-DISCLOSURE BY PROFESSIONAL SOCIAL WORKERS

SANDRA C. ANDERSON AND DEBORAH L. MANDELL

The authors review the literature on the technique of self-disclosure, present guidelines for its appropriate use, and discuss the findings of a survey of its use among social workers in Oregon. The results indicate that self-disclosure is gaining increased acceptance among workers.

The self-referent technique of self-disclosure has gained greater acceptance as a component of a therapist's skill repertoire. Although significant research has been done in recent years concerning the clinical value of this technique, little is known about its pattern of use by social workers and the extent of awareness among social workers regarding principles for appropriate utilization. The present study, a survey of registered clinical social workers in Oregon, attempts to discover the extent of utilization of self-disclosure by professional social workers and to determine relevant variables affecting its use.

LITERATURE REVIEW

More than thirty years ago, Carl Rogers postulated that the therapist's genuineness in the therapeutic relationship was one of six necessary and sufficient conditions for constructive personality change.[1] Since that time, the concept of genuineness has also been referred to as transparency,[2] authenticity,[3] and self-disclosure. In the present study, self-disclosure is defined as "statements referring to the past history or personal experiences of the counselor."[4] The study does not address self-involving responses, defined as "direct present expressions of the counselor's feelings about

or reactions to the statements or behaviors of the client."[5]

The therapist's use of self-disclosure is greatly dependent on his or her theoretical orientation. Psychodynamic practitioners, who rely heavily on analysis of transference, utilize anonymity to foster the patient's projective fantasies and facilitate engagement; they find that self-disclosure contaminates the transference relationship.[6] They also argue that self-disclosure negatively affects both the therapist's neutrality and the ability to maintain an appropriate level of closeness or distance from the client.[7] The recent movement toward humanistic-existential psychology, however, challenges the detached therapeutic stance and espouses a more genuine, personalized relationship with clients.[8]

The primary reason for the use of self-disclosure is to increase client disclosure. Sidney Jourard labeled this the "dyadic effect,"[9] wherein people elicit disclosure in proportion to the amount that they themselves disclose. There is disagreement, however, concerning whether the dyadic effect is due to reciprocity (the exchange of social rewards), to modeling, or to some combination of the two. Morgan Worthy and colleagues found support for the notion of reciprocity,[10] and Lawrence Annis and Donald Perry demonstrated that videotaped modeling was associated with higher rates of self-disclosure.[11] Regardless of the mechanism of operation, however, the dyadic effect has universal empirical support.

The proponents of self-disclosure believe that it projects nurturance and strengthens rapport,[12] enhances client trust,[13] and aids the client in developing a new perspective.[14] Self-disclosure has been found to increase client

Sandra C. Anderson is Professor, Graduate School of Social Work, Portland State University, and Deborah L. Mandell is Family Therapist, Morrison Center for Youth and Family Services, Portland, Oregon. The authors wish to thank Joan Arbuckle, Cynthia Eckersley, Diane Harris, Cathy Hitchcock, Susan Platt, Lynn Rothman, Susie Snyder, and Barbara Waldron for their participation in this study.

disclosure[15] and to be more effective in doing so than are approval, support, or reflective techniques.[16]

Variables Affecting Self-Disclosure

The literature on factors influencing the effects of self-disclosure focuses on client, intervention, and therapist variables.

Client variables. In a study of therapy groups, Richard Wiegel and co-workers found a negative relationship between therapist self-disclosure and the client's perception of the therapist's mental health.[17] They postulated that therapist self-disclosure may violate client role expectations, which have been conditioned by decades of popular exposure to traditional models of psychotherapy. This finding was supported by Valerian Derlega and colleagues, who found that clients' expectations about the appropriate intimacy level of disclosure affected their reaction to a disclosing therapist.[18]

In a more recent study, however, Leon Vande Creek and Lori Angstadt found that self-disclosing counselors were viewed more positively even when clients stated they did not prefer, and were experimentally led not to anticipate, a disclosing counselor.[19] Robert Dies and Lauren Cohen found that group therapy members appear to be more comfortable with therapist self-disclosure than are individual clients.[20] They also found that the longer the client was in group therapy, the less likely it was that therapist self-disclosure would lead to negative client evaluations of therapist stability.

Intervention variables. Much of the original research in self-disclosure focused on variables such as amount (breadth), depth (level of intimacy), and duration (length of time disclosing).[21] More recent studies have examined the effects of favorable vs. unfavorable content,[22] timing,[23] and direct vs. indirect disclosure.[24] Gordon Chelune identified affective manner of presentation as an additional intervention variable,[25] but it has not been studied to date.

Researchers have varied the amount of self-disclosure in an attempt to discover optimum levels for a therapeutic relationship. Findings indicate that there is a curvilinear relationship between the amount of therapist

self-disclosure and the client's willingness to disclose.[26]

Some studies on the depth of self-disclosure indicate that intimacy of disclosure is governed by reciprocity; therapist self-disclosure reinforces client disclosure.[27] Analogue studies have indicated a positive relationship between the intimacy level of the therapist's disclosure and that of the client's.[28] Norman Simonson and Susan Bahr, however, found that although high-intimacy self-disclosure was associated with increased client disclosure for paraprofessionals, demographic (moderate intimacy) self-disclosure was more effective for professionals.[29]

Two studies found that although favorable disclosure effectively increases the client's evaluation of the seriousness of the problem and motivates corrective action, unfavorable disclosure also has therapeutic value, decreasing the client's negative evaluation of him- or herself.[30] John Curtis, however, warns that unfavorable self-disclosure may influence the client to model inappropriate behavior or erode the client's faith in the therapist.[31]

Timing is a critical factor influencing client response to therapist self-disclosure. Therapist disclosure too early in the relationship can be seen as inappropriate or threatening to the client and may inhibit interchange.[32] Most authors caution against using self-disclosure before a therapeutic relationship is established.[33] Ruth Loeb and John Curtis found that therapists making indirect references to their experiences and feelings using the word "we" and nondisclosing therapists were both preferred to therapists who use the word "I" when self-disclosing.[34]

Therapist variables. Therapist variables that may influence the use and/or effectiveness of self-disclosure include flexibility of disclosure pattern,[35] education, gender, and marital status.[36] Therapist use of self-disclosure also influences client perceptions of therapist attractiveness, trustworthiness, and expertise. The effects of other variables such as race, age, and sexual orientation have not been studied.

Self-disclosure flexibility refers to the ability of individuals to vary their disclosure according to subtle social cues and may be increased by training.[37] High-flexibility disclosures were rated higher in levels of empathy and attraction and produced more effective counseling responses than did low-flexibility disclosures.[38]

In a study of self-disclosure by social workers, Linda Bradmiller found that social work education and experience have no significant effect on the amount of worker disclosure to clients.[39] Married social workers, however, tended to disclose more to clients than did unmarried social workers, a fact Bradmiller attributed both to the protection from intimacy and the relative richness of relationship experience offered by marriage.

Although no consistent relationship between therapist gender and self-disclosure is apparent in the literature, clients are more likely to perceive female therapists who use self-disclosure as being untrustworthy than they are to perceive male therapists or female therapists who do not disclose as being untrustworthy.[40] This perception is particularly likely to occur among clients who ascribe to traditional sex-role stereotypes when the therapist is inexperienced.[41]

Numerous studies have assessed client responses to self-disclosure in terms of perceived attractiveness,[42] trustworthiness,[43] and competence of the therapist.[44] The literature is often unclear, however, about the relationship among attractiveness, trustworthiness, and competence and between these variables and treatment outcome.

Three recent analogue studies focused on self-disclosure of specific therapist variables. Steven Fox and colleagues found that therapist disclosure that he or she had been in therapy as a client facilitated the therapeutic relationship.[45] Brent Mallinckrodt and Janet Helms indicated that therapist revelation of a disability generally drew more positive counselor ratings.[46] Stuart Chesner and Roy Baumeister, however, discovered that therapist nonverbal disclosure of religious values through wearing a religious symbol had either a detrimental or neutral effect on client disclosure.[47]

Drawbacks of Research

Criticism of existing research in this area has focused on three factors: (1) lack of uniformity in defining self-disclosure, (2) a resulting lack of uniformity of measurement criteria and methods, and (3) reliance on analogue studies using "normal" college students in a one-time interview format. The first two factors, along with a failure to control for situational variables, have limited comparison across studies and may account in part for the conflicting findings. The reliance of the research on analogue studies with healthy individuals raises questions concerning applicability to ongoing therapist-client relationships.

Leonard Goodstein and Virginia Reinecker questioned the reliability of some instruments used to measure self-disclosure.[48] Concerns have also been raised about the predictive and retrospective validity of self-report of self-disclosure, on which the research is heavily dependent.[49] Although the effects of self-disclosure on variables such as client self-disclosure and client perception of therapist expertness have been documented, these variables are intervening variables and may not, as has been assumed, invariably promote positive treatment outcomes. Finally, the effects of significant variables, such as client diagnosis and therapist's affective manner of presentation, have yet to be studied.

GUIDELINES FOR SELF-DISCLOSURE

Given the current knowledge base, principles for the appropriate use of self-disclosure have emerged. Major considerations are as follows:

• Do not allow self-disclosure to shift the focus of the session from the client to the therapist. Be brief and use a "checkout" phrase to return the focus of the session to the client. It is appropriate to use self-disclosure in response to a direct personal question, unless the question is being asked in order to shift the focus of the session, or unless it would be better to explore the reason for the question in lieu of or in addition to answering.[50]

• Keep disclosures impersonal and to a minimum until trust and rapport have been established.[51]

• Use moderation—avoid too much or too little self-disclosure.[52]

• Take client variables such as treatment goals, frame of reference, role expectations, and cultural and ethnic background into account. Use extreme caution when disclosing with clients who exhibit low self-esteem, weak reality-testing, or other ego deficits that might make them prone to misinterpreting others.[53]

• Do not disclose material representing unexamined countertransference[54] or reflecting instability or incompetence.[55]

• To clarify role expectations, indicate early that therapist self-disclosure is an expected part of treatment.[56]

• Take reasonable risks when disclosing. There is conflicting evidence concerning whether information of high or moderate intimacy value is most effective in eliciting client self-disclosure.[57] Female therapists should use caution in disclosing to clients who ascribe to traditional sex-role stereotypes.[58]

• Be responsive to subtle social cues, for example, client discomfort, by varying amount and type of self-disclosure.[59] Elicit feedback to all self-disclosure and desist if the client reacts negatively.[60]

• Give a balanced view of yourself.[61] Use positive self-disclosure to increase the client's awareness of the seriousness of his or her problem and to increase motivation for change; use negative self-disclosure to "normalize" feelings or behaviors that the client overestimates as problems.[62] Disclose both sides of an ambivalent feeling.[63]

• Display emotions congruent with the content of the disclosure.[64]

• Do not use self-disclosure as a response to client disclosure. Rather, indicate that the disclosure has been heard with empathy.[65]

METHODOLOGY

The present study measured the extent to which self-disclosure was used by professional social workers in Oregon. It also examined the adherence to guidelines that govern the use of this technique.

Subjects

Of 495 practicing clinical social workers registered by the state of Oregon in 1982,

365 individuals were chosen for the study. It was assumed that all respondents met registry requirements of a master's or doctoral degree from an accredited school of social work and a minimum of two years' supervised post-master's experience. Workers were excluded from the sample on the basis of a job title that indicated they were not primarily involved in direct practice, for example, administrator or director. Because of the unavailability of demographic information on social workers in Oregon, representativeness of the purposive sample or of respondents could not be determined.

Of the 365 social workers to whom questionnaires were mailed, 160 (41 percent) responded to the survey. Sixty-five percent of respondents were female. The majority (64 percent) were between the ages of thirty and forty-nine; 35 percent were fifty years or older. The sample was predominantly white (98 percent) and heterosexual (98 percent). Most (68 percent) were currently married, with an additional 11 percent cohabiting. Nearly three-quarters (73 percent) of the respondents had children.

Private practice (36 percent) was the most common mode of employment, followed by practice in a private (26 percent) or public (22 percent) agency. An additional 13 percent of the respondents combined private practice with agency practice, with the majority (9 percent of the total number of respondents) in private agencies. Almost one-half of the respondents (46 percent) provided more than twenty hours of face-to-face counseling per week, with 34 percent providing eleven to twenty hours, 17 percent, one to ten hours, and 3 percent not currently providing face-to-face counseling.

The theoretical orientations represented were eclectic (47 percent), psychodynamic (23 percent), humanistic/client-centered (11 percent), family systems (11 percent), cognitive-behavioral (2 percent), and other (6 percent). As their ages suggest, respondents were highly experienced, with 18 percent having more than twenty years of experience; 43 percent, eleven to twenty years; 33 percent, six to ten years; and 7 percent, two to five years.

Instrumentation and Data Gathering

The researchers developed a 148-item instrument, a portion of which incorporated categories from the sixty-item Jourard Self-Disclosure Questionnaire. The items were designed to obtain demographic information from respondents and to ascertain the extent and content of self-disclosure utilized, reasons for using or not using the technique, and variables affecting its use, including the amount of relevant training received by respondents. After being pretested with experienced MSWs not listed in the registry, the questionnaire was mailed with an introductory letter explaining the purpose of the study and defining self-disclosure.

RESULTS

Respondents were asked to rate their use of self-disclosure on a five-point Likert scale (1 = never; 5 = always). The mean response was 2.95, with a modal response of 3 (sometimes). Of nine different types of self-disclosure, personality, personal history, and current relationships were the most commonly reported and sexuality and money the least commonly reported.

Table 1 indicates the reasons cited as major factors for the use of self-disclosure.

Table 1. Respondents' cited reasons for using self-disclosure, according to frequency (%).

Increases client awareness of alternative viewpoints/options	60
Increases client self-disclosure through modeling	55
Decreases client anxiety	50
Increases client involvement in the relationship	47
Increases client perception of therapist authenticity	47
Increases client self-disclosure through reinforcement	41
Increased client perception of therapist's empathy	33
Decreases client resistance	29
Decreases transference reactions	11
Decreases therapist anxiety	2

Given the debate in the literature concerning whether the "dyadic effect" is due to modeling or reinforcement, it should be noted that the respondents to this study believed that modeling was the more potent mechanism. Table 2 indicates the major factors in limiting use of self-disclosure, the most important of which was its tendency to shift the focus from the client to the therapist.

When the client variables of gender, marital status, age, social class, race, and diagnostic category were taken into account, it was found, not surprisingly, that the most likely recipient of self-disclosure was a married, middle-class white female between the ages of twenty and fifty, in short, a person similar to most respondents. The target individual was also more likely to have anxiety or adjustment disorder than to have a psychotic, personality, substance abuse, or affective disorder. The fact that the most common target was a female appears to be a concomitant of the preponderance of female therapists responding; male respondents disclosed significantly more to male clients than they did in general ($p = .02$). The objective finding, consistent with the literature, that client-therapist similarity is conducive to self-disclosure was supported by the subjective feelings of respondents, the majority (56 percent) of whom indicated that they were more likely to disclose to clients similar to themselves.

Individual clients received slightly more self-disclosure than did couples, groups, or families. The likelihood of self-disclosure was not affected by treatment length.

Table 2. Respondents' cited reasons for limiting the use of self-disclosure, according to frequency (%).

Shifts focus from client to therapist	64
Decreases time available for client disclosure	40
Interferes with transference	39
Creates role confusion	28
Deviates from client expectations of professional behavior	20
Inhibits the placebo effect	8
Personally uncomfortable	6
Creates doubt about the mental health of the therapist	6

Respondents disclosed personal weaknesses more often than they did personal strengths, a phenomenon that is consistent with the reasons most often given for use of self-disclosure (see guidelines). Past and present information were disclosed equally. As dictated by the tenets of good practice, respondents were extremely reluctant to disclose a serious, ongoing personal problem to a client.

Few respondents systematically varied their use of self-disclosure according to phase of treatment. Although fewer than 3 percent noted the intimacy level of their disclosure decreasing over the course of therapy, 71 percent reported that intimacy of disclosure fluctuated or remained the same throughout treatment. Fifty-two percent reported the same likelihood of self-disclosure use in all phases of treatment, and only 15 percent indicated to clients at the beginning of therapy that therapist self-disclosure was an expected part of the treatment.

Therapist Variables

Professional education. Eighty-two percent of respondents indicated that they had had some professional education in the use of self-disclosure, with 45 percent having received at least a moderate amount of such exposure. Thirty-six percent increased their use of self-disclosure due to education, 42 percent reported no change, and 22 percent decreased their use of self-disclosure. Almost all respondents who decreased their use had a psychodynamic orientation.

Gender and Marital Status. Although males tended to use more self-disclosure than did females, this difference was not significant. Male respondents disclosed more to male clients than they did to female respondents ($p = .01$), and were more likely than were females to have had professional education in the technique of self-disclosure ($p = .01$).

In contrast to a previous study, which found that married social workers used more self-disclosure than did their unmarried counterparts,[66] marital status had no significant effect on the use of self-disclosure in the present study.

Theoretical Orientation. The study's major finding was that psychodynamic respondents adhered to the proscription of self-disclosure in the psychodynamic literature. Respondents with a psychodynamic orientation scored consistently lower on all measures of self-disclosure than did respondents from other theoretical perspectives. Psychodynamic respondents scored lower than did their counterparts on overall self-disclosure ($p = .04$), used fewer types of self-disclosure ($p = .03$), and disclosed significantly less about personality ($p = .01$), personal history ($p = .02$), and current relationships ($p = .01$). They also disclosed fewer strengths ($p = .01$) and less past ($p = 0.1$) and present ($p = .01$) information. Results were consistent for all clients regardless of race, gender, age, marital status, social class, diagnosis, treatment modality, or treatment length. As mentioned, psychodynamic respondents were more likely to decrease the use of self-disclosure as a result of professional education, whereas others were more likely to increase use ($p = .01$). As might be expected, when the reasons for limiting use of self-disclosure were examined, psychodynamic respondents were significantly more likely than were others to say that the technique interferes with transference ($p = .01$).

Employment. In the present study, the effects of employment setting were largely mediated by theoretical orientation; psychodynamic respondents were significantly more likely to work in private than in public agencies ($p = 0.1$) and were more likely to be in private practice than in agency practice ($p = .03$). Consistent with this distribution, respondents in public agencies were more likely to use high levels (often and always) of self-disclosure than were those in private agencies ($p = .03$). Respondents in private agencies and private practice were also most likely to identify interference with transference as a reason for limiting self-disclosure ($p = .03$).

Age. Age of therapist, although positively associated with psychodynamic orientation ($p = .03$), had little independent effect on usage of self-disclosure. Respondents older than age forty were more likely than were younger respondents to use self-disclosure with adults aged fifty-one or older ($p = .02$).

DISCUSSION

The differences between the results of the present study and those of Bradmiller's 1978 study[67] suggest that self-disclosure has gained acceptance by social workers in the intervening years. This increase may be due to an increase in the availability of education on the use of the technique or the increased empirical evidence of its therapeutic benefits. Another possible explanation is that the Oregon sample may have differed from Bradmiller's Midwestern sample, particularly in the number of respondents with a psychodynamic orientation.

Overall, Oregon social workers seemed conversant with the principles of self-disclosure. For example, they would not disclose an ongoing, personal problem to a client and were aware of the need to avoid the use of self-disclosure to reduce therapist anxiety or express unexamined counter-transference. Use of the technique was appropriately moderate, and respondents were duly cautious about using the technique with severely impaired clients, for example, psychotic clients. Exceptions to this general knowledgeability were a lack of awareness of the importance of timing in the use of the technique and the need to address client expectations regarding therapist use of self-disclosure.

In general, the results of this study were compatible with the predictions of previous studies and of the theoretical literature. Most notably, psychodynamic respondents were less likely to use self-disclosure than were other respondents, and were more responsive to transference considerations in limiting their use. On the other hand, the present study differs from previous studies in its finding that marital status had no effect on the use of self-disclosure. This finding may be due to an idiosyncrasy of the respondent population or it may suggest that further research is needed before the explanation that marriage provides immunity from misinterpretation of personal remarks can be generally accepted. This finding may be true only for females in that males constituted a relatively high proportion of married respondents in the present study. Finally, a significant contribution to the literature is made by the finding that practicing clinicians see modeling as being more potent than reinforcement as a mechanism by which therapist disclosure promotes client disclosure.

The small size of the sample prevented statistical refinement of some issues involving small subsamples, for example, males. The use of self-report has documented pitfalls; *in vivo* research would be an important contribution to the study of self-disclosure.

In addition to *in vivo* studies, the authors recommend that education concerning the use of self-disclosure be expanded at both the graduate and postgraduate levels. Despite significant clinical experience, 55 percent of the sample population in the present study had little or no training in the use of the technique. As empirical evidence mounts, principles for the appropriate use of self-disclosure become clearer and their communication to practitioners more imperative. Finally, as the present study shows, education does make a difference in that it promotes, for the most part, greater usage of self-disclosure among receptive practitioners and greater sophistication with regard to reasons for its use.

REFERENCES

[1]Carl R. Rogers, "Necessary and Sufficient Conditions of Therapeutic Personality Change," *Journal of Consulting Psychology* 21 (2, 1957): 95–103.

[2]Sidney M. Jourard, *The Transparent Self,* rev. ed. (New York: Van Nostrand Reinhold, 1971).

[3]J.F.T. Bugental, *The Search for Authenticity* (New York: Holt. Rinehart, and Winston, 1965).

[4]Patricia R. McCarthy and Nancy E. Betz, "Differential Effects of Self-Disclosing Versus Self-Involving Counselor Statements," *Journal of Counseling Psychology* 25 (July 1978): 251.

[5]Ibid.

[6]John M. Curtis. "Indications and Contraindications in the Use of Therapist's Self-Disclosure," *Psychological Reports* 29 (October 1981): 449–507; John M. Curtis, "Determinants of the Therapeutic Bond: How to Engage Patients," *Psychological Reports* 49 (October 1981): 415–19.

[7]Joseph Palombo, "Spontaneous Self-Disclosures in Psychotherapy," *Clinical Social Work Journal* 15 (Summer 1987): 107–20.

[8]D. Corydon Hammond, Dean H. Hepworth, and Veon G. Smith, *Improving Therapeutic Communication: A Guide for Developing Effective Techniques* (San Francisco: Jossey-Bass, 1979).

[9]Jourard, *The Transparent Self.*

[10]Morgan Worthy, Albert L. Gary, and Gay M. Kahn, "Self-Disclosure as an Exchange Process," *Journal of Personality and Social Psychology* 13 (September 1969): 59–63.

[11]Lawrence V. Annis and Donald F. Perry, "Self-Disclosure in Same-Sex and Mixed-Sex Unsupervised Groups," *Journal of Counseling Psychology* 24 (July 1979): 370–72.

[12]Linda J. Bradmiller, "Self-Disclosure in the Helping Relationship," *Social Work Research and Abstracts* 14 (Summer 1978): 28–35.

[13]David W. Johnson and M. Patrick Noonan, "Effects of Acceptance and Reciprocation of Self-Disclosure on the Development of Trust," *Journal of Counseling Psychology* 19 (Septempber 1972): 411–16.

[14]Gerard Egan, *The Skilled Helper: Model, Skills, and Methods for Effective Helping* (Monterey, Calif.: Brooks/Cole, 1982).

[15]Charles B. Truax and Robert R. Carkhuff, "Client and Therapist Transparency in the Psychotherapeutic Encounter," *Journal of Counseling Psychology* 12 (January 1965): 3–8.

[16]W. J. Powell, Jr., "Differential Effectiveness of Interviewer Interventions in an Experimental Interview," *Journal of Consulting and Clinical Psychology* 32 (April 1968): 210–15.

[17]Richard G. Weigel et al., "Perceived Self-Disclosure, Mental Health, and Who Is Liked in Group Treatment," *Journal of Counseling Psychology* 19 (January 1972): 47–52.

[18]Valerian J. Derlega, Ron Lovell, and Alan L. Chaikin, "Effects of Therapist Self-Disclosure and Its Perceived Appropriateness on Client Self-Disclosure," *Journal of Consulting and Clinical Psychology* 44 (October 1976): 886.

[19]Leon Vande Creek and Lori Angstadt, "Client Preferences and Anticipations about Counselor Self-Disclosure," *Journal of Counseling Psychology* 32 (April 1985): 206–14.

[20]Robert Dies and Lauren Cohen, "Content Considerations in Group Therapist Self-Disclosure," *International Journal of Group Psychotherapy* 26 (January 1976): 71–88.

[21]Paul C. Cozby, "Self-Disclosure: A Literature Review," *Psychological Bulletin* 79 (February 1973): 73–91.

[22]Mary Ann Hoffman-Graff, "Interviewer Use of Positive and Negative Self-Disclosure and Interviewer-Subject Sex Pairing," *Journal of Counseling Psychology* 24 (May 1977): 184–90.

[23]Valerian Derlega and Alan L. Chaikin, *Sharing Intimacy: What We Reveal to Others and Why* (Englewood Cliffs, N.J.: Prentice-Hall, 1957).

[24]Ruth G. Loeb and John M. Curtis, "Effect of Counselors' Self-References on Subjects' First Impressions in an Experimental Psychological Interview," *Psychological Reports* 55 (December 1984): 803–10.

[25]Gordon J. Chelune, "Self-Disclosure: An Elaboration of Its Basic Dimensions," *Psychological Reports* 36 (February 1975): 79–85.

[26]Vincenzo Giannandrea and Kevin C. Murphy, "Similarity, Self-Disclosure, and Return for a Second Interview," *Journal of Counseling Psychology* 20 (November 1973): 545–48; Brenda Mann and Kevin C. Murphy, "Timing of Self-Disclosure, Reciprocity of Self-Disclosure, and Reactions to an Initial Interview," *Journal of Counseling Psychology* 22 (July 1975): 304–308.

[27]Howard J. Ehrlich and David B. Graeven, "Reciprocal Self-Disclosure in a Dyad," *Journal of Experimental Social Psychology* 7 (July 1971): 389–400; Jon A. Hall, "The Effects of Interviewer Expectations and Level of Self-Disclosure in a Dyadic Situation," *Dissertation Abstracts International* 37B (1976): 2506 (Doctoral diss., University of Arkansas, 1976); S. I. Vondracek and Fred W. Vondracek, "The Manipulation and Measurement of Self-Disclosure in Preadolescents," *Merrill-Palmer Quarterly of Behavior and Development* 17 (January 1971): 51–58.

[28]Worthy, "Self-Disclosure as an Exchange Process," 50–63.

[29]Norman Simonson and Susan Bahr, "Self-Disclosure by the Professional and Paraprofessional Therapist," *Journal of Consulting and Clinical Psychology* 42 (June 1974): 359–63.

[30]Hoffman-Graff, "Interviewer Use of Positive and Negative Self-Disclosure," 184–190; Mary Ann Hoffman and Gregory P. Spencer, "Effect of Interviewer-Subject Sex Pairing on Perceived and Actual Subject Behavior," *Journal of Counseling Psychology* 24 (September 1977): 383–90.

[31]Curtis, "Indications and Contraindications," 499–507.

[32]Derlega and Chaikin, *Sharing Intimacy;* Norman Simonson. "The Impact of Therapist Disclosure on Patient Disclosure," *Journal of Counseling Psychology* 23 (January 1976): 3–6.

[33]Egan, *The Skilled Helper;* Hammond, Hepworth, and Smith, *Improving Therapeutic Communication;* Myron F. Ewiner, "Self-Exposure by the Therapist as a Therapeutic Technique," *American Journal of Psychotherapy* 26 (January 1972): 42–51.

[34]Loeb and Curtis, "Effect of Counselors' Self-References." 803–10.

[35]Gregory J. Neimeyer and Paul G. Banikiotes, "Self-Disclosure Flexibility. Empathy, and Perceptions

of Adjustment and Attraction," *Journal of Counseling Psychology* 28 (May 1981): 272–75; Gregory J. Neimeyer and Margaret L. Fong, "Self-Disclosure Flexibility and Counselor Effectiveness," *Journal of Counseling Psychology* 30 (March 1983): 258–61.

[36] Bradmiller, "Self-Disclosure," 28–35.

[37] Neimeyer and Banikiotes, "Self-Disclosure Flexibility, Empathy, and Perceptions of Adjustment and Attraction," 272–75.

[38] Neimeyer and Fong, "Self-Disclosure Flexibility and Counselor Effectiveness," 258–61.

[39] Bradmiller, "Self-Disclosure," 28–35.

[40] Thomas V. Merluzzi, Paul G. Banikiotes, and Joseph W. Missbach, "Perceptions of Counselor Characteristics: Contribution of Counselor Sex, Experience, and Disclosure Level," *Journal of Counseling Psychology* 25 (September 1978): 479–82.

[41] Thomas V. Merluzzi and Bernadette Merluzzi, "Androgyny, Stereotypy, and the Perception of Female Therapists," *Journal of Clinical Psychology* 37 (April 1981): 280–84.

[42] Patricia R. McCarthy, "Differential Effects of Self-Disclosure versus Self-Involving Counselor Statements across Counselor-Client Gender Pairings," *Journal of Counseling Psychology* 26 (November 1979): 538–41; Merluzzi, Banikiotes, and Missbach, "Perceptions of Counselor Characteristics," 479–82; Neimeyer and Banikiotes, "Self-Disclosure Flexibility, Empathy, and Perceptions of Adjustment and Attraction," 272–75.

[43] John M. Curtis, "Effect of Therapist's Self-Disclosure on Patients' Impression of Empathy, Competence, and Trust in an Analogue of a Psychotherapeutic Interaction," *Psychological Reports* 48 (February 1981): 127–36; Sidney M. Jourard and Robert Friedman, "Experimenter-Subject Distance and Self-Disclosure," *Journal of Personality and Social Psychology* 15 (July 1970): 278–82; McCarthy, "Differential Effects of Self-Disclosing," 538–541; Merluzzi and Merluzzi, "Androgyny, Stereotypy," 280–84.

[44] Azy Barak and Michael B. LaCrosse, "Multidimensional Perception of Counselor Behavior," *Journal of Counseling Psychology* 22 (November 1975): 471–476; Curtis, "Effect of Therapist's Self-Disclosure," 127–36; McCarthy, "Differential Effects of Self-Disclosing," 538–541; Merluzzi and Merluzzi, "Androgyny, Stereotypy," 280–84.

[45] Steven G. Fox, Cynthia A. Strum, and H. A. Walters, "Perceptions of Therapist Disclosure of Previous Experience as a Client." *Journal of Clinical Psychology* 40 (March 1984): 496–98.

[46] Brent Mallinckrodt and Janet E. Helms, "Effect of Disabled Counselors' Self-Disclosures on Client

Perceptions of the Counselor," *Journal of Counseling Psychology* 33 (July 1986): 343–48.

[47] Stuart P. Chesner and Roy F. Baumeister, "Effect of Therapist's Disclosure of Religious Beliefs on the Intimacy of Client Self-Disclosure," *Journal of Social and Clinical Psychology* 3 (1, 1985): 97–105.

[48] Leonard D. Goodstein and Virginia M. Reinecker, "Factors Affecting Self-Disclosure: A Review of the Literature," in *Progress in Experimental Personality Research,* vol. 7, ed. Brendan A. Maher (New York: Academic Press, 1974), pp. 49–77.

[49] Ibid.: Leonard D. Goodstein and Scott W. Russell, "Self-Disclosure: A Comparative Study of Reports by Self and Others," *Journal of Counseling Psychology* 24 (July 1977): 365–69.

[50] Hammond, Hepworth, and Smith, *Improving Therapeutic Communication.*

[51] Ibid.

[52] Giannandrea and Murphy, "Similarity, Self-Disclosure," 545–48; Mann and Murphy, "Timing of Self-Disclosure," 304–308.

[53] Hammond, Hepworth, and Smith, *Improving Therapeutic Communication.*

[54] Ibid.

[55] Weigel et al., "Perceived Self-Disclosure," 47–52.

[56] Derlega, Lovell, and Chaikin, "Effects of Therapist Self-Disclosure," p. 866.

[57] Simonson and Bahr, "Self-Disclosure by the Professional," 359–63; Worthy, Gary, and Kahn, "Self-Disclosure as an Exchange Process," 59–63.

[58] Merluzzi and Merluzzi, "Androgyny, Stereotypy." 280–84.

[59] Neimeyer and Banikiotes, "Self-Disclosure Flexibility, Empathy, and Perceptions of Adjustment and Attraction," 272–75; Neimeyer and Fong, "Self-Disclosure Flexibility and Counselor Effectiveness," 258–61.

[60] Hammond, Hepworth, and Smith, *Improving Therapeutic Communication.*

[61] Ibid.

[62] Hoffman-Graff, "Interviewer Use of Positive and Negative Self-Disclosure," 184–90.

[63] Hammond, Hepworth, and Smith, *Improving Therapeutic Communication.*

[64] Chelune, "Self-Disclosure," 79–85.

[65] Gerard Egan, *Interpersonal Living: A Skills/Contract Approach to Human Relations Training in Groups* (Monterey, Calif.: Brooks/Cole, 1976).

[66] Bradmiller, "Self-Disclosure," 28–35.

[67] Ibid.

Reprinted with permission from *Social Casework* 70(5)(1989):259–267.

6

Fixed Methods: Relational and Longitudinal Research

I s employment related to the amount of care adult daughters provide to their frail elderly parents (Brody et al. 1987)? Are there gender differences in the learning and school performance problems children experience, and do girls and boys receive the same or different amounts and types of supportive services in school to help them with these problems (Anastas & Reinherz 1984)? What are the variations in the way elderly people reminisce, and are these variations related to personality and/or to depression (Daniels 1993)? Is childhood abuse related to teenage pregnancy (Smith 1996)? What is the relationship between socioeconomic status and race and adaptation to a diagnosis of cancer (Ell & Nishimoto 1989)? Or, as in our sample article, is biculturalism related to self-ratings of mental health among Cuban Americans (Gomez 1990)? If you pick up any recent issue of a journal in social work or the social sciences, the pages will be filled with articles addressed to questions that are similar in nature to these. These studies all have one basic thing in common: They are addressed to examining relationships between or among variables as they occur in everyday life. This book terms such studies *relational research*, that is, research designed to describe regularities or patterns in how a predefined phenomenon relates to other predefined phenomena.

The term relational research is one not commonly found in other discussions of types of research. However, what this text is terming relational research questions are very common in social science and human services research.[1] By defining relational designs as a distinct type of study, it is possible to consider their methodology more carefully and to evaluate their findings in light of their

---

1. Although the term "correlational research" is sometimes encountered, it generally refers to research that depends on using correlational statistical techniques in the data analysis, while relational research as defined here may use them or may not.

stated purpose, rather distinguishing them from other types of studies by characterizing them as "less than" or "quasi" something else.

Like experimental research, relational research is a deductive method of inquiry because it begins with a logical hypothesis, or provisional theory, about a specific relationship among phenomena, and the study methodology is also predetermined in advance based on the phenomena to be examined. However, it differs from experimental research in that the phenomena being examined are not deliberately manipulated by the researcher as part of the research; thus it is not possible to say that creating change in one variable can produce change in another.

Relational research is different from descriptive research because instead of describing a static phenomenon in a static context, it examines dynamic, that is, changing or interacting, relationships among phenomena. However, because both are fixed methods of research, relational studies may be built on descriptive research designs that address questions like "What precisely are the characteristics of this phenomenon or population?" to address how several specific characteristics or properties of a phenomenon may relate to each other. For example, in the study of gender differences in children's learning mentioned earlier, the research was designed to address its original question, which was an epidemiological one, and additional analyses were later undertaken to answer relational questions (Anastas & Reinherz 1984). In many cases, however, the study begins with a relational question, and this chapter is about the nature of such studies and how they can best be designed. The studies of reminiscence, caregiving, teenage pregnancy, biculturalism, and coping with cancer cited above were all studies originally conceived and designed to answer a relational question.

Defining Relational Research

Relational studies are designed to show that two (or more) phenomena or features of a phenomenon do, in fact, vary together in regular ways. From the standpoint of fallibilistic realism (Manicas & Secord 1983), the goal of research is to develop observational information about phenomena in reality as it exists in the "real world" and to generate the best possible theoretical explanations of that reality. Relational studies are designed to show how different predefined phenomena or properties of them do (or do not) regularly vary together and, through the use of theory, to describe the nature of the connection between them. Establishing covariation is, in fact, one step in establishing what have traditionally been termed causal arguments, but it is not the only one. Although relational studies cannot demonstrate "causation" (Brigham 1989), they have an essential role to play in showing how different phenomena may (or may not) be regularly linked to each other, and in uncovering dynamic and not just static properties of phenomena in relation to each other. Relational research is also used in building theory by demonstrating that relationships predicted by a theory to exist in fact can be shown to occur (Kuhn 1970).

Experiments also are designed to examine relationships between variables, but they do so by introducing or producing change in one (or more) variable(s) and assessing the subsequent change, if any, in another variable or variables. This study strategy assumes that the variable of interest can be controlled or manipulated, which is not true of many of the variables important to social work theory and practice. For example, status variables, such as race, gender, socioeconomic status, and the like, cannot be changed experimentally except by analogue, meaning they can be changed artificially in a vignette, case description, or videotape. Many other factors, such as the occurrence of cancer, the death of a spouse, or the experience of child abuse, could never ethically be imposed on study participants, even if there were the means to do so. Relational designs provide the means to study these phenomena when manipulation of the variable of interest is not possible or necessary. In traditional terms, relational research is used for *ex post facto* designs involving manipulated variables or interventions, for all group comparisons involving nonmanipulated variables, and for cross-sectional and longitudinal research whenever its purpose is the examination of the associations among variables, whatever the statistical or analytic techniques used.

The goal of relational research is to describe whether or not a phenomenon or a characteristic of it is systematically associated with another phenomenon and, if so, how. Alternatively, a relational question may address how two different phenomena relate to each other. Finally, a relational research question may be conceived of as a question about how one or more dimensions of the observational context relate to observed characteristics of the phenomenon itself.

Relational research is a form of fixed method research for two main reasons. First, theory is used to identify the phenomena and relationships to be examined in advance of implementing the research design. The formal statement of the research question takes the form of a hypothesis, which is then examined in relation to the empirical observations made. This hypothesis may be thought of as a provisional theory that will be examined for its relevance to data drawn from planned observation. It fixes the focus of the research, which remains the same throughout the study.

Second, in relational research the methods and procedures used to conduct observations are fixed before the study begins and remain inflexible throughout the conduct of the study. As with descriptive designs, theory thus drives the design by determining: (1) the characteristics sample members must have or, in other words, the kind of sample that must be sought in order to examine the variations of interest, (2) the characteristics or properties that are to be examined, (3) the way in which each characteristic will be measured or observed, and (4) the point of view that will be taken on the phenomenon. These decisions, once made, result in the design of a specific method of study that is carried out as planned and is not varied during the conduct of the research.

When, as is typical, quantitative data are generated, the analytic methods for a relational study can generally be specified in advance as well. The analysis in relational research may involve correlations between and among variables in a single sample group or it may involve comparisons between or among naturally occurring groups. In addition, the researcher as actor is generally not considered part of the phenomena designated for study in relational research. One reason that study methods and techniques are "fixed" is to hold the observational context as constant as possible, to reduce as much as possible the variation in what is observed that can be attributed to the act of observation itself. However, methodological studies designed to assess variations in observational context in the methods or tools of observation or in observer characteristics are themselves examples of relational research.

Relational research as a concept has several advantages. First of all, as has already been stated, it denotes a form of research that is very common in the helping professions and in the social sciences. Second, its very name does not suggest that it is a method subordinate to any other, as "quasi-experimentation" (Cook & Campbell 1979) does. Finally, the idea of relationships among phenomena is core to theory development. An integral part of developing ideas or theories about how things work lies in the discovery and observation of patterns or regularities in how phenomena relate to each other, or interact, in the observable world. Relational research is designed and undertaken for the express purpose of describing these regularities, patterns, or relationships among phenomena when the goal is not creating change or when the variable or variables under study cannot be manipulated. By describing research designs undertaken for this purpose as a distinctive study type, the importance and usefulness of this kind of investigation is highlighted.

Types of Relational Designs

There are two basic methods for doing relational research: studying associations among different variables in a single sample group or studying group differences on the same variables. In each of the questions listed at the beginning of the chapter, one (or more) properties of the phenomenon is measured in the sample and then examined in relation to another property. This may be done either by examining the correlations between and among multiple characteristics in the same sample (levels of depression and styles of reminiscence, number of hours worked per week and amount of time spent in caregiving, biculturalism and mental health) or by comparing groups (male/females, "minority"/"majority," abuse history/no abuse history) on the same variable(s) (standardized test scores and special education status; pregnancy status).

The one-group kind of question, which involves correlational analysis, may seem the most obvious type of relational research. In it, one phenomenon is examined for how it is associated with another or with some aspect of its observational context. However, studies that proceed by comparing naturally occurring groups are indeed examining the same kind of question. The only difference is that in the latter case one or more of the phenomena is measured in such a way as to produce a categorical, not a continuous or quantitative, variable, and the statistical techniques that are therefore used in developing the study findings are different, although their underlying mathematics are equivalent.

Correlation Versus "Causation"

Relational research examines whether concepts, phenomena, or characteristics of them are or are not connected to one another and, if so, in what way. In traditional terms, however, the matter of establishing causation is a complex one that goes far beyond empirical evidence from any one research study, however carefully it is designed and executed. Traditional discussions of causation have traditionally emphasized that a major step in developing a causal line of argument is to show that two things vary together. Relational research is designed to do just that.

One of the great dangers in relational research is to jump too quickly in interpretation from the observation of a relationship or covariation between variables to assumptions about invariance in the nature of that relationship. How can we know about which variable preceded the other when both were assessed at the same time? Is there any other factor, either one measured in the study or one that might not have been studied at all, that could have produced the pattern observed? Is there some intervening variable, which may or may not have been assessed, through which the two variables are connected rather than being connected directly to each other? Is there a theory that can explain the way the covariation occurs? Is there evidence from other studies showing consistency in the observed relationship? Is there evidence from other studies showing that arranging a change in one variable will produce the expected change in the other?

This last type of question cannot by definition be answered by a relational study. Only experimental studies, prospective by definition, in which an antecedent or "causal" variable is manipulated and then the predicted changes are (or are not) observed in the consequent or "effect" variable can provide evidence of this kind. Even then, the ability to predict change in one variable by manipulating another has to be distinguished from the fact that even such a utilitarian operation may be distinct from the ultimate cause or reason for the working of the mechanism (see chapter 7 on experiments).

Even in the traditional view, "causal" arguments depend ultimately on the theory that explains them and thus on the fact that there are not plausible, competing explanations for how and why a "cause" produces its "effect." Relational studies can show covariation and can suggest the theories that may explain it, but they cannot in their design show the effects of change or "control for" or rule out all competing or alternative explanations for the relationship observed.

The nature and limits of correlation or covariation as a concept can best be shown in a picture. In figure 6–1, let "A" be biculturalism and let "B" be subjective mental health. The arrow that connects the variables points in both directions to indicate a bidirectional relationship: It is not clear whether it is biculturalism that produces a greater sense of mental health or whether those who report a higher level of mental health are better able to embrace the complexities of multiple cultural worlds. Although Gomez (1990) favors the former explanation, there is nothing in the data themselves that can shed any light on the direction of the arrow or on which explanation may have the greater claim to legitimacy.

Consider also "C": It is possible that some other factor, as yet unnamed and unimagined, affects both biculturalism and reported mental health, that both are

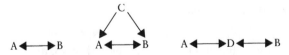

Figure 6–1 Possible Relationships Between Variable A and B

"effects" of some other "cause." Relational study designs often attempt to include as many other factors as possible that might prove to be "Cs" in their designs in order to look for such relationships and, it is hoped to rule them out as competing explanations for the hypothesized relationship. The Gomez study, for example, examined such other factors as age and SES for their effects on the dependent variables (pp. 384). Gomez (1990) used a multiple regression technique to show that the relationship between biculturalism and the measures of mental health remained strong even after variability due to these "C" factors was statistically taken into account (pp. 385–86).

Finally, consider "D," a possible intervening variable. Perhaps biculturalism and mental health only appear to be directly connected, and perhaps biculturalism is related to some other factor, such as self-confidence, that itself is related to mental health. Relational studies are often also designed to include and measure as many "Ds" as possible, and multivariate techniques such as multiple regression and path analysis may be used to determine whether the arrow should go directly from "A" to "B" or whether it should go from "A" through "D" to "B." However, it is not generally possible to measure and assess the potential effects of all the "D" or intervening variables imaginable in any one study.

Given these limitations of relational studies, why are they so often done? First of all, many of the variables that are important to understand in the social and human sciences cannot realistically be manipulated in experimental investigations (Sechrest & Hannah 1990). Sometimes the barriers are practical, as when studying such variables as race, gender, adoption, or early developmental experiences; such characteristics of a person cannot be changed except in analogues, that is, by using and varying the content of documents, videotapes, or other simulations of real situations, which have their own problems of interpretation.

Sometimes the barriers to experiments are ethical, as in studying the antecedents or aftereffects of painful or traumatic conditions or experiences. Another type of ethical barrier to experimentation arises when a treatment or program seems so manifestly superior to an alternative or no treatment that it is unethical to withhold it from the control group participants, a situation that occurs frequently in program evaluation research and sometimes in medical research as well.

Experimental studies rely on randomization to hold constant many of the factors that may precede, accompany, or follow an event (see chapter 7). However, many characteristics, issues, or events are complex, and it may be difficult or undesirable to isolate them from their contexts. Some events, like the occurrence of certain illnesses or medical conditions, as well as other rare events, must be studied in very large samples—groups ordinarily too large for experimental control or too expensive to study—or over very long periods of time. In these circumstances, experiments are costly, impractical, and liable to failure (Sechrest & Hannah 1990). Thus relational studies are the most practical research method available for examining relationships among phenomena in these circumstances.

The inability of relational studies to provide definitive evidence regarding causal statements, however, must always be recognized. It is this limitation that is one of the roots of many contemporary arguments in social science and public policy, such as about the nature of the effects of divorce and various custody arrangements on children. A decision to request or award joint custody of children to two parents is embedded in judicial ideologies and state laws, the nature of the parental relationship, the conflict prior to the divorce, and the nature of the relationship the two parents can manage following it, as well as on geographic and other circumstances. All of these factors, in turn, as well as others, influence each other and also influence the outcomes in terms of the well-being of the children that a study of child custody would seek to assess. Since experimentation in such a circumstance would be unthinkable, relational studies offer the best evidence available—on this and other important issues—even though caution must be used in interpreting their results.

Finally, it is important to emphasize that newer views of science, including fallibilistic realism (Manicas & Secord 1983), emphasize understanding and explanation rather than notions of causation and proof as the ultimate purpose of science. Understanding depends not only on observational data of all kinds but also on the concepts used to make sense of the data and the logical statements connecting them, that is, on theory. Relational studies have a great deal to contribute to theory development because their focus is on theory-building, on showing how phenomena and concepts relate to each other and by suggesting how these relationships may be understood.

An Example of Relational Research

The Gomez (1990) study of biculturalism and mental health in a Cuban American population illustrates the principles of relational research well. It begins with a review of the limited empirical research on biculturalism, describing how the concept of biculturalism emerged replacing former theories of acculturation and noting that the relationship of biculturalism to mental health had yet to be studied within a "healthy" population. A "general" hypothesis is stated: "after controlling for variability due to sex [sic], age, marital status, socioeconomic class, and length of stay in the United States, there would be a positive linear relationship between subjective mental health and one's level of biculturalism" (p. 377). Conceptually, this hypothesis is also rendered as a question, ". . . is optimal adjustment associated with a dual identification with both cultures?" (p. 376), that is, in immigrant communities, is optimal adjustment associated both with the "host" culture and the "ethnic" culture. As the hypothesis reveals, this relational study is of the one-sample type because it will proceed to examine two characteristics, biculturalism and mental health, in one sample of respondents.

Relational research is deductive and fixed in its method. It is deductive because a logically derived hypothesis drives the observations *and* because key aspects of the method are logically driven as well. Once developed, these methods of observation remain fixed throughout the conduct of the study. In this case, rules for the selection and recruitment of a sample were developed, and structured interviews were conducted. Data from the interviews were then quantified and analyzed statistically.

As noted earlier, in fixed method research the first aspect of a study to be developed is the sample, and samples in relational research are designed to provide the best possibility for examining the specific phenomena of interest in a study. Gomez specifies several characteristics of his sample at the outset that will make it useful for answering his specific research question. The first is that it should be a "healthy" or nonclinical sample. This requirement results in using census data to survey community households rather than, for example, going to a community agency and studying those who are seeking help. It also results in screening potential sample members in order to include only people with no history of psychiatric treatment, drug abuse, or use of psychotropic medication (p. 380). As in many descriptive and relational studies that seek to develop generaliz-able findings, random selection was used to identify the blocks within census tracts from which households were surveyed. There were additional criteria for selection as well, namely that the respondent be 18 or older, not acquainted with the interviewer, and, of course, willing to be interviewed.

The next areas of method are also driven by theory, namely, the identification of the specific, predetermined properties to measure and then selection of the specific tools and procedures for measuring them. Because of the importance of these issues, Gomez spends considerable time in his article discussing them. In stating his hypothesis, he identifies four specific aspects of the concept or phenomenon of "subjective mental health" that he will focus on: psychological well-being, self-esteem, marital adjustment, and job satisfaction. He defends each area as important to overall adjustment and also considers the potential role of culture in each; he then goes on to identify the specific measurement tools and procedures used to assess each area. Note that a different way of defining subjective mental health conceptu-ally or selecting different aspects of it to focus on would have led to a quite different study even if the sample and the purpose had remained the same. In addition, he might have retained the same concepts but selected different measurement tools.

The other major concept in the study, biculturalism, is also discussed and defined. In this case as well, an existing measurement instrument was adopted. It should be noted that the tendency to use existing measurement tools when possible is common in fixed method research (see chapter 15 on selecting and using existing measures) because the rules for their use are well known and well developed and because findings from them can be interpreted from a base of knowledge about their prior use.

In addition, various "control variables," as Gomez called them, were also assessed. These variables, like age, gender, marital status, socioeconomic status, and length of residence in the United States, are the "C" factors discussed in figure 6–1, and are some possible alternative explanations for any association observed. Some, like known mental health problems, were eliminated through sampling; others, like these enumerated previously, were taken into account by assessing and examining them in the data analysis. In the end, in this study few of the assessed variables showed any strong relationship to the major study variable, biculturalism. One of the greatest challenges in the design of relational research is deciding what factors like these must be accounted for and what methods to use in dealing with each.

As to point of view, Gomez aligns himself clearly with those thinkers who ques-tion the traditional notion of acculturation, that is, accommodation to the host culture through abandonment of the ethnic culture as conducive to positive adaptation for immigrant groups. In fact, his study is designed to demonstrate that biculturalism rather than monoculturalism in terms either of the ethnic or the host culture is conducive to positive mental health. Thus the results of the study go beyond describing a particular sample or population; through the concepts used to organize and summarize what has been observed, implications for theory also emerge.

In terms of research design, the fact that Gomez has a point of view is not a problem as long as his study methodology allows for any possible empirical result, a confirming one or a disconfirming one. The great detail offered about method in the report of this or any other fixed method study is designed to let the skeptical reader determine for him- or herself whether or not the method of study was fair and unbiased.

The findings of this study, as expected from the overall one-sample design, are expressed principally as correlations, or measures of relationship, among the major variables of interest: scores derived from the measures of the four aspects of subjective mental health assessed and scores on the measure of biculturalism. As predicted, biculturalism did show a positive linear relationship to all of the measures of mental health selected although less strongly with job satisfaction than with others.

Cross-sectional Designs in Relational Research

Most relational studies, like the Gomez study, are cross-sectional in design; that is, they measure variables as they occur at one point in time, as in a snapshot, holding the temporal context constant. This section will summarize common features of cross-sectional relational research designs.

Sampling

Samples for relational research study designs are guided by the nature of the question. If the study is to proceed by examining correlations among variables in a single group, care must be taken to ensure that sample membership will naturally include a full range of variation on each of the variables under study. If the study will proceed by comparing naturally occurring subgroups in the sample, it is essential to ensure that each subgroup is large enough to be representative and to permit reliable statistical comparison. In either case, the goals of sampling in relational research are to encompass variation in the phenomena of interest and produce a sample representative of the population to which the results will be generalized.

The Gomez study of biculturalism and mental health among Cuban Americans illustrates sampling issues in relational research well. The use of census data to select residential tracts allowed for random sampling to be used. As with descriptive research, the more unbiased the method of sample selection, the more confidence one may have in generalizing research findings from a sample to the more general population that the research seeks to represent, in this case, Cuban Americans living in a given community in New Jersey. Since random sampling is the selection method that has proven to be most unbiased (see chapter 10), relational studies that seek to develop generalizable findings often incorporate random methods of sample selection.

The Gomez study also illustrates what can happen when a sample does not contain enough variation to represent a characteristic well. For example, one of the measures initially selected to describe subjective mental health was a scale of marital satisfaction. This scale could only be meaningfully completed by study participants who were involved in an intimate relationship. However, because of variability in marital and relationship status in the sample, which accurately reflected diversity in the population, those respondents who were not in intimate relationships could not complete the scale. Therefore, part of the original question about the relationship between biculturalism and self-reported marital satisfaction had to be dropped from the multivariate analysis of relationships among study variables (p. 385). The question of how all of the correlates of marital satisfaction, including biculturalism, may relate to each other must then be pursued in some later study using a representative sample of Cuban Americans limited to those who are married or involved in intimate relationships.

If a relational study is to proceed by examining the relationship between group membership and another variable, the goal of the sampling plan is to ensure adequate representation of each of the groups to be compared. If subgroup samples are not adequately large, analysis may become impossible or attenuated. If the subgroups are not of equal size in the population there are special sampling techniques, such as proportional sampling and weighting, discussed in the chapter on sampling, that should be considered for ensuring that groups that are smaller are adequately represented in study results.

This problem of ensuring that small or underrepresented groups are adequately reflected and described in studies has often been discussed in relation to the study of people of color (see chapter 10). When studying race or ethnicity, for example, it may be easy for majority researchers to succumb to the tendency to see each group itself as monolithic or homogeneous. However, African Americans vary among themselves in national origin, class, and religion, among other factors. Latino/as and Asian Americans vary markedly by these factors and by generation of migration as well. Native Americans differ by nation, religion, specific historical experience, and amount of experience with reservation life, among other factors. Language differences may occur in all groups as well. Samples of these groups must be designed to include and record variability on these and other relevant dimensions; small or undifferentiated samples from these groups may invalidate the generalizability of the research.

No one study can presume to isolate, measure, and discuss every variable of possible interest. Each study must, of necessity, focus on only a limited number of variables or factors. Others must be taken account of or "controlled for" in some other way. Still others—many others—must be acknowledged as existing and as having potential effects but as not controlled or not addressed by the particular study at hand. A careful review of the literature (see chapter 2 on problem formulation) is an important source of information about variables that may need to be taken into account one way or another.

There are two basic methods of "control" used in relational designs. One is to measure other known and suspected influences or variables as part of the study and then to include them in the analysis (see below). The other is to concede that the study will not address variation in certain characteristics and to control for these by making the sample studied homogeneous with respect to those characteristics. In other words, *selection criteria* are developed that deliberately eliminate some specified variation. Such a sample will not then be representative of the entire range of possibilities as they might naturally exist in the population, but it does afford a lens through which to see clearly how the variables studied interact without "muddying the waters" with variation due to other factors. For example, as noted earlier, Gomez (1990) screened sample members and included only those with no prior history of mental health treatment so that scores on subjective mental health would not be lowered by respondents with specific illnesses. Thus his findings may be generalized to Cuban American city residents with no history of mental health or substance abuse problems but not to Cuban American city residents as a whole.

In another example, the Ell and Nishimoto (1989) study of socioeconomic and racial differences in adaptation to cancer selected sample members based on age, specific types of cancers newly diagnosed, and the absence of other major illnesses or psychiatric or central nervous system disorders. Thus the sample obtained is not representative of all cancer patients, but the data on coping are not confounded by other factors that could have an effect on coping itself. Thus samples used for relational research often have a delimited nature based on the selection criteria, although methods for drawing a trustworthy sample from within such a delimited population must still be designed to be representative through the use of unbiased selection techniques. For example, in the Ell and Nishimoto study (1989), all available patients meeting the sampling criteria were invited to participate.

Data Collection

The first issue in data collection is to decide what characteristics of the sample(s) need to be assessed or taken account of in order to answer the research question. It is obvious that those variables directly implicated in any hypothesized relationship between variables should be assessed. For example, in the study of gender and children's emotional and behavioral problems, measures are obviously needed of gender, a relatively simple matter, and of emotional and behavioral problems, a complex one. What characteristics will best inform us about behavioral problems? About emotional ones? From whose perspective should these characteristics be assessed—the parent's? the teacher's? a mental health professional's? the child him- or herself? Informed choices must be made and defended in relation to all of these questions.

While it is essential to measure accurately the characteristics directly involved in the guiding question or hypothesis of the research, this alone is not enough. One of the ways to establish credibility for an explanation of a pattern is to cast doubt on competing or alternative ideas. Thus if there are other factors that might better explain the variation observed (the "Cs" and "Ds" in figure 6–1), these factors should also be taken into account in the research design, either by eliminating those sources of variation through sample selection or by including them in the data collection and analysis.

For example, in the study of gender differences in emotional problems, since having experienced a parental divorce is thought to be related to children's emotional and behavioral problems, it is important to establish that the boys and girls in the study were equivalent with respect to the occurrence of divorce. The problem could have been handled by limiting the sample either to children from intact marriages or to children who had experienced a parental divorce. Alternatively, the experience of divorce could be allowed to vary; if so, it must be assessed: boys and girls must be compared as to their divorce experience and, if the groups differed, any difference between them must be handled in the data analysis. What is essential here is that the variable—the occurrence of divorce—must be taken into account. If not eliminated as a factor through sample selection, it must be measured as part of the study so its potential relationship to the observed variations in emotional and behavioral problems can assessed. Without that, there is no way to defend the study's conclusions about gender from the challenge of a competing explanation.

Many of the variables of interest in relational research, like subjective mental health or the emotional and behavioral problems of children, are complex conceptually and provide challenges to reliable and valid data collection. Relational studies, like all fixed methods of research, require the specification and definition of the variables of interest in advance of collecting the data. In these studies, a traditional approach to quantitative measurement is generally used (see, for example, chapter 15 on selecting existing measures). Relational study designs are often considered stronger when existing, well-validated instruments and measurement procedures are used (Sechrest & Hannah 1990). As long as measures can be found that adequately reflect the concepts and theories used in the research, it can simplify the research process and the defense of study results if the measures used do not require development and/or defense in and of themselves. The capacity to apply efficiently the measures selected in large samples and to derive quantified results from them contributes to the effectiveness and precision of the analysis that can be undertaken once the data have been collected.

Data Analysis

Although relational studies have in the past been termed "correlational" (Cook & Campbell 1979), in fact a variety of statistical techniques can be used to examine relationships among variables. The first are correlational: all the measures of association that can be used to assess whether and how strongly two (or more) variables are related to each other in the same sample. The specific correlational measure to use, of course, depends primarily on the level of measurement of each variable and how it is distributed in the actual sample (see chapter on 17 on descriptive statistics). Measurement at the interval or ratio level is generally preferred because the range of techniques available is greatest, and the measurement can always be reduced to a simpler form (ordinal or nominal) if, for example, the distribution should turn out to be bimodal or markedly skewed. When possible, the ability to specify, based on theory, the direction of a relationship in advance makes it possible to use one-tailed rather than two-tailed tests of statistical significance, which are more powerful.

Relational questions are also answered, of course, by examining differences between sample groups, as in the case of status variables like race and gender. The specific statistical technique to be used for these comparisons depends on the number of sample groups to be compared and on the level of measurement of the variable(s) on which they are compared. Again, interval or ratio levels of measurement are often preferred because the techniques available for working with them are more numerous and in some cases more powerful. Statistical methods of group comparison work best when there are sufficient numbers within each group; in some cases, as with two-group comparisons using the t-test, balanced or equal-sized groups usually make it possible to use a more powerful version of the test. This possibility must be planned for when the study, especially its sampling method, is originally designed. As with correlational techniques, when making two-group comparisons, if the direction of group difference can be specified in advance, the tests of statistical significance can be made more powerful by using the one-tailed version (see chapter 18 on inferential statistics).

Often it is impossible or undesirable to isolate just two variables from their context in order to examine the relationship between them. For example, in the study of boys and girls in school, boys and girls did not enter school looking the same, so comparisons of them at third grade had to control for the initial differences between them so as not to confound differential outcomes with preexisting differences. This "control" was accomplished using a multivariate technique: analysis of covariance (Anastas & Reinherz 1984). While discussion of multivariate statistical techniques is beyond the scope of this book, the techniques are not that difficult to understand conceptually and are now widely available to researchers through the various computerized statistical packages in use today. In fact, some are designed to generate and test "models" from descriptive data; techniques exist for working with both continuous and categorical variables in this fashion. There are several excellent resources available to guide the researcher in how to use the techniques and how to interpret the analyses that result. These include Afifi and Clark (1984), Grimm and Yarnold (1995), and Stevens (1996). Now that the complexities of calculation can be solved by the computer, multivariate techniques offer the researcher the possibility of designing relational studies and data analyses that more accurately reflect the complexity of individual and social behavior as it exists.

It should be noted, however, that it is often necessary to have a relatively large sample size available in order to legitimately use multivariate statistical techniques. In the case of multiple regression procedures, including factor analysis, in which many variables are commonly used, overall sample size is often a limiting factor in what analyses can be done, especially when missing data on specific variables is taken into account. Therefore it is important to plan for an adequate sample size for such analyses when the study is being designed and implemented.

Longitudinal and Developmental Research

Relational research has been discussed up to this point as examining variables as they might relate to each other at essentially the same point in time. Often, however, theory and observation suggest that earlier developmental experiences or contextual factors are predictive of later characteristics or events. Retrospective, cross-sectional studies that examine earlier experiences by means of history or recall can be used to study such issues and would be classified as relational. However, it makes a more powerful argument to study the effects of historical or developmental events prospectively rather than rely on recall or reconstruction of the past, which are often influenced by the present.

Studies that follow the same individuals over a period of time are called *longitudinal*. These studies may precede an event, experience, or life stage of interest and then examine how the event unfolds differentially based on prior characteristics or experiences. These studies can also be designed to follow an experience, event, or life stage of interest, seeking information about how that experience is related to subsequent characteristics and events during some period of short or long-term follow-up.Some longitudinal studies may seem to be simply descriptive if they are designed only to picture the unfolding of developmental or maturational processes. However, such *longitudinal research* can be thought of as studies in which time and maturational processes vary systematically, and the phenomenon or phenomena of interest is studied in relation to this variation in context. Most such studies are more focal, though, concentrating on some limited or specific behaviors or on specific historical or developmental events or experiences and then seeking to explain variation in how such events or experiences are negotiated, how such behaviors emerged, or what their short- or long-term correlates may be. Such longitudinal studies are quite obviously a special form of relational research.

Even program evaluation research may be considered longitudinal when clients who participated in a program or treatment are followed over a period of time. For example, in social work and public health, programs designed to reduce the incidence of repeat teen pregnancies typically use a two-year follow-up period because it has been found that most teens who become pregnant again do so within a two-year period after the first birth. Programs designed to prevent teen pregnancy altogether might require even longer periods of follow-up if the programs are initiated early, such as during the junior high school years, because former clients of those programs will remain teens and "at risk" for teenage pregnancy for a considerable period. In these cases, patients and clients (or their families or physicians) must be regularly contacted and assessed for the entire follow-up period in order for rates of pregnancy, morbidity, and/or mortality to be accurately assessed. Typically, considerable resources must be expended on the follow-up process alone in order to ensure adequate rates of retention of sample members in any longitudinal study.

Developmental research can be done focussing either on problems or potentially problematic experiences, or on positive outcomes and processes. For example, Judith Wallerstein and her colleagues recruited families who were undergoing separation and divorce and followed them and the children in those families for a ten-year period (Wallerstein 1984, 1985; Springer & Wallerstein 1983). She divided the children in her sample into various age groups and studied the differing effects of divorce on these children according to the developmental stage of the child at the time of the separation and at five- and ten-year follow-up. While her studies have been criticized for lacking a control or comparison group of children who had not undergone a divorce experience, they were among the first to examine children's functioning following a divorce systematically and in depth over a long period of time. In addition, they were designed to relate the descriptions children gave of the effects of divorce on them with known differences in developmental capacity connected with the age of the child.

Special Issues in Longitudinal Research

While longitudinal research may be the best method for examining developmental and other specific kinds of relational questions, it is a complex and demanding form of research. Special problems must be addressed at all levels of design in order for the research to be a success, and addressing these problems can make longitudinal research quite expensive. This section will outline some of the special challenges in conducting longitudinal research and suggest methods that have been used to meet these challenges.

Sample attrition. Sample attrition, or the tendency for people to be lost to follow-up in longitudinal studies over time, is probably the greatest challenge in such research. The longer the period of follow-up needed, the higher the rate of attrition from the sample is likely to be. For this reason, studies that are planned from the outset to be very long-term undertakings often are done in locations chosen because the populations within them are geographically stable and accessible. Werner's research on child development was done on one Hawaiian island, an area with a finite and stable population falling into one administrative unit for health services (Werner, Bierman, & French 1971; Werner & Smith 1977, 1982, 1992); similarly, Earl's research was done on the permanent population of an island off the New England coast (Garrison & Earls 1981). While these populations may differ from others in part because of their geographic isolation and stability, they have traditionally afforded ideal locations for long-term research because it has been possible to remain in touch with almost all sample members over a very long period of time. Centralized systems of record keeping about health and social services are also a great advantage in this type of research, systems more common in Europe, for example, than in the United States.

Aside from selecting a finite and stable population for the research when possible, wherever longitudinal research is undertaken there are methods that can be used to increase rates of follow-up and reduce sample attrition. When beginning research that will incorporate follow-up procedures, it is essential to get permission for future contact as part of the original consent procedure when people are first recruited to the study. Without this consent, contact with the client in future will not be assured even if the client can be found. It is often helpful as well to get names of friends, neighbors, relatives, or professionals from the client at the outset and to secure permission to contact them if the client cannot be located directly at some future follow-up point. This list of contact people should be updated from time to time if contact is to be maintained for a very long period.

Repeat contacts with sample members should be made as frequently as possible just for purposes of tracking. If people are to be studied in depth every five years, for example, it may be useful to make contact by phone or mail annually, just to keep current about people's location.

A reliable system for tracking clients and for keeping track of when each client is due for follow-up contact is essential to any longitudinal research project. Regular contact with research participants is a product both of the willingness of participants to remain involved and of the initiative of the researchers in reaching out to make connection. Often large numbers of respondents are being followed in a single research project, each on a somewhat different schedule for follow-up contact based on differing initial data gathering points. It is essential that some system, preferably a computerized one, be developed that will reliably indicate each month, quarter, or year the sample members who are due for contact. Such a system requires constant updating, of course, to ensure that up-to-date information about how to make contact and when the sample member was last contacted is included. Without such a system, it is inevitable that some data collection will be missed or will take place off-schedule in such a way that results may be compromised.

Sample sizes in longitudinal research should be planned from the outset to permit some attrition and still yield a sample size viable for the analyses needed. Because attrition will generally increase the longer the time period of study, studies should be designed to use the shortest time period possible for achieving worthwhile results.

People can be lost to follow-up either because they subsequently withdraw their participation from the research voluntarily or, more often, because they are "lost"—not contacted, found to have moved so far away that data collection is no longer possible, or simply not found when an attempt to make contact was made. The validity of longitudinal research results rests in large measure on the integrity of the sample over time. However, it is impossible to prevent some attrition from samples because we live in a mobile society on a national and even global level and because vicissitudes of life will intervene in the form of morbidity, mortality, and other life crises that may compromise a person's ability or interest in research participation.

When sample members are lost to follow-up, as will inevitably happen, the reasons they were lost should be recorded and reported in the results. Unexplained loss from the sample may raise greater concerns about the adequacy of the follow-up efforts and the representativeness of the remaining sample than when low but predictable rates of geographic mobility are shown to contribute to the attrition. Because some attrition is inevitable, it is also inevitable that a comparison between sample members remaining and those lost to follow-up be made and reported based on their initial characteristics. The hope, of course, is that no significant difference in known, initial characteristics will be found between those who remained in and those who were lost from the sample. If differences are found, however, these need to be acknowledged and taken into account in analyzing or interpreting results based on those who remain.

Data collection. In relational research of any kind, it is important to include and assess as many of the variables that might affect the outcomes of interest as possible. For example, if the question is about what negative effects divorce might have on children, it would be important also to assess those factors that might either exacerbate or mitigate those effects as well. Otherwise true correlates of divorce might be overstated, masked, or missed.

The longer the period of the research, or the longer the follow-up period, the larger the number of alternative factors that might occur and that might intervene to affect outcomes. These factors may also differ at different follow-up points. While longitudinal research depends most on repeated measures at different points in time, it may be necessary to include different variables as well as they become salient at different follow-up points or developmental periods. These intervening variables must be studied carefully or must be controlled for via sampling restrictions.

A special characteristic of data collection in longitudinal research is that the same or similar procedures are often repeated with the same respondents at intervals over the lifetime of the study. Data collection tools for longitudinal research must therefore be selected or developed with this demand in mind. Some data collection tools are designed to measure stable characteristics of individuals ("trait" versus "state" anxiety, for example) and thus would not be expected to show much variation even if readministered over long intervals. If the goal of the longitudinal research is to describe and study variation over time, instruments designed to measure stable characteristics would be a poor choice. Conversely, especially when administered at short intervals, measures can show changes based on their previous administration (a "retesting" effect) rather than on changes in the characteristic being assessed. Finally, over time, interviewers or other aspects of data collection may change, which might also affect results.

Close attention to the time frame cues given to respondents in the wording of questions is especially important in longitudinal research. A question that asks "Have you ever . . ." as opposed to one that asks "In the last 30 days have you experienced . . ." may give a different result and will look different when analyzed for changes over time. In the second instance, answers may vary each time the question is asked; in the first instance, one could go from a "no" to a "yes" answer over time, but it would be theoretically impossible to go from a "yes" to a "no" one.

Measures suitable for longitudinal research, then, should be designed to measure traits or behaviors that could reasonably be expected to vary over the time frame of the study, be sensitive to such changes when they occur, and be relatively impervious to the effects of repeated administration. Technical descriptions of available standardized instruments may often indicate whether or not the tools are suitable for use as repeated measures; longitudinal research should employ data collection tools that are.

Naturally, it is also important to use the same data collection personnel over time whenever possible. Certainly, standardized procedures should be developed and training in them undertaken when personnel must change. Even when the people collecting the data remain the same, however, without continued monitoring of the data collection process, considerable "drift" in method can occur when a study is ongoing over a long period of time. If changes in personnel or adjustments in procedure need to be made, these should be acknowledged and their effects assessed quantitatively when possible as part of the data analysis.

Despite what has been said about trying to find measures in longitudinal research that are not too prone to testing effects, the fact is that particpation in data collection is an event in people's lives. Like any event, it may have its own effect on responses in ways that may influence findings. The continuted attention from program personnel in follow-up research done for purposes of program evaluation, for example, may feel to clients like a continuation to some extent of the caring they experienced when active program participants. By contrast, the repeated contact might be experienced as an intrusion and cause the assessment of the program to become less positive. There often is no way to assess or control for these influences completely, but the various possibilities must be borne in mind when findings of the research are interpreted.

Repeat contacts for study should also offer some benefits to clients. One obvious strategy is to pay a cash stipend or to offer some other tangible reward for participation in follow-up data collection, especially if this data collection may be intrusive or time-consuming. There is some controversy about the payment of stipends in that offering large payments may be seen as coercive, especially to very impoverished respondents. Even when payments are kept relatively modest, however, response rates in follow-up research have been improved, and the payment can be seen as making some kind of statement about the fact that the data the respondents can provide has a real value to the research and to the researchers. In-kind rewards, such as a party or reunion for former group members or program participants or gifts of developmentally appropriate toys or books for children being assessed, can also be offered in lieu of cash.

Contacts with researchers should also be opportunities to asses the well-being of clients with some regularity. While the main purpose of the contact must remain data collection, when a sample member or family is found to be in acute distress or need at the time of a research contact, provision should be made to at least discuss with the respondent the possibility of referral for additional assessment or assistance. All of the legal and ethical obligations and constraints on professionals are operating whether the initial professional contact is for research or for other purposes. If the research staff members having contact with sample members are not themselves professionals, the parameters of these obligations and the options available must be explained to them so they can handle matters appropriately with sample members, and supervisory backup must be provided for them as well. Any feedback that can be provided to clients on their own health or well-being or on that of their children based on the data gathering will often be perceived by them as a real service and can provide a powerful positive incentive for continued participation in the research.

Analytic methods. Longitudinal research requires special methods for data analysis. While a thorough review of advanced statistics related to repeated measures, causal modeling, and time series analysis is beyond the scope of this book, it is important to note that even the simplest of procedures in inferential statistics must be undertaken differently when longitudinal data are employed. Even when data are restricted to a before-and-after assessment of the same group of clients on the same measure, the problem of statistical independence on which the assessment of probabilities and differences between groups rests must be understood differently. Statistical procedures of this kind dealing with group differences over time (repeated measures) are called correlated group techniques. Versions of them exist for both the two-group and multigroup situation. When dealing with correlational designs, the same problem is labelled intercorrelation, and techniques exist for assessing and dealing with this situation as well. Log-linear techniques can also be applied successfully to longitudinal data that are expressed in nominal form. The point here is simply to note that powerful techniques exist for the analysis of longitudinal data but that they may differ somewhat from those used when analyzing data that are only cross-sectional in nature.

Summary

Relational, including longitudinal, research designs are powerful tools for examining all kinds of research questions about patterns of covariation among phenomena, even when the phenomena cannot ethically or practically be manipulated. Social scientists and human service professionals commonly think in relational terms. Relational studies can be of two broad types: correlational studies, which proceed by examining how two (or more) variables covary in a single sample, or group comparison studies, in which members of sample subgroups are compared on the same variables. Relational designs are deductive in their logic and fixed in their methods and thus share some features with descriptive research, on the one hand, and with experiments on the other. Despite the widespread use of relational studies and their great utility for the field, caution must be used in interpreting results so that the language of correlation and causation are not confused. Longitudinal research, which is a special form of relational research, employs a variety of special techniques to deal with sample attrition, repeated measurement, and data analysis when the same sample members and variables are assessed repeatedly over time.

By defining relational research as a distinct type of design, it has been possible to discuss the unique contributions these designs can make to the building and testing of theories explaining stable relationships observed among phenomena and their features. When the goal of research is to find out not just whether variables vary together but rather how to create change or what the effects of changing one variable are on another, however, experimental designs are needed, which are discussed in the next chapter.

BICULTURALISM AND SUBJECTIVE MENTAL HEALTH AMONG CUBAN AMERICANS

MANUEL R. GOMEZ
Florida International University

This study seeks to determine if adopting a bicultural perspective affects an ethnic individual's subjective mental bealth. The ethnic group studied was the Cuban-American community of West New York, New Jersey. A sample of 151 healthy Cuban Americans was interviewed. Multivariate multiple regression analysis indicated that biculturalism predicted a significant amount of the variability in the indicators of subjective mental bealth even after variability due to background factors was partialed out.

In clinical social work it is now assumed that to be well adjusted, members of an ethnic group living within a dominant culture must not only assimilate the larger culture but simultaneously maintain their own roots.[1] This duality is commonly referred to as biculturalism. However, this axiom has been accepted only ideologically and has limited empirical validation. Although this twofold burden is increasingly implied in the literature, it is seldom recognized formally.

José Szapocznick and William Kurtines have challenged the traditional view that, for ethnic individuals such as Cuban Americans who live in bicultural communities, acculturation is a linear and unidimensional process. According to the traditional view, an ethnic individual's identification with his or her original culture slowly fades as he or she gradually becomes assimilated into the host culture. These authors suggest that, among Cuban Americans, acculturation should be studied as an accommodation that takes place along two independent dimensions. One dimension involves the acquisition of the host culture, the second dimension involves the retention of the original culture.[2]

Yoel Camayd-Freixas and Hortensia Amaro view biculturalism as a balance in this accommodation.[3] In this study, it was assumed that monoculturalism is represented by either

of the two extremes of a continuum of acculturation. At one end of this continuum, monocultural ethnocentrism implies a rejection of the host culture in favor of a total or almost total identification with the ethnic culture. At the other end of the continuum stands monocultural assimilation, which implies a rejection of the original culture in favor of a total or almost total identification with the host culture. Biculturalism is found at the middle ranges of the continuum.

Most empirical studies that explore the relationship between psychological adjustment and acculturation follow the traditional view of acculturation. An awareness of the personal effect of cultural transition on members of an ethnic group has led these investigators to predict that the better people are able to assimilate, the fewer psychological and interpersonal problems they will experience in their adjustment. The results of these studies have invariably contradicted their expectations; level of acculturation has not been found to be related significantly to psychological adjustment.[4] These contradictions lead to the hypothesis that biculturalism rather than assimilation is positively related to subjective mental health. The term "subjective mental health" is used here to refer to subjects' own evaluations of their experiences in different, but specific, aspects of their lives.[5]

In two studies by John Lang, Ricardo Munoz, Guillermo Bernal, and James Sorensen, and by Szapocznick and Kurtines, it was concluded that biculturalism, not higher

Social Service Review (September 1990). © 1990 by The University of Chicago. All rights reserved.
0037–7961/90/6403–0006S 01.00

levels of acculturation, is significantly related to psychological adjustment.[6] The Lang et al. study was flawed by the failure to screen out subjects with histories of mental health problems, and the Szapocznick and Kurtines study was based on a clinical population. Subjects known to suffer from mental health problems might score at the extremes of acculturation scales because of their mental health, not their acculturation problems. Thus, neither study addressed the overall relationship between acculturation and mental health. The present study was designed to clarify the relationship between biculturalism and subjective mental health within a healthy population.

Among the research questions that have not been asked are, Is the subjective mental health of a healthy ethnic group member related to the degree of identification he or she maintains with his or her own ethnic group? If such a relationship exists, which individuals report better adjustment—those who identify most with their ethnic culture or those who identify most with the dominant culture? Or, as some evidence suggests, is optimal adjustment associated with a dual identification with both cultures? This study was designed to answer these questions.

The study's general hypothesis was that, after controlling for variability due to sex, age, marital status, socioeconomic class, and length of stay in the United States, there would be a positive linear relationship between subjective mental health and one's level of biculturalism. This general hypothesis generated a specific hypothesis for each of the four variables used to measure subjective mental health: psychological well-being, self-esteem, marital adjustment, and job satisfaction. Each of the variables used in this study has been shown to be related significantly to mental health in the past.

These variables were explored using a sample of Cuban Americans who have no history of psychiatric problems, drug abuse, or psychotropic medication use. The Cuban-American community is the third largest Hispanic group in the United States. Cubans were chosen because a body of data exists from other studies that investigated the relationship

between level of acculturation and psychological adjustment.[7] These data allow the comparison of results of this study with other studies of the same population that have employed different measures in different locations.

VARIABLES

Overall psychological well-being.—Norman Bradburn has defined overall psychological well-being as the relative combination of positive and negative affect in the same individual. He has shown that a person's psychological well-being is related significantly to an excess of positive affect in an individual's life.[8]

Corrective feedback from members of the dominant culture is essential to becoming bicultural. Diane de Anda has noted that negative feedback generates negative affect, which interferes with the discriminative learning of complex behaviors and concepts. An excess of negative feedback may drive the individual to withdraw from the socialization process and reject the dominant culture. An excess of negative feedback may also lead the individual to reject his or her ethnic background to avoid the punishment experienced for being different from others. Retaining the original ethnic culture while simultaneously acquiring the dominant culture is a difficult and complex task that can be accomplished only when the individual experiences positive affect in the socialization experience.[9] This is why we expect bicultural individuals to report experiencing more positive than negative feelings.

Self-esteem.—Self-esteem is defined as the expression of the ability to perceive oneself and to evaluate these self-perceptions according to a variety of standards.[10] A negative perception of self has been seen traditionally as a sign of emotional problems, as well as a symptom of mental illness. A positive perception of self has been linked to happiness[11] and subjective mental health.[12] The individual acquires from within the context of his or her family the basic criteria from which to evaluate him- or herself. However, the larger social environment in which the family lives also influences the individual. It can complement or contrast with the family's values, supporting or challenging them.

Individuals who have acquired a positive sense of self from within their family context begin to feel strange and devalued when the larger social environment does not support the family's criteria for self-evaluation. Morris Rosenberg's work with individuals raised in Catholic, Jewish, or Protestant homes but who live in communities that do not share their religious values has shown that those individuals have lower self-esteem than those who live in communities in which the majority share their religious views.[13] Harriet McAdoo's work with blacks supports these findings.[14] The implications of these studies suggest that a sense of continuity and belongingness bolsters self-esteem. Support from the family and larger society appear to be necessary sources of self-worth.

Ethnic individuals who live in a society that does not understand their language and often does not support the ethnic values learned at home can be expected to experience feelings of low self-worth. The degree of acculturation they acquire is likely to be related to their level of self-esteem.

Monocultural individuals who reject their original culture acquire a sense of belonging to the host culture, but at the expense of having to devalue the ethnic values learned from their families. These individuals lose a primary source of self-esteem when they break their ties with the culture that originally provided value and worth. Monocultural individuals who reject the influence of the host culture retain a sense of continuity with their original values, but at the expense of never feeling that they belong to the society in which they live and work. These individuals are missing the necessary support from their social environment to retain their self-worth. Bicultural individuals accept the presence and influence of the host culture without devaluing their original ties to the ethnic family. They recognize the differences between the two cultures, but they learn to accept the host culture in spite of the differences. Learning the language, attitudes, and beliefs of the host culture and accepting its values improve their chances of

being accepted since they no longer appear so different. They gain a feeling of belonging without ever losing continuity with their ethnic origins. Both sources of self-esteem are maintained, mitigating the negative impact of environmental dissonance on their self-esteem. It is for these reasons that we expect bicultural individuals to have higher self-esteem than monocultural individuals.

Marital adjustment.—Graham Spanier and Charles Cole define marital adjustment as the outcome of several factors, including marital satisfaction, dyadic cohesion, and dyadic consensus.[15] They found these variables to be interrelated dimensions of marital adjustment. Ed Diener notes that marital satisfaction has been found to be the strongest predictor of subjective well-being.[16] The ability for consensus and cohesion are the hallmarks of intimacy and mutuality in a relationship that is possible only between mature and healthy individuals.[17]

Culturally determined gender roles are part of the repertoire of attitudes and behavior that ethnic group members bring with them when they enter the host culture. The literature on Cubans describes the aggressive, dominant, and provider role of the Cuban man and the passive, submissive, and dependent role of the Cuban woman.[18] An ethnic couple could avoid conflict between the traditional gender roles and the more egalitarian values of the U.S. culture by isolating the traditional relationship from the new influence. However, financial need often makes this isolation impossible. The woman is forced to assume the role of coprovider and to be less financially dependent on the man. The inevitable conflict created by this violation of the traditional gender role has led Bernal to predict emotional difficulties and marital disharmony among Cubans.[19] Yet for some the conflict may not be as severe as originally expected. There is evidence that many Cuban women who work have not given up their belief in emotional dependence and male dominance.[20] The violation of gender roles has more severe consequences for the men in social condemnation and psychosocial stress.[21] However, these negative consequences are likely to be minimized under conditions that improve the financial situation of the family while allowing the man to still feel needed by his wife. He could then be expected to be less rigid in his adherence to the traditional gender role, resulting in a reduction of marital conflict and disharmony. Bicultural individuals are more likely to achieve this type of accommodation in their marriages since it involves both the acquisition of behaviors sanctioned and approved by the dominant culture and the retention of the ethnic philosophy that governs relationships between men and women. It is for these reasons that bicultural individuals were expected to be more satisfied with and better adjusted to their marriages.

Job satisfaction.—The meaning of job satisfaction varies according to what each individual values in his or her work. Psychological satisfaction in the job is often defined in terms of the sense of accomplishment the individual derives from his or her labor and the extent to which the job matches the worker's interests and abilities.[22] Job satisfaction is known to be related to overall happiness,[23] and Diener notes that it is a predictor of subjective well-being as well.[24]

Ethnic individuals tend to participate in the economic institutions of a society to the extent that their work ethic is similar to that of the majority group. The discrepancy between the work ethic of the ethnic individual and that of the majority group must not be too big. If it is, then the ethnic individual must be willing to accept the dominant work ethic in order to find and maintain a rewarding job.[25] In the case of Cubans in the United States, this means accepting the North American emphasis on work as an end by itself instead of the Cuban view of work as a necessity.[26]

There are three options for ethnic individuals facing these value conflicts: economic separatism, assimilation, and biculturalism.[27] Monocultural separatism is not a solution for Cubans. They lack the numbers and the resources at a national level to create their own economy. Like others who reject the work ethic of the dominant culture. Cubans are likely to experience cultural dislocation, social alienation, and low job satisfaction.[28] Assimilation is also a poor alternative. Cultural

assimilation has not been found to be a predictor of job satisfaction among Cubans.[29] It is for these reasons that bicultural Cubans were expected to report greater job satisfaction.

METHOD

Sample

The sample used in this study consisted of 151 Cuban-American citizens 18 years or older from West New York, New Jersey. The participants had no history of psychiatric treatment or drug abuse and had never used prescribed psychotropic medication. The sample was drawn using a combination of random and accidental sampling procedures based on census tract mappings.

West New York is divided into nine census tracts of different sizes. Three square blocks were selected at random from each tract. Thus, regardless of size, each tract contributed the same number of square blocks (three) to the final selection of the sample. All homes or apartments in each block were visited to determine how many of them were occupied by Cuban Americans. Each tract contributed a different percentage of subjects to the sample. This percentage was the same as the percentage of the population residing in the tract.

Once all subjects were identified, an interviewer went to each address selected and requested an interview of the first person 18 years or older who met the research criteria. If the subject refused the interview, changed her or his mind, or knew the interviewer, the next person available at home was approached. In cases in which no one in the home agreed to be interviewed, no one met the criteria, a member of the family knew the interviewer, or no one was at home, the closest Cuban-American home in that square block was approached. On many occasions the interviewer had to schedule an appointment with a subject to interview her or him at a more convenient time.

In the 207 homes visited, 12 refusals were encountered. In addition, nine people could not be interviewed because they knew the interviewer. While 45 potential subjects did not meet the research criteria, in only 10 of the cases was another person from the same household used. For the other 35 cases, the interviewer proceeded to the next closest home. The total number of interviews completed was 151.

The obtained sample was heterogeneous. The age range was from 18 to 72 years, with a mean age of 41 years. All subjects were employed. Although 17 were officially retired, they continued to work *por la izquierda* (under the table). The sample contained 25 subjects (16.6%) who were single, 109 (72.2%) who were married, and 17 (11.2%) who were separated, divorced, or widowed. There were 86 male (57%) and 65 female (43%) subjects in the sample. Subjects' educational and occupational levels were diverse, with every Hollingshead category from highest to lowest represented. The periods of residence in the United States ranged from 5 to 40 years. The largest percentage of respondents (54%) reported from 20 to 24 years of residence in the United States, representing the first wave of migration from Cuba following the revolution. The second largest (17.2%) reported from 5 to 9 years of residence in the United States, representing the last wave of migration during the Mariel boat lift.

Measurements

Psychological well-being.—The Affective Balance Scale (ABS) developed by Bradburn and David Caplovitz has 10 items, five that measure positive affect and five that measure negative affect.[30] The difference between scores on positive and negative affect has been found to be the best predictor of overall well-being.[31] Bradburn has reported a 3-day test-retest reliability coefficient of .90 for the ABS. Validity estimates for the ABS include gamma coefficients between .45 and .51 when the ABS scores are correlated with selected indicators of happiness and life satisfaction.[32]

Self-esteem.—A modified version of the Rosenberg Self-Esteem Scale was used in this study.[33] Rosenberg's original scale included items designed for use with adolescents. The items in the modified version can be used with any population. Rosenberg reports a Guttman-

scale reproducibility coefficient of .92. Earle Silbert and Jean Tippett reported a 2-week test-retest reliability coefficient of .90.[34]

Marital adjustment.—A modified version of a measure of marital adjustment developed by Spanier is used in this study.[35] The Dyadic Adjustment Scale (DAS) was designed to measure marital adjustment, but it is also applicable to unmarried couples living together. The modified DAS is composed of three subscales and a total of 27 Likert-type items. The subscales are Dyadic Consensus, Dyadic Cohesion, and Dyadic Satisfaction. An alpha coefficient of .96 was reported for the DAS. Alpha coefficients reported for the subscales were Dyadic Consensus, .90; Dyadic Cohesion, .86; and Dyadic Satisfaction, .94. The scale discriminates between married and divorced couples.

Job satisfaction.—The "Job Satisfaction Blank Number Five" scale (JSB) developed by Robert Hoppoch was used in this study.[36] The JSB is an overall measure of job satisfaction, applicable to any occupation. The instrument is composed of four items, with seven response options for each item. When the scale is adapted to an interview, respondents are asked to say which of the seven possibilities for each item applies to them. Each of the possibilities represents different degrees of satisfaction with the current job. The scale is scored by adding the scale values of respondents' choices. Hoppoch reported a split-half reliability coefficient of .93 for a sample of over 300.

Biculturalism.—Biculturalism was measured by using an adaptation of the biculturalism scale of the Latino Bicultural Assessment Questionnaire (LABIA) developed by Camayd-Freixas and Amaro and designed to be used with any Latino population.[37] The scale used in the present study is a 45-item questionnaire using a five-point Likert-scales format. It measures three factors selected from a review of previous studies on acculturation on the basis of their repeated presence in many of those studies. These factors are language use and preference, ethnic identity and cultural contact, and ethnic social interaction.

The scale produces an overall measure of biculturalism in which extreme scores represent monoculturalism (either Latin or North

American) and middle scores represent bicul-turalism. The scoring procedure for the scale is modified for the purpose of the present study. In order to obtain a single interval scale in which higher scale values represent greater biculturalism and lower scale values represent greater monoculturalism, the extreme scores are combined for each item. For example, in items designed to identify language prefer-ence, respondents answer by choosing one of the following values: (1) always or almost always Spanish; (2) more Spanish than English; (3) both Spanish and English approx-imately equally; (4) more English than Span-ish; (5) always or almost always English. The two scores 1 and 5 are combined into the sin-gle score, 1. The two scores 2 and 4 are com-bined into the single score, 2. This yields a scale that goes from 1, representing the great-est degree of monoculturalism, to 3, represent-ing the greatest degree of biculturalism. The averaged sum of all item responses provides an overall measure of biculturalism.

Standardized alpha coefficients were cal-culated for the three factors, based on the study data. These coefficients were .94 for lan-guage use and preference, .92 for ethnic iden-tity and cultural contact, and .80 for ethnic social interaction and contact. The validity of the instrument was determined by comparing the scores of a group of self-identified Latinos, a group of North American bilinguals, and a monolingual group. Significant differences were found between the groups on the overall measure of biculturalism.

The control variables used in this study have been identified in the literature as possi-bly related to the dependent variables alone (i.e., marital status) or both the dependent and independent variables (i.e., age, sex, socioeco-nomic status, and length of residence in the United States).

Diener has identified marriage as one of the strongest predictors of subjective well-being.[38] In terms of age, younger persons have been found to be happier[39] and to experience higher levels of joy than older persons.[40] Diener notes little difference between the sexes on measures of subjective well-being, but he reports an interaction of sex with age. Younger women appear happier than younger men, and older women appear less happy than older men.[41] There is evidence to show that socioeconomic status[42] and length of residence in the United States have an indirect effect on subjective well-being.[43]

Szapocznick, Mercedes Scopetta, and Kurtines report that the longer a person lives in the United States, the more acculturated that person becomes. Younger individuals accultur-ate faster than older ones, and females accul-turate slower than males.[44] Eleanor Rogg and Rosemary Cooney have found that the higher the education and the occupational status, the higher the score of respondents in some mea-sures of assimilation.[45]

RESULTS

Table 1 shows the mean, standard deviation, and the matrix of bivariate correlations among the five independent and dependent variables. The table shows that the four dependent vari-ables were substantially intercorrelated. The

Table 1. Means, Standard Deviations, and Intercorrelations of Independent and Dependent Variables (N = 151)

Variables	Mean	SD	(1)	(2)	(3)	(4)	(5)
1. Biculturalism	5.87	1.46					
2. Psychological well-being	5.73	2.38	.86***				
3. Self-esteem	8.88	2.90	.87***	.86***			
4. Marital adjustment	77.74	32.53	.89***	.87***	.87***		
5. Job satisfaction	20.34	5.88	.38***	.35***	.38***	.27***	

Note.—Column numbers correspond to the numbered variables.
*** $p < .001$.

range of correlations between these four indices of subjective mental health indicate that subjective mental health may in fact be a unitary concept, tapped by affective balance, self-esteem, and marital adjustment. Job satisfaction would appear to be a related, but distinct, dimension. A principal components analysis showed that one factor accounted for 70 percent of the variability of scores in the four variables. The factor loading for psychological well-being was .93; for self-esteem, .94; for marital adjustment, .84; and for job satisfaction, .46.

To determine whether any of the demographic characteristics measured in the study were related significantly to the dependent measures of subjective mental health, t-tests were performed for the two dichotomous variables, sex and marital status (categorized as married vs. not married).

Pearson product-moment correlations were calculated between the dependent measures and the interval-scale control variables (age, years of residence in the United States, and socioeconomic status). The results of the first set of tests showed no significant differences between men and women on any of the four indices of subjective mental health. Married respondents expressed greater job satisfaction than unmarried respondents ($t = 3.60$,

$p < .001$, df = 134). Table 2 shows the correlations between the dependent measures and the continuous demographic variables. Weak but significant negative relationships were obtained between age and self-esteem and between age and psychological well-being. This indicates that there was a tendency for older people to experience less positive affect and less self-esteem. Also, a weak but significant positive relationship was found between age and job satisfaction. This suggests a tendency for older subjects to be more satisfied with their work than younger subjects. Weak but significant relationships were also obtained between socioeconomic status and the four indices of subjective mental health. Since lower numerical scores on the Hollingshead Two-Factor Index signify higher socioeconomic status, the negative signs on these correlation coefficients show a tendency for higher socioeconomic status subjects to have greater job satisfaction, greater psychological well-being, higher self-esteem, and better marital adjustment. Period of residence in the United States was related significantly to only one measure, job satisfaction.

Thus, all of the relationships between indices of subjective mental health and subject's background variables were found to be weak.

Table 2. Intercorrelations Between Dependent Measures and Continuous Demographic Variables

Variables	Age	SES	Years in the United States
Psychological well-being:			
r	−.14	−.26***	.05
p	.040	.001	.258
Self-esteem:			
r	−.15*	−.26***	.09
p	.025	.001	.128
Marital adjustment:			
r	−.01	−.19*	.07
p	.460	.025	.232
Job satisfaction:			
r	.19*	−.28***	.19*
p	.016	.001	.013

Note.—In the Hollinghead system, lower numerical scores indicate higher socioeconomic status (SES).
* $p < 0.5$.
*** $p < .001$.

Because several of the relationships were significant, a multivariate multiple regression analysis (MANOVA) was employed to control for variability attributable to these factors while the effects of biculturality were tested. However, the Statistical Package for the Social Sciences (SPSS-X) MANOVA program used for this analysis excludes all individuals with missing data on any variable. In this study, those respondents who were not living in an intimate relationship or who were unmarried did not have scores on the marital adjustment measure and therefore would have been excluded by the SPSS-X MANOVA program. To avoid this undesirable consequence, marital adjustment was excluded from the analysis so that all subjects could be used; losing 42 unmarried subjects not only would have reduced the sample size considerably but also would have restricted the sample to married individuals.

The results of the multivariate multiple regression analysis are presented in Table 3. The multivariate Pillais test indicated a highly significant relationship between the predictors and the dependent variables of subjective mental health (F (approx. 28,488) = 6.34, $p < .001$). The univariate tests for the significance of each dependent variable on the predictors were all highly significant ($p < .001$). This indicates that the predictor variables explained a significant amount of the variability in each of the three indices of subjective mental health.

The data in table 3 indicate that biculturalism explained a highly significant ($p < .001$) portion of the variability of each index of subjec-

tive mental health, even after variability due to the other predictors was partialed out. Another finding indicated in table 3 is the significant ($p < .01$) relationship between socioeconomic status and job satisfaction. When all other predictors were controlled for, there was a tendency for respondents with higher socioeconomic status to report greater job satisfaction. Age was also related significantly ($p < .05$) to job satisfaction. There was a slight tendency for older respondents to report greater job satisfaction. Finally, marital status was found to be related significantly ($p < .05$) to psychological well-being. There was a slight tendency for married respondents to report greater psychological well-being.

DISCUSSION

This study sought to determine whether subjective mental health is related to an ethnic group member's degree of biculturalism. It was expected that biculturalism would be related to overall psychological well-being. The results support this hypothesis. The more bicultural the Cuban-American subjects were, the higher their psychological well-being. These results support those of Lang et al., who found that bicultural Latinos reported greater psychological adjustment when the ABS was used to measure the affective component of their life experience.[46]

A positive relationship was anticipated between biculturalism and level of self-esteem. The results obtained support this hypothesis. The more bicultural the Cuban-American subjects, the higher their self-

Table 3. Multiple Regression of Subjective Mental Health Indicators on Biculturalism and Background Variables: Test for Individual Dependent Variables

| Variables | R^2 | Standardized Regression Coefficients | | | | | |
		Biculturalism	Age	Sex	Marital Status	SES	Years in the United States
Psychological well-being	72***	.73***	.14	.11	.36*	−.13	.03
Self-esteem	75***	.74***	.06	−.16	.14	−.24	.31
Job satisfaction	26***	.51***	.31*	.01	−.12	−.46**	.22

Note—SES = socioeconomic status.
* $p < .05$.
** $p < .01$.
*** $p < .001$.

esteem. These results support those of Judith Klein, who found self-esteem improved in young affiliated Jewish individuals as they integrated their Americanism with their Jewishness, about which they had previously experienced many negative feelings.[47]

A positive relationship was expected between biculturalism and degree of job satisfaction. The results support this hypothesis. The percentage of variability in job satisfaction explained by biculturalism, however, was relatively small (9%) when compared to psychological well-being (54%) and self-esteem (61%).

The discrepancy between the findings on job satisfaction and those obtained with respect to psychological well-being and self-esteem may be explained by a higher degree of job specialization. It seems quite possible that a craftsman or skilled worker could transfer his or her work from one culture to another and continue to derive satisfaction from this activity, whether or not that worker adopted a substantial portion of the new culture. In contrast, psychological well-being and self-esteem appear to be factors that are tied to a broad range of interactions the individual may have with his or her environment. As such, it is difficult to imagine that these factors could be determined without reference to the influence of the dominant culture.

A positive relationship was expected between biculturalism and level of marital adjustment. Since 42 subjects did not respond to the question on marital adjustment because they were not married or living in an intimate relationship, the marital adjustment measure was excluded from the multivariate analysis. However, the bivariate correlation between biculturalism and marital adjustment presented in table 1 indicates that, among married individuals, marital adjustment was related significantly ($p < .001$) to biculturalism.

The results of this study support the work of Szapocznick and Kurtines with Cubans in Florida and the work of Lang et al. with Latinos in California.[48] Both of these studies suggest that effective acculturation and psychological adjustment entail adaptation to the majority culture and retention of the ethnic culture. Further research is needed, however, to apply this conclusion generally to all Cuban Americans and other culturally similar and dissimilar groups regardless of geographical location and clinical status.

The results of this study can be used to empower the Cuban-American community with the knowledge that a culturally sensitive mental health service that supports the establishment and development of biculturalism is better equipped to help those with mental problems than a service that neglects the bicultural dimension. Mental health planners and administrators need to be aware not only of the differences among the ethnic composition of the community that a program is intended to serve but also of the style of cultural adaptation that the community has chosen.

These results are also particularly relevant for the mental health assessment and treatment components of social work practice. My findings suggest that an assessment of an ethnic group member is not complete without an evaluation of the client's level of biculturalism.

NOTES

[1] Monica McGoldrick, John K. Pearce, and Joseph Giordano, eds., *Ethnicity and Family Therapy* (New York: Guilford, 1982), p. 43.

[2] José Szapocznick and William Kurtines, "Acculturation, Biculturalism and Adjustment among Cuban Americans," in *Acculturation: Theory, Models and Some New Findings,* ed. Amado Padilla (Boulder, Colo.: Westview, 1980), pp. 139–59.

[3] Yoel Camayd-Freixas and Hortensia Amaro, *The Measurement of Hispanic Bilingualism and Biculturality in the Workplace* (Boston: Massachusetts Department of Social Services, Office of Human Resources, 1984).

[4] Fernando Ruiz, "Effects of the Interpretation of Acculturation and Generational Membership on the Mental Health of Hispanics" (doctoral diss., California School of Professional Psychology, 1981); John G. Lang, Ricardo F. Munoz, Guillermo Bernal, and James L. Sorensen, "Quality of Life and Psychological Well-Being in a Bicultural Latino Community," *Hispanic Journal of Behavioral Sciences* 4 (1982): 433–50; Eleanor M. Rogg and Rosemary S. Cooney, *Adaptation and Adjustment of Cubans: West New York, New Jersey* (New York: Hunter University, Hispanic Research Center, 1980), p. 59.

[5]Joseph Veroff, Richard A. Kulka, and Elizabeth Douvan, *Mental Health in America* (New York: Basic, 1981); Joseph Veroff, Elizabeth Douban, and Richard A. Kulka, *The Inner American* (New York: Basic, 1981).

[6]Lang et al. (n. 4 above); Szapocznick and Kurtines (n. 2 above).

[7]Rogg and Cooney (n. 4 above), p. 59; Szapocznick and Kurtines (n. 2 above).

[8]Norman M. Bradburn, *The Structure of Psychological Well-Being* (Chicago: Aldine, 1969).

[9]Diane de Anda, "Bicultural Socialization: Factors Affecting the Minority Experience," *Social Work* 29 (March–April 1984): 101–7.

[10]Charles Zastrow and Karen K. Kirst-Ashman, *Understanding Human Behavior and the Social Environment* (Chicago: Nelson-Hall, 1987), p. 483; Edith Jacobson. The Self and the Object World (New York: International University Press, 1980), p. 72; Eleanor E. Maccoby, *Social Development* (New York: Harcourt Brace Jovanovich, 1980), pp. 270–75.

[11]Warner Wilson, "Correlates of Avowed Happiness," *Psychological Bulletin* 67 (1967): 294–306, esp. 294.

[12]Veroff. Douvan, and Kulka (n. 5 above), pp. 112–14.

[13]Morris Rosenberg, *Conceiving the Self* New York: Basic. 1979). p. 32.

[14]Harriet P. McAdoo. "Racial Attitude and Self-Concept of Young Black Children over Time," in *Black Children: Social Educational and Parental Emironments,* ed. Harriet P. McAdoo and John L. McAdoo Beverly Hills, Calif.: Sage. 1985), pp. 213–42.

[15]Graham B. Spanier and Charles L. Cole, "Toward Clarification and Investigation of Marital Adjustment." *International Journal of Sociology of the Family* 6 (Spring 1976): 121–46.

[16]Ed Diener. "Subjective Well-Being," *Psychological Bulletin* 95 (1984) 542–75, esp. 556.

[17]Jay R. Greenberg and Stephen A. Mitchell, *Object Relations in Psychoanalytic Theory* (Cambridge, Mass.: Harvard University Press, 1983), p. 189.

[18]Magaly Queralt. "Understanding Cuban Immigrants: A Cultural Perspective," *Social Work* 29 (March–April 1984): 115–21, esp. 117; Guillermo Bernal, "Cuban Families," in McGoldrick. Pearce, and Giordano (n. 1 above), 193–95.

[19]Bernal (n. 18 above), p. 194.

[20]Marie L. Richmond. *Immigrant Adaptation and Family Structure among Cubans in Miami, Florida* (New York: Arno, 1980).

[21]Joseph H. Pleck, *The Myth of Masculinity* (Cambridge, Mass.: MIT Press, 1981).

[22]Herbert C. Morton, "A Look at Factors Affecting the Quality of Working Life," *Monthly Labor Review* 2 (October 1977): 64.

[23]Edward Noll, "Adjustment in Major Roles II: Work," in Bradburn (n. 8 above), pp. 202–4.

[24]Diener (n. 16 above), p. 555.

[25]Genevieve De Hoyos, Arturo De Hoyos, and Christian B. Anderson, "Sociocultural Dislocation: Beyond the Dual Perspective," *Social Work* 31 (January–February 1986): 61–67, esp. 63.

[26]Queralt (n. 18 above), p. 118.

[27]De Hoyos, De Hoyos, and Anderson (n. 25 above), p. 65.

[28]Ibid., p. 64.

[29]Rogg and Cooney (n. 4 above), p. 59.

[30]Norman M. Bradburn and David Caplovitz, *Report on Happiness: A Pilot Study of Behavior Related to Mental Health* (Chicago: Aldine, 1965).

[31]Bradburn (n. 8 above), p. 67.

[32]Ibid., p. 69.

[33]Morris Rosenberg, *Society and the Adolescent Self-Image* (Princeton, N.J.: Princeton University Press, 1965).

[34]Earle Silbert and Jean Tippett, "Self-Esteem: Clinical Assessment and Measurement Validation," *Psychological Reports* 16 (1965): 1017–71.

[35]Graham Spanier, "Measuring Dyadic Adjustment: New Scales for Assessing the Quality of Marriage and Similar Dyads." *Journal of Marriage and the Family* 38 (1976): 15–28.

[36]Robert Hoppoch. *Job Satisfaction* (New York: Harper, 1935).

[37]Camayd-Freixas and Amaro (n. 3 above).

[38]Diener (n. 16 above), p. 556.

[39]Wilson (n. 11 above).

[40]Diener (n. 16 above), p. 554.

[41]Ibid., p. 555.

[42]Ibid.

[43]Thanh Van Tran and Roosevelt Wright, Jr., "Social Support and Subjective Well-Being among Vietnamese Refugees," *Social Service Review* 60 (September 1986): 449–59.

[44]José Szapocznick, Mercedes A. Scopetta, and William Kurtines, "Theory and Measurement of Acculturation," *Interamerican Journal of Psychology* 12 (1978): 113–30.

[45]Rogg and Cooney (n. 4 above), p. 54.

[46]Lang et al. (n. 4 above).

[47]Judith Klein, *Jewish Identity and Self-Esteem: Healing Wounds through Ethnotherapy* (New York: Institute on Pluralism and Group Identity, 1980).

[48]Szapocznick and Kurtines (n. 2 above); Lang et al. (n. 4 above).

Reprinted with permission from *Social Service Review* 64 (3) (1990):375–389.

7

Fixed Methods: Experimental Research

Experiments are generally regarded as fundamental to the accumulation of new information in science. In fact, the notion of experiments is so central to traditional conceptions of science that to some the terms research and experiment are interchangeable. Some researchers, in fact, including some in the helping professions (see for example Thyer 1993), regard experiments as the most credible means of generating new information for practice. Contemporary thinking, however, regards experiments as the preferred form of generating information only about certain types of questions, namely, questions about whether the introduction of a specific controllable event tends to be followed by the occurrence of one or more other predictable events. Such questions have traditionally been said to ask about causal connections.

A number of important areas of research in social work and the human services have been addressed through group experimental studies. Perhaps of greatest importance to the helping professions have been treatment outcome studies demonstrating that certain interventions can, at least with some types of problems, result in greater improvement than would occur in the absence of help (Gorey 1996; Williams & Ell 1998). This kind of evidence can be very important in convincing cost-conscious organizations that funds expended on social work and other services are not wasted or frivolous.

Results from good experiments are quite persuasive: They offer highly credible answers to questions about "If I do this, what most likely will happen next?" In terms of fallibilistic realism (Manicas & Secord 1983), this question can be restated as "Will manipulating phenomenon A result in the observation of a predicted change in phenomenon B in the context of a closed observational system?" Because fallibilistic realism emphasizes explanation and understanding, experiments are defined as useful for explaining certain kinds of situations, namely situations involving planned changes or manipulations, rather than as essential for making causal arguments, as in the traditional view. In addition, falli-bilistic realism empasizes the importance of having a theory adequate to explain the connection between the manipulation and the change observed.

Experiments rely heavily in their design on deduction. Logic is used both to derive the theoretical questions or hypotheses that guide the research and to derive the method of investigation, the design of the research. Experiments are a form of fixed method research because the method of observation is determined based on this deductive logic before the study itself begins and is implemented as designed. Perhaps nowhere are the rules of how to conduct research more fully articulated and formalized than they are for the design of experimental research.

What is unique to experiments as opposed to other forms of fixed method research is that the investigator enters the observational field by making a planned alteration in a predefined phenomenon of interest, that is, he or she manipulates one or more predefined variables in order to assess what changes, if any, are observed in one or more other predefined variables. Unlike in flexible method research, however, the researcher's interaction with the observational field is intended to be iimited to making the planned manipulation. In all other respects, the observational context is fixed; thus the experiment takes place in a closed observational system.

The Classical View of Experiments

Answers to questions about what will happen next have traditionally been inter-preted as indicating whether one event causes another on the basis of a logic developed by the philosophers David Hume (1748,1988), John Stuart Mill (Nagel 1950), and Karl Popper (1959). Their logic, summarized below, provides the rules for when it is considered scientifically acceptable to conclude that the manipula-tion of variable A "causes" a change in variable B. Because this logic has tradi-tionally been so influential not only in defining experiments but also in defining research itself, it is worth reviewing it in some depth.

The logic of experimental designs is rooted in philosophy, specifically episte-mology. The philosopher Hume, for example, considered the conditions that result in the commonsense belief that one thing causes another and identified three. The first is contiguity between events: Using symbols, if A is presumed to cause B, then it must be true that A and B touch one another in time. Hume's first condition clarifies an important distinction between science and philosophy: Science is concerned only with the immediate, not ultimate, causes of things.

Hume's second condition also concerns the temporal relationship between presumed causes and effects, and has to do with order in time: If A is presumed to cause B, then A must precede B in time. This second condition at first seems intu-itively obvious: Of course event B cannot be caused by event A if event A occurs after it, since that would mean B was caused by something that did not yet exist when A occurred.

Hume's third condition is the most demanding, and the most important: "constant conjunction." Constant conjunction between a presumed cause and a presumed effect means that the presumed cause must be present whenever the presumed effect occurs. By this third condition, if one is to be able to argue that A causes B, then every time B occurs, A must be observed to immediately precede it. Hume's condition of constant conjunction, while pointing the way toward some important logical considerations, was somewhat problematic. Among other difficulties, it was unable to handle events that were multiply caused, such as sneezes, for example, which can be preceded either by inhaling pepper, exposure to pollen (for an allergy sufferer), or incubation of a cold virus.

It remained for the philosopher John Stuart Mill to elaborate Hume's logic. Like Hume, Mill argued that three conditions must be met in order to justify concluding that one event caused another. Mill's first condition was identical to one of Hume's: The presumed cause must precede the presumed effect in time. Mill's second condition was an expansion of Hume's principle of immediate contiguity. While Hume had argued that a cause and effect must touch each other in time, Mill's second condition was less restrictive: Mill argued that there must be a demonstrably regular temporal relationship including, but not limited to, immediate temporal contiguity between a presumed cause and a presumed effect.

Mill's third condition was the most complex and the most important. It can be stated simply: arguing that A caused B requires ruling out other potential explanations for why B occurred. Mill's third condition, while simple to state, is hard to fulfill: In practice it is generally very difficult to arrange observational conditions that rule out other reasons for an observed change. In addition, in the end an argument that is causal depends on theoretical explanation for what has been observed.

Mill articulated three methods for fulfilling this third condition. The first, called the Method of Agreement, requires that the presumed effect be observed to be present whenever the presumed cause is made to occur. Returning to symbols, if A is the presumed cause and B the presumed effect, the Method of Agreement requires that the presumed effect be observed to be present every time the presumed cause is made to occur. Returning to symbols, if A is the presumed cause and B the presumed effect, the Method of Agreement requires that "whenever A, then B" must be observed.

The second method is called the Method of Difference. This method requires that whenever the presumed cause does not occur, the presumed effect will be observed to not happen. Using symbols, if A is again the presumed cause and B the presumed effect, the Method of Difference requires that "whenever not A, then not B" must be observed.

Mill's third method, the Method of Concomitant Variation, ties the first two methods together. According to the Method of Concomitant Variation, when the first and second methods are observed simultaneously, and under otherwise equivalent conditions, potential explanations *other than* the presumed cause for why the presumed effect occurred can be ruled out. Again using symbols, where A is the presumed cause and B the presumed effect, Mill's argument implies that observing "when A, then B" and "when not A, then not B" simultaneously, under otherwise identical conditions, offers strong evidence that A was the cause of B.

Hume also argued strongly that a logical case for a cause and effect relationship can only be made for events in the past. Even when a strong argument can be made that an event caused another event in the past, there is no empirical reason to argue that the same causal connection will hold in the future. While it is common practice to believe that causal connections regularly observed in the past will continue to hold true in the future, there is no logical reason for doing so, and Hume and Mill were careful to make this point clear.

This logical qualification had profound implications for the development of a science for the helping professions. Presumably, the primary aim of a science of the helping professions is to identify causal connections that will enable helpers to produce change. But change must take place in the future; if identified causal connections are logically relevant only to the past, they are of no use to change agents, or practitioners.

Fortunately the philosopher Popper contributed thinking that permits the development of a science of helping. Popper conceded that because Hume's position that observed past cause cannot logically be taken as proof of future cause is true, it is not enough to expect science only to accumulate collections of causal observations in the past. Popper argued that science must develop an articulated *theory* that includes certain causal connections reasonably expected to hold true in the future. The role of research, then, is to determine whether specific theoretically derived explanations of causal connections can be observed to be true in reality, that is, empirically. However, it is not the repeated *observation* that the sun "comes up" each morning that gives us confidence that it will "rise" again; it is the explanation for its regular appearance that is convincing.

In Popper's view, theory is given support to the extent that its implied causal connections are observed to hold true, assuming that those same connections are not more simply, or parsimoniously, implied by a different theory. However, the overarching theory cannot be proven, even when its implied causal connections are observed, since those same connections could potentially be understood or explained by a better but as yet unknown theory. Fallibilistic realism (Manicas & Secord 1983) also holds that theory is a critical organizer of understanding and central to the scientific enterprise even though the notion of "proof" or certain (as opposed to approximate or probabilistic) knowledge is rejected.

According to Popper, the role of experimental research, then, is twofold. Its first role is to discredit false theories, which it does when experiments fail to produce results clearly implied by the theory under test. Popper termed this role for experimental research "falsification," and although disconfirming data are not always or unambiguously regarded as falsifying the theory from which they derive, the notion that carefully collected unexpected or anomalous results will call theories into question is generally accepted (Kuhn 1970). The second role of experimental research is to provide support for overarching theories, which it does by implication: If data collected in the context of an experiment do not falsify a theory, by implication they provide support for it.

The logic of experiments, then, following Hume, Mill, and Popper, may be seen in traditional terms as following this course:

1. The researcher begins by stating a theory. From this theory will be deduced one or more specific statements about an implied causal connection between two (or more) phenomena: the hypothesis.

2. The researcher will presume this implied causal connection is true and will arrange conditions to demonstrate this presumption.

3. The demonstration will involve arranging two sets of circumstances identical except for one feature: the presence or absence of the presumed causal phenomenon.

4. After arranging these circumstances, the researcher will observe what happens under them. If the presumed effect occurs when the presumed cause is present *and* the presumed effect does not occur when the presumed cause is not present, the researcher will conclude that the original theoretical statement has received support. If the presumed effect does not occur when the presumed cause is present, or if the presumed effect occurs when the presumed cause is not present, the researcher will conclude that the original theoretical statement may be false.

These four steps form the underlying logic of experimental design and provide the ground rules for distinguishing between credible and flawed experimental studies.

Conducting an experiment, then, involves being able to make two arrangements. First, the experimenter must be able to introduce or withhold (or control the amount of) the causal phenomenon, termed the *independent variable*, at will. Only when this is the case is the independent variable truly free to vary, that is, truly independent, so that its presence or absence, but more importantly what is seen to occur contingent on its presence or absence, cannot be held to depend on or result from anything else, such as another, hidden causal variable. Second, the experimenter must be able to arrange, or gain access to, at least two sets of circumstances that in the ideal case are identical or, more realistically, at least do not differ from one another in any important respect. In this case, what is important is what happens with the phenomenon that is expected to be changed, that is with the *dependent variable*. It turns out that arranging for the absence or presence (or amount) of the independent variable, while not always possible, is the easier of the two to arrange. Creating or gaining access to identical or equivalent sets of circumstances, which is essential for making uncontaminated comparisons between "what happens to the dependant variable when, versus what happens when not?" is often quite difficult.

Early on, it was believed that since the best way to compare identical circumstances would be to compare the same ones, the purest comparisons would involve seeing what happened under a given set of circumstances before versus after the introduction of an independent variable event. As will become clearer in a later section of this chapter, however, it cannot be argued that circumstances before and after the introduction of an independent variable "stay the same" except for the introduction of the independent variable. Just because the experimenter has not done anything else to make them different does not mean that they aren't different. And in fact, circumstances before and after the occurrence of an independent variable will always also be different in at least one respect: the after circumstances will always occur at a later point in time. This time difference turns out not to be unimportant. For this reason, it is considered much better to make comparisons across sets of circumstances occurring at the same point in time.

The research exemplar in this chapter includes just such a comparison. Before examining this illustration, it must be noted again here, as it was in the context of discussing other types of research designs, that there is no such thing as a perfect experiment. All experiments involve making compromises between ideal design principles and actual conditions. No matter: An experiment need not be perfect to be valuable. It needs only to be carefully designed, carefully done, and honestly reported.

An Example of Experimental Research

The El-Bassel et al. (1995) study of an intervention to assist drug-using women in prison reduce their risk of contracting HIV disease illustrates the usefulness of the experimental method. As the HIV epidemic continues in the United States, increasing numbers of women, especially young women, have been diagnosed with AIDS (Center for Disease Control [CDC] 1998), and ways to help slow the spread of HIV disease among women are urgently needed. The study's literature review cites studies showing that women in prison in particular are at high risk of HIV infection. In addition, the literature review is used to show that both interpersonal skills and social support can reduce sexual risk-taking, although there were at that time no studies examining the use of these techniques to help drug-using women in prison. The researchers wanted to know whether or not a program designed to enhance these skills—interpersonal skills and social support—would or would not help these women in reducing their risk-related behavior after release. The idea is that information alone is not enough; people need to know how to put that information effectively to use and to get support for doing so.

The experiment was organized to examine a specific hypothesis: ". . . that women in the [treatment] group would exhibit higher rates of safer sex practices (consistent condom use or abstinence), perceived vulnerability to HIV/AIDS, improvement in coping skills, perceived emotional support, and sexual self-efficacy at follow-up one month after release" (p. 132) than women receiving a more limited intervention. According to the logic of experiments, then, the research design must allow for a comparison of the "outcome" phenomena or dependent variables under two conditions: in this case with a "standard" information-based treatment or with an experimental one that also aimed to enhance interpersonal skills and social support. The nature of the treatment received must be controlled by the researchers, and the way the participants in both groups are observed must be the same or at least equivalent. The outcome of an experiment is a statement about whether or not the hypothesis was supported by the evidence.

The intervention studied, the group designed to reduce high-risk behaviors, was carefully defined. A detailed description of the groups and how they were conducted is included in the study report. The description emphasizes how the groups addressed the enhancement of interpersonal skills and social supports specifically. This relationship of the intervention studied to the concepts selected as important in theory, and to the outcomes assessed is critical to any analytic generalization that can be made from such a study.

The logic of experimental design also requires that the groups being compared be the same to begin with so that any differences observed after treatment can logically be attributed to the intervention received. This requirement is generally addressed by using *random assignment*. Indeed, in the El-Bassel (1995) study all the women in one particular prison who met study criteria and who consented to participate were randomly assigned to the experimental group, which offered 16 skill-building sessions, or a "control" group, a 3-session AIDS information group. In this way, differing motivations to undertake a more or less demanding treatment were ruled out as an explanation for the results.

The sample in the El-Bassel et al. study (1995) was characteristically specialized. First of all, they were women in prison, who certainly are not statistically representative of all women at risk for HIV infection. In addition, only some women in the prison were eligible to participate; they had to be "between 18 and 55 years of age, convicted and serving a sentence between three months and one year, scheduled for release within 10 weeks [to certain parts of New York City], and self-reported drug users . . ." (p. 132). These criteria were designed to involve women in the study who had a history suggesting risk, who could consent to participate in the research for themselves, and who would soon be in a position to deal with high-risk sexual situations in the community. Thus it was a sample in which the phenomena of interest—changes in risk-related behavior—could best be observed.

In the El-Bassel et al. (1995) experiment, several distinct outcomes involving both behavior and attitudes were assessed. In addition, one of the outcome, or dependent, variables, coping skills, was measured in a specific, predefined way using a previously developed instrument, a Coping Skills Questionnaire. The others were based on answers to self-report questions that were quantified in specified ways. Data were collected and analyzed in the same ways in both groups of study participants—those who did and did not get the experimental intervention.

As is common in experiments, multivariate statistical analyses were conducted, in this case logistic regression analysis, a form of multiple regression analysis that allows for independent variables that are categorical, like marital status and treatment received, as well as continuous, like the number of sessions of treatment attended. The authors state that their hypothesis received "some support" (p. 138) because only some of the outcome variables—safer sex behavior, coping skills, and perceived emotional support—were shown to differ according to whether or not the participants had received the experimental treatment. The fact that no difference was found in AIDS knowledge was not surprising since both groups, experimental and control, had been exposed to this information. The fact that safer sex behaviors changed as a result of the group treatment although perceptions of risk did not "seem[s] to challenge a central tenet of the health belief model," the authors concluded. Thus both practical and theoretical implications of the results are considered.

As the El-Bassel et al. (1995) study illustrates, experimental designs are logically simple but complex to conduct. Retention of study participants was a challenge. Nevertheless it illustrates well the logic of experimental design and the standards traditionally used to judge how well any experiment has satisfied the logical conditions that lead to confidence in the conclusions drawn.

The Logical Validity of Experimental Designs

Because so much attention has been paid to the experiment as a method of empirical research, there is a great deal of special terminology used in the discussion of experimental designs. The experimenter's theoretically derived statement concerning a change-result relationship, or the presumed "cause-effect" relationship, is called a hypothesis. More precisely, it is called a *hypothesis of difference,* because it is a hypothesis that the presence or absence of the presumed cause will make a difference in the occurrence or nonoccurrence of the presumed effect(s), which is determined by comparing outcomes in two (or more) groups.

Hypotheses of difference, then, make theoretically based statements about links between a manipulation, the presumed "cause," and a predefined observed change, the presumed "effect." The manipulated variable is known as the independent variable; it is a variable, since its values can vary, and it is independent, presumably, of everything except the experimenter's decision about whether it will be absent or present and to what degree. The phenomenon expected to change is known as the dependent variable; it is a variable, again, since its values can vary, and it is called dependent to signify that it presumably depends on the independent variable for its presence or absence. In the El-Bassel et al. (1995) study, the independent variable is the intervention received; the dependent variables were safer sex behavior, coping skills, perceived availability of emotional support, sexual self-efficacy, perceived vulnerability to HIV/AIDS, and AIDS knowledge. Clients who did and who did not receive the experimental treatment were compared on the dependent variables holding all other things equal—in Latin, ceteris parabus.

As mentioned earlier, ceteris parabus is an important qualifier. The comparison between the two conditions is valid only to the extent that all other things, that is, all factors other than the deliberately varied independent variable, were in fact equal. If there were other inequalities, differences observed in the dependent variable(s) might result from those other differences rather than from the arranged difference in the independent variable. Recalling Mill's logic, the other differences become rival hypotheses explaining observed differences in the dependent variable that cannot logically be ruled out. Therefore, inequalities between the compared conditions compromise the value of an experiment for establishing a link between an independent and a dependent variable. The coexisting, unintended inequalities are called *confounds* because they are mixed up, or confounded, with the independent variable.

Confounds threaten what is known as the *internal validity* of an experiment. An experiment's internal validity refers to the extent to which it is legitimate to attribute observed dependent variable differences unambiguously to independent variable differences. Internally valid experiments permit concluding unequivocally, following the logic of Hume, Mill, and Popper, that the independent variable and dependent variable are linked. When the design of an experiment lacks internal validity, it is impossible to determine whether dependent variable differences were caused by variations in the independent variable or whether they were caused by the other factors.

A hypothetical example will serve to illustrate this point. Suppose a researcher believes that therapy A is more effective than therapy B for the treatment of depression. Testing this hypothesis would involve dividing a group of depressed clients into two equivalent subgroups, administering therapy A to one of the subgroups of depressed clients, administering therapy B to the other subgroup of depressed clients, and then comparing the average depression levels in the two subgroups posttreatment. The experimenter hopes that there will be a specific posttreatment difference in the dependent variable, namely that the group of clients who received therapy A will be less depressed than the group of clients who received therapy B. If this difference in the dependent variable is, in fact, observed, the experimenter would like to attribute it to the deliberate difference in the independent variable (i.e., therapy A versus therapy B).

Now suppose for a moment that the two therapies were administered by different therapists. And suppose that the therapists for therapy A were well-respected, seasoned clinicians while the therapists for therapy B were barely-trained but well-intended undergraduate paraprofessionals. Clearly, under these circumstances it would not make sense to suggest that the dependent variable difference could be unambiguously attributed to the intended independent variable difference. Since there were two major differences in the treatment given the two groups, that is, the type of therapy and the experience of therapists, it is not possible to determine whether it was the first or second of them, or the combination, that caused the posttreatment dependent variable difference.

In general, this same ambiguity is found whenever an additional variable changes along with the intentionally altered independent variable. The ravages confounds introduce into experiments, in terms of weakening the legitimacy of the independent-dependent variable link that can be made on the basis of them, are profound. The impact of confounds is so great, in fact, that not having them is considered by some methodologists to be the single most important criterion of a good experiment.

Confounds in Experimental Design

In a famous 1963 monograph, Campbell and Stanley provided an in-depth discussion of the confounds encountered in experimental research. Each of these confounds, discussed below, is a difference that varies alongside the intended difference in the independent variable. When present, each undercuts the internal validity of an experimental design by permitting an alternative explanation, or rival hypothesis, other than the independent variable difference, for why dependent variable differences might be observed.

These common confounds are most easily understood through example. Suppose that El-Bassel and colleagues had only enrolled women in the experimental treatment to enhance social supports and interpersonal skills and then studied them after release, finding that the women had gained in social support and other measures at the second assessment point. Notice that this study strategy involves making a before-and-after comparison using only one group of people. This type of design is often called pre-post. *Pre-post designs* are not internally valid because the pre- and postconditions are not identical except for the occurrence of the independent variable. We will now consider why this is the case—what may be different in addition to the presence versus absence of the independent variable and therefore what else might be explaining any dependent variable differences observed before and after intervention.

History. The first rival hypothesis, introduced inherently with the passage of time, is termed history. These other events, whether they are known or not, represent confounds, and the passage of time always allows for the occurrence of additional historical factors that could account for observed pre-post independent variable effects. For example, a major public education campaign about HIV disease might have taken place in the home community to which the women had been released. The street supply of an illegal drug commonly used by the women may have been reduced, resulting in fewer occasions for intoxication and unsafe sexual encounters. Such developments might provide alternative explanations for any positive changes in outcome observed.

Maturation. Campbell and Stanley (1963) termed the second rival hypothesis maturation. Linguistically, maturation refers to the process of becoming older; in psychology it also refers to the emergence of personal and behavioral characteristics through processes of experience and growth. In the example of the drug-using women in prison, it may be that the process of conviction, imprisonment, and release alone helped move them along on average to better functioning. In addition, there is evidence that some people "age out" of addiction. These factors rather than the experimental treatment could be alternative explanations for post-treatment change arising from within the individuals involved. Again, with the passage of time, there is always the possibility that some naturally unfolding developmental process might account for observed differences; maturation becomes a rival hypothesis to explain pre-post gains.

Repeated testing. Whenever independent variable effects are monitored through pre- and posttesting, the effects of repeated testing become a potential confound. In the El-Bassel et al. (1995) example, women were asked questions about themselves and their behavior before and after they had treatment. It is possible on hearing the same questions a second time that the study participants consciously or unconsciously gave more positive answers about themselves because they had time to reflect on what the researchers might think about their answers. Repeated testing, then, is another confound; like history and maturation, it introduces a rival explanation for apparent pre-post intervention changes in the dependent variable(s).

Instrumentation. The fourth common confound Campbell and Stanley (1966) discussed is instrumentation. This term refers to score shifts that result from changes in the measure rather than changes in the measured: Scores look different because the measuring instrument has changed. In the El-Bassel et al. (1995) study, for example, the same interviewers were used at all data collection points. It is possible that the interviewers, once they got to know the women, consciously or unconsciously "helped" the women they interviewed give more positive answers at follow-up because they had come to care about them. Where instrumentation changes are a possibility, it is not possible to determine whether the independent variable (in this case, participation in the skill-building group) or the confound (in this case, changes in interview practices) resulted in the higher spring grades.

Regression to the mean. The fifth common confound is called *regression to the mean*. This confound is easy to understand intuitively, despite the fact that it is a statistical concept. Scores on any measure of a phenomenon, including behavioral self-report measures, are unfortunately imperfect: All scores are comprised of some truth and some degree of error. This error component, when not due to systematic bias, is assumed to be randomly distributed. Therefore some of the scores at either extreme, that is, some of the scores that are extremely low and some of the scores that are extremely high, will be extreme partially because of the influence of error. Upon retesting, that error will be more likely to cancel itself out than it will be to reoccur; the result of this fact is that on retesting extreme scorers are more likely to get less extreme scores than they are to get equally or more extreme scores.

As applied to our example, regression to the mean might apply. Because women's self-reported behavior was being compared to what it had been in the month before imprisonment, their posttreatment behavior was being compared to the point in their lives when it had been the worst, the point at which they got into trouble with the law. Extreme scores always tend to normalize, that is, to move or regress toward the average score, called the mean, upon retesting. In the case of a pretest, a score's regressing toward the mean (i.e., normalizing) would ordinarily be taken as indicating improvement. Therefore, whenever working with those most in need, which we often do as helping professionals, unless we take special design precautions, it is not possible to attribute improved scores to the treatment rather than to regression to the mean.

The Use of a Control Group

Fortunately, in experiments special design precautions can be introduced to neutralize the possible effects of regression to the mean and the other potential confounds just described. Without question, the most important special design element that can be introduced into an experiment is what is known as a *control group*. Control groups provide a basis for comparison. Theoretically, including a control group in an experiment should provide a basis for a pure, that is, unconfounded, comparison between what happens when the independent variable is introduced in one way (e.g., when it is present) versus what happens when the independent variable is not introduced in exactly that same way (e.g., when it is absent). In fact, the use of a control group can eliminate all of the threats to the internal validity of an experiment so far discussed.

The El-Bassel et al. (1995) design involving two equivalent groups of women studied during the same period of time eliminates history as a confound. If events other than the experimental treatment that might affect the dependent variables occurred during the study period, they would be likely to affect both groups; thus if differences between the groups had been found, it would have been hard to argue that historical events had affected one group but not the other. Similarly, maturational processes can be expected to have affected both groups. In addition, the fact that both groups of women—those who got the experimental and those who got the standard treatment—completed the same assessment controls for the effects of testing and of instrumentation. If testing or instrumentation effects were occurring, they should have affected both experimental and control groups equally. On the other hand, a finding that two groups that were the same before the intervention but different after it would suggest that testing or instrumentation did not create the difference—if they both underwent the same testing procedures. As to regression to the mean, the inclusion of two equivalent groups of "low scorers," that is, of women in trouble, eliminates regression to the mean as a competing explanation for the results.

These precautions that preserve internal validity do not eliminate possible effects from these confounds; what they do is ensure that all study participants remain equally susceptible to them. This equal susceptibility means that experiments really make the following comparison: what happens when the independent variable is introduced under a set of conditions that include some factors in addition to the independent variable that may have an effect on the dependent variable, versus what happens when the independent variable is not introduced under a set of conditions that include the same factors other than the independent variable that may have an effect on the dependent variable. Experiments demonstrate that independent variables make differences above and beyond whatever differences result from other, confounding factors.

This requirement, that is, that experiments must make comparisons between effects observed under conditions equally susceptible to effects from confounds, includes both a freedom and a constraint for the researcher. The freedom is found in the fact that it is not necessary to be able to arrange a sterile, static environment to demonstrate independent variable effects. It is hard to imagine how experimental design would have any relevance to the helping professions without this freedom since many, if not most, of the most pressing questions facing social workers and other human service professionals can be meaningfully asked only in the ever-changing and certainly not sterile world of practice, rather than in the static, sterile conditions sometimes possible in the laboratory.

Balanced against this freedom is a constraint: Whatever the factors are that were part of the context when the effects of the independent variable were demonstrated become potential boundary conditions, that is, conditions that limit when the independent variable can be expected to exert those same effects. These boundary conditions include what have traditionally been called confounds affecting *external validity* due to the interaction of the treatment or manipulation itself and the process of study (Campbell & Stanley 1963). So, in the case of the El-Bassel et al. (1995) study, for example, this single experiment cannot "prove" that the same effect of the experimental treatment would be found in the absence of participation in the other pre- and posttesting that took place as part of the study or if the selection of participants had been made from some entirely different group. However, its internal (within itself) logic, or validity, is clear.

It does not detract from the value of experiments, or any form of research, to recognize that most scientific observations hold true only under certain conditions. What matters is recognizing what those boundary conditions are so that effects will not be anticipated in the absence of them. What is essential here is to note that this problem of boundary conditions affects all kinds of research and not just experiments and that theoretical logic and independent replications of observations have always been acknowledged to be essential for generalization from experiments and other forms of research (Campbell & Stanley 1963).

Other Forms of Control in Experiments

The term control actually has several meanings in experimental design. All are variants of the idea of allowing a valid comparison, that is, a comparison uncontaminated by effects from extraneous variables—from variables that are not of primary interest in the study. For example, when considering control groups, the term control means equally susceptible to the effects of the kinds of confounds that were described above.

Sometimes experimenters will speak of "controlling for" a variable when they mean to prevent a variable from having an effect. This variant of control is analogous to the type of precaution exercised in the legal system when a judge sequesters a jury to prevent media accounts and others not part of the jury from being able to exert an influence on the jury's decision. Sometimes experimenters arrange an experiment in such a way as to prevent a potentially influential variable from having an effect on the participants under study and their responses. When this is done, the experimenter is said to have "controlled for" the effects of that excluded variable.

Persons not very familiar with research often believe this second meaning of control is the only meaning researchers have for the term. That is, lay people usually assume that to control for a variable always means to eliminate its effects. This elimination is one meaning of the term control and in fact is the meaning that justifies asking questions about human behavior in the laboratory rather than in the "real world," since certain variables can only be eliminated in the laboratory, where the experimenter has more control over the situation. However, it is only one meaning of the term, and it certainly is not the most fundamental one.

There is a third way in which the term control is used in experimental design. Sometimes it is clear that an extraneous variable has had an effect on some research participants and not on others, and that different numbers of participants were affected in the experimental than in the control group. In this circumstance, the extraneous variable is confounded with the independent one. That is, participants in the two groups were different in two ways at once. First, they were different with respect to whether or not they were administered the independent variable. Second, they were different by virtue of being affected by some extraneous variable: More of the people in one of the groups rather than the other were affected by it, so that the groups were not equally susceptible, or exposed to, the effects of that extraneous variable. It is possible to control for the effects of such an extraneous variable in a variety of ways, including through multivariate statistical analysis like that used in the El-Bassel et al. (1995) study. For example, marital status and the number of treatment sessions attended were examined along with treatment group participation when examining the outcome of maintaining safer sex practices. This analytic strategy controls for the effects of those potentially confounding variables, rendering the main comparison ceteris parabus.[1]

---

1. Note: There are statistical techniques for mathematically adjusting for the effects of variables that differ between groups. These techniques essentially use mathematics to derive adjusted values for the dependent variables, values free of the measured effects of the confounding variable(s), that can then be directly compared. While legitimate mathematically, these techniques may not result in adequate conceptual control because it may not be reasonable to expect that variables can be completely freed from one another.

The Functions of Control Groups

The notion of control, then, implies making comparisons ceteris parabus, which is usually done by including an appropriate control group in an experimental design. Useful control groups are ones that are as susceptible to the influences of all variables other than the independent one as is the experimental group. This equal susceptibility allows study of the effects uniquely attributable to the presence of the independent variable. The comparison between experimental and control groups is useful only when the conditions described in the Latin phrase ceteris parabus are met, that is, only when all other things are equal. If ceteris parabus, then it will be permissible to use the logic of experimental reasoning to argue that observed differences between the experimental and control groups in what happens are definitively attributable to the experimenter-manipulated independent variable.

Although the inclusion of a control group can help strengthen the internal logic of an experimental design, there are factors that can render a control group not useful. In essence these factors are ones that destroy the fundamental comparability of the experimental and control groups. This fundamental comparability can be destroyed before, during, or after the occurrence of the independent variable. The way participants in an experiment are assigned to experimental and control groups within a study turns out to be essential to making them useful and to avoiding some additional potential confounds to the logic of the design.

Random Assignment

The method of determining group assignment that has the best chance of ensuring comparability between the experimental and control group is just that: chance. Chance, or pure randomness, is ultimately indifferent; if indifference is used as the basis for assigning participants to groups, then chances are that nothing will favor one group over the other, which is what results in inequality. Using chance to assign participants to groups is of fundamental importance in working toward ceteris parabus, which is of course the condition that legitimizes attributing observed differences to the manipulated independent variable. There are several methods for achieving random assignment that are discussed in chapter 10. All of them employ some unbiased, chance-based method, like drawing names or numbers from a container, as in a lottery, or using tables of random numbers.

When random assignment, either simple or stratified, is used, several additional potential confounds are either eliminated or minimized. The first of these is called selection. Selection is a confound that arises when some procedure other than chance is used to assign participants to groups and that procedure results in initial group differences (which will almost always be the case when some nonrandom procedure is used to determine group assignment). Initial group differences, as has been mentioned many times, preclude arguing that observed after-the-fact differences arose because of the treatment rather than because of the initial group difference or some correlate of it.

Selection effects. Studies confounded by selection effects are ones in which the experimental and control groups are not comparable from the outset by virtue of the fact that they were selected using different criteria. As an example, suppose an administrator wants to evaluate the effects of supervising student interns on social worker morale. Experimental design would imply conducting that evaluation by comparing the morale of social workers who are supervising student interns against the morale of social workers who are not supervising student interns. Now, suppose the administrator identifies the workers who will be given student interns by asking for volunteers. Is there not reason to believe that the workers who volunteer to supervise students might systematically differ in important ways from those who do not volunteer? This preexisting difference would be just as likely to explain any differences in morale after supervising as would the presence or absence of the student supervise. It is not possible to untangle the factors that would be responsible for any dependent variable differences or whether dependent variable differences were attributable to the joint effects of the preexisting difference—the willingness to volunteer—and the impact of the independent variable. The comparison is not ceteris parabus: All other things, that is, things other than the independent variable, were not equal since the groups were different both in terms of the independent variable, the presence or absence of the student intern, as well as whatever other differences preexisted between the group of workers who had volunteered for the supervision versus the group of workers who had declined to volunteer (Rosnow & Rosenthal 1982).

It may seem that the best way to arrange comparability between experimental and control groups is to work at it. Put differently, it may seem that the best way to ensure that the experimental and control groups are equal at the outset is to study all the eligible participants and then deliberately assign some of them to the experimental group and others to the control group, using care to make sure that overall, the two groups are well matched. And in fact, sometimes this is the best strategy: If there is one very important known variable that must be equal between the two groups before the treatment is applied, stratified random assignment can be used, as described in the section on sampling below.

In general, however, while matching may seem a logical strategy, very rarely can an experimenter identify before the study all the variables important that groups are equivalent on. Also, even when these variables can be identified, usually there is more than one so that identifying matched participants becomes quite cumbersome. Nevertheless, whether an important matching variable can or cannot be identified, the question remains of how to determine whether each subject should be assigned to the experimental or the control group.

It turns out (and many methodologists have debated and studied this question) that the best way to ensure original, before-the-fact comparability between an experimental and a control group is not matching. Even the best-intended researcher cannot be fair: Biases in group assignment always enter in, whether the researcher is or is not aware of them. It also turns out that there is no way to guarantee that experimental and control groups will be equal before the fact: There is always a chance that, no matter what precautions are taken, they will be different in some important known or unknown way.

Differential attrition. Random assignment to groups has been said to provide some protection against another confound, although random assignment by no means affords the same level of protection against this confound that it does against selection.

This confound is termed *differential attrition*. Attrition refers to loss of participants during the conduct of the research. Attrition always presents a threat to the generalizability of a study in that what is observed can be considered generalizable only to the sort of people represented by the participants who remained in the study. With *differential attrition,* the degree of participant loss is different between the treatment and control conditions: More participants are lost in one of the conditions than in the other. As a result, ceteris parabus is lost: The two groups are no longer equal because of the differential loss, so comparing them is not appropriate. The El-Bassel et al. (1995) study discusses this problem and how it was handled on page 135.

Consider also the following example. Suppose a psychiatrist wants to compare the effectiveness of a traditional drug to the effectiveness of a new drug for the treatment of depression. And suppose that the new drug turns out to have many more unpleasant side effects than does the traditional drug. It is quite likely that under these circumstances many more of the patients receiving the new drug will drop out of the study. If this happens, the end comparison will be between patients receiving the old treatment and the few patients receiving the new treatment that tolerated the drug well enough to remain in the study. The fact that more patients in the treatment group dropped out during treatment renders the two groups noncomparable after treatment, and this would be the case even if random assignment had been used to initially assign participants to groups. So while random assignment provides some protection against differential attrition (in that factors other than ones associated with treatment that might induce attrition will be unlikely to differ between groups), it cannot prevent it.

Verifying the Independent Variable

A final issue in drawing valid conclusions from experimental studies has to do with verifying the independent variable. El-Bassel et al. (1995) do this in two ways. First of all they describe the nature of the experimental intervention in some detail. Omitting from the study this information about the independent variable makes an experiment difficult to replicate. This leads to what is called the "black box" approach, in which the content of the treatment that proved effective remains an unknown.

Verifying the independent variable also means making some assessment of its actual use as part of an experiment. El-Bassel et al. (1995), for example, recorded the attendance of the women in both the treatment and control groups. This information is termed dosage, that is, the amount of exposure to the intervention of interest. However, the analyses they reported did not show a statistically significant relationship between the number of treatment sessions attended and outcome. The conceptual link between intervention and outcome is strengthened when the amount of exposure to a treatment is shown to have an impact on outcome.

Ethical Issues in Implementing Control Group Designs

Given the power that a well-designed experiment has to demonstrate the effects of manipulated factors on specific outcomes, including interventions or treatments, it is somewhat surprising that experiments are not more often undertaken in social work and the human services. There are no doubt many explanations for this fact. Experiments are very expensive and demanding to conduct, and they are intrusive in method. They also require, of course, that both the intervention being studied and the effects of it that are expected must be specific and specifiable, which requires a level of theory development that is often difficult to attain.

Perhaps the greatest barrier encountered to the conduct of experiments to study practice, however, has to do with an essential element of their design: the control group. Imagine approaching a group of practitioners and asking them to participate in a study of a promising intervention that may help the clients they are already serving. Imagine their reaction when told that as part of the study a control group of potential clients that will *not* participate in the treatment must be recruited and studied as well. To many practitioners this suggestion will seem an unethical one. How is it possible to defend withholding a potentially useful treatment from someone who wants and might benefit from it? Debate about this kind of study procedure is now, in fact, quite widespread in medicine, especially when trials of experimental treatments for serious and life-threatening conditions like HIV disease are being discussed (Epstein 1996).

The defense of the use of the control group or "no treatment" condition in an experiment is basically simple: Experiments are only useful when there is a genuine question about the usefulness, or even the potential harmfulness, of a treatment or intervention (see chapter 9). If a program or service is known to be useful, there is not an ethical justification for withholding it. Research, however, is conducted at the boundaries of knowledge, when there is a genuine question about whether an intervention will or will not be effective under certain conditions or for whom. For example, if the El-Bassel et al. (1995) study had found that the experimental treatment had strong positive effects on all the outcome measures assessed, it would naturally be hard to justify a future study in which some clients were not permitted to participate while others were. Even so, both theory and preliminary research findings like theirs suggest that solely educational approaches to HIV prevention may not be effective, at least in some high-risk groups.

There are some specific adaptations that are sometimes made to experimental designs in real-world practice settings, however, that can help to reduce potential ethical problems with them. Sometimes an agency or program has more clients available and seeking its services than it can accommodate at any one time. In this circumstance, some way of selecting clients to receive the service must be found. Random selection of clients into treatment and control groups from a waiting list can work quite well. Every client on the waiting list has an equal chance of receiving the experimental treatment, and those who are not getting it initially could not have been accommodated anyway.

In fact, not using random selection in such a circumstance will often introduce confounds into a study. It is not difficult to imagine examples. Suppose limited funds are available for a study of the effects of a school breakfast program on children's school performance; would a teacher or social worker selecting participants for the study not be tempted to be sure the hungriest children were included in the treatment group? However, by comparing an experimental group composed of the hungriest children to a control group composed, by default, of the better fed, the groups would not be comparable to begin with. In fact, in such a circumstance it may become *less* likely that the intervention will show an improvement in performance because the experimental group will be full of those at greatest risk.

Once a study period is over, however, participants in a control group can be made eligible to receive services, only at a later time. In fact, experiments can be planned to provide treatment or services to successive waves of eligible clients. This kind of successive treatment design is termed a staggered baseline design in which those initially excluded are later included and studied as a successive group, and it can be used whether or not a waiting list exists at the beginning of the first study period or not.

Finally, experimental studies often opt for an alternative treatment comparison group rather than a control group. In such designs, a new and innovative intervention is added to or substituted for a standard or traditional one rather than consigning a group of study participants to no treatment or services at all. In fact, this is the approach used in the El-Bassel (1995) study. It would have been considered unethical not to offer the standard educational intervention about HIV disease in order to achieve a "no treatment" condition even though there were doubts about its effectiveness.

Whatever the design used, however, once an experimental study has accumulated data that suggest an intervention is truly helpful or if some new effective treatment for the problem under study were to become available from somewhere else, it is always necessary to revisit the question of the use of a control group. It is only ethical to ask people to participate in an experiment with a control group, or even a comparison group, if there is real doubt about the effectiveness or potential harmfulness of the intervention under study. Even medical studies are often stopped in their tracks when the accumulating evidence suggests that the treatment being studied is effective enough that withholding it from some can no longer be considered right.

Generalizing from Experiments

In experiments, researchers deliberately introduce a certain describable set of circumstances and then note what unique effects those circumstances are observed to have. The circumstances are introduced into a carefully controlled context of other circumstances. Those other, background circumstances provide the context for what the researcher is studying; those background circumstances determine the boundary conditions of whatever causal connections the experiment can be taken to establish. Of course, they also must be held constant across both the experimental and control groups.

Clearly, then, conclusions drawn from experiments seem quite restricted. However, researchers are very rarely interested in drawing conclusions only about the circumstances they studied. In fact, the typical impetus for studying a certain set of conditions is interest in a broader set of conditions the studied one is thought to represent. Consider the El-Bassel et al. (1995) study: Clearly the purpose of the research was not simply to show that in that particular prison, those particular women selected for treatment had changed for the better. As the literature review suggests, women, especially drug-using and incarcerated women, are at high risk of dying from AIDS and there is "mounting evidence . . . that increasing AIDS knowledge by itself will not lead to significant behavioral changes" (p. 131). Thus the study evidence is meant to contribute to a wider discussion of what works in the prevention of HIV disease, not just to assist women in one particular prison at one point in time.

One important basis for the credibility of any study, including experiments, is the theory that is used to explain the results. Efforts to enhance internal validity in experiments helps to rule out alternative explanations for the findings. However, the general credibility of the original hypothesis and the theory on which it is based is important as well. Experimental findings lend credibility to a theory by showing that the theory can predict certain observations and events. However, it is rare in the psychological, social, and medical sciences to encounter experimental findings that are compatible with only one theory. Therefore the credibility of an experimental study must also rely on evaluations of theory that are external to the study itself.

The Importance of Replication

The generality of any study's conclusions, including the ones that can be drawn from an experiment, has been termed its external validity. In terms of the traditional framework for understanding causality, externally valid experiments are ones in which the inferred causal connections are also valid under conditions external to those studied. No single study, no matter how well it is designed and how carefully it is executed, can be assumed to have complete external validity. The science of the helping professions, like all other sciences, has precious few universal laws (see Hawking 1988), that is, generalizations, theories, or propositions that have been shown to hold true under any and all conditions and circumstances. However, the external validity of a study is typically enhanced by including conditions in it that fairly represent circumstances outside of it.

The external validity of a conclusion is most convincingly enhanced by demonstrating it again. This repeated demonstration is called a *replication*. It refers quite simply to conducting the same study again. Because repeated demonstrations and observations are necessarily conducted under different conditions (since it is never possible to literally recreate the exact circumstances included in the first study), each successive replication provides more reason to believe that the "effect" observed will reoccur following the manipulation under still other sets of different conditions.

The enhanced belief afforded by replication in an effect's wider applicability is greater to the extent that successive replications are independent and different from one another, that is, conducted by different experimenters, in different geographical locations, or using somewhat different measures. If similar results are obtained across all the variations—especially if those variations have been systematically selected so as to be deliberately wide over the most relevant circumstantial variables, as is the case in large-scale, national, multisite collaborative studies typically sponsored by federal agencies such as NIMH—the conclusion drawn from them can be held with a great deal of confidence.

It should also be noted that replication is important in all forms of research, not just in experiments. However, some forms of research, such as descriptive and relational studies, typically can employ larger and more varied samples than experiments can, which adds to the credibility of the generalizations made from them. Fixed method studies in which samples are small, such as in experiments and single-subject designs (see chapter 8), thus are more often replicated. Unfortunately, however, replication research is not conducted or published as often as it should be, which is a serious problem for knowledge development in general.

Issues in Experimental Design

There are several additional issues in experimental design that are useful to consider when planning or evaluating experimental research. The experimental design paradigm that has been discussed in this chapter and illustrated in the El-Bassel et al. (1995) article is that of the classical group experiment, although one taking place in the field rather than in a laboratory setting. Important variations of this design exist and there are issues in sampling, data collection, and data analysis that are of particular importance in experimental designs.

Variations in Designs

As the discussion of experimental designs has illustrated, an experimental design itself is complex and involves many elements. Key design elements include the use of two groups for comparison, random assignment of participants to groups, repeated measurement (before and after), and the introduction of an intervention or manipulation. Any one of these design elements may be altered, although changing them may affect the conclusions that can be drawn if confounds are introduced.

So far, experiments have been discussed primarily in terms of the comparison made between the experimental and the control groups. The design can also involve comparisons within groups, however, that is, in each group from the time before the manipulation or intervention was made to the time after. Campbell and Stanley (1963) point out that the posttest-only design, as long as it includes random assignment to treatment and control groups, may be just as strong in internal validity as the pre- and posttest design. A posttest-only design involves only between group comparisons; the pre- and posttest design involves both between and within group comparisons.

Other variations, however, have greater effects on the internal validity of the design. For example, a study may examine a change before and after some event that was not in the control of an investigator. Measurements may or may not be repeated. Group membership may or may not be randomly assigned. No group for comparison may be included and only a within-group comparison over time may be made. Since each part of the experimental design is there specifically to eliminate confounds, any of these changes in fact introduces one or more confounds into the design. For that reason, such designs are termed quasi-experiments (Cook & Campbell 1979) because they do not fully adhere in all respects to the logic of a true experiment. *Quasi-experimental designs* are quite common, especially in applied fields such as education, social work, and human services research. While they confer some disadvantages on the clarity of the conclusions that may result, they can be quite useful, especially if viewed as a form of relational research (see chapter 6).

When a true experiment cannot be used because the variable of interest cannot be manipulated by the researcher, an analogue experiment may be conducted. That is, the variable of interest may be manipulated by analogy rather than in real life. For example, the helping professions have been quite concerned about the effects of racism on practice, especially on the assessment of clients. Since the race of a client cannot be manipulated for study, case materials, such as a case history, written vignette, or videotape, can be developed and the race of the client manipulated to see if the social workers' responses to the case are the same or different depending on the race of the client described. The Paviour (1988) study of social work students' assessment of cases is a good example of just such a study. These designs are true experiments, but they present a problem of interpretation in that there is no way to know whether or not responses to case materials or a written vignette differ from how the same respondents would react when confronted with real clients. However, analogue experiments can be useful tools for addressing questions when manipulation is not possible in the real world.

Sometimes in an experiment more than one intervention may be made and compared, or the intervention may be varied, thus involving more than two groups in the experiment. Similarly, an intervention may be made (and withheld) in groups that differ systematically on some other variable or variables of interest. What results in either of these cases is termed a *factorial design,* that is, one in which more than one independent variable, or factor, is compared. One question that such designs must address is whether each factor by itself seems to have an effect on the outcome variable(s), termed a *direct effect,* or whether some combination of the factors may have a unique effect together. These combined effects are termed *interaction effects.* Sophisticated techniques of analysis are available that can separate direct from interaction effects, and these should be utilized whenever factorial designs are employed (Hays 1981; Bryman & Cramer 1990).

One variation in design that has already been mentioned is the single-subject experiment (see chapter 8). The fundamental differences between single-subject designs and the type of experiments thus far considered is the context of the comparison. In the type of experiments discussed so far, termed group experiments, independent variables or interventions are examined by comparing what is observed in two groups of participants deliberately treated differently. In single-subject experiments, independent variable effects are tested by comparing what happens in an individual participant before and after the intervention is made. Single-subject experimental designs originated in biology and medicine where the primary interest is in treating the individual case. For this reason, many helping professionals have advocated single-subject experimental methodologies as especially suited to the clinical situation, where treatment is directed toward individuals or individual cases, not toward groups (see chapter 8).

Sampling

The hallmark of an experimental design is manipulation: some change is introduced affecting one or more groups of people. Experimental research thus demands quite intensive involvement with and study of participants as well as a high degree of access to and control in the observational situation. For these reasons, samples in experimental studies are often relatively small and/or carefully chosen. Experimental studies thus do not depend, as descriptive and most relational ones do, on large, representative samples. Rather, the ability to generalize from the results of experimental studies depends instead on the strength of the theoretical explanation of the observations made and on replication.

The key issue in sampling in experimental research, then, is the way in which assignment of study participants is made to experimental and control groups. Random assignment to experimental and control groups is essential to the logic of the comparison that an experiment is designed to make. If more than one factor is being manipulated, of course, the randomization procedure must include all the groups. Random assignment can be done in a variety of ways, from drawing numbers to using a random number table or computerized random number generator (see chapter 10 on sampling). What is essential is that it take place in order for a study to be considered a true experiment.

Data Collection

In general, data collection issues in experiments are no different than in any other form of fixed method research. There are only two additional points to be made. The first is that if the experimental design involves a pre- and postcomparison, data collection procedures must be used that work well with repeated use. Experiments are no different in this respect, of course, from any other form of longitudinal research.

Some experiments are designed to be "blind" experiments; that is, people involved with study participants during the course of the study are not supposed to know whether a given individual is in the experimental or the control group. Data collection procedures and any data revealing who is in which group must be carefully safeguarded in such circumstances. For example, in Applegate's (1992) study of the effects of client self-monitoring on treatment outcome, some therapists learned from the spontaneous remarks of their clients that they were participating in the self-monitoring (experimental) process. While the researcher elected to gather and use these unexpected, spontaneously generated data as part of the findings, there is a possibility that a therapist's knowledge that a client had participated in the self-monitoring affected the Global Assessment Scale ratings given after eight interviews, which was one of the study's outcome measures. However, the presence of other client-based outcome measures seemed to validate the overall finding of no significant difference in therapist ratings of treatment outcome.

Data Analysis

However carefully an experiment is designed, its observed results rarely reflect the hypothesized outcome perfectly. In most cases, the results of an experiment or a study of treatment in social work and the human services are not expected to be deterministic or exactly as predicted in every case. In reality, the are expected to be *probabilistic,* that is, likely on average. El-Bassel et al., for example, hypothesized that those clients who participated in the skills-building group would do better one month after release from prison than those who did not. However they did not expect that every client in the experimental (skills-building) group would be rated more positively on every outcome measure than every client in the control (or educational) group. Logically, given the complexity of human psychological life, it is unreasonable to assume that every person will react in the same way to any event. In addition, the methods available for assessing effects, such as, for example, self-reports of high-risk behavior, are not so precise and accurate that even if perfect improvement were obtained the questions used to measure it would necessarily capture the change. The question then is: how *likely* is it that the empirical results obtained do or do not support the study hypothesis?

Often, then, hypotheses of difference are examined at the data analysis stage using *inferential statistics* (see chapter 18). Inferential statistics require that the original hypothesis of difference be divided into two sub-hypotheses called the research hypothesis and the null hypothesis. The alternative hypothesis of difference and the null hypothesis are arranged so as to be mutually exclusive, which means that only one of them can be true. It is the null hypothesis that is then tested statistically, with the hope of rejecting the null hypothesis and thereby providing support for the alternative hypothesis of difference by implication. Inferential statistics, which are based on assessing probabilities, are the tools used to examine the probabilistic nature of experimental results.

The statistical analysis of data from experiments uses a set of inferential techniques for examining hypotheses of difference termed the *analysis of variance* (see chapter 18). When factorial designs are used (see above), it is necessary to employ the multivariate versions of these techniques in the analysis. Finally, when pre- and post-comparisons are included in an experimental design, the specific statistical tests to be used are different from those used when the groups compared are independent of each other. Many experimental designs employ both within-group (pre- and post-) and between-group comparisons. The statistical procedures used in such a circumstance are termed mixed models because they incorporate the comparison of both independent and correlated groups.

Conclusions: The Strengths and Weaknesses of Group Experiments

Experiments are the method of choice when a variable of interest can be manipulated at will by the experimenter and when the research question asks about whether one or more manipulatable variables can produce change in one or more prespecified effects. Under these conditions, well-designed and well-executed experiments can offer highly credible answers to the specific question, including information about treatment techniques, service delivery, and social programs. Because experiments have traditionally been considered the pinnacle of scientific method in the social sciences, the rules of method for the design and conduct of experimental studies have been described in great detail. In particular, since experiments aim to demonstrate a logical connection between one event and another, a great deal of attention has been paid to designing experiments in a way that will support such a conclusion. Experimental studies are therefore often quite elaborate in method and demanding to conduct, especially in field settings.

Experiments have limitations. They can be applied only to phenomena that the experimenter can completely control. Moreover, since they rest on comparisons, they can be applied only to outcomes that predictably and generally occur. With group experiments, questions are answered by examining what happens on average under certain conditions, rather than what happens in any one individual case. While an unimportant feature for many purposes, this characteristic of experiments can become a real limitation when the primary interest is in generating knowledge about how to best work with particular people or cases. Such questions are best examined with the kind of research introduced in the next chapter: single-subject designs.

PREVENTING HIV/AIDS IN DRUG-ABUSING INCARCERATED WOMEN THROUGH SKILLS BUILDING AND SOCIAL SUPPORT ENHANCEMENT: PRELIMINARY OUTCOMES

NABILA EL-BASSEL, ANDRÉ IVANOFF, ROBERT F. SCHILLING,
LOUISA GILBERT, DEBRA BORNE, AND DUAN-RUNG CHEN

Despite escalating rates of human immunodeficiency virus/acquired immune deficiency syndrome (HIV/AIDS) among incarcerated women, few jails provide more than minimal HIV prevention programs. This pilot study tested the efficacy of a skills-building and social support enhancement intervention designed to reduce the spread of AIDS among 145 incarcerated women with recent histories of significant drug abuse. Participants were randomly assigned to either informational group sessions on HIV/AIDS prevention or group sessions on skills building and social support enhancement. Six major outcomes were used to compare the efficacy of the two interventions: safer sex practices, perceived vulnerability to HIV infection, sexual self-efficacy, coping skills, AIDS knowledge, and perceived emotional support. Participants in the second group showed modest improvement in three outcomes. This study confirmed the feasibility of implementing a skills-building intervention for drug-using women in jail.

Key words: drug abuse; HIV/AIDS; jail; offenders; women

Acquired immune deficiency syndrome (AIDS) has become the leading cause of death among female inmates (Brewer & Derrickson, 1992). The rate of human immunodeficiency virus (HIV) infection among women in 10 selected U.S. jails and federal and state prisons ranged from 3.2 percent to 14.7 percent in 1991, substantially higher than the 2.3 percent to 7.8 percent reported for their male counterparts (U.S. Department of Health and Human Services, 1992). In 1993, 25.8 percent of the women incarcerated at New York City's Rikers Island Jail, where this study was conducted, were HIV positive, compared with 16.0 percent of their male counterparts (Weisfuse et al., 1991). The higher HIV infection rates among female inmates may be attributed to their wider prevalence of substance abuse; exchanging sex for money or drugs; and, at least in Western countries, the apparent greater efficiency of male-to-female HIV transmission (Centers for Disease Control, 1989; Graham & Wish, 1994; VanHoeven, Stoneburner, & Rooney, 1991; Weisfuse et al., 1991).

Despite these escalating HIV/AIDS rates among incarcerated women, few jails provide more than minimal HIV prevention programs consisting of informational sessions or videos (Brewer & Derrickson, 1992; Stevens, 1993). Mounting evidence suggests that increasing AIDS knowledge by itself will not lead to significant behavioral changes (Kelly, Murphy, Sikkema, & Kalichman, 1993; O'Leary, 1985).

Several studies have indicated the effectiveness of skills-building approaches in reducing HIV risk behaviors among various populations (El-Bassel & Schilling, 1992; Kelly, St. Lawrence, Hood, & Brasfield, 1989; Rotheram-Borus & Koopman, 1991; Schilling, El-Bassel, Schinke, Gordon, & Nichols, 1991; Valdiserri, Arena, Proctor, & Bonati, 1989). HIV/AIDS risk reduction requires both self-management and interpersonal management skills. Self-management skills, consisting of

Nabila El-Bassel, DSW, is assistant professor, André Ivanoff, PhD, and Robert F. Schilling, PhD, are associate professors, and Louisa Gilbert, MS, CSW, and Debra Borne, MSW, are research associates, School of Social Work, Columbia University, 622 West 113th Street, New York, NY 10025. Duan-Rung Chen, MPh, is research associate, Department of Sociology, Columbia University. Please direct correspondence to Nabila El-Bassel.

personal awareness, problem-solving, and coping skills, are needed to enhance perception of risk and motivation to reduce risk behavior, to identify high-risk situations and recognize prospective situations that are likely to lead to unsafe sex (including the ability to avoid or rearrange those situations so that they do not lead to risky behavior), and to work through high-risk situations by developing and maintaining alternative coping behaviors. Interpersonal skills enhance the ability to assert a commitment to safer sex, to reduce a partner's opposing reactions, and to develop and maintain relationships that are supportive of safer sex (Kelly et al., 1989).

A growing number of studies underscore the importance of social support and social networks in the acquisition of HIV/AIDS protective behaviors among drug users and gay men (Des Jarlais, Friedman, & Strug, 1986; Des Jarlais et al., 1993; El-Bassel & Schilling, 1992; Kelly et al., 1992). Most drug abusers lack adaptive social support (El-Bassel & Schilling, 1992; Hawkins & Fraser, 1983; Nurco, Stephenson, & Hanlon, 1991; Rhoads, 1983). Rhoads (1983) suggested that drug-using women tend to lack the support systems that are available to men. Through focus groups and developmental work conducted before this study, we learned that this population of incarcerated drug-using women is particularly lacking in social support from family and friends who do not use drugs.

Although skills-building and social support enhancement approaches hold promise for reducing sexual risk behavior among incarcerated women, the efficacy of these approaches with this population has not been tested. With a captive and for a time relatively drug-free audience, jail may provide an ideal context for engaging women who would otherwise be beyond the reach of prevention programs. Yet information and skills-based approaches may not be effective in controlled settings in which participants are removed from the normal environment of sexual risk taking and drug use. Also, skills-building approaches favor participants who are at least willing to contemplate changing their behavior, rather than inmates who are beleaguered

with more immediate problems. Studies are needed that test the effectiveness of these and other approaches in reducing HIV risk behavior among incarcerated women.

This pilot study was conducted to inform the design of AIDS prevention intervention and measurement protocols of subsequent randomized trials. Specifically, we sought to compare the efficacy of a skills building and social support (SS) enhancement intervention with a standard AIDS information (AI) intervention with respect to the acquisition of safer sex behavior and attitudes among incarcerated women with recent histories of significant drug abuse. For this study 145 incarcerated women with such histories were randomly assigned to SS and AI groups. Participants in the SS condition attended 16 two-hour group session in jail and six monthly booster sessions starting one month after release. Participants in the AI condition received three two-hour educational sessions about HIV/AIDS prevention, typical of most jails.

We hypothesized that women in the SS group would exhibit higher rates of safer sex practices (consistent condom use or abstinence), perceived vulnerability to HIV/AIDS, improvement in coping skills, perceived emotional support, and sexual self-efficacy at follow-up one month after release than women in the AI group. Although we also compared increases in AIDS knowledge, we anticipated that such gains would be similar across the SS and AI conditions. To our knowledge, this is the first experimental investigation of a HIV risk-reduction intervention in a jail setting.

METHODS

Participants

Female drug users incarcerated at Rikers Island in New York City were recruited by means of posted notices and staff referrals. To be eligible to participate in the study, inmates needed to be between 18 and 55 years of age, convicted and serving a sentence between three months and one year, scheduled for release within 10 weeks to one of four boroughs of New York City (excluding Staten Island), and self-reported drug users (cocaine, crack, or heroin) three or more times a week during the three months before arrest. Self-reported drug use was corroborated by review of correctional or medical intake records documenting drug abuse before arrest. Of the approximately 200 women who were recruited, 159 met eligibility criteria and completed the pretest.

Informed consent was obtained by project staff before the pretest. All project procedures were explained, and women were informed that participation in the project in no way affected their status in the jail or in the larger criminal justice system. All potential participants were provided the opportunity to ask questions before signing the informed consent form; a copy of the form was given to each participant listing the investigator's telephone number should additional questions arise.

At pretest all participants were randomly assigned to either three two-hour HIV/AIDS informational group sessions or to 16 two-hour skills-building group sessions that met twice a week in jail followed by six booster sessions that met monthly in the community. The effects of the six booster sessions were not assessed in this study because they occurred after the one-month follow-up interview.

At pretest 75 participants were assigned to the SS condition and 84 participants to the AI condition. Between pretest and the first session of the intervention, 14 participants were lost because of unplanned release or transfer to another facility, leaving a total of 145 participants, 67 assigned to the SS condition and 78 to the AI condition.

Measurement

Major outcome variables used to assess the effectiveness of the skills-building and social support enhancement intervention are safer sex behavior (consistent condom use or abstinence), coping skills, perceived availability of direct emotional support, sexual self-efficacy, perceived vulnerability to HIV/AIDS, and AIDS knowledge. Safer injection behavior was not included as a behavioral outcome because few participants had injected within 30 days of their arrest.

Demographic Characteristics. Demographic characteristics were considered as mediating factors in this study. Variables included were age, ethnicity, marital status, number of children, and level of education.

Drug Use. Participants were asked about their use of heroin, marijuana, cocaine, and crack cocaine. For each substance, respondents were asked whether they had ever used it and how often they had used the drug during the month before arrest.

Condom Use. Condom use was measured by asking participants about the frequency of condom use during vaginal sex in the 30 days before arrest. Likert-type responses were measured by a five-point scale on which 1 = never, 2 = less than half the time, 3 = about half the time, 4 = more than half the time, and 5 = always.

Change in Safer Sex Practices. This variable, created to assess intervention effects on condom use or abstinence, was coded in four categories: 0 (worse) = participant always used condoms or was abstinent the month before arrest at pretest but at follow-up reported having vaginal intercourse without using condoms during the past month postrelease, 1 (no change) = participant did not always use condoms during vaginal intercourse at pretest and at follow-up, 2 (continued safe sex) = participant was abstinent or always used condoms at pretest and at follow-up, and 3 (improved) = participant had vaginal sex without always using condoms at pretest but always used condoms during vaginal sex or was abstinent at follow-up. For the purpose of measuring safer sex behavior, this ordinal variable was recoded dichotomously as "continued or improved" and "worse or no change."

Number of Sexual Partners. This variable was measured by one question: "How many different people did you have vaginal sex with in the 30 days before arrest?"

Sex Exchanging. This variable was assessed by asking participants if they had exchanged vaginal, oral, or anal sex for money or drugs in the past and in the 30 days before arrest. The women responded either yes or no.

Perceived Vulnerability to Contracting HIV. This variable was measured by asking, "What would you say your chances are of getting the HIV virus?" Responses on the item were measured by a five-point Likert-type scale on which 1 = almost certainly will not, 2 = small chance, 3 = very great chance, 4 = almost certainly will, and 5 = have AIDS/HIV positive.

AIDS Knowledge. This variable was measured by eight true-false items concerning the transmission and prevention of HIV.

Coping Skills. Coping skills were assessed using the Coping Skills Questionnaire (CASK) (El-Bassel & Schilling, 1993). The CASK uses seven items with four-point Likert-type responses ranging from 1 = never to 4 = always to assess positive and negative coping behaviors (for example, "When you are angry or upset, do you talk to friends?" and "When you are angry or upset, do you yell?"). The time periods for measuring coping behaviors were the month before arrest for pretest and the month after release for follow-up. To measure the intervention effect on coping behavior, we dichotomously assessed changes in participants' use of positive coping behavior from pretest to follow-up. Those who improved their frequency of positive coping behaviors one or more points on the Likert scale and those who maintained the highest frequency of positive coping behavior from pretest to follow-up were categorized as 1; all others were categorized as 0.

Emotional Support. Emotional support was measured by eight items assessing direct emotional support. Participants were asked, for example, "Do you have someone to listen to you when you need to talk?" "Do you have someone who understands your personal problems?" or "Do you have someone to turn to for advice?" Responses were coded on a five-point Likert scale ranging from 1 = none of the time to 5 = all of the time. The time period for measuring emotional support focused on the month before arrest for pretest and on the month after release for follow-up. For the purpose of measuring the intervention effect on perceived emotional support, this study dichotomously assessed the change in direct emotional support from pretest to follow-up. Participants who increased their perceived level of emotional support one or more points on the Likert scale and those who maintained

the highest frequency of perceived availability of emotional support from pretest to follow-up were categorized as 1; all others were categorized as 0.

Procedure

Participants were interviewed several times during the study period: at pretest; at the exit interview two to seven days before release; in the community within two days of release; and at one, three, six, and 12 months following release. These pretest, exit, postrelease, and follow-up interviews were administered by the same interviewer, who maintained contact with each participant.

Exit Interview. The exit interview served two functions. The first function was to prepare participants for the community follow-up interviews. The second function was to obtain locator information such as frequent hangouts, names and addresses of significant others, and social services and treatment agencies used by the women. The postrelease interview was scheduled and its location determined. A business card with the program telephone number and address and the interviewer's pager number was given to the participants.

Postrelease Interview. The postrelease interview was conducted in the community within the first two days after release for both the experimental and control groups. In the postrelease interview, the interviewer updated locator and social network data. The women were reminded of their first follow-up interview and, as appropriate, their first booster session. A business card was again given to the participant.

More than a few inmates were homeless, and their release without discharge planning made it difficult to follow them over time. However, several strategies such as meeting with the women just before release and then again two days postrelease, using the same interviewers for interviewing participants from pretest to the last follow-up, updating locator information at each contact over time, and giving out business cards and pager numbers all increased rates of follow-up interviews with this transient population. Follow-up rates for experimental and control groups in this study were similar.

One-Month Follow-up Interview. Among the 145 participants, 101 (69.7 percent) were located and participated in the follow-up interview one month after release. Follow-up interviews lasted approximately one hour and were conducted in the participant's neighborhood, frequently in fast food restaurants or other safe public places.

Interventions

Skills-Building and Social Support Enhancement Intervention. The SS participants attended 16 two-hour group sessions that met twice weekly in prison and six group booster sessions that met monthly in the community. Conducted in structured groups of 10 participants, SS sessions were led by two group facilitators selected for ethnic similarity to the participants, experience in substance abuse, and structured group work methods. Before leading groups, facilitators participated in three full days of training. Weekly individual and group supervision was provided to all facilitators.

The HIV/AIDS prevention strategies were based on several overlapping theoretical areas, including social cognitive theory, self-efficacy (Bandura, 1989), the health belief model (Janz & Becker, 1984; Rosenstock, 1974), behavioral and cognitive skills training (Lazarus, 1971; Meichenbaum, 1972), problem solving (D'Zurilla & Goldfried, 1971; Nezu & D'Zurilla, 1981; Platt, Taube, Metzger, & Duome, 1988), social support and help seeking (Fraser & Hawkins, 1984; Froland, Pancoast, Chapman, & Kimboko, 1981; Wills, 1982), and empowerment (Levine et al., 1993; Simon, 1994). The skills building and social support enhancement intervention aims to bolster participants' awareness of HIV/AIDS risk behaviors and their ability to anticipate high-risk situations; to enhance their self-efficacy, problem-solving, and coping skills in high-risk and other life problem situations; to enable participants to assess their social networks, strengthen ties to drug-free support networks, and use supportive individuals in reducing

HIV/AIDS risk behavior and solving life problems; and to help participants gain access to formal and informal help to support their efforts to acquire and sustain protective behaviors. Although injection-related risks were included, few participants had a current injection history. Accordingly, more attention was given to safer sex practices.

Skills were introduced, defined, modeled, and reviewed by group facilitators. Skills were conceptualized as either cognitive-behavioral (problem-solving or social skills) or technical (condom use and needle cleaning). Participants practiced skills in role plays and simulated situational exercises, receiving coaching and feedback from the facilitators and other members. Homework assignments were reviewed in each subsequent session. As part of this education, participants practiced putting condoms on penis models and learned techniques to eroticize condom use as well as safer sex alternatives to intercourse.

During the first session participants identified at least one drug-free person in their network of friends and family whom they could turn to for advice, support, and help with their recovery. Between sessions, participants were encouraged to call and establish contact with supportive people. Participants also explored and identified their needs for social services, housing, drug treatment, and other services on release. Using a resource handbook designed specifically for female drug-using offenders, facilitators assisted participants in selecting services that best met their needs. Participants were encouraged to make appointments for intake interviews and speak with contact people and thus, in effect, learn to manage their own discharge planning. In group sessions, participants shared their successes and problems carrying out these tasks. Through role plays, they learned to use problem-solving and social skills under challenging circumstances (Schilling, Ivanoff, El-Bassel, & Borne, 1993).

AIDS Information Intervention. Over three two-hour sessions, HIV/AIDS information was presented, primarily focusing on transmission-related issues and safer sex and drug alternatives. Participants asked questions and discussed personal concerns about AIDS.

Data Analysis

Demographic characteristics, patterns of drug use, and sexual characteristics of the participants are described using univariate frequency distributions. Intervention effects were first analyzed using chi-square tests with the baseline Likert-scale variables and follow-up counterparts, categorizing changes as worse, no change-remain bad, no change-remain good, and improved. We dichotomized the outcome variables as improve-maintain and worse-no change. Logistic regression models were then used to compare the efficacy of SS and AI interventions, controlling for the confounding variables (attendance of sessions and demographic and criminal history variables).

To estimate group membership effect, univariate logistic regression analyses were first conducted by entering the group membership variable with each outcome variable, unadjusted for other factors. Then, the group membership variable was entered with each outcome variable, adjusting for each confounding variable in separate equations. Confounding variables considered included number of sessions attended; age; ethnicity; level of education; marital status; number of children; number of prior incarcerations; whether they had ever injected; and regular crack use, cocaine use, and heroin use one month before arrest. We used the change-in-estimate method, a common alternative to stepwise regression, to select confounding variables (Hosmer & Lemeshow, 1989). This method selects variables based on relative or absolute change in the estimated exposure effect (in public health terms, group membership is the exposure variable). If entering a confounding variable resulted in more than a 10 percent increase or decrease in the change in estimate of the group membership effect, and if a confounding variable significantly improved the goodness of fit over the unadjusted model, it was retained for the final model of that outcome variable.

Pretest Comparisons

SS and AI groups were compared at pretest on sociodemographic and drug and sexual risk variables. No significant differences were found (see Table 1). In addition, no significant differences were found on the pretest outcome variables of coping skills, emotional support, AIDS knowledge, perceived vulnerability to AIDS, and sexual self-efficacy.

Participant Retention

Attendance. Among those who participated in the SS group ($n = 67$), more than half (52.2 percent) attended 13 or more sessions, 28.4 percent attended between four and 12 sessions, and 19.4 percent attended three or fewer sessions. Among those assigned to the AI group ($n = 78$), 85.9 percent attended all three sessions.

Pretest to Intervention. Analyses revealed no significant differences regarding age, education, ethnicity, marital status, or parental status between the 14 women who were lost before intervention and those who remained. However, lost participants did have more prior incarcerations than those who participated in either condition ($M = 16.9$ versus $M = 7.5$, $t = -2.57, p < .01$).

Follow-Up. We were unable to locate 44 women (30.3 percent) from pretest to follow-up—18 (26.9 percent) experimental group participants and 26 (33.3 percent) control group participants. Dropouts and retained participants did not differ significantly on age; ethnicity; marital status; level of education; number of prior incarcerations; frequency of condom use or abstinence from sex; HIV status; coping skills; perceived emotional support; or regular use of heroin, cocaine, or crack. To reduce the likelihood that experimental mortality differentially influenced outcome results between SS and AI groups, between-group differences were controlled for in outcome analyses.

RESULTS

Univariate

Sociodemographics. The sample was composed primarily of African American, unemployed, single mothers who did not com-

Table 1. Sociodemographic Characteristics, Drug Use, and Sexual Risk Behavior among 145 Incarcerated Female Participants at Pretest Comparing Social Support Enhancement (SS) plus AIDS Information (AI) Conditions

Characteristic	Total Sample (N = 145)		SS Condition (N = 67)		AI Condition (N = 78)		
	M	SD	M	SD	M	SD	p
Age (years)	32.8	6.48	32.2	6.68	33.3	6.34	.307
Education (years)	10.9	2.1	10.9	2.79	10.9	2.02	.982
Number of previous incarcerations	3.72	4.72	3.87	4.87	3.63	4.64	.761
	n	%	n	%	n	%	n
Marital status							
Single, never married	97[a]	67.4	50	74.6	47[b]	61.0	.208
Common law or married	21[a]	14.6	7	10.4	14[b]	18.2	
Separated or divorced	26[a]	18.1	10	14.9	16[b]	20.8	
Ethnicity							
African American	93[a]	64.6	45	67.2	48[b]	62.3	.548
Latina	27[a]	18.8	10	14.9	17[b]	22.1	
White	18[a]	12.5	8	11.9	10[b]	13.0	
Other	6[a]	4.2	4	6.0	2[b]	2.6	
Have children under 18	111	76.6	50	74.6	61	78.2	.512
Drug use							
Regular crack use[c]	91	62.8	44	65.7	47	60.3	.565
Regular heroin use[c]	33	22.8	15	22.4	18	23.1	.888
Regular cocaine use[c]	50	34.5	22	32.8	28	35.9	.657
Injected 30 days before arrest	25	17.2	10	14.9	15	19.2	.474
Sexual risk factors							
Used condoms always or was abstinent in 30 days before arrest	67	46.2	28	41.8	39	50.0	.287
Exchanged sex for money or drugs in 30 days before arrest	34	23.4	16	23.9	18	23.1	.943
Self-reported HIV positive	23	15.9	9	13.4	14	17.9	.473

[a]N = 144. [b]N = 77. [c]Used drugs three or more times per week during the 30 days before their arrest.

plete high school (Table 1). Most were repeat offenders.

Drug Use and HIV Risk Behavior. Almost two-thirds of the total sample of 145 (62.8 percent) reported using crack three or more times a week during the month before arrest, and almost one-quarter (22.8 percent) reported using heroin three or more times a week during the month before arrest. Only 17.2 percent indicated they had injected drugs during the month before arrest (Table 1).

Slightly less than half of the sample (46.2 percent) reported that they were abstinent or used condoms every time they had vaginal sex during the month before arrest. Almost one-quarter (23.4 percent) indicated that they had exchanged sex for money or drugs in the month before arrest. Among the total sample, 15.9 percent reported that they had tested HIV positive (Table 1).

Sexual Behavior. About one-tenth of the sample (11.7 percent, $n = 17$) reported they had sex with women during the month before arrest. Almost three-quarters of the total sample (72.4 percent, $n = 105$) indicated they had vaginal, anal, or oral intercourse the month before arrest. Those who had vaginal sex in the month before arrest averaged 2.87 partners. Frequency of condom use varied by type of sexual partner. Only 16.0 percent ($n = 13$) of those having vaginal sex with a steady, noncommercial partner in the past month indicated that they had always used condoms, compared with half of those having vaginal sex with casual partners (50.0 percent, $n = 7$) and two-thirds of those having sex with commercial partners (66.7 percent, $n = 24$). Almost one-fifth of the sample (18.6 percent, $n = 27$) indicated that they had been abstinent in the past year. One-half (52.4 percent, $n = 76$) reported that they had contracted a sexually transmitted disease at some time in the past. Despite these factors, more than half of the women (58.6 percent, $n = 85$) believed that they had little or no chance of contracting HIV/AIDS.

Statistic Regression Analysis

The major outcomes were modeled to compare the efficacy of the SS and AI interventions: safer sex (constant condom use or abstinence), perceived vulnerability to HIV, AIDS knowledge, sexual self-efficacy, coping skills, and perceived emotional support. Safer sex behavior, coping skills, and perceived emotional support were significantly associated with group membership in the adjusted logistic regression models. A greater proportion of the 48 SS participants at follow up (one participant did not respond) indicated improvement on these three outcomes: 70.8 percent ($n = 34$) of the SS participants indicated that they improved or maintained safer sex behavior, compared with 61.5 percent ($n = 32$) of the 52 AI participants at follow-up; 37.5 percent ($n = 18$) of the SS participants indicated that they improved or maintained their coping skills, compared with 21.2 percent ($n = 11$) of the AI participants; and 72.9 percent ($n = 35$) of the SS participants improved or maintained their emotional support, compared with 53.8 percent ($n = 28$) of the AI participants. No significant association was found between group membership and perceived vulnerability to HIV, sexual self-efficacy, or AIDS knowledge in unadjusted or adjusted logistic regression models.

Model 1 tested the association of the intervention variable with change in safer sex behavior, unadjusted for other variables. Participants in the SS group were not significantly more likely to increase safer sex behavior. The maximum likelihood ratio test indicates that the unadjusted model with the group membership variable does not have a statistically better fit than the null model of no association [$X^2(1) = 1.05$, $p = .3$], suggesting consideration of possible mediating factors (see Table 2). Potentially confounding demographic, drug use, and criminal history variables were then entered along with the group membership variable in separate equations. Only number of sessions attended and marital status were found to change the estimate of the group membership effect by more than 10 percent; these variables were therefore entered into model 2. This model revealed that after adjusting for marital status and number of sessions attended, intervention group participants were 3.8 times more likely to increase their safer sex behavior from pretest to follow-up at an almost significant level ($p < .09$). Participants who were married or living with their significant other were significantly less likely to report improving safer sex behavior. The maximum likelihood ratio test indicated a significant improved fit of model 2 over model 1 [$X^2(3) = 12.3, p < .01$].

In Table 3, model 1 tested the univariate logistic regression association of the group membership variable and change in coping skills from pretest to posttest. SS group participants were 2.14 times more likely to improve or maintain positive skills than AI group participants at an almost significant level ($p < .09$). The maximum likelihood ratio test indicated an improved fit over the null model of no association at a level approaching significance [$X^2(1) = 2.87, p < .08$]. Prior incarcerations, the only confounding variable that resulted in a more than 10 percent change in estimate of the group membership variable, was entered in model 2. Model 2 indicates that SS group participants were 2.83 times more likely to improve their coping skills than AI group participants. Those who had a greater number of prior incarcerations were less likely to

Table 2. Correlates of Improving or Maintaining Safer Sex Practices (*N* = 100)

Model and Variables	Estimated Log Odds	SE	Estimated Odds Ratio	*p*
Model 1: Exposure variable only (experimental versus control group)[a]				
Constant	0.521	0.289		
Experimental group	0.366	0.429	1.44	.39
Model 2: Exposure variable and confounders[b]				
Constant	0.993	0.413		
Experimental group	1.389	0.794	3.83	.09
Number of sessions attended	−0.119	0.808	0.89	.11
Marital status				
Married	−1.473	0.625	0.229	.02
Separated or divorced	0.779	0.702	2.18	.26

[a]−2 log likelihood = 125.3. Model improvement from null model = .73, *df* = 1, *p* < .30.

[b]−2 log likelihood = 113.034. Model improvement from model 1 = 12.3, *df* = 3, *p* < .01.

Table 3. Correlates of Improving or Maintaining Coping Skills (*N* = 101)

Model and Variables	Estimated Log Odds	SE	Estimated Odds Ratio	*p*
Model 1: Exposure variable only (experimental versus control group)[a]				
Constant	−1.239	0.342		
Experimental group	0.762	0.455	2.14	.09
Model 2: Exposure variable and confounders[b]				
Constant	−1.034	0.371		
Experimental group	1.043	0.472	2.83	.02
Number of times previously incarcerated	−0.029	0.025	0.97	.25

[a]−2 log likelihood = 114.745. Model improvement from null model = 2.87, *df* = 1, *p* < .08.

[b]−2 log likelihood = 105.219. Model improvement from model 1 = 9.53, *df* = 1, *p* < .00.

improve their coping skills, but not at a significant level. The maximum likelihood ratio test indicated a significantly improved fit over the null model of no association [$X^2(1) = 9.53$, $p < .00$].

In Table 4, model 1 tested the univariate logistic regression association of the variable and change in perceived emotional support from pretest to posttest. SS group participants were 2.3 times more likely to improve their emotional support from pretest to posttest than AI group participants. The maximum likeli-hood ratio test indicated a significantly improved fit over the null model of no association [$X^2(1) = 3.94$, $p < .04$]. Number of prior incarcerations, which was again the only confounding variable resulting in a more than 10 percent change in estimate of the intervention variable, was entered into model 2. In model 2, those in the SS group were 2.71 times more likely to improve their emotional support from pretest to posttest than those in the AI group. Number of prior incarcerations, however, had a reverse effect with this outcome: Those who

Table 4. Correlates of Improving or Maintaining Emotional Support (N = 101)

Model and Variables	Estimated Log Odds	SE	Estimated Odds Ratio	p
Model 1: Exposure variable only (experimental versus control group)[a]				
Constant	0.154	0.278		
Experimental group	0.836	0.427	2.31	.05
Model 2: Exposure variable and confounders[b]				
Constant	−0.203	0.335		
Experimental group	0.996	0.459	2.71	.03
Number of times previously incarcerated	0.043	0.028	1.04	.13

[a] −2 log likelihood = 127.85. Model improvement from null model = 3.94, $df = 1$, $p < .04$.

[b] −2 log likelihood = 114.28. Model improvement from model 1 = 13.57, $df = 1$, $p < .00$.

had more previous incarcerations were more likely to report improving their emotional support, although not at a significant level. The maximum likelihood ratio test indicated a significant improved fit over model 1 [$X^2(1) = 3.57, p < .00$].

DISCUSSION

The results of this pilot study lend some support to the hypothesis that a skills-building and social support enhancement intervention is more effective than AIDS information alone in facilitating safer sex behavior, coping skills, and direct emotional support. These findings are consistent with other studies supporting the efficacy of skills-building and social support enhancement approaches (El-Bassel & Schilling, 1992; Kelly et al., 1989; Malow, Corrigan, Pena, Calkins, & Bannister, 1992; Schilling et al., 1991). Beyond these encouraging, if relatively modest, observed outcomes, the process of conducting this novel pilot study confirmed the feasibility of implementing a brief skills-building intervention for drug-using women in the context of a jail setting.

Participation was high, and the intervention was well received by participants and jail staff. Follow-up rates were adequate, especially considering the multiple difficulties of tracking this population. We were able to maneuver successfully through numerous logistic, political, and ethical barriers cited by others as potential impediments to implementing HIV prevention programs in prison (Baxter, 1991; Stevens, 1993).

As expected, no difference was found between SS and AI groups with respect to AIDS knowledge. Contrary to our expectations, however, there was no significant difference between the SS and AI groups in perception of vulnerability to AIDS or sexual self-efficacy. These results, although disappointing, are consonant with other studies (Gibson, Lovelle-Drache, Young, & Sorensen, 1991; McCusker, Stoddard, Zapka, & Lewis, 1993; McCusker et al., 1992) that have not found substantial differences between skills-building and informational approaches in improving safer sex behaviors and attitudes among drug users over time.

Consistent with previous evidence on female inmates (Temple, 1993; Weisfuse et al., 1991), the HIV-related risk profile of this sample was high. For example, less than one-fifth of the sexually active women reported using condoms during vaginal sex with regular partners one month before arrest, and about one-quarter of the sample reported exchanging sex for money or drugs one month before arrest.

Despite these risk factors, more than half of these women believed that they had little or no chance of getting AIDS. The discrepancy between perceived and actual risk found among this sample is consistent with findings of other individuals who engage in high-risk behaviors but do not perceive themselves as being at risk (Kalichman, Hunter, & Kelly, 1992; Memon, 1991; Wettrich, 1993). The failure of the SS intervention to significantly increase perception of risk may be due to intervention strength, measurement error, or inability to detect significant differences in a small sample. Alternatively, our finding of no observed effect may reflect the reality that HIV risk issues are less salient for this population than are the more immediate problems of housing, regaining child custody, and basic daily survival. The SS intervention had a significant effect in improving safer sex practices after adjusting for confounding factors without significantly increasing perception of risk. These paradoxical findings seem to challenge a central tenet of the health belief model (Janz & Becker, 1984; Rosenstock, 1974).

The lack of group membership effect on increasing sexual efficacy may also be due to measurement error. It is possible, however, that any intervention gain in sexual self-efficacy may be delayed until participants have sufficient opportunity to practice safer sex negotiation and condom use skills in the community rather than in the simulated situations in jail. Community-based booster sessions may directly bolster sexual self-efficacy and help participants generalize and transfer skills by working through the myriad problems they confront after release. Analyzing follow-up results from the 6–, 12–, and 18–month measurements in the full-scale trial will yield data to assess the relative effect of the intervention and booster sessions on acquisition and maintenance of sexual self-efficacy and other desired outcomes. Such data will be helpful in determining the most efficient mix of initial incarceration-based and community transfer and maintenance strategies with this population.

Women with more incarcerations were more likely to drop out of the study after pretest and less likely to improve their coping skills, albeit not at a significant level. These preliminary findings suggest that women with multiple incarcerations may be less motivated or less able to change their behavior. Married or common law and single participants also differed in treatment response with respect to

safer sex behavior change: Women in legal or common law marriages were significantly less likely to increase safer sex behavior. Analyses of future follow-up data will reveal the extent to which obstacles to change in these subgroups merit tailoring an intervention to their specific interpersonal skill deficiencies and situational demands.

Several limitations must be considered in interpreting these results. As in most research on HIV-related behavior, this study relied on self-reported sexual behavior. Confidentiality assurances and private interviewing conditions were used to minimize response bias, and other studies have established the validity and reliability of similar HIV risk behavior self-report procedures (Coates et al., 1988; Kelly et al., 1992). Nonetheless, biological markers, such as sexually transmitted disease incidence, are needed to corroborate findings in future studies. Although efforts were made to minimize contamination across conditions in this study, it is possible that participants in the enhanced intervention shared their experiences from the group with control participants, thus diluting the observable effect of the skills-building intervention. About one-fifth of the skills-building participants attended three or fewer sessions and thus received the same or less intervention time as the AIDS information group. Although there were no differences between those who dropped out and those who were retained on outcome variables at pretest, participant attrition from pretest to intervention and follow-up may have biased outcome results. Finally, the generalizabilty of these results is limited by the small, nonrandomly selected sample.

Notwithstanding these limitations, the findings of this pilot study may help in developing and implementing future HIV risk reduction efforts with incarcerated women. First, the sexual behavior of these women is diverse: Some are not sexually active, some are exchanging sex for money or drugs and have multiple partners, and some are bisexuals or lesbians. Any intervention should address this range of sexual activities, and didactic and interactive role play material should address HIV prevention issues related to woman-to-woman as well as heterosexual sex. Second, the findings suggest that the skills-building and social support enhancement approach may be more efficacious than an AIDS information approach with respect to improving safer sex behavior, coping behavior, and social support. The extent to which these gains will be maintained over time remains a critical issue to be addressed in future follow-up studies.

Third, it appears that marital status and number of previous incarcerations influenced treatment response. Future research—exploratory, developmental, and interventive—will lead to sound, empirically derived intervention strategies designed for the specific needs of married women and women with histories of repeated incarcerations. Fourth, women in the skills-building and social support enhancement group improved their safer sex practices without increasing their perception of vulnerability to AIDS, possibly raising questions about the importance of perceived susceptibility to AIDS in promoting safer sex behavior. Although some studies have suggested a strong association between perceived susceptibility and safer sex behavior (Aspinwall, Kemeny, Taylor, Schneider, & Dudley, 1991; Yep, 1993), others have failed to find a clear relationship between these two variables (Eversley et al., 1993; Malow et al., 1992; Schilling, El-Bassel, Gilbert, & Glassman, 1993).

Finally, this study raises questions about the salience and temporal importance of sexual self-efficacy in safer sex behavior change. We look forward to analyzing future data in hopes of providing some answers to these questions.

REFERENCES

Aspinwall, L. G., Kemeny, M. E., Taylor, S. E., Schneider, S. G., & Dudley, J. P. (1991). Psychosocial predictors of gay men's AIDS risk-reduction behavior. *Health Psychology, 10,* 432–444.

Bandura, A. (1989). Perceived self-efficacy in the exercise of control over AIDS infection. In V. M. Mays, G. W. Albee, & S. F. Schneider (Eds.), *Primary prevention of AIDS* (pp. 128–141). Newbury Park, CA: Sage Publications.

Baxter, S. (1991). AIDS education in the jail setting. *Crime and Delinquency, 37,* 48–63.

Brewer, T. F., & Derrickson, J. (1992). AIDS in prison: A review of epidemiology and preventive policy. *AIDS, 6,* 623–628.

Centers for Disease Control. (1989). Update: Heterosexual transmission of acquired immunodeficiency syndrome and human immunodeficiency virus infection—United States. *Journal of the American Medical Association, 262,* 463–471.

Coates, R. A., Calzavara, L. M., Soskolne, C. L., Read, S. E., Fanning, M. M., Shephard, F. A., Klein, M. H., & Johnson, J. K. (1988). Validity of sexual histories on a prospective study of male sexual contacts of men with AIDS or an AIDS-related condition. *American Journal of Epidemiology, 128,* 719–728.

Des Jarlais, D. C., Choopanya, K., Fischer, J., Lima, E., Friedman, P., & Friedman, S. R. (1993, June). *Cross cultural similarities in AIDS risk reduction among injecting drug users* (Abstract WS-DO9–3). Paper presented at the Ninth International Conference on AIDS in affiliation with the Fourth STD World Congress, Berlin.

Des Jarlais, D. C., Friedman, S. R., & Strug, D. (1986). AIDS and needle-sharing within the IV drug use subculture. In F. D. Johnson (Ed.), *The social dimensions of AIDS: Methods and theory* (pp. 111–125). New York: Praeger.

D'Zurilla, T. J., & Goldfried, M. R. (1971). Problem solving and behavior modification. *Journal of Abnormal Psychology, 78,* 107–126.

El-Bassel, N., & Schilling, R. F. (1992). 15–month follow-up of women methadone patients taught to reduce heterosexual HIV transmission. *Public Health Reports, 107,* 500–503.

El-Bassel, N., & Schilling, R. F. (1993). *The coping skills questionnaire (CASK).* Unpublished manuscript, Columbia University, New York.

Eversley, R. B., Newstetter, A., Avins, A., Beirnes, D., Haynes-Sanstad, K., & Hearst, N. (1993). Sexual risk and perception of risk for HIV infection among multiethnic family planning clients. *American Journal of Preventive Medicine, 9,* 92–95.

Fraser, M., & Hawkins, J. D. (1984). Social network analysis and drug misuse. *Social Service Review, 58,* 81–97.

Froland, C., Pancoast, D., Chapman, N., & Kimboko, P. (1981). *Helping networks and human services.* Beverly Hills, CA: Sage Publications.

Gibson, D. R., Lovelle-Drache, J., Young, M., & Sorensen, J. L. (1991, June). *Does brief counseling reduce HIV risk in IV drug users? Final results from a randomized clinical trial* (Abstract Th.D. 59). Paper presented at the Seventh International Conference on AIDS, Florence, Italy.

Graham, N., & Wish, E. D. (1994). Drug use among female arrestees: Onset, patterns, and relationships to prostitution. *Journal of Drug Issues, 24,* 315–329.

Hawkins, J. D., & Fraser, M. W. (1983). Social support networks in treating drug abuse. In J. K. Whittaker & J. Garbarino (Eds.), *Social support networks: Informal helping in the human services* (pp. 357–380). Hawthorne, NY: Aldine de Gruyter.

Hosmer, D. W., & Lemeshow, S. (1989). *Applied logistic regression.* New York: John Wiley & Sons.

Janz, N. K., & Becker, M. H. (1984). The health belief model: A decade later. *Health Education Quarterly, 11,* 1–47.

Kalichman, S. C., Hunter, T. L., & Kelly, J. A. (1992). Perceptions of AIDS susceptibility among minority and nonminority women at risk for HIV infection. *Journal of Consulting and Clinical Psychology, 60,* 725–732.

Kelly, J. A., Murphy, D. A., Sikkema, J. K., & Kalichman, S. C. (1993). Psychological interventions to prevent HIV infection are urgently needed. *American Psychologist, 48,* 1023–1034.

Kelly, J. A., St. Lawrence, J. S., Hood, H. V., & Brasfield, T. L. (1989). Behavioral intervention to reduce AIDS risk activities. *Journal of Consulting and Clinical Psychology, 57,* 60–67.

Kelly, J. A., St. Lawrence, J. S., Stevenson, Y., Hauth, A. C., Kalichman, S. C., Diaz, Y. E., Brasfield, T. L., Koob, J. J., & Morgan, M. G. (1992). Community AIDS/HIV risk reduction: The effects of endorsements by popular people in three cities. *American Journal of Public Health, 82,* 1483–1489.

Lazarus, A. A. (1971). *Behavior therapy and beyond.* New York: McGraw-Hill.

Levine, O. H., Britton, P. J., James, T. C., Jackson, A. P., Hobfoll, S. E., & Lavin, J. P. (1993). The empowerment of women: A key to HIV prevention. *Journal of Community Psychology, 21,* 320–334.

Malow, R. M., Corrigan, S. A., Pena, J. M., Calkins, A. M., & Bannister, T. M. (1992). Effectiveness of a psychoeducational approach to HIV risk behavior reduction. *Psychology of Addictive Behaviors, 6,* 120–125.

McCusker, J., Stoddard, A. M., Zapka, J. G., & Lewis, B. F. (1993). Behavioral outcomes of AIDS educational interventions for drug users in short-term treatment. *American Journal of Public Health, 83,* 163–165.

McCusker, J., Stoddard, A. M., Zapka, J. G., Morrison, C. S., Zorn, M., & Lewis, J. (1992). AIDS education for drug abusers. *American Journal of Public Health, 82,* 533–540.

Meichenbaum, D. H. (1972). Cognitive modification of testanxious college students. *Journal of Consulting and Clinical Psychology, 39,* 370–380.

Memon, A. (1991). Perceptions of AIDS vulnerability: The role of attributions and social context. In P. Aggleton, G. Hart, & P. Davies (Eds.), *AIDS responses, interventions and care* (pp. 157–168). London: Falcon Press.

Nezu, A., & D'Zurilla. T. (1981). Effects of problem and formulation of the generation of alternatives in the social problem-solving process. *Cognitive Therapy and Research, 5,* 265–271.

Nurco, D., Stephenson, T., & Hanlon, T. E. (1991). Aftercare/relapse prevention and the self-help movement. *International Journal of the Addictions, 25,* 1179–1200.

O'Leary, A. (1985). Self-efficacy and health. *Behavior Research and Therapy, 23,* 437–451.

Platt, J., Taube, D. O., Metzger, D. S., & Duome, M. J. (1988). Training in interpersonal problem solving (TIPS). *Journal of Community Psychology, 2,* 5–34.

Rhoads, D. L. (1983). A longitudinal study of life stress and social support among drug abusers. *International Journal of the Addictions, 18,* 195–222.

Rosenstock, I. M. (1974). Historical origins of the health belief model. *Health Education Monograph, 2,* 328–335.

Rotheram-Borus, M. J., & Koopman, C. (1991). Sexual risk behaviors, AIDS knowledge, and belief about AIDS among runaways. *American Journal of Public Health, 81,* 208–211.

Schilling, R. F., El-Bassel, N., Gilbert, L., & Glassman, M. (1993). Predictors of changes in sexual behavior among women on methadone. *American Journal of Drug and Alcohol Abuse, 19,* 409–422.

Schilling, R. F., El-Bassel, N., Schinke, S. P., Gordon, K., & Nichols, S. (1991). Building skills of recovering women drug users to reduce heterosexual AIDS transmission. *Public Health Reports, 106,* 297–304.

Schilling, R. F., Ivanoff, A., El-Bassel, N., & Borne, D. (1993). *Project WORTH: Women on the Road to Recovery* [Unpublished intervention manual]. (Available from Columbia University, School of Social Work, 622 West 113th Street, New York, NY 10025)

Simon, B. L. (1994). *The empowerment tradition in American social work.* New York: Columbia University Press.

Stevens, S. (1993). HIV prevention in a jail setting: Educational strategies. *Prison Journal, 3,* 379–390.

Temple, M. T. (1993). Patterns of sexuality in a high-risk sample: Results from a survey of new inmates at a county jail. *Archives of Sexual Behavior, 22,* 111–129.

U.S. Department of Health and Human Services. (1992). HIV prevention in the U.S. correctional system. *Morbidity and Mortality Weekly Report, 41,* 391.

Valdiserri, R. O., Arena. V. C., Proctor, D., & Bonati, F. A. (1989). The relationship between women's attitudes about condoms and their use: Implications for condom promotion programs. *American Journal of Public Health, 79,* 499–501.

VanHoeven, K. H., Stoneburner, R. L., & Rooney, W. C. (1991). Drug use among NYC prison inmates: A demographic study with temporal trends. *International Journal of the Addictions, 26,* 1089–1105.

Weisfuse, I. B., Greenberg, B. L., Back, S. D., Makki, H. A., Thomas, P., Rooney, W. C., &

Rautenberg, E. L. (1991). HIV-?? infection among New York City inmates, *AIDS, 5,* 1133–1138.

Wettrich, M. (1993, June). *Perception of risk for HIV/AIDS, self-efficacy for behavior change and sexual behaviors among STD clinic clients* (Abstract PO-D23–4121). Paper presented at the Ninth International Conference on AIDS in affiliation with the Fourth STD World Congress, Berlin.

Wills, T. A. (1982). *Basic processes in helping relationships.* New York: Academic Press.

Yep, G. A. (1993). Health beliefs and HIV prevention: Do they predict monogamy and condom use? *Journal of Social Behavior and Personality, 8,* 507–520.

The contributions of Barbara Grodd are acknowledged. This research was funded by grant DA 7059 awarded to Robert Schilling and André Ivanoff by the National Institute on Drug Abuse.

Original manuscript received August 25, 1994
Final revision received February 1, 1995
Accepted February 22, 1995

8

Single-Subject Designs

Research in social work and the other helping professions can have a variety of purposes. One is to examine ideas or theories about individual human behavior; another is to examine the interventions that social workers and other human service professionals use in helping individuals, families, groups, or organizations to change. Most researchers study groups of people for these purposes. However, there is one type of fixed method research, termed single-subject or single-system design, which uses the intensive, prospective study of single cases over time to examine how they may change when interventions are made or to learn more about human behavior in general by studying what can make it change in an individual. Single-subject research of this kind is often described in the social work literature as using a practitioner-researcher or practitioner-scientist model, which enables the individual social work professional to function as both helper and investigator at the same time. Although Manicas and Secord (1983) do not discuss single-subject designs, fallibilistic realism is as useful in understanding the strengths and limitations of single-subject research as it is for group designs.

Single-subject research as a method was developed by behavioral psychologists as a way to study the effectiveness of various techniques for producing behavior change in individuals (Barlow, Hayes, & Nelson 1984). Behavioral theory has traditionally posited that behavior is shaped most strongly by its immediate antecedent and consequent contexts and that observable behaviors rather than the feelings and motivations that may accompany them are the most important aspects of a person to consider. Using this theoretical framework, interventions, and the changes associated with them thus could be studied over relatively short periods of time by observing and recording the specific behaviors of an individual before and after an intervention designed to change the behavior was made, looking for patterns of change that coincided with when specific interventions had occurred.

The logic of single-subject designs thus shares several features with group experimental designs. First of all, there is a manipulation, intervention, or treatment done that is posited to produce a change in some predefined phenomenon or characteristic(s) of the individual. In addition, there is a comparison made; that is, one or more prespecified characteristics of an individual are observed, and the observations made before and after the intervention is introduced are compared. In fact, because of these features, single-subject designs are most often compared to group experiments and, like them, are frequently used in the study of treatment effectiveness.

Single-subject designs also share something with longitudinal methods of research in that a case is followed over time and repeated measurements of the same behaviors or characteristics are made. It is a prospective method of study; observation begins before the treatment or manipulation does, and the assessment of change is made by comparing what is observed when the treatment is present to what is observed without the treatment being present.

Rather than compare groups of clients to each other, however, single-subject design uses a *case-control* method in which the participant in the research serves as his or her own "control." The term "control" in this context has a meaning similar to its meaning in group experiments: a method for making a comparison under equivalent circumstances.

Single-subject research differs from other fixed methods of research discussed in several essential ways. First of all, it is designed and developed for the intensive study of individual cases one at a time. The *case-control* method is substituted for the control group method for reducing ambiguity in drawing conclusions from comparisons. In experiments using control groups, the method is designed to produce two (or more) groups of people who are equivalent through randomization. As in one group, pre- and posttest experimental designs, in single-subject designs the same aspects of behavior are observed in the same circumstances over time, a change is introduced into those circumstances in the form of a planned intervention, and then the observations made before and after the change are compared. However, in single-subject designs, behavior is studied in only one person or one case although multiple observations pre- and postintervention are made. The case or person studied, the person doing both the studying and the intervening, and the focus of the observation remain the same throughout.

In addition, traditional group experiments depend on comparing group averages before and after or with and without treatment. Aggregating information from groups can mask considerable variability in how individuals within the treatment or control group have fared, whatever the outcome for the group as a whole. Clinical practitioners are often most intensely interested not in how a treatment will work "on average" but on how it will work for a specific individual. Single-subject studies are designed to answer just such questions: What changes can be observed in an individual or in a particular case when a specific intervention is introduced?

Group experimental designs also depend on being able to collect sufficient numbers of comparable cases and control group members for the research, and it often requires access to a very large number of potential cases in order to recruit an adequate sample with the required characteristics. Single-subject designs proceed with just one case. However, as in experiments, the selection criteria for the study must be clearly specified, and the individual participant in a single-subject study is often carefully selected based on specified characteristics that make him or her a useful case in which to examine the research question guiding the study.

An additional way in which single-system designs differ from other research methods is their use of the practitioner-researcher model. The practitioner-researcher model posits that the practitioner shall function as the scientist, deciding how research to evaluate practice should be conducted, the relevant dimensions of the case, and the treatment process to assess. In addition, by developing a model for evaluation that is more feasible for the individual practitioner to employ than the group experiment, it is hoped that social workers and human service professionals will begin to produce more practitioners who actually do research and who are more regularly guided in their practice by the results of evaluation research.

The ideal of the "scientist-practitioner" undergirds education in all the helping professions, and single-subject research designs have been advanced by many in social work as a means to achieve better education for and research about practice. Debates in social work about the wisdom of the practitioner-researcher model and about some of the ethical and practical issues it raises are still ongoing (Bloom & Orma 1993; Corcoran 1993; Nelson 1994; Rosen 1996; Thomas 1978). Although some have observed, for example, that the practitioner is hardly a disinterested observer of the outcome of his or her own work, fallibilistic realism posits that theoretical perspective and the investigator's standpoint are influences in all kinds of research. As in practice, then, or in traditions of flexible method research, bias regulation is to be accomplished through bias recognition (Heineman Pieper 1989; Tyson 1992).

Because of their relative feasibility, single-system designs are thought by many in the social work profession to have promise for producing research on practice effectiveness and for making evaluation research and the generation of knowledge more feasible for the average practitioner. They are certainly among the most useful designs available for answering questions about the effects of interventions on single individuals or cases and for using studies of individual cases from practice to examine theories about how people respond to specific efforts to help them.

Single-Subject Research Designs

Single-subject designs have not previously been defined from the perspective of fallibilistic realism. Single-subject designs are classified as a form of fixed method research because the standpoint of the researcher, the focus of observation, and the methods of observation are all defined in advance of making the observations and remain fixed throughout the conduct of the study.

As in many group experiments—in single-subject designs the researcher enters the observational field and typically, after a period of time, introduces an intervention, then continuing the observational process after the intervention has been made. However, unlike in flexible method research, the focus and nature of the observations made do not typically change during the course of the study based on results from it. Thus, if any additional, spontaneous observations are made, these are characterized as the addition of a flexible or qualitative component to an otherwise fixed or quantitative method of study (see, for example, Nugent 1991).

In fact, the sequence of observing, acting, and then observing may be repeated more than once in the course of a single-subject study. The scope of the observation, however, is limited to one individual or entity. Theories about the individual's behavior and/or the expected effects of the intervention to be tried guide the selection of the intervention, the planning of the observations to be made, and the conclusions drawn from what was observed.

All single-system research designs share several distinctive features. As the name suggests, the focus of study is a *single case*. It should be noted, however, that the single case, or system, while normally referring to an individual person, can also be conceptualized as a couple or dyad, a group, a family, an organization, or a community if the intervention is designed for a collectivity of that kind. For example, research on the outcomes of family therapy is no further developed than that on psychotherapy, and single-case research designs hold promise for that field as well (Rabin 1981). Group treatment can be studied by examining the group as a whole or by tracking the progress of individual group members concurrently (Edelson, Miller, Stone, & Chapman 1985). However, single-subject designs are most often used for the study of individuals.

The logic of single-subject designs is not based on the idea of generalizing from a sample to a population as descriptive and relational studies do. Rather, like experiments, they depend for their credibility on the internal logic of the design and on the theories used to make sense of the observations made. Like experiments, then, they also depend on replication, or repetition of the same study with different cases, for generating support for the theories and propositions they advance. However, results of the replications are not aggregated but rather presented alongside one another in order to determine whether results are consistent or inconsistent across individual cases.

Types of Single-Subject Studies

Single-subject research is a prospective, time-series method that uses repeated measures. Conclusions are drawn about the effects of treatment on the case studied based on continuing assessments of the same characteristics or phenomena during a *baseline* or pretreatment period *and* during the time that the formal intervention or treatment is being undertaken. By convention, the baseline or "no treatment" period is labeled "A" and the treatment period is labeled "B." Analysis of the data is undertaken to determine whether or not there was a change in the assessed characteristic(s) between the baseline and treatment periods of study.

As in all research, the design of a single-subject study must take into account from the beginning what data analysis is planned. In the case of single-subject

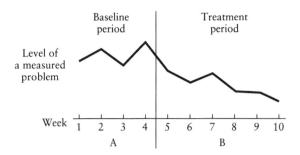

Figure 8–1 The A/B Single-Subject Design with Hypothetical Data

research, the first problem that must be considered is the length of the baseline period. In order to determine whether or not an intervention has changed a problem, it is necessary to have an accurate assessment of the problem as it was before treatment. In single-subject research, the baseline period must be long enough to develop a reliable picture of the problem as it existed before treatment. If the problem fluctuates little, a short baseline period with only 3 or 4 data points may be sufficient; if it seems to fluctuate substantially, more data points will be necessary to capture the natural range of variation in the problem accurately. Sometimes retrospective assessment may be used to establish a sufficient number of baseline data points, especially when there is some urgency to initiating treatment because of the nature of the problem and when the nature of the problem is concrete enough to permit reasonably accurate recall. For example, it is not ethically acceptable to ask a client who may be dangerous to him- or herself or others to wait to begin treatment simply to accumulate adequate baseline data for research; in the Edelson et al. (1985) study of group treatment for men who batter, therefore, retrospective rather than prospective data on battering incidents were collected so that treatment could begin right away. However, in general, retrospective data are not considered as accurate and reliable as data collected prospectively as they are during the treatment period.

Documenting a difference in the phenomenon of interest in the treatment period as compared to the baseline period of study is essential to the logic of single-subject studies. Although demonstrating such a difference is necessary for making the argument that introducing an intervention was related to the change observed, it is not sufficient. As in group experiments, alternative explanations for the observed change must also be ruled out. As with group experiments, many of the design elaboration in single-system research are employed to try to do just that.

A scientifically skeptical thinker will bear in mind that any change observed in a single-subject experiment could have occurred without the intervention for any one of a variety of reasons. As with group experimenters, two other possibilities are inherent in the passage of time itself. Observed changes could result from maturation, or the unfolding of ongoing developmental processes. They could also result from the influence of some event in the contexts of the study's participants but external to the focus of the study, termed a history effect. Other possibilities seen in group experiments can occur, such as the effects of repeated measuring or drift in how phenomena are evaluated over time, confounding results that can be attributed to the intervention itself with changes in the assessments themselves. Even regression to the mean can occur or the natural tendency of extremely low or extremely high scores to not be observed again.

One safeguard against these alternative explanations for change is to have a baseline period long enough in which to establish a stable picture of the phenomenon of interest. If repeated assessments of the phenomenon—a specific behavior or affect, for example—are essentially the same throughout a baseline period of observation, it is harder to argue that these competing explanations, or confounds, explain any subsequent change that occurs in the treatment period. Trends due to maturation or regression to the mean, for example, if present, would likely be seen during such a baseline period because scores would be changing during that time. However, while extending the baseline period helps, it is still possible to assert that a maturational, historical, or measurement change took place exactly coincident with the implementation of the intervention being studied and not before.

There are many varieties of single-subject designs used in an effort to eliminate alternative explanations for results observed. These designs vary according to whether or not they are termed experimental (utilizing a withdrawal or reversal period), whether or not multiple baselines are used, whether or not multiple measures of different problems or outcomes are incorporated, and whether single, multiple or changing intensity treatments are incorporated and assessed (Bloom, Fischer, & Orne 1995).

Single-subject experiments. Some single-system designs may include a withdrawal or reversal period: After the treatment has begun to take effect, it is stopped to see if the problem then reverts to its baseline level (A/B/A) and then often reinstituted (A/B/A/B) to see if the initial treatment effect can be reproduced. These designs are termed single-subject experiments because the reversal or withdrawal period is meant to serve as a "control" or no treatment condition comparable in function to the control group used in group experiments. The logic behind these designs is simple: If it is the treatment or manipulation that "causes" the change observed between baseline and treatment periods, when the treatment is stopped, continuing observation will show that there will be another change back to things as they were during the baseline or pretreatment phase of the study.

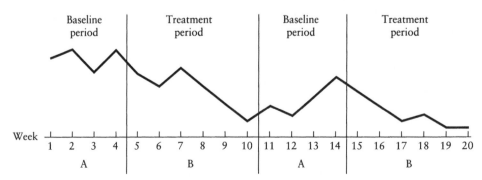

Figure 8–2 The A/B/A/B Single-Subject Design with Hypothetical Data

If the observed change were due to some other explanation, like maturation or the other alternatives described above, stopping the treatment would not result in any additional change because maturation (or some other "cause" or confound) would still be continuing. The prediction is that observations made during a withdrawal period will resemble those made in the baseline period.

Because single-subject designs are so often used to study treatments that are designed to be beneficial to clients, in single-subject experiments the treatment is generally restarted or reinstituted again after the withdrawal phase is over while observations continue (A/B/A/B design). Resumption of the treatment is expected to be associated with an additional change back to observations like those made during the first treatment period. Each time changes in the ongoing observations made of the study participant can be shown to covary in time with changes in the presence or absence of the intervention being studied, the argument that the two are related to each other is strengthened.

Most psychosocial interventions have as their goal, of course, that clients will ultimately be able to maintain positive changes without treatment. Therefore studies of the effects of treatment that assume that any positive effects of treatment might disappear once treatment were withdrawn are generally conducted at the beginning of a course of treatment. An analogy might be drawn to antibiotic treatment of a bacterial infection: At the beginning an antibiotic is needed and an infection will worsen again if the medicine is withdrawn shortly after it has been started. If the medicine has been taken long enough, however, in an otherwise healthy person the infection will not be likely to return even when treatment ends. For this reason, single-subject designs must be planned so that baseline, treatment, withdrawal, and re-treatment periods all occur in fairly rapid succession near the beginning of a course of treatment so variation in client response can realistically be expected.

The inclusion of withdrawal periods in single-subject designs, like the use of control or "no treatment" groups in experiments, always raises some concerns about ethical issues. While this issue is discussed in depth in the chapter on ethics in research, it should be noted here that seeing what happens during a brief cessation of treatment can affirm for both client and therapist that a chosen course of treatment indeed is working well. If it is not, it is important to know that, too, so a new and better one may be tried. In sum, as in group experiments, single-subject research as opposed to an unvarying treatment approach is only appropriately used when there is an open question about whether or not a given technique will be useful with a particular client or for a particular kind of problem.

Multiple baseline designs. Sometimes a multiple- or staggered-baseline approach is used in single-system designs to help rule out testing, history, and maturation as alternative explanations for any change observed. Multiple-baseline designs can be used with a single case when multiple problems exist. Each of the several problems is assessed simultaneously, and the intervention is first targeted to one of the problems. It is expected that the one problem should then change while the others do not; they in turn should change only when interventions targeted specifically to them are subsequently introduced. Multiple-baseline designs are also useful when more than

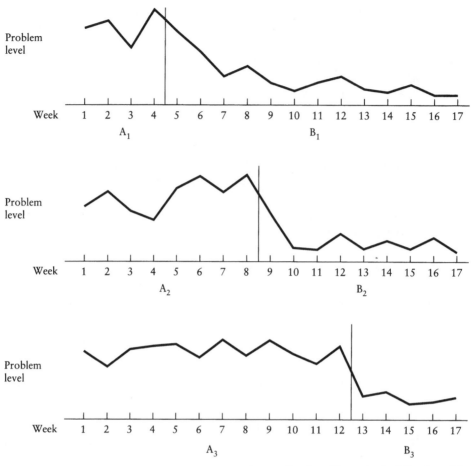

Figure 8–3 Example of a Multiple Baseline Single-Subject Hypothetical Study, with Different Baseline Periods for Different Problems or Clients

one similar case is being studied. If the intervention is applied at different points in time to different people, the change in outcomes can be shown to correspond in time to the implementation. Note that all participants are observed for the same or similar periods of time prior to the beginning of the intervention period. History, maturation or testing effects would likely occur at the same time or in the same way across individuals rather than at different times corresponding to when the intervention was implemented in each case. Thus the argument that it was the intervention and not some other factor that is associated with any changes observed is strengthened.

Sometimes multiple treatments or interventions may be employed with a single case, either because the initial treatment was not successful or because the several problems being assessed (multiple baselines) may require differing interventions. Such an additional treatment is typically labelled "C" (or "D" or "E" as numbers mount). An A/B/A/C or A/B/C/A/C design might easily be imagined. Thus single-subject designs can be made quite complex, lending themselves to the examination of complex or staged models of treatment.

Interaction effects

One major question in the logic of single-subject designs remains: How can the effects of treatment be untangled from the effects of studying that treatment? Did the treatment used interact with the study of that treatment to produce the changes observed? The truth is that there is no way within any single study of treatment to make this separation of "causes" of change; if effectiveness is found, it is effectiveness due to treatment-coupled-with-study-of-the-treatment. Only replication of the treatment under different study conditions can suggest that it is not the study activities but the treatment activities that made the difference. However, the general condition of "study" still remains, raising the possibility of what is termed the "placebo" effect. This paradox exists in all forms of evaluation research and is not unique to single-system design.

Specifying Outcomes and Interventions

As in all flexible method research, specification and assessment of the behaviors, feelings, or problems that the treatment can be expected to change is essential to single-system designs. Theory, past research, previous clinical experience and observation, and the client's presenting complaint may all be used as guides in selecting the focus for assessment. Clinical theory in particular may be useful as a guide not only to the relevant outcomes to assess but also to the interventions needed to meet the target problem(s) and to what may be expected in response to a given course of treatment. In fact, single-subject designs, like group experiments, may be designed as much to test theoretical propositions about treatment as to answer pragmatic ones about what will work with a specific client.

As in any kind of study of treatment processes or outcomes, specification and assessment of the interventions used is also essential to single-system designs (Nelson 1985). Informed use by readers and replications by other investigators are only possible when the intervention itself has been well documented. Single-subject studies are often notable for the care with which the intervention being studied is described. However, as in any human interaction, what the practitioner experiences him- or herself as doing and what is actually being done may not exactly correspond. When the researcher and the practitioner are one and the same person, observation and self-examination are as important with respect to the actual nature of the treatment being implemented as in documenting client outcomes.

An Example of Single-Subject Design

A recent study reported by Richey and Hodges (1992) illustrates how single-subject designs can be effectively used even by a student for evaluating practice. The study begins with a review of the literature on family caregiving for frail elders and the kinds of burdens that such caregivers often experience. Respite care, or the use of limited amounts of professional help for the purpose of relieving strain on a family caregiver, is the intervention recommended and studied.

The caregiver in the case studied was a 69-year-old daughter who lived with and cared for her 99-year-old mother, who had several cognitive and physical difficulties. The focal problems for the caregiver were: (1) her feelings of entrapment, including her lack of freedom to leave her home, and (2) her resentment toward her mother because of it, which represented a troubling change in her relationship with her mother. The concepts that were measured in the study were directly related to these focal complaints. They were: the amount of time the client spent away from home, the self-reported level of enjoyment she was able to experience during those times, and a standardized scale measuring negative attitudes toward her mother. This standardized scale was one designed for use in single-subject studies, although its use with an adult child and an elderly mother was a new application of the tool. The three areas assessed were all problems delineated in the literature as often being part of the burden of caregiving as well as being focal complaints of the client.

The intervention studied, the use of respite care, was both an emergent, understudied resource in work with the elderly and their caregivers and a form of service acceptable to the client. The program under which this care was made available is well-described in the study report. However, exactly what the respite care worker did while present is not depicted in detail and, in fact, the respite care worker changed during the course of the study.

In addition, the use of respite care was taking place concurrent with twice-weekly case management visits by a social worker; thus the intervention studied was not respite care in isolation but respite care in combination with case management services and client self-assessment as required for the research. The biweekly case management visits served as the occasions for the completion of the scale on attitudes toward the mother by the client and for review of the daily logs kept by the client to record the amount of time she had spent away from home and her level of enjoyment of it.

Unlike the case management component of the intervention, the respite care itself was arranged by but not undertaken by the researcher. Thus this study departs somewhat from the practitioner-researcher model in its purest form. However, case management services and monitoring of the client's self-assessment activities were indeed undertaken by the practitioner-researcher herself.

This single-subject study artfully used the natural vicissitudes of practice in its design. The intervention, respite care, took some time after the start of case management visits to arrange. This period of assessment and waiting for service was used as a baseline period during which self-assessment by the client began. Periods of client assessment and of waiting for services because of eligibility or referral issues are common in practice. Baseline periods of data collection for the purposes of single-subject research are then not periods of a contrived withholding of treatment; rather these naturally occurring periods of study or delay can be put to use for research provided that measurement begins and continues during them.

Although planned as an A/B design, this study became an A/B/A/B design when after several weeks the respite care worker resigned and a new one had to be found, resulting in a week's cessation of service. Client self-assessment continued during this week, resulting in a second baseline or no treatment period. The study then continued for another two weeks once the new worker was in place; this became the second treatment period.

Note that although multiple indicators of the client's problem were used, this study is not a multiple baseline design. The baseline and treatment periods were literally the same for all of them, and there was no prediction that any one variable would change on a timetable different from any other.

The results of the study, displayed graphically, showed that the weekly average hours of time away from home and the levels of enjoyment of them went up when respite care was in place and down when it was not. It is noted, however, that while the client's time away from home increased when respite care was available, her total time away was small and represented only a small fraction of the time that the respite care worker was present. The clients' self-ratings of her negative attitudes toward her mother gradually came down after respite care was instituted, went up again when it was absent, and came down again when it was in place the second time.

Rather than rely entirely on visual display, the authors used the two-standard deviation band approach to data analysis (see data analysis section below). A range of scores expectable during the treatment periods was projected based on a range around the average scores obtained during the initial baseline period. While this approach might be criticized here because the number of data points during baseline was relatively low (2-4), the use of such an approach provides a standard beyond a subjective one against which the amount of change observed between baseline and treatment periods can be assessed. Based on this method, the results showed that many data points outside of the range expected were observed during treatment periods but not during baseline ones. Thus the authors conclude that the presence or absence of the intervention, respite care, was regularly associated with changes in the client's complaints. The general conclusion to be drawn is that the evidence from this case study supports the idea that respite care can reduce particular aspects of caregiver burden.

Elements of Single-Subject Designs

Although single-system designs do not depend on groups of participants as most other designs do, it is useful to consider the usual design elements—sample, data collection, and data analysis—in planning and evaluating them. In particular, techniques for statistical data analysis are different when only one case is used; since the chapters on statistics do not include this material, it is covered in some depth here.

Sampling

Sampling in single-system design is not a question of how to assemble a group for study; rather it is a question of how to select the individual case or cases to study one at a time. As with group designs, it is necessary to specify the *selection criteria* or characteristics that an individual must possess in order to be included in the research. These criteria often involve at a minimum the nature of the problem or complaint that the client has and for which the treatment is designed. When the purpose of a single-subject study includes a larger theoretical component, the selection of the client (and the intervention) must be made logically based on the kind of client and/or problem to be studied that will offer the best lens on the theory in question. For example, Richey and Hodges (1992) show that the client and caregiving situation they studied was very much like the typical caregiver one in the literature: a daughter who was herself elderly caring for a very old and frail mother needing increasing amounts of care. However, they do not explain how (or why) this particular case was selected for study.

When multiple individual clients are to be included in a series of single-subject studies, it must be ensured that the clients are homogeneous with respect to the problem or problems they have and to any other characteristics that might make a difference in how the treatment will work. For example, in the Edelson study of the effectiveness of group treatment for men who batter, only those individuals referred to the group who had physically abused women were included in the study; those who were abusive only verbally were not because it was thought that their problems and the interventions needed to change them were somewhat different (Edelson et al. 1985). However, it is also useful to collect additional demographic and other relevant descriptive data about each client because these may prove useful in trying to interpret outcomes, especially unexpected or unusual ones.

One concern about the practitioner-researcher model is that the interest of the practitioner in showing a positive outcome to the treatment will affect the conduct of the research. One way in which this might happen is in the selection of cases to study or report on. With a sample of one, there is no way to know what a "typical" case is. However, choosing a case for study can be done in ways that are more or less explicit. Unfortunately, many reports of single-subject studies in the social work literature do not report how or why a given case was chosen for study or report.

Because single-subject designs do not aim to generalize from a sample group to a population of interest, replication, or repeating the study with additional cases, is therefore an essential means for demonstrating the generalizability of the results of single-subject studies. Knowing how a case was selected for a study will help inform subsequent ones. When multiple cases are studied and reported on, it is also essential to describe the basis on which they were chosen and the characteristics they had that were both similar to and different from each other.

Data Collection

Data collection issues in single-subject designs are the same as those in other kinds of fixed method studies: deciding what should be measured; how it should be assessed; in what context to assess it; and by whom. Because single-subject designs rely on comparing assessments over time, methods of data collection that stand up to frequent use and repetition must be chosen or developed. Results from the assessment methods chosen must be stable; that is, in the absence of change in the phenomenon, the data collected should not show change. However, they must be sensitive as well; that is, when the phenomenon changes, the data collected must show change too. Some data collection procedures that produce stable results are not sensitive, and some that are sensitive are not stable. Nevertheless, because the passage of time is so central in the logic of single system designs, it is important to develop observational and data collection procedures that have both qualities.

Assessing the independent variable. Most attention and interest in measurement in single-subject designs has been focussed on assessing client problems or outcomes. However, it is equally important to measure the treatment being implemented to ensure that it is in actuality what was intended (Nelson 1985). This point is dramatically illustrated by a single-subject study of the use of a cognitive-behavioral intervention for anger control (Nugent 1991). In this study, qualitative data gathering was used in addition to quantitative; these narrative, self-report data allowed the client to describe both the problem and the treatment in greater depth as she experienced them. While the planned quantitative data analysis suggested that the intervention was successful in reducing incidents of anger or "blowups" by the client, the narrative data revealed that the planned intervention, a triple-column, structured technique for writing down, analyzing, and altering specific thoughts, had been modified by the client within a few days. Instead the client began daily journal writing in unstructured descriptive prose to "write down what I was feeling and thinking about what was going on" (p .7). Thus the intervention planned and what was actually used turned out to be quite different. However, because information was provided in the study about what the nature of the intervention actually turned out to be, the reader can then interpret the results independently and draw his or her own conclusions about which version of the intervention—planned or actual—to credit with the positive outcome.

Assessment of the nature of the intervention can be undertaken in a variety of ways. The Nugent study (1991) used client self-report because the planned intervention was taught to the client during meetings with a mental health professional but implemented by the client at home. If the intervention is itself applied during individual or group meetings with clients, tape-recordings of sessions can be made and, if necessary, transcripts prepared from them for content analysis. If an intervention is implemented in a hospital, at work, or in other settings, it can be monitored in the setting by the client, worker, or other reliable informant.

Unless the intervention is a standardized one, it is unlikely there will be an existing tool for measuring it. Some effort must be invested in designing efficient and reliable ways to document and describe the nature of the treatment as it actually occurred, rather just relying on what was intended. However, when there are preexisting paradigms of treatment, such as the Hollis typology of psychosocial interventions (Hollis & Wood 1981), they should be used where suitable.

Assessing client outcomes. A great deal has been written about the assessment of client outcomes in single-subject research. Chapter 11 reviews in detail principles of data collection in research; in many ways these are no different in single-system research than in any other type of fixed method study except for the fact that measurement procedures are typically repeated a number of times in the course of the study. This section will briefly review selected measurement issues as they are likely to present themselves in a single-subject design study.

Who the informant(s) shall be is an important question to address, as in all fixed method studies. Should the practitioner assess the outcome? Should the client assess him- or herself? Are there other informants who are in frequent contact with the client—family members, teachers, other helping professionals—who might be enlisted in the assessment? Can multiple assessments by different informants be considered? Each type of informant may be considered to have a different kind of stake in the outcome of the study that could affect the reports each gives, but each can potentially offer a unique and valuable perspective on the outcomes of an intervention.

Client self-report measures, which are frequently used, can take a variety of forms, standardized or qualitative, normed or self-anchored (Bloom, Fischer, & Orme 1995). However, the self-monitoring a client does also may also have an impact on the treatment itself. The experiment conducted by Applegate (1991) and included in the previous chapter in fact was designed to answer questions about the effects of client self-assessment on a particular kind of social work treatment. How client self-reporting may enhance or detract from the treatment being studied must therefore be considered in any study of treatment processes or outcomes, including single-system designs. For example, in the Nugent (1991) study of anger control, the client self-reporting was both an integral part of the treatment and the method of documenting outcome. Self-monitoring thus served both therapeutic and research purposes.

Finally, a third party—someone other than the practitioner-researcher or the client—may be used for recording treatment outcomes. When a child is in treatment, a parent, teacher, or other professional may serve as a useful informant about changes in the child. For example, Dean and Reinherz (1986) describe a single-subject study in which nurses reported on the state of mind of a terminally ill client in a chronic care setting who was receiving psychodynamic treatment from a social worker for depression. In such an instance, using a third party for assessment reduced the burden on the ill client of participation in the study and involved the people who initially noticed the problem and referred the client for social work treatment, the nurses, in assessing whether or not the help offered was having the desired effect.

In the Richey and Hodges (1992) study, while eligibility for respite services was based on the mother's income and problems, the "real" client was the daughter, whose capacity to continue to care well for her mother was being threatened by the need for her constant presence and by her increasing resentment of the demands she faced. Thus the daughter's feelings, not the mother's condition, were both the presenting problem and the focus of measurement.

In fact, whether to rely on client self-report or on the reports of significant others can be a matter of some controversy, as in the Edelson et al. (1985) study of group treatment for men who batter. While the men in treatment reported weekly on the number of instances (if any) in which they had engaged in specified forms of violence toward their female partners, no corroboration was obtained from their wives. While this strategy has been criticized, the potential risk of retaliation against spouses who served as informants for the study may have been considered in making this choice.

In addition to deciding who will make the best informants, the nature of the outcome or outcomes to be assessed must also be considered. In practice, of course, these two dimensions must be considered together, and the choice of informant may depend a great deal on what qualities, characteristics, feelings, or behaviors are to be measured. What behaviors, feelings, skills, or other characteristics of the client are the targets of change as a result of the intervention? What are the presenting complaints or concerns of the client at the beginning of treatment? What are the goals of the client and/or the practitioner for the intervention? Are there short-term or intermediate goals that the client must achieve in order to meet the long-term objectives of treatment? How can these target feelings or behaviors be efficiently assessed in a way that will enhance and not detract from the aims of the treatment itself?

As with all types of research, it is never possible or feasible to measure all of the dimensions of possible interest in a single-subject study. The literature on the problems the client may have and on the specific treatment approach being tried will suggest where the priorities in assessment will lie. The Richey and Hodges (1992) study uses the literature well to show how the problems selected for study were both common and critical ones and why the intervention used, respite care, was likely to prove useful for them.

Intimately connected to the question of *what* to measure is the question of *how* to measure the characteristics in question. As single-system designs have become more popular in social work, considerable effort has gone into identifying and developing assessment tools that can be used efficiently and effectively in the treatment context. Emphasis has been on tools that are short and that can be repeated in relatively short intervals of time. Fischer and Corcoran (1994) have assembled a source book of existing measures of this type for use in clinical social work practice; the assessment tools reviewed can be used with adults, children, or couples and families and cover a range of problems, symptoms, and personal attributes. Hudson (1982) has developed a set of assessment tools of his own specifically for use in single-subject studies of practice; one of these, the Child's Attitude Toward Mother Scale, was in fact used in the Richey and Hodges (1992) study. However, any one of the many standard reference works on existing scales and measures may be consulted when planning a single-subject study, although attention must be paid in selecting a measure to ease administration and repeated application of the scale (see chapter 15 on selecting an existing measure).

Single-subject studies, like other fixed method studies, must address the dilemma of whether to use existing scales and measurement procedures or whether to develop new ones tailored to the needs and circumstances of the study at hand. The chapters on choosing among existing measures and on developing new measures should be consulted when making such a decision. As already noted, the sensitivity and stability of a measurement technique in repeated use must be considered for a single-system design in addition to all the other factors always taken into account.

Data analysis. The logic of single-system designs depends on assessing differences between one or more baseline and treatment periods, and therefore the analysis of data in single-system designs is focused on demonstrating whether or not such a difference exists. The essential question that the analysis must grapple with is "How much difference is enough difference to be considered real and not just apparent?" A real difference in observations made between baseline and treatment periods is taken to represent evidence that the introduction of an intervention produced a change.

Visual display. Most often, the presentation and analysis of data in single-subject designs is centered on the visual display or graphing of the data obtained. All of the basic principles of graphing must be adhered to when preparing a display of repeated measures. As with all graphs, care must be taken to label clearly the metric of the measure on the vertical axis and to show the full range of the measure, including the zero point, if any. The horizontal axis of the graph is used to indicate the time points when assessments were made; these points should be spaced proportionally to the time periods indicated, or a visual indication, such as cross-hatching, should be made when this cannot be done. A vertical line is used to indicate any change in phase from baseline to treatment period.

A point is plotted on the graph to correspond to the score on each measure at each data collection point; these points are connected to create a line showing the trends in measurement over time and between baseline and treatment period(s). When a data collection point is missed, a broken line is used to indicate the estimate of change between the data points that were available.

Sometimes straightforward criteria exist for evaluating the success of an intervention. For example, the first goal of any treatment for battering is the cessation of all battering behavior; gains short of that absolute standard may be encouraging but are not enough. Simple visual inspection of data from the treatment period will be enough to determine whether or not incidents of battering have ceased.

In other, less dramatic instances, there may be explicit standards of clinical success that can simply be looked for in the data. Some assessment tools have psychometrically derived norms or criteria separating problematic or clinically significant behavior from normal or average expectable behavior. The goal of a treatment may be to bring measured behavior into a predefined normal or desirable range. Such norms can be indicated visually on the graph, and outcome may be evaluated based on whether or not all (or most) of the data points during treatment meet the preestablished criteria. This reasoning simply says that when there are measurable clinical criteria of success, outcomes of treatment can be evaluated visually to determine whether or not these criteria of success have been achieved.

When no clear criterion of success exists, conclusions from single-subject design studies may sometimes still be drawn based only on the visual inspection of graphical data. A discontinuity of a line in level or direction between baseline and treatment periods is the most convincing graphical evidence of change that there is. For example, if a problem had been stable (level line) or worsening (rising or falling line) during the baseline period, a line that distinctly changes level or direction during the treatment period provides compelling evidence of a significant change in the phenomenon assessed. Bloom, Fischer, and Orme (1995) and Jayaratne (1978) provide exhaustive illustrations of the varieties of patterns that can appear in such graphs, along with guidelines for interpreting them.

Simple statistical approaches. Often, however, it is not possible to state with certainty what a criterion of success is or that apparent differences between baseline and treatment periods are so marked that a discontinuity in trends between the baseline and treatment periods unequivocally exists. In the situation of undefined norms or of trends that might be interpreted in more than one way, there are some very simple statistical techniques that may be used with single-system designs to distinguish significant differences from minor variations. A few of them will be described here for the purpose of illustrating their usefulness, although the reader is referred to other texts and articles for greater detail, such as Bloom, Fischer, and Orme (1995) and Jayaratne (1978).

The *two standard deviation band* approach relies on the idea of averages and standard deviations and can be used when the measure applied is interval or ratio level (see chapter 17) and when enough baseline and treatment data points are present to permit the calculation of means and percentages. The mean and standard deviation of the scores observed during the baseline period are calculated; and a range of two standard deviations above and below the mean at baseline is then calculated as well. Lines to represent the baseline mean and the baseline range are then projected into the treatment period on the graph. Scores actually obtained during the treatment period are plotted and examined to see how often they fall within or outside this range of expectable scores based on baseline measurements.

It is reasoned from laws of probability that if no change has taken place, scores during the treatment period will remain within this band and may even fall outside it about 5 percent of the time. If scores obtained during the treatment period fall outside the range of the two standard deviation band more than 5 percent of the time, it is concluded that the difference reflects real change rather than chance or expectable fluctuation. The two standard deviation band method thus provides a yardstick for assessing how much change is enough change to draw a conclusion of effectiveness. This technique was the one used in the Richey and Hodges (1992) study above.

A similar method for data with limited variability is called the proportion/ frequency approach. Instead of using the standard deviation, the middle two-thirds of the range of scores observed during baseline is used to project what might be expectable during the treatment phase if no change were to occur (Bloom & Fischer 1982). A similar approach would be to indicate on the graph a range of scores defined through norming as ordinarily expectable. As in the two standard deviation band approach, scores actually obtained in the treatment period are then examined to see how often they fall within or outside the range projected based on baseline assessments.

These analytic techniques are best used when baseline data are relatively stable. When baseline data seem instead to describe an ongoing course of change—a trend upward or downward on the graph—it is better to analyze the data using a *celeration line* approach. In this technique, a trend (rather than a stable average) is described for the baseline period, often by dividing it in half, calculating a mean for each half, and then constructing a trend line from these two means. This line is then projected into the treatment period, continuing to rise (or fall) as it had during the baseline period. Data points during the treatment period are then classified as to whether they fall above or below the trend line forecast, and a statistical table is used to see whether the proportion obtained is statistically significant or not (Bloom, Fischer, & Orme 1995). The logic here is the same as with the two standard deviation band approach, except that what is projected is a trend or a rate of change predicted from the baseline period rather than the continuation of a stable rate (also predicted from the baseline). The choice between approaches really depends on whether the data obtained during the baseline period were stable or changing and on how they were measured.

All of these statistical methods of analysis depend in the end on the presence of multiple data points during both baseline and treatment periods. As with all kinds of research design, the requirements of the data analysis process must be anticipated and planned for when data are collected and the research design is put in place.

Issues in Single-System Design

Applicability to Nonbehavioral Interventions

As already observed, single-subject research designs were brought into social work from behavioral psychology, and the logic of the designs seems to depend on the idea that specific behaviors can be isolated, measured, and observed to change in a fairly short time period when interventions targeted specifically to them are used. However, practitioners interested in communication theory (Nelson 1981) and in psychodynamic theory (Dean & Reinherz 1986) have discussed the adaptation of these designs to these other models of social work practice. Part of the challenge in this adaptation is in measurement: How can such concepts as defenses, coping, or expression of affect be adequately operationalized? How can interventions that depend on such concepts as empathy or relationship be assessed?

Clearly, some of the things that nonbehavioral and specifically psychodynamically oriented practice may seek to change are often more difficult to observe directly than the specific behaviors that are the target of other forms of treatment (Dean & Reinherz 1986). Psychodynamic treatment can be defined as efforts to support, promote, and increase the internal, psychological resources of people (Applegate 1992), and internal resources are by nature subjective. Proponents of the use of single-subject study methods with such forms of practice argue that creative assessments of the outcomes of such interventions can be focussed on how a client learns to use treatment (the amount of talk about feelings in sessions, for example), subjective states as self-reported by the client, or the judgements of others about the mood states and relevant characteristics of the client that might be expected to change. Even structured existing instruments can be used if they are addressed to the specific issues, feelings, or attitudes that the treatment seeks to address. Part of the challenge may be met by considering partial or intermediate goals in treatment rather than long-term or ultimate outcomes, and the study method can be adapted to changing goals and interventions as needed (A/B/C designs; see Bloom, Fischer, & Orme 1995). Often the focus of study when psychodynamic treatment is used is on the treatment process itself, and methods of data collection and analysis that can accommodate unstructured data can be useful in capturing the somewhat more diffuse or abstract concepts that may be involved without subjecting them to quantitative operationalization before the fact. However, to qualify as single-subject design, methods of data collection must be fixed before the study begins even if the coding of data may not be fully worked out until afterward.

Feasibility

Single-subject studies, for all these problems, have been considered to have special promise for the profession of social work because they are feasible for the individual practitioner to undertake. Certainly a single-subject study may be somewhat easier and less expensive to mount than a large-scale follow-up survey or a classical evaluation experiment using treatment and control groups. However, that does not mean that tensions between research and service may not exist.

Several of the points of tension that can arise in conducting single-subject research in a practice setting have already been mentioned. These include the problem of potentially withholding treatment during a baseline period, which can be solved by using a retrospective baseline or by using naturally occurring periods of delay in implementing service, such as a planned assessment period, as the baseline. In general, of course, ethical considerations must outweigh all others, and some single-system studies have short or nonexistent baseline periods as a result. In addition, doing research of any kind on treatment or service delivery always imposes greater record-keeping requirements on the practitioner and sometimes even on the client. Naturally, care must be used to ensure that these data collection efforts, especially those that involve clients, are not unduly burdensome.

Subjecting a treatment or a case to systematic study is demanding and time-consuming no matter what the method used. Despite the relative feasibility of single-system designs, studies of social workers who were educated in the use of single-subject designs have had mixed results, some showing that more research and practice evaluation was being done and others showing little evidence of such a trend (Penka & Kirk 1991). Finding encouragement in the work place, formal and informal, for undertaking research of any kind, including single-subject study, is essential for doing the research on practice effectiveness that the profession needs.

Summary

The past 15 years have seen the introduction of a special form of single case research, the single-subject design, into social work and the human services. Single-subject designs have to date been widely used in social work education but not very often published. This form of research has much in common with group experimental designs, but its logic relies on a case-control, repeated measures approach to the study of individual cases rather than on the comparison of groups. As such, single-subject designs, while demanding to design and undertake, offer the practitioner a realistic way to generate answers to questions about the effectiveness of interventions and how best to effect change one case at a time.

EMPIRICAL SUPPORT FOR THE EFFECTIVENESS OF RESPITE CARE IN REDUCING CAREGIVER BURDEN: A SINGLE-CASE ANALYSIS

CHERYL A. RICHEY
VANESSA G. HODGES
University of Washington

This article examines the effectiveness of respite care in reducing feelings of entrapment and resentment experienced by a 69-year-old daughter who was sole caregiver for her frail, 99-year-old mother. Outcome measures collected weekly over a 2-month period included caregiver reports of amount and enjoyment of time away from home and attitude toward mother. An experimental single-system (ABAB) design allowed comparison of caregiver burden during times when respite care was and was not available. All measures evidenced statistically significant changes in predicted directions when respite care was in place. Issues discussed include operationalization of burden and the clinical significance of findings. The case study offers an exemplar of how empirical support for respite care can be garnered to promote social welfare policies and programs that are responsive to the needs of families pursuing caregiving functions.

People are living longer, resulting in increasing numbers of older citizens. In the United States the proportion of people aged 65 years and over has doubled since the beginning of this century and is expected to triple within the early part of the next century (Siegel & Taeubex, 1982). In 1980, the elderly represented slightly over 11% of the population (American Association of Retired Persons, 1986). With greater life expectancies, percentage increases have been particularly marked among the old-old (75 and over), a group especially vulnerable to ill health and consequent dependency (Archbold, 1983). Furthermore, demographic trends suggest that the majority of older persons will continue to be women, resulting in an aged population that is primarily a female society (Hooyman, 1987).

These population trends, along with the policy shifts of deinstitutionalization and diversion (Briar & Ryan, 1986), raise serious questions regarding society's continuing ability and willingness to address the needs of its older members and their home-based caregivers. Indeed, the increase in the proportion of older persons coupled with a decline in federal funds for formal, comprehensive programs has led to forecasts of increasing demands on the family to provide support services for their older members (Stoller, 1983). As a result, parent-caring, the provision of needed services to functionally impaired elderly parents, is increasing proportionately with the number of frail elderly in the population. Contrary to popular belief, the immediate family remains the major source of support for dependent older persons (Lang & Brody, 1983). Further, women, who themselves may be 60 or 70 years old, constitute about 80% of the family members providing support for elderly relatives (Brody, 1985).

Despite the positive rewards of caregiving, for example, facilitating a comfortable and loving environment for one's mother, achieving one's personal standards of familial or intergenerational duty, or developing closer, more intimate family relationships (cf. Hooyman & Lustbader, 1986), taking care of a chronically ill or incapacitated elderly person is nevertheless a progressively difficult, all-consuming activity. Enormous effort is

Authors' Note: This article describes a study based on an MSW student research project conducted by Phyllis L. Norwood, now deceased. Appreciation is extended to John Gibson, Naomi Gottlieb, Nancy Hooyman, Judy Kopp, and Elizabeth Roberts for helpful comments on an earlier version of this article. Correspondence may be addressed to Cheryl A. Richey, School of Social Work, JH-30, 4101 15th Avenue, N.E., Seattle, WA 98195.

required to feed, dress, and bathe another adult, who may be unresponsive or even hostile to such assistance. These physical caregiving tasks do not include the additional responsibilities that come from providing close supervision and interpersonal stimulation to the elder.

The demands, stress, risks, and costs associated with caregiving have been discussed by many authors (e.g., Biegel, Sales, & Schulz, 1991; Cantor, 1983; Johnson, 1983; Montgomery, Gonyea, & Hooyman, 1985; Moroney, 1980; Pearlin, Mullan, Semple, & Skaff, 1990; Pruchno & Resch, 1989; Sheehan & Nuttall, 1988; Soldo & Myllyluoma, 1983; Zarit, Reever, & Bach-Peterson, 1980). Caregiver burden, although defined and measured somewhat differently across studies, is generally accepted as a multidimensional concept, which can be divided into two broad categories. The first category, termed "objective burden," "caregiving impact" (Poulshock & Deimling, 1984), or "primary stress" (Pearlin et al., 1990), involves strain associated with caregiver responsibility for providing personal care and for managing specific tasks related to activities of daily living (ADL) and supervision of family members who are extremely confused or tend to wander as a result of their disability. These effects largely focus on the concrete or instrumental impact of caring on caregivers' daily lives, including family relationships and social activities. The second broad category of burden identified as "subjective burden" (Poulshock & Deimling, 1984) or "secondary stress" (Pearlin et al., 1990) involves caregivers' perceptions, appraisals, and interpretations of their experiences as tiring, difficult, or upsetting, which can be influenced by such feelings as low self-esteem, loss of self, and role strain.

Caring for severely impaired older parents often begins when the caregiver is herself in middle age or early old age, thus marking the beginning of another "caregiving career" (Briar & Ryan, 1986, p. 23). For example, a recent study of 50 caregivers and their frail relatives reported that 48% of the caregivers were adult daughters, and the mean caregiver age for the entire sample was 60.34 years (Marks,

1988). In a British study of 41 adult daughters caring for mothers on a co-resident basis, 44% reported beginning their full-time caring responsibilities when they were between 50 and 59 years old (Lewis & Meredith, 1988). Like child rearing, meeting the dependency needs of a parent is extremely demanding physically and psychologically. Unlike child rearing, in which the child's physical and emotional dependence gradually diminishes, parent-caring demands continue or increase over time (Archbold, 1983).

Indeed, the toll of caring appears high. Whether propelled by love, concern, and/or guilt, caregivers frequently provide nonstop care, without respite, until they become emotionally, financially, or physically impaired themselves (Briar & Ryan, 1986). Cantor (1983) observed that family supports tend to erode and strain on the giver tends to increase over time, especially when the older family member suffers from severe, chronic conditions. Numerous studies now document caregiver feelings of burden and stress (Archbold, 1983; Arling & McAuley, 1983; Cantor, 1983; Clark & Rakowski, 1983; Pearlin et al., 1990; Pruchno & Resch, 1989; Stoller, 1983). Caregivers themselves often report feeling physically and emotionally drained (Poulshock & Deimling, 1984). Over 80% of the caregivers surveyed in one study reported role stress, and half saw their stress as a serious problem (Johnson, 1983).

Other hazards of parent-caring that have been identified by caregivers include decreases in their own independence and mobility, for example, limited opportunities to pursue activities outside the home, such as shopping, maintaining social contacts, and engaging in recreational or cultural events (Moroney, 1980). Some have suggested that the most prevalent and most severe impact of family caregiving is this restriction of freedom for the caregiver (Archbold, 1983; Cantor, 1983). Not surprisingly, one effect of these restrictions for caregivers of the elderly is feeling entrapped (Moroney, 1976).

Because family members providing continuous care make numerous personal sacrifices, it is not uncommon for intense, negative emotional reactions to develop, including bitterness about their situation (Doll, 1976) and resentment, hostility, and even violence toward the elderly person (Clark & Rakowski, 1983; Hickey & Douglass, 1981). When physical, economic, or emotional burdens reach intense levels, the caregiver's recognition of and sensitivity and responsiveness to the needs of a frail elder are greatly reduced. Thus adult caretakers, overtaxed by caregiving demands, may be at greater risk for elder neglect and abuse (Hickey & Douglass, 1981).

Although there is increasing recognition of the multifaceted burden that accompanies in-home caregiving, ways to reduce the burden have not received commensurate attention (Gallagher, 1985; Zarit, Reever, & Bach-Peterson, 1980). Several authors have urged that research and service agendas include a systematic examination of the effects of respite or substitute care and other support services with high-risk, highly stressed family caregivers (Briar & Ryan, 1986; Zarit, Todd, & Zarit, 1986). Respite care has been defined as temporary care of a disabled person that provides relief to the primary caretaker or individual responsible for ongoing patient well-being (Bader, 1985; Salisbury & Intagliata, 1986). The most fundamental purpose of respite care is to provide rest for caregivers (Foundation for Long Term Care, 1983; Montgomery & Prothero, 1986). Respite services are generally short-term and time-limited, and can include companionship, homemaking services, and total personal care. Location of respite services also varies, based on client needs and agency capacity. Some services are provided in the family home, whereas others are provided in hospitals or community care facilities.

Respite care has a brief but important history in maintaining chronically ill and disabled family members in their family homes. Formal respite services were first provided in the 1970s for deinstitutionalized developmentally disabled children (Cohen, 1982). Studies evaluating the outcome of these services support their effectiveness (Intagliata, 1986; Joyce, Singer, & Isralowitz, 1983; Upshur, 1983; Wikler, Hanusa, & Stoycheff, 1986). For example, families caring for developmentally disabled persons report improved levels of

functioning, including getting along better with each other, improved marital relationships, reduced social isolation, greater satisfaction with interactions with the disabled family member, and reduced likelihood of institutional placement (Joyce et al., 1983; Pagel & Whitling, 1978; Wikler et al., 1986).

Because the application of respite care services with geriatric populations is relatively recent (Crossman, London, & Barry, 1981; Lawton, Brody, & Saperstein, 1989), few large-scale empirical studies have been conducted to evaluate the impacts of formal respite care (Gonyea, Seltzer, Gerstein, & Young, 1988). However, one recent quasiexperimental study, comparing 25 families receiving formal respite service with 25 families waiting for service, offers beginning evidence that respite care can significantly reduce caregiver stress among families providing full-time, in-home care to a frail elderly relative (Marks, 1988). The present case study, which employs an experimental single-system design methodology (ABAB), attempts to garner additional empirical support for the effectiveness of respite care as an intervention to reduce caregiver burden. *Burden* for this caregiver included being homebound or trapped by caregiving responsibilities and feeling resentful and angry toward a frail, dependent, elderly mother.

METHOD AND PROCEDURES

Client

The client, Anne, a 69-year-old Caucasian woman, widowed for 7 years, was sole caregiver for her 99-year-old mother, Mrs. N. Anne had been caring for her mother for 12 years when the referral was received by a hospital-based elder care project for inhome evaluation and case management follow-up. The referral was initiated by Mrs. N's physician because of the "stress" created for Anne by her mother's progressively greater care needs. Anne complained of tension, heart palpitations, and fatigue.

A BA-level social worker, who functioned as case manager, made an initial visit to Anne's home, which was located in a rural-suburban community about 45 miles from a major northwest city. Assessment of Mrs. N's physical condition, ability to complete ADL, and mental status revealed her marked dementia and cognitive loss. The care situation was further complicated by the mother's recently fractured wrist secondary to a fall. A history of cardiac arrythmias also was noted. Mrs. N was functionally dependent on her daughter for all her personal care, such as bathing, dressing, and toileting, and she needed standby assistance when ambulating. The mother revealed minimal awareness of her surrounding environment. She recognized her daughter and knew she was "at home," but she was unable to provide specific information regarding past or present events. Despite these impairments, Mrs. N was not prone to disoriented wandering or to verbally or physically abusive behavior. She was calm and composed during home visits and expressed positive feelings about her daughter. Although expressing unawareness of any problems or concerns, Mrs. N verbalized agreement to case management services.

An inventory or list of concerns was generated with Anne during subsequent discussions. She also completed the 13-item Caregiver Strain Index (CSI) (Robinson, 1983), which was used as an assessment tool to determine problem magnitude and to pinpoint and operationalize specific target concerns. The CSI assesses the level and source of caregiver stress among adult children who are primary caregivers for their aging parents. Data have been reported that suggest high reliability (.86) and construct validity. Responses to the CSI range from 0 to 12, with a mean and standard deviation both of 3.5, suggesting that a score of 7 or more indicates higher stress. Anne scored 8 on the CSI, denoting marked caregiver stress. Anne identified a number of specific strains, including her mother's bladder incontinence and need for 24-hour supervision, resulting in Anne's feeling "trapped," "a prisoner in my own home." Further assessment revealed that Anne typically experienced many conflicting and troubling thoughts both when preparing to leave the house (e.g., "I need to get away" and "I shouldn't leave Mom alone") and when she was out of the house, even for a short time (e.g., "I should be home" and "I'm

not a good daughter"). She reported experiencing high levels of tension and anxiety and low levels of enjoyment or satisfaction during these ventures away from home. Often she would return home earlier than originally planned, feeling tired, weepy, and resentful of Mom (e.g., "I feel cheated" and "I feel trapped"). Thus, for Anne, caregiver burden included feelings of entrapment and lack of freedom to leave her home, as well as resultant negative feelings about herself and her mother.

The central target problem, jointly identified by Anne and the social worker, was lack of freedom to leave home because of the absence of substitute caregivers and her mother's need for constant supervision. Several service options, including nursing home placement for mother and stress reduction or relaxation training for Anne, were initially discussed but later dismissed. These alternatives were unacceptable to Anne, as they did not address the core issue as she perceived it. Anne wanted her mother to remain at home, and she desired some actual relief from her caregiving responsibility. She reasoned that having substitute home care would free her from the worries and guilt that now plagued her whenever she left her mother alone and that increased personal freedom and mobility would alter her growing negative attitude toward her mother. Her resentment and antagonism toward her mother was especially troubling to Anne, as she reported a history of a strong mother-daughter relationship. In consort with Anne's conceptualization of the problem, three specific outcome goals were selected and monitored. These included increasing the duration and enjoyment of time spent outside the home and improving Anne's attitude toward her mother.

Outcome Measures

Repeated collections of data on Anne's out-of-home behavior and feelings and on her attitude toward her mother constituted the outcome measures obtained over an 8-week period. Not only can multiple measures increase confidence in the validity of results from single-system design studies (Bloom &

Fischer, 1982), but they can also facilitate interpretation of differential changes across behavioral, emotional, and cognitive response modalities (Levy & Richey, 1988).

Amount of Time Away From Home. Increasing Anne's time away from home was viewed as an operational measure of greater personal freedom. Anne agreed to monitor in a daily log the amount of time she spent outside the home. Log entries were reviewed and discussed during semiweekly (Monday and Thursday) sessions, and weekly totals in hours were entered in the client's file and plotted on a graph.

Enjoyment of Time Away From Home. Anne was also asked to enter in her daily log the level of enjoyment she experienced when away from home. Enjoyment was rated on a 5-point, self-anchored scale (1 = *not at all enjoyable,* and 5 = *very enjoyable*). Along with duration data, these ratings were also reviewed and summarized during sessions, with weekly aggregate scores entered in the case file and graphed. All raw, self-monitored data on daily logs were retained by the client. In an effort to enhance validity of client self-monitored data—in addition to apparent face validity—the social worker attempted to reduce the possibility of socially desirable responding by telling Anne there were no correct responses and that honesty in completing the daily log was the most important dimension of record keeping.

Attitude Toward Mother. Anne completed the Child's Attitude Toward Mother (CAM) scale during each Monday and Thursday session throughout the 2-month service period (Hudson, 1982). The CAM scale, like other standardized questionnaires in Hudson's Clinical Measurement Package, contains 25 positively and negatively worded items that are rated on a 5-point scale (1 = *rarely or none of the time,* 5 = *most or all of the time*). Items include, for example, "I feel very angry toward my mother" and "I really like my mother."

The Hudson scales were designed for single-system research (Bloom & Fischer, 1982). All scales include instructions to discourage courage socially desirable responding; are relatively easy to administer, score, and interpret;

and have high internal consistency and test-retest reliabilities (.90 or better) and high face, concurrent, and construct validity (Bloom & Fischer, 1982).

The use of the CAM to gauge the degree or magnitude of a relationship problem experienced by an adult child with her mother is a relatively innovative application of the scale that was tested for reliability and validity with much younger populations. However, examination of individual scale items indicated a high correlation between the issues it addresses and those thought to be major areas of concern in assessing the caregiver role for this client. Thus, although the scale has not been used extensively with adult children, its application in this study seemed appropriate and yielded interesting results.

Social Work Intervention

Intervention largely consisted of case management, with the hospital-based social worker taking central responsibility in assessing, planning, arranging, coordinating, evaluating, and advocating for services (Gambrill, 1983; Johnson & Rubin, 1983). In this case, concrete community resources, in the form of home-based respite care, were procured in order to alleviate caregiver burden and to prevent deterioration of familial bonds and quality of home care. Over the course of 8 weeks, the practitioner spent an estimated total of 27 hours performing tasks related to accessing, coordinating, and monitoring respite care services. These activities, when added to the 16 hours of face-to-face client contact, resulted in a total service output of 43 hours by the social worker.

After the initial assessment, both the practitioner and Anne identified respite care as the primary need for case management services. Steps were taken to (a) obtain COPES (Community Options Program Entry System) subsidization of a substitute caregiver and (b) locate a suitable care provider. Because Mrs. N received public assistance (SSI) benefits, she was eligible for a community-based care Medicaid waiver from the federal Department of Health and Human Services. These waivers were made possible through Section 21.76 of the 1981 Omnibus Reconciliation Act (PL95–35). Basically, this is a welfare program, jointly funded by federal and state governments, designed to meet the needs of low-income persons for health care. During the 2 weeks required to determine COPES eligibility and to locate a suitable care provider, home visits continued, and baseline data were collected. With Anne's endorsement, provision was made for respite care in the home Monday through Friday, 6 hours daily, from 10 a.m. to 4 p.m. Despite Anne's enthusiasm for the intervention plan, the social worker continued to encourage her utilization of these outside resources by reassuring her that relying on substitute care was not a sign of personal weakness or failure (Briar & Ryan, 1986; Gonyea et al., 1988; Lewis & Meredith, 1988).

Research Design

Originally, a basic AB single-system design was planned to reflect a 2-week baseline observation period (A) and a 6-week intervention period employing respite care (B). It should be noted that the A phase in this study was not entirely intervention free, as supportive home visits continued semi-weekly throughout the course of service contact.

The AB design was altered after 5 weeks, when the COPES provider was unable to continue. The required change in the substitute caregiver resulted in a natural return to baseline (A_2) while an alternative provider was located. This unplanned shift during intervention created an experimental replication design (A_1, B_1, A_2, B_2,) that provided stronger support for the causal efficacy of the intervention, respite care, than could the more simple AB design (Bloom & Fischer, 1982).

RESULTS

All three outcome measures, amount and enjoyment of time out of the house and attitude toward mother, evidenced rather dramatic changes in predicted directions when respite care was introduced, withdrawn, and reintroduced.

Amount of Time Away From Home

The caregiver's self-monitored daily log of time outside the home was used to calculate weekly totals. As illustrated in Figure 1, baseline levels in the A_1 phase were very low, with weekly totals of less than one hour ($M = 0.7$, $SD = 0.14$). With the institution of respite care (B_1), weekly totals more than doubled to 2.2 hours after the first week of in-home care. The mean for B_1 phases was 1.7 hours, which indicated a 147% improvement over baseline. When respite care was not available during Week 6 (A_2), the client largely stayed at home ($M = 0.6$ hours). Out-of-home behavior again increased in B_2 when respite care was reinstituted ($M = 1.9$ hours). With the exception of Week 3 in the B_1 phase, which was the first week of respite care, introduction and withdrawal of intervention appeared to clearly coincide with changes in the amount of time the caregiver was away from home.

To determine whether changes in time away from home were statistically significant, two standard deviation bands (Shewart Charts) were calculated from baseline data (Bloom & Fischer, 1982). This procedure was judged appropriate because baseline data were not autocorrelated ($r = .5$), and there were limited observations. Based on this statistical procedure for time-series data, any two consecutive data points that fall beyond two standard deviations above or below the baseline mean indicate significant differences beyond the .05 level. As noted in Figure 1, the increases in time away from home during Weeks 4 and 5 (B_1) and Weeks 7 and 8 (B_2) were statistically significant ($p < .05$), as they were well above the upper two standard deviation band.

Bloom and Fischer (1982) note that autocorrelation is a complex statistical problem with time-series data. Although computational steps are available for detecting autocorrelation, these may not be sensitive with small baselines. Hence results of the r formula with baseline data in this case must be cautiously interpreted (Bloom & Fischer, 1982). However, testing for autocorrelation may be unnecessary, if the statistical test is interpreted as only a rough indicator of association between

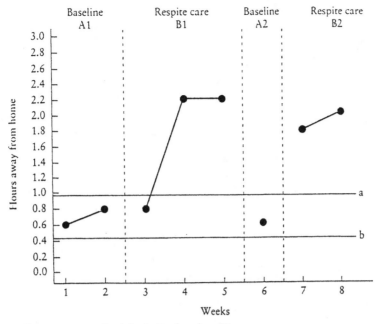

a. Upper two standard deviation band = .98.
b. Lower two standard deviation band = .42.

**Figure 8–1 Total Number of Hours Caregiver Reports Being Away
from Home Each Week**

intervention and subsequent data patterns (Blythe & Tripodi, 1989).

Enjoyment of Time Away from Home

Figure 2 summarizes weekly averages of the client's rating of her enjoyment level while away from home. Again data patterns reflect marked changes in predicted directions when respite care was and was not in place. Mean enjoyment level during the first 2 weeks of baseline (A_1) was low ($M = 1.8$, $SD = 0.35$), suggesting that the brief excursions made during that time offered very little satisfaction. Enjoyment plummeted to a very low level again ($M = 1.5$) during the 6th week, when the substitute caretaker was unavailable (A_1). The first introduction of respite care (B_1) appeared to occasion a marked and sustained increase in enjoyment of time away from home ($M = 3.3$). When respite care was reinstated during Weeks 7 and 8, enjoyment of time away again increased noticeably ($M = 3.6$).

An initial test for autocorrelation revealed the absence of serial dependency in baseline

data ($r = -.5$), so the two standard deviation band approach was again utilized. All enjoyment ratings during the respite care conditions (B_1 and B_2) were statistically significantly above baseline levels ($p < .05$). These findings strongly support intervention effectiveness.

Attitude Toward Mother

Figure 3 summarizes scores on the CAM scale obtained during weekly Monday and Thursday sessions over the 2-month service period. The data reveal an average score of 36.5 ($SD = 4.5$) during the initial A_1 baseline phase. This score is above the clinical cutting point of 30 recommended for all Hudson scales, thus suggesting a clinically significant problem in Anne's attitude toward her mother before the introduction of respite care. Although attitude began to improve slightly during baseline, notable score decreases occurred during the initial 3 weeks of respite care (B_1), with an average CAM score of 26.8. This decrease is greater than the 5-point standard error of measurement for

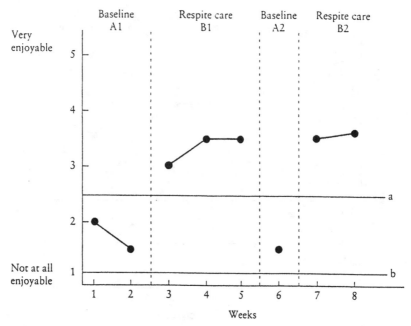

a. Upper two standard deviation band = 2.45.
b. Lower two standard deviation band = 1.05.

Figure 8–2 Weekly Averages of Caregiver Employment When Away from Home

the Hudson scales, so it likely represents a "real" change in Anne's attitude. Consistent with data patterns from the other two measures, CAM scores spiked during the A_2 phase ($M = 38$), confirming apparent deterioration during the nonrespite week. More positive attitude scores emerged again during B_2, with all scores falling below the clinical cutoff ($M = 22$).

DISCUSSION

The unintended ABAB design in this case study supports the positive impact of respite care on caregiver burden. Despite the fact that the B_2 was not an exact replication of B_1 (each phase employed a different COPES provider), the core intervention, provision of an alternate caregiver, remained constant. Apparently, intervention effects were not limited to a particular respite care worker. Along with the experimental replication design, the statistically significant results also offer strong empirical evidence of intervention effectiveness.

The study was strengthened and practice knowledge increased by the use of multiple outcome measures, reflecting client behavior, feelings, and attitudes. The caregiver was highly motivated to improve her situation and remained an active participant by recording and discussing information throughout the study. The client's active involvement in collecting data might be challenged by some practitioners as disruptive to the development of a therapeutic relationship. On the contrary, participation of the caregiver in this study through self-monitoring and questionnaire completion represented an empowerment strategy, as well as a way to document change (Kopp, 1989). Self-assessment can provide a source of positive feedback and support to clients who may be unaware of small changes on a day-to-day basis. For instance, a series of single-case design studies with 66 home-based caregivers reported that caregivers enjoyed recording and graphing behavioral data and that the figural depictions of progress had great clinical value (Pinkston, Linsk, & Young, 1988).

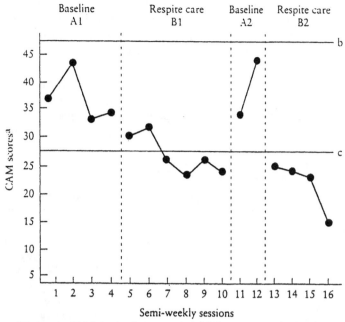

a. Hudson's Child Attitude Toward Mother (CAM) Scale. Higher
   scores = greater problem severity; clinical cutting score = 30.
b. Upper two standard deviation band = 45.5.
c. Lower two standard deviation band = 27.5.

**Figure 8–3 Caregiver Attitude Toward Mother on CAM Scale Assessed
During Monday/Thursday Sessions Over 2 Months**

A potential weakness of the study was the operationalization of a multifaceted problem such as burden. Although the definitions selected were supported by the caregiver, they nevertheless represented only a small part of the construct burden. Other variables of interest could have readily included depression and social isolation. Goal selection could represent another weakness. Although goals of increased time and enjoyment away from home and improved regard toward mother reflect pressing client concerns, these outcomes appear to emphasize relatively short-term changes that are primarily related to Anne's role as caretaker for another. To reduce possible gender bias and increase clinical relevance of goals selected, it might be important in casework with adult female caregivers to take time to focus on additional goals that are longer range (preparing Anne for a life without mother) and more personal (enhancing Anne's self-esteem and friendship networks; Gambrill & Richey, 1986).

The issue of clinical relevance must also be raised in this study with respect to levels of goal attainment, especially for duration of time away from home. Despite the statistical significance of increases in this measure, the clinical or practical significance of change must be addressed. Given the expanded opportunities to leave the house afforded by respite care (up to 6 hours daily, 30 hours weekly), a high of 2.2 hours a week away from home (or 7% of time available) seems a small respite indeed. Although these breaks from caretaking are important, they allow limited opportunity for extended interaction with friends or participation in community events. Perhaps Anne, like many caregivers whose opportunities to engage in reinforcing and pleasurable activities erode over time, was unable to think of things she would enjoy doing outside the home (Pinkston et al., 1988). On the other hand, it may be erroneous to conclude that Anne's time at home was unpleasant. Solitary activities, like reading, knitting, listening to music, or talking on the telephone may be more common "pleasant events" among caregivers than social activities requiring time away from their caregiver role (Lovett & Gallagher, 1988). Thus the presence of the respite care worker in the home not only allowed Anne the freedom to leave the house if she chose to, but it also relieved her of constant care responsibilities during most of the day, so she could pursue solitary activities at home without interruption. Future research could examine more specifically how relieved caregivers spend their respite time. For example, is time spent in activities that are active or sedentary, social or solitary?

A further limitation of the study involves the failure to systematically assess and document the quality of and satisfaction with caregiving provided by the respite care worker. Although the social worker routinely checked on Mrs. N during each home visit, no ongoing evaluation of the care itself was performed. Future research could contribute significantly to our understanding of respite care by studying the quality, appropriateness, and satisfaction of alternative care from the viewpoints of both the elder and the respite worker (Barer & Johnson, 1990).

As the number and proportion of older people increase, the importance of understanding and meeting the needs of caregivers also increases. Public policies supporting accessible and affordable community-based services for caregivers must become a high priority if we are to provide sound alternatives to institutionalization (Kane, 1985) and alter our narrow cost-containment mentality, which justifies cheap rather than humane long-term care options (Pilisuk & Parks, 1988). Because the family will continue to play an important support role with vulnerable individuals, it is imperative that the material, social, and emotional strains placed on relatives be recognized and addressed programmatically. This study offers one example of how empirical support for respite care and other support services can be collected by individual practitioners for purposes of both case and class advocacy (Hepworth & Larsen, 1990). Individual case data can be used to acquire, continue, or expand needed benefits and services for specific clients. To promore social policy change, ideographic data can be amassed and aggregated to form compelling evidence of intervention feasibility, efficiency, and efficacy for family caregivers as a group. Such evidence can boost efforts to develop social welfare policies and programs that support all family members in the pursuit of their caregiving roles.

REFERENCES

American Association of Retired Persons. (1986). *A profile of older Americans.* Washington, DC: Author.

Archbold, P. G. (1983). Impact of parent-caring on women. *Family Relations, 32,* 39–45.

Arling, G., & McAuley, W. J. (1983). The feasibility of public payments for family caregiving. *Gerontologist, 23,* 300–306.

Bader, J. (1985). Respite care: Temporary relief for caregivers. *Women and Health, 10,* 39–51.

Barer, B. M., & Johnson, C. L. (1990). A critique of the caregiving literature. *Gerontologist, 30,* 26–28.

Biegel, D. E., Sales, E., & Schulz, R. (1991). *Family caregiving in chronic illness.* Newbury Park, CA: Sage.

Bloom, M., & Fischer, J. (1982). *Evaluating practice: Guidelines for the accountable professional.* Englewood Cliffs, NJ: Prentice-Hall.

Blythe, B. J., & Tripodi, T. (1989). *Measurement in direct practice.* Newbury Park, CA: Sage.

Briar, K. H., & Ryan, R. (1986). The anti-institution movement and women caregivers. *Affilia. 1*(1), 20–31.

Brody, E. M. (1985). Parent care as a normative family stress. *Gerontologist, 25,* 19–30.

Cantor, M. H. (1983). Strain among caregivers: A study of experience in the United States. *Gerontologist, 23,* 597–604.

Clark, N. M., & Rakowski, W. (1983). Family caregivers of older adults: Improving helping skills. *Gerontologist, 23,* 637–643.

Cohen, S. (1982). Supporting families through respite care. *Rehabilitation Literature, 43,* 7–11.

Crossman, L., London, C., & Barry, C. (1981). Older women caring for disabled spouses: A model for supportive services. *Gerontologist, 21,* 464–470.

Doll, W. (1976). Family coping with the mentally ill: An unanticipated problem of deinstitutionalization. *Hospital and Community Psychiatry, 27,* 183–185.

Foundation for Long Term Care. (1983). *Respite care for the frail elderly: A summary report on institutional respite research* (Monograph 1). Albany, NY: Author.

Gallagher, D. (1985). Intervention strategies to assist caregivers of frail elders: Current research status and future research directions. In M. P. Lawton & G. Maddox (Eds.), *Annual review of gerontology and geriatrics* (Vol. 5, pp. 249–282). New York: Springer.

Gambrill, E. D. (1983). *Casework: A competency-based approach.* Englewood Cliffs, NJ: Prentice-Hall.

Gambrill, E. D., & Richey, C. A. (1986). Criteria used to define and evaluate socially competent behavior among women. *Psychology of Women Quarterly, 10,* 183–196.

Gonyea, J. G., Seltzer, G. B., Gerstein, C., & Young, M. (1988). Acceptance of hospital-based respite care by families and elders. *Health and Social Work. 13,* 201–208.

Hepworth, D. H., & Larsen, J. A. (1990). *Direct social work practice.* Chicago: Dorsey.

Hickey, T., & Douglass, R. L. (1981). Mistreatment of the elderly in the domestic setting: An exploratory study. *American Journal of Public Health, 71,* 500–507.

Hooyman, N. R. (1987). Older women and social work curricula. In D. S. Burden & N. Gottlieb (Eds.), *The woman client: Providing human services in a changing world.* New York: Tavistock.

Hooyman. N. R., & Lustbader, W. (1986). *Taking care of your aging family members: A practical guide.* New York: Free Press.

Hudson, W. W. (1982). *The Clinical Measurement Package: A field manual.* Homewood. IL: Dorsey.

Intagliata, J. (1986). Assessing the impact of respite care services: A review of outcome evaluation studies. In C. L. Salisbury & J. Intagliata (Eds.), *Respite care: Support for persons with developmental disabilities and their families* (pp. 263–287). Baltimore, MD: Brookes.

Johnson. G. L. (1983). Dyadic family relations and social support. *Gerontologist, 23,* 377–384.

Johnson, P. J., & Rubin, A. (1983). Case management in mental health: A social work domain? *Social Work, 28,* 49–55.

Joyce, K., Singer, M., & Isralowitz, O. (1983). Impact of respite care on parent's perception of quality of life. *Mental Retardation, 2,* 153–156.

Kane, R. A. (1985). A family caregiving policy—should we have one? *Generations, 10,* 33–36.

Kopp, J. (1989). Self-observation: An empowerment strategy in assessment. *Social Casework, 70,* 276–284.

Lang, A. M., & Brody, E. M. (1983). Characteristics of middle-aged daughters and help to their elderly mothers. *Journal of Marriage and the Family, 45,* 193–201.

Lawton, M. P., Brody, E. M., & Saperstein, A. R. (1989). A controlled study of respite service for caregivers of Alzheimer's patients. *Gerontologist, 29,* 8–16.

Levy, R. L., & Richey, C. A. (1988). Measurement and design issues in behavioral medicine with women. In E. A. Blechman & K. Browell (Eds.), *Handbook of behavioral medicine for women* (pp. 421–438). New York: Pergamon.

Lewis, J., & Meredith, B. (1988). *Daughters who care: Daughters caring for mothers at home.* London: Routledge.

Lovett, S., & Gallagher, D. (1988). Psychoeducational interventions for family caregivers: Preliminary efficacy data. *Behavior Therapy, 19,* 321–330.

Marks, R. (1988, June). Families with frail elderly: An examination of family life, mechanisms of support and long-term care policy. In E. Rayne (Ed.), *Families in transition: Implications for social work and practice* (Tulane Studies in Social Welfare Vol. 17, pp. 149–167). New Orleans: Tulane University.

Montgomery, R., Gonyea, J., & Hooyman, N. (1985). Caregiving and the experience of subjective and objective burden. *Family Relations, 34*(1), 19–26.

Montgomery, R. J. V., & Prothero, J. (Eds.), (1986). *Developing respite services for the elderly.* Seattle: University of Washington Press.

Moroney, R. M. (1976). *The family and the state: Considerations for social policy.* New York: Longman.

Moroney, R. M. (1980). *Families, social services and social policy: The issue of shared responsibility.* Rockville, MD: National Institute of Mental Health.

Pagel, S. E., & Whitling, B. (1978). Readmissions to a state hospital for mentally retarded persons: Reasons for community placement and failure. *Mental Retardation, 16,* 164–166.

Pearlin, L. I., Mullan, J. T., Sempie, S. J., & Skaff, M. M. (1990). Caregiving and the stress process: An overview of concepts and their measures. *Gerontologist, 30,* 583–591.

Pilisuk, M., & Parks, S. H. (1988). Caregiving: Where families need help. *Social Work, 33,* 436–440.

Pinkston, E. M., Linsk, N. L., & Young, R. N. (1988). Home-based behavioral family treatment of the impaired elderly. *Behavior Therapy, 19,* 331–344.

Poulshock, S. W., & Deimling, G. T. (1984). Families caring for elders in residence: Issues in the measurement of burden. *Journal of Gerontology, 39,* 230–239.

Pruchno, R. A., & Resch, N. L. (1989). Aberrant behaviors and Alzheimer's disease: Mental health effects of spouse caregivers. *Journal of Gerontology, 44,* 177–182.

Robinson, B. C. (1983). Validation of a caregiver strain index. *Journal of Gerontology, 38,* 344–348.

Salisbury, C. L., & Intagliata, J. (1986). *Respite care: Support for persons with developmental disabilities and their families.* Baltimore, MD: Brookes.

Sheehan, N. W., & Nuttall, P. (1988). Conflict, emotion, and personal strain among family caregivers. *Family Relations, 37*(1), 92–98.

Siegel, J. S., & Taeubex, C. M. (1982). The 1980 census and the elderly: New data available to planners and practitioners. *Gerontologist, 22,* 144–150.

Soldo, B. J., & Myllyluoma, J. (1983). Caregivers who live with dependent elderly. *Gerontologist, 23,* 605–611.

Stoller, E. P. (1983). Parental caregiving by adult children. *Journal of Marriage and the Family, 45,* 851–857.

Upshur, C. C. (1983). Developing respite care: A support for families with disabled members. *Family Relations, 32,* 13–20.

Wikler, L. M., Hanusa, D., & Stoycheff, J. (1986). Home-based respite care, the child with developmental disabilities, and family stress: Some theoretical and pragmatic aspects of process evaluation. In C. L. Salisbury & J. Intagliata (Eds.), *Respite care: Support for persons with developmental disabilities and their families* (pp. 243–261). Baltimore, MD: Brookes.

Zarit, S. H., Reever, K. E., & Bach-Peterson, J. (1980). Relatives of the impaired elderly: Correlates of feelings of burden. *Gerontologist, 20,* 649–655.

Zarit, S. H., Todd, P. A., & Zarit, J. M. (1986). Subjective burden of husbands and wives as caregivers: A longitudinal study. *Gerontologist, 26,* 260–266.

Reprinted with permission from *Research on Social Work Practice* (2) (1992):143–160.

Part III
The Elements of Research Design

This section of the text discusses three basic elements of research design—ethics, sample selection, and data collection. How research participants are chosen has always been considered central to the research design process. However, attention to ethical issues is also an indispensable and integral part of research especially in the human services.

Basic principles of data collection as they affect both fixed-method and flexible method research are reviewed in this section. Details of the specific methods used to collect original data for social work and human services research—observation, interviewing, and questionnaires—are covered in part IV. This general chapter on data collection should be read in conjunction with any of the more specific chapters in part IV.

9

Research Ethics for the Helping Professions

The profession of social work shares with other human service professions, like clinical psychology and others, a primary concern with furthering the well being of the people it endeavors to help. The ethical principles that guide research in the helping professions thus have a dual source and focus: on the ethics that have traditionally guided all sciences and on the ethical principles that underlie all professional helping relationships with people. While these two sets of principles sometimes seem not to cohere, at best they work together to enhance both the product and the process of research. As Sieber (1992) has stated, "the ethical researcher creates a mutually respectful, win-win relationship with the research population; this is a relationship in which subjects are pleased to participate candidly, and the community at large regards the conclusions as constructive" (p. 3). While researchers sometimes view addressing ethical issues as an obstacle to be overcome, in fact care taken in addressing the ethics of conducting research involving human beings actually results in sounder research findings.

Some sciences, like astronomy, geology, or chemistry, are directed toward the study of nonliving things. Such fields need only rules governing scientific responsibility. Scientific responsibility concerns conventions about what one must do to enter and remain an accepted member of the scientific community and about the responsibilities of the scientific enterprise toward society as a whole.

When people are studied, however, they inhabit complex social and historical environments that they share, of course, with the professionals who plan and carry out research. The obligation to the other person who is also a participant in the study, with whom the researcher has a professional relationship for the purposes of knowledge-building, is the foundation on which ethical principles in research rest.

This chapter will provide an overview of ethical issues in research in the human service context. Consideration of the ethics of a proposed study should be as central to the research design process as any of the elements traditionally discussed, such as problem formulation, sampling, data collection, or data analysis. In fact, when a study cannot be done ethically, it simply is not done. Similarly, consideration of the ethics of a published research study should be an integral part of any critique.

In the general framework used in this text to understand research, research ethics can be considered a special set of principles and rules, written and unwritten, that place particular parameters on the relationship of the researcher to the people who participate in or who may be affected by the research. These people include those who are studied, fellow researchers, and those who may encounter or make use of the products of the research. In other words, ethics address research activities in their human and social context. They have to do with how researchers enter and conduct themselves in the field of investigation, as well as with how researchers conduct themselves toward fellow professionals and research consumers of all kinds. This chapter will discuss these parameters and explain why they are important, giving particular attention to how they are understood in the context of social work and the other human service professions.

Ethical Principles in Research with Human Beings

There are ways in which ethical matters are of special concern to social work and other human service fields, like clinical psychology, that have the mandate to relieve human suffering. This mission has two clear implications. The first is that these fields are not just professions or subdisciplines; they are callings. People who do not have as their primary concern improving the lot of others and of society are unlikely to be found in such professions. The second is that social work, clinical psychology, and other human service professions are respected both because of the credibility earned and afforded by science and because of the value placed on activities directed toward helping others. Such professions therefore have a responsibility to be both helpful and scientific, which gives rise to special ethical considerations above and beyond those applying to research in other disciplines.

There are three general ethical principles that should underlie research activities: *beneficence,* which means maximizing benefits and minimizing harm or risk; *respect,* which means respecting the autonomy of individuals and protecting those who cannot protect themselves; and *justice,* which means ensuring reasonable, nonexploitative and fair procedures, including "fair distribution of costs and benefits among persons and groups" (Sieber 1992:18). When people and groups who participate in research are treated with respect and fairness and when they can trust in the benign outcome of the enterprise, the result is cooperative and productive relationships between researchers and participants. Any extra care spent on ensuring ethical conduct in research therefore results in more trustworthy data and results.

Historical Problems in Research Ethics

The field of clinical psychology was the first of the human service professions to develop a detailed set of codified principles with the explicit purpose of protecting the rights of human subjects in research. However, many people believe this activity was prompted by some retrospectively controversial or even questionable pieces of psychological research that were done in the branch of psychology called social psychology. The one most often mentioned was conducted and reported by Stanley Milgram at Stanford (1963).

Milgram's research addressed the question of what might be called obedience. He was interested in what one person would be willing to do to another if told to do it by a respected authority. To examine this matter he created a laboratory setting in which he could present a plausible situation calling for obedience. Study participants, who were themselves students, were told that they were engaged in a study of learning and that their part in the work involved serving in the role of teacher. They were further told that another volunteer, whom they could see and hear through a one-way mirror, was serving in the role of learner and would in fact be his/her student. The research task was presented as teaching the learner a set of word associations. The teaching method to be used was punishment: Every time the student gave a wrong answer, the "teacher" was to shock her or him using a simulated shock machine controlled by the teacher but apparently hooked up to the student.

Unbeknownst to the person in the role of teacher, the student was in reality an experimental confederate—a person working with the researcher to mislead the real object of study, the teacher, into believing that the situation was something other than it really was. So while in reality the "learner" was not just another research volunteer whose part in the study happened to involve being expected to learn a set of words and being shocked for every learning error, the real research subject was actively led to believe that this learner was in fact the object of study. This deception obscured from the person in the role of the teacher that he or she in fact was the real object of study in the research.

After being misled about the focus of the study by the experimenter, the real experiment began. The learning task was started, and the confederate/student made deliberate (but the teacher thought preventable) errors. When an error was made, the researcher told the teacher to administer an electric shock to the learner. The teaching task continued and so did the deliberate learning errors. With each successive error, the researcher told the subject/teacher to administer shocks at higher and higher levels. In fact, the experimenter made a deliberate effort to get the subject/teacher to administer shocks in a range labeled on the control panel with the words "warning—dangerous levels."

The experimental situation was arranged so that the subject/teacher could see the confederate/learner throughout. The research plan called for scripted acting on the confederate/learner's part. When an error was made and a shock was administered as per instructions, the learner acted as if a shock had actually been experienced. As the lessons, and therefore the errors, continued, the teacher was encouraged to deliver shocks of increasing intensity and to believe that increasing shocks were given. To help create this illusion, the confederate/learner acted as if he/ she were in progressively greater physical and emotional pain. In fact, after a certain point was passed on the shock intensity scale, the confederate/learner by design simulated very great distress, as is illustrated by this description from Milgram's original article (1963): "Well, it's not fair to shock the guy. . . . These are terrific volts. I don't think this is very humane. . . . Oh, I can't go on with this; no, this isn't right. It's a hell of an experiment. The guy is suffering in there. No, I don't want to go on. This is crazy . . ." (pp. 375–76). Milgram himself commented, "These subjects were frequently in a highly agitated and even angered state" (p. 376).

While the Milgram study was presented to subjects as researching teaching methods, it was in reality researching obedience. The dependent variables recorded and analyzed were the maximum shock level administered and whether or not the participants administered all thirty shocks planned. The study's primary finding was that most people are far more willing to follow the instructions of authorities, even those that went against their principles, than was previously assumed. This finding was clearly a very important one that helped answer some of the questions people had been left with after the Nazi Holocaust in Europe.

However, there were tremendous costs to making this discovery. One was the impact participating in the research had on some of the subjects/teachers in the study, who found themselves feeling enormous guilt after seeing what they had been willing to do to another person just because they were told by a trusted authority to do it. Another was the damage done to the reputation of researchers. Knowing that a researcher would deliberately lie to research participants under-mined the public's sense of researchers as humanitarian and instead showed them to at least sometimes be people who could not be trusted to protect the well-being of those they worked with in the pursuit of knowledge.

Milgram's study raises what is perhaps the most fundamental set of questions raised in research ethics, namely: (1) What information are researchers ethically obligated to provide to participants when soliciting their participation in a piece of research? and (2) When there is any potential for harm to study participants, what if anything, justifies conducting the study?

Experiments are not the only kind of research in which deception or less than complete candor about research activities can arise. Ethnographic and participant observation research can on rare occasions involve deception as well (ASA 1997; Fine 1993; NASW 1997). Rollins's (1985) study of household domestic work involved the author taking a job as a domestic worker in order to conduct her study and not revealing the fact that she was doing research on the woman who employed her in the privacy of the woman's own home. As Rollins commented:

> My participant observation as a domestic worker raised an ethical question. Deception was, after all, a fundamental element in this phase of the research. . . .
>
> [M]y research led me to repeatedly treat other humans, the subjects of my research, in a way that I would have under other circumstances considered immoral. What justification is there for the research situation to change one's morality? (p. 11)

The purposes of Rollins's research were clear: to explore the relationships between domestic workers and the women who employ them, and she believed that experiencing the situation herself was an essential part of studying it. In fact, both large and small issues of deception arise almost inevitably in ethnographic and participant observation research, most obviously when deciding whether the process of observation itself will be overt or covert, but often subtly even when the observational role has been made explicit (Burgess 1989; Fine 1993).

Psychology and ethnography are not the only fields in which questions about research ethics have been raised. One of the most infamous examples of ethical problems in research comes from medicine: the Tuskegee Syphilis Study. This United States Public Health Department study of the stages of syphilis began in 1932; poor African American men were recruited as participants and were offered an annual physical examination, free health care, and the promise of treatment for "bad blood" in return for their participation. The study's focus was on the manifestations of second and third stage infection in previously untreated African American men, a group in which the disease had not previously been studied. The project was undertaken in a rural county in which medical care of any kind had not previously been available to the poor and in which rates of syphilis infection among African American residents had been found to be high.

The study was originally planned to last only a few months, and some medical treatment was in fact provided at first. However, the longer the study lasted, the more deceitful the researchers became in recruiting, testing, and withholding treatment from participants. One major study activity in fact became obtaining the bodies of those who died for autopsy study, and families were offered burial money in return for their permission to conduct an autopsy.

By the 1940s, the discovery of penicillin for the first time provided an inexpensive, effective, and short course of treatment for syphilis, replacing the earlier, costlier, protracted and dangerous methods of treatment previously used. However, study participants were not informed of or offered this new treatment although the research continued until 1972 (Bowman 1991; Jones 1981). Treatment that could have cured them and prevented the spread of the disease was withheld from the men only because they were part of the study. Over nearly forty years, participants suffered and died needlessly in part because there were no ethical norms for scientific research on human beings that the physicians, nurses, and public and private organizations involved in funding or carrying out the research could use to evaluate it. In addition, contemporary accounts of the study make clear that race and class were major factors contributing to the way in which the study was designed and carried out (Bowman 1991; Jones 1993).

Norms and practices have changed a great deal in the world of research since these studies were undertaken. Professional codes of ethics now include specific content related to the conduct of research. In addition, due largely to federal legislation passed in the 1970s, mechanisms for the review of the ethics of research studies involving human beings have been developed and implemented in academic, medical, and human service settings. Any ethical issues raised by a proposed study are discussed and debated before the study can begin, and studies are often reviewed and monitored while they are ongoing and once they are complete before there is any dissemination of results. In fact, many believe that the scandal that occurred when the Tuskegee study was uncovered contributed to the implementation of ethical reforms in medical research (Bowman 1991; Jones 1993; Sieber 1992).

However, controversies about research ethics still occur. In social work, for example, a social worker was recently charged with ethical violations because of a study he undertook to evaluate the review process in social work journals (Feinberg 1988; Goleman 1988). This researcher sent altered versions of a previously published article to 140 journals in social work and related disciplines; the versions varied only by whether or not the social work intervention described was found to have a positive effect on the client. The results of the study showed that among the 33 social work journals surveyed, the version reporting a positive effect was accepted for publication more often than the version reporting a negative effect, revealing a bias in the review process toward articles favorable to social work treatment.

A group of journal editors, led by one whose reviewers had recognized the article as a copy of an earlier one and which therefore had rejected it, lodged a formal ethics complaint against the researcher protesting the ethics of the study. The complaint was based on two grounds: (1) that no consent had been obtained from the journals in question to participate in the study, and (2) given the rules of research publication that require that previously published work not be submitted and that an article be sent to one journal at a time, the study methodology was based on deceiving the journal and its reviewers about the fact that this was a previously published work. The counterargument made was that the study of bias could not have been conducted any other way and that the journal review process is so important to what knowledge gets legitimated in the profession that journal review processes must be regularly scrutinized. What are the ethical principles by which this or any other study should be evaluated?

In addition, controversies about the ethics of experimental designs persist, especially in medicine. For example, AIDS activists pressured government agencies for more rapid approval and patient access to promising treatments for HIV disease. They also pushed for wider representation of populations at risk, such as women and people of color, in clinical trials (Epstein 1997). Like advocates for cancer patients and others with life-threatening illnesses, they raised important questions about the ethics of randomized experiments in which only some people received promising new but unproven treatments. Thus discussions continue about how to ethically and responsibly balance the need to develop sound knowledge about diseases and their treatments with the needs of patients.

Ethical Standards in Research

Both the National Association of Social Workers (NASW) (1997) and the American Psychological Association (APA) (1992), among other groups, have general codes of ethics that also address ethics in research. The APA code emphasizes deception as an issue because experiments are so often used in the field. The code in sociology (American Sociological Association 1997) emphasizes confidentiality based on the relatively greater use of survey methods in the field. The code in anthropology (American Anthropology Association 1997) tends to stress the protection of the whole communities being studied based on the comparatively greater use of ethnography in that field (Bowman 1991). This text will focus on the codes in psychology and social work for purposes of illustration and because of their practice focus. However, it should be noted that most of the ethical principles governing research contained in these various codes are similar.

The principles set forth in codes of ethics are necessarily written at a fairly abstract level. Therefore they are not prescriptive: They do not provide unambiguous instruction about what specific practices should and should not be done in every specific situation. Instead they provide guidelines whose applicability and meaning must be interpreted in each specific case.

The most widely used code of ethics in social work is that of the NASW (1997). Anyone who becomes a member of the association agrees to practice in accordance with the code. One section of the Code pertains to evaluation and research, setting forth a number of principles that should guide any research study (see figure 9–1). For purposes of comparison, elaboration, and emphasis, the 10 general principles adopted by the APA (1992) governing research with human participants are given in figure 9–2.

The first principle that guides research ethics is that the *potential consequences* of any piece of research for people must be considered (NASW 1990). This principle is meant to address consequences for human beings in general as well as for those directly participating in a study. Stated another way, research in social work should contribute to furthering the overall goals of the profession of service to people and to society. In this standard, the specific mission of social work and other helping professions unites with what is often taken as an obligation of the scientific enterprise whatever the discipline. In ethnographic research, this principle has been described as the "classic virtue" of being "the kindly ethnographer," one who is sympathetic to those she or he studies and wishes them well (Fine 1993). The 1997 NASW code addresses this idea of beneficence in its stipulation that all social work professional activities, including research and evaluation, should contribute to the common human good.

The Tuskegee study described above, for example, did not conform to this principle, both because treatment was withheld from participants who could have been helped by it and because furthering the description of end-stage syphilis obtained in this way cannot easily be shown to have had any compelling social or scientific benefit. Although the Tuskegee example seems obvious in retrospect (and is by today's standards), the ethical issues do not always seem so clear when research is actually being done.

The challenge encountered when putting this principle into practice is in having the imagination to anticipate what all the potential findings of a study might be and to consider the uses, political or professional, to which its findings might be put. In addition, different people may evaluate the consequences of a study quite differently, as many of the recent controversies about research into AIDS and its treatment illustrate (Epstein 1997). Where there is legitimate question about the potential usefulness of a study or about any damage that it may do, there is an obligation to seek advice and sanction for the study before it is begun, as the APA standards (1992) state explicitly. Continued monitoring of such studies

4. **SOCIAL WORKERS' ETHICAL RESPONSIBILITIES AS PROFESSIONALS**

4.01 Competence

(a) Social workers should accept responsibility or employment only on the basis of existing competence or the intention to acquire the necessary competence.

(b) Social workers should strive to become and remain proficient in professional practice and the performance of professional functions. Social workers should critically examine and keep current with emerging knowledge relevant to social work. Social workers should routinely review the professional literature and participate in continuing education relevant to social work practice and social work ethics.

(c) Social workers should base practice on recognized knowledge, including empirically based knowledge, relevant to social work and social work ethics.

4.08 Acknowledging Credit

(a) Social workers should take responsibility and credit, including authorship credit, only for work they have actually performed and to which they have contributed.

(b) Social workers should honestly acknowledge the work of and the contributions made by others.

5. **SOCIAL WORKERS' ETHICAL RESPONSIBILITIES TO THE SOCIAL WORK PROFESSION**

5.01 Integrity of the Profession

(a) Social workers should work toward the maintenance and promotion of high standards of practice.

(b) Social workers should uphold and advance the values, ethics, knowledge, and mission of the profession. Social workers should protect, enhance, and improve the integrity of the profession through appropriate study and research, active discussion, and responsible criticism of the profession.

(c) Social workers should contribute time and professional expertise to activities that promote respect for the value, integrity, and competence of the social work profession. These activities may include teaching, research, consultation, service, legislative testimony, presentations in the community, and participation in their professional organizations.

(d) Social workers should contribute to the knowledge base of social work and share with colleagues their knowledge related to practice, research, and ethics. Social workers should seek to contribute to the profession's literature and to share their knowledge at professional meetings and conferences.

5.02 Evaluation and Research

(a) Social workers should monitor and evaluate policies, the implementation of programs, and practice interventions.

(b) Social workers should promote and facilitate evaluation and research to contribute to the development of knowledge.

(c) Social workers should critically examine and keep current with emerging knowledge relevant to social work and fully use evaluation and research evidence in their professional practice.

(d) Social workers engaged in evaluation or research should carefully consider possible consequences and should follow guidelines developed for the protection of evaluation and research participants. Appropriate institutional review boards should be consulted.

(e) Social workers engaged in evaluation or research should obtain voluntary and written informed consent from participants, when appropriate, without any implied or actual deprivation or penalty for refusal to participate; without undue inducement to participate; and with due regard for participants' well-being, privacy, and dignity. Informed consent should include information about the nature, extent, and duration of the participation requested and disclosure of the risks and benefits of participation in the research.

(f) When evaluation or research participants are incapable of giving informed consent, social workers should provide an appropriate explanation to the participants, obtain the participants' assent to the extent they are able, and obtain written consent from an appropriate proxy.

(g) Social workers should never design or conduct evaluation or research that does not use consent procedures, such as certain forms of naturalistic observation and archival research, unless rigorous and responsible review of the research has found it to be justified because of its prospective scientific, educational, or applied value and unless equally effective alternative procedures that do not involve waiver of consent are not feasible.

(h) Social workers should inform participants of their right to withdraw from evaluation and research at any time without penalty.

(i) Social workers should take appropriate steps to ensure that participants in evaluation and research have access to appropriate supportive services.

(j) Social workers engaged in evaluation or research should protect participants from unwarranted physical or mental distress, harm, danger, or deprivation.

(k) Social workers engaged in the evaluation of services should discuss collected information only for professional purposes and only with people professionally concerned with this information.

(l) Social workers engaged in evaluation or research should ensure the anonymity or confidentiality of participants and of the data obtained from them. Social workers should inform participants of any limits of confidentiality, the measures that will be taken to ensure confidentiality, and when any records containing research data will be destroyed.

(m) Social workers who report evaluation and research results should protect participants' confidentiality by omitting identifying information unless proper consent has been obtained authorizing disclosure.

(n) Social workers should report evaluation and research findings accurately. They should not fabricate or falsify results and should take steps to correct any errors later found in published data using standard publication methods.

(o) Social workers engaged in evaluation or research should be alert to and avoid conflicts of interest and dual relationships with participants, should inform participants when a real or potential conflict of interest arises, and should take steps to resolve the issue in a manner that makes participants' interests primary.

(p) Social workers should educate themselves, their students, and their colleagues about responsible research practices.

Figure 9–1 Excerpts from the NASW Code of Ethics Related to
Evaluation and Research

PREAMBLE

Psychologists work to develop a valid and reliable body of scientific knowledge based on research. They may apply that knowledge to human behavior in a variety of contexts. In doing so, they perform many roles, such as researcher, educator, diagnostician, therapist, supervisor, consultant, administrator, social interventionist, and expert witness. Their goal is to broaden knowledge of behavior and, where appropriate, to apply it pragmatically to improve the condition of both the individual and society. Psychologists respect the central importance of freedom of inquiry and expression in research, teaching, and publication. They also strive to help the public in developing informed judgments and choices concerning human behavior. This Ethics Code provides a common set of values upon which psychologists build their professional and scientific work. . . .

From the section on General [Ethical] Standards

1.14   Avoiding Harm

Psychologists take reasonable steps to avoid harming their patients or clients, research participants, students, and others with whom they work, and to minimize harm where it is foreseeable and unavoidable.

1.23   Documentation of Professional and Scientific Work

(a) Psychologists appropriately document their professional and scientific work in order to facilitate provision of services later by them or by other professionals, to ensure accountability, and to meet other requirements of institutions or the law.

(b) When psychologists have reason to believe that records of their professional services will be used in legal proceedings involving recipients of or participants in their work, they have a responsibility to create and maintain documentation in the kind of detail and quality that would be consistent with reasonable scrutiny in an adjudicative forum. (See also Standard 7.01, Professionalism, under Forensic Activities.)

1.24   Record and Data

Psychologists create, maintain, disseminate, store, retain, and dispose of records and data relating to their research, practice, and other work in accordance with law and in a manner that permits compliance with the requirements of this Ethics Code. (See also Standard 5.04, Maintenance of Records.)

From the section on Privacy and Confidentiality

5.01   Discussing the Limits of Confidentiality

(a) Psychologists discuss with persons and organizations with whom they establish a scientific or professional relationship (including, to the extent feasible, minors and their legal representatives) (1) the relevant limitations on confidentiality, including limitations where applicable in group, marital, and family therapy or in organizational consulting, and (2) the foreseeable uses of the information generated through their services.

(b) Unless it is not feasible or is contraindicated, the discussion of confidentiality occurs at the outset of the relationship and thereafter as new circumstances may warrant.

(c) Permission for electronic recording of interviews is secured from clients and patients.

5.04   Maintenance of Records

Psychologists maintain appropriate confidentiality in creating, storing, accessing, transferring, and disposing of records under their control, whether these are written, automated, or in any other medium. Psychologists maintain and dispose of records in accordance with law and in a manner that permits compliance with the requirements of this Ethics Code.

From the section on Teaching, Training, Supervision, Research and Publishing

6.06   Planning Research

(a) Psychologists design, conduct, and report research in accordance with recognized standards of scientific competence and ethical research.

(b) Psychologists plan their research so as to minimize the possibility that results will be misleading.

(c) In planning research, psychologists consider its ethical acceptability under the Ethics Code. If an ethical issue is unclear, psychologists seek to resolve the issue through consultation with institutional review boards, animal care and use committees, peer consultations, or other proper mechanisms.

Figure 9–2 Excerpts from APA Code (1992)

Reprinted with permission from the *Ethical Principles of Psychologists and Code of Conduct.*

(d) Psychologists take reasonable steps to implement appropriate protections for the rights and welfare of human participants, other persons affected by the research, and the welfare of animal subjects.

6.07 Responsibility

(a) Psychologists conduct research competently and with due concern for the dignity and welfare of the participants.

(b) Psychologists are responsible for the ethical conduct of research conducted by them or by others under their supervision or control.

(c) Researchers and assistants are permitted to perform only those tasks for which they are appropriately trained and prepared.

(d) As part of the process of development and implementation of research projects, psychologists consult those with expertise concerning any special population under investigation or most likely to be affected.

6.08 Compliance With Law and Standards

Psychologists plan and conduct research in a manner consistent with federal and state law and regulations, as well as professional standards governing the conduct of research, and particularly those standards governing research with human participants and animal subjects.

6.09 Institutional Approval

Psychologists obtain from host institutions or organizations appropriate approval prior to conducting research, and they provide accurate information about their research proposals. They conduct the research in accordance with the approved research protocol.

6.10 Research Responsibilities

Prior to conducting research (except research involving only anonymous surveys, naturalistic observations, or similar research), psychologists enter into an agreement with participants that clarifies the nature of the research and the responsibilities of each party.

6.11 Informed Consent to Research

(a) Psychologists use language that is reasonably understandable to research participants in obtaining their appropriate informed consent (except as provided in Standard 6.12, Dispensing With Informed Consent). Such informed consent is appropriately documented.

(b) Using language that is reasonably understandable to participants, psychologists inform participants of the nature of the research; they inform participants that they are free to participate or to decline to participate or to withdraw from the research; they explain the foreseeable consequences of declining or withdrawing; they inform participants of significant factors that may be expected to influence their willingness to participate (such as risks, discomfort, adverse effects, or limitations on confidentiality, except as provided in Standard 6.15, Deception in Research); and they explain other aspects about which the prospective participants inquire.

(c) When psychologists conduct research with individuals such as students or subordinates, psychologists take special care to protect the prospective participants from adverse consequences of declining or withdrawing from participation.

(d) When research participation is a course requirement or opportunity for extra credit, the prospective participant is given the choice of equitable alternative activities.

(e) For persons who are legally incapable of giving informed consent, psychologists nevertheless (1) provide an appropriate explanation, (2) obtain the participant's assent, and (3) obtain appropriate permission from a legally authorized person, if such substitute consent is permitted by law.

6.12 Dispensing With Informed Consent

Before determining that planned research (such as research involving only anonymous questionnaires, naturalistic observations, or certain kinds or archival research) does not require the informed consent of research participants, psychologists consider applicable regulations and institutional review board requirements, and they consult with colleagues as appropriate.

6.13 Informed Consent in Research Filming or Recording

Psychologists obtain informed consent from research participants prior to filming or recording them in any form, unless the research involves simply naturalistic observations in public places and it is not anticipated that the recording will be used in a manner that could cause personal identification or harm.

6.14 Offering Inducements for Research Participants

(a) In offering professional services as an inducement to obtain research participants, psychologists make clear the nature of the services, as well as the risks, obligations, and limitations. (See also Standard 1.18, Barter [With Patients or Clients].)

Figure 9–2 continued

(b) Psychologists do not offer excessive or inappropriate financial or other inducements to obtain research participants, particularly when it might tend to coerce participation.

6.15   Deception in Research

(a) Psychologists do not conduct a study involving deception unless they have determined that the use of deceptive techniques is justified by the study's prospective scientific, educational, or applied value and that equally effective alternative procedures that do not use deception are not feasible.

(b) Psychologists never deceive research participants about significant aspects that would affect their willingness to participate, such as physical risks, discomfort, or unpleasant emotional experiences.

(c) Any other deception that is an integral feature of the design and conduct of an experiment must be explained to participants as early as is feasible, preferably at the conclusion of their participation, but no later than at the conclusion of the research. (See also Standard 6.18, Providing Participants With Information About the Study.)

6.16   Sharing and Utilizing Data

Psychologists inform research participants of their anticipated sharing or further use of personally identifiable research data and of the possibility of unanticipated future uses.

6.17   Minimizing Invasiveness

In conducting research, psychologists interfere with the participants or milieu from which data are collected only in a manner that is warranted by an appropriate research design and that is consistent with psychologists' roles as scientific investigators.

6.18   Providing Participants With Information About the Study

(a) Psychologists provide a prompt opportunity for participants to obtain appropriate information about the nature, results, and conclusions of the research, and psychologists attempt to correct any misconceptions that participants may have.

(b) If scientific or humane values justify delaying or withholding this information, psychologists take reasonable measures to reduce the risk of harm.

6.19   Honoring Commitments

Psychologists take reasonable measures to honor all commitments they have made to research participants. . . .

6.21   Reporting of Results

(a) Psychologists do not fabricate data or falsify results in their publications.

(b) If psychologists discover significant errors in their published data, they take reasonable steps to correct such errors in a correction, retraction, erratum, or other appropriate publication means.

6.22   Plagiarism

Psychologists do not present substantial portions or elements of another's work or data as their own, even if the other work or data source is cited occasionally.

6.23   Publication Credit

(a) Psychologists take responsibility and credit, including authorship credit, only for work they have actually performed or to which they have contributed.

(b) Principal authorship and other publication credits accurately reflect the relative scientific or professional contributions of the individual involved, regardless of their relative status. Mere possession of an institutional position, such as Department Chair, does not justify authorship credit. Minor contributions to the research or to the writing for publications are appropriately acknowledged, such as in footnotes or in an introductory statement.

(c) A student is usually listed as principal author on any multiple-authored article that is substantially based on the student's dissertation or thesis.

6.24   Duplicate Publication of Data

Psychologists do not publish, as original data, data that have been previously published. This does not preclude republishing data when they are accompanied by proper acknowledgment.

6.25   Sharing Data

After research results are published, psychologists do not withhold the data on which their conclusions are based from other competent professionals who seek to verify the substantive claims through reanalysis and who intend to use such data only for that purpose, provided that the confidentiality of the participants can be protected and unless legal rights concerning proprietary data preclude their release.

6.26   Professional Reviewers

Psychologists who review material submitted for publication, grant, or other research proposal review respect the confidentiality of and the proprietary rights in such information of those who submitted it.

Figure 9–2   continued

is also helpful. These days it is common to read of biomedical studies that are halted or modified once data about effective treatments becomes available.

The principle that participants in any research should be protected from any unwarranted harm extends this idea and spells out its common implications. In addition to physical harm, psychological distress such as that experienced by some of Milgram's "subjects" is to be avoided or minimized. Nor can potential research participants be deprived of any service or treatment they might otherwise be entitled to based on whether or not they agree to be part of a study. Legal risks may also occur for research participants. Sieber (1992) gives several examples of research and program evaluation with urban residents who are HIV positive, where both discrimination based on HIV status and the risk of arrest for illegal drug use were obstacles to recruitment that had to be sensitively overcome.

In addition, the NASW (1997) code recommends that access to supportive services be available to any research participant who has need of them. This is to address any discomfort or distress that research participation may engender. It is also suggested because researchers in community and human service settings sometimes simply encounter people in need in the course of doing their research.

Another major concept guiding research with human beings is that the consent of participants in the research be voluntary and informed. Each of the terms in this statement deserves careful definition. As Sieber (1992) states:

> Voluntary means without threat or undue inducement. Informed means that the subject knows what a reasonable person in the same situation would want to know before giving consent. Consent means explicit agreement to participate (p. 26).

All parts of this injunction are important. In many instances, it is a simple matter to inform a potential research participant of what will be requested of him or her as a participant. For example, it is relatively easy to ask an adult selected from the general population about whether or not he or she is willing to participate in a 20-minute telephone interview to answer questions on some social policy issue such as welfare or health insurance reform. However, very difficult circumstances often arise in the case of clinical research when obtaining informed consent from vulnerable populations, including some whom it would not be fair to regard as necessarily capable of protecting themselves or acting in their own best interests. It is easy to think of instances of this latter circumstance, such as in studies of children, mentally retarded people, or elders with Alzheimer's Disease. In addition, there are often tensions in all forms of research, including ethnography (Fine 1993), about how candid to be with participants about research questions and processes when doing so might affect the findings.

In some cases, a researcher must also decide how to explain a study in ways that participants can understand or decide who, ethically and legally, can act on the participant's behalf in consenting. Individual communication difficulties, differences in sensory capacity, cultural differences, and language differences must all be taken into account when consent is sought. Sometimes, as in the case of children, the law stipulates that they cannot consent for themselves and that the consent of a parent or guardian must be substituted. When studying adolescents, the consent of a parent and the assent of the participating teen are often both sought. Social workers and other human service professionals have the communication skills and the ability to convey respect to potential participants that can both help make participation in the study seem appealing and make the potential participant feel respected from the outset.

Whoever is making the decision about participation, any risks that might occur must be explained, and any provisions that have been made to assist participants in dealing with any research-related problems that might occur must be spelled out as well. The activities involved in participation must be explained, and the nature of the data to be generated and its dissemination should be described as well. Only in this way will a consenting individual know exactly what she or he is agreeing to.

In addition to being informed, consent must be voluntary. In most cases, this criterion is easy to meet. However, it is important to consider how vulnerable a potential research participant (or family member) may feel when approached. In the face of a refusal, will services be affected? Can an individual client who is approached by his or her helping professional feel free enough to say no? Will a student or employee in reality be comfortable saying no to a teacher, employer, or supervisor? Will some negative judgement be made by the more powerful professional? Are any payments or services offered for participation an "undue inducement" given the situations of those approached? For example, Williams (1992) reports sometimes paying small sums of money to informants who were crack-addicted for the service they provided, namely information about themselves. Is this undue inducement?

Finally, how much control, if any, will the participant have over how he or she or his or her community or reference group will be represented when the study is completed (Burgess 1989; Bowman 1991)? Williams (1992) speaks of the control that participants can exercise by altering the information they provide. In the end, however, it is generally the researcher, who is most often not part of the community studied, who decides how an individual or community will be depicted (Bowman 1991). In fact, it is most often those who are vulnerable because of race, class, or lack of power politically or in the context of study, like students, who have been exploited in the research situation (Engram 1982; Bowman 1991; Burgess 1989). Any socially sensitive research, that is, any study "in which there are potential social consequences or implications, either directly for participants in the research or for the class of individuals represented by the research," requires special attention to ethical issues (Sieber & Stanley 1988:49).

It is important to note that consent to participate in research is not irrevocable. In fact, it is common practice to tell potential research participants explicitly that they may withdraw consent at any time during or after conduct of the study and that, if they do so, any data describing them will be destroyed. This stipulation protects a participant from continuing to engage in a process that turns out to be problematic in ways that he or she did not anticipate when making the original agreement. The concept that consent can be withdrawn also means that a participant is not required to answer all questions or agree to total or continuing participation just because consent to participate was originally given.

In some rare situations, procedures to obtain written consent are not employed. The first such situation is when maintaining a written record of the consent would pose a greater potential threat to participants' well-being than the lack of one would (Sieber 1992); one situation might be when data are kept about illegal activities that could be connected with a name through the consent form. As Sieber points out, however, the fact that written consent is not obtained does not mean that an oral consent procedure should not occur. A second such situation is when the consent process itself would jeopardize the study process itself, as was claimed in the case of the study of journal review processes summarized earlier. This kind of situation is a special case of the more general problem of whether and in what circumstances deception of any kind is acceptable when conducting research (see below).

An additional major principle of research ethics addresses a risk that accompanies participation in virtually all research: the invasion of privacy and threat to confidentiality. Responsible researchers often devote considerable energy to protecting the privacy of the people they study. Anonymity in research means that the identity of the person participating is unknown to the researcher and that it cannot be inferred by anyone else from the data presented. In fact, anonymity can only be achieved when there is no face-to-face contact between researcher and participant and when no identifying data are available. This circumstance is rare except in some survey research.

More commonly, the issue is confidentiality. Often the researcher knows, or could know, the identities of the research participants but keeps this information confidential. Confidentiality also requires that data describing respondents be presented in such a way that the identity of participants cannot be inferred from it. In addition, as with clinical records, ensuring confidentiality also requires that data be stored during and after the conduct of the study in such a way that any identifiable information is protected.

It is not only individual participants in research who have something at stake when it comes to confidentiality. Agencies, programs, and program personnel may be at risk when evaluative studies are conducted, and data from such studies must be treated professionally and confidentially as well.

In addition, ethical standards in research address relationships among researchers. Responsibility to those whose prior and current work is used includes adherence to the conventions of scholarly inquiry, including standards regarding plagiarism:

(a) Social workers should take responsibility and credit, including authorship credit, only for work they have actually performed and to which they have contributed.

(b) Social workers should honestly acknowledge the work of and contributions made by others (NASW 1997:24).

This means that the work of all those who contribute to a study should be acknowledged in an appropriate way. When undertaking team or collaborative research, it is generally helpful to make explicit agreements about the forms of participation and acknowledgement to be granted, including authorship of any articles and reports that may result.

Finally, research, for both good and bad reasons, often focuses on groups defined as disadvantaged, vulnerable, or deviant. Because of past abuses, as epitomized in the Tuskegee Study, cynicism and resistance to research, however well-intentioned, are now often encountered in communities of color and in other vulnerable groups. For example, Puerto Rico was the site of the first field trials of early oral contraceptive medications, and the many side effects women there experienced are still sometimes reflected in attitudes both to research and to reproductive health care services in Puerto Rican communities on the mainland.

Bowman (1991) has suggested two additional principles of beneficence that should be considered in research in vulnerable communities: *significant involvement* and *functional relevance*: "*Significant involvement* calls for members of the group under study to have a central role in the entire research process. *Functional relevance* dictates that studies should operate to promote the expressed needs and perspectives of the study population" (p. 754).

Significant involvement in a piece of research can be achieved in a variety of ways. The use of indigenous interviewers, community consultants (both individuals and groups), trade-off and exchange agreements, including payments to participants, and attention to the relevance of the study to the community studied rather than just to "knowledge development" in general have become fairly well-accepted strategies for enhancing community participation in research. However, Bowman (1991) points out that these strategies are most effective when they include the formulation, planning and design phases of the research rather than just the implementation and reporting phases of a study. Significant involvement of community members, of course, is the strategy; functional relevance is the outcome desired to which researchers and community members must be committed. Taking these principles seriously is likely to affect both the content and the process of the research in profound ways. However, adapting research efforts to the needs of the communities and populations studied in fact is likely to improve the quality and relevance of the research produced.

The Role of Research Ethics Committees

In recognition of the importance and complexity of ethical decision making in research, the helping professions, in part because of requirements of the federal government, have developed the practice of relying on Human Subjects Committees, or Institutional Review Boards (IRB) to evaluate whether specific proposed studies would or would not be, if actually conducted, ethical. These Institutional Review Boards, required by law at any institution receiving federal monies, are comprised at minimum of researchers as well as members of the community. The researchers on such committees have as one responsibility bringing the perspective of the scientist to the dialogue. The members of the community have the dual roles of representing how the general public is likely to feel about specific procedures and how the study procedures as proposed would be likely to impact on the people who might participate in it.

These boards are provided by researchers with detailed descriptions of planned studies. Most of the IRB considerations revolve around evaluating two matters: (1)

the adequacy of the voluntary informed consent procedures to be used when inviting people to participate in the study, and (2) the cost/benefit ratio of the proposed study. This cost/benefit ratio examines the risks any research participant might encounter from being a part of the proposed study and weighs them in relation to the benefits that might be anticipated were the study to be completed as proposed. However, all ethical issues raised by a proposed study will in fact be considered. Often this deliberative process is helpful in identifying potential ethical problems before the fact and in helping a researcher to make the most of a proposed study design.

As already stated, voluntary informed consent is a fundamental principle in research with human beings. It stipulates that research can be done only when a person has been informed of the nature of what participating in the research will entail and has freely agreed to participate. One of the more difficult circumstances involving informed consent was represented in Milgram's study: It is difficult to obtain informed consent when the study design requires withholding some information from the participants or even deliberate deception about what is going on. In the case of the study of journal review processes, the investigator argued that the process of obtaining consent at all would have rendered the study useless by alerting editors and reviewers to an impending study and thus altering their normal reviewing behavior. An IRB reviewing either of these studies would have to decide whether or not the circumstances and purposes of the research warranted the absence of any consent or fully informed consent procedures in each instance.

The ethical guidelines of both the APA and NASW emphasize that studies involving deception should only be conducted when the yield in knowledge is expected to be great and when no alternative study strategy for addressing the question can be used. When deception is used, the APA requires that disclosure and explanation be made to participants as soon as possible, but no later than the conclusion of the study (APA 1992).

When preparing material for IRB review, the methodology of the proposed study must be described in detail. Any recruitment letters, advertisements, and data collection instruments must be included. In this way, committee members will know exactly what a participant will encounter and be exposed to. In addition, the specific tools and procedures used to obtain informed consent from participants must be explained as well.

Often a written consent form is used and submitted for review. This form records the description of the study's purpose and exactly what participation in the study will entail. Such consent forms are provided to each study participant; participants' signatures document that participant consent was actually given. Copies of such forms should be retained by both researcher and participant. Federal law specifies a number of elements that must be part of any consent form (see Sieber 1992:33); all Human Subjects Committees or IRB can provide either guidelines or standardized formats to be used.

There are some instances when such consent forms are not necessary. A mailed survey with anonymous returns and covering a nonthreatening topic is one such case because the respondent can simply ignore the survey or throw it away. The telephone survey is another, since it is assumed that refusal to participate can be conveyed at any time by hanging up the phone. The return of the survey or the completion of the telephone interview are considered evidence of consent to participate. However, this procedure requires that the cover letter that accompanies the survey or the introduction to the phone call must inform all potential respondents about the purpose of the study, its sponsorship, any assurances about confidentiality of the data obtained, and the uses to which the data will be put.

The matter of evaluating the cost/benefit ratio of a study is even more difficult. There is always some cost to study participants that arises from being part of any study. This cost may be as minor as the loss of the time taken to participate in the study, which could certainly be otherwise spent. However, it may be as major as suffering a crisis of self confidence, as happened to some of the participants in Milgram's experiment, or agreeing to refrain from receiving alternative treatment for a specified period of time. Ethical research requires that efforts be made to minimize the costs and enhance the benefits of any research, and IRB work with researchers on both of these dimensions.

Reducing costs. There are many ways to address any costs to participants that might arise in research. The first and most important step is to consider any design alternatives that could answer the research question without running the risk of harm to participants. Only when no alternative design exists will a high risk study be approved. Studies that pose more than minimal risk to participants, such as those that involve deception and those that involve working with vulnerable populations, will naturally be scrutinized much more closely by IRB than others.

Any IRB will want to know what measures will be taken to maintain the confidentiality of data. These measures will range from attention to how data are recorded, to how they will be stored, with access by whom and for how long, to how they will be described and disseminated once the data analysis is complete. Identifying information or material from which the identities of participants can be inferred will require the most care in handling. The researcher also has the responsibility to inform him- or herself about state and federal law as it may limit confidentiality, as through court subpoena, and inform the participants of these laws as they may affect them by limiting the protection that can be offered.

Some specific potential harms can be met with special assistance. For example, debriefing of participants after any research involving deception is now standard practice (see APA standards above). When research of any kind is done on sensitive or potentially painful issues, such childhood experiences of sexual abuse, it is common to offer to provide professional help to participants who may require it following the data gathering process.

Whatever the ethical issues are that can be anticipated before a study is approved and undertaken, there are many subtle dilemmas around confidentiality that can arise in the conduct of participant observation and other research that may need careful handling (Burgess 1989). These include how well all of those whom the researcher may encounter in the field are informed of the nature of the research and the observer's role and how even information explicitly labeled "confidential" or "off the record" will or will not inform the research. Burgess (1989) states a principle for ethnography that actually applies to reducing the risks or cost to participants in all research: ". . . a review of ethical problems and dilemmas should be at the heart of reflexive practice by those ethnographers who are working in the field" (p. 74). Social workers and other human service professionals have habits of self-examination and experience in dealing with ethical dilemmas in the practice situation that can serve them well as researchers.

Evaluating benefit. In any methodologically sound and carefully executed study, there is always some benefit. At the very least, as in a replication study, there will be an additional demonstration of support for some previously held belief. And on occasion there is a genuine advance in real knowledge: Something new is discovered or understood. However, if a study is poorly designed, its results will be of questionable intrinsic value. If a study is never completed and reported, the results will never get communicated to those who might benefit from the knowledge gained. If there will be no yield in knowledge, no benefit, there is no justification for even minimal risk to participants. In evaluating the risk/benefit ratio of a study, therefore, an IRB will look carefully at the proposed study methodology and at the qualifications of the investigator to carry out and complete the research.

One of the ways an IRB may work with a researcher, then, is to suggest methodological changes in a proposed research design. This kind of response may seem inappropriate at first to an applicant for approval to conduct a study. However, remembering that risk is understood as acceptable only in the context of benefit from the project, this kind of response from an IRB should be seen as aimed at enhancing the benefit side of the equation.

Problems can arise, though, when a given IRB holds a narrow or idiosyncratic view of what constitutes a valuable study. For example, if experimental designs are seen by an IRB in the traditional way as at the pinnacle of the design hierarchy, someone proposing a flexible method study may find it difficult to secure approval for the research simply because the committee sees little benefit to any piece of research of this kind. This book takes the position that both flexible and fixed methods of research are valuable; thus an IRB should include people with expertise in all types of research, and its comments should be directed to maximizing the methodological soundness and conclusions of whatever type of study is proposed.

In summary, it is the task of Institutional Review Boards to determine whether participants' rights to refuse to take part in a study, or to discontinue participating in it, are protected in the study protocol and whether the anticipated benefits from a study are sufficient to outweigh all reasonably expected, potential harm. These questions are weighed by boards who discuss specific study protocols; their considerations are guided and informed, although not directed, by the ethical principles of whatever helping profession is the professional affiliation of the person primarily responsible for managing the research.

A Study of IRB Decisions

The review process, like any human activity, is of course not perfect. Ceci, Peters, and Plotkin (1985) conducted a carefully designed study to examine the nature of the review process as it operated in practice. They asked various IRB around the country to conduct an ethical review of one of several versions of a specific study.

The methods of all the studies reviewed were identical. What varied between them was the political sensitivity of the topic studied. First, Ceci et al.'s (1985) research found that boards tended to form different sets of local standards. Even when following the same set of guiding principles for their reviews, different boards often made different decisions about the same studies, and analyses of the review sheets indicated that these differences were primarily attributable to differences in local standards rather than differences in interpretations of the guiding principles.

To some extent, this finding should probably not be surprising. It is well known that local standards vary, so it is not unexpected that individual IRB would develop their own sets of practices for given circumstances. For example, one IRB established a practice for handling research protocols involving deception: Whenever procedures required misleading research participants, investigators were required to provide full disclosure to participants at the earliest possible moment and to re-obtain informed consent to use the data just collected after full disclosure had been made.

Ceci et al.'s (1985) second finding was that the ethics of studies with identical procedures but addressing different research questions were evaluated differently. In general, they found that it is more difficult to obtain ethical approval to conduct a study whose findings are perceived to be potentially hurtful to vulnerable populations or to programs designed to help them. For example, a study that might have generated findings that children of mothers who work outside the home fare more poorly than children of mothers who do not, or that the school performance of "disadvantaged" children is not helped by early educational enrichment programs, are less likely to receive IRB approval than are other studies using identical research procedures.

This second finding reported by Ceci et al. may seem unfair. After all, if it is the job of an IRB to simply evaluate the possibility of risk to research participants, what difference does the nature of the research question make? On deeper analysis, however, their finding is reassuring on two counts. First, it indicates that IRB are at least implicitly evaluating the potential risk of a particular piece of research to members of society in general as well as to those particular members of society who happen to be participating in the study. This beneficence principle is reflected in the human welfare content of both professional codes presented here.

In addition, the finding makes it clear that IRB take their role of evaluating the cost/benefit ratio quite seriously. It will be recalled that one of the two overarching principles guiding research ethical reviews is that the anticipated cost to study participants must be clearly outweighed by the potential benefit the research will have to society. From this vantage point, it is appropriate that the ethical review of individual pieces of research would be influenced by both the nature of the research methods and the nature of the research question to which those methods are to be applied. It is also quite different from the practice uncovered in the study of journals mentioned above: accepting or rejecting a study after the fact simply because the findings did not support a favored opinion or belief.

Ceci et al.'s (1985) findings again demonstrate that research and science in general are not value free. Research is a human activity that occurs in a social and political context. Community values influence the conduct of research at a great number of points, including whether a specific piece of research will receive funding and whether a piece of work once completed will be accepted for publication. In like manner, values influence research from the very beginning, including IRB activity: Values and sociopolitical contexts thus play a role in whether a particular research question can even get addressed.

Ethical reviews are both valuable and necessary. Despite the fact that they impose an additional administrative requirement on investigators, they can offer helpful feedback to the researcher that in the end are likely to enhance the process and the product of a study. Human subject reviews take place in the same fashion as does the rest of the scientific enterprise, namely, they draw conclusions that reflect the scientific community's collective or collaborative best judgment made on the basis of an explicated and explicit rationale.

Special Ethical Considerations in the Helping Professions

Research in the helping professions is always directed toward solving some individual or social problem either directly, by studying interventions or programs, or indirectly, by examining and/or developing new theories of human behavior or of creating change. Because of this focus, special considerations must be taken into account that follow from ethical principles but that have specific methodological implications for human services research. In a sense, except for the first one, they may be thought of as ethically implied methodological principles for conducting professionally responsible research.

The first special consideration that applies to research in the helping professions is that individual helping professionals have a moral obligation to do research. This moral responsibility is not fulfilled solely by reading research but requires doing it. In the NASW Code of Ethics (1997) this principle is reflected in a general statement under the heading of "the social worker's ethical responsibility to the social work profession":

> Social workers should contribute to the knowledge base of social work and share with colleagues their knowledge related to practice, research, and ethics. Social workers should seek to contribute to the profession's literature and to share their knowledge at professional meetings and conferences (NASW 1997:24).

Conducting research is essential for two reasons. First, it is only by doing research collectively that practitioners can base interventions, services, and programs on data rather than on expectation or theory or on appeal to authority and tradition. Having theoretically sound methods of intervention that have demonstrated their usefulness is a prerequisite to arguing that a field is scientifically based. In fact, some have argued that clients have an ethical and legal right to treatments that have been empirically demonstrated to be effective (Bloom & Orme 1993; Myers & Thyer 1997).

In addition, by remaining active in research an individual can retain personal humility in the role of clinician or professional. Involvement in research promotes the retention of healthy skepticism. This skepticism involves the continuing realization that every belief is always only an hypothesis that is held with greater or lesser degrees of confidence depending on how much support has been demonstrated for it.

The remainder of the points in this section are directly prescriptive about research design. They reflect some ways in which the special charge of the helping professions has direct implications for the nature of the methods that should be used to generate a science of helping. Because relational studies comparing groups, group experimental designs, and single-subject designs are the ones most commonly used to study professional interventions, most of the methodological points in this section pertain to these forms of research.

When hypothesis-testing research is done on practice, researchers in the helping professions should always examine nondirectional alternative hypotheses. In the helping professions, which have as their explicit aim enhancing human welfare and relieving human suffering, the researcher's favored hypothesis, left only to preference, would always be directional. For example, a hypothesis is likely to be stated as that a treatment will be helpful or that the preventive program will work. However, it is very important to examine *non*directional hypotheses for the simple reason that, unless nondirectional alternatives are examined, iatrogenic effects (i.e., harmful effects of interventions) may not be detected. Helping professionals must always stay attuned to the fact that interventions intended to help may hurt or that, even if they help in some respects, unanticipated negative effects may also occur. Examining nondirectional alternatives is how this awareness translates into hypothesis-testing terms. Such a hypothesis would be about differences, positive or negative, that might occur as the result of any intervention that is made.

Researchers in the helping professions must always remain especially attentive to serendipitous findings. No researcher can always correctly anticipate every way in which a desirable or undesirable change may occur. In fixed method designs, unanticipated dependent variables by virtue of their having not been identified before the fact cannot be formally measured. However, a good researcher does not narrow his or her vision to the observation of only those variables formally measured. Informal observations also take place during the conduct of a study. Especially in the case of treatment research, it is essential to stay attentive to unanticipated variables that change, in either a positive or negative direction. For example, it would have been unethical for Nugent (1991) not to report that the seemingly successful behavioral intervention he studied had been altered by the client to a journal-writing exercise.

In fixed method research in the helping professions, a demonstration of statistical significance is necessary but by no means sufficient for claiming real significance; clinical significance must be empirically demonstrated as well. A statistically significant result only justifies claiming that a difference between groups or a relationship between variables is nonzero (see chapter 18 on inferential statistics). But in the helping professions, just being able to make some difference is not necessarily good enough. Clinical significance means that the change produced is large and positive enough to represent a real clinical benefit.

Any research in the helping professions that draws its conclusions by comparing groups, as in experiments, must examine differences in variability (i.e., variance) as well as differences between means. When studying treatment response, the helping professions, perhaps more than other branches of psychology, must pay attention to what Cronbach (1957) termed the two disciplines of scientific psychology, that is, the study of general (i.e., nomothetic) theory, and the study of individual (i.e., idiographic) differences. Unless variability is examined and an attempt to explain it is made, treatment that results in marked deterioration for some clients but improvement for most may be regarded as generally beneficial. Moreover, failure to study variability obscures understanding of which clients are likely to benefit from a specific treatment.

There is another way in which methodology can obscure important findings in such clinical research: when the issue of statistical power is not taken into account in comparative research designs. When groups are compared—a group that experienced an intervention and a group that did not, for example—relying on standard statistical procedures can obscure differences that might be substantively significant even if they are statistically not significant (Crane 1976). Using the traditional .05 level of significance in fact increases the chances of making what statisticians term a *type II error,* failing to recognize a difference that exists (see chapter 18 on inferential statistics). Statistical power analysis shows what risk of a type II error is being run for a given alpha level, sample size, and statistical procedure. In clinical or other evaluation research, failing to detect that an intervention works (making a type II error) is at least as bad as falsely claiming effectiveness (making a type I error). In fact, it may perhaps be worse, since ineffective interventions will be found out on replication (if alpha = .05 in two independent replications, the probability of falsely claiming treatment effects in both drops to .01), but effective interventions not recognized as such may never be given a chance again. In designing and evaluating such studies, then, there is an obligation to consider both possibilities for error and to design studies that will effectively address both issues.

Research in the helping professions must give as much weight to what has traditionally been termed external validity (Campbell & Stanley 1963) as it does to the traditional concept of internal validity. The helping professions are of course interested in developing theories explaining the change process, but what most matters is theory in practice. This concern requires that helping-professional research always be designed with an eye toward generalizability by, for example, working hard in descriptive or relational studies to study random samples that can be reasonably expected to represent their larger (parent) group.

Sample selection, however, is not the only way in which to demonstrate generalizability. Any of the dimensions sampled in a piece of research—the particular people who serve as the change agents, the specific measures used to assess treatment effects, the specific treatment protocol used, and the specific point in space or geography and time or history when the finding was demonstrated—presents a potential boundary condition on the study. And, as discussed previously, generalizability must be demonstrated through replication rather than assumed. For example, examining the maintenance of treatment effects over time has become expected.

While these methodological principles may at first seem somewhat unrelated to research ethics as they are usually discussed, they do relate to the general obligation of every social worker and every helping professional to develop sound knowledge for responsible practice. In addition, attention to excellence in research design enhances the benefit side of the cost/benefit equation, making committee review easier and ensuring that the efforts of participants will result in the most useful findings possible.

Ethical Issues in Single-Subject Research

There are a few specific ethical issues that pertain only to single-subject research studies. For example, some have questioned the need for specific consent or human subjects review procedures when single-subject studies of practice are carried out. However, because of the importance of client self-determination as a value in social work practice, practitioner-researchers should seek specific consent of their clients before involving them in single-subject research (Bloom & Orme 1993; Nelson 1994). On the dimension of privacy alone, single-subject studies almost always entail more record keeping, documentation, and wider dissemination of information about the treatment than is usual during the helping process (Bloom & Orme 1993). As with other forms of research, the consent procedure can include discussion of how confidentiality will be maintained and of the potential publication of results at the same time. Both client and practitioner do know throughout treatment that research is being conducted, and thus the treatment process cannot be considered quite "ordinary" in nature. However, this problem is the general one of the interaction of treatment with the study of treatment that would exist with or without a consent procedure. Therefore, the research should be done in a way as to minimize its impact on treatment (Bloom & Orme 1993).

Publishing the results of single-subject studies can present special ethical challenges even when client consent has been obtained, especially if only a single case is used and if narrative data are used to describe the case. Any description in detail of an individual client (or program) can result in the client being identified or identifiable to the reader of the study, even if a name is never used. One solution is to resort to disguise of the descriptive material, such as by altering some demographic data, although this strategy raises its own questions, then, about the reader's ability to make informed or accurate inferences about which other clients might be likely to benefit from the treatment under study. Whether or not disguise is used, it is essential to review all written materials describing single cases carefully to be sure that confidentiality is not inadvertently breached.

It should be noted that when consent to participate in research is sought for single-subject designs, it is usually the client's present or potential helper who is doing the asking. To the extent that the client wants the potential help to be offered or is afraid of beginning the relationship by saying "no" to the professional's request, questions may be asked about whether or not any consent given is free of undue inducement. Certainly assurance should be offered in any consent procedure that a client's right to receive services will not be affected and that participation in the research is entirely voluntary. Clients who receive mandated treatment should still have the right to refuse research participation even when they must accept service. However, those who consider transferential reactions to be common and powerful in clients as well as those concerned about systemic power differentials between professionals and clients may question whether or not clients should ever be approached with requests to participate in research from their clinicians. Although this general problem is common to all forms of evaluation research, it may be highlighted when the researcher and the practitioner are the same individual, the person on whom the client must depend for service. Because no consensus has emerged on how to handle the ethical dilemmas raised by this situation, different agencies, human subjects committees, and researchers will take different positions on the issue.

Summary

Attention to ethical issues in research is the obligation of every professional and an intrinsic part of the research design process. In part because of past abuses, contemporary researchers are now aided by the existence of written codes of ethics governing research, federal guidelines on research ethics, and formal review mechanisms for proposed studies. The principles that guide research in the helping professions are clear, but sometimes weighing the costs and benefits of specific study practices can be difficult. Knowledge of the principles and standards that guide ethical decision making in research, consultation with other professionals, formal and informal, about any ethical dilemmas that may arise, and constant self-examination are the best safeguards that the researcher can offer to participants that they will be protected and respected in the research process. The experience that social workers and other human service professionals have in dealing with ethical issues in the practice situation will serve them well in dealing with ethical issues in research. While upholding ethical standards in the conduct of research is a laudable end in itself, the kind of relationships that ethical research practices foster with participants, colleagues, and communities will enhance the products and usefulness of the research.

10

Who Will Be Studied: Sampling

Sampling, or using a carefully selected group to study an issue, has become such a common practice in research that its use is an everyday feature of public and scientific discourse. In fact, there is an active debate about whether or not the Year 2000 United States Census should use sampling methods for greater accuracy. Because sampling is now so widely used, research results based on samples are sometimes accepted quite uncritically, while at other times they are greeted with an equally unwarranted suspicion. The truth about sampling is that when a good sampling plan is carefully considered and meticulously carried out, the research gains immeasurably in efficiency and soundness of results.

Sampling plays a different role in different kinds of research designs. Traditional views of research have emphasized fixed method designs, some of which depend heavily on sampling logic for their conclusions. It is by generalizing from the description of a phenomenon within a finite sample to a larger population that many descriptive and relational research studies accomplish their goals. What has been termed scientific sampling is thus central to those methods. While samples are used in flexible method research, such studies depend more for their persuasiveness on conceptualization and on how well sample members turn out to embody the phenomena of interest in the research. Group experiments and single-subject studies depend primarily on internal logic and replication to support their conclusions. Nevertheless, samples of one kind or another are used in all of these form of research.

This chapter will review the reasons that sampling is used and then discuss in detail the sampling techniques employed both in fixed method and in flexible method research. As with all other aspects of research methodology, the choice of sampling technique must be coherent with the total research design, its logic, and its purposes. Because of the variety of designs encountered in social work and human services research, there is a range of sampling techniques to consider and a variety of sampling issues to take into account when planning, conducting, or evaluating research.

This chapter is written from the point of view of someone planning a research project who has the freedom to develop a sampling plan for it. It is often the case in practice, however, for research to be done using an available sample, such as a case or client group encountered in practice about which the researcher needs to know more. In these circumstances, it is perhaps even more important to understand principles of sampling; only with this knowledge can one determine what the actual value and limitations of such a sample are.

In general, the chapter will use the language of individual people because this situation is the most common one in social work and human services research. However, it should be noted that groups of people, such as couples, families, or organizations; geographical or political entities, such as communities, states, or nations; events or time periods; or things, such as case records or professional documents, have been and can be used as the units studied in social work research. While the language may change in these circumstances, the process of sampling, or selecting and examining illustrative parts to understand the whole, remains the same.

The Goals of Scientific Sampling

The logic of scientific sampling has been developed primarily for survey and other forms of descriptive and relational research. Nevertheless, the terminology and basic concepts of sampling as developed for such studies form an important framework for thinking about sampling in any design context.

Usefulness of the Data Source

The first goal of sampling is to identify and gain access to the most effective sources of information possible to suit the purposes of the research. The utility of a study's results depends in large part on the quality of the information generated and thus on the selection of the sources of information for the research. This general concept is best expressed in the philosophy of those flexible method researchers who describe their respondents as the "experts" on the research topic.

Who will be the most useful informants for the study? What will these informants be like? Where can they be found? Answering these questions means developing selection criteria, or a list of the characteristics a person (or organization, community, event, or document) must have in order to be included in the study. This list then provides the rules used for assembling sample members.

It should be noted that the most useful source of information for a study may not always be an available source, and choices based on feasibility are often made in developing a sampling plan. For example, a preschool child's parent may be the most feasible source to use for gathering retrospective information about the child's developmental history. This may be true even though the parent's report might differ from that of a trained observer, had there been one, or from the report the child herself might make were she able. The parent is, however, the expert on *his or her own experience* of the child's developmental course.

Efficiency

Another goal in sampling is to maximize the efficiency of the research. The idea is to select and study some subgroup of individuals from a larger population of interest, reducing the effort that would otherwise be needed for the research. Census studies are studies of whole populations, and whole population studies are rare in part because they are so costly. However, efficiency is gained at the loss of certainty regarding the accuracy of conclusions drawn from sample data about some aspect of a larger population or about a phenomenon in general.

Much of the technology of scientific sampling is designed to quantify or reduce the uncertainty, the amount of error, and imprecision, introduced into a study's conclusions by relying on a sample. Sample size is one key factor in determining the accuracy of the information derived from a sample, although all samples, however large, remain only population estimates. While the element of uncertainty can never be entirely eliminated, it can be reduced.

Representativeness

A problem inherently related to selectivity in sampling is concern about representativeness. This feature of a sample is especially important in descriptive and relational research that aims to provide large-scale descriptions of phenomena or the relationships among them. The sample for such a fixed method study may be large, but it still may be misleading in its results. A commonly cited example of this kind of problem is the *Literary Digest* poll that in 1936 predicted the landslide victory of Alf Landon over Franklin D. Roosevelt in the presidential election that year. The sample, although large, consisted only of readers of that one particular magazine, a group of survey respondents who did not resemble or represent voters in general. *Literary Digest* readers did support Landon; the American electorate as a whole supported Roosevelt.

Another common kind of problem with representativeness in psychological and other social science research has been to generalize results from research using samples of white males to all people. Carol Gilligan's work (1972), for example, showed how theories of moral development were severely distorted by applying norms developed on all-male samples to women, picturing women as inferior in moral development as a result.

People of color also are typically excluded or underrepresented in research samples. As a result, their experiences may be missing or incompletely rendered in the description, distorted by the application of assumptions about whites to them, or simply assumed to be reflected in the data describing the whites without evidence that they are similar or different. Some of the problems of sexism, racism, and heterosexism in research design described in chapter 3 are the result of inadequate sampling.

One of the problems with a sample that is not representative is that in the absence of knowledge about the population it is impossible to detect the nature or direction of the distortion resulting from its use. The infamous *Literary Digest* poll may have represented the magazine's readership well; in retrospect, the error was in generalizing from the readership to the general electorate. An important goal of good sampling, then, is to ensure that it will yield a legitimate basis for the conclusions drawn.

In some kinds of research, however, such as flexible method studies, group experiments, and single case studies, the validity of the conclusions drawn does not depend on sampling logic as much as on replication logic (Yin 1994). The usefulness of the results depends on the general applicability of the theories and conceptual frameworks developed or examined in them. This generalizability can also be empirically demonstrated by conducting additional studies with other samples and in other settings; hence the term replication logic. In fact, replication research has much to contribute to knowledge development in social work and the human services and should be conducted and published more often than it is.

If a study depends on replication logic, the issue of whether or not its sample represents some larger population of participants accurately becomes less important. Although flexible method, experimental, and single case studies may not claim a sampling representativeness they do not have, samples for such studies, especially for group designs, must still be carefully considered. However, the focus of the selection of participants in these forms of research should be on the utility of the sample for the examination of the specific theories or treatment techniques under study rather than on demographics. Participants and the research situation should illustrate the theories, concepts, phenomena, or techniques of interest well, not necessarily the population at large.

In addition, because of the volume of data collected or the need to control the research situation, samples in flexible method and experimental studies are often fairly small. In these circumstances, it is often difficult to study gender, racial, ethnic, or class variation systematically because the numbers in each subgroup are so small that only one or two people may stand in for a large, heterogeneous group. In this situation, it is impossible to distinguish individual from subgroup variation, and a homogeneous or focal sample concentrating only on one subgroup may be the preferred study strategy. However, in such a circumstance, the specialized nature of the sample must be taken into account when conclusions are drawn. Such studies depend on analytic generalization for their validity rather than on demographic representativeness as reflected in the specific sample studied (Gilgun 1994; Strauss & Corbin 1990).

Selection Bias

An often-cited goal of scientific sampling is to reduce selection bias. Bias differs from other sources of error or uncertainty in sampling because it is directional, that is, it operates systematically, if unconsciously at times, to tilt results in a particular direction. Even if the nature and effects of the bias cannot be predicted with certainty, what is certain is that the errors introduced will tend to be replicated across all members of the sample.

Scientific sampling is designed to reduce selection bias by introducing rules into the sample selection process and, through describing sampling methods and procedures explicitly, by subjecting sampling decisions and procedures to critical examination. Sampling methods include a variety of techniques that reduce selection bias, that is, choose sample members in such a way as to maximize the likelihood that the sample will fairly represent the larger population or illustrate the phenomenon that it intends to.

To speak of bias in sampling is to speak of lack of representativeness. However, the term "bias" is useful because it has meaning both in the context of fixed method studies that rely primarily on sampling logic for their generalizability and in the context of other studies that rely on replication logic instead. In both situations, the need to be explicit and to think critically about the sample selection methods used remains central.

Fitting Sampling to Design

Different kinds of research have different purposes. In particular, although most research employs samples for efficiency and all studies seek sources of useful, relevant data, the importance of the representativeness of a study's sample may vary considerably depending on the type and purpose of the research design as a whole. As mentioned, by their nature some studies rely more heavily on replication than on sampling logic for generalization of their results. Put in other terms, their potential utility rests more on the universality of the concepts generated or employed than on the scope of the sample that was examined. Case studies are limited in the sample by definition, and yet a case study may effectively explicate concepts or describe techniques that can then be replicated or demonstrated again empirically (see chapter 8). Flexible method studies may rest on similar logic as they generate theory from what typically are samples limited in size and chosen primarily for theoretical efficiency. For example, Feagin (1990) studied discrimination in public places only among middle-class African Americans because of a specific theoretical formulation—that structural economic deprivation in the underclass and not racism per se was the contemporary problem for African Americans—that he viewed as problematic.

On the other hand, descriptive and relational studies that seek to make generalizations about specific populations require samples that are representative of that population. For this reason, for example, Gomez (1990) used random samples of blocks from each of the census tracts in the city being studied and visited all households on those blocks to identify ones in which Cuban Americans resided. The first person eighteen years or older who was encountered in that household was asked for an interview. Stratifying by census tract ensured that all areas of the city would be included; sampling blocks randomly from within each stratum ensured that selection was unbiased; and sampling blocks (rather than households) ensured that the in-person data collection could be efficient and that all current residents, even those not officially listed, had a chance of being included. The goal was clearly a representative sample of Cuban Americans, at least from that city, so that general inferences about the relationship of biculturalism to mental health among Cuban Americans could be made.

Sampling Terminology

Several key terms must be understood in order to plan or analyze a sampling strategy. In sampling, the term *population* is used to indicate every individual in

278 • Part III: The Elements of Research Design

the entire group of interest to which the results of the study may be generalized. This population will have some definable set of distinguishing characteristics, such as social workers in private practice, American corporate employees who regularly care for an aging relative, or Cuban Americans living in West New York, New Jersey. Each element or member of the population will have in common the population distinguishing characteristics of interest, although they may differ markedly in many others. These elements are the units of analysis of the study.

Care in delineating the distinguishing characteristics of the population of interest is essential. For example, social workers in private practice and licensed social workers in private practice will not be the same populations in reality, even if they are intended to be in law, and the methods needed to recruit samples representing the two groups would necessarily be different.

A *sampling frame* is a list of all the members of the population of interest. A carefully selected sample is only as good as the frame from which it is drawn. Often no adequate sampling frame exists for the population of interest, and feasibility issues often dictate that researchers use whatever sampling frames are available. To illustrate, in the case of social workers in private practice, a list of licensed social workers in a state, which is a matter of public record, will contain the names of all licensed social workers doing private practice as well as those not doing private practice. A second step would be required to eliminate from the sampling frame those licensed social workers who are not in private practice. Such a list will not include *un*licensed social workers, if that is part of the group of interest, and another strategy to identify and reach them would have to be developed.

Sometimes the target population or ideal population of interest is so difficult to describe or gain access to that an approximation is used. In such a case, it is important to make clear what compromises have been made in defining the group to be studied so a judgement can be made about the effect of the compromise on results. A classic example of this problem arises when discussing homeless people, and many policy debates center on differences of opinion about just how many homeless people there really are and how many of them are getting services. The target population may be all homeless people; the available population to count or study may be homeless people living in shelters, even though those who are being temporarily sheltered by friends and relatives and those who refuse, are denied, or will not seek shelter services are not included. Differences between a target population and the population actually used to develop a sample must, of course, be recognized when conclusions are drawn.

The term "sample" has so far been used without formal definition. In research, a *sample* is the subgroup of elements of the population that has been included as the source of information in a study. The selection criteria are the distinguishing characteristics of the population as applied to each member of the sample. Sometimes exclusion criteria are also stated, as in the Gomez (1990) study that excluded respondents who were already acquainted with the researcher or those who had ever received mental health and substance abuse services. When, as is common, no sampling frame exists for a population of interest, it is the selection and exclusion criteria that are intended to ensure population membership at the point of recruitment to the study. While these criteria define the sample and the population, it is the nature of the sample selection methods that determine how representative the sample will be. There are a variety of sampling techniques that have been developed in order to select a sample from a population of interest in unbiased ways.

Sampling Techniques

Sampling techniques, or the methods for drawing a sample, can be divided into two broad groups depending on whether or not chance has been used systematically in selecting the sample. *Probability samples,* sometimes termed statistical samples, involve chance systematically; *nonprobability samples* do not.

Multilevel and *multistage sampling* are the terms used when two or more selection steps are necessary to obtain a sample. For example, to study nursing home residents, it is necessary to select nursing homes and then to select residents. There are various methods of developing multilevel or multistage sampling plans employing probability or nonprobability techniques.

Probability Sampling

Research that has as its purpose the generalizable description of a phenomenon or of relationships among phenomena using sampling logic should employ probability sampling. In the logic of fixed method designs, probability sampling methods are the only ones that legitimately permit generalizations to be made from a sample to a population. Since all samples by definition include only incomplete knowledge about the population, the error of estimation of any sample is a concern. With *random sampling,* the likely magnitude of this error can be estimated with a specified degree of confidence. Finally, random sampling reduces selection bias and thus maximizes the likelihood of representativeness within the limits of the sampling frame from which the elements are drawn.

The technical definition of a random sample is that it is one selected in such a way that every element in the population (or in the sampling frame) has an equal probability of being included in the sample, and every sample of a given size has an equal probability of being selected. This probability is the fraction created by dividing the sample size by the size of the population.[1] This probability may be very low if the sample to be drawn is modest in size and the population itself is large, or it may be high if the sample is large relative to the population.

Sample Size

Because the likely error of a population description inferred from a random sample can be estimated mathematically, with random sampling it is possible to plan the size of a sample to yield the degree of precision of results needed. In

---

1. For the sake of simplicity, this discussion of random sampling does not treat the differences between random sampling with and without replacement. In general, the description assumes sampling with replacement even though this technique is in fact rarely used. With large populations, of course, the differences between the two are trivial.

general, the larger the sample, the more precise the estimates that can be made from it, or the smaller the calculated range in which population parameters estimated from the sample will fall. Figure 10.1 shows the relationship of sample size to precision. As it illustrates, the relationship between sample size and precision is not a linear one, so that there are diminishing returns from successive increments in sample size.

Calculating an estimate of a population parameter from a random sample is covered briefly in chapter 18 (inferential statistics). In general, the precision of the estimate that can be obtained depends on the amount of variability within the sample on the characteristic of interest, known statistically as the standard deviation or variance within the group, as well as on the size of the sample itself. For simplicity's sake, what the table in figure 10–1 does not show, then, is that a more precise population estimate can be made from a relatively homogeneous sample than from a heterogeneous one.

Given a random method of sample selection, bigger is always better, that is, more precise, providing that the volume of data can be adequately managed. However, bigger is also more expensive, and a lot bigger may not be much more efficient than a little bigger. In practice, then, in planning the size of a sample the researcher seeks a trade-off between precision and feasibility. Also, note that if the method of selection of the sample is not a random one, increasing the size of the sample does nothing to increase its accuracy. A bigger sample under these circumstances will only be more precisely inaccurate.

By sample size, of course, is meant the number of respondents actually heard from. Therefore planning the size of a sample must include consideration of the response rate or the percentage, for example, of mailed questionnaires that are likely to be returned (see chapter 14 on questionnaire design). To illustrate, if 300 respondents will be needed to achieve the degree of precision of estimation desired and a 50 percent response rate is expected, an initial sample of 600 must be drawn and surveyed to achieve this result. In longitudinal research, which is discussed later in the chapter, the additional problem of attrition of a sample over time must be considered. However, it must be remembered that whenever people are lost from a probability sample, whether through nonresponse or through attrition, the representativeness of the sample has been compromised, and it is advis-

Sample Size

Standard error of:	10	15	20	30	40	50	100	200	300
Mean[a] ($\bar{x}$)	5.00	4.01	3.44	2.79	2.40	2.14	1.51	1.06	0.87
Correlation coefficient[b] (r)	0.38	0.29	0.24	0.19	0.16	0.15	0.10	0.07	0.06

a. Assumes a sample standard deviation of 15.
b. Based on a transformation of the correlation coefficient (z_r) and its standard error (s_r).

Figure 10–1 Sizes of the Standard Errors of Sample Means and Sample Correlation Coefficients Relative to Sample Size

able to learn as much as possible about what systematic differences may exist between those who remained in and those who were lost from the group.

Probability Sampling Techniques

Having decided on a random sample, how is a random sample actually obtained? The most basic form of random sample is the simple random sample. The most common examples of simple random sampling may be the names drawn in a raffle or the numbers generated each day or week in state lottery systems.

The easiest method of drawing such a sample is to use a computer with the capacity to generate random numbers. Using appropriate software, the computer is programmed or commanded to generate a list of random numbers in the range from 1 to the size of the sample. If 300 people are to be selected from a list of 1500 names, the computer is instructed to select 300 4-digit numbers in the range from 0001 to 1500. These numbers are then used to identify the corresponding elements from the sampling frame, or list of eligible population members, that has been numbered sequentially for the purpose.

This same result can be obtained manually with a random number table. Such tables are commonly found in the appendixes of statistics texts. The tables consist of rows of blocks of digits in random order. To use the table, make up a rule of selection. An example of such a rule would be to select the first 4 digits from the left in the second row of each block of digits. If the sample size is to be 300 from a pool of 1500, use the table to compile a list of the first 300 nonrepeating numbers between 0001 and 1500 that are encountered in reading the table according to the rule. These are the numbers used to select the elements from the list, as above.

A *systematic random sample* is an approximation to a simple random sample that can be used when there is a sampling frame or population list. This method requires, however, that the sampling frame, or the list from which sample members are to be drawn, is not in any systematic order that might be expected to affect study results. First, based on the size of the sample needed and the size of the sampling frame, the proportion of the population needed is calculated by dividing the desired sample size by the population size. For example, a sample of 300 to be drawn from 1500 names is a 20 percent, or 1/5, sample. A random number table (or roll of a die or some other random, unbiased method) is used to select a number between 1 and 5 in the case of a 20 percent sample (or 1 in 10 in the case of a 10 percent sample, etc.). This person becomes the first name selected

08425	65259	19137	99585	95462	18381	60672	85371	85743	51832
70880	29136	73527	63465	68509	58548	72900	55802	45819	06653
78709	46697	97289	18568	48303	99486	61650	15469	98139	57038
08168	67125	78084	77402	40905	06494	31908	75149	85052	89520
12779	95960	25920	39177	14051	42682	10086	17736	89177	95177
61548	27226	04191	53097	13739	56957	77947	18478	05516	93751
80867	95863	18035	23682	95091	98410	49819	07466	26695	16051
07117	12800	93806	57732	55399	33934	87499	93185	19549	95323

Figure 10–2 Portion of a Random Number Table

from the list of potential sample members. Every fifth (or tenth, etc.) name thereafter is subsequently chosen. The result is a systematic sample with a randomly selected starting point, a convenient method often used as an equivalent to a simple random sample.

The use of this technique is not appropriate when there is order to the list (people listed by street or institution, etc.), especially if the selection interval is large (e.g., every one-hundredth entry as opposed to every fifth) and the sampling fraction small. In that case there may be too few elements selected from some subgroups. In these cases, either the list should be randomly reordered before selection or simple random sampling should be employed.

Multistage Random Samples

More than one step is often involved in obtaining a sample, and it is important to consider each step in the sampling process carefully. For example, drawing a careful random sample of clients from an agency that is handy produces a representative sample of the agency's clients but does not address the effects of convenience in choosing the agency.

Elaborations of the simple random sample method are often used when there are subgroups in the population that must be systematically represented in the study or for efficiency when very large, heterogeneous samples are used. These techniques may employ various methods to select or define sample subgroups, but they can only be termed random samples if at the initial stage groups are randomly selected *and* at the final stage there is random selection of elements within groups.

Multilevel samples are useful not only for planning comparisons but also for the incremental development of the sampling frame itself. In most instances, sampling frames for a population of interest do not exist, and a major part of the research effort must be expended in developing and maintaining one. A sample, even a random sample, is only as good as the sampling frame from which it is drawn. Using cluster sampling techniques, for example, to focus the scope of the research can result in the development of more adequate sampling frames for the subpopulation to be targeted for study.

Stratified samples. A stratified random sample means that elements of the sampling frame are first ordered into sets of subgroups or subpopulations according to some known characteristic(s) before the random sample is drawn. This technique is useful when comparisons are planned between the subgroups and when adequate representation of each subgroup must be ensured. The subgroups can be sampled in equal or different proportions.

For example, because there are more females than males in the social work profession, comparing the salaries of male and female social workers may be aided by randomly selecting a higher proportion of males than females from a licensing list. The comparison can then be efficiently accomplished with a smaller total sample. This procedure involves breaking down a list of social workers into two lists, or *strata*, one of males and one of females, and then drawing two simple random samples, as outlined above, at different proportions to yield sample groups equal in size. Stratification can also be extended to more than one dimension, such as gender and level of licensure, for example, to create cells representing each of the possible combinations of the stratification variables.

Stratification techniques can only be used when it is possible to determine accurately at the point of drawing the sample who on the sampling frame belongs in each subgroup. For example, while the stratification technique is potentially useful in ensuring adequate representation of people of color in research samples, the information to make the stratification in advance is not always available. One then must draw a total random sample large enough to represent adequately on a percentage basis the smallest group of interest within the whole.

When proportional sampling is used among strata, the proportion of cases from each stratum deliberately differs in the obtained sample from what it is in the population. Because of this unnatural proportioning in the sample, so useful for planned comparisons, accurate estimates from the sample to the total population cannot be made without taking this disproportion into account by a procedure known as weighting. With weighting, a multiplication factor is applied to the cases before population estimates are made.

Taking the example of males and females in social work, assume that the proportion of females to males is approximately 4:1 as it was in the national NASW membership in 1995 (Gibelman & Schervish 1997). Therefore a stratified sample might well include four times as many of the men in the population as women to achieve a study sample with balanced numbers of men and women for purposes of comparison. To make a population estimate from this sample, perhaps of overall social work salaries, each female case should be weighted, or multiplied, by a factor of 4 in developing the population estimate to correct for their underrepresentation in the study sample. Conversely, the responses from males could be given the inverse weighting of 1/4 or .25. Without weighting, given what is known about wage differentials in general and about social work in particular, there is likely to be an overestimate of social work salaries as a whole from a sample in which half of the salary information comes from males. With weighting, an accurate population estimate can be obtained. However, only an analysis of gender differences can show that this average wage is not equally shared by men and women in the field. (See, for example, Kalton [1983] for a more complete discussion of the uses of weighting in survey research.)

Cluster sampling. A *cluster sampling* technique is used when it is necessary to gain access to people across geographic or institutional boundaries. For example, while there is no national register of people living in long-term care facilities at any point in time, there are national lists of such facilities. To develop a nationally representative sample of such people, as was done in 1976 for the national Survey of Institutionalized Persons (SIP), clusters, in this case institutions, were first selected and sampling frames then developed for each. Sample members were then randomly selected from within each cluster. The use of cluster sampling greatly increases the efficiency of both sampling and data collection procedures without sacrificing randomness and can be used if there is a population listing of clusters but not of elements within clusters. The use of city blocks within census tracts in the Gomez (1990) study, discussed above, is another example of this kind of cluster sampling.

Strata versus clusters. Clusters differ from strata in that clusters are considered equivalent to each other, and elements from only some of the clusters are used in the final sample. If a given cluster is not selected, no person from that cluster can be included in the sample, but it is assumed that residents of other equivalent clusters can represent them. In addition, all clusters and cluster residents initially have similar chances of being included in the final sample. Strata, on the other hand, are defined by their differences from each other, and elements belonging to all strata are included in the final sample although perhaps in different proportions.

Complex multistage sampling designs. While stratification or cluster sampling methods are by definition multistage sampling plans, sometimes strata and/or clusters are combined in more complex multilevel sampling designs. Multistage or multilevel sampling designs, as the name implies, involve several steps from population to sample members. These steps may involve both clusters and stratification. They are typically designed both for feasibility and for efficiency in accomplishing certain goals of the research design, such as permitting particular comparisons among sample members to be made.

The national Survey of Institutionalized Persons (Bureau of the Census 1978) illustrated this multistage design well. First, institutions were stratified by type; nursing homes, facilities for the mentally retarded, and facilities for the mentally ill were three of the types included. Within each of these strata, facility lists were compiled by state, and one state was randomly chosen from within each of six regional clusters to represent the region as a whole. Further development of the sampling frames and data collection was thus made more efficient by focussing on one state in each region. Because it was expected that the characteristics and care of residents would vary between small, medium, and large facilities, adequate representation to permit comparison by facility size was needed. Facilities in the selected states were therefore stratified both by type and by facility size (small, medium, and large as defined by bed capacity). A higher proportion of the small facilities was included in the survey in order to balance the numbers of residents from each type of facility available to the study. Finally, sampling frames of residents were developed for each selected facility, and individual residents were selected for study by simple random sampling from each of them.

As in any stratified sampling plan, when differing sampling proportions are used for different strata, differing weights must be assigned to sample members from each stratum if estimates of the total population are to be made. With multilevel sampling designs, the weighting becomes more complex because it must reflect factors multiplied for each level at which proportional sampling was used. Data describing a person who was a resident of a small residential facility for mentally retarded persons, for example, would have a different weight assigned to it than data obtained from a person living in a large nursing home facility, because of the different proportions of residents actually interviewed in each type of facility relative to their numbers in the total population of people living in residential facilities at the time.

Nonprobability Sampling Techniques

Despite all of the obvious virtues of random sampling methods, there are nonrandom sampling techniques that have their place in research as well. In fact, nonrandom samples are much more commonly used than random ones in social work and human services research. Not all research is or should be directed primarily at the general description of widespread phenomena. Nor is the validity of all research conclusions determined exclusively by the representativeness of the sample from which they are drawn. In many situations, nonrandom sampling methods can be used to identify research participants efficiently and effectively.

Flexible method research studies in particular tend to depend on the richness in their data and its closeness to the experience of participants more than on the representativeness of the sample as the determinants of the value of the conceptual descriptions derived from them. Often in order to understand thoroughly a complex or unusual phenomenon, a sample large enough to be representative is impossible to work with simply because of the volume of data that would be generated. Data collection methods such as intensive interviewing and participant observation, for example, often produce very large volumes of data even when very small samples are employed. Experimental designs, too, in order to achieve the degree of control needed to conduct the experiment, may utilize small samples; in addition, these samples are often not random but are randomized, which ensures the internal equivalence of groups but not their representativeness compared to a general population (see chapter 7).

This section of the chapter will describe some of the nonrandom techniques used to develop samples. The same issues—fitting the sampling plan to the overall purposes of the research, minimizing selection bias, enhancing the efficiency of the research effort by gaining access to useful information, and acknowledging the limits of the representativeness of any sample obtained—must be considered in nonrandom sampling as in any other kind of sampling design.

Sample Size in Nonprobability Samples

Any sample that is very small is unlikely to generate a stable, and therefore precise, population estimate even if it is randomly selected. Small-scale studies employing samples limited in size are therefore the ones in which the use of nonprobability sampling techniques can be most easily justified.

Determining an adequate size for a nonrandom sample is not as clear-cut a matter as it is for a random sample. Because errors of estimation cannot be calculated without random sampling, sample size cannot be planned based on the mathematical precision of estimation desired. In general, the sample should be as large as possible and, in any event, large enough to give a picture of both typical and atypical features of the group. If the recruited sample is quite homogeneous with respect to the phenomena under investigation, then the general tendency of the group may be describable with only a few sample members. If the group recruited is heterogeneous, however, the sample may need to be larger in order to distinguish individual idiosyncrasy from sample, or group, variability.

In some kinds of flexible method research, the exact size of the sample cannot be determined until the data collection and analysis are underway. In this situation, a useful guiding principle may be the concept of diminishing returns. When and only when successive interviews or encounters are consistently yielding little or no new information or insight, the sample obtained is large enough. If, on the other hand, new and unexpected insights continued to be generated from new people contacted, there is a need to continue to include additional respondents and/or to gather more data until predictable patterns can be articulated and confirmed.

Haphazard, Convenience, or Accidental Samples

The type of nonprobability sample termed a haphazard, *convenience,* or *accidental sample,* entails the use of research participants chosen primarily because they meet the study selection criteria and they are easily available. Clients of a given agency or social worker, "person on the street" interviews, and magazine readership surveys are common examples of accidental samples.

The major advantage of such a sample is its feasibility. The major disadvantage of convenience samples is that, of course, being in such a sample because of being in a given place at a given time is not at all a random event for researcher or study participant. The factors that might cause a respondent to be on a particular street corner at a certain hour of the day, to read a particular issue of a magazine and to fill out its survey, or to be seeking services from a particular agency at a given point in time cannot be adequately known. Hence there will be influences on the results of a study employing such a sample that cannot be adequately discerned and that may then affect the study findings.

Volunteer samples are a special example of this problem. When populations (and samples) for study are hard to find because of the special characteristics members must have, researchers often resort to advertising for volunteers. Although this sampling strategy solves the problem, it leaves unanswered the question of who among those who read the advertisement and met the study criteria volunteered and who did not. This unknown "volunteer factor" may introduce some bias into study results of a kind that is impossible to assess or define.

If the decision has been made to use a sample of convenience, it is useful to consider what can be done to keep those biases that can be anticipated to a minimum. What Bogdan and Taylor (1975) have said about the selection of a study site in participant observation research can be generalized to all kinds of convenience sampling: Researchers should only get involved in situations in which the research participants are otherwise unknown to them and in which they have no particular professional or personal self-interest.[2] It is impossible to predict the kind

---

2. The practitioner-researcher paradigm recently prominent in social work research that advocates that individual social workers conduct studies of the effectiveness of their own work with individual clients (Bloom & Fischer 1982) represents a major exception in principle to this prescription. The practitioner-researcher model is discussed in detail in chapter 8 and later in this chapter in the section on case study methods.

of difficulties in the work that personal connection to research participants will inevitably inject into the process. Sometimes the problems do not appear until well into the data gathering, data analysis, or report-writing phases of the project. Just as physicians and therapists should not treat, researchers should not research, friends.

Perhaps especially when seeking a sample of convenience, it is essential to specify carefully the selection and exclusion criteria that are used, the characteristics that a site for sample recruitment or a sample member must have. Each alteration in the individual selection or exclusion criteria or in the sampling site potentially changes the scope of the study results.

An example drawn from the study of work and caregiving conflicts in women caring for an aging mother will illustrate the point. In studying working women who are caregivers for elderly mothers, going to an elder service agency or to an employer for recruitment will make a difference in the sample obtained. In the former case, all the older people in the study will have the characteristics necessary to be eligible for the agency's services, such as frailty (Anastas, Gibeau, & Larson 1990; Gibeau & Anastas 1989). The sample will be homogeneous with respect to the characteristics of the elderly person bearing on service receipt but heterogeneous with respect to other characteristics, such as the nature of the caregivers' work. Conversely, a work-site sample is apt to be more heterogeneous with respect to the older people and their functioning but more homogeneous with respect to the caregivers' work (Gibeau, Anastas, & Larson 1990). Each of these variations in sampling design is potentially useful, but each will be more or less efficient for examining different aspects of the work and caregiving situation. Finally, whatever site is used, making caregiver employment a criterion for selection, any woman who has already given up her job in order to care for her mother is excluded from the study by definition.

Finally, when an accidental sample is used, everything that is known about the process of obtaining the sample should be explicitly described so that judgements can be made about the potential limitations of the sample. If a specific agency is used to recruit sample members, what is known in general about the agency and its clients? If volunteers are sought, what is the size of the obtained sample relative to the number of people contacted or who might potentially have responded, and what if anything is known about the nature of the larger group? If there are local, regional, or national data describing people like those sought in the study, that information should be presented and the obtained sample should be compared to it, even if informally.

Given all of these cautionary notes, what is the good of convenience samples? As already emphasized, not all studies have as their purpose developing generalizable descriptions of a phenomenon. Studies with other purposes may not be unduly affected by a convenience sample. In addition, selecting a convenient site for a research study enables the researcher to obtain access to informants efficiently and to concentrate on other aspects of the research design, including the selection of sample members within the site. For example, Gomez (1990) seems to have chosen the city where he conducted the study as a matter of convenience and then to have used his knowledge of the community to carry out a sophisticated sampling plan within it. However, given the single city included, his study report would have been improved by discussing the characteristics of the community chosen.

Quota Samples

A quota sample technique is sometimes used to introduce planned variation into a sample of convenience. For example, if 40 people are to be recruited for a study, a quota of 20 males and 20 females may be set if it is thought that comparisons by gender might be made or that the systematic inclusion of both men and women might improve the overall usefulness of the data obtained. Quota sampling is thus similar to stratified random sampling *except* that strata are designated and predetermined from an existing known sampling frame from which sample members are randomly selected, while quota sampling sets target numbers guiding the recruitment of people not previously identified and who are not selected randomly. Both quota and stratified sampling permit efficient and direct comparisons between sample subgroups of particular interest. As with stratified sampling, if the planned sample is large enough, quotas can be set using several dimensions, such as age and gender and income level, for example, to permit more complex comparisons to be made.

Quota sampling techniques might be best used in needs assessment research and can add considerably to the efficiency of haphazard sampling recruitment. Caution must be exercised in planning a quota sample in that each sample subgroup must be large enough to have a chance of adequately reflecting the variability within that group. If sample subgroup sizes are very small, individual differences observed may be confounded with subgroup variation. On the other hand, with an adequate number in each sample subgroup and several dimensions defining the subgroups, the total sample can become quite large, raising the question of the importance of representativeness in the design and whether some form of random sampling might then serve the study better.

Theoretical sampling is a term used in some flexible method research to indicate a sampling plan that purposefully builds variation into a nonrandom sample along dimensions theoretically relevant to the study issue (Glaser & Strauss 1967; Strauss & Corbin 1990). In that sense, it is like quota sampling, but it usually does not involve specification of a target number of respondents of each type, and it is a technique used when the sample size is indeterminate at the beginning of the project. As with quota sampling, the definition of the theoretical categories relevant to the study will differ depending on the nature and focus of the research, and it is important to develop subgroups of adequate size to be meaningful.

Purposive, Judgment, Focal, or Expert Samples

Aside from samples of convenience, the other most common kind of nonrandom sample is the *purposive*, judgment, *focal,* or *expert* sample. These terms are applied to samples that have been selected not to approximate representativeness but because the respondents are atypical in some way that specially equips them to be useful as study informants. For example, one might naturally turn to identified professional experts in a newly emerging field of practice to gain insight into that field. When crisis intervention was a new concept in mental health, Bloom (1963/1976) wanted to study the effectiveness of crisis intervention but found that the concept of a mental health crisis had not been adequately defined. Using a set of vignettes designed to elicit definitions, he recruited a small sample of mental health professionals conversant with this then-emergent public health concept for his study, which resulted in the specification of what was and was not a crisis situation in mental health, a working definition of the field provided by those who then knew it best.

Two issues are key in focal sampling: defining the selection and exclusion criteria and gaining access to the people who meet these criteria. As with samples of convenience, the description of the selection and exclusion criteria must be carefully wrought, as seemingly minor variations in the criteria can change quite markedly the scope of the phenomena actually under study. For example, Bloom (1963, 1976) recruited staff of the community mental health program at the Harvard School of Public Health for his study, people who could be assumed to know a lot both about mental health and public health and who were practicing in the kind of setting in which the crisis intervention concept was designed to be employed.

Selection and exclusion criteria must be designed with feasibility in mind as well. The more detailed the sampling criteria, the more difficult it will be to find and gain access to people who can meet them all and the more specialized and therefore potentially restricted in generalizability the results will be. Access to such samples is often gained via group membership, institutional affiliation, or networking, as in snowball sampling.

Snowball Samples

One nonprobability technique that deserves special mention is the *snowball sample*. This technique is used either with convenience or purposive samples when there is initial access only to a very limited number of identifiable sample members. These few people who meet the sampling criteria are recruited, and they in turn are requested to identify other people like themselves who would be eligible to participate in the study. Since those nominated share either a personal or professional network with the original respondents, whatever biases were in the original sample may be reflected or even magnified in the snowball method. However, the longer the chain of referral from the original sample members to the last members recruited, the more attenuated the original connection will be and the more potentially diverse the result.

Because of this limitation, this method of sample recruitment is normally recommended when access to all but a very limited number of study participants at the start is impossible. Snowball sampling remains the method of choice for reaching "deviant" or hidden groups, such as those who participate in illegal behavior because for obvious reasons it is often hard to gain initial access to those groups. For example, the Waldorf, Reinarman, and Murphy (1991) study employed snowball sampling to examine heavy cocaine use among workers in high-tech industries in northern California in the 1980s.

Snowball sampling is, of course, the sampling method inherent in participant observation research in the field when the point is to get to know a social system, formal or informal, by networking among its members. The implicit ties that unite the respondents in knowing about each other, the network, is itself often the phenomenon of interest in such a study. Williams (1992) briefly describes how his earlier contact with a group of teenagers involved in the cocaine trade (Williams 1989) led to later contacts with people who introduced him to a variety of crack houses in the area, one of which became the focus of his study of crack house life.

Sampling in Case Study Research

Until now, this discussion of sampling has focussed on the recruitment of groups of research participants. Case study research, which uses by definition single individuals (or families or organizations), then, would not seem relevant in a discussion of sampling. Nevertheless, conclusions are often drawn, if tentatively, from case study research—conclusions that are expected to have applicability beyond the single case in question. For this reason, principles of sampling can be useful to consider in planning case study research and in describing the limits of such studies.

It is obvious that no one person can be assumed to fully represent any group, and case studies depend more than other kinds of research on replication and on producing meaningful theory for their validity. As in small-scale or flexible method research, then, the nature of the sample is not the basis on which claims to generalizability rest. However, the general principle of providing a demographic description of the case and an account of how and why the case was selected for study or presentation holds true in case study research as in other kinds of research employing nonrandom sampling. This description allows the reader to form a judgement about the nature and potential relevance of the case studied to cases of their own. It should be noted, however, that in case study research, care must be taken that the description of an individual case not be so explicit that the identity of the person, family, or organization being studied is unwittingly revealed to the informed reader.

When the case study design is a prospective one, as in single-system research designed to evaluate practice (Bloom & Fischer 1982), principles of scientific sampling can be used to guard against selection bias. Since the purpose of such a study is the evaluation of the investigator's own effectiveness in working with the case, selecting the case for study so as to show only favorable results is a hazard. When there are several similar cases available for study, the case to be studied can be randomly selected from among them. Similarly, a systematic method of selection could be used, as in stating that the case to be studied will be the next case referred meeting certain selection criteria for the type of problem or intervention needed. Either method of case selection, when feasible, would tend to reduce selection bias by introducing explicit, impersonal rules for choosing the case.

Replication of case and single-system studies is the best means of demonstrating the general applicability of the results, even though each successive case is still treated as an individual. Aggregation of case study results may obviate some of the benefits of the single-case approach by masking important individual differences within the group (see chapters 4 and 8).

Sampling Issues in Longitudinal Research

There is an additional issue of representativeness of samples that occurs in longitudinal research: the problem of attrition. In panel and other longitudinal designs in which the same people are restudied at selected intervals over a longer period of time, it is essential that the sample representativeness be evaluated both at the beginning and *at the end* of the period of data collection. It is unlikely however that all people initially included will be retained throughout the study course. The percentage of cases lost to follow-up is called the rate of *attrition*. Obviously, the lower the rate of attrition the better. The problem of attrition must be addressed in two ways: (1) building in procedures to keep attrition to a minimum by enhancing follow-up efforts, and (2) describing and analyzing the effects of the attrition that has occurred.

When a sample for a longitudinal study is initially drawn, procedures for follow-up must be built into the consent procedure and into the initial data collection. Names, addresses, and telephone numbers must be carefully recorded, and it is useful to obtain information about friends or relatives who are likely to know where the study participant is in the future as well. If the period between data collection points is long, regular contact in the intervals may be useful just to keep track of the whereabouts of the participants. Sometimes, with appropriate consent, access to the records of organizations to which the sample members are connected can also be used to assist in locating people who have moved.

Despite retention efforts, however, some sample members are inevitably lost to follow-up over time. Data describing the people who were lost to follow-up and those who remained in the sample should be compared as of the beginning of the study. This comparison will reveal the ways in which people lost to follow-up were similar to or different from the group remaining. Published longitudinal studies must describe the rate of attrition from the sample and report the comparison of sample members lost and remaining so the reader can at least consider the possible effects of sample attrition on the study results.

Randomization in Experiments

So far, sampling has been discussed in terms of selecting and recruiting participants for a given study. In group experiments, however, there is an additional sampling issue to consider: how to deploy sample members between groups within the study. In fact, as the chapter on experiments has demonstrated, experiments depend on their internal logic and often on their ability to achieve equivalent groups within the study sample at least as much as on how people were selected to participate in the study to begin with. This process of obtaining equivalent sample groups is called randomization.

The actual way to achieve randomization is quite simple. If there is no known variable that it is very important to match participants on, then identifying information about each participant, such as the name and a unique identification number, is written on a slip of paper. The slips of paper are then mixed up (analogous to shuffling a deck of cards) and drawn out, one at a time. Assuming two groups in the design, the participant on the first slip is assigned to one of the groups; the participant on the second slip is assigned to the other group; the participant on the third slip is assigned to the first group; and the process continues until all the slips have been drawn and therefore all the available participants have been assigned to one of the two groups. When this process is used, there is absolutely no reason to expect that there will be any systematic difference between the two groups, since it was chance and chance alone, which is by definition random or indifferent, that determined membership in them.

Assigning participants to groups purely by chance maximizes the likelihood, but cannot guarantee, that the groups will be equal. Literally by chance, sometimes they're different. Therefore it is customary to include a statistical examination of the groups obtained to determine whether or not the groups are the same, at least on their known characteristics.

Of course, computerized randomization may be used in place of the manual technique of drawing names if that is more convenient. As with drawing a random sample, the specific technical method used to achieve randomness is not essential; the fact that a random technique is used in some form to constitute it is because that is the only way to be sure that selection bias has not occurred.

Issues in Sampling

Whatever the type of research being undertaken and whatever the purpose of that research, certain core sampling issues must always be addressed. While these topics have all been discussed for each type of sampling described, each issue deserves its own comment as a way to summarize sampling concerns.

Size

With all studies except perhaps single-case designs, one of the most common questions asked of a sample is whether or not it is large enough. Understanding principles of sampling and of research design allows for a more informed answer to this question. If the purpose of the study is to produce a generalizable description of some phenomenon or of how two or more concepts or phenomena may relate to each other, then a bigger sample is probably better because it allows for greater precision of estimation. However, if random or probability sampling cannot be employed, estimates may not be precise in any case.

In addition, many kinds of studies do not have this goal as primary. Experiments depend for their findings on the internal validity of the design and on randomization of sample groups as part of that design, not on the size of the sample. Flexible method studies most often have samples limited in size in order to permit the in-depth data collection and analysis they require. One danger of larger samples under these circumstances is that the investigator can become overwhelmed by data or too selective in the data actually used and reported on. In sum, bigger may often be better when it comes to samples, especially probability samples, but not all studies require or even benefit from samples that are large in size.

Precision Versus Cost

With random sampling, size does permit greater precision of estimation of population parameters. However, larger sample studies are, of course, more expensive to conduct. It costs money simply to find and recruit participants and then, of course, to collect data from them. Thus even when description is the purpose, precision must be weighed against cost, especially as increases from large to very large samples only yield small increases in precision (see figure 10–1).

One solution to the cost problem when a large or nationally representative sample is desired is to use existing data sets for secondary analysis. Various branches of the federal government conduct regular surveys and special studies with representative samples, and many of these surveys are made available in electronic form for additional analysis by other researchers. In some fields of study, there are other organizations developing archives or collections of electronic data on specific topics for research purposes. Some of these data sets include longitudinal data collected, which are prohibitively expensive and time-consuming for individual researchers to assemble on their own. While the information contained in existing data sets are already shaped and structured by the original study, it is often possible to adapt these studies to additional and creative use.

To conclude that size is the best or only criterion of importance in developing or assessing a study's sample, however, is a mistake. A biased sample will not be improved by being larger. As already noted, many studies depend on the concepts, theories, and internal logic of the design for their results, not on the size or diversity of the sample they employ.

Homogeneity Versus Heterogeneity

A tension that often arises in planning a sample, random or nonrandom, is whether to make it homogeneous or heterogeneous. In an increasingly diverse society, it is essential to include traditionally underrepresented groups in research samples and thus in the knowledge base of the professions. However, especially when the size of the overall sample will be limited, including only a token number of respondents from particular groups may be of little advantage. As with other elements of research design, the decision of about whether to use a homogeneous or a heterogeneous sample depends in the end on the purpose of the research. When homogeneous or demographically unrepresentative samples are used this limitation must be acknowledged when study results are described and discussed.

Summary

Deciding whom to study is a key part of the research process, one that, especially with descriptive and relational designs, will determine in large part the generalizability of the results obtained and, in all studies, will determine how well effective sources of information have been identified and recruited for study. Whatever the type of study to be undertaken, knowledge of the principles that underlie scientific sampling in fixed method designs is useful in thinking about sampling in other design contexts as well. Probability and nonprobability sampling methods both have their place in social work research. Careful consideration of whom to study and of how those who participate are actually contacted, recruited, and retained during the study process can add immeasurably to the credibility of study conclusions drawn whatever type of research design is used.

11

Basic Issues in Data Collection

Because research is a method of knowing that is built on empiricism, data collection is at the heart of all research. The importance of data collection in research flows from the importance of the observational process itself: of someone systematically examining phenomena in the real world and then recording and reporting on that examination in conceptual or theoretical terms, focussing on some defined question or issue. The question or issue guiding the research may be quite broad or it may be quite narrow and specific. The research as a whole may proceed largely inductively, from observation to concept, or deductively, from concept to observation. However, while data collection of some kind is part of all research, in fact there is great variety in the kinds of data collection procedures used in research in social work and the human services.

This chapter will present the basic issues in data collection that affect all of kinds of social work research. It will give an overview of data collection methods used and of the issues that must be considered when planning a data collection effort of any kind. In particular, it will focus on the context of research and data collection efforts, showing that how the context for data collection is viewed and handled is one of the defining characteristics that distinguishes the two broad types of research—flexible and fixed methods—from each other. This chapter provides essential background for the individual chapters on specific data collection methods—observation, interviewing, and the use of written self-report methods—that follow in next section of the book.

In planning and carrying out any data collection for research, several questions must be answered. *What* data will be collected, or what concepts will be the focus of the data collection, whether deductively or inductively defined? Under what circumstances, *where and when,* can such data best be obtained? While this question in part is a sampling issue, it also directs attention to data collection activities themselves and to defining the context in which data can best be obtained. Similarly, deciding *who* will supply the needed information is in part a sampling question, but it is a data collection question as well when deciding *how* and *from whom* data describing designated research participants can best be obtained. Of these questions, how data are to be collected—by interviewing, observation, or written self-report—is generally the one most often discussed. However, this chapter will focus on how the answers to these other questions also shape all data collection efforts and ultimately the findings of a study.

The traditional view of data collection for research in social work and the human services has been based on *measurement theory*. Methods of data collection are considered methods of measurement, and the language of instrumentation is often used—calibration, precision, and the like. The image is of a scale or a thermometer used to measure specific physical properties of phenomena "objectively," that is, with presumably perfect agreement in observations among observers using the same tool under the same conditions. Fallibilistic realism, of course, takes a different view: that observations are not only the product of what exists in the real world but also of the observer, the relationship of the observer to the observed, the process of observation itself, and the theories and concepts that form the lens through which the world is seen and that set the terms in which it is then described.

The traditional way of thinking about data collection has introduced two basic concepts into the literature on data collection or "measurement"—reliability and validity. Researchers in the flexible method or qualitative tradition have instead used the term *trustworthiness* when evaluating data collection efforts. This chapter will discuss these key concepts but will do so from the framework of fallibilistic realism in order to consider their applicability to the full range of social work research methods—flexible and fixed.

Deciding What to Observe

The first question that must be answered in any data collection effort is what information is needed, what phenomena or characteristics of phenomena should be observed. All data collection in research is focussed by the research question or questions: The data to be collected are those that will provide an answer to the research question or that will be useful for evaluating the hypothesis. Thus all data collection in research is focussed, although this focus can be developed in strikingly different ways. Like all other forms of professional activity, data collection for research is also purposeful, that is, undertaken for specific reasons, and this purpose helps to define the focus of the research.

One of the key ways in which flexible and fixed methods of research differ from one another is in how this question of what to observe is answered. In flexible method research, the focus of any data collection effort is only broadly defined at the beginning of the research, so it may change somewhat as the process of being in the field and learning about the informants and the setting continues. The concepts around which the report of findings is organized are often emergent and are not even named or defined until the data have been analyzed, that is, coded according to the meanings they reveal. The concepts that organize the observations thus emerge inductively from the data.

Williams's (1992) study of the world of the crack house illustrates this process. A central conclusion of the work is that the society of the crack house represents "a culture of refusal" (p. 88). This conceptualization emerges from two main sources: the documentation in his data of an organized culture in the seemingly disorganized crack house, with its own members, mores, language, patterns of living, and rituals; and his informants' commentary on the economics of the cocaine trade and of the communities in which he studied it. The culture of refusal expresses a relationship that its members take both toward mainstream norms of everyday living and toward the very limited, socially sanctioned economic options that exist in the communities in which the crack trade flourishes. The concept he develops—the culture of refusal—is then turned back on the data to illuminate it, such as in describing one reason why safer sex practices are not followed by crack house residents. His conclusion was that crack house residents did not trust the information and standards of safer sex behavior received from mainstream medicine, which represented to them the larger culture and its economic institutions that they have rejected and refuse to participate in.

Although data collection in flexible method research often begins with an area of interest rather broadly defined, it is nevertheless focussed by the purposes and questions that guide the research. In flexible method research, this purpose and focus may shift somewhat, and generally does, in response to the data as they incrementally emerge and as the interpretations of them are developed and explored in further data collection or analysis. However, there is always some degree of focus to the data collection effort if only because it is impossible to observe, record, and make sense of every feature of an encounter or interaction.

One key way in which research-based observation differs from everyday observational experience even in flexible method research is that the focus of the observational effort is made explicit at the outset, however general the focus may be. In flexible method research, it is possible to enter the field and begin data collection with only a general notion of what the key concepts of interest will be. The hard work of identifying and defining the concepts relevant to understanding what has been observed is then carried out during the concurrent data collection and data analysis processes (Strauss & Corbin 1990).

In fixed method research, however, the question of what to collect data about is answered differently, that is, before any data collection actually begins. Fixed method research designs are defined as such in large measure because the phenomena to be studied are preselected, preidentified, and predefined. In fixed method research, once a phenomenon has been identified as a focus of study in the research question or hypothesis it becomes a focus of data collection. In framing the research question, then, the major phenomena to be studied are identified, and data collection methods are derived deductively.

Any phenomenon that will be a focus of data collection efforts in fixed method research must therefore be carefully defined. The process of explicit definition has two related purposes: to clarify what will be studied so that it can be examined efficiently and effectively and to clarify for others who will read the study exactly what is meant when the defined term is used. The concepts or phenomena to be studied are traditionally defined at two levels: the conceptual and the operational. The *conceptual definition* locates the idea theoretically; the operational definition identifies the specific procedures or operations—the actual data collection activities—that will be used to identify the phenomenon in the research. *Operational definitions* in fixed method research are often standardized, that is, drawn from previous studies or from preexisting instruments developed specifically for use in research (see chapter 15).

Definitions useful for fixed method research are ones that specify unambiguously the criteria by which instances of the defined phenomenon can be recognized. These definitions serve to distinguish observations that fall under the definition of the phenomenon from observations that do not. Using such a definition, it can be deduced whether or not an observation fits into a conceptual category, the definition of the phenomenon of interest. The concept is then operationally defined by the method used to measure it.

The Gomez (1990) article illustrates well the process of moving from a concept to an operational definition. Gomez translates the term "subjective mental health" in the title of his article as the concept of "overall psychological well-being," defined as the excess of positive to negative affect in a person's life (p. 377). Note that the very general concept of mental health has been qualified from the start as subjective mental health, that is, a sense of mental health as experienced and reported by the individual rather than as assessed objectively against some predefined clinical or other external standard. Defining mental health in this way fits well with the data collection method chosen for the study: interviewing using questions that are self-descriptive of the person being interviewed. Gomez is also careful to explain why, since his interest is in biculturalism, psychological well-being and the balance of positive and negative affects makes sense as a definition of subjective mental health in the context of this study (see p. 377).

The problem remains, however, of how to gather data that will determine the relative amounts of negative and positive affect in the life of each person to be interviewed for the study: the problem of the operational definition. Psychological well-being, therefore, is further defined by Gomez as scores derived from an existing instrument called the Affect Balance Scale (Bradburn & Caplovitz 1965), a scale with "10 items, 5 that measure positive affect and 5 that measure negative affect" (p. 381). The operational definition of psychological well-being in this study is the score obtained from people's responses to questions on the Affect Balance Scale. The very general concept of subjective mental health, then, has been defined for the study in a specific way—as overall psychological well-being—and then a particular way to measure it has been selected: a specific 10-item scale. In addition, Gomez measures other variables—self-esteem, marital satisfaction, and job satisfaction—that he argues are often major components of psychological well-being, selecting specific operational definitions for each of these as well.

The strength of this traditional way of defining concepts in terms of their operational definitions is that once an operational definition has been developed and accepted, there is clarity about whether or not or how much of a phenomenon has been observed if the operational definition has been adhered to in the data collection process. In addition, by making the operational definitions public and explicit, the data collection procedures can be replicated, compared between studies and critiqued.

However, the limitations of this approach are also apparent: data collection operations, that is, their operational definitions, will invariably be more restricted than the general or conceptual definition of a phenomenon. For example, there are many existing scales designed to measure depression, but each of them captures a different, specific, and ultimately limited aspect of the phenomenon. Beck's Depression Inventory (Beck & Steer 1987), for example, focuses on the thought patterns that often characterize depression, while the symptom checklist (SCL-90) (Derogatis 1983) concentrates on the symptoms of depression as an illness. Since each data collection method elicits different information, scores obtained by the same person at the same time on these two instruments might be quite different. Each specific data collection procedure thus reduces the concept of interest, depression, to a predefined, limited subset of information that is then taken to represent the phenomenon as a whole—or at least the aspects of the phenomenon most relevant to a specific piece of research.

In discussing operational definitions, it should be noted that while they may consist of quantitative measures, they need not always be quantitative. There are also standardized data collection procedures designed to elicit narrative data or subjective judgements in predetermined ways. In addition, it should be noted that standardized operational definitions can be developed or applied to interviewing, observation, or self-report procedures. For example, the Ainsworth measure of attachment in young children (Ainsworth, Slater, Behar, Waters, & Wall 1978) is an observational procedure from which standardized categories describing styles of attachment behavior are derived.

Operational definitions need not be standardized; in fact, any repeatable way of making an observation is an operational definition, including "Rate your own anxiety about research: Is it very high, high, moderate, or low?," which is a very subjective and idiosyncratic one. However, this question is an operational definition if it is used in the same way with all research participants and its answers are interpreted similarly in developing the findings of the research. Thus each question or set of questions on a survey defines operationally the characteristics or phenomena that the survey findings will describe.

In fixed method research, the conceptual and operational definitions are specified before any data collection actually begins. The researcher must then identify or develop an operational definition for each major concept or phenomenon defined as part of the scope of the research. The best operational definition to use is the one that most closely fits the phenomenon as conceived to exist by the researcher, best suits the participants in the research, and best fits with the data gathering situation as it will occur, that is, be most feasible. In flexible method research, on the other hand, the formal definitions of the phenomena of interest are the products of the data analysis, and the challenge in designing the data collection effort is to develop a general strategy and focus that will best permit the information needed for analysis to emerge.

The Data Collection Context

Only recently have researchers begun to understand the importance of the observational context in research. For many years, except in the literature on ethnographic and some other forms of flexible method research, the research context was considered to be like the placebo effect in treatment: Everyone knew that it was important, but its influence was regarded in the traditional framework as a contaminant of the real thing.

One reason that experimental methods have traditionally been considered the apex on a continuum of value among fixed method research designs is that such designs attempt to isolate two or more variables from all other influences to study them in closed systems in order to examine how change can be produced. A key feature of experimental designs is therefore that they hold the observational context constant, which has also meant making the experimental context an artificially controlled one relative to the practice or real world situation. However, it is only outside of the experimental context that phenomena exist in their natural states and settings and in which theories and knowledge for professional practice must prove themselves. In fact, much of the debate about the usefulness of particular research designs, especially experiments and their alternatives, has focussed on the usefulness of knowledge derived in artificially controlled observational contexts, like in laboratory experiments or double-blind treatment studies, rather than in the everyday social or practice world (see, for example, Epstein 1996).

Embracing a wide range of research designs and methods confers both the freedom and the responsibility to choose the best context for data collection and for research. In fact, in research, ". . . choosing and creating settings demands much in the way of imagination, ingenuity and critical thought" (Aronson, Ellsworth, Carlsmith, & Gonzales 1990:183). The researcher always exercises choice in selecting the context to use for gathering information. And there are often many additional choices to be made about whether and how much to intervene in that research context beyond the tampering inherent in simply arranging to collect data within it and about how much of the context to invite "in" to the study itself.

Context and Control

Some of the questions about the context of research most properly belong to questions of research design rather than to data collection. However, it is in sampling and data collection activities that research design encounters the real world, bringing questions of context to the forefront.

There are two ways in which research designs can deal with controlling the observational context directly: whether or not manipulation is used as part of the design, as in single-subject studies and in group experiments, and in how much of an effort goes into holding the observational context constant.

When manipulation is used in a research design, the researcher (and/or others) actively does (or does not do) things that are expected to affect the people who are being observed. For example, in the El-Bassel et al. (1995) study discussed in chapter 7, some women received a standard preventive intervention and others received a more intensive one. The same observations were made of all study participants before and after release from prison—those who did and those who did not receive the innovative treatment—and the results were then compared. As this study illustrates, the experimental intervention introduced both the treatments and control over who got which treatment into the prison context, which was otherwise the same for all of the women in the study.

To make such a comparison of groups of study participants valid and meaningful, of course, the second type of experimental control also comes into play: the need to hold constant all other things that might affect the comparison through various controls. In the El-Bassel et al. (1995) study, for example, this control consisted in setting criteria governing who was eligible to participate in the treatment and the research, in randomly assigning people to the two study groups, and in collecting all the data needed from both groups in exactly the same way. These efforts to hold the context in which the treatment takes place constant are often what gives rise to controversy about this kind of research (Epstein 1996). For example, decisions made about who is offered a promising treatment is rarely randomly made in the practice setting. In fact, the more normal practice is to offer a treatment first to those considered most in need. However, in an experiment, such a practice would tend to make it harder to show that a new treatment was effective because of the more serious problems that the participants getting the experimental treatment would have.

The most often-cited controversy about research conducted in controlled contexts has been framed in terms of artificiality. For example, practitioners are sometimes skeptical of the findings of research that has been conducted under special and contrived circumstances and uncertain about whether or not the results of such studies would turn out to hold in the context of everyday practice. El-Bassel et al.'s (1995) primary purpose in conducting the experiment, for example, was to demonstrate the effectiveness of a specific preventive intervention in reducing risky behavior in a group of drug-using women in prison once they returned to the community. These women did not only get the treatment; they were also intensively studied and followed in prison and upon release into the community. However, the average reader of his study is likely to be more concerned with what the effects of such a treatment might be when applied under nonresearch, uncontrolled circumstances. This problem has traditionally been called the problem of *external validity* or *generalizability,* that is, how much it is reasonable to depend on the validity of a study's findings in contexts different from those originally studied. In flexible method research, this quality is called transferability (Drisko 1997).

While this problem of generalizability has most often been discussed in relation to experiments, the general problem is true of any piece of research in that no two pieces of research are ever conducted in exactly the same context, if only because the historical moment may be different. The problem of generalizability, then, cannot ever be solved by logic or through debate about what kind of research to do or about how much to try to strive for an artificial or a "natural" context for research. Rather it is an empirical question that can be answered only through additional research, specifically through replication.

Whatever the kind of research that is being done, however, there is an unavoidable distinction between research and nonresearch settings. This distinction exists, if for no other reason, because the research setting is always somehow observed, always somewhat constrained, and sometimes even manipulated. Thus the question of artificiality in research is a relative one, not an absolute one. This relative distinction is real, however: Research designs do differ in how rigorously they attempt to "control" contextual influences on the phenomena they are focussed on.

Context Versus Content

One way to describe this difference in research designs, suggested by Manicas and Secord (1983), is in terms of open versus closed systems. Experimental designs, for example, work by creating closed systems that isolate some phenomena as much as possible from their contexts in order to study them. Flexible method and other more naturalistic designs, at the other extreme, operate as open systems, including the context in which phenomena are found and the process of observation itself in the field of study. One major way in which research designs and data collection strategies differ, then, is in how much of the research context is treated as *content* that itself may be subject to study in the research.

In fixed method research, the general issue of what will be treated as context, outside the scope of the data collection effort, and what will be treated as content, within the scope of the data collection effort, is generally settled at the problem formulation stage when the research question and design are developed. Relational research designs, for example, are often directed toward studying how variations in specific phenomena, sometimes including specific contextual characteristics, may relate to each other. Gomez (1990), for example, includes information on several key demographic factors that might be expected to affect an individual's psychological well-being, such as gender, age, socioeconomic status, and number of years of living in the United States. Those contextual factors that were found to be correlated with the measures of psychological well-being used, such as age and socioeconomic status, were controlled for statistically in the data analysis (see page 385). It is essential when planning any data collection effort, then, to identify deductively or from the literature those contextual factors that might be expected to affect the major variables under study and then to collect data on them so their effects can be taken into account as findings are developed.

When undertaking any data collection effort, however, it is also important to understand clearly the research context and the full range of what ought to be included as content in the research, including content that defines and describes the context of the study. For example, had the Gomez study employed multiple interviewers as many large-scale descriptive or survey studies do, it would be essential to record who the interviewer was in each instance. The data collected could then be analyzed initially for interviewer differences in case some tended to elicit or record more or less positive self-ratings from participants than others.

In flexible method research, by contrast, the boundary between context and content may be fluid. For example, in a participant observation study, it may only be after spending time in a given setting that the features of the context that affect the phenomena of interest can be identified. As with other aspects of the data collection, then, the determination of what is relevant to observe and record about the observational context may only emerge inductively as the study proceeds. In addition, flexible methods of inquiry like participant observation are often employed specifically when it is assumed that understanding a phenomenon in its "natural" context is important. The assumption is, then, that context is often a central part of what needs to be described and understood in a flexible method study.

The Observer as Context or Content

One key feature of the research context is the observer, the person or people whose experiences of those being studied form the basis of the research. The traditional view of research emphasizes "objectivity," or the idea that the well-trained observer can function as a neutral or transparent medium for apprehending an unchanging reality. Fallibilistic realism, on the other hand, views observation as an act and the observer as an actor who provides a specific account of what has been observed based on his or her experience of it. Fixed method research strives to standardize the process of observation and thus hold the context of the observations made constant by defining the observer as outside the boundary of what is being studied. Flexible method research, by contrast, generally allows the process of observation to vary at least to some extent and thus includes the observer and process of observation itself within the boundary of what is being studied.

Within the fixed method tradition, observational processes are considered important and have been studied as well. In this tradition, studies of the effects of the observational context on what is observed are termed methodological studies and are usually undertaken and/or reported separately from substantive ones. For example, the literature is replete with studies comparing telephone and in-person interviewing, variations in responses to mailed surveys depending on characteristics of the material mailed or the methods of eliciting responses used, how interviewer characteristics affect what participants in a study may say or do, and the like. These studies are aimed at providing information useful to researchers who will be designing the relatively standardized or unvarying ways in which to collect data for any given fixed method study. They may also be used to identify factors in the data gathering context that will have to be taken into account as variables when analyzing and interpreting the findings of a study, that is, when deciding what must be treated as content and what as context for a specific study.

Rather than treating specific, predefined aspects of the observational context as potential subjects for systematic study in the traditional sense, flexible method studies tend to include the observer within the boundary of what is to be observed in each study as it is conducted. In other words, some degree of reflexivity is inherent in the way the observational context is usually handled in most flexible method research. The investigator in a flexible method study often treats his or her own experiences in the data gathering process as data that are part of the whole phenomenon being studied. Stated differently, the reactions of the studier are considered part of the information available about the studied. These spontaneous observations about the observational process may include perceptions of the setting and of the self as observer, and they may be incorporated on the spot to inform the ongoing activity from which further observations are generated. This kind of integration of the observer into what is observed is most clearly illustrated in participant observation and ethnographic research in which the investigator joins in the social life of a group in order to learn more about it. While an investigator in such a tradition is free from preplanned constraints on how data are to be gathered or how observations are to be made, the responsibility for the intensive self-examination that is required is great. Continuously documenting this self-reflective process is essential through diaries, field notes, memos, and other techniques that encourage reflection not only on the content of the study but on the process of it as well (Padgett 1998).

The Political Context of Research

Except in the field of evaluation research, the political context of research is an aspect of the broader context of data collection that is rarely discussed except by those with a critique to make of the status quo. There are always various stakeholders in any piece of research, however, and these stakeholders may have similar or different interests. Some of these interests may affect aspects of the data collection process from access to a site to selection of the questions to ask to selection of who will do the asking, as well as the uses to which the results of a study may be put when it is done.

Conducting any data collection effort requires resources, money, or the equivalent in time and effort. In addition to material resources, intangible resources, such as sanction, encouragement, and moral support, are often needed as well. Whoever provides the resources for a piece of research usually has a stake of some kind in its outcome. This stake may be in one aspect of the effort rather than in any one specific outcome or finding. However, it is important to know about any piece of research who the stakeholders are, especially if they are the sponsors or others who provided resources.

When views on a subject are polarized, people sometimes think that scientific or research-based information can be used to "settle" the dispute, but few findings in research are so unequivocal or open to only one interpretation that such a strategy will work. In conducting any data gathering effort, it is essential that any political conflicts among those designing and conducting the research be identified, aired, and resolved or set aside. For example, when two groups of people have an interest in the findings of an interview study but they disagree about some aspect of the problem being studied, it is not wise to have members of either group conduct the interviews because members of one group may not trust the information provided by members of the other. Getting them to agree on someone whom they both trust to gather the data and on how the data will be gathered will ensure that the findings from the interviews will be accepted and used.

Finally, it is important to anticipate the political uses, positive or negative, intended or unintended, to which any findings can be put before data collection is begun. Often there is little control that can be exercised after the fact over how and by whom research results will be used. As far as is possible, then, representatives of any groups, organizations, or communities that may be affected by the anticipated findings should be consulted before data collection begins (Bowman 1991).

Selecting a Research Setting

All of the considerations discussed so far in relation to the context of research have been fairly abstract. The selection of a setting in which to conduct a study and in which to gather data, however, is also a very practical one. The following set of questions reflects both the theoretical and the practical dimensions that must be considered when choosing a setting for research.

What context, setting, or situation(s) will be most likely to allow for the phenomena of interest to be seen or to emerge? This question comes first because it is by far the most important one. Whatever the method of data collection to be used when observing or interacting with people, the setting in which they will be seen or spoken with may have a great impact on what they do or say and thus on what can be observed in the research. For example, if the focus of an observational study is on how residents of a nursing home do or do not interact with each other, it might make more sense to observe people in the common or dining rooms rather than in their individual bedrooms or bathrooms because those are the places in which they are most likely to encounter each other. However, to the extent that residents are accustomed to visiting each other and socializing in their own rooms, that behavior would be lost to study. In an interview study of marital satisfaction, for example, interviewing couples at home or in an office, alone or in the presence of others, together or separately, are all likely to affect the kind of information that is shared.

Will the setting contemplated allow for the kind of data collection needed to be done? Will it allow for the kind of recording of information that is needed as well? Once the kind of setting that will best allow the phenomena of interest to emerge has been identified, it is also important to consider how well the setting will accommodate the kind of data gathering that is contemplated. For example, when studying the social interactions of nursing home residents through observation, the common rooms might most easily accommodate that form of data collection; in an individual room, much time might pass without any interactions to observe. If, on the other hand, the plan is to interview the residents about their social lives and their satisfaction (or dissatisfaction) with them, it might be better to conduct the data collection in rooms with greater privacy, perhaps leading to greater candor. It might also involve less background noise, making hearing the questions and answers easier for participants and interviewers.

The setting chosen for data collection must also be able to accommodate whatever means of data recording that will be used if the recording is taking place on site. Traditional methods of participant observation research, for example, have involved the generation of extensive field notes *after* each period of time spent in the setting. If such a method is to be used, the periods of data collection on site must be planned in such a way as to allow for periods of recording directly afterward.

When the recording of observations will take place on site simultaneous with the data collection itself, planning must allow for that as well. If videotaping or audiotaping will be used, will the data collection setting accommodate it? And how will be it be explained to and experienced by participants and others in the setting? Paper and pencil recording may often seem less intrusive, but even the presence of a person with clipboard, paper, and pencil in hand may have a meaning and impact in the setting that should be anticipated and addressed. Finally, in some cases portable computers are now used for recording information on site; again, if used, a data gathering setting that can accommodate this method must be selected.

Is the setting contemplated for the data collection accessible? Can the researcher count on being able to gain access to the site? This question is one both of *can* and of *may*. The "can" part speaks of feasibility for the researcher; the "may" part speaks to consideration of ethical issues and of the permissions that may be necessary for legitimating the conduct of the data gathering effort. To return to the example of the nursing home study, a researcher is likely to select a nursing home that is geographically convenient in which to conduct the research. This strategy makes sense; energy can then go into observation itself rather than into travel to the site.

Once the nursing home has been selected, however, although an observer can most likely enter a nursing home's common areas to make observations under the guise of being a visitor to a resident, this strategy would not be ethical or prudent. The permission of those who own or have responsibility for the setting in which any data collection will take place should be sought not only for ethical reasons (see chapter 9) but also to legitimate the research. There are very few spaces that are truly public. In conducting research, as in any other professional encounter, sanction for the activity based on its purpose is very important to obtain. The choice of specific sites for data collection, then, are often based on whether or not legitimated access to the facility or setting for research purposes can easily be obtained or not.

How can the setting be described so that it can be compared with others that are similar and distinguished from others that are different? How representative is the setting of others that might be assumed to be like it? An area that is often neglected in reports of research studies is how the sites for the data gathering were chosen and what they were actually like. The issue of how well a given sample of individual study participants represents some larger population is commonly considered, but the fact that a given setting may (or may not) represent some larger population of possible settings is not often discussed. Except in large scale survey studies, settings are rarely sampled in the way that individual participants are. Even so, a description of the setting and of the data gathering context is necessary for the reader of a study to determine how applicable the results might be in other contexts or how the context of the data gathering may have affected what was learned. All phenomena are studied in a context, and the context influences what is observed. Therefore, describing the contexts of any data gathering effort is essential.

How to Collect Data

There are three basic methods used for the collection of original data in research: observation, interviewing, and written self-report. Each of these has a long tradition of use in the social sciences and in human service research, and each has its advantages and drawbacks that make it better suited for gathering some kinds of data than others. While these advantages and drawbacks are described in depth in the chapters devoted to each method, an overview of them is given here.

Observation

The term *observation* has two uses in the literature on research: the process of experiencing and recording information for research in general based on some kind of sensory experience of it and, more specifically, the process of gathering visual information. As a specific data collection method in research, observation is currently underutilized in social work research despite the fact that when appropriately used the data that flow from it are often very convincing.

Observation as a specific data collection method covers a range of activities. At one end is the passive, noninteractive process of watching—and perhaps also listening—to what is transpiring in the research setting. At the other, the reasearcher might take a much more active stance by participating in some interaction or performing some planned intervention and then watching—and perhaps also listening to and experiencing in other ways—what transpires before and after the intervention. What is observed may be carefully and precisely predefined prior to the data collection process, or it may be only loosely defined to begin with and then further articulated by the observer once in the setting itself or as a product of the data analysis.

Observation as a data collection method is often best suited to the study of behavior, observable actions, and interactions. What people say they do and what they actually do can differ. Direct observation is often the most effective way of learning about people's behaviors, individual or interactive, as distinct from intentions, motivations, or the recollections of them. Jarrett (1992) (see chapter 4) used observation effectively in her case study to ascertain who really was involved in the family life of one household, discovering that many more people participated regularly in it than data on residence would have suggested. However, some behaviors are normally very private and thus difficult to observe. There are often limitations to learning about intimate or illegal behaviors, for example, through direct observation.

Observation has traditionally been termed a reactive method of data collection. Reactivity is the tendency to evoke a response in those being studied to the data gathering process itself. This reactivity arises from the fact that unless the observational method involves concealing the process from participants, as through one-way mirrors, hidden cameras, or covert observation, the observer(s) and perhaps also observational equipment, such as cameras, are on site, visible, and known to those being observed. Those being observed, therefore, are assumed to have reactions to this presence, and those who observe must acknowledge this potential and react to it in turn. How an observer is introduced into a setting, how the observer appears, what explanation for his or her presence is given, what kinds of interactions do and do not take place during the process of observation, how the observer reacts to questions or challenges about the role, and how the observer leaves the setting—all of these factors are likely to affect the kinds of reactions that those in the setting will have to the data gathering process itself and should be considered when the data collection is planned and when the data are analyzed.

Observation as a data collection method lends itself to the collection of either structured—specific and quantified—or unstructured data. There are protocols in existence to guide the collection of observational information about specific phenomena in a predetermined way. There is also an extensive literature on participant observation and ethnographic research and the techniques used to gather observational information in an unstructured way. In this tradition, observation is often combined with interviewing, with the questioning of participants about events observed, reflecting the flexibility of data gathering in these traditions. Observation, then, while especially useful for the study of nonverbal behavior, can also embrace the study of verbal behavior as well.

Interviewing

Interviewing is probably the most common method of data collection used in social work research. An interview is a conversation conducted for the purpose of eliciting information from someone else. As with observation, interviewing can be used to collect data that are either structured—specific, predefined, and quantified—or unstructured, also called narrative. Interviews can effectively be done both face-to-face or over the telephone. However, because an interview is a verbal medium, a sophisticated understanding of all the factors that influence verbal interactions is essential (Foddy 1993).

Interviewing as a data collection method is focussed on verbal behavior, on the words used by people to describe events, recollections, opinions, attitudes, feelings, motivations, intentions, and meanings. These are essential aspects of people's psychological and social lives that in fact cannot usually be directly determined, but only inferred, from behavior; they are aspects of another person's internal and interpersonal world that often can best be apprehended through their words, through their own verbal description of them. A person's face may express sorrow; tears may be seen to flow. In most cases, however, the explanation of why the person is crying or what the feeling being expressed through the tears is can only be described based on the person's answer to a question about it. Written accounts may also be used to capture the words that people use to describe these internal experiences—feelings, meanings, attitudes, and the like. However most people find it easier to express what they mean orally rather than in written form, especially when the answers or descriptions sought are open-ended or structured only by the participant or, in some cases, when the information sought is of a complex or sensitive nature. However, transcripts of research interviews or other verbal interactions, such as treatment encounters, can be valuable data sources for research.

Interviewing is used in social work and other helping professions all the time for purposes other than research. The knowledge that most helping professionals have about interviewing can provide a foundation for research interviewing, which is similar in some ways and different in others from interviewing for other purposes (Bunin et al., 1983). Skills in establishing rapport, in asking questions that can further illuminate what has already been said, in conveying an accepting and nonjudgmental attitude toward what is said that encourages further explanation, and in modulating personal reactions to what is said—all of these are assets in most research interviewing situations. However, since the purposes of the data gathering are different in research than in the helping situation, adaptations must be made to keep the interview process focussed on the aims of the research: to gather in a structured or unstructured fashion information limited to answers to the general research question that guides it.

Interviewing, like observation, is a fairly reactive method of data gathering. When interviewing, especially in face-to-face interviews, the observer and the participants in the research encounter each other directly and react not only to what is said but to how it is said, to who the interviewer is, to how he or she looks, and to how he or she behaves. Even in telephone interviews, assumptions may be made about who the interviewer (or participant) is and what he or she intends based on the sound of the voice rather than just on what is explicitly said. Specific behaviors, aspects of appearance, and phrasing and tone of voice can be consciously used in the interview situation to aid in the effectiveness of the data gathering by establishing a positive rapport between interviewer and participant. On the other hand, some reactions and responses cannot easily be anticipated. When planning an interview study, therefore, careful consideration should be given not only to the explicit content of the interview encounter, to the questions that will be asked and the explanation that will be given for them. It is also important to consider the other aspects of the encounter that may naturally affect the kind of data that are gathered.

Written Self-Report

Written forms of data collection are also very common in social work research, especially in the form of mailed surveys or questionnaires. In addition, standardized measures of specific psychological, attitudinal, and other characteristics exist that are often incorporated into social work research as the Gomez (1990) study illustrates. This method of data collection is distinguished from others by the fact that the research participants contribute by writing down the needed information. Although this occurs most often by checking off fixed, predetermined responses to preformed questions, written data that is narrative in form can be collected as well, as in journals, logs, or answers to open-ended questions.

The ability of anyone to participate in research that relies on the collection of written data depends, of course, on being able both to read and write in the language of the materials prepared. This factor can be a major one limiting the use of this form of data collection. In addition to those with limited literacy or without knowledge of the language being used, children and, in some cases, those with visual or motor problems also may not be able to participate effectively in providing written data. Sometimes when open-ended data are needed for interpretation, children may be asked to express themselves through drawings—a specialized and interesting form of data collection in itself.

In addition, a researcher wishing to collect verbal data in written form is generally limited to using the languages that he or she knows well. Although the problem of having a common language can affect interviews and even observation as well, there are people who can communicate well orally in a given language who are not as comfortable or effective in written communication in it and thus who might have difficulty with a questionnaire.

One of the great advantages of collecting data in written form is that, if needed, it can be done anonymously, that is, without any direct contact between those who gather the data and those who provide it. The mailed questionnaire or the survey voluntarily picked up, filled out, and dropped in a box are examples of anonymous data collection procedures. Mailed surveys, of course, can be identifiable, and it takes a special effort to keep them anonymous. However, the written self-report is the only form of data collection in which complete anonymity is even possible because the participant is not seen or heard and cannot be located through the response. Although the telephone interview may seem anonymous, the identity of the interviewee can often be determined through knowing the telephone number that has been dialed; in the truly anonymous situation the identity of the participant is both unknown and unascertainable.

The potential anonymity of written data collection means that it is often used for topics that are sensitive or that address illegal, socially sanctioned, or intimate behavior, when it is believed that participants will disclose more in an anonymous situation than when they are identifiable. Information about drug use or sexual behavior, for example, is generally collected in this way.

In addition, although it is possible to use written forms of data collection for narrative data or unstructured responses, because writing at length is generally difficult and time-consuming, data collected in written form are usually prestructured and fixed in form. This requires, of course, that considerable effort be devoted in advance to developing or selecting the questions and response categories that constitute the survey or other data collection form. Unlike in observation or interviewing, then, there is generally little flexibility to the data gathering process once it is underway. Therefore the collection of data in written form is generally associated with fixed rather than flexible method research. However, existing written materials are often incorporated into flexible method studies (Padgett 1998).

One of the major questions to be answered when collecting written data in fixed method research is whether to develop an instrument for this purpose that is unique to a given study or whether to identify and use existing instruments to measure the concepts of interest in the study. With a data collection tool developed specifically for the study at hand, the nature of the data to be gathered can be tailored exactly to the purposes of the study and to the ways of conceptualizing and defining the phenomena of interest that seem most appropriate. However, because of being new and unique, these methods of eliciting data will not have been previously examined for their effectiveness. Much effort will be required to refine and pilot the questions and response categories developed, and flaws that lead to incomplete or ambiguous information are often encountered. For these reasons, researchers often seek out "tried and true" instruments in order to benefit from the prior work of others in developing and debugging easily interpretable measures (see chapter 15). Use of an existing measure, however, requires that the phenomenon it purports to capture is in fact the same as the concept or phenomenon of interest as defined in the present study, and it may or may not be easy to identify an existing instrument that fits the study well. However, there are many tools available to assist in identifying measures that exist and evaluating them for use in a particular study or with a particular type of participant.

Other Aspects of How

So far, the discussion of how to collect data has focussed on the mode of data collection—observation, interview, or written self-report—to be used. There are other questions about "how" to answer, however, especially when structuring questions in fixed method research. In most cases, the goal in gathering data for fixed method research is to be as direct, precise, and unambiguous as possible about the information that is needed when asking a question. Yet there are times, such as when exploring complex feelings or motivations, that some ambiguity in a question is desirable in order to give the participant the scope to answer it in a variety of ways or in the way that best describes a complex response or situation.

In addition to structuring the question, of course, there are the problems of how and how much to structure the response. In general, prestructuring the responses or types of observations to be made increases the comparability of the data recorded for or by each person. It forces the participant or the observer to reduce the natural variation in expression to the categories that exist. The chapter on questionnaire design (chapter 14) later in the book goes into some detail on the choices to be considered in prestructuring both questions and responses, concepts that pertain to interviewing and observation as well in the context of fixed method research.

Who Will Collect the Data

Along with consideration of the content to be covered in the data gathering effort, the context in which the data might best be gathered, and the method of data gathering that should be used, the question of who might best provide the information that is needed should also be considered. Asking this question does not intend to open the question of the best sample to employ in the research (see chapter 10).

Rather it asks, given the nature of the sample, who might best provide the information needed about the people in it: the people themselves or someone else? It also asks, especially in fixed method research, if data are to be gathered from sample members in person, what characteristics and training should this person or people possess?

The question of who might best provide the data is a question of choosing an informant. Suppose, as in an earlier example, there were a study being planned to examine the social activities of a group of nursing home residents. There are several possibilities for informants in such a study. These informants might include the residents themselves about themselves, the residents themselves about each other, staff in the nursing home, visiting friends and family members of the residents, or research observers with no other relationship to the residents or the staff.

Each of these potential informants provides information that is conceptually distinct. All can potentially provide information about behavior either as directly observed, as summarized and reported verbally, or (the residents themselves) through self-report. All can provide information about the motivations for that behavior or the feelings accompanying it, most as inferred but only some, the residents themselves, as directly experienced. Some groups, such as the residents themselves, may have functional characteristics that potentially limit their usefulness as informants, such as perceptual or memory problems. Some may be able to provide written information if that is needed; some may not. All of these potential informants will have a particular point of view on the study issue: Staff and family members, for example, may differ in their perceptions of the adequacy of the opportunities for socializing that the nursing home provides, which may in turn be reflected in the information about residents' social behavior that is furnished to the study.

The choice of an informant for such a study must depend on all these factors: what the specific data needed are, how they can best be collected, what form they will be collected in, the capacity of the various potential informants to provide it, and the points of view that the various informants might bring to the process. The most important determinant of the choice must be the nature of the phenomena to be studied, what the specific data are that are needed. The other choices—of informant and of ways of collecting the data—are made in order to get the specific information needed in the most direct and efficient manner possible. Often trade-offs are made; for example, even though data from residents directly might be preferable, if the group to be studied includes many frail or sick individuals, using other informants might be the most feasible way to proceed although the point of view of the residents themselves would be lost.

When resources are adequate or the decision about informants is difficult to make, multiple informants are sometimes used. This strategy often affords excellent opportunities to understand a phenomenon from more than one perspective and to assess it in more than one way, resulting in a fuller picture of a phenomenon. In studying children, for example, it is commonly acknowledged that parents and teachers often do not describe the same child in exactly the same way but that both often have valuable information to contribute about the child's behavior and functioning. When using multiple informants and when their perceptions differ, it can be difficult to determine how to reconcile their accounts of the phenomena of interest. Conversely, when the reports of different informants agree, the data obtained tend to gain in credibility.

When data are collected and the findings of a study are reported, it is essential that the data be described in a way that makes the nature of the informant clear. For example, data from this hypothetical nursing home study might be described as "nursing home residents' self-reported patterns of socialization" or as "staff perceptions of residents' socialization patterns," depending on who provided the data. While the content of the study in these two cases is in some respects the same—residents' patterns of socialization—the basis for describing it is quite different and must be made explicit. This procedure is one way in which an aspect of the observational context is commonly made clear in reporting the results of fixed method research.

Subjectivity and "Objectivity" in the Data Gathering Process

Choosing the informant for a study is one way of determining whether subjective or "objective" data will be used. By objective data in this instance is meant only that the data are furnished by someone different from the one having the experience of primary interest. Returning to the nursing home residents, a resident's own account of his or her own socialization is subjective; someone else's account of the resident's socialization is not and may be termed objective by contrast. In this sense, neither of these two forms of data is any more inherently trustworthy (or not) than the other. A person may try to deceive others about his or her own activities or may have engaged in self-deception about what he or she really does; similarly, an observer may consciously or unconsciously perceive, or report on his or her observations of, another accurately or not. In this sense, subjective data and objective data are neither inherently better nor worse; they are simply different from each other.

There is another sense, of course, in which the terms objective and subjective are used evaluatively when describing data. Subjective data are often defined as existing only in the mind, without reference to external reality and not trustworthy for that reason. There are some phenomena of interest in social work research, such as feelings and other internal psychological states, such as motivations, that are inherently considered to exist by definition only in the mind. The challenge is to find ways to convey and record such subjective phenomena, by definition not directly observable, for the research. By contrast, however, the term objective can mean both having actual existence in reality and "being uninfluenced by emotions or personal prejudice" (American Heritage Dictionary 1992:1247). It can thus mean observable, as objects or behaviors are in contrast to emotions, for example. However, it can also mean unbiased, that is, a description as close to the reality experienced as possible. In this latter sense, even subjective data can be more or less objectively rendered. Much of the effort that goes into any data collection process, of course, is designed to produce information, whether about subjective or objective phenomena, that are as objective, that is, unbiased, as possible.

However, some question the idea that any data are unbiased in the sense of being uninfluenced by the standpoint and culture of the person doing the observing or providing the data (Landrine, Kolonoff, & Brown-Collins 1992).

For any observer in the research context, there is one final level on which to consider the objectivity and subjectivity of what is observed. In fixed method research, many studies and most forms of interaction between those who gather data and those who are the participants in the research are designed so that only specific verbal or behavioral data are to be noticed and recorded. In some flexible method research, however, the observer enters the research setting and enters into interaction with the participants in the research in a fuller way, through, for example, participant observation or unstructured or intensive interviewing processes. In such situations, there may be many subjective responses evoked in the observer by the data elicited or the situations encountered. These subjective responses of the observer may either be dismissed, considered as contaminants of the observational process, or considered to be part of the data, although subjective, that the observer has that might inform the interpretations made of the data. In other words, these subjective reactions in the data gathering situation may either be defined as part of the data available to the study or not. Although not commonly acknowledged, these subjective reactions to the data gathering process can occur in the context of a fixed method study as well, but they are especially likely to occur when contact between the researcher and the researched is intensive, prolonged, and/or interactive.

If such subjective reactions are to be used as data, they must be treated as such during the data gathering process. If, for example, a structured interview is being conducted, written notes can be made on the interview guide, perhaps at the end of it, recording the observer's responses to the situation for later analysis. In intensive interviewing and participant observation research, it has long been acknowledged that considerable time is needed after each data gathering episode to record in depth the full range of responses of the interviewer or observer along with the data that were gathered about the participants.

The Use of Multiple Observers

Returning to the issue of who will collect the data, there are particular issues to be considered in data gathering when the informants for a study are in the setting only as researchers and when more than one of them is involved. The situation of multiple observers or reporters is, in fact, quite a common one in fixed method research, especially in survey research and other large-scale fixed method studies in which multiple observers or interviewers are used. The problem that this situation poses is, quite simply, that of distinguishing variations in the data collected that arise from differences in what was observed from those due to who the observer or reporter was.

As has already been noted, in most fixed method research the effort during data collection is to hold the observational context constant as much as possible throughout the process. Even when a standardized way of gathering data has been developed, the fact that different people are involved in actually doing the data collection is an obvious source of possible unintended variation in the data. The first strategy used to deal with this problem is to record who the person gathering the data was in each instance in a systematic way. When the data have been gathered, they can then be analyzed to see whether or not there are any systematic differences evident in the findings generated by different observers or recorders.

Before any data are collected, however, it is essential to orient and train all of the people who will be gathering data to the data collection process being used in the study, emphasizing the importance of conducting the data gathering in as consistent a way as possible. While rules to guide the data gathering are important, unanticipated situations always arise whenever data are actually being collected. One benefit of having a number of people engaged in data gathering in the field is the information they can bring back to the study about how the data collection process is actually working out in practice. In particular, they can inform those who are directing a study about the situations they encounter that do not fit well with what participants actually seem to be saying or doing or with the rules for data gathering that have been developed. It is essential, then, not only to work with those who will gather the data at the beginning of a study but to continue to work closely with them during the data collection process so that adjustments can be made across the board based on information coming from the field. Only in that way will the most consistent and trustworthy data be collected.

Evaluating the Usefulness of Data

Whatever the method used to collect data in research and whoever may provide it, in the end the ultimate question that must be asked about any data gathered is how useful they are for answering the research question(s) asked. This broad question about data collection has generally been broken down into two parts based on traditional notions in measurement theory: Are the data reliable? And are they valid? Although traditional measurement theory has depended on logical positivist assumptions that are not the same as those of fallibilistic realism, the concepts of reliability and validity, if more broadly defined, remain useful and important ones to consider when planning or evaluating a data collection effort. Together they really address the general question of how useful and trustworthy the data generated by any given study are.

Validity and especially reliability have more often received formal discussion in fixed method research than in flexible method traditions. From the standpoint of fallibilistic realism, however, the importance of both concepts rests on certain assumptions that apply to both kinds of research:

> There is a world of empirical reality out there. The way we perceive and understand that world is largely up to us, but the world does not tolerate all understandings of it equally (so that the individual who believes that he or she can halt a speeding train with his or her bare hands may be punished by the world for acting on that understanding). There is a long-standing intellectual community for which it seems worthwhile to try to figure out collectively how

best to talk about the empirical world, by means of incremental, partial improvements in understanding. Often these improvements come about by identifying ambiguity in prior, apparently clear, views, or by showing that there are cases in which some alternative view works better. . . . "Truth" (or what provisionally passes for truth at a particular time) is thus bounded both by the tolerance of empirical reality and by the consensus of the scholarly community (Kirk & Miller 1986:11–12).

Concepts of reliability and validity have been essential in guiding discussion of data collection methods both in terms of how well any data tolerates a meaning or interpretation assigned to it and the consensus that is likely to be achieved in the scholarly or professional community about the trustworthiness of those data. Following Kirk and Miller (1986), reliability is defined as the degree to which a reported observation is independent of the accidental circumstances of the data collection process, and validity is defined as the degree to which the data have been interpreted in the right way. Viewed in this way, the concepts of reliability and validity clearly have relevance to data collection for research that is flexible or fixed in method. However, in constructivist traditions of qualitative research the concept of trustworthiness is often used to embrace and expand on traditional notions of both reliability and validity (Lincoln & Guba 1985; Padgett 1998).

Reliability

The concept of reliability has had much more attention in fixed method research than in flexible method traditions. Reliability as traditionally defined in fixed method research has to do with how repeatable or replicable a given observation is. In traditional measurement theory, any given observation made in research is considered to be made up of two components: "truth," the way the thing observed "is" in some absolute way in the world, and "error," the degree of distortion inevitably introduced by any measurement process. This inevitable error inherent in the act of measurement is assumed to be randomly distributed, to distort perceptions of it in no particular direction. Errors of perception or measurement that have a direction are defined as *bias* because they introduce a systematic rather than random inaccuracy into the data collected.

Reliable measurement is defined as having a high proportion of truth and a low proportion of error, either random or systematic. Reliability in measurement is generally described as repeatability or agreement. If there is a high degree of error in a measurement, no two (or more) people making the same measurement of the same thing using the same tool or data collection method are likely to come up with the same observation, or score, in quantitative terms. If there is only a small amount of error in the measurement, however, their observations are likely to agree quite closely.

In everyday life, when dealing with the physical environment, there are many illustrations of this concept of reliability that come easily to mind. Everybody knows that most bathroom scales, for example, operate using a spring mechanism and that such mechanisms are often not very reliable. However, properly calibrated scales that use weights and a balancing mechanism are more reliable. They are much more likely on repeated use to show the same weight for the same person on the same occasion than an ordinary set of bathroom scales will. Similarly, thermometers that use a column of mercury generally give more reliable (and more accurate) measurements of air temperature in general than do thermometers that use a metal coil.

The concept of accuracy is a bit different from that of reliability. Suppose that the truth of an observation, perhaps the air temperature, can be known absolutely. The most accurate measurement is the one that comes closest to what the true temperature actually is. It is possible in theory to have a reliable measurement that is not accurate; for example, there might be a thermometer that registered an air temperature that was always exactly three degrees too high. Such a thermometer has a bias toward a high temperature. It would be considered reliable, giving a consistent reading under the same conditions, but it would not be considered accurate, that is, reflective of the true temperature. Nevertheless, the concept of reliability is generally used to include accuracy as well: A measurement is most apt to be consistent or repeatable when it is also accurate, or reflective of the true phenomenon.

Sensitivity is another characteristic of a measurement tool. A sensitive measurement is one that can detect even small changes in the phenomenon when they occur. By contrast, *stability* in a measurement tool is the quality of being able to show consistency when the phenomenon itself does not change across occasions of assessment. While both of these qualities are desirable in an ideal data collection procedure, they are in some ways opposite from each other. A data collection tool designed to be sensitive may not show stability well; one designed to be stable may not be sufficiently sensitive to change. The formal assessment of the reliability of any data collection procedure must be undertaken knowing that the accuracy, sensitivity, and stability of the measurement, and of the phenomenon it measures, must also be considered.

Redefining Reliability

This conceptualization of data collection as measurement clearly implies that the thing observed is separate from the observer and that there can be one "best" or most "truthful" version of reality developed. Fallibilistic realism holds that there is a real world separate from the observer, but it emphasizes the fact that all descriptions of it are a product of the thing itself, the concepts used to define and describe it, and the standpoint of the describer. This framework is not a relativistic one in which all descriptions are necessarily of equal merit or, as Kirk and Miller (1986) put it, "tolerated" equally well by real world events. Understanding how to evaluate descriptions or data collection in this framework involves understanding science as a collective and social enterprise and the role that observations play in it.

The concept of reliability is about multiple observations and/or multiple observers. Science itself, like any profession, is a social institution made up of those credentialed and viewed in any given society at any given time as the experts in specific and socially defined areas of knowledge. It is also, of course, a set of methods generally accepted in the scientific community as the most useful for developing new knowledge. In this context, reliability in data collection can be understood as consistency or repeatability in the observation of a phenomenon based on the amount of agreement or consensus achieved or achievable among expert observers using common definitions and methods of observation. This idea is also called confirmability (Drisko 1997). This longer definition simply makes explicit some of the assumptions that in fact are embedded in reliability as defined in the traditional framework.

Trustworthiness is the construct used more often by qualitative researchers than reliability to describe the quality of data. Padgett (1998) describes three main threats to the trustworthiness of data in qualitative research: researcher bias, respondent bias, and reactivity. These refer to conscious or unconscious distortions in the information gathered that arise from the researcher, the research participant(s), and/or the interaction between them. Padgett (1998) also describes a variety of techniques that can be used in the data collection and analysis processes to reduce specific threats to trustworthiness, such as prolonged engagement, triangulation, peer consultation, member checking, negative case analysis, and creating an audit trail. However, the concept of trustworthiness and these methods of enhancing it also embrace ideas related to traditional notions of validity, discussed below.

Traditional Types of Reliability

In traditional measurement theory as applied in fixed method research, several different types of reliability have been defined. The most common statistical measures of reliability define it as internal consistency and express it as an *alpha coefficient*. This concept applies to data collection instruments that have many individual questions or items that are meant together to measure a single concept, as in scales of self-esteem, depression, and the like. The idea is that if all the constituent items that make up the scale are actually addressing the same concept or phenomenon, they will be highly correlated with one another. However, if in fact some are capturing aspects of some other phenomenon, they will not be as highly correlated with each other, and the group of items as a whole will not be as highly intercorrelated on average. Statistics such as Chronbach's alpha, then, give an average intercorrelation among all the items that make up a single scale or unidimensional data collection tool as a measure of reliability.

This form of reliability, of course, is by definition applicable only to quantified observations of one particular kind. There are other forms of reliability of this kind such as what is termed *split half reliability*. This method of assessing the internal consistency of a scale consists of dividing its constituent items in half, either the first half compared to the second half in order or by taking alternating items and then comparing the scores obtained on the halves to each other. The idea is that if the items on the scale all assess the same thing, the scores derived from each half of it should be very highly intercorrelated; if they are not, it suggests that the items in the halves may each be assessing different things. Again, this form of reliability has application only to specific forms of quantitative data collection: the development and use of multiple item scales.

The concept of *test-retest reliability,* developed originally in the field of psychometrics, has more general application. This form of reliability can be generally defined as consistency in observations made of the same person and/or phenomenon on two occasions, at two different points in time. The assumption is, of course, that the person or phenomenon itself will be unchanged with respect to the characteristic(s) in question despite the passage of time and that the conditions and context of the observation are also repeatable. If these things are true, then consistency of observation over time is considered strong evidence of the reliability of a reported observation.

While the concept of test-retest reliability was developed and articulated in terms of fixed method research and quantitative measurement, it has its place in some flexible method research as well, although not formally described as such. In some forms of flexible method research like participant observation, observation may be conducted over some period of time. In selecting the most salient features of the many phenomena encountered to describe, one criterion that is often used, explicitly or not, is that the phenomenon be observed consistently, that is, on more than one occasion, if it is to be taken as characteristic of the situation or the group. Although not quantified or quantifiable, such a phenomenon can be said to have been consistently and recurrently observed, also called confirmability (Drisko 1997). That is why in qualitative research prolonged engagement is often cited as a way to enhance the trustworthiness of data (Padgett 1998).

In the traditional framework, there is a major principle affecting test-retest reliability that must be remembered: The longer the interval between the occasions of data collection, the lower the consistency, or reliability, of results is likely to be. This principle expresses the fact that even when a salient and stable phenomenon has been identified and observed, the real world is a constantly evolving context in which things observed are always changing. This is especially true of phenomena or observations at the extremes; it has repeatedly been observed that extreme states and observations are even less likely to repeat themselves than are others, a concept known statistically as regression to the mean.

A final and major form of reliability as traditionally defined is termed *interrater* or *interobserver reliability.* This form of reliability makes explicit the idea of consensus in observations among different people making observations or judgements about what has been observed. This consensus assumes, of course, that the content and conditions of the observations made are the same, that all that differs is the individuals making the observations. If a thing exists in the real world and if its presence or the amount of it present can be assessed by an observer using a specific definition and making certain observations in a specific way, then if another person using the same definition and procedures observes the same thing, the original observation can be said to be reliable. Because there is always some variation, traditionally termed error, in any observation process, the two or more observations are not necessarily expected to be exactly the same; rather they are expected to be similar or highly correlated with each other. If they are not, there is no way to determine which observation, if any, is the more accurate one; if they are similar, however, each separate observation enhances the reliability of the other.

The idea of interobserver reliability is more general than some other types of reliability, like those that apply only to quantitative scales. In participant observation research, for example, concepts or observations obtained from more than one informant in the setting or noted by more than one person involved in the research in the setting may be said to have been repeated. However, flexible method research is less likely to involve multiple investigators or data collectors than some forms of fixed method research. In addition, to the extent that observations may be the result of complex social interactions among specific actors at a particular historical moment or in a particular context, they may not be repeatable at other times or with other participants and observers. While this lack of repeatability may not negate the existence of the first observation, it does speak to the generality of the phenomenon or observation that was made. Interobserver agreement is sometimes used when analyzing records from flexible method research; when more than one observer of the record, or coder, can agree that a concept or theme appears in the data, the credibility of the conclusion may be enhanced. Hence the concepts of triangulation in data collection and peer consultation in both data collection and data analysis are cited as ways to enhance the trustworthiness of data in qualitative research (Padgett 1998).

Finally, the comprehensiveness of the documentation of the data collection process may help to support the believability of the observations made and reported (Kirk & Miller 1986). Even if never repeated, documented observations may be seen as more credible because they show how the data were generated in the first place or how variations in them can be explained. In addition, the observer/reporter will gain in credibility with other scholars simply by making the basis of the conclusions drawn as clear as possible. Padgett (1998) and others refer to this technique as creating an audit trail.

Validity

Validity has been another essential concept in measurement theory. It addresses another neccessary part of scientific observation: the concepts by means of which phenomena are identified or named and then connected to theory. Validity means that the tie between evidence, sensory data, and concept or theory has been defensibly made. Reliability addresses what was seen or observed; validity addresses the meaning attributed to the observation. Simply put, validity is calling things by their right names (Kirk & Miller 1986).

As already noted, the traditional view of research has seen concept and evidence as wholly separable and as tied together by an operational definition derived from a conceptual one. Fallibilistic realism, on the other hand, also views evidence itself as shaped by concepts. Both the traditional point of view and fallibilistic realism recognize that the "fit" between evidence and the concepts used to explicate that evidence can be better or worse. Evaluating validity therefore depends on examining the correspondence between specific observations and either different observations thought to represent the same concept or, simply, the concepts themselves. As with reliability, however, fallibilistic realism reminds us that both the perception of what counts as data and the definition of the concepts of interest are the product of consensual processes generally confined to some community of experts that is socially defined. In assessing validity, then, both the data and the meanings assigned to them are matters of discussion and agreement whether explicit or not.

In fixed method research, the assessment of validity involves assessing the operational and conceptual definitions of the phenomena studied to see how well they correspond. It may also involve identifying multiple types of evidence that can be considered to identify the same concept or phenomenon and then examine how well these multiple indicators of the same thing cohere. In flexible method research, while formal, preformed operational definitions do not exist, the examination of validity tends to proceed in two different ways. One way is through the grounding of conclusions drawn and the interpretations made in a convincing degree of detail from the data, often detailed enough that the reader can draw independent conclusions about them. It can also involve consulting with research participants about how the data should be interpreted, a technique called member checking (Padgett 1998). Sometimes, as in fixed method research, the trustworthiness of data can be enhanced by seeking multiple instances or indicators of the same phenomenon, called triangulation (Padgett 1998). It is also done by contrasting it with different phenomena, as in negative case analysis and other ways of seeking out potentially disconfirming data (Drisko 1997; Padgett 1998).

Traditional Types of Validity

In fixed method research, the most common way of examining validity is by assessing *face validity*. Face validity simply considers whether the manifest content of a data collection instrument or question actually seems to address the concept used to label it. It asks the question, "On the face of it, does this question really seem to capture the concept intended?" A question about caregiving that asks "How many times per week do you prepare meals for your mother?" would be considered to have greater face validity than "Do you love your mother?" or even "How often do you visit your mother?" The latter questions might or might not be relevant to caregiving, but the first question clearly is. It is said to have face validity because the content of the question clearly fits well with the general concept that the question is designed to capture.

Notice that a question does not intrinsically have face validity or not; it does or does not have face validity in relation to the specific concept that is being examined at the time or to the specific context in which it is being asked. The question above about visiting, for example, might have great face validity in a study of social contacts and support among adult family members even though it may not be the best one to ask when caregiving specifically is the focus. Questions without face validity can be considered intrusive, offensive, or deceptive by those who are asked to answer them. Therefore, it is important to consider face validity when asking questions in any form of inquiry, whether flexible or fixed in method.

The apparent face validity of a question can be deceptive. For example, Landrine, Klonoff, and Brown-Collins (1992) conducted a study in which a multiracial group of women responded to a series of items drawn from a standard self-report measure of sex role stereotypes. Afterwards, they were also asked to indicate which of several possible definitions of key words in the items they had in mind when they answered the question. As a whole, there was no difference in how white women and women of color answered the original questions. However, for several items there were differences between the white women and the women of color and between women of different ethnic groups in what definition of the question they reported using when they answered. For example, the item "I am assertive" was sometimes defined as "saying whatever is on my mind," "standing up for myself," "expressing myself well," or being "aggressive." Women of color were more likely to define being "assertive" as "saying whatever is on my mind" and white women were more likely to mean "standing up for myself" or "expressing myself well." This kind of study, exploring what is *meant* by questions and answers, should be done more often. The original result—the finding of no group difference—is true because all of the specific definitions do correspond to accepted meanings of assertiveness. However, important nuances of meaning in responses can be overlooked even when face validity seems clear.

The concept of face validity is applicable both to individual questions used to collect data and to scales and measures composed of multiple items taken as a whole. When dealing with educational testing or assessment in particular, for example, the term *content validity* is also used. This concept deals with the face validity of a whole scale or measure and with the idea that its constituent items taken together adequately sample or cover all of the content relevant to the area being assessed. Consider the tests required to obtain a driver's license: an eye examination, a written test consisting of questions about the state's rules of the road, and a road test in which observations are made of the person driving in real world conditions and in which certain specific maneuvers, such as backing up and parallel parking, must be performed. The test has many parts specifically in order to assure that it has content validity, that all of the areas relevant to safe and competent driving are covered.

Both face validity and content validity address only the correspondence between data and concept through examination of the literal content of the data obtained. Another way to approach the issue of validity, however, is through examining multiple indicators of the same concept when they are available. The ways of evaluating validity that proceed in this way are termed *criterion-related validity*. A question or scale is said to have criterion-related validity when answers or scores derived from one question or scale are compared to other observations that have already been conceded to measure the concept in question. Clearly, as traditionally articulated this kind of assessment of validity is relevant only to fixed method research in which concepts can be predefined and measured in predetermined ways. Triangulation can be seen as a method used in qualitative research to address similar validity issues.

There are several forms of criterion-related validity. Establishing *concurrent validity* means that the answers to a question or set of questions are compared with a separate, often behavioral or real world measure of the same concept that the questions are designed to tap at the same point in time. For example, people might both fill out a questionnaire designed to measure depression and be interviewed and assessed by a mental health professional on the same visit to a clinic. The assessment of depression made by the mental health professional might be used to validate the depression questionnaire. If there were generally a high rate of agreement between the questionnaire results and the professional assessment (the criterion), this would be taken as evidence of concurrent validity. *Predictive validity* proceeds in the same way as concurrent validity except that the real life or other criterion does not occur until some time after the original data have been gathered. The questions are answered at one point in time; the criterion they are designed to measure does not occur until later. However, the logic is the same: The closer the correspondence of the answers to the questions with the criterion they are designed to predict, the higher the predictive validity is said to be.

Criterion-related validity, both concurrent and predictive, is most relevant when the phenomenon of interest can be tied clearly and unequivocally to a single, specific criterion, generally a behavioral one. Examples of such instances are the relationship of the SAT scores of college-bound high school students to the grade point averages earned in college or of a measure of perceived health risk to smoking behavior. However, many of the phenomena of interest in social work and the other helping professions are complex, socially determined, and difficult to relate to any one clear criterion in the present or in the future. In fact, many of the concepts of interest are by definition not directly observable. Consider "aggression," for example: A comprehensive definition of that phenomenon would likely include a consideration of action, context, and motivation or intent. As with the study of answers to a question about assertion discussed above, it can often be difficult to be sure that a specific behavior observed unequivocally is (or is not) evidence of aggression.

When considering complex phenomena that derive their meaning as much from theory as from any one piece of data, validity may need to be considered in relation to several other complex indicators, none of which may provide a perfect match conceptually or behaviorally with the phenomenon being measured. This form of establishing validity through comparing multiple measures with similar meanings is termed *construct validity*. It consists of comparing findings based on one imperfect measure of a phenomenon with others, both those that are considered much like what was originally measured (to show *convergent validity*) and those that measure things that are somewhat different from it (to show *discriminant validity*). Negative case analysis as used in qualitative data collection and analysis can be seen as a procedure that addresses issues of discriminant validity.

These concepts are very important in fields such as psychometrics in which the effort is to develop measures of psychological phenomena that can be used in fixed method research (see chapter 15 on selecting existing measures). Often evidence from measures using different methods of data collection—self-report compared with observation, for example—is used in establishing the construct validity of a measure in this way. Evidence for the construct validity of an existing instrument accumulates gradually based on reports of all the studies in which it has been used and compared to other indicators.

In the end, all the methods of assessing the validity of a data collection procedure are dedicated to determining what the data collected in a certain way mean, what theoretical concept or phenomenon they most accurately represent, what name the phenomenon observed should best be called by. In fixed method research, where methods of data collection can be standardized and repeated, a variety of ways of assessing validity—some data-based and some not—have been described. In flexible method research, the assessment of validity can occur both in the data gathering and in the analysis process. In the data gathering process in participant observation research, for example, the total experience that the researcher has of asking questions, listening, and observing helps to determine what the data mean. An answer to a question delivered with a smirk or without much feeling can be detected and a new approach to the topic devised until the researcher is convinced that the information offered is trustworthy and truly relevant to the topic at hand.

The process of data analysis, discussed at length in chapter 16, is as central to establishing the validity of data in flexible method research as is the process of gathering the data to begin with. In flexible method research, the processes of data collection and analysis or interpretation are often ongoing simultaneously; for example, a statement in the data found on reflection to be ambiguous can sometimes be explored and clarified on a subsequent occasion of data collection. Strauss (1987) speaks of an "indicator-concept model" of analysis in which multiple indicators or pieces of data are connected to a single given concept through *coding*. The names of the codes or categories of meaning used to organize the data may be *in vivo,* that is, supplied by one or more participants, or they may be constructed, that is, invented by the coder (Strauss 1987). In flexible method research, then, validity is a product not only of the data collection process but of the analysis process as well because that is when the concepts used to define the phenomena observed are designated.

Summary

Data collection is at the heart of all research, and there are many things to consider when planning, conducting, or evaluating any data collection effort. This chapter has covered the dimensions of decision making about data collection: the what, where, when, who, and how. Most important, of course, is determining what data will be collected, a decision that is determined by the purpose and focus of the research—its design, guiding question, and conceptual underpinning.

In particular, concepts of reliability and validity and the trustworthiness of data have been emphasized. These ideas are both simple and profound. Are the observations made and reported the products of the accidental or specific circumstances of the data collection or do they reflect some more essential features of the phenomena being studied? Are the phenomena that are described called by the right name, that is, are the observations connected with concepts in a way that seems defensible? What do the data actually represent? Data collection of any kind must be designed and carried out in a way that results in the gathering of information that is trustworthy, both reliable and valid. The next set of chapters in the book discuss in depth the three most common methods for collecting original data in social and psychological research—observation, interviewing, and questionnaires—in light of the basic principles of data collection outlined here.

Part IV
Methods of Data Collection

This section of the book discusses in depth the three main methods of collecting original data in social work and human services research—observation, interviewing, and using questionnaires and other forms of written self-reports. These chapters are written from the point of view of someone who is planning to do research and thus to develop methods and tools for data collection. The final chapter in the section discusses how to find, select among, and use existing measures instead. Chapter 11 in the previous section of the book, "Basic Issues in Data Collection," presents the framework and key terminology used in these chapters. It should be consulted prior to using any of the material in this section of the text.

12

Observation

I n some ways, all research rests on observation. Research is after all always empirical, and empirical by definition means perceived through the senses, that is, observed. In research, however, the term observation has come to mean something more restricted; it refers to data collected by direct visual experience of the study participant(s) by the researcher. Observation as a data collection method is underutilized in social work and human services research. Nevertheless, it is a vital tool for research that has been widely used in psychology and in such theoretically crucial areas as infant and child development. It has also been used to study social processes in formal organizations, informal groups, and even households.

In most cases, the person whose characteristic(s) are observed and the person doing the observing are different people. For this reason, observation as a data collection method is often assumed to be less biased than other methods of data collection based on self-reports. Stern (1985), for example, has commented that we live in an age in which observations are often the preferred form of evidence. As will become clear later on, however, even with observers who have no apparent reason to have a personal interest in the outcomes of their observations, expectations, and other characteristics of the observer can exert a powerful influence on what is thought to be "seen."

There is something quite compelling about observational data. Critics may object to the manner in which observational data were collected or the interpretations that were made of them, but even the most skeptical critic of a researcher's work is unlikely to discount totally data that were seen. In an enterprise where evidence is everything, observational evidence is often considered the most valuable of all.

None of the social sciences can lay claim to special expertise in observation as a data collection method. This measurement form is as old as science itself. What the social sciences can lay claim to, however, is refinement of this data collection method for assessing psychologically and socially defined abstract phenomena.

This refinement has been no easy task. The social sciences typically study phenomena that do not exist apart from conceptual and social judgments about them. This statement is especially true of the helping professions, which tend to study things when there is a socially defined need to do so.

Consider the act of striking a child. Once considered proper discipline in school and at home, this act is now considered abusive. It is relatively easy for someone who is present at the time to decide whether or not a child is being hit. It may be less easy to decide whether or not a bruise or other mark observed on a child's body is evidence of having been hit or of some other kind of event, and it is even more difficult to decide what is good discipline in general and what is not. Even legal definitions of child abuse may be difficult to tie unambiguously to observational data. In social work, definitions of key phenomena can change over time and in different contexts, and the kind of data needed to provide irrefutable evidence even of an often-defined concept like child abuse may be hard to provide unambiguously. For example, Southeast Asian American women may use "cupping" and burning as folk cures for colds, remedies and acts of caring that are standard and accepted in their cultures. The marks these practices may leave on the body of the child may be seen as evidence of abuse although the same evidence would be labeled by others in their own communities as evidence of nurturance (Landrine, Klonoff, & Brown-Collins 1992).

This chapter gives an overview of observation as a data collection method as it used in both flexible and fixed methods of research. In flexible method research the observations made are formative of the understandings and explanations generated. In fixed method research, by contrast, the phenomena to be observed are specified and defined before data collection begins, and the observational process is structured in light of those specifications and definitions. In fact, the observational traditions in fixed method research and in flexible method research are based on sharply divergent assumptions about research, the nature of useful evidence, and the role of the researcher in observation. What observation has in common in both design contexts, however, is its focus on nonverbal, visual data and the dilemmas that are raised by the observation process itself.

Basic Principles of Observation

In the helping professions, observational methodologies have largely been developed and refined by clinicians and researchers working within the behavioral tradition. This connection is not surprising: Behavioral theorists traditionally held that practitioners should address what can be seen, that is, overt behavior. As a consequence, their measurement methods, largely directed toward assessing the observable, have been predominantly observational ones. Behavioral research has generally followed traditional models and used fixed methods of research.

In traditional behavioral terms, observation is a process by which an instrument is used to calibrate certain predefined properties of an observed and distinct other. The instrument of observation may be mechanical, such as a machine to measure galvanic skin response, reflecting perspiration as an index of physiological anxiety.

Actually, the term *detection* rather than *observation* should be used when instruments function to record phenomena that would ordinarily be imperceptible.

More often than not, however, the instrument of observation is a person, and any instrument used, such as a videotape recorder, functions only to make a record of what human senses would perceive. However, when people function as observers in the behavioral tradition, they are instructed do so as precisely and objectively as a machine. That is, the human observer makes a record of what is observed by rules that must be invariantly applied, and he or she also must minimize the impact on or interaction with the observed above and beyond what may be inherent in the act of observation itself.

To some extent, however, observation involves making judgments. Traditionally, observers are therefore trained in applying some clear rules to their observations, rules that specify:

1. The circumstances of observation, when and where observations will take place, and how much control will be exercised over the observational context;
2. The period of time over which observations will be made and with what frequency, including whether and how to sample times of observation;
3. Precisely who will be observed and what will be observed about each person; and
4. How the observations will be recorded.

Even when observations are less structured, decisions are made about each of these dimensions. Participant observational research, however, is opportunistic (Jorgensen 1989), meaning that these decisions are often made in context in the field and adjusted as the process unfolds. In fixed method research, decisions about these dimensions are made before data collection begins. Whatever the form of the research, however, the guiding principle used when answering these questions, of course, is the purpose of the research prompting the observation.

Context and Circumstance

With respect to the question of when observations should be made, the optimal circumstances of observation in flexible method research are whatever ones present themselves in the setting that are relevant to the study question(s). The principle of prolonged engagement (Padgett 1998) indicates that observations are often made over an extended period of time. In fixed method research, the question of when to observe is essentially a matter of deciding on the context(s) in which the phenomena of interest can best and most efficiently be assessed.

The question of how long to observe really breaks down into two different questions, depending on whether the researcher intends to observe a few people over an extended period of time (as is often the case in flexible method research and single case designs) or many people at one or only a few points in time. In the first case, the question remains how long these few people should be observed. In the second the question becomes how many people to observe; since each person will be observed for a roughly equivalent amount of time, the total amount of observation time will be determined by the number of different people observed.

In flexible method research, it is not possible to specify for certain how much observation will be enough before the fact. Leaving such matters open is inherent in this form of design, since the method must remain flexible enough to respond to the data as they come in. With flexible method research, then, the answer to the question of how long to collect observations is at the same time simple and demanding: Until enough data have been gathered to answer the questions to be addressed with convincing data to defend the answer, or at least until additional observation time is yielding little or no new data or insights. That is why how much observation will be enough cannot be specified exactly beforehand.

This inability to specify before the fact how much observation will be enough, which is inherent in flexible method research, is also inherent in single-subject studies (see chapter 8). As will be recalled, single-subject designs set out to document specific changes in behavior that occur following an intervention. In these designs, as in flexible method research, the length of time over which data must be collected is determined not a priori, but rather by the form the data are taking as they occur: Data collection in single-subject designs must continue until the response to the intervention becomes clear. And while sometimes there is an immediate and dramatic reaction to an intervention, more often than not data collection must continue for some period of time until any trends or changes in behavior during the intervention period can be adequately documented. In both single-subject designs and flexible method designs, then, the answer to the question "How much should I observe" is the same: you should observe until you have an answer to the question or hypothesis you set out to address, and until you have data in hand that you can present to others that will give them reason to believe you and agree with your conclusions.

The question of how long to observe can be answered before the fact more easily in descriptive, relational, and group experimental designs. The question really is a conceptual one that boils down to whether or not the phenomena being studied require a longitudinal approach to answer the question or whether a cross-sectional design can serve the purpose (see chapter 6).

Time is only one element of the observational context. The circumstances or settings in which the observations will take place must be considered as well. In any type of research, then, the researcher must decide before initiating the observations what the observational circumstances will be.

Whether planning a fixed or flexible method study, preliminary work is often done to determine which of several alternative available observational circumstances may present the best ones for the research. In field research, this work typically involves finding naturally occurring settings where the behavior of interest is likely to occur and that will accommodate the observation process. In fixed method research, the goal may also be to identify or arrange a setting that will remain sufficiently stable and available to allow making meaningful comparisons of behavior across repeated observations made in it.

Since fixed method research is often directed toward making some form of comparison, it frequently requires repeated observations either over time or across people. Comparing what is observed in these repeated observations in a way that permits drawing conclusions about the people who were observed rather than the circumstances of observation means that influential elements of the observational context must remain the same or at least be equivalent. If constancy or at least equivalence of the observational context is not maintained, what is observed can be expected to literally look different, not because it is in fact different in some intrinsic way, but rather because the circumstances under which it is being studied have changed.

Since comparability of observational setting can be so important to fixed method researchers, sometimes the researcher decides to create the observational circumstance rather than using a naturally occurring one. Consistency in the observational context can be arranged either within or outside the laboratory. When it is arranged within the laboratory, the form of the observation is typically called controlled, because the researcher is controlling not what the person being observed is doing but the circumstances within which the participant can do whatever he or she is doing. When it is arranged outside the laboratory, it is called contrived. There is no functional difference between controlled and contrived observation: Both involve standardizing the observational context. The difference between them is that one takes place within a laboratory, and therefore always with the knowledge of the person being observed, while the other takes place outside the laboratory, and therefore potentially without the knowledge of the person being observed.

One example of this use of a controlled observational context is in attachment research (Ainsworth, Blehar, Waters, & Wall 1978). Their strange-situation procedure was carefully designed to assess the attachment of one-year old babies to their primary caretaker, the mother. Using a one-way mirror observation is made of the mother. Two chairs for adults, one for the child, and some toys are arranged in a standardized way in an office-like room. A fixed sequence of events takes place, beginning with the mother and baby alone in the room, the entry of a stranger who approaches the baby and then leaves, the leaving of the mother, the return of the stranger, and the final return of the mother. Babies react in quite different ways to this sequence of events. Their contact with the adults, their movement around the room, and their affect are all observed by two people who are not in the room. A system of categories has been developed to describe the various styles of reactions that babies have displayed in this standardized set of circumstances. This classification system for styles of attachment in infancy, in turn, has subsequently been studied as a predictor of many aspects of later development. This is only one example of how controlled observational circumstances have been used in the study of infant and child behavior and development.

Whom and What to Observe

Whom to observe would at first seem obvious: Certainly the people chosen to be participants in the research should be observed. As will be recalled from the sampling chapter, these participants should be ones in whom the research phenomenon is expected to appear in clear, even exaggerated form or people representative of the larger group to which one hopes to generalize.

Given this, the question becomes "Who else to observe?" When the research question involves inquiry into the context surrounding the primary participant's behavior, it is often appropriate to observe people other than the primary participant as well. From this perspective, these other people become important as potentially interesting features of the interpersonal context for the primary participant's observed behavior. These other people become part of the "what" that is observed, the Jarret (1992) study in chapter 4 illustrates.

The behavioral tradition has given rise to a form of observation in which the observer and the observed are one and the same. This form of direct observation is called *self-monitoring* or *self-observation*. Typically self-monitoring is used with one of two types of behaviors: Ones that are easily defined and counted, such as the number of cigarettes smoked each day, and subjective experiences that are otherwise inaccessible to outside observers, such as the number of self-critical thoughts while smoking a cigarette. This chapter, however, focuses on observation by another and thus on how to capture behavior and interactions, those things that are observable by someone else.

Of the several questions that must be answered when designing or choosing an observational methodology, it is the what question that has received most careful attention, but this attention has tended to be technical. Much has been written about characteristics that distinguish between phenomena that can be observed successfully and those that cannot. In general, physical objects, nonverbal behaviors, facial expressions, gestures, and social interactions lend themselves best to observation. On the other hand, subjective experiences, ideas, meanings and other intangibles can only be inferred from observational data, and other modes of data collection may be preferable for studying such phenomena. However, children and others who cannot give a verbal account of themselves understandable to the observer cannot be interviewed, and observation is often used to study them instead. In addition, what people do and what they know or say they do may differ markedly. Much social and interactive behavior may be unconscious and unexamined by the participants, and observational methods can be more effective for studying them than relying on some form of self-report.

A major challenge in observing an abstract phenomenon is developing a definition for the phenomenon that discriminates between when that phenomenon as defined is present and when it is not. In fixed method research, it is assumed that the phenomenon to be observed has been adequately defined, at least at a conceptual level. It should be remembered, however, that the nature of the definition critically and indelibly influences the nature of the data subsequently collected. As is always the case in data collection, the what that is being measured can never be assumed to be correct only on the basis of the "how."

Observational data describing well-defined, observable phenomena, however, only *seem* self-evident; the complexity of the act of observation has traditionally been overlooked. The logical positivist tradition in social science research maintained that observers could see what they were observing in an objective and undistorted fashion. Moreover, they assumed that when they made observations, what they could see was raw reality, so that what they believed they saw would reflect what was objectively really there.

This belief reflected two underlying assumptions. The first was that human observers could be made to function as reliably and predictably as would a mechanical recorder: Human observers could be trained well enough so that they would perform just like a reliable thermometer, which if used repeatedly in the same fashion—located correctly and left in place for the proper amount of time—would calibrate the temperature of a feverish person with the same result given the same level of fever each time.[1] This first assumption turns out to be true only sometimes. In fixed method research, it has been shown that human observers are reliable only when rigorous design guidelines are followed when both developing and applying whatever observational methodology is being used.

There is a second assumption embedded in the logical positivist tradition, however, which turns out to be much more problematic: Human observers can be passive receptors of their external worlds. Observations are only what the observer makes of them. Stern (1985), for example, speaks of the "observed infant" described in developmental psychology as "a special construct, a description of capacities that can be observed directly" (p. 17). Such a view of the infant is formed both by what the observer notices and by what the observer *can* notice; the infant's subjective experience, for example, can only be inferred.

The way in which observations are processed influences what is seen. This effect is more subtle, but its impact is more profound. For a moment, force your attention away from the words you are reading in this text. Without changing positions, let your eyes move around the space in front of you. No matter where you are sitting, there will be a great number of objects and surfaces before you. Had you noticed them when you were reading the text? Probably not. The point is that when we observe, we engage in a process similar to the one you were using earlier when reading this text: We see only a portion of what is in front of us, the parts we choose to focus on.

It is easy to see how this form of perceptual selection bias could exist when evaluating a very focussed, specific observational system. In fact, there is some reason to believe that the more focussed an observational system is, the less possible it is to notice phenomena that were "unexpected." By defining what is to be observed, constraints are placed on what can be observed. Observers are unlikely to see what they are not looking for.

Decisions about what to observe, then, are of profound importance. They must be made so that the observational system chosen will be consistent in principle with the properties of the research design. In flexible method research, observational systems must start out as very unfocussed. The observations are always guided by a general notion of what is being looked for, but to have specific notions of what will form the phenomena of interest would likely preclude the observer's being sensitive to the unexpected. And since flexible method research has as its intent understanding things that are poorly or incompletely understood, which implies seeing the unexpected, to use an observational system with preconceived parameters would not work. Mutual development of method and data thus characterizes the observational process used in flexible method research.

---

1. This is, of course, an oversimplification. As was emphasized in chapter 11, there is some error inherent in all measurements, including observations. It would be more technically accurate to note that thermometers, when they are functioning reliably, give approximately the same temperature readings given the same level of fever each time they are used.

At this point it should come as no surprise that it may be easier to conduct observations within the frame of descriptive, relational, and experimental research than in a more open-ended fashion. These three research designs all require specifying fixed methods, methods framed around specific research questions or hypotheses, before the data are in hand. It follows, then, that the specific variables that will be observed not only can but should be specified and defined beforehand.

Recording Observations

The question of how observations should be recorded is, of course, a technical one with a general answer that applies in all cases, regardless of the type of research or the observational methodology employed. The method that preserves as much of the available relevant data as possible with the greatest degree of accuracy and permanency and the least degree of intrusion on the data preserved is the one that should be used. Since most observations are collected and recorded by human observers, we have grown accustomed to collapsing the several stages in an observe-record-code complex into one in our thinking, but they are really separate stages, each of which merits attention.

Consider the situation in which observation is accomplished by a video camera. When the camera is running, observation is taking place in the situation, even if there is a mechanical problem precluding making a record of what is observed. If there is no mechanical failure, there will be a record on the tape. However, what will be recorded is limited to the times when the camera was running and the part of the scene on which the camera was focussed. In addition, not until those data are coded, or translated into meaning units in some fashion, is the observation of them complete. It clarifies the issues involved in the observation-record-code complex to consider each of the facets in it separately.

The recording process refers to the technology used to make a permanent record of what is observed. This technology is most clearly illustrated by the photographic methodology of video cameras when video observation is used or the magnetic recording processes of audio recorders when audio observation is used. Often, however, the recording methodology involves arranging for a human being to serve in the role of an audio and/or video recorder by providing that human observer with a set of rules indicating what record to make when a certain event is observed to occur.

There is a clear analogue between the mechanical and human processes in observation. Mechanical technology works by virtue of the translation of information from one form to another. In the case of audiotape recordings, for example, sounds issued within a certain frequency range and greater than a certain volume will be recorded using a machine that enters electrical impulses onto magnetic tape, which then becomes a symbolic representation of the event transpired. In like fashion, when human observers make records of what is observed, they follow a set of rules that results in their entering symbols usually onto paper such that these symbols are recognized as representing the event recorded.

In some circumstances, researchers prefer using mechanical rather than human observers. With human observers, there are lapses in attention or motivation and misunderstandings or differences of interpretation about how to implement the recording rules. In addition, human recorders have been shown to change over time: As they observe a certain phenomenon more often, they can become immune to noticing minor instances of it, which has been termed "calibration shift" (Kent & Foster 1977).

Unlike humans, mechanical recorders are consistent. However, they lack some capacities that make human recorders an indispensable part often of the data recording and always of the data reduction process. These capacities include selectivity in recording what is observed, sensitivity to what was not expected to be observed, flexibility in changing focus when needed, and the capacity for following recording rules that involve higher order processing of information.

Machines record indiscriminately. For example, a machine will, and can only, record an entire conversation, while a human observer can be instructed and trained to record only those parts of a conversation characterized by a certain content, for example, those parts relevant to the expression of affection. Humans, are thinking recorders, and having a judging being making records can be an asset in observation.

Research questions often concern complex phenomena that are difficult to define simply. Quite often determining whether the researched phenomenon has occurred requires making complex judgments. Machines will only record what they are sensitive to recording. An audiotape, for example, will miss whatever nonverbal communication is taking place, and a video camera will record only what is focussed on and only for the period specified. Human recorders, on the other hand, do not lose their more general awareness when following a set of recording rules. Unexpected or complex phenomena that strike the human recorder as important can be noted, observed, and passed on to the investigator.

The process of coding is always a human activity. It involves selecting specific features of the observation record to classify conceptually. Observational systems that rely on human observers typically complete the record and encode components of the observation-record-encode complex simultaneously; in fact, typically only codable features of what is observed are recorded as part of the observation process. Observational systems that rely on mechanical recorders, on the other hand, accomplish the recording and encoding components separately. The former is handled mechanically while the latter is managed by a person after the fact.

The Observer and the Observed

There is a final, critical feature of observation that must be addressed: the relationship between the observer and the observed. In the traditional view, observation implied that there was no relationship, that the observer was related to the observed only through passively receiving and accurately recording information about the behavior of those observed. There are of course very few observational circumstances that approximate this situation.

Consider what can happen when making observations of two children interacting with one of their parents. The observer's role involves sitting quietly in a corner, clipboard and pencil in hand, observing and recording any event that seemed important in understanding the parent-child interaction. The children had a different take on the circumstance. The observer was not to be allowed to remain in the role of passive, uninvolved environmental feature. Questions ranging from "Who are you?" to "What are you writing?" are asked continuously. When the questions go unanswered, the observer is subjected to nose pulls, shin kicks, and lap climbs. Under such circumstances, an observer will usually find it impossible to maintain a totally passive stance.

Reactivity

In general, the process of observation involves introducing something into a situation that would not otherwise be there. As has been mentioned many times, the introduction of this feature constitutes making a change in the circumstances surrounding the researched phenomenon. And since we are typically interested in studying phenomena in people who are responsive to their environments, the process of observation can be expected to affect the person being observed and often the feature(s) of interest in the person being observed. This effect is termed reactivity; it refers to change induced in what is observed by the process of observing it.

The reactivity inherent in observation troubles many researchers: No one likes to think that he or she is getting an invalid picture of what is being studied. It is distress over this nettling reality that has led some researchers to strive for concealed means of observation. An example of such concealed observation is presented by the work of Humphreys (1970), who entered public restroom facilities frequented by men who came there to engage in impersonal acts of homosexual sex to systematically gather data on their activities. People observed in the rest room were traced by means of their auto license plate numbers and found to include middle class, married members of the community. The use of a concealed observational method was defended on the basis of reactivity: Given the nature of the behavior being observed, the phenomenon studied would never have been evidenced in the presence of a known observer. Humphreys took on a role in the setting—of lookout—that justified his presence as an otherwise nonparticipating observer, a strategy he defended as "passing as deviant to avoid disrupting the behavior he wished to observe" but not for the purpose of gaining access to a space that was private, since he was already entitled to access (Golden 1976).

This study presents a dramatic and controversial example highlighting the troubling ethical issues raised by the question of whether researchers ever have the right to observe others without their knowledge and informed consent. Most Institutional Review Boards believe that such observation is permissible only when studying innocuous behaviors as they naturally occur in very public situations and when the persons observed are not identified or affected by the observers. Concealed observation in other cases is more controversial and represents a clear example of the important role Institutional Review Boards, or consultation with community members and colleagues not invested in the research plan, have to play in monitoring research activities.

The observer-observed relationship distills into a single question: How much and what kinds of interactions will occur within it? Some observational systems try to minimize or standardize them. In these systems, the observer is to function in a manner analogous to a mechanical instrument. As much as possible, the observer is to be affected by but not to affect the observed. Any effect is to be only temporary and is to extend only as far as is necessary to make a record of whatever observed event was just noticed. However, other observational systems allow for, expect, and in fact make use of observer-observed interaction to further the research. One such form of observation is called *participant observation,* which is discussed in more detail below

Examples of Observation in Use

In recent decades the use of observation, generally of a quite structured kind, has revolutionized the field of early infant research and the theoretical understanding of psychological development in infancy. Fraiberg's (1970) research on blind infants illustrates the use of observation, structured and unstructured, in developmental research. Stern (1985) describes the new developments in infant research as follows:

> The revolution in research consisted of turning the situation on its head, by asking not, what is a good question to pose to an infant? But what might an infant be able to do (like sucking) that would serve as an answer? With this simple turn-around, the search for infant abilities that could be made into answers (response measures) began, and the revolution was set in motion. . . . Good infant "answers" have to be readily observable behaviors that are frequently performed, that are under voluntary muscular control, and that can be solicited during alert inactivity. Three such behavioral answers immediately qualify, beginning at birth: head-turning, sucking and looking (pp. 38–39).

Infants, for example, have been shown, using electronically wired pacifiers, to be especially interested in the human voice as compared to other sounds of the same pitch and loudness. They also demonstrate by turning their heads that they prefer the smell of their own mother's milk to the milk of another woman (Stern 1985). From the accumulation of many such observational studies of infants' early abilities, preferences, and interests, new theoretical understandings of infant development and parent-child interactions have emerged.

Infant research is not the only area in which observational data are useful, however. Jarrett's (1992) case study, reprinted in chapter 4, gave one example of observation in use. As an another example, Hochschild's (1989) study of how two-career couples handle the work of caring for a home and young children used in-home observation to supplement the extensive data collected through interviewing. The purpose of Hochschild's study was to explore whether or not married men were contributing any more to household work than the early studies in the 1960s and 1970s had shown. She also explored the various tensions that were occurring in couples because of class norms, ideologies about how things "should" be that didn't match with day-to-day necessity, and the effects of earnings differentials in couples in how work at home was shared.

In particular, she wished to examine how well people's accounts of themselves and how they shared domestic responsibilities meshed with reality. In part this was accomplished by interviewing both members of a couple, but observation of selected couples at home was done as well:

> I also watched daily life in a dozen homes during a weekday evening, during the weekend, and during the months that followed, when I was invited on outings, to dinner, or just to talk. I found myself waiting on the front doorstep as weary parents and hungry children tumbled out of the family car. . . . I sat on the living-room floor and drew pictures and played with the children. I watched as parents gave them baths, read stories, and said goodnight. Most couples tried to bring me in to the family scene, inviting me to eat with them and talk. I responded if they spoke to me, from time to time asked questions, but I rarely initiated conversations. I tried to become as unobtrusive as the family dog. . . (Hochschild 1989:6–7).

Note that this brief description offers a sense of the "time sampling" attempted with each family. It also speaks to the particular role that she as observer elected to play in each setting.

What did such an observational strategy yield? In many cases, subtle effects could be seen of the strains and tensions between husbands and wives about housework (and other issues) that they might not even be aware of. A brief vignette from one family may illustrate:

> After a long day, mother, father, and son sit down to dinner. Evan and Nancy get the first chance of the day to talk to each other, but both turn anxiously to Joey, expecting his mood to deteriorate. Nancy asks him if he wants celery with peanut butter on it. Joey says yes. "Are you sure that's how you want it?" "Yes." Then the fidgeting begins. "I don't like the strings on my celery." "Celery is made up of strings." "The celery is too big." Nancy grimly slices the celery. A certain tension mounts. Every time one parent begins a conversation with the other, Joey interrupts. "I don't have anything to drink." . . . By the end of the meal, no one has obstructed Joey's victory . . . (Hochschild 1989:35).

If nothing else, such observation illustrates vividly the vicissitudes of daily life in the family. Hochschild uses such data, however, to make the point that inequities in the division of child care and housework responsibilities set up complicated dynamics among all family members that help to perpetuate whatever arrangement exists. Based on the interview data, the mother and father in this family had a wholly different explanation for "Joey's problem" that he wouldn't go to bed at night, as "normal," stage-related behavior. Whatever the framework that might be used to explain the interactions observed, the observational data make the nature of them quite vivid and clearly suggest, based on an interpretation of the observer, that Joey's behavior is related to dynamics between his mother and father. Thus observational data can reveal aspects of a situation that even the participants in it may not see or articulate clearly.

Developing or Selecting a Structured Observational Tool

As is true with all data collection methods, a researcher has two options when planning observational research in the context of a fixed method study. He or she may choose to employ a measure, in this case an observational system, previously developed by another investigator, or he or she may choose to develop a new observational system specifically tailored to the requirements of his or her research circumstance. Chapter 15 covers how to locate and select an existing measure.

Naturally, whenever the research design is a flexible one, the form of the research requires developing the observational system as the research goes along. Hochschild (1989), for example, found that talking to a family's babysitters and child care providers and even doing some observation with them was an unexpected and useful source of information, and she then added this to her plan of data gathering for each family. A skilled researcher, then, should know how to invent an observational methodology. Considering how a new observational system has to be developed will clarify many of the issues that should be attended to when deciding whether someone else's system is good enough to use.

Developing an Observational System

The first step in observation is specifying the purpose of the observation, what question(s) the observation is supposed to inform. In flexible method research, this purpose will usually be to define and understand the phenomena of interest more clearly. In other forms of research, this purpose will be to describe and/or show connections between some already well-defined research phenomena. In the latter cases, this first step implies clearly specifying the definition of the phenomenon to be researched or observed. In the beginning, this definition properly remains an abstract, conceptual one. The definition will be narrowed to an operational one, that is, to a set of rules for deciding whether or not or how much of a phenomenon has been seen in response to what is observed.

It may be of interest in this context to note that developing a new observational system for any research purpose often requires conducting what might most easily be described as flexible method research at the outset. While there is a general idea of what is to be observed, an idea that is used to guide the observation process, specific notions of what is to be noticed are left open until the data are given an opportunity to inform and shape them. The Fraiberg (1970) studies of the development of infants blind from birth illustrate this evolution well when she uses her observations of a particular case to shape her later observations of a group of blind babies.

Any research study takes place in a specific context. That is, the question or hypothesis will be posed not in the abstract but under some narrowed or restricted set of circumstances. These circumstances must also be defined at the outset of developing an observational system. Just as the research purpose guides what is to be noticed, the context defines the circumstances under which observations will be made.

Practical considerations enter into the selection of an observational context as well. Suppose one is interested in studying intimacy. Optimal circumstances for making observations relevant to this construct would most probably be private (i.e., intimate) ones. However, short of developing a mechanical observation system that can run continuously in such circumstances (and this procedure has in fact been used), arranging observations in private circumstances is quite difficult and can raise important ethical questions.

Once the researcher has specified the purpose of the observation, which in the case of descriptive, relational, and experimental work will include stating an explicit conceptual definition of the phenomenon to be observed and the circumstances under which observations will be made, unstructured observations should take place. In unstructured observations the researcher enters the observational situation armed only with a clipboard and a pen or pencil or a portable computer and the guiding notion of the research purpose. The observer's initial task is to literally observe, to notice everything taking place in the circumstance that seems even remotely related to the research purpose as stated, and to record as completely as possible a narrative description of what he or she sees.

The observer's task does not involve interpreting or making sense of what is noticed at this point. As much as possible, the observer is to function as a probe, an instrument of observation sufficiently sensitive to notice whatever important is there to be observed. Preconceived notions and theoretical biases should exert as minimal an influence as possible on what is noticed.

Although there is no such thing as a "naive observer," since without some sophistication an observer would be incapable of discriminating between what information it is important to attend to and what information is not, observers will necessarily have different perspectives. In some cases, these perspectives can be dictated strongly by preconceived notions. To the extent that they are, they become biases, that is, predispositions to "see" events in a certain way, even when the events are seen in a different way by others with a different perspective. It can even be useful to employ multiple observers selected so as to vary importantly from one another. When research is done by a team, it is always a good idea for the person directing the research, who may have the strongest preconceptions about what should or will be seen, to conduct some of this informal observation as well.

In fixed-method research, the data obtained in this way are regarded not as an end in themselves but instead as preliminary. The records from these observations must be studied carefully to identify observations that are concrete instances of the research phenomena to be studied. The descriptions of these observed events are then used to derive statements identifying how to recognize instances of the researched phenomenon and how to distinguish between observed events that are instances of it and similar events that are not.

For example, suppose a fixed method study was aimed at observing "aggression." A conceptual definition for this research phenomenon might be "actions with the apparent primary intent of coercing another or expressing anger toward them." While this conceptual definition might be acceptable to a variety of researchers studying aggression in a variety of contexts, concrete definitions of aggression would be expected to vary widely across subject types and observational situations. What is aggressive behavior among four year olds, for example, is quite different from what is aggressive behavior in adults. Similarly, the form adult aggression may take at work typically differs from the form adult aggression may take at home. Variations in concrete definitions might also arise because of differences in theoretical or political perspectives: what appears to be aggression from one person's perspective might appear to be self-defense from another. Sorting through narrative records from unstructured observations, then, allows a fixed method researcher to clarify what the distinguishing features of the research phenomenon are, given his or her interpretation of the conceptual definition and given the people and setting that will be observed.

Once these distinguishing features are identified, the statements describing them become the operational definitions of the research phenomenon. These definitions then form the basis of what observers will be trained and expected to recognize. The purpose of the initial unstructured observations is to generate information that will allow the researcher to create an informed system for structured observations. In this way, an observational system can be tailor-made to fit the observational circumstances, making it more likely that the structured system will be sensitive to the research phenomenon as it is conceptually defined and as it is manifested in the particular circumstances that will be studied.

Once the definition has been clearly stated, the technology surrounding how the defined phenomenon will be observed, recorded, and coded must be specified. The observation technology will typically be either mechanical or human. Sometimes the phenomenon can be operationally defined such that a mechanical device can reliably detect it, such as defining "making too much noise in the house" as "sound episodes or events that exceed 70 decibels for three or more seconds." In such a case, if the appropriate mechanical apparatus is both available and acceptable to those who will be observed, then a mechanical observational system is often preferable.

Sometimes, however, the phenomenon as operationally defined is either too subtle or too complex to be mechanically detected. This is particularly likely to be the case in two circumstances. First, many psychological phenomena are difficult to detect mechanically: these phenomena are typically quite subtle, and their indicators can vary widely across different people or even within the same person at different points in time. Second, many interpersonal phenomena can only be detected by human observers, since recognition of the occurrence of such phenomena typically cannot occur without a knowledge and understanding of the interactional context within which particular events are occurring.

Where a mechanical observational system can be arranged, developing the observe-record-code technology is quite straightforward. The apparatus is positioned optimally, that is, so as to have most complete access to the circumstances of observation, and an observation schedule is set. The observation schedule can be continuous, which is most appropriate when a research phenomenon both rarely occurs and is no more likely to occur at certain times than others. If one were researching how two-worker families with school-age children manage morning tasks, however, it would be inefficient to record all day—continuously— rather than just during the morning hours when the research phenomenon is present. But if one were researching all the ways in which such parents coped with both work and family responsibilities, it would be optimal to record continuously at various times in the day except, of course, when both were at work, as Hochschild (1989) did.

Sampling Observational Periods

In general, with any circumstance where the research phenomenon appears often, observations can be conducted on a schedule rather than all the time; they can be sampled. The assumption under these circumstances, of course, is that the times that are observed give a representative picture of what happens during the times that are not observed. This assumption, it will be recalled, is similar to the assumption always made whenever a sample is used to draw conclusions about a larger population. In other words, study participants are not the only feature sampled in research designs; occasions for observation may be another. In this case, the assumption is that what is observed during those times that observation takes place represents fairly what would have been observed at other times that observation might or could have taken place.

As in sampling individuals, when the interest is in generalizing from the sample observations to some larger population of observations, the only or at least primary determinant of when observations occur should be chance. Optimally, then, one would decide on the duration of single observation sessions (for instance, 45 minutes), write each possible 45-minute observation period on a slip of paper, and then randomly select slips to determine when observations will be made each day.

Practical constraints typically impinge on this ideal. Especially with human observers, their schedules must be at least as influential a determinant of when observation sessions take place as is chance. And in certain settings, such as schools, hospitals, nursing homes, or homeless shelters, there are organizational schedules that dictate when observations can be made. It is not bad research when these practical considerations, rather than chance, determine when observations occur. But the conclusions drawn from research where observation schedules were determined by practical considerations must take into account the limits of these practical features on the generality of what was found.

Most fixed method observation systems or schedules specify short time periods during which the observer will work, followed by short time periods during which the observer will make a record of what was just seen. The length of both these intervals varies. The length of the observation cycle will depend on how much observation time is required to see enough of what is going on to be able to detect the research phenomenon as defined. This length of time will obviously need to be longer for phenomena that themselves take longer to occur, as well as for phenomena that cannot be identified without knowledge of what else is going on when they do or do not occur. Someone observing compliance with authority figures, for example, would be unable to code a particular action as an instance of compliance without knowing whether or not the action had been preceded by an authority figure request to do it. Recording cycles are usually short. They need only be long enough to permit the observer to make a record of whether the observation target events did or did not occur.

Recording Data

An observation record can be either mechanically or humanly produced. In the case of mechanical observation, the record will of course be made mechanically. A video recorder will produce a videotape record, an audio recorder will produce an audiotape record, and a polygraph will produce a written polygram.

In the case of human observation, the record can be made either with or without the assistance of mechanical aids. In the simplest case, the human observer will keep track of what was observed by making marks on an observation sheet. A set of codes will appear for each observation period or cycle. At the end of each cycle, the observer will mark various codes to reflect which of the observed behaviors did and did not occur during each of the observation intervals. If available, mechanical or computerized recording methods can be used to facilitate this process.

When the observations have been made by humans, the observe-record-code complex has been completed with the creation of the record, assuming that the recording system involves making a record by coding whether specific, predefined phenomena were or were not observed during the observation cycle. Thus in structured observation systems, to record *is* to code. When unstructured observations are made mechanically, however, the observation record, such as a videotape, will itself typically require review and coding by a human observer. In other words, only the observe and record parts of the observe-record-code sequence have occurred.

Having a videotape certainly provides certain research advantages. It is no small contribution, for example, to have a permanent record of the events of interest that can be examined and reexamined, permitting a greater degree of depth in what is understood about them. Alongside this decided advantage is a disadvantage. The videotape record is no more informative than were the events as they originally occurred. Usually, then, mechanical observation requires a human observer who must later execute the observe and code components of the observe-record-code complex during a coding process.

Whether using a mechanically assisted observation technology or one that relies only on human observers, the end product of the observe-record-code process is information about whether the phenomena as defined did or did not occur during each of a series of observation intervals. This information is typically translated into a frequency score, reflecting the number of times the research phenomenon was seen during the observation period. As with any structured data collection method, the resulting data are then analyzed for reliability and validity as described below.

The advantages of developing a new observational system are clear: the system can be tailored to conform exactly to the new investigator's conception of the researched phenomenon as well as the specific research circumstances involved. But this luxury comes at some cost: It takes a lot of effort to develop an observational system, as is the case with any new measure.

Using an Existing Observational Measure

Having discussed the steps that one must go through to create a good structured observational tool, it may seem obvious why fixed method research often uses existing measures. First, the quality of the observational system, in terms of its reliability and validity in other studies, will already have been established. It is generally easier to demonstrate a measurement tool's usefulness in a new context than to demonstrate the reliability and validity of one that has never been used before.

There is a second reason for the use of preestablished systems whenever possible: Doing so allows comparisons of results across studies having measurement methods in common. Using a preestablished observational measure creates a connection between a new study and others that have used the same measure before. It is this interlocking of method, as well as of question, that makes research a collaborative rather than an isolated activity across investigators. Familiar methods yield results more easily interpretable by other researchers.

How to find and select among existing measures is covered in detail in chapter 15. In general, there is little difference between selecting an existing measure for observation as compared to an interview or questionnaire measure. However, there are a couple of additional points to consider. The first is that in addition to the content of the observations, the observe-record-code process must also be suited to the circumstances of the present investigation. The recording system in particular deserves review; some may be too demanding or complex for easy use in all settings. The training requirements for observers should also be considered. In general, when multiple observers are used, a rate of interobserver agreement of 85 percent is considered minimally acceptable.

As with other preexisting measures, the reliability and validity of any observational measure adopted for a study must be established in the new context of use and checked throughout the duration of the data gathering. In addition, it is also useful to arrange checks on what has traditionally been called "calibration slippage," which refers to the fact that observers may unintentionally alter their standards of observation over time. This sort of slippage occurs, for example, when there is a certain event that strikes observers as a blatant example of what is being observed when the study first begins but as not a real example of what is being observed after they have watched things for a while, becoming "jaded" or "desensitized" to what they see.

Of course it is not always possible to use a previously developed observational system. Sometimes one is not available. Sometimes the ones available do not suit the circumstances, sample, or conceptual base of the research. In this latter circumstance, sometimes the existing system can be modified to make it acceptable: Observation intervals can be lengthened, recording technologies can be added, and so forth. Whenever such changes are made, however, the observational method is in reality a new one, and its reliability and validity should be again examined and reported.

Reliability and Validity in Observation

It is interesting to note that, because observational data can *seem* so inherently credible, the reliability and validity of observational data collection systems have not always been examined as carefully as other types. There is increasing acknowledgement even among traditional measurement specialists that this failure is unfortunate: Every data collection method must be shown to be good and not assumed to be so.

The most usual form of reliability examined with observational data collection is called variously interrater reliability and interobserver agreement. This kind of reliability requires demonstrating that different raters or observers are making or would make the same recordings about the same events. Most often interrater reliability is demonstrated by arranging for two or more observers to make records of the same situations or events. In the case of live observations, this would involve being in the same place at the same time as Fraiberg (1970) and her coinvestigators were, for example. When working with audio or videotapes, the observers need not be working at the same time.

In fixed method research, double-coding by observers in order to assess interobserver reliability must be done independently. That is, the two observers should not be influenced in their ratings by seeing how the other observer has classified a particular event. Given this requirement, mechanical records have a clear advantage in that it is easy to make sure observers are not working together when they are coding.

After each observer has prepared his or her observation record, their records are compared to see how much agreement there is between them. If there is a high level of agreement, the system can be regarded as reliable. If agreement is not good, it may be because the operational definitions provided for the observers were not clear enough, because the observational task was too demanding (the observers were being expected to notice too many different things at once), or because the observer training was not adequate. Each of these problems is of course correctable. Unless the problem is fixed, the resulting observational data cannot be regarded as trustworthy or repeatable.

Observer agreement can be calculated in several ways. The simplest involves counting the number of observation intervals during which the observers agree and dividing that number by the total number of observation intervals in the study. This method is generally regarded as acceptable when whatever is being observed occurs about half the time. However, when the phenomenon to be observed occurs either very often or very rarely, this method will make it look like observers are agreeing very closely when in fact they may not be agreeing at all.

Consider, for example, the following situation. Suppose two observers observe a child for 20 observation intervals, and suppose the first observer records a single instance of the research phenomenon in the third interval, while the second observer records a single instance of the observed phenomenon during interval 17. Computing their agreement by counting the number of agreements by the number of agreements and disagreements would produce a very high agreement index: They produced the same record 18 times (agreeing that the observation target was not seen in intervals 1, 2, 4, 5, 6, 7, 8, 9, 10, 11, 12, 13, 14, 15, 16, 18, 19, and 20) and different records twice (intervals 3 and 17). Their coefficient of agreement, then, would be 18 divided by 20, or 90 percent, but in reality they would have had absolutely no agreement at all on when the phenomenon occurred. Coefficients of rater agreement must be calculated in such as way as to genuinely reflect the degree of agreement between the two observers.

With observational data, interrater reliability is generally regarded as the most important form of reliability to demonstrate. When it has been demonstrated, the researcher can legitimately argue that the research phenomena as operationally defined are being observed similarly by two (or more) independent raters. Other forms of reliability, such as demonstrating consistency across times or across settings, may also be examined. Consistency in observation must be demonstrated and not assumed.

It is also just as important to demonstrate that a new observational system is valid as it is to demonstrate that any new data collection procedure is reliable. Reliability addresses the degree to which whatever is measured is repeatedly observable. Validity addresses whether whatever is measured has been defensibly understood. In other words, the validity of a measure relates to how data can be interpreted or to what sense can be made of the data.

When the conceptual and operational definitions guiding the observation have been carefully developed and articulated, observational data are generally regarded as easily having face and content validity (see chapter 11). Of course neither face nor content validity involves an empirical demonstration of the meaning of a score. However, criterion-related and more general construct validity must be empirically demonstrated for new observational systems just as they must for any new measurement procedure (see chapter 11).

Particularly if an observational system is to be used in additional studies by other researchers, it is important to demonstrate the criterion and/or construct validity of the method. Past demonstrations of interrater reliability, for example, only show that the system *can* be used reliably, not that it *is* being used reliably in the current work. Thus it is necessary to demonstrate rater reliability with each new scale application, in part because the observational system itself is only one component of the observational methodology. The observers are also an integral component of the methodology, and there is no guarantee that new observers will perform reliably using the same system other observers were able to use successfully.

It is also wise to collect evidence bearing on an observational system's validity, and most well designed studies will afford these data as a matter of course. As will be recalled from the chapter on data collection in general, random error in measurement is inevitable. Therefore, it is often prudent to include multiple measures of key phenomena in any study. To the extent that important findings are replicated across different measures, a more compelling argument can be made for the apparently significant result.

Well-designed fixed method studies, then, often include more than one measure, or operationalization, for the central research phenomena. These several measures, while not properly interchangeable, should be meaningfully related; it follows that scores from them should be significantly correlated. To the extent that scores on an observational measure are correlated with scores on other measures of the same variable, the observational measure can be regarded as a valid indicator of the phenomenon under study.

Participant Observation

Participant observation is a flexible method of research widely used in sociology to examine social interactions, small groups, and organizational or community life. It involves the observer becoming a part of and a participant in the groups and communities being observed so that the role taken with those observed is less distant and more "inside." Participant observation includes the same basic processes as seeing, recording, and coding or analyzing what is seen although adapted to the role the observer takes in the research setting. The Humphreys (1970) study and some parts of the Hochschild (1989) study, as well as the Rollins (1985) and Williams (1989, 1992) studies described in earlier chapters, are examples of participant observation research.

Observation, however, is often only one part of the participant observation process. For example, ethnomethodological studies, and others, typically include data gathering through both observation and intensive interviewing for the purpose of understanding the culture of a particular group or society. Even outside of formal interviewing, asking and listening take place as the observations are made. Documents and other artifacts may be collected at the site as well. Participant observation is above all opportunistic (Jorgensen 1989); therefore observation is not as clearly separated from other methods of data gathering as in other kinds of research.

Participant observation as a method is defined by the fact that the researcher is both a participant and actor in the situation being studied and an observer of it. However, the participant-observer role can be thought of as a continuum (Williamson et al. 1982). This continuum ranges from situations in which the observer is overtly identified as and acting almost always as a researcher with relatively little other interaction with those being observed (see Hochschild example above) to situations in which the observer is an active group participant, perhaps initially known as a group member and not as a researcher, whose research activities, such as record keeping, are designed to be covert or at least as invisible as possible in the setting.

Jorgensen (1989), for example, discusses three styles of participant observation: the active participant, who has a job or other social role in the setting in addition to the research; the privileged observer, who is known and trusted and has access to private information; and the limited observer, the most common one, who has no role other than researcher and who works to build trust in the setting over time. When multiple roles are occupied, as in the first two styles, managing and negotiating them can be a challenge.

In fact, major issues in any participant observation study concern how the observer will gain access to and enter the group or social system to be observed, whether and how the research is represented to others, and what role(s) the observer will engage in in the setting. In general, observations and other data gathering activities in the setting go from being very unfocussed in the beginning to being more focussed as data accumulate and potential answers to the research questions begin to emerge (Jorgensen 1989).

Participant observation research uses reactivity as a tool in the research. How those who are being observed react to the research and/or to the observer form part of what is learned about them, their social systems, and their view of the world. How the researcher reacts personally to those she observes are also data that inform her about the people and situations she studies. For example, like any traveler, a newcomer to a group or social setting will notice patterns of behavior that seem odd but that to a group member are so familiar and taken-for-granted they would never be commented on as unique or of any importance.

Like other forms of observation, participant observation is an expensive data collection method. It requires long periods of contact with the groups being studied, in part because over time initial atypical responses due to the presence of an outsider fade as the "outsider" becomes an "insider." Although there is much to gain in knowledge from such familiarity, there is a risk in such long exposure that the researcher will begin adopting uncritically the views and perspectives of those who are studied and of failing to take adequate notice of things to which the observer is no longer naive.

During the course of a participant observation study, an observer is typically exposed to many sources of information and to many informants. Often, for example, a key informant will serve as a guide or a person who can help the researcher gain access to a particular group or social setting. Williams (1992) reports having such a "guide" in his study of crack houses in New York. This relationship requires careful nurture and can be quite rewarding to both parties. However, no one informant can be assumed to be typical of a group in every way, and no one informant can be assumed to be trustworthy and nonpartisan at all times and on all issues.

Triangulating data obtained on different occasions and from different sources is an important technique that can both validate information obtained and, when data are discrepant, suggest new dimensions of inquiry to pursue in order to explain apparent inconsistencies (Fetterman 1989). Seeking out and using multiple contacts and sources of information in the setting is thus an important step in determining which data are credible and worthy of report. Given the complexities involved in any individual entering, negotiating roles in, and leaving the field of study, the use of multiple data sources to validate information is much more common in participant observation than the use of multiple observers.

Recording the observations made is essential. Sometimes recording in the form of note-taking can go on in the setting, and sometimes it cannot. In either case, the researcher must plan adequate time for preparing the narrative records, generally called field notes, of what has been observed (Taylor & Bogdan 1984). These field notes should contain as much detail about who and where the recorded events took place as well as about the events themselves as possible. There is always a great deal of detail observed in any interaction, and it may take a great deal of time before it is possible to distinguish important and relevant information from the unimportant. In fact, the analysis stage may be well underway by then. Recording data is generally less compelling and interesting than collecting it, but keeping the record complete and up-to-date is an essential discipline in participant observation research. While the notes must be as complete as possible in describing the events observed, they usually include interpretive material as well. Recording the subjective reactions of the observer brings them into awareness and makes them part of the data to be used in understanding the events studied. Thus observer and observed not only interact with each other; they are both "inside the frame" of the research itself.

Summary

Observation is involved whenever a recorder, human or mechanical, observes events for the purpose of collecting information about and making a permanent record of them. This is a broad definition, for observation is a versatile data collection method. Observation has been used as the data collection method both in highly structured forms of research and in flexible method studies in the form of participant observation. In fact, its use illustrates extremes in assumptions and styles of research. It can appear as the most "objective" or as the most "subjective" and reactive form of data gathering. Because visual data are so compelling, however, observational research has been essential to knowledge-building in many important areas of inquiry.

In some senses, observation captures the spirit of true empiricism. The greatest limitation of observation is probably practical: Done correctly, it is an expensive and time-consuming assessment methodology to use. Standing alongside this limitation is great strength: Done correctly it produces highly credible data especially when information about nonverbal and social behavior is needed.

13

Interviewing

T he interview is so common in research that it is often taken for granted as a data collection method, but interviewing is in fact a complex, varied, and frequently misunderstood data collection technique. Despite these complexities, however, the research interview has certainly proven itself in use. In fact, it has been estimated that 90 percent of social science data have been obtained via interviews of one kind or another (Briggs 1986). However, as an eminent British sociologist observed, "Interviewing is rather like a marriage: everybody knows what it is, an awful lot of people do it, and yet behind each closed front door there is a world of secrets" (Oakley 1981:41). Recently insights from ethnographic interviewing and such disciplines as sociolinguistics have significantly enriched our understanding of the research interview as a data gathering method.

In the interview, a researcher and an informant meet in person or interact on the telephone, engaging in a conversation that has as its purpose the generation of data useful for research. This conversation may be a highly structured or an unstructured one; that is, it may be overtly guided almost wholly by the interviewer or by the informant. It may cover a wide range of information or only a narrow or specific topic. It may elicit in-depth content or relatively superficial information. The interview data may be recorded in summary on paper or verbatim on audiotape. Its purpose may be to collect information in order to examine preexisting hypotheses, to provide precise or in-depth description of selected phenomena, or to explore new or poorly understood phenomena.

Given the variety of its uses and of the forms that the research interview may take, the techniques used in interviewing also vary considerably. In fact, while there are some commonalities in all interviewing, it is really necessary to consider interviewing as it is done in fixed method and flexible method research separately. However, there are some commonalities that underlie all uses of the research interview. Knowledge of the strengths and weaknesses of interview techniques in general and of the various types of interviewing in particular will help in selecting the best data gathering method for a study and in evaluating studies that use interview methods.

Uses and Advantages of the Interview

Actions can be observed directly in the present; subjective experiences—motivations, feelings, meanings, and interpretations and memories of events from the past—cannot. However, these essential aspects of human behavior can be apprehended in words through interviewing. Written accounts may be used to capture these phenomena as well, but writing typically takes an informant more time and energy than speaking, and of course it requires literacy skills. People are often more willing and able to reflect at length on complex feelings, understandings, and past experiences through the spoken word than the written one.

In many ways, flexibility in the data gathering situation is the greatest strength of the interview. The degree of flexibility used will depend on whether the general approach to data gathering will be highly structured or unstructured. However, some degree of adaptability in the interaction is both necessary and desirable whatever form an interview takes. For the interviewer, there is always an element of being there with the respondent, which can afford the opportunity for observation above and beyond what the interview itself is designed to call forth.

The interview is an encounter and interaction between interviewer and interviewee. From the standpoint of the researcher, there are many advantages to being present as the informant encounters the interview questions. Pauses, hesitancies, and facial expressions may affect how a verbal answer should be interpreted. Outright questions from the interviewee or responses that seem "off the mark" may indicate that the interview questions have not been understood as intended. Unlike with the mailed questionnaire, often it is possible to interpret, explain, repeat, or redirect an interview question on the spot to obtain the information that the question was designed to elicit. Similarly, informants can be asked to elaborate on responses that are surprising or that seem incomplete, irrelevant, or hard to understand. Such flexibility in the moment may be greater or lesser depending on how structured the interviewing process is, but even in the most structured of interview approaches the interviewer can draw on observational data from the interaction to better understand the responses offered.

From the standpoint of the respondent, the presence of the interviewer may make it easier or harder to convey the information intended. With a skilled interviewer, the respondent will feel a sense of rapport, of being listened to and understood without judgement, and of focus on their own rather than the interviewer's ideas, all of which can make it easier to talk. The interviewee also has a chance to "size up" the interviewer and the research itself through asking his or her own questions and discussing his or her own expectations about the interview and subsequent use of the data. Thus the research interview shares with many other kinds of professional encounters the quality of being a social interaction with a defined purpose and its own social rules that are both like and unlike those of ordinary conversations.

Even in survey research using highly structured interview protocols, there are some situations in which interviewing conveys specific technical advantages. Data gathering in which the sequence or nature of the specific questions to be asked depends on the answers to previous questions, termed *contingency questioning,* is best handled through interviewing. Only a well-trained and experienced interviewer can reliably follow a complex sequence of questions through multiple contingencies. Respondents to questionnaires that require taking complex and different paths through the questions often have difficulty completing them, however clear the arrows and other written directions may be. Those who are interviewed, however, may never realize that questions that don't apply to them have not been asked and that the interviewer is working hard to follow complex and differing paths through all the possible questions.

Similarly when exhaustive enumeration and coverage of a geographic sample or population is needed, there is no substitute for trained interviewers on the street for unit-to-unit canvassing of a given residential area, including identifying living spaces and respondents not previously known or officially recorded. The Gomez (1990) study of Cuban Americans in West New York, New Jersey, used survey interviewers to canvass the community in just this way. Only by going door to door in a specified block could all the households in which Cuban American residents lived be identified.

Disadvantages of Interviews

As with all data gathering techniques, the advantages and disadvantages of the interview are closely related. Anonymity for the informant is not possible in a face-to-face interview. Confidentiality is usually offered, but once a person has been located and seen, his or her identity is known. This lack of anonymity is usually not a problem, but if issues of stigmatized or illegal activity should come up, it must be remembered that research interview data are not legally privileged and are certainly not immune from court subpoena. Any project in which data bearing on criminal matters or on mandated reporting issues such as child abuse might emerge must consider and deal with these limits on confidentiality (Herek et al. 1991, and see chapter 9 on ethics). Data generously given must be scrupulously recorded and safely used.

For the informant, an interview is a fairly intrusive form of data collection. It takes time, it may take place in the life space of the informant, and it may touch upon issues that are somewhat painful or difficult to discuss with a stranger. Interview procedures must deal thoughtfully with the impositions made on participants and must afford the informant the autonomy to decide whether or how completely to participate.

From the point of view of the interviewer, an interview is also a time-consuming endeavor. For each hour of contact with an informant, several hours of training, scheduling, and traveling before and of recording, data checking, and coding afterward may be necessary. Inevitably some interview appointments are cancelled and must be rescheduled. This intensity of effort makes interviewing a relatively expensive form of data collection, especially if large samples are involved.

Finally, while the interview encounter may result in a rapport that enhances the quality of the information obtained, factors known and unknown in the encounter between interviewer and respondent may affect the data in unpredictable ways. When face-to-face, interview responses can be affected by the race, gender, class, and appearance of the interviewer. In general, people may be most open in their responses when they perceive the interviewer to be someone like themselves. At other times, however, this may not be true; Herek et al. (1991) speculate, for example, that in AIDS research, gay male respondents who perceive their interviewers to be part of the gay and lesbian community may self-protectively underreport their unsafe sexual practices. Thus in survey research or other studies using multiple interviewers, care is often taken in the assignment of interviewers or in the management of their appearance and presentation to try to enhance the reliability of the data they gather. Even when there is only one interviewer, consideration must be given to all the factors in the interaction that might affect results.

The social rules of conversation can interfere with research interviewing. Respondents may only say what they think will be acceptable to the interviewer. For example, in conversation people prefer to express agreement rather than disagreement. "Yes, but . . ." answers may therefore be used in the research context to express a difference of opinion rather than a "no" response. The interviewer must then decide whether or not a "yes" or a "no" response was really intended from the point of view of the study.

Interviewing in Flexible Method Research

The interview designed to gather unstructured data, which includes what is termed clinical, focussed, qualitative, intensive, or ethnographic interviewing, is a common data gathering method used in flexible method research. In flexible method research, intensive interviewing is generally used because the research question springs from a desire to explore and learn more about some phenomenon that has not been previously studied or has been poorly understood. In this situation, the assumption is that the informant's knowledge and experience of the phenomena of interest should guide the dialogue. Often the focus of flexible method study such as the psychological meaning of an event to a respondent is such that, by definition, it could only be captured in the respondent's own words. Weiss (1994), for example, suggests using open-ended interviewing for developing detailed descriptions; eliciting multiple perspectives on an event, organization, or situation; understanding internal, interpersonal, or social processes; learning about how events are interpreted; and helping readers to understand a situation from a different point of view.

In ethnographic research, interviewing is often used in conjunction with participant observational techniques in order to elicit participants' views and interpretations of the events that have taken place. Sometimes these narrative data are later reduced through content analysis either to a categorical or quantified form (see, for example, Miller 1990), but most often they are analyzed in narrative form (see chapter 16 on coding narrative data).

In flexible method research, the content of the interview itself is always developed as an integral part of the research process. Available instruments are not generally used because this would defeat the basic purpose of the research: to learn inductively about a phenomenon that was previously unknown or poorly understood. Often, however, an *interview guide* may be developed as a general map of the content and form of the questions to be asked (Padgett 1998; Weiss 1994).

Interviews in flexible method research vary in the extent to which control of the interview process and content is shared between interviewer and interviewee. At one extreme are ethnographic-style approaches in which the interviewee is treated as the expert who guides the interviewer toward increased knowledge of the cultural, social, or psychological phenomenon under study. In this way, the risk of imposing the researcher's preconceptions on the phenomena reported is minimized. Such interviews will be as varied as the respondents who take part in them. The danger in such an approach is that the researcher will become so caught up in the view of reality offered up by the informant that he or she may adopt uncritically whatever typical or atypical rendition of reality the interviewee sets forth. However, even in ethnographic research, there are times when the researcher may choose to ask some preplanned or pointed questions, for example, to be sure to cover certain material, to check out inconsistencies in reports from different informants, or to explore emerging interpretations of the data. Patton (1980), for example, describes such approaches as "the informal conversational interview" as compared to the "general interview guide" (p. 197).

At the other extreme are interviews that are preplanned in almost all respects and conducted in the same way for each respondent even though the answers to the questions asked are unstructured ones. Patton (1990) terms this "the standardized open-ended interview" approach (p. 197). Care taken in advance about how each question is asked can yield useful data and may be an especially productive interviewing strategy to use when more than one interviewer will be used. The data gained from such similar interviews may also be more amenable to comparison between individuals and between groups of respondents. However, the danger in such an approach is that the researcher, in controlling the flow of the data, may miss some worthwhile information although it may reduce individual interviewer bias or variability in how questions are asked.

In fact, the interview may best be viewed as a special case of the conversation, an event in which two participants are to one extent or another mutually influencing the interaction and thus the data it will yield. In some interview situations, the interviewer will play the role of expert most of the time; in other instances, the respondent will be asked to play the role of expert predominantly, as in the life history interview. However, in no case must the interviewer fail to consider that her or his actions will wittingly or unwittingly shape the data the interview will yield. Verbal and nonverbal cues will either encourage an interviewee in a given line of conversation or discourage her. This influence cannot be willed or wished away. Rather it must be understood and used in a way that will enhance the credibility of the results.

Briggs has written eloquently about this problem in anthropology:

> Growing up in a given speech community presents the language learner with innumerable opportunities to discover the rules that relate form, context, and meaning. When a researcher leaves her or his own native speech community and establishes contact with another group of human beings, however, no such common body of experience is available to smooth the initial encounters. The same problem arises when investigators work with a different social class or ethnic group within their own society. In filling this gap, researchers often draw on the communicative device their speech community views as the best means of obtaining large bodies of information in the least amount of time—the interview. The implicit reasoning seems to be that interviews allow the researcher to assume control of the type and quality of information being conveyed. This enables him or her to circumvent the usual constraints on the transmission of knowledge (e.g., kinship, age, degree of intimacy, gender, initiation, etc.) (Briggs 1986:39).

Whatever the form of the interview, the interview situation must be appreciated as a type of communicative event in which the participants, interviewer and respondent, may have concordant or discordant understandings about their roles and goals in the interaction. Making referents clear and helping respondents understand the scope of the response that is desired are essential. In addition, the interviewer must be careful to interpret responses contextually and not assume that his or her frame of reference is necessarily that of the respondent.

Social workers bring valuable practice skills to the research interviewing situation (Bunin et al. 1983). Fraiberg (1970), for example, deliberately sought out experienced clinicians for the observation and interviewing of blind babies and their mothers in her pioneering study in Michigan because of their ability to focus, to distinguish trivial from essential information. In addition, most practitioners are skilled in developing rapport with people, a skill that is also useful in research interviewing. Conveying an interested neutrality and a nonjudgmental attitude can be very useful as well.

Patton (1980) offers the following comments on the interview process:

> Neutrality means that the person being interviewed can tell me anything without engendering either my favor or my disfavor with regard to the content of their responses. I cannot be shocked; I cannot be angered; I cannot be embarrassed; I cannot be saddened—indeed, nothing the person tells me will make me think more or less of them.
>
> At the same time I am neutral to the *content* of what is being said to me, I care very much about that the person is willing to share with me what they are saying. *Rapport is a stance vis-á-vis the person being interviewed. Neutrality is a stance vis-á-vis the content of what that person says.* Rapport means that I respect the people being interviewed, so what they say is important because of who is saying it. I want to convey to them that their knowledge, experience, attitudes and feelings are important. Yet, the content of what they say to me is not important (Patton 1980:231).

Conveying these essential attitudes—of regard for the person in combination with neutrality toward the content of what is said—is very familiar to social workers and other human service professionals. Their skills in these areas help to make them very effective interviewers for research as well.

Sensitivity to the needs of any participant in an encounter—for example, to begin by getting oriented to and comfortable in the interaction before dealing with sensitive material and to have some opportunity for closure at the end of the interview experience—all of these are fostered by clinical experience. It is also essential that the interviewer monitor his or her own subjective reactions to the interview material and work to keep these reactions from intruding unduly upon the data gathering process, just as is necessary in any clinical interview (Bunin et al. 1983; Padgett 1998).

Weiss (1994) suggests that the interviewing relationship be based on an implicit contract that includes, in addition to the general ethical guidelines for research, the following clauses:

1. The interviewer and the respondent will work together to produce information useful to the research project.
2. The interviewer will define the areas for exploration and will monitor the quality of the material. The respondent will provide observations, internal and external, accepting the interviewer's guidance regarding topics and the kind of report that is needed.
3. The interviewer will not ask questions out of idle curiosity. On the other hand, the interviewer will be a privileged inquirer in the sense that the interviewer may ask for information the respondent would not generally make available, maybe would not tell anyone else at all.
4. The interviewer will respect the respondent's integrity. This means that the interviewer will not question the respondent's appraisals[,] choices, motives, right to observations, or personal worth (p. 65).

He also notes that the interviewer may take the role of student to that of the respondent's expert or may present him- or herself as the means by which the respondent can tell his or her story. Both respondent and interviewer have important responsibilities in the interaction. Nevertheless, problems can arise during an interview, and Weiss (1994) has many suggestions about how to deal with them.

Preparation for conducting an interview designed to gather unstructured data may be less time-consuming initially than when a completely structured data gathering tool and procedure must be designed to fit all eventualities. Much care must be taken in advance, however, to consider both the content and process of such an interview in relation to the issues outlined above. Pilot testing, or conducting trial interviews, is as useful in clinical or intensive interviewing as in questionnaire design. Are there key interview questions that can or should be specified in advance? How may they best be worded so as to facilitate the most discursive or focussed response? Asking a "yes-no" question, for example, is not a very productive way to proceed. How will each interview begin and end? In what order might the content be presented in order to make the process comfortable, comprehensible, and efficient for the respondent? How will the research and the respondent's participation be explained or described? Some informants may need help in staying focussed on the issue at hand or in limiting their remarks; others will be more reticent and may need to be drawn out. What kinds of probes and other questions can be used to help respondents to focus, elaborate on, or clarify their responses? How can questions be worded to make their meanings clear? What data will be recorded and how? Will data analysis occur concurrent with or after data collection is complete? Weiss (1994) and Patton (1980) provide excellent examples of how and how not to frame interview questions when interviewing in the context of a flexible method study.

Using probes, or questions about the answers given, in open-ended interviewing is an essential tool for deepening understanding and following up on unexpected answers. Padgett (1998) gives an excellent example of this technique from her study of health beliefs and practices related to mammography among low-income African American women using questions like, "Could you tell me more about that?" As she reported,

> we queried respondents regarding their beliefs about what caused breast cancer to spread in the body and several mentioned their belief that "air" is responsible. Intrigued, our interviewers probed further. Respondents explained that opening up the body during surgery exposed "dormant" cancer cells to the air and precipitated their spread throughout the body (p. 61).

Since a focus of the study was why these women did not often get follow-up care following a mammogram with abnormal findings, this kind of information might help to explain why recommendations for biopsies and other procedures were not followed (Padgett 1998). Health beliefs like these that differ from mainstream medicine are of course common throughout the population.

Whatever the preparation, much time is usually needed for the data gathering itself and for preparation and analysis of the data after the fact. Formal or informal review of the data from early interviews may be used to guide subsequent ones, or analysis may not take place until all the data are in hand. The grounded theory method of qualitative research is one in which the interview process is continually revised as data are concurrently analyzed (Strauss & Corbin 1990). However the analysis is approached, as in observation, data gathering through interviewing is not complete until the data have been recorded and analyzed as well. In structured interviewing, most of the recording and coding of responses takes place as soon as the question is answered. In flexible method interviewing, including when conducting standardized interviews that elicit open-ended data, the recording and analysis of the interview data typically require considerable additional effort.

When narrative data are being collected, the main challenge lies in recording the data completely and in detail. In general, there is no substitute for the audiotape in recording such interview data. Written notes should be limited to recording other data, such as facial expressions and other nonverbal behavior, unspoken interviewer reactions, or thoughts about the data as they emerge. In addition, audiotaping frees the interviewer to focus on participating fully in the interview conversation rather than having to worry in addition about preparing an adequate written record of what is being said.

If interviewing and participant observation are being combined, it may be useful to prepare written field notes immediately after each period of data gathering, recording the setting and experience of the interview in addition to the verbatim detail of what was asked and what was said. Such notes provide an additional source of valuable data to inform or constitute part of the analysis itself. Those accustomed to providing process recordings of clinical interviews, for instance, know that with experience and prompt recording recall of the details even of complex interactions can be quite good.

Often typed transcripts are prepared from audiotapes of interviews. The use of written transcripts can make the review and analysis of verbal data more rapid and more complete. In any case, the demands of the data analysis process must be anticipated when planning and conducting interviews so that effective recording of data will occur.

The narratives drawn from each interview, however, are generally the most important data. In the richness of the words as spoken lies the very reason for asking open-ended questions to begin with: the possibility of discovery of the unexpected and the convincing nature of people's own accounts of their social and inner experiences described in their own terms. Because these data emerge in interaction, it is essential that the entire interaction—the questions and other remarks as spoken by the interviewer as well as the "answers" as given by the respondent—be part of the record used in analysis. Only in its context can the real meaning of the data emerge.

An Example of Flexible Method Interviewing

Feagin's (1991) study of discrimination in public places illustrates the uses to which unstructured data gathered in flexible method interviews can be put (see chapter 3). In the Feagin study, 37 African American respondents in a larger study spontaneously described instances of discrimination they had encountered in public places. Feagin makes the point that the interviewers were also African American, which may have facilitated the emergence of this (and other) information during the interview.

Some of the analysis of the interview data was quantitative: The number of incidents reported, the specific actions reported, and the site of the incidents, in the street or in public accommodations, were enumerated. Incidents of discrimination were analyzed separately depending on which kind of site they occurred in. Although the results were quantified and categorized, the advantage of the open-ended interview approach in this instance was that the categories were not imposed by the interviewers in advance; rather they were developed inductively after the fact based on the information volunteered by the study's informants.

Most of the analysis, however, was based on use of the interview data in narrative form. For example, two fundamental strategies in response to incidents occurring in public accommodations were identified—verbal confrontation and withdrawal—and then illustrated with verbatim accounts from the transcripts. In many of the passages quoted, the specific questions and probes used by the interviewer to elicit data about the incident are included in the quotations in brackets, allowing the interviewer's contribution to the telling of the story to be assessed. The validity of the interpretations made of the incidents can then be evaluated in context by the reader, at least for the specific examples provided. Feagin's basic point—that even middle-class, successful African Americans face incidents of discrimination in public places—is illustrated in the narratives. Samples of the interview responses are given in enough detail in the report to allow the reader to judge whether or not the interpretation of them as acts of discrimination and the classification of the types of responses to them, for example, are warranted.

Interviewing in Fixed Method Studies

While the use of the face-to-face interview as a tool in survey research seems to be declining (Salant & Dillman 1994), structured interviews are still often used in descriptive and relational research in special populations or when particular topics require in-depth but flexible delineation. Interviewing in fixed method research is generally designed to elicit standardized, comparable responses from the interviewees so that answers can be reliably quantified for statistical analysis. In fact, in structured interviewing, available interview guides or questionnaires that can be adapted to the interview situation are often used in preference to developing new measures of complex phenomena. When large samples are needed, multiple interviewers may be hired and trained in the use of the specific, predefined interview protocol and the data they collect pooled for analysis.

Standardization in interviewing often covers all aspects of the interviewing process, including the manner in which respondents are recruited, the ways in which the interview encounters are begun or ended, and the instructions that are given to respondents to guide their participation. The questions themselves may be designed to elicit unstructured, structured, or "semi-structured" data, which means they elicit some combination of open-ended and close-ended responses. The order of questions, the exact wording of each, definitions of the terms used in them or in the response categories, and the exact wording of probes and/or clarifying remarks are usually all determined in advance and in detail. Often not just the questions but the response categories as well are predefined or standardized (structured questions), and codes or numerical values may be assigned to responses in advance of the interviewing itself.

Because standardized questions are most often used in mailed questionnaires, specific guidelines for writing structured questions and designing predefined data gathering protocols are given in the chapter on questionnaires (chapter 14). Use of these guidelines is essential to any successful structured interviewing effort. This section will address the application of these standardized data gathering techniques in the face-to-face interview situation.

The Gomez (1990) study of biculturalism and mental health among Cuban Americans illustrates how content is often developed in structured interviewing (see chapter 6): by taking advantage of existing scales. The interview protocol for this study was in fact composed of several preexisting measures of specific phenomena of interest to the study. These included separate measures of psychological well-being—Affective Balance Scale; the Rosenberg Self-Esteem Scale; a "modified" version of a Dyadic Adjustment Scale to measure marital adjustment; and a job satisfaction measure, which was adapted from a self-administered questionnaire to an interview format—and a Latino Bicultural Assessment Questionnaire (see the reprint in chapter 6 for citations to the authors of each instrument). In addition, of course, there were questions asked to gather demographic data about each respondent. The interviewer had to obtain data in the same way from each respondent using all of these discrete measures. Each measure, of course, would have come with its own instructions for administration, and the interviewer would have had to be trained in the use of them all.

The decision to use an available instrument for a structured interview is made in the same way as it is in observational and questionnaire studies: by deciding whether or not the measures that exist are compatible with the concepts of interest, the theoretical perspective of the present research, and the population to be studied. The Gomez (1990) paper, for example, spends considerable time defining each study variable, such as self-esteem, conceptually and showing its relevance to the topic, mental health. Biculturalism itself, a key concept, is posited as a new and better approach to understanding patterns of adaptation in immigrant groups than the more familiar ones, such as assimilation. Biculturalism is therefore discussed at considerable length, both conceptually and operationally, in measurement terms. Even a sample item from the scale is included to show concretely how this less familiar concept was measured in the research. For each other major concept, such as psychological well-being, there is a separate discussion of how the available instrument selected relates to the conceptual area already described and a description of its measurement properties as shown in prior research.

Although the Gomez article does not address this issue, it is likely that all but the biculturalism measure had to be translated into Spanish for use with at least those members of the population who were monolingual in Spanish. The translation of an available instrument into a different language can be a difficult undertaking (Rogler 1999). It is often recommended that after the initial translation, back-translation into English be undertaken as a precaution; the retranslated items can then be compared to the original ones to be sure that there has not been much drift in meaning from one version to the next. Once an instrument has been translated an additional advantage of interviewing in cross-cultural research is that, if bilingual interviewers and interview materials are used, a respondent can be offered the choice of participating in whatever language is the most comfortable. Unfortunately, the Gomez article does not provide any information about how the language issue was handled in his study.

In terms of content, using available instruments in cross-cultural studies can present other challenges in addition to language. An example of this comes from a program evaluation following low-income African American and Puerto Rican pregnant and postpartum women who were clients of a drug treatment program (Anastas 1997). The funding agency and treatment providers were interested in the "parenting skills" of the women, since one of the goals of the program was to prevent problems in their babies by supporting the women in their mothering.

Review of the available instruments for measuring parenting skills showed that all were either deficit-based, that is, focussed on uncovering "abuse potential," for example, or they had not been developed and used on similar low-income women of color, thus missing key cultural and environmental issues affecting them. In this instance, translation alone could not solve the problem; instead, it was decided to develop an interview guide, in part unstructured, that would not stigmatize and that might better capture the experiences of the program's clients, rather than use what was available. Program staff who were themselves members of the communities from which the program's clients came were intimately involved in determining the content and types of questions to be included in the interview.

In addition to dealing with content issues, process must be addressed as well. The assumptions of the interview situation are more often taken for granted in the structured interview than they may be in the unstructured interview. It is often assumed, for example, that the well-designed interview is a "neutral measurement instrument" to the extent that it is conducted outside of the norms and practices of ordinary conversational events. It is now being argued, however, that the failure to consider even structured interview data as a process and in context reduces rather than enhances the reliability and validity of the data obtained and the interpretations made of them (Foddy 1993; Suchman & Jordan 1990).

If questions can so carefully be crafted in advance of the data gathering event, why use interviewers at all? As Suchman and Jordan note, "Successful communication is not so much a product of the avoidance of misunderstandings as of their successful detection and repair" (1990:238). An interviewer skilled in communication—in both speaking and listening—may be able to detect the points where the worldview of a respondent and the research may differ or where a term or concept is not being used in the same way by respondent and researcher (Landrine, Klonoff, & Brown-Collins 1992). When misunderstandings or inconsistencies seem to occur in a standardized interview, the interviewer faces a dilemma about whether or not to depart from the preplanned protocol to seek the elaboration or clarification needed. When the interviewer is not the principal researcher, it is possible that the interviewer as well as the respondent may misunderstand or misconstrue the intent of the research, affecting the usefulness of the data obtained even if training has occurred.

In each study using structured interviewing, there is a need to strike a balance between the demands of standardization on the one hand and "local control" between the interviewer and the respondent on the other (Fine 1990). Without some degree of standardization, variation in the data will increase and responses will lose comparability, which is often necessary for relational and other comparative research designs. Without some degree of "local control," however, error of other kinds will be introduced when respondents "misunderstand" or do not accept the terms of discourse set forth in the interview questions. A skilled communicator on the scene, the interviewer, who understands the intentions and demands of the research on the one hand and who witnesses and tries to convey the real experience of the respondent on the other, is often in a position to bridge these gaps in understanding and to increase the reliability and validity of the data obtained with judicious use of a little flexibility in the interview situation.

Finally, it should be noted that interview questions designed to elicit unstructured data may also be used in descriptive or even relational research when the nature of the phenomenon being described is more complex than answers to structured questions can capture. In other cases, unstructured questions are used in interviews simply because there is insufficient knowledge on which to base the structuring of questions. In fact, some interviews consist wholly of a set of standardized questions that elicit open-ended responses only (Patton 1980). Sometimes questions eliciting unstructured data are included in an interview that also seeks structured data; the answers to such questions are often used to amplify, verify, or explain answers to the structured ones. In fact, using a combination of fixed response and open-ended questions in interviews is often recommended (Foddy 1993).

Telephone Interviewing

Telephone interviewing is now being used more frequently in research, especially in marketing research (Salant & Dillman 1994). As access to a telephone becomes more common among American households, telephone interviewing is generally considered a reasonable alternative to structured face-to-face interviewing in survey research. There have even been reports that open-ended or clinical interviewing can be conducted successfully by phone as well (Tausig & Freeman 1988). Before discussing the interview process itself, however, some implications of using telephone interviews for sampling must be considered.

Sampling Issues

The telephone survey can only be as representative as the ownership of a telephone is. This issue does not speak to the effectiveness of the telephone interview for data gathering; rather it addresses a *sampling limitation* imposed when all respondents must have a telephone in the household in order to participate. For many pieces of research, it may be quite reasonable to assume that all potential respondents would have a telephone. For other samples of interest, it may not. Telephone interviewing can only be used when all respondents do have a phone.

There is another issue to consider, however: whether or not the telephone numbers of all potential sample members are available. If the study is a follow-up of former agency clients (Tausig & Freeman 1988), for example, telephone numbers should be available for all clients from the agency record except for those who may have changed their residence or phone number since leaving the agency. Otherwise recourse is often to the telephone directory or to random digit dialing methods. The former has the advantage of efficiency; except for changes since the directory was published, only real, active telephone numbers are called. The latter has the advantage of including households with unlisted or unpublished numbers, households that probably differ systematically from others (Salant & Dillman 1994).

Other sampling challenges occur in telephone interviewing. The telephone number gains the researcher access to a household. It does not say anything about how many people, related or unrelated, or of what ages, are part of that household.

This information can be sought in the interview, but there is no guarantee that the person who answers the phone will be the respondent desired. Time of day will affect which household member answers; employed household members, for example, are not likely to answer except in the evenings or on weekends. Calls at the dinner hour, for example, are not likely to result in respondents who are prepared to answer multiple questions or to elaborate on their answers. Answering machines result in a billable call but no useful information. Thus surveys addressing the household as the unit of interest and treating any adult respondent as a spokesperson for the household unit might be among the best candidates for the telephone interview. Otherwise, time for repeat calls at convenient hours must be planned to enhance respondents' cooperation or if a particular household member is to be targeted. For long interviews, it is best to schedule them as individual, preplanned appointments in order to keep time pressures from interfering with the data gathering effort.

There is at least one major sampling advantage in the use of telephone interviews: geographic diversity. An advantage that the mailed survey has always had over the in-person interview has been its capacity to reach samples of people over great distances. Long distance telephone service means that interviews can be conducted with people who live great distances from each other with much less cost than is incurred in sending interviewers out in person. There are many issues and questions in which regional or residential diversity among respondents may prove important. The telephone interview may then offer the "best of both worlds": more flexibility in data gathering than the mailed questionnaire combined with greater geographic scope at a cost less prohibitive than in-person interviewing.

Interviewing on the Telephone

Most telephone interviewing consists of questions calling for structured or at least semistructured responses. All of the preparation needed for conducting the structured in-person interview is thus required for the telephone interview as well, and the principles underlying structured interviewing apply. Physical appearance may not be an issue, but an impression of the interviewer is conveyed by voice, intonation, and manner over the phone line as well. These need to be considered as influences on the interview conversation in the telephone interview situation in much the same way as voice, manner, and appearance shape the in-person interview.

In the telephone interview, some anonymity is gained but some communication may be lost. When a person is interviewed over the phone, he or she must rely solely on hearing the spoken question in formulating answers. Therefore, much care must be taken to ensure that questions are simply worded and intelligible, even if the electronic connection is not very clear (Salant & Dillman 1994). Certain consonants, "f" and "s," for example, are often hard to distinguish over the phone. A strong regional accent may confuse a listener or interviewer not used to it. There are no visual cues from the lips or expression of the interviewer or from the printed page to help the respondent understand the questions. The interviewer, in turn, can only rely on inconsistencies in answers, pauses, or tone of voice to guess when the respondent may be uncertain or may be responding in a way different from that anticipated when the question was written. Thus care in preparing the questions, in rehearsing their delivery, and in seeking clarification when needed are all essential to conducting the successful interview by phone.

Focus Groups

A final form of interview that deserves brief mention is the focus group. This form of inquiry has recently been widely used in marketing research, advertising, and political campaigning. Its origins go back to Thomas Merton's technique of focussed interviewing conducted with groups as part of his research in the 1940s and 1950s on the effects of propaganda (Merton, Fiske, & Kendall 1956; Merton 1987). Today's techniques are in some ways similar to and in other ways different from Merton's original use of the group interview (Merton 1987).

In the focus group, a number of people who share specific characteristics of interest to the researcher are assembled, and questions are posed or materials are presented to elicit their reactions. Group members may be chosen because they are typical in some way or atypical, as when community leaders are chosen to share their reactions to a political or business initiative. In political research, for example, likely voters of similar or differing demographic characteristics and/or political affiliations might be gathered in a small group or series of groups and asked to comment on selected campaign issues or possible campaign materials or advertisements. Not only their opinions and reactions but their reasons for them as well are elicited. Focus group members react not just to the materials and questions presented by the researchers but to each other's ideas and comments as well. The responses of the group members are used to predict the reactions of voters at large and may even become part of the campaign verbatim. In evaluation research, groups of clients, former clients, or community members can be assembled to discuss a program and how it might be improved.

Focus groups have proven to be very effective devices for eliciting and elucidating the complex and differing feelings and opinions that may underlie such actions as voting, purchasing, or participating in a program. The stimulation of the group members and their reactions to each others' opinions and challenges can result in more revealing responses than a series of individual interviews might make possible. Because of the potential for multiple reactions and a rapid flow of responses and information from members, such groups are usually convened and led by more than one person. Careful recording of the event is also essential, and videotaping is often used for this purpose so that words, gestures, and simultaneous responses can be carefully analyzed after the fact.

There are some limits, of course, to the usefulness of data obtained from focus group interviews. As in any research, the sponsorship of the focus group may influence profoundly what and how much participants are willing to share of their experiences and opinions. Because information shared by group members who begin as strangers is immediately public to some extent, discussion of very personal or sensitive topics may not be appropriate to this method. Contributing, purchasing, and voting, for example, are all somewhat public behaviors to begin with and thus lend themselves well to the focus group technique. Clearly leaders of focus groups must be skilled and experienced in handling group dynamics to protect participants from runaway debate or too much conflict. The leaders must also ensure that all group members get a chance to have their opinions heard. As with any research encounter with people, the ground rules about confidentiality, the limits on conflict within the group, and the uses to which the data will be put must be shared and respected.

Fontana and Frey (1994) sum up the advantages and disadvantages of group interviewing very well:

> The group interview has the advantages of being inexpensive, data rich, flexible, stimulating to respondents, recall aiding, and cumulative and elaborative, over and above individual responses. This type of interview is not, however, without problems. The emerging group culture may interfere with individual expression, the group may be dominated by one person, the group format makes it difficult to research sensitive topics, "group think" is a possible outcome, and the requirements for interviewer skills are greater because of group dynamics (p. 365).

When there is a good fit between what the technique can do and the kind of data a study needs, however, focus group interviews are a highly effective data gathering tool.

The Interview Process

So far this chapter has analyzed various types of interviews: the open-ended interview as used in flexible method research; the structured interview used in descriptive and other fixed research designs; the telephone interview; and the focus group. In actually conducting research using interviews, there are several matters of process that must be considered. It is easiest to understand these process matters by distinguishing the situation when the researcher him- or herself will conduct all the interviews, as is common in ethnographic, thesis, and dissertation research, from the situation in which multiple interviewers are hired to carry out larger scale projects.

Because interviewing is so common the greatest danger is that the process will be taken for granted and not seen as potentially problematic. It can easily be assumed that the interviewer understands and controls all aspects of the data gathering, even to the point of rendering her or his own participation in the data gathering invisible. The reality is that the interview encounter is mutually shaped by both (or all) participants. Thus the conduct of each interview in a study can never be entirely routine and must be approached thoughtfully.

Preparation for the Interviewer-Researcher

The interviewer who is conducting her own research has many advantages. She understands the background, content, and purposes of the research intimately. She can then make any decisions or judgements that may be required in the field with full knowledge of these issues. The more flexible the design of the research or the plan for the interviews, the more such judgements may be called for and the greater the advantage that accrues from having the researcher herself in the field.

By the time the actual interview takes place, there is much that has preceded it. How the preparations for the interview are handled can have a great effect on the interview process and the usefulness of the data gathered. This preparation must extend beyond the interview itself to an appreciation of the entire context in which it takes place and an examination of the individual and cultural assumptions interviewer and respondent are bringing to the situation.

The respondent's experience of the interview and his or her understanding of the research begins with the first contact. This contact may be a letter, telephone call, or printed advertisement soliciting participation. How the research is represented will affect how it is understood and thus forms part of the context in which the interview questions and answers must be understood. Great care must therefore be taken to ensure that how the research is represented is true to its purposes, clear about the requirements of participation, and not overly suggestive of the shape the data to be offered should take. For example, a study of how students cope with the stresses of graduate school might best be represented as a study of students' experiences in graduate school so as not to suggest to respondents that only the negative experiences and not the positive ones are of interest. Tausig and Freeman (1988) report, for example, that repeatedly emphasizing the fact that there were no right or wrong answers to the interview questions seemed to add to the candor of the responses offered in their follow-up study.

How the researcher conducts herself also makes an impression on respondents from the first contact to the last. Even if the initial solicitation to participate is relatively impersonal, such as by mail, at some point researcher and respondent must speak together to schedule and arrange the data gathering encounter. In order to feel motivated to give time and careful attention to the research, participants must feel respected and be convinced that they have something valuable to offer. They must also feel confident that they and the information they will offer will be correctly understood and that they are in the hands of a knowledgeable and competent professional who will handle them and their confidential data sensitively. If interviews are to be tape-recorded, for example, this fact should be made clear at the outset.

It is quite likely that potential respondents will ask questions about the research, how they were selected to participate and why, how the research data will be used in the end, and/or exactly what will be required of them. The interviewer who is also the researcher will clearly be well-equipped to answer these questions knowledgeably. In fact, the risk may be to assume too much rather than to seek out the underlying questions that may be on the potential respondent's mind. Preparing answers in advance to some of these common questions will be of great help.

Setting up a schedule of interviews can be a considerable challenge. Each interview requires time for planning the encounter, traveling to and from the chosen interview site (unless the telephone is used), doing the interview, and reviewing the data and record made of it after the fact. It is important to consider interviewer fatigue: There is a limit to the number of hours of interviewing that can be conducted effectively in any one day, especially if the time to record data and review the collected data are considered as well.

It is also useful to consider travel efficiency whenever possible in developing a data gathering schedule. Interviewer and respondent must each have a way to contact the other in the case of an emergency or if plans must change. If anyone is traveling to the interview, and that is most often the interviewer, clear directions must be available as well. Despite these scheduling pressures on the interviewer, the goal must be to plan the interview for a time and place convenient and agreeable to the respondent.

Finally, it is important for the interviewer to take a little time before each encounter to review the interview guide and the questioning process to be used, even if that is to follow the lead of the respondent. The preconceptions and expectations that the researcher brings to the situation should be remembered and set aside. The attitude to be cultivated is one of openness and genuine interest in what each new data gathering opportunity may yield.

The researcher-interviewer may be more tempted than others to take short-cuts in preparing for or processing data after the interview, but this temptation should be resisted. Events that seem indelible will fade in memory, and the apparent opportunity to work information in later, during analysis, will in actuality become a wish for a more detailed record from the field.

When the interviewer and the respondent differ in such characteristics as race, ethnicity, gender, or social class, researchers must consider the possibility that the interviewer and respondent may not share the same worldview, language about, or understanding of the phenomenon under study or of the interview situation itself. For example, in a needs assessment survey of a diverse community, it was noted that Navajo respondents consistently expressed fewer needs for services than those in other groups. However, to the Navajo person it is extremely rude to speculate upon the wishes or needs of others, to presume to know their desires and actions. Thus the person answering the survey for each Navajo household was not including his or her assessment of any other family member's needs as respondents from other groups did and as the question invited the respondent to do (Briggs 1986). Without the clarification of this cultural and linguistic difference, the data might have been interpreted to mean that there were fewer service needs among the Navajo in this community. The Navajo respondents did not "misunderstand" the question; they simply approached its answer within the cultural and linguistic norms of their own community and not those of the researchers.

While most common in the situation of cultural difference, such differences in understanding about process and substance are possible in any interview encounter. Briggs (1986) uses a sociolinguistic analysis of ethnographic interviewing to formulate a few suggestions for use in all types of interviews: (1) First learn through prior observation or reports in the literature about how the particular group of respondents typically express themselves; (2) Apply this knowledge to the design of the total interview encounter, including what means of recording to use; (3) Employ the reflexivity of the interview encounter to the advantage of the research by recording the interviewer behavior as carefully as that of the respondent and inviting comment on the interviewer as well as the interviewee after the fact; and (4) Carry this contextual understanding of the interview itself over into the analysis and interpretation of the data. While the analysis of the interview process need not overtake the analysis of its content, Briggs' injunction to "listen before you leap" is a helpful one.

Conducting the Interview

As the actual interview begins, the first order of business is usually a review of the ground rules for the conversation, such as those regarding the general purpose and scope of the research and those governing the interview data and their uses, such as confidentiality (see chapter 9 on ethics). Even issues discussed before, such as the use of a tape-recorder, should be reviewed again to ensure that the respondent is comfortable in the situation. Respondents have the right to change their minds about participation even after the interview is complete. Thus review and clarification of the ground rules is the only protection the researcher has against a "wasted" effort.

The early phase of the interview encounter, which often consists of the review of the ground rules and the gathering of more routine data, such as demographics, functions as the nonthreatening beginning during which rapport is built (Bunin et al. 1983). This phase is used by the interviewer and the respondent to learn and adjust to each other's conversational and cognitive styles. In flexible interviewing, as concepts and actors are introduced into the conversation, a mutual understanding of who or what is being named must be developed. For example, the graduate student asked about stresses may talk about "hassles," and this term may become the one used by both respondent and researcher if the latter becomes convinced that "hassles" to this respondent denotes what the researcher or another respondent might call "stresses." Making these adjustments can help the respondent to express feelings or describe experiences in a more powerful or realistic way.

These subtle adjustments that the interviewer makes to a respondent can be the source of problems as well. The less structured the interview method, the more likely that the interviewer as an actor may shape the data by what is asked and what is not asked. Conversely, the more structured the interview method, the more likely that a miscommunication or misunderstanding of the interview question or response will go uncorrected. Interviewer judgement and self-discipline are the only protection against both kinds of distortion in the data. The researcher-interviewer, whose knowledge of the research is thorough but whose investment in its results may also be very strong, may be especially challenged in keeping the flow of information in tune with the respondent's reality rather than the researcher's expectations. The capacity for self-observation and self-criticism, that is, an appreciation of the reflexivity of the interview situation, as well as anticipation of the standards of critical review by others, are the best safeguards in the interview process.

All interviews will come to an end, and care must be taken that the interviewee is allowed a period of closure especially if the interview material discussed has been sensitive or emotion-laden (Bunin et al. 1983; Tausig & Freeman 1988). It may be useful to include some questions specifically designed to help the respondent gain perspective or a sense of mastery of the material before the interview ends. Leave-taking may also be a time for new questions from the respondent or for recapitulating understandings reached earlier about the research. The respondent must always be provided with a way to reach the researcher after the fact.

Some researchers will offer respondents the opportunity to review data (tapes or transcripts) and to offer commentary or elaboration on it. More often, respondents may be offered some kind of summary report on the finished research or the chance to review any direct quotation used in a published report. Arrangements for any of these follow-up contacts are typically made at the end of the interview.

The period just following an interview is an important one for the researcher. Notes, observations, or impressions from the encounter should be recorded as soon after the fact as possible. The interview protocol or tape on which data have been recorded must be reviewed for completeness. Transcripts to be prepared must be complete, including the contributions of interviewer and respondent, and carefully done. Data recorded and prepared for analysis close to the time of the original interview can be reviewed with the actual interview still fresh in the researcher's mind.

Using Multiple Interviewers

When a large number of interviews is undertaken, it is often necessary to hire people to gather the data. This situation raises problems of reliability in addition to all of the problems of validity addressed above: The concern is that the interview data obtained by different interviewers from many different respondents be as similar in form and as comparable as possible. More structured methods of data gathering are generally used in this situation, both to aid in standardizing the data and in quantifying the data for analysis. Structured interviewing by multiple interviewers does not obviate the interactional variability of the interview situation. Orientation, training, and processing of the experience with the interviewers are all necessary for enhancing data collection and interpreting the data gathered.

Preparation for Interviewing

Interviewers hired to participate in data gathering need first and foremost to be oriented to the background, goals, and purposes of the research they will be contributing to. Even when the interviews to be conducted are highly structured, there will inevitably be situations in the field in which they will be called upon to make judgements and decisions affecting the data. These judgements are best when made with a full understanding of the issues under study and of the interview situation itself.

Training and orientation meetings for interviewers must include attention to both areas: the substance of the research and the nature of interviewing as a data gathering technique. Role playing and other participatory techniques are excellent training tools that can also be used to anticipate the problems or issues that may arise during the course of an interview in the field. Patton (1980), for example, gives excellent illustrations from training that he has conducted about ways to convey the importance of the wording of questions to interviewers.

It is best to begin training interviewers in the use of an interview protocol before the design of the interview guide is final. Pilot testing with various interviewers is as useful as pilot testing with a variety of potential respondents. Many useful suggestions for the improvement of interview protocols come from those who must use them every day in the field. Taking the input of interviewers seriously at the interview development stage also encourages conscientious reporting of problems and reactions later once the final data collection has begun. Only an attitude of acceptance and respect on the part of those directing the research will elicit full cooperation and information sharing from interviewers. Only complete contextual information, in turn, will allow accurate and valid interpretations of the data obtained.

The training of interviewers must also include sensitizing them to the interview context as outlined above. The interview is affected by everything from first recruitment contact to final farewell, and the interviewers must be taught to handle all parts of the encounter thoughtfully. The nature of their participation is indeed critical to the outcome of the research, and reminding them of this fact frequently can be highly motivating. To fail to do so, in turn, can be greatly demoralizing, leading to turnover and/or risking the quality of the data obtained.

Pay for interviews is typically made only for completed ones and must be generous enough to be fair when travel, a certain percentage of cancellations and rescheduling, and review and/or coding of the data after the fact are all taken into account. If people feel unfairly treated, the quality of the work is likely to suffer. As with respondents, the nature of the contract—what time will be paid for and what will not—must be clearly spelled out. It is customary to pay for time spent in training sessions and in meetings to underscore the importance of this part of the work.

Monitoring and Feedback

Once the interviewing process has begun, it is vital to continue close and regular communication with the interviewers. A large number of interviews and interview situations will mean that no matter how careful the pilot testing and preparation, new and unexpected challenges will occur in the field. All interviewers should be encouraged to bring these situations to the attention of the principal researcher for discussion, review, and mutual problem solving. The various solutions and improvised responses devised by the interviewers in the field should also be fully discussed and debated. It can be as dangerous to assume too much about what an interviewer may be experiencing or perceiving in the situation as it is to do so with a respondent. In either case, an important reality from the field may be missed.

If data gathering continues over a long period of time, it may be useful to revisit the interview role-play on occasion to ensure that there is not undue "drift" from methods and understandings worked out earlier. Any changes or adaptations uncovered should be considered messages from the field and not merely "mistakes" on the part of the interviewer whatever the response to them might ultimately be. Similarly, how the data are being reviewed and coded after the fact should be reviewed periodically as well. If the coding is not being done by the interviewers, questions arising in that process should be brought back to the group so the interviewers are aware of what happens to the data at the next stage and so that coders may learn what the interview experience actually was in a questionable situation.

When multiple interviewers are used to gather unstructured data it may be useful to have the interviewers review the transcripts for accuracy and completeness. Where part of a tape has been unintelligible to a transcriber, a participant in the original event who has spent some time listening to the voice of the respondent may be able to fill in the blanks. Particularly when multiple interviewers are used, it is essential that the interviewers' contributions, questions, and remarks be part of the record. Only then may the respondents' answers to questions be correctly understood in the context in which they were given.

Summary

Interviewing is probably the most widely used data gathering technique in social work and human services research. Because of its familiarity, its ubiquity in modern professional life, and the variety of forms it can take, the interview can be taken for granted and therefore misunderstood. The goal of any data collection technique is to yield reliable and valid data for analysis. New insights about the research interview drawn from sociolinguistics, ethnography, and other forms of flexible method research show great promise for increasing the validity of the information generated in all kinds of interviews. Whether conducted in person, by telephone, or in small groups, whether structured or unstructured in form or in the responses it elicits, the interview is an interaction shaped by both interviewer and respondent. By careful attention to context and by disciplined and reflective use of self by the interviewer, rich and meaningful data may be obtained to inform research of all kinds.

14

Questionnaire Design

Questionnaires and their derivatives, standardized checklists and rating scales, are among the most commonly used methods of data collection in social work and human services research, second only to interviews. Their popularity is at least in part a function of their compatibility with some fundamental American values, namely their coincidence with "rational" methods of mass production institutionalized in this country during the industrial revolution. The use of questionnaires also reflects the somewhat mechanistic views of research predominant in the social sciences in this century. However, as in other areas of research, concepts of questionnaire design have recently been changing based both on changing epistemologies and advances in the scientific understanding of how people actually respond to questionnaires (Aday 1989; Foddy 1993; Sudman & Bradburn 1982).

Standardized questionnaires were first developed as substitutes for assessment interviews. In psychology the first such questionnaire was the Woodworth Personal Data Sheet (PDQ), developed during World War I by Woodworth and his associates. This questionnaire was developed at the request of the United States Army, which was faced with the task of screening thousands of young men before sending them into combat in an effort to identify that subset who would be at special risk for psychological difficulties under the extreme stress of battle conditions in the trenches.

Woodworth and his colleagues used a very simple strategy to develop their screening questionnaire: They listed all those questions ordinarily asked during a standard psychiatric interview and expected the recruit to answer each honestly and validly. Examples of items from this scale include questions such as "I sometimes wet the bed" and "I frequently have nightmares." Although Woodworth's PDQ was never put to the test because World War I ended just as the instrument was being prepared for wide-scale application, its development did usher in a new era in research. A precedent had been set for gathering personal information using an impersonal technique. Moreover, a data collection method had been developed that was more efficient for mass application than the interview.

Today, however, understanding of the questionnaire is multifaceted, and sending out a questionnaire is seen as an occasion for interaction between the researcher and the participant rather than as a mechanical or impersonal process. Dillman (1978), for example, speaks of designing survey instruments to address a variety of intangibles: to enhance the rewards of participating, to reduce the costs of participating, and to build trust between researcher and participant. While much of this exchange may be between people who do not actually meet, these relationship factors should not be underestimated.

A *questionnaire* is simply a set of written questions that is self-administered, that is, answered by the person whom the data are meant to describe. A *rating scale* is a similar data collection instrument, that is, a set of written questions, but its purpose is to elicit a written description of one person by another. Some questionnaires are designed for one-time use in a particular study; others, termed standardized questionnaires or *scales,* are designed for use in any research situation to measure a specific concept or phenomenon.

Questionnaires can be administered in person, both individually or in groups, or mailed out. They are most often associated with survey research, that branch of descriptive research that aims to develop detailed information about a sample of respondents in order to make generalizations about a population of interest. A questionnaire or rating scale is always based on selected, predefined concepts or phenomena of interest to the research, and therefore questionnaires and rating scales can be used in any form of fixed method research: descriptive, relational, experimental, or even single-subject designs.

Because questionnaires are often used for efficiency when studying large groups, the responses they invite are usually structured rather than open-ended.[1] However, many elements of the questionnaire contribute to how it is perceived, how it is responded to, and the nature of the information it will yield. These include the content of the questions themselves, the nature of the response categories or the ways in which the respondent is invited to express the answers to the questions, the instructions provided, and the way in which the questionnaire is administered to or encountered by the respondent. Both advances in cognitive psychology and studies of how people have responded to questionnaires in past research have contributed to our present understanding of the questionnaire (Aday 1989; Foddy 1993). The questionnaire is now understood as part of a complex encounter between the researcher in absentia, the questionnaire itself, and the participant who is invited to respond and who may or may not take up that invitation in the way the researcher anticipated.

---

1. It should be noted that there are forms of written data collection that utilize open-ended responses. These are most often projective methods of psychological assessment that invite a respondent to "project" essential and even unconscious information about him- or herself in response to ambiguous or emotionally charged questions, such as to complete an unfinished story or to supply a written description of someone. While these techniques can be useful in some forms of research, they are not covered in this book because they generally require trained specialists for proper administration and interpretation.

When to Use a Questionnaire

Like all the methods used for gathering data in fixed method research, developing a structured questionnaire requires that the phenomena of interest be specified and defined before data collection begins. Developing a conceptual definition of each phenomenon to be studied is an essential first step. The questions on the questionnaire itself form what is traditionally termed the operational definition of the concept or concepts of interest.

Questionnaires, like interviews, are a form of verbal report. Questionnaires are often addressed to attitudes, opinion, and beliefs. They are also used to ask about behavior, especially behavior in the past or behavior that occurs in situations in which direct observation would be difficult or impossible. Nevertheless, it must be remembered that questionnaires (and interviews) provide *reports of behavior.* They capture what people *say* they do, which may or may not be the same as what they *actually* do or did.

A self-administered questionnaire can be used only when the phenomena of interest can be conceptually and operationally defined in a way that permits a written self-report to be given and the phenomena are in fact available to the respondent for self-report. Similarly, a rating scale can only be used when the phenomena of interest can be observed or are known by the rater. In fact data on a wide range of phenomena can indeed be gathered in this way, even some that do not initially appear to lend themselves to the method. The operational definition need not be confined to one question; it is often the answers to a whole series of questions that taken together define a concept or phenomenon. However, there still are some things that are very hard to capture in written self-reports. In these cases some other method of data collection, like interviewing or observation, should be employed instead.

In general, it often seems that the simplest way to find out about something is to ask someone about it, either through a questionnaire or through an interview, and often direct inquiry is the most appropriate way to extract information about a particular variable. Sometimes, however, it is not, and the researcher must make sure at the outset that the phenomenon to be measured will be accessible through the data collection method planned. For example, if what is being measured is thought to be unconscious or inaccessible to the person in whom it is being measured for any reason, then it would not be appropriate to expect a self-report methodology to be capable of measuring it directly. For example, consider the absurdity of inviting someone to "Please list in rank order your three most important unconscious conflicts."

Advantages of Questionnaires

The self-administered questionnaire as a data collection method is most often compared to structured telephone and face-to-face interviews, which also generally ask about things directly using a question and answer method. One major advantage a questionnaire confers in data collection is cost: It is by far the cheapest method for asking questions of large groups of people. Costs of printing and mailing, even when repeat or follow-up mailings are used, are never as great as the cost of interviewing would be. An additional advantage of the questionnaire that relates to cost is geography: If the goal of the study is to include a sample from a wide geographic area, a mailed questionnaire is always the cheapest way to do so.

The other most important advantage of the self-administered questionnaire is that it is sometimes easier for people to answer threatening questions privately on paper than to speak the answers aloud to someone else. Examples of areas that are usually considered threatening to respondents are questions about intimate or sexual behavior, illegal or socially sanctioned activities, or any opinion or behavior that the respondent may believe would occasion disapproval or punishment from others.

The relative safety of the questionnaire response stems from its anonymity: The respondent is not seen or heard and is usually guaranteed that he or she will not in any other way be identified with the specific responses made. Answering even nonthreatening questions can be easier when responses are anonymous. Because trust between researcher and respondent is essential in getting the most out of any data collection procedure, including the use of questionnaires, anonymity promised must be respected and delivered even when it makes conduct of the research more difficult or more costly.

However, whatever promises of anonymity may be made it is unreasonable to expect people to answer freely questions that they feel might put them in jeopardy. People in institutional settings are often justifiably concerned about the privacy of their responses. Questions about illegal activities or reportable problems like child abuse may not always be answered honestly for obvious reasons. This limitation is inherent in any self-report method.

In some ways, a questionnaire may seem a less reactive method of data collection than some others. After all, at least with mailed questionnaires, there is no observer or interviewer present for the respondent to react to positively or negatively. In addition, all copies of the questionnaire are identical. The questions and response options are standardized. Everyone who receives and responds to the questionnaire is encountering exactly the same material when they respond.

Finally, a questionnaire can be visually accessible. It can even incorporate visual aids and materials to illustrate its content or to aid in guiding responses. There has been a great deal of work done recently on how to make questionnaires visually appealing. The increasing accessibility of advanced graphic design and printing capabilities through the use of computer hardware and software has also contributed to raising standards for the appearance and visual appeal of questionnaires.

Disadvantages of Questionnaires

Questionnaires also have some major disadvantages. First, a self-administered written questionnaire can only be used with people who are literate. Even if the respondent can read, the type and level of language used must be as accessible as possible. If the questions are not comprehensible, they will not be answered or the answers given may reflect a misunderstanding of the text. In addition, the language in which the questionnaire is written must be considered as well.

Not all kinds of content can be easily translated or rendered in accessible language. Complex questions and the complex sequencing of questions, such as including many contingent questions to be answered depending on the responses to previous ones, create problems in self-administered questionnaires. These kinds of questions are generally handled more easily with trained interviewers. However, some techniques for making contingent questions as easy to follow as possible have been developed. In addition, including definitions of key concepts and terms used in questions and explanations of what is meant by specific response categories in the questionnaire itself can help enhance the accuracy of responses.

The *amount of data* to be gathered may be limited with a mailed or other written questionnaire because people are unlikely to respond at all to a thick, multipaged document. To read, think about, and write responses to many questions is often fatiguing for respondents, and the questionnaire as a whole may be rejected if respondents think it will involve too much work. Very lengthy data gathering seems to be most easily accepted when done by an interviewer in person (Aday 1989). Similarly, open-ended questions, especially those requiring the respondent to reply at length in writing, are difficult and tiring for most respondents to questionnaires. Often such questions on questionnaires are left unanswered or answered incompletely. However, higher response rates can be obtained with long questionnaires if sufficient attention is paid to the design of the instrument and to follow-up procedures (Dillman 1978).

The anonymity of the questionnaire, which can be such an advantage when sensitive data are needed, is a disadvantage, too: It is very easy for someone who receives a questionnaire in the mail simply to disregard it, to leave it partially answered, or to fill it out and fail to mail it back. Nonresponse rates are therefore quite high with mailed questionnaires. For this reason questionnaires are sometimes administered in person even though this obviates the potential advantages of complete anonymity and geographic flexibility. For example, questionnaires may be distributed in a classroom or at a meeting to be filled out and returned on the spot. However, even when filled out with a researcher present, the specific responses that the participant records can often be concealed, such as through use of a "ballot box" for their return, and in some circumstances this method can be successfully used to enhance response rates. With mailed questionnaires, too, a variety of techniques have been developed that have proven effective in enhancing response rates.

A final major disadvantage of the questionnaire compared to the interview is that there is no way to clarify or check on the respondent's understanding of the questions as the data are being provided. The response to each question is written down in isolation and later interpreted to mean what the researcher understood the question and specific response to mean; there is no way to know if the response intended by the participant was the one expected and assumed by the researcher. Often in interviews if a respondent looks puzzled or if later comments make it clear that a question was not understood as intended the interviewer and respondent can discuss and clear up the matter before the answer is recorded. Obviously this cannot be done using a mailed, self-administered survey.

In a self-administered questionnaire, a question not understood may be left unanswered, answered randomly, or answered inaccurately simply because the respondent did not understand the intent of the question. For this reason, use of a self-administered questionnaire requires the most exhaustive preparation, review, and testing of the data collection instrument prior to use of any data collection method. The work done in advance is designed to detect and correct as many potential misunderstandings before the fact as possible. It also requires that considerable energy be invested after the fact in reviewing the responses received and checking them for internal consistency and completeness before proceeding with any data analysis.

An Example of Using a Questionnaire

The Anderson and Mandell (1989) study of the use of self-disclosure among professional social workers illustrates the kind of situation in which survey questionnaires can be effectively used. Whether, when, and under what circumstances professionals should talk about themselves to clients, self-disclosure, has been a controversial topic. The first step in studying an issue and developing a structured data collection instrument to study it, such as a questionnaire, is to define the concept(s) of interest. Self-disclosure has been defined in a variety of ways. The literature review in the study describes and discusses how self-disclosure had previously been defined and measured and differentiates it from similar concepts, in particular the "self-involving response." Questionnaires can only be used effectively when the phenomenon of interest is both defined in itself and distinguished from other related phenomena, as it was in this study.

In addition, prior research was used to identify other factors, such as characteristics of the social worker, the stage of treatment, and characteristics of the client, which had previously been observed to bear on how self-disclosure is used. These factors, too, needed to be included in the questionnaire's content in order refine the description of how, when, and under what circumstances social workers reported using the technique.

Self-disclosure has historically been a controversial issue in the profession. The questionnaire format, then, not only made it easier to reach a statewide sample of social workers cheaply; it also afforded the respondents anonymity in reporting on a practice that they might potentially have been unwilling to discuss candidly in person.

When studying a professional group, some of the potential limitations of self-administered questionnaires may not obtain. Such respondents are literate; they are also likely to be familiar and comfortable with writing tasks and research procedures. The researchers most likely felt confident that respondents understood the questions asked and gave responses reflective of their actual experiences based on shared professional norms and commitments to knowledge development. However, Anderson and Mandell are careful to note that the key concept under study, self-disclosure, was defined in the cover letter that accompanied the questionnaire to help ensure that respondents and researchers were using the same frame of reference on the phenomenon being studied.

Nevertheless some of the disadvantages of questionnaires were still evident. For example, the overall response rate to the questionnaire was not especially high; only 41 percent of those surveyed returned the questionnaire. No information is offered on how complete the questionnaires received were. Nor does the article state whether or not any attempts were made to enhance response rates through follow-up mailings, as will be described below.

One strategy that Anderson and Mandell (1989) did use to enhance their study was to adapt parts of a preexisting instrument. The next chapter will discuss in depth how to go about selecting an existing instrument for use. Because it is so difficult to create standardized questionnaires, it is generally a good idea to take advantage of existing instruments when it is possible to do so. It is also important to note that Anderson and Mandell (1989) pilot tested their questionnaire on some experienced social workers who were not in the sample before mailing it out, an essential step. Pilot tests are done to identify questions that respondents find confusing and other problems with the questionnaire, which can then be rectified before data collection begins.

The Elements of a Questionnaire

There are several elements that must be considered when putting together a self-administered questionnaire. These include (1) the questionnaire itself, which may take the form of a booklet (Salant & Dillman 1994), including its content, the instructions for its use, and its appearance, such as its covers and decoration; (2) envelopes for the initial mailing and return of the questionnaire; (3) a cover letter or introductory statement on the questionnaire that speaks to the purposes and auspices of the study; and (4) any materials and procedures used for follow-up mailings to enhance the response rate in a survey. Attention to all these elements of question-naire design will improve the response rates and completeness of information obtained through self-administered questionnaires (Salent & Dillman 1994).

Creating Questions

Questions are the heart of any questionnaire. It is through the questions asked that the concepts and phenomena that are the focus of the research are represented to the informants who will participate in the research. Participants' efforts to describe their attitudes, opinions, knowledge, or experiences will only be successful if the questions on the questionnaire and the response choices offered can convey the information they wish to share effectively to the researcher. The principles outlined here for writing questions are no different when a structured interview protocol is being designed, and some of them apply as well to asking interview questions in flexible method studies when a standardized set of ques-tions is used (Patton 1980).

Defining the content. The initial definition used in developing questions about the phenomena of interest in a study should be a conceptual one, the definition that gives the abstract idea of each phenomenon to be measured. Several sources should be consulted when developing this definition. The first, of course, is the researcher's own notion of what the study, and hence the measure being constructed for it, is intended to find out about. For example, consider the situation of a student interested in measuring internalized homophobia (Rodriguez 1992). Available measures all indexed this phenomenon by measuring attitudes toward homosexuality, which this perceptive student recognized as conceptually and perhaps empirically quite distinct from attitudes about homosexuality with reference to oneself.

When first starting work, this student set down a working definition of internalized homophobia. In it he addressed matters such as whether the phenomenon was primarily conscious or unconscious, unitary or multidimensional, stable or situationally variable, and so forth. At first he considered only his own ideas about each of these matters. When developing a new measure, it is important to clarify one's own ideas and to describe clearly how they differ from others.

His next step, then, involved extensive reading and consideration of what other researchers said or implied about the concept. Some of what he needed to read was easy to find. Doing so involved only looking in the introductory sections of articles and books addressing the general topics of homosexuality and the sequelae of oppression. Other material was less accessible. This less accessible material included conceptual definitions offered by researchers who had developed related measures in the field, such as measures of attitudes toward homosexuality. It also included "reading between the lines" of other measures of homophobia to get a sense of how the concept might have been defined conceptually given the operations used to measure it.

Tracking down how other researchers or theorists conceived of a phenomenon will be more or less useful depending on how concordant one's own thinking is with the notions expressed by others. This step is indispensable; it is the step that ensures that one is taking advantage of whatever collective wisdom has accumulated in the field. This is not to say that a new study will adopt whatever even partial definition is suggested by prior work. In fact, especially if one is developing a new measure because of dissatisfaction with available ones, it is likely that there will be significant disagreement with previous definitions. However, existing definitions can suggest useful features to consider when developing a more satisfactory conception.

This conceptual definition is of more than academic importance. Frequently the conceptual definition will imply which of several possible data collection methods is more appropriate to use in measuring it. In the case of the work to measure internalized homophobia, for example, the decision about whether the phenomenon was primarily conscious as opposed to unconscious had major implications for whether it could be measured using self-report.

Recent attention to the importance of language itself in how ideas and experiences are understood has reminded us that the professional literature need and should not be the only source consulted to develop conceptual definitions. Particularly with words in both common and professional use, dictionaries can provide valuable information about how concepts should be defined. Since dictionaries capture natural language, they include popular denotations of terms. In some fields this information might not be useful, but in the social sciences where so many terms are socially defined dictionaries as repositories of the consensually held meanings of terms can be an invaluable resource for understanding common implications of terms and crafting the wording of questions.

A final source to consult when developing one's conceptual definition is people familiar with the concept in use. Two perspectives are equally essential: the perspective of those who engage in or are characterized by the concept to be measured, and professional experts familiar with those persons. In the case of internalized homophobia, for example, gay men and lesbians would be an important group to ask for definitions of the term, as would therapists and advocates with special expertise in working with gay male and lesbian clients.

On occasion it is important to insure that the conceptual definition in use successfully discriminates between the phenomenon to be measured and related but distinct ones. For example, when Poulin and Young (1997) developed the measure of the helping relationship in social work practice, they considered the ways in which such relationships are similar to the concept "working alliance" (Horvath & Greenberg 1989), "therapeutic alliance" (Hartley & Strupp 1983), and "helping alliance" (Luborsky et al. 1983) as discussed in the content of psychotherapy. However, they also concluded that the conceptualization of clinical social work includes a broader range of activities than does psychotherapy. Therefore they concluded that a new instrument was needed that captured both clinical social work and psychotherapy practice. Sometimes commonalities and differences between empirical procedures can be used in testing distinctions between definitions or measures, as when Poulin and Young (1997) compared client responses on their Helping Relationship Inventory to responses given by the same clients on existing scales measuring the working alliance in psychotherapy. Even if it is not feasible to use empirical procedures, it is still prudent to be sure that one's conceptual definition successfully distinguishes between the concept to be researched and other related but distinct terms. In all fixed method research, it is wise to consider whether one's definition is useful for both excluding what is not a part of the concept and including what is a part of the concept to be measured.

Writing Questions

Once the concepts under study have been carefully defined, the next step is to frame the questions that will represent it empirically. Sometimes a series of questions together represent some general concept in a scale; often, however, each question is written to capture a distinct piece of information and is separate conceptually from the others. Whether part of a scale or standing on its own, each question on a questionnaire must be crafted carefully in order to represent concepts accurately and make answering the question accurately as easy as possible.

Questions are, quite simply, composed of words, phrases, and sentences, and every word in a question counts. The words and phrases to be used in research questions should each be carefully chosen. Simple language is the best. Jargon, technical, and professional terms should be avoided or at least carefully defined for the respondent if a specialized term is used. When possible, the words used in questions should be those of everyday life that the respondent might use spontaneously to represent her or his experience or opinions. Slang, however, should be avoided because it changes so rapidly and is used differently among different groups. Inflammatory terms must never be used; racist or sexist language must also be avoided.

Questions should be phrased so that a full range of responses can be made. Because people usually find it easier to express agreement than disagreement, *leading questions* must be avoided:

Don't you think that the president is doing a good job?

This particular example is an easy one to detect. Yet, because the researcher typically has a point of view on the topic of the research, questions that subtly lead respondents toward one particular response rather than another can quite easily find their way onto a questionnaire.

Social desirability can also affect how people answer questions; people may find it easier to give an answer expressing an opinion or attitude that they think others are likely to approve of than one they might not. In such a situation, it can be helpful to phrase the question in such a way as to invite a range of responses:

Some people think that it is better for children with disabilities to attend school in the same classrooms as other children. Other people think that it is better for them to have separate classes. Do you favor or oppose combined classes?

The question is carefully framed to let the respondent know that any answer to this question will be viewed as acceptable. This example illustrates the point that while in general short questions are generally preferable to long ones, it may be better to use long questions when they are potentially threatening ones.

When people are answering a series of questions on a similar issue, a *response set* can develop. In particular, many people have a tendency automatically to say yes to questions rather than no. The problem of a response set can be corrected by altering the questions so that some require a yes, agree, or positive response to express an opinion and others require a no, agree, or negative response to express a similar opinion. For example:

Access to abortion should be restricted except when a mother's life is in danger.   [ ] AGREE   [ ] DISAGREE

Women should be able to obtain an abortion in the first trimester upon request.   [ ] AGREE   [ ] DISAGREE

Sometimes questions on a questionnaire can be worded in such a way that it is unclear what the response to the question means and unclear to many respondents exactly how they should answer. Double-barrelled questions in particular can cause problems:

Do you exercise regularly and limit what you eat?

The respondent who does both things can say yes, and the respondent who does neither can say no, but the person who does only one or the other might not know what to say. In addition, the researcher will never be entirely sure what each yes or no response means: Was it answered based on one (and which one?) or both of the weight management practices mentioned?

In general, long questions and sentences can be harder to understand than short ones. Keeping questions shorter may help avoid such problems as the double-barrelled question. Though in some cases the need to invite a range of responses or to explain concepts clearly may add to the length of the question. In short, there are no inviolable rules for writing good questions except in their result: that they be clear, to the point, and uniformly comprehensible to all of those who will encounter the questionnaire.

Overly complex wording of questions can result in inaccurate findings. When the Roper polling organization in a 1992 survey asked "Does it seem possible or does it seem impossible to you that the Nazi extermination of the Jews never happened?" 22 percent of respondents said it was "possible" it never happened. This finding that one in five Americans apparently doubted the existence of the Holocaust caused considerable concern. However, a revision of the question used by Roper in a 1994 poll yielded quite different results. When asked, "Does it seem possible to you that the Nazi extermination of the Jews never happened, or do you feel certain that it happened?" only 1 percent responded that it was "possible" (Kagay 1994), a result considered more representative of actual public opinions on the matter. The first version of the question contained what is termed a double negative, when the word *impossible* was paired with *never*. Questions containing double negatives are notoriously difficult to understand and to answer accurately.

The length of the questionnaire as a whole must be considered as well. Length can be expressed in two ways: the number of pages and the number of questions included or responses required. There are usually many things that the researcher would like to know about the people involved in a study. The difficulty usually lies in narrowing the questions down to a manageable number. In general, the shorter the questionnaire is, the easier it is to fill out and the higher the response rate will be. Specifically, it appears that once a questionnaire gets over 10–11 pages in length, response rates go down (Dillman 1978). Focusing the content on the main questions and purposes of the research is of course the best guideline for separating essential questions from those that are merely interesting and could be eliminated. Questions should be included because they are needed to answer the overarching research question, not just because it would be nice to know the answer (Salant & Dillman 1994). Naturally, much of the energy spent in designing mailed questionnaires is designed to make even long ones easy and inviting to complete.

Finally, a great deal of useful information can be gained by reserving some space at the end of the questionnaire for respondents' spontaneous comments. These may be comments on the survey itself, of course, but often they address some issue raised by the questions asked. In addition this option allows respondents who are feeling hemmed in by the prepared response categories to provide information about specific issues that might otherwise be missed entirely.

Shaping Responses

One factor in how questions are answered is the question; another is how the responses to the questions are shaped. Sometimes open-ended questions or partially open-ended questions are used in questionnaires when it is important to allow the respondents to supply unexpected answers or when elaboration of a specific response is needed. Most often, questions on questionnaires have structured, prespecified response categories.

When structured response categories are used, it is important to set off response options visually from the text of the questions. Note that the convention for response options recommended by Salant and Dillman (1994)—that questions be written in upper- and lower-case letters and that response options be written in uppercase letters only—is followed in these illustrations.

When structured response categories are used, an often-stated rule is that the categories be mutually exclusive and collectively exhaustive. Categories that are mutually exclusive are designed so that a respondent can place him- or herself in *one and only one* of the response categories listed. Categories that are collectively exhaustive means that there should be a category for everyone who will encounter the question.

Take the question commonly asked about marital status:

What is your marital status? (Check one.)

SINGLE	[ ]
MARRIED	[ ]
SEPARATED	[ ]
DIVORCED	[ ]
WIDOWED	[ ]

First of all, the question is somewhat ambiguous, since it does not specify *current* marital status. Therefore, the response categories will not be mutually exclusive for those respondents who have occupied more than one marital status in their lifetimes. A person who was once single and then married may now be divorced. While people tend to answer with their current status, one cannot be certain from the wording of the question that they have done so.

If asking about lifetime legal marital statuses, the question would have to be presented differently:

Have you ever been married?	[ ] YES	[ ] NO
Have you ever been separated?	[ ] YES	[ ] NO
Have you ever been divorced?	[ ] YES	[ ] NO
Have you ever been widowed?	[ ] YES	[ ] NO

Note that there is no question about being single since everyone begins life in that legal status. If a respondent were to answer no to all of the questions above, it could be correctly inferred that the respondent had never been married or in any other marital status.

The response categories in both questions above about marital status would be experienced by some respondents as not collectively exhaustive. People who are in committed relationships without being married, such as partners in gay, lesbian, or some heterosexual relationships, might not see themselves as single in the sense of being unattached or without an important social support even though they are not legally married. An alternative way to word a question might be:

How do you describe your current relationship status?

[ ] **NEVER MARRIED, NEVER IN A DOMESTIC PARTNERSHIP**
[ ] **MARRIED OR IN A DOMESTIC PARTNERSHIP**
[ ] **SEPARATED OR DIVORCED (INCLUDE DOMESTIC PARTNERSHIPS)**
[ ] **WIDOWED (INCLUDE DOMESTIC PARTNERSHIPS)**

Such a question includes a greater range of relationship situations, but it depends, in turn, on an understanding of the phrase, "domestic partnership," which is generally defined as a homosexual or heterosexual relationship involving cohabitation. If the phrase were unknown to respondents or if a respondent objected to a relationship classification system based either on legal definition or cohabitation, problems might still arise. Those who are formally engaged to be married might have difficulty deciding what to say, especially if they were not living together. Inclusion of an "other" response category, especially if accompanied by a request to specify what the "other" situation was, is a common technique used to ensure that the response options are exhaustive:

[ ] **OTHER (Please specify.)** _____

Several points are illustrated here. First of all, the way a question should be phrased depends entirely on the research context and its purpose. For example, if the study were about attitudes toward divorce laws, legal marital status and whether or not a respondent ever had a direct experience of a legal divorce might be the most important information to have. On the other hand, if it were important to know about social support, some form of the question that captures whether or not the respondent defines him- or herself as partnered may be more important. To ask such a question about partnering without including the range of possibilities would yield misleading data as well as create problems in answering for some respondents. Clearly the terminology to be used and the categories to include depend as well on the population group to whom the questionnaire will be administered. Even an apparently simple question can have a great deal of complexity, complexity that must be considered and worked out when the questionnaire is written, before the data are collected.

Response categories should always be designed so that some written response must be given. Otherwise an item left blank will be ambiguous, representing either a "not applicable" response or an item omitted. For example, a question on health services utilization could be worded as:

In the past six months, have you had an office visit with any of the following health care professionals? (Check all that apply.)

[ ] FAMILY DOCTOR OR PRIMARY CARE PHYSICIAN
[ ] MEDICAL SPECIALIST (DOCTOR WHO SPECIALIZES)
[ ] NURSE OR NURSE PRACTITIONER
[ ] DENTIST
[ ] DENTAL HYGIENIST
[ ] OTHER HEALTH CARE PROVIDER (Please specify.)

_____

If no visits had taken place, no responses would be marked, but the researcher would be unsure whether that was the case or the data were simply missing because the question had been skipped.

It might be better to write the question as:

In the past 6 months, have you had an office visit with:

a family doctor or primary care physician	[ ] YES	[ ] NO
a medical specialist (a doctor who specializes)	[ ] YES	[ ] NO
a nurse or nurse practitioner	[ ] YES	[ ] NO
a dentist	[ ] YES	[ ] NO
a dental hygienist	[ ] YES	[ ] NO
other health care provider	[ ] YES	[ ] NO

(Please specify.) _____

In the second version, nothing except perhaps the "specify" line is left blank unless a question has been skipped.

Response categories have a lot to do with how vague or precise the information gained from a question will be. For example, when asking about use of dental services, one might ask:

How often have you been to the dentist to have your teeth cleaned?

[ ] NEVER   [ ] A FEW TIMES   [ ] OFTEN

Only in the case of "never" is the meaning of the answer unambiguous. A more precise version of the question might be:

In the past two years, approximately how often have you been to the dentist's office to have your teeth cleaned?

[ ] NEVER
[ ] 1–2 APPOINTMENTS
[ ] 3–4 APPOINTMENTS
[ ] 5–6 APPOINTMENTS
[ ] MORE THAN 6 APPOINTMENTS

On the other hand, it may or may not be necessary to gain complete precision:

Exactly how many visits have you made to the dentist to have your teeth cleaned in the past two years? _____

Including the phrase "in the past two years" is referred to as a *bounded recall* (Sudman & Bradburn 1982), a technique that generally aids people in remembering accurately by putting some concrete limits on the task.

Note that the amount of precision demanded is a product both of how the question is worded and how the response categories are designed. The improved wording of the question in the second version wouldn't help much without improved response categories as well.

It is often harder for the respondent to come up with exact or precise information rather than more general responses. Respondents are not generally able to make finer discriminations when responding to a questionnaire than they ordinarily use when thinking about a topic. On the other hand, the researcher may have more flexibility in working with the data when more precise numerical information is available. The needs of the research in general and the data analysis in particular must therefore be weighed against the demands on respondents when deciding how much precision in answering to seek.

When questions are threatening, being *less precise* often helps people to answer questions more honestly. Even the dental question above could be seen as indicating whether or not the respondent was a "good citizen" (Sudman & Bradburn 1982) and thus be somewhat threatening, leading to overreporting of "good" behavior. Income and assets, for example, are generally underreported, and the use of categories rather than asking for exact income or wealth figures can make responses more accurate.

The question of precision comes up in a different way when using *Likert scales* for responses. A common example of these scales is found in the ubiquitous "satisfaction" questions, which often appear in the following general form:

How satisfied with X are you?

VERY DISSATISFIED				VERY SATISFIED
1	2	3	4	5

One issue in framing responses for questions like this one is how many points to include on the response scale. There is a great deal of difference for both respondent and researcher between giving only a **SATISFIED/DISSATISFIED** option and a 3-point, 5-point, or 7-point choice. This quality is termed *response latitude*. The larger the number of response points, or the greater the response latitude, the finer the distinctions that can be made between answers to different questions, but too few or too many possible responses will make it hard for the respondent to represent herself easily.

Using an odd number of response categories in scaled responses allows for a midrange or neutral response. Giving an even number of choices does not.

Respondents often like the neutral option, but the researcher may wish that respondents were more willing to commit to an opinion one way or the other and thus may prefer to use an even number of points on the scale.

The text that is used to describe the points on such a response scale are called *anchoring terms*. Note that in the example above anchoring words are given only for the end points on the scale; the meaning assigned by respondents to the other points on the continuum is inferred. It is possible, of course, to give anchoring terms for each point on the scale. For example, the response categories can appear simply as words to be circled rather than as numbers:

VERY   **VERY**

DISSATISFIED   **DISSATISFIED**   **MIXED**   **SATISFIED**   **SATISFIED**

The examples of Likert scale response categories given so far are *bipolar;* that is, the responses range from one extreme, of dissatisfaction, to another extreme, of satisfaction. It is also possible to write *unipolar* responses, ranging, for example, from **NOT AT ALL SATISFIED** to **EXTREMELY SATISFIED**. The absence of satisfaction may not be the same as the presence of active dissatisfaction. In addition no midpoint or neutral response is possible on a unipolar response continuum.

In general, the precoding of responses on questionnaires, that is, of assigning numerical codes to answers in advance and printing these along with the responses on the questionnaire itself, is no longer necessary. Because of advances in computer technology, data entry screens reproducing the questionnaire itself are now most often used, and coding, the assignment of numbers to specific responses, can be done by computer at the time of data entry.

Open-ended questions offer essentially infinite response latitude. Such questions are generally used on questionnaires only when it is impossible to specify in advance what the range of responses might be. An example already given is the **Please specify** question that follows an **OTHER** response. A risk in asking such a question is that the fact that a particular response was not mentioned may mean that it did not apply or that it simply did not occur to the respondent to mention it. Therefore if there are any particular responses of interest, these should be asked about directly.

Ordering the Questions

The *order* in which questions are presented on a questionnaire also has a great deal to do with how easily and accurately questions can be answered. Dillman (1978) makes the point that a questionnaire should begin with questions that will interest respondents and draw them into the process. Thus while routine demographic questions frequently begin interviews, they are often placed at the end of questionnaires.

It is generally said that questionnaires should begin with easy content. A questionnaire can appear like a test, suggesting right and wrong answers and a potentially difficult task. Encountering a few questions that are easy and interesting to answer at the beginning will encourage a respondent to begin and then complete the questionnaire.

The first question in particular is crucial. In addition to being interesting, it should be neutral and applicable to everyone, because no one wants to feel left out or uncomfortable in answering to begin with. Also, the first question should be related in some way to the main issues addressed in the study, which is what has drawn the respondent to participate in the first place.

There are no firm guidelines for the order in which to set items on a questionnaire, but responses will be affected by whatever has come before them, so that early items and the reactions to them will influence how later items are perceived and reacted to.

The content of the questionnaire, as in an interview, should lead the reader logically through the range of content to be covered. Questions on the same or similar content should most likely appear together on the questionnaire. If the questions refer to different time periods, questions about the same time period should be placed together. It might be helpful to the respondent to ask the questions in chronological order. In short, questions should be arranged so that recalling and organizing the information needed to give a response is as easy for the respondent as possible. As topics or time periods change, some text briefly providing transition for the respondent can be helpful as well.

A *funneling* technique is often used to order opinion or attitude questions. First, the broadest and most general question is asked, followed by more specific ones. For example, in asking questions about attitudes about abortion, one might first try to determine whether or not a respondent supports access to abortion in general and then follow with a series of more specific questions about particular circumstances or situations in which he or she might qualify his or her general opinion. Asking the specific questions first might influence the answer to the general one; in asking them afterward, they can be interpreted as qualifying (or not) the general opinion expressed to begin with.

Sometimes certain questions are only to be answered by some respondents based on an answer to a previous one. These contingency questions can create problems in guiding the respondent through the questionnaire. Visual aids, such as arrows and the placement of questions on a page, can make it much easier for a participants to find the specific questions that pertain to him or her. For example, if there are two options or sets of questions, presenting them in parallel columns on the page can be very effective. Arrows can be used to guide the respondent to the correct column.

Presentation of the Questions

The first step in developing a questionnaire is to write the questions and responses. Once the content of the questionnaire has been developed, it is necessary to present it visually in a way that is inviting and efficient. Principles of questionnaire design have as their goals enhancing both response rates and the accuracy of the data recorded.

Dillman (1978) suggests preparing a mailed questionnaire as a booklet with pages smaller than the standard 8.5" × 11" size. Whatever the size, a booklet format presents a polished-looking product in which a respondent will be expecting to find content on both sides of the page, an important bulk-saving feature of a good questionnaire. In addition, by folding the booklet, part of the back cover can be used for the mailing address, saving an envelope. The return envelope can be stapled in with the pages. The idea is that the questionnaire not look bulky, which may translate to the recipient as demanding.

Visually, each page of the questionnaire must be vertically organized, leading the eyes of a reader from one question downward to the next. Sometimes double columns are used to make maximal use of space while adhering to the principle of vertical organization. The layout of each page should also be carefully planned to avoid empty spaces or overcrowding of content.

While type size can be manipulated to save space and get more content onto each page, the type should not be so small as to present problems for the reader. Older people, for example, may have greater difficulty with small print than some other groups. Differing type sizes and styles can be used to set off sections of the questionnaire and to indicate clearly which parts of the text are *questions,* which are *responses,* and which are instructions or *transitions* between sections. Salant and Dillman (1994) recommend using upper- and lowercase type for questions and all uppercase type for response categories. While there is no universal standard for this currently in use, in every questionnaire questions, responses, and instructions should be consistently presented so that each is instantly recognizable visually for what it is.

Instructions are a key element in questionnaire design. In addition to educating the respondent in how to respond to the questions, they provide the context within which the answers will be given. There may be general instructions for the whole questionnaire:

> **Please answer the following questions candidly. There are no right or wrong answers. Answer by circling one of the responses next to each question. Please add any comments you may have on the last page.**

There may also be brief instructions limited to a single question: **CHECK ALL THAT APPLY** or **IF YES, GO TO QUESTION 32**. As already mentioned, an instruction like **GO TO QUESTION 32** should generally be accompanied by a visual aid, such an arrow, to make the transition easier.

In general, instructions should be kept to a minimum. As far as possible, questions should be clear and self-explanatory, requiring little special direction for answering. The layout of the questionnaire should make it easy to follow from one question to the next without a lot of instruction. However, simple directives can be a vital ingredient in helping a respondent complete a questionnaire with ease. In an interview, there would be "natural" conversational guidance for the participant; in a structured questionnaire, general guidance in how to approach the questions and explicit directions for how to answer them can be very helpful.

The *cover letter* that accompanies a questionnaire is also an essential element of the questionnaire. This letter describes the purpose of the research in such a way that the potential respondent can decide whether or not it deserves her or his participation. Explaining how results of a survey will be used to influence decisions that may matter to a respondent, for example, is likely to enhance response rates. Knowing the purpose of the research will also influence how the respondents interpret and answer the questions that are asked. Exactly how the purpose is explained is therefore important to consider.

Respondents should also be told in a cover letter that their participation is important to the success of the study. Knowing why they were chosen and how the information they provide will be used can help to explain to participants that their thoughtful participation is needed and that their responses will be put to good use. A statement like, "It is important to us to know what the people who use our services think about them," for example, can be used in an agency's client satisfaction survey for encouragement.

Who is sponsoring the research must also be stated in the cover letter. This information, too, can influence how questions are answered. For example, people might be moved to answer questions about their use of illegal substances differently in surveys sponsored by a law enforcement agency than by a health care organization. Overall response rates can also be affected by who is sponsoring the survey: A trusted local agency might have a higher percentage of questionnaires returned from a given community than a university-sponsored or governmental survey would. Visually, sponsorship can also be effectively conveyed through symbols, logos, and letterheads, which are additional assurances of the legitimacy of the enterprise.

Consent to participate in a mailed questionnaire study is generally given by the act of returning the questionnaire. Therefore, the cover letter must include any information about consent issues that the respondent should consider when deciding whether or not to complete and return the questionnaire. These include at a minimum whether or not the data will be anonymous or handled as confidential and the uses that will be made of it. If any sensitive information will be requested, a more formal consent procedure should be used (see chapter 9 on ethics).

In general, the cover letter is really the *invitation* to a potential respondent to contribute to the research. Like a consent form, it includes a kind of contract offered to the respondent by the researcher: If you will provide the kind of effort and information I am asking for here, I will indeed use the data in the way and for the purposes discussed. In reading the letter, the respondent should feel that she has something important to offer that will be of value not only to the worthwhile people sponsoring the research but to the larger issues that the study will address. Cover letters should be individually signed by the sender to emphasize the importance of each response.

The cover letter may not actually be a separate document. It can be printed right on the front cover of the booklet containing the questionnaire. Because the content of the cover letter is essential to the questionnaire itself, it might as well be an integral part of it. But if space in the booklet itself, which will be returned, is tight, a separate letter can be included.

Pilot Testing

Before a questionnaire is mailed out, it must be given a *pilot test,* given an extensive trial use. While pilot testing is necessary with all forms of data collection, it is especially vital with questionnaires because everything is preset before the instrument is used and because the participant does not have the chance to interact with the researcher once the data collection is underway.

Once the questionnaire materials have been perfected, a set should be prepared exactly as for its ultimate use. This set should first be administered in person to volunteers as much as possible like those who will receive the mailing, but who agree to give feedback as well as fill out the forms. After they have completed the questionnaire, they should be asked in detail for their candid reactions to the questions and the other materials. It is inevitable that some questions that seemed clear will be ambiguous or misunderstood, that their tone or wording may need to be changed, and that some response categories will prove unsatisfactory.

In addition to seeking the comments of those who used the instrument, the written responses should be carefully reviewed. Were responses clearly recorded? Were they internally consistent? Can they be coded and computer-entered readily in the form they were received? Were any parts of the questionnaire missed consistently? Revision of the questionnaire based on verbal feedback and the written pilot test responses will prevent costly mistakes in the final product.

Managing a Mailing

The low response rates to mailed questionnaires may be their greatest drawback. Therefore, the mailing of a questionnaire has as its goal achieving as a high a return as possible. The first and most important tool in getting a mailed questionnaire returned is to provide a *stamped, self-addressed envelope* to the respondent along with the questionnaire. The reason for this is obvious: The easier it is for the respondent to return the questionnaire, the more likely he or she is to do it. Salant and Dillman (1994) suggest that stamped return envelopes may get a slightly higher return rate than business reply mail envelopes do. Note that if the questionnaire is lengthy, additional postage may be required.

Another technique that has been used successfully in mailed surveys is to send reminders to nonrespondents. The problem is, if the questionnaire is truly anonymous, there is usually no way to know who has mailed the questionnaire back and who has not. Therefore, one good strategy is to send a *postcard reminder* out to everyone about a week after the survey is first mailed. This card should inform the recipient that the survey was sent; after all, it could have been lost in the mail. It should thank the recipients for sending back the questionnaire if they have already done so and remind them to do so if they have not. It should give a telephone number to call if a new copy of the survey is needed or if questions about the survey have come up. While mailing such a postcard is an additional expense, the return for this investment in additional questionnaires received is usually considerable.

Naturally, care must be taken in how such reminder cards are worded. A respondent has the right to refuse participation in the survey, and this right must be respected. On the other hand, most questionnaires that do not get returned do not represent a refusal but rather a lapse in the intention to return it. Any postcard reminder must be inviting and courteous with the goal of helping each respondent do what they wanted and intended to do anyway.

One way to determine who has responded to a mailed survey and who has not without compromising the anonymity of the questionnaire is to send a postcard with the original. This stamped, preprinted postcard simply states that the questionnaire was returned and bears the respondent's name. The respondent is to mail it back at the same time as the questionnaire but *separately,* simply to indicate that the survey was answered without attaching a name to the questionnaire itself.

When it is possible to identify whose questionnaires have been returned and whose have not, that is, when the separate postcard system has been used or when the survey is not anonymous, it is possible to send additional reminder mailings to nonrespondents. Salant and Dillman (1994) recommend that a second copy of the questionnaire be sent to identified nonrespondents with a shorter cover letter on the assumption that the first mailing may not have reached the intended recipient. A survey that is not returned in a couple of weeks is likely to be set aside indefinitely. This mailing is therefore scheduled for about three weeks after the original. Sometimes additional mailings to nonrespondents may be undertaken as well, all designed to ensure that as large and representative a sample as possible is obtained (see Salant & Dillman 1994).

Summary

Questionnaires have been successfully used for a number of years in social work and human services research, and recent advances in knowledge about questionnaire methods and data entry technology have made them even more effective. Although seemingly impersonal, the questionnaire method is best understood as an opportunity for interaction with a participant even though the interaction is not face-to-face. What is conveyed to the respondent in the wording of questions, the design of response categories, and the process of administering the questionnaire are all essential to a successful data gathering effort.

This chapter has given an overview of questionnaire design especially as it is used in mailed surveys. The principles of question writing are little different when applied to structured interviews conducted by telephone or in person. Because so much care must go into designing questions that people can answer easily and accurately, when possible it is helpful to use or incorporate existing questionnaires and scales when they are available. The next chapter covers how to select and evaluate such instruments. With careful attention to the design of the total process, questionnaires can be an efficient and effective method of data collection in fixed method research.

15

Selecting an Existing Measure

Developing structured data collection methods, whether for observation, interviews, or questionnaires, requires a great deal of hard work. Although in many cases data collection instruments unique to one specific study must be developed, because in fixed method research the data collection method is predefined it is often possible to use data collection instruments that already exist.

Given how difficult it is to develop structured ways of collecting data that describe many psychological, social, and interpersonal phenomena, many data collection instruments have been developed that are designed for use in a variety of studies. These existing instruments can often be adopted or adapted for use in social work research (Fischer & Corcoran 1994). Some, in fact, have been specifically designed for studying social work practice (Hudson 1982). The Gomez (1990) study reprinted in chapter 6 used existing measures, and the Anderson and Mandell survey (1989) reprinted in chapter 5 adapted an existing measure for use, illustrating how common this strategy is in social work and human service research. This chapter will cover the use of existing measures in social work and human service research: when to employ them and how to select among them.

While most standardized data collection instruments are *questionnaires,* that is, *written self-report* measures, other forms of data collection are represented as well. Some available instruments are *rating scales,* designed for either general or observational report on others. There are also standardized *interview* protocols widely used, for example, for diagnostic screening and epidemiological studies in health and mental health. Any of these data collection methods can be useful in fixed method studies by providing a predetermined way to describe a specific characteristic or phenomenon.

Whatever methods of data collection are used and whether the tools are designed for describing self or other, existing instruments have several features in common: they are standardized both in their content and how they are meant to be used and interpreted. Some are *normed,* that is, they include information about how some previous group or groups of respondents has scored on the measure, providing a standard against which an individual's score or a group's average score can be assessed.

Most of these measures are indexes or scales, that is, measures that use multiple questions or items to assess a single phenomenon or construct, or they may be *unidimensional,* assessing a single concept or phenomenon. Others are *multidimensional,* having one or more *subscales* or *factors,* each of which measures a distinct aspect or part of the total phenomenon. All of these characteristics, and others, must be considered whenever a data collection toll is selected for use. However, before going on to discuss the selection of such an instrument, it is important to consider how such data collection tools are developed in the first place.

Concepts in Instrument Development

Standardized measures "fix" or hold constant four things. The first is the content and wording of the items or questions themselves. The second is the set of response options that will be offered to respondents for reporting their "answers" to the questions. The third is the measurement context, including the instructions that will be given, time limits (if any), and all the other details about how the instrument is to be used. The fourth is the manner in which responses are to be handled in the analysis, that is, quantified or scored.

When selecting an existing measure, attention must be paid to how the instrument was first developed and for what purpose. The steps in developing a new measure are much like those described in the preceding chapters on observation, interviewing, and questionnaires. The major difference lies in the fact that, rather than relying on a set of single items to tap a variety of different attributes of respondents, as in the typical survey questionnaire, existing measures are generally designed to be indicators of complex characteristics, requiring many items or questions to assess each one.

Defining the Phenomenon

As in all measurement, definition of the concept or characteristic to be assessed is essential. A phenomenon like depression, for example, can be defined and viewed in a variety of ways, and how it is defined will, of course, affect how it is measured. Depression can be viewed as a clinical condition marked by symptoms; the Self-Rating Depression Scale (Zung 1975), for example, treats depression in this way, offering a checklist of the most common physical signs and symptoms. The Beck Depression Inventory (Beck & Steer 1987), by contrast, focuses on cognitive concerns, the typical thought patterns and ideas that people have when they are depressed. The Depressive Experiences Questionnaire (Blatt, D'Afflitti, & Quinlan 1979) offers yet another approach: It treats depressive feelings and moods as a potentially transitory but almost universal part of human emotional experience and seeks to differentiate between types of depressed mood. Finally, from the medical or psychiatric perspective, there are full-blown diagnostic tools such as the Schedule of Affective Disorders and Schizophrenia (SADS) interview (Endicott & Spitzer 1978) that are designed to diagnose a range of affective disorders, including depression. This list is by no means exhaustive as there are literally scores of existing measures for depression. It is only meant to illustrate that even when a concept of interest has been named and identified, exactly how it is defined will determine which, if any, existing measure may serve to measure it in a given study. In addition, the cultural context exerts a powerful effect on how a syndrome is defined that must be taken into account in cross-cultural research (Rogler 1999).

With phenomena that have a medical or psychiatric nature, it is important to recognize the difference between diagnostic and screening instruments and between research and clinical uses of them. Clinical diagnosis ordinarily takes place after careful in-person individual assessment; in fact, in all professional disciplines it is generally considered unethical to diagnose an individual outside of the context of a professional helping relationship including face-to-face contact. However, for research purposes there are a few existing instruments, generally standardized, in-depth interview protocols, that are indeed used for establishing a diagnosis for research purposes. Most instruments, however, can at best be considered screening tools, instruments, often for rapid assessment, that can identify people who *might* be found to carry a clinical diagnosis as compared to others who most likely would not. In fact, clinical diagnosis is often the criterion against which research and screening tools are measured when medical and psychiatric syndromes are assessed.

This notion of a criterion to which measurement results will be compared is a crucial one. In the helping professions, unlike many other fields, the phenomena studied are often intangible and subjectively defined. Affects like anxiety and depression, attitudes like authoritarianism or homophobia, behaviors like aggression and leadership, and cognitions like self-concept and body image are all designated on the basis of someone's subjective judgment. Much of what standardized questionnaires, interviews, and rating scales do, then, is make explicit and formalize a process to use that mimics other ways of classifying individuals on these subjectively determined dimensions. In addition, medical and mental health diagnosis is itself an inexact procedure. It is valuable not to lose sight of the fact that the success of some of the most well-developed, standardized data gathering tools is often based on identifying which subjectively defined and perhaps poorly understood category best characterizes the person on whom the measure is gathering data.

For example, there is consistent empirical evidence that the relationship between the helper and the client is a powerful contributor to successful results in psychotherapy and other forms of interpersonal helping. Therefore there has been great interest in assessing it for research purposes. One example of such an instrument is the Working Alliance Inventory (WAI) developed by Horvath and others (Horvath 1984; Horvath & Greenberg 1989). This instrument illustrates well how defining the concept to be measured is essential in developing and selecting a measurement tool. The WAI is based on a specific conceptualization of the helping relationship that is designed to be pantheoretical, that is, to be relevant whatever the theory—behavioral, psychodynamic, cognitive, or other—that is guiding the intervention. It draws on a theory that suggests that psychotherapeutic relationships have key aspects: bonds, goals, and tasks (Horvath & Greenberg 1989). Because worker and client perspectives on the relationship do not always agree, two versions of the measure were developed, one for use by therapists and one for use by clients (Horvath & Greenberg 1989). In deciding whether or not to use the WAI in a particular study, knowing about its theoretical origins is essential. For example, this tool was created based on theory and research about psychotherapy as a specific form of helping. This conceptual and definitional background, together with an examination of the items themselves and a review of subsequent research done using the instrument, is essential knowledge in deciding whether or not the WAI would be worth using in a given study.

The Content of the Instrument

Once the phenomenon to be measured has been defined, the next step is generating an item pool. This collection of items is generally much larger initially than it will be at the end of the process. The idea is to examine a large number of potentially useful items and then determine which of them will work the best to describe the phenomenon of interest and differentiate it from others.

A common strategy for item generation involves inventing potential scale items or questions based on the theoretical understanding of what the instrument is to measure. For example, in creating the WAI, a large pool of items was generated by using words and phrases from writings about the guiding theory about the working alliance (Horvath & Greenberg 1989). This pool of possible items was then narrowed down by asking for both expert psychologists and psychologists in practice to rate the relevance of each proposed item to the concept in question and to each of its three dimensions. The 36 items that most raters agreed were relevant were then edited and included in the instrument. A related strategy involves asking recognized experts on the topic to be studied to generate the potential items.

Another strategy in instrument development involves borrowing items from existing measures that seem to stand a good chance of working. This strategy is by no means plagiarism; it is a common practice, and credit is always given to the authors of the instrument from which items are drawn. Rather it reflects a process in which each new measurement effort attempts to improve upon previous ones.

For example, Poulin and Young (1997) used this strategy in developing a tool, the Helping Relationship Inventory (HRI), for assessing the strength of the helping relationship in social work practice. Conceptually, the authors of the new scale argued that the wording of the items in the various measures of the relationship based on psychotherapy, including the WAI, did not take into account the more varied activities, including advocacy and service linkage, that are part of what a social worker does. They also explicitly drew on self psychology as a theory when developing some of the items for the scale. Again, both client and worker forms of the instrument were developed (Poulin & Young 1997). Despite these important conceptual differences, there are some similarities in the concepts guiding these two scales, so older scales were consulted in developing the new one (Poulin & Young 1997). Therefore, the wording of some items is very similar (client items): "I am clear about what my responsibilities are in therapy" (WAI) and "How clear are you about what is expected in your work together?" (HRI) In this way, as new instruments are developed, they tend to build on each other, both conceptually and even in terms of what items are included.

It should be noted that some measures regard some items as being more important to, or saturated with, the quality being assessed than are others. These measures provide numbers, called scoring weights, to use for taking into account the differential importance of individual items in determining the final scale score. The Michigan Alcoholism Screening Test (MAST; Selzer 1971), for example, assigns a weight of 2 to the item quoted below about stopping drinking. In other words, when scoring, a "yes" response to an item about stopping drinking without a struggle counts for twice as much as a "yes" answer to an item with a weight of one, such as **Have you gotten into fights when drinking?** However, it counts for less than an item with a weight of 5, such as a "yes" to **Have you ever been in a hospital because of drinking?**. These weights are based on ideas about how important each item is in deciding whether or not, in this case, the respondent is likely to have a problem with alcohol that is serious enough to warrant treatment.

Response Options

After generating the item pool, the next task is designating what response options will be offered to respondents. In multi-item scales, these response options are generally the same across all or many of the items. This practice, which is designed to make responding easy, presents an additional challenge in writing the questions that will make up the instrument or scale since the wording of all of the questions must fit the response pattern to be used.

Standardized measures can offer a variety of response options. In general the various options vary along two features: the number of response dimensions offered and the number of response categories offered per dimension. The most restrictive response option format offers only one dimension and only two response categories on that dimension. The familiar **YES/NO** response format is a good example of this situation:

YES   NO   (2)   4. Can you stop drinking without a struggle after one or two drinks?

As this item illustrates, the response options offered on the Michigan Alcoholism Screening Test (MAST) (Selzer 1971) do not include any opportunity to indicate variability (sometimes yes, sometimes no) even though that may be common. Restricted response options like these are designed to force the respondent to commit to an answer despite some reluctance to do so, which seems appropriate to a screening device for a characteristic like alcoholism in which denial of the problem often plays a role.

In general, the more response dimensions one offers subjects, the more information one obtains, and the more response categories one offers respondents per dimension, the more precisely one is measuring the dimension being assessed. However, by including 25 different questions on the MAST screening instrument, many dimensions of drinking behavior are covered, and no one answer to any question is taken to represent the whole picture of the respondent's possible alcoholism.

There is another tool to measure substance use, the Chemical Dependency Assessment Profile (Honacker, Harrell, & Cimienro 1986) that illustrates a multidimensional response:

How many times have you stopped drinking and then started back?

(1) once	**(4) four times**
(2) twice	**(5) more than four times**
(3) three times	**(6) never**

Such a set of response choices is clearly designed to capture quantity rather than just a **YES/NO** response. A response of "once" or "four times" conveys a more nuanced picture than a simple "yes."

Some response options actually allow for multiple responses to the same question or item. Another item from the Chemical Dependency Assessment Profile (Honacker et al. 1986) illustrates such a question:

I have been arrested:*
(1) for being drunk and disorderly
(2) for driving under the influence of alcohol [DUI/DWI]
(3) for driving under the influence of drugs
(4) for buying drugs
(5) for selling drugs
(6) for other crimes committed while drinking or using drugs
(7) for reasons other than alcohol or drugs
(8) never

The asterisk references initial directions on the questionnaire that state: "A star * indicates that multiple options may be selected." For an item like this one, in fact, each answer option is treated in the analysis as a separate variable, and the question is handled by indicating whether or not each answer option was chosen in each case. However, to the participant, the item appears as one question to which multiple answers may be given.

Defining Subscales

The complex personal and interpersonal characteristics of importance to human service professionals are often considered to be multidimensional, that is, to have distinct but related aspects. For example, the theory on which the WAI is based suggests that the working alliance in psychotherapy has three dimensions: tasks, bond, and goals (Horvath & Greenberg 1989). The HRI, on the other hand, conceptualized two rather than three dimensions to the relationship: a structural one involving goals and tasks, and an interpersonal one reflecting the psychological bond between worker and client (Poulin & Young 1997). Every individual item or question on each of the scales is associated with one of the two or three dimensions, factors, or subscales that make up the whole.

Subscales are usually defined empirically as well as conceptually. For example, Poulin and Young (1997) used a common multivariate statistical technique called factor analysis to study whether the items they had developed for the HRI actually divided into two factors in the way theory had suggested. In fact they found that in both worker and client versions of the HRI, each of the two conceptual dimensions—structural and interpersonal—had two parts. For example, the structural dimension could be divided into items that were called planning (e.g., "How much have you and your social worker discussed the specific problem(s) with which you want help?") and action (e.g., "To what extent have you and your social worker discussed the specific actions you will take to address your difficulties?"). However, not all HRI items seemed to be strongly associated empirically with either factor, and a few items were statistically associated with both factors. This finding suggests, not surprisingly, that this new tool may require further work if the subscales are to be considered wholly useful.

Using the Instrument

An essential element of an existing instrument is the instructions that are given to those who will use it. Just like the questions that make up the scale, the instructions for use are always given in the same way each time an existing scale is used. For example, the instructions on the therapist version of the WAI (Horvath 1984) read:

> **On the following pages there are statements that describe some of the different ways a person might think or feel about his or her client. As you read the sentences mentally insert the name of your client in place of _____ in the text.**
>
> **Below each statement there is a seven-point scale:**
>
> | 1 | 2 | 3 | 4 | 5 | 6 | 7 |
> |---|---|---|---|---|---|---|
> | **Never** | **Rarely** | **Occasionally** | **Sometimes** | **Often** | **Very Often** | **Always** |
>
> **If the statement describes the way you *always* feel (or think) circle the number 7; if it *never* applies to you circle the number 1. Use the numbers in between to describe the variations between these extremes.**
>
> **Work fast, your first impressions are the ones we would like to see. (PLEASE DON'T FORGET TO RESPOND TO EVERY ITEM.)**
>
> **Thank you for your cooperation.**

Notice that these instructions do many things. They explain what the response categories should be used to represent and how to mark them (by circling a number). They explain what to do with items that look like this:

5. I feel I really understand _____.

1	2	3	4	5	6	7
Never	**Rarely**	**Occasionally**	**Sometimes**	**Often**	**Very Often**	**Always**

They also let the respondent know that it is first impressions that should be given, and they encourage completion of the whole instrument.

Matters in addition to the instructions have to be fixed. Perhaps most important is the order in which the questions are presented. It is intuitively obvious that the order in which questions come will have an effect on the answers that are given. The fact that a given question has been asked will influence how one reads and responds to all the questions that follow.

Standardized measures present the items or questions in a standard order; whatever these order effects are, then, becomes a property built into the measure. This property, that is, the influence of question order, is only one of the properties that must be understood about a measure. In fact, perhaps the greatest advantage standardized measures have to offer is the information that is available on them from prior research about their various properties.

Reliability and Validity

Once an instrument has been developed, its reliability and validity must be demonstrated and reported. A reliable instrument is one that gives a consistent result when the phenomenon being measured is not changing and which is also sensitive enough to show change when change has occurred. Measures that are multi-item scales or indexes also must have a form of reliability called internal consistency; that is, items that together constitute indicators of a whole should vary similarly, and, conversely, items that are part of different scales or subscales should show different patterns of variation or correlation. Validity means that the scores obtained reflect something substantive and that they reflect the specific phenomenon that was intended. The various forms of measuring the reliability and validity of multi-item measures are described and discussed in chapter 11.

An existing measure is often chosen for use because its reliability and validity have already been demonstrated in use. However, these properties—reliability and validity—are not necessarily the same under different conditions of use. They must be examined again, study by study, each time a scale is used.

Other Features of Existing Instruments

As computers have become more common, many scale developers have invented ways to computerize the data entry, scoring, and, in some cases, even the administration of existing measures and the interpretation of results. In addition to facilitating the efficiency with which existing scales can be scored, computerized data entry and scoring systems often also include mechanisms to check on the accuracy of the data that has been entered. In addition, when the calculation of subscale scores is automated in this way, they are ensured of being accurate. Report-writing functions, including often the graphical display of results, are often incorporated as well.

Once an instrument has been standardized, detected problems can only be acknowledged, not fixed. Therefore, many standardized instruments that have been used for a number of years have undergone revisions. Most popular measures that stay around for a while are eventually subjected to revision, if for no other reason than to update the language used in the item wording. For example, one widely used assessment tool related to alcohol and drug use, the Addiction Severity Index (ASI), originally developed using a sample of men, has recently been revised to incorporate content that improves its applicability to women (McLellan et al. 1992). The advantages of such a revision are expected to outweigh the disadvantages of losing the value of all the data accumulated with the prior forms (i.e., the special scales, normative data, etc.). Whenever measures are revised, work on demonstrating their properties, their reliability and validity, must be done again because what was true of the older version may not be true of the instrument as revised.

In addition, some measures will offer various forms. For example, the well-known measure of children's emotional and behavioral problems, the Child Behavior Checklist, has three versions: a parent report form (Achenbach & Edelbrock 1983), a teacher report form (Achenbach & Edelbrock 1983), and even a Youth Self-Report form (Achenbach & Edelbrock 1987) that can be used by children aged eleven or older. Item content and the subscales derived from them are similar although not identical in the three different versions. Intelligence tests and other similar measures, on the other hand, often come in different versions or editions that are meant to be scored and interpreted identically.

The Problems with Standardized Measures

The advantages of using existing instruments in fixed method research should by now seem obvious, but there are a number of serious problems that can occur with their use. The history of the measurement of intelligence provides some the best-known examples of the kinds of problems that can occur in using standardized tests and measurements. As has been illustrated, standardized measures are often developed incrementally, reflecting concepts that have acquired a specific meaning and set of implications, and then tested against criteria that have their own meanings and implications. In the case of intelligence, for example, Gould (1981) has argued that the concept of intelligence itself was invented at least in part to capture that quality of human beings that was thought to differ by race, itself a problematic concept. Although some would disagree with him, racist thought, Gould asserts, is built in to the very concept of intelligence as well as into the measures invented to assess it. He also discusses some dramatic historical instances of scientific error and fraud that have tended to justify a view of intelligence as race-based or heritable in any way.

Most concepts that have been studied using standardized measures have not proven as controversial as intelligence has. However, as has already been noted, the usefulness of an existing measure depends primarily on how the concept it assesses is defined. Qualities may be defined in ways that tend to stigmatize certain groups (Herek et al. 1991). If so, any measure based on them will have limited, if any, real utility.

Another way in which existing instruments can be limited is by the population groups used when they were developed and on which they have been used since. For example, the ASI (McClellan et al. 1992) already mentioned, is an instrument widely used to measure the severity of the problems a person is encountering as a result of substance use. It was originally developed in the Veteran's Administration system in the 1970s. As such, the population used in its development was largely male. Was the question about hospitalization meant to include childbirth or not? If included, it could contribute to making childbearing women look more "impaired" than otherwise comparable males. How could part-time employment be recorded? Where was any content on a history of childhood sexual or physical abuse, widely acknowledged to be a precursor to substance use in many women? Subsequently additional work had to be done to make the ASI more applicable to women and the ways in which substance use problems may manifest in them, work that is being reflected in newer editions of the instrument (McLellan et al. 1992). In this case, it is not the very concept itself, addiction, that has been questioned; it is the fact that addiction and its problems may be manifested in different ways in different population groups, in this case men and women.

This problem, of the representativeness of the groups on which instruments are developed and normed, is a very common one. Most measures are developed using European American, middle-class samples that are assumed to be heterosexual, reflecting the groups most easily accessible to those typically doing the research and the assumptions that many researchers have traditionally brought to their work. When studying groups that differ in composition from those originally used or assumed, it is essential that measures developed and/or validated for use with such groups be employed. However, it should be noted that the definitions of concepts or phenomena may not be transferable in exactly the same form across different cultural or social groups, therefore making adaptation impossible (Rogler, 1999).

The use of the results of standardized tests to allocate resources or access, as, for example, in using intelligence testing to decide what kind of schooling a person may receive, makes knowing about any biases that may be embedded in such measures essential. In the research context, measurement is not performed for the purpose of decision making about individuals, as in some testing situations. However, population groups or program outcomes may be characterized by what an existing instrument shows in research. For example, a program using the ASI to measure its success in treating clients' addiction must ensure that the kinds of problems and outcomes its clients are likely to encounter are indeed reflected in the measure used to assess them.

There is one final disadvantage in using an existing instrument, one that grows from an advantage: that the method has been used before, allowing comparison across studies. This tradition of use can feed a tendency to reify the measurement, that is, to treat the measure or the score derived from it as directly representative of a concept or thing. Measurement in science is only approximate; in the social and psychological sciences, this approximation is often very evident. The use of existing or standardized measures, however, can tend to obscure that fact. It is easy to forget that the concept is not there exactly in the measure, even in ideal use, and that the use of a measure in any particular instance is never an exact rendering of reality on that occasion either. In particular, the concept and the instrument may need some adaptation in cross-cultural research (Rogler 1999).

Why Standardize?

Despite these potential disadvantages, it turns out that there can be certain advantages to having and using standardized measures. One situation in which standardized measures are enormously useful is in providing a common metric for describing disparate individuals and groups of individuals. When such instruments are administered in a standardized fashion, comparisons across individuals and across studies can be more reliably made than when differing measures are used.

There is one special circumstance for which such comparisons are especially useful. It is becoming more and more common to conduct what is known as meta-analysis. In this kind of research, there is an interest in combining and analyzing results across multiple, separate studies in order to determine what the overall research in a specific area of research shows. To the extent that different studies include common measures, such comparisons are more direct.

Most standardized measures and rating scales have been subjected to intensive study of their previous use. Their reliability and validity has been documented by the instrument developer and in other prior studies. The strength of these measures, then, lies in the fact that they are to some extent known quantities.

Weighing the Pros and Cons of Measures

There are many factors to consider in deciding whether or not to use a given standardized measure. The first and most important is how closely the developer's concept of the phenomenon being measured matches the conceptualization used in the present study. Generally the fit is not perfect. An existing instrument may only approximate the definition of the phenomenon the researcher actually wants to study. Where the correspondence in definition is very close, it is generally better to use the already developed measure. Where the fit is not close and in fact is unacceptably distant, it is generally better for the researcher to develop a novel measure.

Even when a developer's conceptual definition of the measured variable may be a close fit with the conceptual definition used in a new study, the operational definition may be quite different. For example, even when two instruments purport to measure similar things, the way the idea is languaged can be quite different. For example, similar content in the WAI (Horvath 1984) and the HRI (Poulin & Young 1997) illustrates this well. The WAI asks a question worded **I feel comfortable with** _____. The HRI has an item worded **Do you enjoy meeting and talking with your client?** One is a statement that invokes the client's name and should be answered on a 7-point scale of "never" to "always." The other is in the form of a question that is to be answered on a 5-point scale ranging from "not at all" to "a great deal." Both items are clearly meant to assess the emotional bond that the worker or therapist feels toward the client. However, the connotations of "feeling comfortable with" and "enjoying meeting and talking with" may be quite different. The WAI includes items that are worded in the positive and the negative: **I have doubts about what we are trying to accomplish in therapy** and **I am confident in my ability to help** _____. The HRI puts all of the items in the positive, perhaps in part because it contains fewer items (20) than the WAI (36). In sum, then, it is important when selecting an instrument to be sure that there is a close match between the measured variable(s) as operationalized and the phenomenon to be studied.

As already emphasized, who the measure is appropriate for is also an essential consideration. When there is no history of developing, adapting, or using a particular instrument with the specific population to be studied, it is generally considered risky to use an existing measure. This is a judgement call, however, depending both on knowledge of how the phenomenon is conceptualized in the original measure and how it might be expected to be evidenced similarly or differently in the new group to be studied. Sometimes existing measures can be adapted for use in the new context, but the instrument must then be treated to some extent as a new one since changes have indeed been made. However, when a measure has successfully been used in groups and contexts like the one being studied, it is best to adopt it rather than to try to create a new one from scratch, a considerable piece of work in itself.

When an instrument includes norms, or scores against which to compare individuals or groups, the question of who the measure has been used for becomes especially important. Interpretations of scores on such a measurement are standardized by placing obtained scores in the context of the distribution of scores obtained by the normative sample on which the measure was standardized. The value of a particular standardized measure for a particular piece of research is at least in part, then, a function of whether the sample on which the normative data were gathered is relevant to the intended study sample. If not, the measure or at least the norms should not be used.

When a new measure is used or a measure is being used in a new context, it is often wise when possible to include at least one existing, accepted measure in the study as an anchor for legitimizing the new one. At the least, the old measure will provide some accepted and generally meaningful descriptive information about the sample studied in the work. Poulin and Young (1997), for example, administered the WAI as well as their new HRI to both clients and workers in their study. They found that correlations between how workers and clients rated the relationships on the HRI and the WAI were high, which in this case suggests that the HRI as a whole taps into something similar to what the WAI measures in the clinical social work practice situation. This strategy is only possible, of course, if there is an existing measure suitable to the group to begin with.

There are other characteristics of a potential measure to consider, such as its dimensionality. In every measurement situation, there is a limit to the amount of information that can be gathered. Given this constraint, any researcher must make the decision about how much territory to try to cover with a given measure. The more territory that a measure covers, the less detailed the picture of any given piece of it will be. In audiophile terminology, if one is interested in accessing a broad band or wide range of frequencies, one must sacrifice clarity or fidelity in the reproduction of the specific sounds. The opposite also holds true: If one is willing to assess only a narrow range of functioning, one can typically obtain a much more precise (i.e., accurate) measure of that narrow band.

This phenomenon has several implications for selecting an instrument. Almost every phenomenon can be measured on a very broad scale, and many can also be broken down into subdimensions as well. The Child Behavior Checklist (Achenbach & Edelbrock 1983), for example, offers both broad band factors, or scores to measures general dimensions of functioning such as internalizing and externalizing behavior, and narrow band factors, or scores to measure specific behavior problems, such as aggressivity. The dimensionality of a possible instrument is thus one other characteristic that must be considered when a choice is made.

Another characteristic to consider is the *range* of the phenomenon that a measure can best capture. An instrument will be useful for a given researcher only if that measure is sensitive to variations at the point in the scale where the study sample is likely to fall. For example, an intelligence test that is very good at discriminating between persons who are gifted and those who are of average intelligence may be of very limited value in a study designed to measure differences in aptitude in a sample of persons all of whom are very bright. The Achenbach measures of child behavior problems (Achenbach & Edelbrock 1983), for example, work better for distinguishing nonclinical from clinical populations of children than for discriminating among the problems experienced by severely disturbed children.

There is another implication of this point for selecting a measure. Some instruments, like Achenbach's Child Behavior Checklist (Achenbach & Edelbrock 1983), were designed to be what is known as omnibus measures. Such measures were designed to measure, as the name implies, a little bit about almost everything, in this case every possible aspect of childhood behavior problems. Such instruments have attained respectability but as omnibus measures, not in parts. If a particular researcher is interested in measuring a component from such an omnibus measure, that is, a subscale from it, it is important to evaluate that subscale's separate psychometric properties and to be sure they are sufficient for the measurement purpose. It would be wrong to assume the value of a particular scale only on the basis of the value of the overall measure from which it is drawn.

Another key feature to consider is the stability/sensitivity balance. As was discussed in chapter 11, a key characteristic of any measure is reliability: Scores can only be useful to the extent that they are consistent when there has been no real change. In like manner, however, when a measure is being used to detect differences, whether differences between people or in the same person at different points in time, scores from it will be useful only to the extent that they are different when differences occur. Some measures are built to capture enduring phenomena, to be more resilient and therefore to provide more consistent scores; others are built to capture changing states, to be more sensitive to change. For those familiar with the history of testing and measurement, this continuum has been described as the trait-state. Trait anxiety, for instance, is considered to be relatively immune to momentary changes, while state anxiety is considered to fluctuate markedly within relatively short periods of time. When evaluating a measure, it is important to determine whether the instrument's point on the stability/sensitivity continuum matches the researcher's need, given the study's intent.

Some existing measures are quite long; others are short, often termed rapid assessment instruments. Longer instruments are useful only in some situations and generally when administered only once. In other situations, and often when administered repeatedly, as in single-subject designs, shorter, rapid assessment measures are preferable.

When a self-report measure is being considered, does it have an appropriate mix of subtle and obvious items? There are some situations that are unusually sensitive, and in which the use of terms that are somewhat subtle and indirect can be important. If saturated with obvious items, that is, items whose intent is very clear, a measure that has great value in a benign situation may be much less valuable in an emotionally sensitive one. It is unreasonable to expect people who encounter a measure to behave in ways that they do not perceive to be in their own best interests. In such a situation, the inclusion of subtle items and other ways to handle sensitive responses (see chapter 14 on questionnaires) may be important.

There are many pragmatic issues to consider when selecting a measure as well. One of them is what the instrument *costs*. Many well-known standardized measures have been copyrighted and are marketed by for-profit publishing companies. Sometimes these companies, or the authors of the instruments they are publishing, will forego all but nominal charges if they know an individual is interested in using one or more of their measures for research purposes, particularly student research (provided, of course, that appropriate acknowledgment is given to the authors and publisher). Such generosity is by no means, however, universally the case. There may be considerable cost involved when it is not.

There may be additional, less obvious costs to using a published measure as well. Manuals to guide the use and interpretation of measures must be purchased. Computer programs for data entry or analysis may also be available for sale. In addition, many individually administered, standardized tests, including projective measures, often require skilled, and therefore expensive, examiners or training. Skilled scorers may also be required. When considering whether to use a published measure, then, the cost of the use of the measure in addition to the cost of its purchase must be considered.

It should be noted that some instruments, notably those developed using public funds, are in the public domain and thus available for use at nominal or no cost. Other instruments are developed for research purposes only and are not commercially or privately published. The holders of copyrights to such instruments normally require that another researcher obtain written permission for their use and of course require acknowledgement of the source but do not charge for copies or manuals (except, perhaps, for the cost of duplication). Such individuals may request or require a report on the instrument's subsequent use and on the results of the study, however.

Finally, a practical but basic and essential characteristic of an existing measure to consider is the language used (see chapter 14). If it is a self-report measure, are the questions written at a level that respondents can readily read, understand, and relate to? Is it in the language they customarily use? Most people read and understand best when the words and sentence structures used are relatively simple.

Where to Find Existing Measures

Given the obvious importance of selecting good measures, it is important to consult as many sources as possible to identify all the alternatives available. There are many things to consider when selecting an existing measure, and no available measure will fit the researcher's needs perfectly. The task at hand, then, is not to find the perfect measure or set of measures; it is to find a good enough measure. Being good enough means providing credible data that bear meaningfully on the research question as the researcher has framed it.

Locating possibly useful measures and then determining whether each specific instrument is or is not good enough requires considerable effort. While it can seem tedious, expending sufficient effort on this phase of planning a piece of research is an enormously important and prudent investment. The best research idea in the world will come to naught if mistakes are made in the nature of the measures used to assess the major variables in a given piece of research.

It will be recalled that "looking to see" is at the heart of empiricism and therefore of the scientific method. It is the instruments chosen that provide the researcher's method of "looking to see" in fixed method research. If the methods chosen are not good, that is, if they work like a pair of dirty eyeglasses, then the data they generate will not provide a good image of what is there to be seen. More than one well designed study has failed because the measures it included were not good enough to detect what was there in reality.

There are a variety of resources for finding preexisting measures. A number of reference books have been published as guides to existing instruments. Some guides are specialized in some way and include both commercially published and research instruments. There are guides for instruments on social functioning (Lake, Niles, & Earle 1973); depression (Marsella, Hirschfeld, & Katz 1987); attitudes (Robinson & Shaver 1973); gender roles (Beere 1990a) and gender issues (Beere 1990b); for African American poplulations (Jones 1996) and psychotherapy change (Waskow & Parloff 1975), to name only a few. A good reference librarian can be invaluable in identifying sourcebooks and bibliographies of existing measures.

Some guides to existing measures merely compile them. Others offer reviews or critiques of the measures themselves. These reviews are typically written by researchers knowledgeable about psychometrics and the specific content of the measure; their intent is to provide an unbiased, and often slightly critical, assessment of the measure's strengths and weaknesses as an instrument. Whenever possible it is valuable to find and compare the content of more than one review of a given measure, since different reviewers will evaluate it from different perspectives.

Reviews are enormously valuable in helping someone unfamiliar with a measure evaluate the probable value of that measure for their own purposes.

In social work there are two guides to measures that deserve mention. The first is Hudson's *Clinical Measurement Package* (1982), a guide to a series of rapid assessment measures developed by the author for use in a variety of direct practice situations. The instruments are short and designed for rapid and repeat assessments as might be necessary in single-subject research. The other is *Measures for Clinical Practice: A Sourcebook*, two volumes edited by Fischer and Corcoran (1994). This book includes scales from a number of authors covering a range of characteristics and issues, some designed for use with adults, children, couples, and families.

When planning a study in an unfamiliar content area, one of the first things any researcher should do is carefully study what data collection methods have been used by other researchers also working in the field. If the area is a new one, that is, one where not much research has been done before, then it is important to consult the literature for the methods that have been used to study related questions or areas. It is particularly important to consult carefully the part of the methods section of published studies that describes the measure(s) used to assess the study variable(s). In addition, some journals publish articles reviewing individual or collections of measures. These articles can be located in the same way as other kinds of articles using guides to the literature (see chapter 2).

As promising measures are located, one should not stop at finding the written description of them. It is often useful, when possible, to get in contact with the person(s) who developed the instrument as well as with other researchers who have used it, to ask directly about their experiences with and professional evaluation of the strengths and weaknesses of the measure. This person-to-person contact is crucially important, since much more is usually known by people familiar with a research area than can ever be, or is, communicated in written research reports. While it is lamentable that professional publication styles have evolved such formal rules that more of this information about researcher impressions is rarely published, researchers are often eager to share it with one another, since only by taking this first-hand, informal knowledge into account can better research be planned.

For most standardized measures, certainly all copyrighted ones, a formal manual is available. This manual of course provides information about how to administer and score the instrument. Most importantly, it also usually provides information about its development. The developer's definition of the measured construct and a description of the procedures used to generate and select items, to assign items to subscales (if applicable), and to determine the scoring procedure should all be reported in the manual. Information concerning the measure's reliability and empirical (as opposed to face) validity should also be reported. It is also important to know something about the people on whom the measure was first used when it was developed. Preferably, some of the research evaluating the psychometric properties of the measure should have been conducted by researchers other than the one(s) who developed it, and for well-established measures reference to such studies is often also included.

An essential part of evaluating a measure's value for a particular study is, of course, carefully examining an actual copy of the instrument. In addition, a measure should be informally tried out in use. For example, a researcher can administer a self-report measure to him- or herself to get firsthand knowledge of what it might feel like to use the measure. It is also useful to ask others to self-administer the measure and provide feedback on the experience. Similarly, a rating scale should also be tried out personally before deciding to adopt it.

It should be noted that guides to existing instruments and journal articles usually do not contain copies of actual measures, and it often requires an extra step to acquire them. Companies that publish copyrighted instruments commercially usually will supply an examination copy free or at nominal charge. Theses and dissertations, by contrast, almost always include copies of any instruments used as appendix materials.

In addition to how it feels in use, there are other matters to consider when examining the measure. One is the item content, their face validity: Do the questions ask what the researcher is interested in finding out about? There are also practical concerns: Are the items written in a language and at a reading level appropriate for the people who will be using the measure? Is the item content likely to seem acceptable or offensive in the setting where the measure is to be used? How long does the instrument take to complete? Are the instructions clear and in language consistent with the tone the researcher wishes to set in the new study?

A final valuable resource for locating existing measures, including actual copies of them, is faculty in relevant departments in nearby colleges and universities, who can be consulted. Faculty typically remain abreast of the most current research in their particular areas of study. Even if a particular member of the faculty is not at the moment actively doing research, he or she generally knows where relevant current research is available or knows which of his or her colleagues would be likely to offer relevant help. It is always valuable to consult with knowledgeable others, both for their suggestions about possible instruments and for their opinions about the value of instruments being considered for use. One would not dream of beginning work with a new type of practice problem without seeking consultation from a trusted professional more familiar with the dilemmas presented; the same should be true of beginning a new direction of research study.

Finally, professional networking at conferences and with other professionals working in the same or similar research areas can be a very fruitful means of identifying potentially useful measures. Some instruments that are in development and not yet published or widely available can, in fact, be found only in this way.

Assessing the Measure in Use

Once a measure has been located, evaluated, and selected, how it is actually working out in use must be assessed. As Lyerly and Abbott (1970) remarked in their classic early review of psychiatric rating scales, there is no such thing as *the* reliability or validity of a scale as a permanent or invariant property of it. Just because a scale has proven reliable or valid in prior use does not mean that it will have those qualities in a different context. Therefore the reliability of any scales or subscales must be formally assessed with each new use. Ways to examine the reliability of scales are discussed in detail in chapter 11.

If possible, any ways available to examine validity of an instrument in the context of the new study should be employed as well. If more than one indicator of the concept is available in the study, this can be done by examining the degree of agreement between or among them. For example, if the ASI were to be used to assess substance use, practitioners' impressions of the client's substance use problems and their effects might be compared to scores obtained from it. If a high level of agreement were obtained, it suggests a valid result. If the assessments do not agree, however, there is no way to determine empirically which assessment, if any, to believe or disbelieve. In sum, while selecting an available measure can add a great deal to the efficiency and effectiveness of a fixed method study, attention must still be paid to the basic issues in data collection confronted in any empirical study once it is in use.

Summary

In fixed method research, there can be many advantages to using an existing instrument to measure the phenomena of interest. These include providing a common measure of a phenomenon across different studies, the fact that the strengths and weaknesses of such instruments are often well known at the point of use, and, of course, efficiency. However, using an existing instrument works best when it has been previously used with people similar to those to be studied and when the explicit and implicit content of the measure fits well with the conceptualization that guides the study in which it will be used. Therefore, the most important question to address in deciding whether to use an existing measure and in selecting which one to use is how closely the conceptual definition that guided the construction of the measure fits the way the concept is defined in the context of the present or proposed study.

Finding and evaluating existing measures can be a time-consuming process, but developing a new one may be even more difficult. There are a number of dimensions to consider in selecting a measure, some of them conceptual and others more practical, but there are also resources, such as print- and computer-based compendia of measures, that can aid in the process. While the fit between a study and an existing tool is rarely if ever perfect, using existing measures when possible is an efficient and effective strategy that is widely used in social work and human services research.

Part V
Methods of Data Analysis and Dissemination

It is common when doing research to underestimate the time it may take to analyze the data that has been collected, whatever the form it is in, and to communicate research findings to others. Generally data analysis requires doing, thinking, then doing some more. The data analysis process is an important one because it leads directly to drawing conclusions based on what was observed and presenting the results of the research to others.

This part of the text covers methods of data analysis, including how to work with data in both narrative and numerical form. The content on working with numerical data is divided into two parts: descriptive and inferential statistics. It also includes a chapter on using the computer, which includes discussion of both quantitative analysis and the analysis of qualitative data. Since the scientific method depends on the scrutiny of others, describing research effectively and submitting the conclusions drawn to critique by other members of the professional and scientific communities is essential. The final chapter in this section discusses how to present the results of a research project to others.

Reliability and Validity

Strictly speaking, the discussion of reliability and validity belongs to the topic of data collection. Mirroring the flexible method research process in which data collection and data analysis are often intermingled, however, the discussion of content analysis must begin with measurement issues. While the concepts of reliability and validity have been discussed in chapter 11, the way they are applied in content analysis deserves specific attention. Analysis of any form of data, including narrative data, must be directed to using it as efficiently and effectively as possible to advance the aims of the research without transgressing its limits.

Narrative or qualitative data can be very valuable scientific data. To achieve scientific usefulness, however, what Lincoln and Guba (1985) term "trustworthiness" must be achieved.[1] To make a claim of trustworthiness, attention must be given to issues of reliability, or the reproducibility of observations or results under the same or similar conditions, and validity, or the defensible assigning of meaning to what was observed. In the context of working with narrative or qualitative data, "reliability is the degree to which the finding is independent of accidental circumstances of the research, and validity is the degree to which the finding is interpreted in the correct way" (Kirk & Miller:20). In flexible method research, the selection of stable and relevant phenomena to record—and some interpretation of them—take place in the field during the data collection process, but consideration of reliability and validity is also important in the data analysis process. Another way to look at it is that in flexible method research the measurement process includes both data collection and data analysis activities (Drisko 1997).

While fixed methods of research depend on rules and procedures to keep the researcher's influence at a minimum, flexible methods of research tend to view all information as contextual and to deal with issues of bias and interpretation by "inviting them in." It is not assumed that objectivity in the form of an uncontaminated observer can be achieved. To revert to standardization of behavior in a series of interviews or field encounters would obviate the very purposes of flexible method research: to explore and understand the situation in depth and in its variety. The report is not about some people; it is about a person encountering and making observations of some people. Therefore it is also assumed that the only useful safeguard to objectivity is that the context of the data analysis (and of the data gathering) be made explicit and taken into account in interpreting results.

The nature of a qualitative analysis springs quite directly from the specific materials at hand. There are few precodified rules or procedures to depend on. For this reason, the spirit of skepticism and the self-awareness intrinsic to the scientific method are essential in the analysis of narrative data. The stance of self-awareness and the need to find ways to keep personal biases and reactions from interfering with the flow of information is familiar to every social work practitioner. The habit of skepticism and the need to submit ideas to efforts at disproof before accepting them as new knowledge may be less so. Both skepticism and self-awareness are essential, however, to the building of knowledge that will endure.

---

1. Trustworthiness includes ideas analogous to traditional notions of "external generalizability" and "objectivity" as well.

Flexible methods of study are usually associated with inductive processes of generating knowledge. They are often used by those suspicious of the conceptual or attitudinal limitations of existing research who seek instead data uncontaminated by old ideas. The goal is to discover new insights, understandings, or theories based directly on the words and behavior of the people being studied (Drisko 1997). The irony is that this form of inquiry immerses the inquirer directly and personally in the data gathering situation. This contrast can be seen at its most obvious in comparing the author of the mailed questionnaire with the intensive interviewer or the participant observer. The nature of the researcher's influence on the information gathered is more continuous and variable in the latter situations than in the former. In data analysis as well, the personal reactions of the data analyst can interfere. Attention to issues of reliability and validity is one safeguard against drawing idiosyncratic conclusions from data.

Reliability in content analysis refers to replicability: Would another person using the same materials in pursuit of the same question or issue reach the same conclusions or coding decisions? This assumes, of course, that the phenomenon, at least as captured in the data, is a stable one. It also assumes, however, that the person doing the analysis is seeking defensible, that is, reliable, and valid results. Boyatzis (1998) defines reliability in as consistency of judgment in observation, labeling, and/or interpretation. He notes that this can be based on "consistency of judgment among different viewers" or coders and/or "consistency of judgment over time, events, and setting" (p. 147). This idea has also been called dependability (Boyatzis 1998) or confirmability (Drisko 1997).

When data are prepared or transformed for analysis, reliability must be considered. Field notes that seemed intelligible at the time they were made may seem confusing months later when details of events have been forgotten. Additional written documents that supplement or summarize the notes may be useful. Tape recordings must be of adequate quality to make relistening and accurate transcription possible. Transcriptions must be accurate. In fact, once they have been made, transcriptions should be compared to the original tapes and edited for accuracy and readability. Errors in transcription can easily lead to significant mistakes in describing and interpreting what research participants have said, as Poland (1995) has dramatically illustrated.

Transcriptions of audiotape recordings are extremely useful in content analysis because they allow for rapid, nonsequential access to the data. However, it should be noted that transcriptions include only verbal data, and the emotional tone that enlivens and adds meaning to the spoken word can be lost. Some idiosyncrasies of speech, such as an accent or other form of unusual pronunciation, are likely to be lost as well. Qualities of speech that can be captured in print, such as pauses and interjections like "ummm's" and "ah's", should be included in the transcription as they may bear on how a remark should be interpreted.

Coding of data, another form of transformation, presents important issues of reliability and validity, which are discussed in detail below. Techniques used to ensure reliabilty in the coding of narrative data often involve other people. Someone else may be asked to read an interview transcript or to code some of the data, and the coding decisions obtained or the conclusions and interpretations made are compared. Specific suggestions for when and how to use multiple coders or raters are made in the section *Ensuring the Trustworthiness of Codes* below. It is the principle of replicability that is important to emphasize here.

Validity is often considered the strong point of the narrative data generated from flexible method studies. Apparent validity (Kirk & Miller 1986:22) is generally shown by anchoring concepts closely to detailed descriptions from the field. Validity may also be described as "calling things by their right names" (Kirk & Miller 1986). Concepts may be labeled by using language supplied by the research participants themselves, termed in vivo codes by Strauss (1987). Content may also be relabeled by the researcher in terms connecting the content to theory or specific concepts, what Strauss, a sociologist, would term sociological codes. As Boyatzis (1998) notes:

> A theme may be identified at the manifest level (directly observable in the information) or at the latent level (underlying the phenomenon). The themes may be initially generated inductively from the raw information or generated deductively from theory and prior research. (p.vii)

However generated, the codes must be anchored clearly and illustrated repeatedly in the verbatim data from which they arise to tie them to the evidence from which they are derived.

Flexible research methods are often used in research aimed at discovery and the generation of new ideas from the in-depth observation of experience. Remembering, however, that one case may "disprove" or limit the generalizability of a proposition, the usefulness of flexible methods may extend to the generation, demonstration, or verification of theory as well. For example, the constant comparative method of Glaser and Strauss (1967) is a style of flexible method research deliberately designed for theory development and testing. When the purpose of the research is to generate or demonstrate the applicability of theory, validity, or the question of what the data mean, becomes an essential issue. In flexible method research, theoretical validity (Kirk & Miller 1986) has to do with evidence that the correspondence asserted between observation and concept or theory is defensible. This idea is analagous to what is traditionally termed construct validity in fixed method research. Demonstration of a defensible link between data and meaning has also been called credibility (Drisko 1997). It suggests that the data and the interpretation of it are believable and not shaped or reshaped by the researcher.

Flexible method research is often described as "experience near" and as such is seen as having a high degree of apparent or face validity. However, words are symbolic communications, and the same word or term may be used when quite different things are meant or implied. Because the process of analysis overlaps with data collection, a key concept or term emerging in an analysis can be taken back to the field for further exploration of its meaning in use or for a more pointed explanation. Sometimes it is even necessary to challenge the explanations or formulations offered to get beyond official or formal responses that may mask what is really meant (Drisko 1997; Kirk & Miller 1986). Also, the volume of data frequently generated can afford opportunities for checking out a formulation with another case or in another situation already described in the data at hand. As with quantitative data, when different ways of describing or demonstrating something converge on a single explanation or pattern, validity, or credibility, has been demonstrated.

The Analysis Process

When working on flexible method studies, data analysis activities commonly overlap with the period of data collection. Early results of the analysis are often fed back into the data collection process itself to make the process more efficient. This differs markedly from the analysis of quantitative data in fixed method research when the two phases of activity are quite distinct and separate. In both kinds of studies, however, the data analysis period always extends well beyond the end of data collection. In fact, the time that is required to complete the analysis of narrative data is often seriously underestimated.

Miles and Huberman (1984) describe the analysis of narrative data as consisting of three concurrent activities: *data reduction,* data display, and conclusion drawing or verification. These three functions of analysis are also found in quantitative work, but their application is quite different when narrative data are being used. Each of these functions of the analysis will be discussed in some detail.

Data Reduction

One of the most urgent problems which the analysis of narrative data typically presents is its volume. A few hours of interviewing or field observation can yield many pages of transcribed data or field notes to be analyzed. Clearly the first and most important line of defense against an overwhelming mass of data is to have a data collection plan which will yield an amount of data which is manageable for analysis. While no research project is efficient enough to use every scrap of data collected, it is essentially unethical to gather data from people that will go unused simply because there is too much of it.

When the content analysis of available documents is undertaken, systems of sampling may be employed to select only parts of the data for intensive analysis. For example, specific issues or pages of publications may be chosen for thematic analysis while a larger amount of material is subjected to less intensive review. Such a procedure, although it takes place at the data analysis rather than the data gathering phase of the research, must conform to the logic of sampling for data gathering. It must also make sense in light of the unit(s) of analysis chosen (words, phrases, paragraphs, pages, editions, etc.) and of the purposes of the research.

However voluminous the data collected are, it is wise to begin an analysis with a review—relistening, rereading, relooking—of all the available data. This review will often cast the data in a new light and suggest an initial focus for the analysis. In fact, this kind of impressionistic reexamination of the data as a whole is useful to repeat more than once in the course of the analysis.

Even though it expands the amount of data available, it is often extremely useful to keep formal written notes to oneself, or memos, at the analysis stage as well as during the data collection process. Themes and ideas emerging from the data should be noted along with their source or referent(s) for future use. There is nothing more frustrating than remembering a passage or case but being unable to relocate it in the data when needed.

Some data collected in free-floating form may be more fruitfully and efficiently apprehended and presented if quantified. This strategy is often used with sample demographics and similar descriptors of the research situation. Content analytic techniques can be fruitfully used to reduce verbal descriptions to numerical ones. Miller (1990), for example, has developed an innovative technique for assigning ranks or scores to individuals based on the relative ranking given to narrative passages based on a quality or set of qualities in each passage.

When any system of quantification is used, care must be taken to develop and record the operational definitions used to transform words to numerical codes. The effort of transcription and analysis can then be focussed on those remaining data where the original unstructured form is essential.

It should be noted, however, that the quantification of narrative data has its limits, particularly when the research is exploratory in purpose. Geis and Fuller's (1985) study of the responses of hospice workers to the first AIDS patients they were called upon to care for illustrates this point well. They found three main themes expressed by the hospice workers they observed and interviewed. These were fear of the contagious quality of this then poorly understood disease, unresolved feelings about sexuality and sexual orientation, and consequent embarrassment about irrational responses to AIDS patients in their care. In the presentation of their findings, Geis and Fuller deliberately did not give the frequency with which each theme was encountered in the data. Their reasoning was that the sample was small and their research was exploratory. They chose instead to note that all three themes were encountered more than once and to provide data showing how each was manifested. They deliberately left the problem of estimating their relative frequency to future studies with a more descriptive purpose and design.

In many cases, the degree to which the amount of the data analyzed can be reduced through sampling or quantification is quite limited because to do so would obviate the very purposes for which the research was originally designed. Coding, however, which is primarily designed to demonstrate the meaning of and to display the data collected, also have a part to play in making the data more manageable.

Coding

The coding of narrative data in fact incorporates all of the aspects of the analysis: data reduction, data display, and conclusion drawing. It is the primary method of reducing narrative data to conceptual categories into which parts of the text can be grouped and in terms of which the text can be described or displayed. Much of the creativity in flexible method research takes place in the analysis in the development of coding schemes.

In coding data, the problem of the unit of analysis must first be answered. What is the unit that will be coded: the word? the line of text? the phrase? the paragraph? the theme or idea? Research designed to study the structure of verbal expression, as in some forms of narrative analysis, often uses the phrase or the line of text as the unit of analysis. In addition, political scientists often analyze documents for the frequency of occurrence of specific words in a text or analyze the same word as it may be used in a range of contexts.

In social work and human service research, it is most often the theme or idea that is the unit of analysis, whether that idea is expressed in a phrase or a paragraph. A theme has been defined as a "chunk of meaning" (Marshall 1981). Lincoln and Guba (1985) note that a theme should be heuristic, that is, useful in terms of the aims of the research, and parsimonious, that is, as small a unit as can stand alone.

In an analysis based on themes, coding is the process of assigning a name to a theme. As Boyatzis (1998) describes it:

> A good thematic code should have five elements:
>
> 1. A label (i.e., a name)
> 2. A definition of what the theme contains (i.e., the characteristic or issue constituting the theme)
> 3. A description of how to know when the theme occurs (i.e., indicators on how to "flag" the theme)
> 4. A description of any qualifications or exclusions to the identification of the theme
> 5. Examples, both positive and negative, to eliminate possible confusion when looking for the theme
> (p. 31)

Coding categories should not be too broad or too narrow. If nearly everything fits in a category, it has no specific meaning. If it is so specific that there are few instances of the category found, it may not be a relevant code. On the other hand, an unusual response or idea may be a very illuminating one, so a coding category of high apparent relevance should not necessarily be abandoned just because it does not crop up very often.

As stated earlier, codes or theme categories can be named by the research participants themselves, termed in vivo or indigenous codes (Strauss & Corbin 1990), or by the researcher. They may be very concrete or rather abstract. They may address the manifest, the obvious or directly stated, meaning of the words on the page, or they may be designed to capture latent meanings, those hidden or based on some inference drawn by the coder or listener. Codes may cluster; that is, there may be subdivisions of a broad category into narrower ones. What do women say about their work? What do they say about its satisfactions? Its frustrating aspects? These questions might be answered with a code name or number signifying work themes with subtypes to indicate positive and negative aspects of work embedded within it.

In coding the data from a specific study, there should be as many coding categories developed as are needed to capture the major ideas and meanings in the data. Given the complexity of human communication, a given piece of narrative data may in fact be classifiable or codable in more than one way. A passage in which a woman tells about her feelings when her elderly mother calls her at work because she is having a problem and wants some help could be coded as bearing on both frustrations of working and on family responsibilities. If the woman is talking about how being at work prevents her from having to respond to constant demands for help from her mother, it may be coded as a benefit of working. Glaser and Strauss (1967) and others speak of saturating the text with codes until all the meanings relevant to the study have been extracted from it (Drisko 1997).

Coding categories work well when there are many clear instances of the theme in the data and when it is relatively easy to decide in most instances what does and what does not belong in the category. The specific codes or coding categories are typically developed gradually, by developing and trying out some provisional categories and then further developing and refining them in use (Beeman 1995; Boyatzis 1998). Feagin (1991), for example, classifies his participants' responses to discrimination that occurred in public accommodations into two broad types: verbal confrontation and withdrawal. Sometimes the categories may spring from theories or conceptualizations from outside of the study and imposed on it. Feagin (1991) first divided all of the incidents of discrimination reported into two groups—those that occurred in places legally classified as public accommodations, such as hotels and restaurants, and on the street—because the patterns of discrimination and response reported seemed quite different in each. However the coding categories for the analysis are derived, however, it should be possible to develop in writing a description of what each coding category means, and referring to this description, in turn, will help to determine how to code additional material or ambiguous passages.

Recording the Codes

Concretely, coding narrative data means recording on a copy of the data, such as an interview transcript, marks to indicate the codes that apply to each part and then assembling copies of all the data in a given code category together. For example, in Feagin's study, each passage in a transcript describing an incident of discrimination would be marked at a minimum to show where the incident took place—public accommodation or the street—and the type of response made.

There are both computerized and paper systems that have been developed for marking and storing coded data. The computer-based packaged systems for analysis are discussed in chapter 19, but they are only mechanical aids. The conceptual work cannot be automated.

Paper-based systems typically use multiple copies of text. Working with text copies requires documents with wide margins for the recording of coding marks. Colored highlighting pens or brackets with numbers or symbols to represent each code can be used. The coded text is then reproduced, and coded passages are cut from the copies and stored together in folders, one for each category. Each coded passage must be marked with its source in case the context needs to be checked at a later point. It is essential to retain on file a complete coded but uncut copy of each transcript or piece of text. Thus paper files are created for each code category, and the files are used for studying the code and for writing up the results.

Using a personal computer, word processing packages can be employed very effectively in place of paper files when coding narrative data. Texts, such as individual interview transcripts, are entered into the computer as documents and then scanned and coded. An electronic file can be created to correspond to each code. Block, move and save, or cut and copy features can be used to copy coded chunks of text from each transcript into a file that will contain all the passages from all the transcripts that have been given the same code. Each piece of text extracted and saved must, of course, be labeled as to its source. When the coding process is complete, electronic files containing all the examples of each specific code have been created for use in presenting the findings.

Because of the contextual nature of the data themselves, the connection that can be made between coding and further data collection and the theoretical refinement that is often needed in developing and applying codes—the work of coding narrative data, unlike in quantitative data—is rarely delegated. When multiple coders are used, there needs to be frequent discussion, communication, and cross-checking among them to make sure that coding categories are being consistently understood and applied.

Ensuring the Trustworthiness of Code

Lincoln and Guba (1985) outline some of the problems that may distort the analysis of narrative data. The first of these has already been mentioned: the sheer volume of the data generated that taxes the memory and energy of the analyst. Data not easily retrieved may be overlooked or underutilized, and the potential importance of missing data may be underrated. The order in which information is encountered is also an influence; in particular, first impressions may take on an undue importance. Once an idea has taken hold, cases or formulations that contradict it may be discounted too easily and those that confirm it may be too easily accepted. Novel cases or explanations may be either under- or overvalued. Finally, co-occurrences of codes may too easily be interpreted as correlations or connections between phenomena.

Many of these potential problems require that conclusions drawn be "checked out" with others as data analysis proceeds. This checking may be with research participants ("member checking") or with colleagues (Padgett 1998). These consultants may be interested or disinterested parties, but they must be people willing and able to provide a different perspective to the analyst.

Investigators working in the naturalistic paradigm often recommend "member checks" (Lincoln & Guba 1985; Padgett 1998), or verifying the codes and the conclusions with the original participants in the research. The participants are invited to comment on whether what has been represented in the codes corresponds with what they intended to convey. Clearly this method has limits in that what people legitimately convey may well go beyond what they intended or are willing to admit to directly.

If data collection is complete and a conceptual model is being examined, codes can be developed on part of the data and then applied to the remainder (see Beeman 1995, for an example of using this procedure). As already noted, the order in which the data are encountered may have an undue effect on what is perceived as salient. Therefore it can be useful to select randomly or systematically a few cases on which to develop coding categories. Once defined using these data, the codes can then be applied and "tested" on the remaining cases. If they hold up well in use, they may be considered reliably and validly defined.

Other methods of ensuring the trustworthiness of codes involve other investigators or peer commentators. Especially when data are being coded in broad categories that involve judgements about latent meanings, reliability and validity checks using multiple coders are advisable. If multiple coders are used, the degree of agreement they were able to achieve should be reported. Krippendorf (1980) presents elaborate models for calculating reliability coefficients based on interrater coding agreement under a variety of conditions.

Complete records of the investigation, the data, and the coding process should be made and maintained. This responsibility is, of course, common to both quantitative and content analysis. However, it is often seen as more important in flexible method or qualitative research because the techniques used and judgments made are often study-specific. This practice is referred to as enhancing accountability (Beeman 1995; Padgett 1998) through creating an audit trail. It is part of the scientific discipline to make one's data and methods available to outside scrutiny if requested, even though these requests are rarely made. Taking the time to develop and maintain an efficient system for storing and retrieving raw and coded data and recording how this was done are essential.

The Grounded Theory Method

The "grounded theory method" of Glaser and Strauss (1967) is probably the most commonly used system for the generation of theory from flexible method research. The grounded theory method, recently elaborated in relation to data analysis in particular by Strauss (1987) and Strauss and Corbin (1990), was originally developed as a corrective to what its authors saw as an overemphasis on grand theory in sociology. As its name suggests, the goal of the method is to ensure that theory is adequately grounded in "reality" or empirical data, particularly in the complex, contextual data that are generated by flexible method research. Its method is addressed to systematizing rigorous approaches to qualitative, or flexible, methods of inquiry. Because it is so well developed and well known, its description of coding, the heart of any narrative analysis, is worth review.

The bedrock of the grounded theory method as it applies to data analysis is what is termed *constant comparison*. As in all flexible method research, however, analysis is not separated from data collection, so the constant comparative method includes theoretical sampling (see chapter 10 on sampling). This section will address itself to the method of constant comparison as it applies to coding in particular.

In the grounded theory method, coding is used to move from the data of experience to concepts:

> Grounded theory is based on a concept-indicator model, which directs the conceptual coding of a set of empirical indicators. The latter are actual data, such as behavioral actions and events, observed or described in documents or in the words of interviewees and informants. These data are indicators of a concept the analyst derives from them, at first provisionally but later with more certainty (Strauss 1987:25).

The first step in the method of constant comparison is that of comparing indicators with each other. As described in the section on coding above, indicators (feelings, attitudes, events, statements) that are similar to each other and different from others are joined together in categories or codes. In examining the indicators, the coder confronts "similarities, differences, and degrees of consistency of meaning" (Strauss 1987:25).

In the grounded theory method, coding takes place in overlapping stages. The process of data analysis begins with open coding, in which the analyst "opens up" the data by assigning provisional codes to all the indicators discernible in the data. Strauss recommends that the data be scrutinized minutely and densely coded. Total precision in categorization or interpretation need not be the goal at this initial stage because the codes will be further elaborated and verified as the process unfolds. Both the data themselves and the concepts the analyst brings to the process from experience and from the literature contribute to the coding process: "Open coding quickly forces the analyst to fracture, break the data apart analytically, and leads directly to the excitement and the inevitable payoff of grounded conceptualization" (Strauss 1987:29). Thus even at an initial stage, the coding should go beyond mere description and move toward theoretical analysis.

The next stage in the process is termed axial coding. At this stage, coding is done intensively around one axis or category at a time. This process forces specification of the parts of a concept and of the relationships between one concept and another. The analyst may go back and forth between open and axial coding processes.

The grounded theory method assumes that a core category will emerge from the coding process and becomes the major focus of the analysis. Coding then becomes selective as the analyst works "systematically and concertedly" on the core category and gradually "delimits coding to only those codes that relate to the core codes in sufficiently significant ways as to be used in a parsimonious theory" (Strauss 1987:33). Selective coding around the core category comes to predominate as the process of analysis proceeds. Some characteristics of a core category are that it be central to as many of the categories discovered in the data as possible, that it appear frequently in the data, relate easily to other categories, and account for maximum variation in the data. In short, the category must have "clear implications for a more general theory" if it is to serve as a core concept.

Glaser and Strauss (1967) recommend that the analyst constantly write "memos" during the coding process, a term they introduced into the literature on content analysis. These memos are running notes and reflections that help to capture thoughts, associations, and interpretations made of the coding categories. In other words, the memos are the record of the constant comparisons being made as the coding proceeds. They are especially useful in identifying relationships among categories. The memos and the data are kept separate; the memos are, in a sense, the data describing the conceptual analysis that takes place during coding. Whether or not formal memos are written, some way of keeping track of hunches, interpretations, and ideas during the analysis process is often recommended (Boyatzis 1998; Taylor & Bogdan 1984).

An Analysis Using the Grounded Theory Method

From the social work literature, the Dudley (1989) study of how administrators of community-based residential programs for developmentally disabled people deal with neighborhood issues shows the grounded theory method in action. Controversy often surrounds a decision to locate a community residence in a neighborhood. However, a key reason to locate such residences in communities is to afford residents a greater chance for interaction with ordinary people than institutional life affords. In order to explore the nature and quality of community relationships achieved, in-depth interviews were conducted with the administrators of several community residences and then analyzed using Glaser and Strauss' techniques.

Based on descriptions of how the administrators tended to respond to complaints from neighbors, a core category emerged. Dudley concluded that administrators could be divided into those who tended to take a "bend over backwards" or "bob" approach and those who were more "middle of the road" or "mor." Those who ascribed to the "bob" approach tended to consider potential community reaction to almost all programmatic decisions; the "mor" administrators did not. One "bob" administrator, for example, referred to a "good neighbor policy" and another even described providing counseling to an angry neighbor. A "mor" administrator, by contrast, was quoted as saying, "We won't jump through hoops for neighbors . . . [even though] . . . reasonable complaints had to be responded to" (Dudley 1989:102).

This distinction in administrative stance turned out to be related both to responding to and complying with perceived neighborhood norms, even down to staffing practices, and to the degree to which the programs were proactive in reaching out to their surrounding communities. Although he did not relate this distinction in strategy to any larger body of theory, Dudley used the grounded theory method to uncover and describe differing patterns in how in real life administrators met a common challenge. He also described the unexpected ways in which this set of practices affected other aspects of program functioning, including staffing decisions.

Other Forms of Selective Coding

The grounded theory method relies largely on generating codes inductively from the data. Depending on the nature of the study, however, it may be useful to code selectively for categories predetermined before the data are collected or at the beginning of the data analysis process. Such a strategy may be termed selective coding because the coding process is selectively focussed on categories deemed theoretically important. A common example of selective coding is when transcripts of interviews are coded based simply on the topic areas expressed as major questions on an interview guide. It is unusual to see such a process used exclusively, however, because to do so would be to overlook the possibility of other, perhaps more relevant, concepts to emerge from the richness of the data at hand.

One illustration of this kind of a priori selective coding can be seen in the analysis of social work treatment processes. Based on intensive analysis of many casework interviews, Florence Hollis, for example, developed a detailed classification of the kinds of interventions made by caseworkers (Hollis & Woods 1981). The categories developed reflect certain assumptions about social work practice and client functioning, notably that it is the person-in-situation configuration that is important but that functioning in the present can, at least at times, reflect developmental influences. The six categories used in this typology to classify client-worker communications, as distinct from environmental interventions, were:

A. Sustainment
B. Direct influence
C. Exploration, description, ventilation
D. Person-situation reflection concerning:

  1. Others, outside world in general, client's own health.
  2. The effects of one's own behavior on self and others.
  3. The nature of own behavior.
  4. Causative factors that lie in interactions of the self with others or in situational provocation.
  5. Self-evaluation.
  6. The worker and treatment process.

E. Pattern-dynamic reflection (discussion of dynamics of response patterns or tendencies)
F. Developmental reflection (discussion of developmental aspects of response patterns and tendencies)
(Hollis & Woods 1981:104–105)

Transcripts of verbatim worker-client interactions can be analyzed line-by-line using this system to examine treatment and its effectiveness and the differential use of self by a social worker. This kind of analysis, when preexisting categories are applied to narrative data, is not commonly discussed as part of "qualitative" analysis but is, in fact, fairly commonly used (Boyatzis 1998).

Presenting Results

Coding leads directly to the presentation or display of the data. While the process of coding is carried out individual by individual or record by record, the presentation of conclusions is made concept by concept. The coding categories are the concepts or variables that form the basis for the description of the findings.

The validity of the codes or concepts derived from the content analysis of narrative data is generally demonstrated in the research report by the inclusion of examples of the codes or concepts in the words of the research participants. The illustrations chosen may include the most eloquent of the responses, but the examples together should give a picture of the range of the phenomena the code is thought to indicate. Thus data reduction, categorization, and "display," or presentation, are all accomplished by means of the codes.

An Example of Data Display

The analysis presented in the Feagin (1991) article on discrimination against middle-class African Americans, reprinted in chapter 4, is a good illustration of coding and the presentation of data to illuminate the conceptual categories identified as relevant in the analysis. Feagin concludes from his data that one strategy employed by his respondents to protect themselves from acts of discrimination is to "use the resources of middle-class occupations" (p. 109). He offers the following quotation from an interview with a professor at "a major white university" to illustrate this point:

> If I'm in those areas that are fairly protected, within gatherings of my own group, other African Americans, or if I'm in the university where my status as a professor mediates against the way I might be perceived, mediates against the hostile perception, then it's fairly comfortable . . . but it's fairly consistently unpleasant at those sites where there's nothing that mediates between my race and what I have to do. For example, if I'm in a grocery store, if I'm in my car, which is a 1970 Chevrolet, a real old ugly car, all those things—being in a grocery store in casual clothes, or being in the car—sort of advertises something that doesn't have anything to do with my status as far as people I run into are concerned.
>
> Because I'm a large black women and I don't wear whatever class status I have, or whatever professional status [I have] in my appearance when I'm in the grocery store, I'm part of the mass of large black women shopping. For most whites, and even some blacks, that translates into negative status. That means they are free to treat me the way they treat most poor black people, because they can't tell by looking at me that I differ from that (Feagin 1991:109).

This is an example of in vivo coding because the interpretation it has been given, having to do with using professional or class status to ward off discrimination, is already explicitly there in the words of the respondent.

Whether a coding category already seems to be explicitly stated in the data themselves or not, the display of narrative data is almost always organized to give at least one direct illustration from the verbatim data of any important category utilized in the analysis. This display allows the reader to draw his or her own independent conclusions about the validity of the code or concept as it was applied in at least one instance of the use of the code.

There are, however, other methods of data display that are very useful both in the analysis process and in reporting results. One of these is the matrix or *data array.* A data array is simply a chart on which the rows represent cases and the columns represent characteristics, codes, or variables. It corresponds exactly, of course, to the form quantitative data take when coded for computer entry, except that the content of the array includes text and not just numerals. A data array is a very useful tool for developing an overview of the patterns in narrative data in the sample as a whole. When the data are extremely simple and straightforward, the data array may be the major product of the analysis, and entries to the array may be made directly from an audiotape. More often, however, a data array is constructed from all or part of the data after a more exhaustive coding process has taken place.

The data array, however, is ordinarily a tool to be used in developing an overview of patterns in the data. It is often too large and detailed to report as a whole. In addition, the data in an array may be readily identifiable because data about and comments of the respondents are connected with each other in the rows of the array. Confidentiality can be easily compromised if data are presented in this form.

Matrices of other kinds, however, can be very useful in exploring, summarizing, or communicating study results. Using rows and columns for categories of different concepts or codes, matrices can illustrate relationships between dimensions in the data very effectively. Rows and columns may describe time segments, roles, conditions, dimensions of a situation, or any category useful and relevant to understanding the variation being depicted. An extended discussion of using matrices to examine flexible method study results is found in Miles and Huberman (1984).

Other kinds of graphic illustrations can be useful as well. If the research has been aimed at the explication of behaviors or processes, and if the coding has resulted in the generation of theory that connects the concepts, diagramming these theoretical relationships can be the most effective means of putting the ideas across. Strauss (1987) gives several useful illustrations of the kinds of diagrams that can be used to display study findings of this kind.

It should be noted that the assumption most often made in discussing the results of a narrative analysis is that the result will be the identification of the relevant concepts or variables at play in the situation and perhaps the specification, through theory, of the relationships among them. Sometimes, however, what seems to emerge most clearly is a typology of cases, or subgroups in the sample. Defining the nature of the subgroups or subtypes, then, may be the easiest road to understanding the sources of variation in the sample. Careful exploration of the subtypes can bring the investigation back to the conceptual understanding of the phenomena. Matrices describing the subtypes, not individual cases, can be very useful in uncovering the relevant dimensions defining the typology, and describing the subtypes clearly in the report of results.

Case illustrations are another major strategy for "displaying" the results of a content analysis. Putting the study issues into human terms in someone's story can be a compelling way to convey the meaning of the data. Cases and the information given about them must be chosen carefully both in relation to the substance of the study and to issues of confidentiality. It is surprising, however, how often case illustrations are used that give only weak or limited support to the theoretical points the author is trying to make.

There may be a case in a sample, for instance, that seems to encompass all or most of the points the study can illustrate. This case may be a typical or an atypical one, and this should be made clear. Often, however, no one real case incorporates all the dimensions worthy of comment. In this instance, a composite case may be invented and described consisting of all of the modal features artificially assembled into one portrait. Again, this circumstance must be made clear, that is, that the case is not "real" but is a composite.

If the case illustration used is a real one, care must be taken with identifying information. If confidentiality was promised, no one should be able recognize the case from the description in the report. For example, it is important to note in the Feagin illustration given above that only limited demographic information about the person quoted is given to guard against inferred identification. Sometimes disguise of identifying information is used, but care must be taken that the characteristics transformed do not change the meaning of the illustration. If case information is disguised, that fact should be stated. Sometimes people whose case materials are being used are invited to read and approve the version of their words that will appear in print, and it is both respectful and a useful safeguard to obtain their approval and consent.

Drawing Conclusions

All phases of a content analysis involve both data reduction as the material is reduced to manageable and meaningful chunks and interpretation as the "researcher brings meaning and insight into the words and acts of the participants in the study" (Marshall & Rossman 1989:114). The process of interpreting narrative data also involves testing the emergent hypotheses and formulations against the data, searching for alternative explanations of the data, searching out and examining negative cases, and stating the qualifications that must apply to the conclusions, or what Taylor and Bogdan (1984) have termed "discounting the data."

The Negative Case

Whatever the approach used to drawing conclusions from research data, no theory, even a provisional one, can be advanced without subjecting it to the possibility of disconfirmation. Theories cannot be disproven simply from data; they can only be compared to competing formulations and constructions of the phenomena in question. However, in the scientific method, theories, explanations, or understandings cannot be advanced uncritically or without reference to whether or not there are any empirical data describing the real world that either tend to support or contradict them. Even if the "facts" seem consistent, there is usually more than one way to explain them.

Analysis of the negative case is a concrete technique for incorporating scientific skepticism into the analysis of narrative data (Drisko 1997; Padgett 1998). It has been described as part of the grounded theory method (Strauss & Corbin 1990) as well as in other techniques for analytic induction (Taylor & Bogdan 1984) as a key technique for strengthening theoretical formulations. As a theory or pattern begins to emerge in a content analysis, it is essential that the data be thoroughly searched for any case or situation that is not consistent with them. If data gathering is still ongoing, an effort must be made to try to find cases that seem different and to learn more about them by adding them to the sample. If not, the available data must be scrupulously reviewed to find any evidence of individuals or statements that don't fit. In the grounded theory method, this step is most essential, of course, for any code or category advanced as core.

The study of the negative case may have several results. The emergent theory may have to be rejected entirely and a new line of inquiry pursued. The theory may be seen to be bounded in its application or qualified by the circumstances exhibited in the case. The original theory may need to be modified or elaborated or the definition of the phenomenon may have to be revised until the contradictions posed by the negative case are resolved. Analysis of the negative case must never be simply omitted or excluded; its inclusion always results in the end in the strengthening of the theoretical argument made from the data.

Refining the Analysis

Because the results of a content analysis are so specific to the actual materials under study, it is difficult to set forth clear rules for any part of the analytic process. In addition to negative case analysis, however, there are a few guidelines in refining the analysis that should be mentioned.

Because content analysis requires such immersion in the data, as the coding proceeds it is often useful to check out the ideas that are emerging with others. These others may be fellow coders, colleagues, or experts in the field. It may also be useful to return to the literature, perhaps even the literature of a different field, to search out information on the concepts emerging. Codes and concepts that hold up after examination by others or in relation to the literature are also likely to bear up well after publication. On the other hand, codes or concepts that are novel, as in the Dudley (1989) study, or that contribute to debate in a field, as in the Feagin (1991) study, make a clear contribution as well.

Once coding is completed, it is essential that the analyst review the data and examine any sections or passages that have been left out. Although no study uses all the data collected and data should not be forced into categories, this review is a safeguard in case there was premature closure on categories which do not in fact capture all that there is of interest in the data.

In general, conclusions drawn directly from the data may have more validity than those that are based on an inference from the data. In other words, in vivo codes may have more apparent validity than others. For this reason, multiple raters are more often used when inferences are drawn. Even if raters agree on the inference, however, it may not be a valid one. The more direct evidence of the conclusion that can be identified, the better.

Discounting the data (Taylor & Bogdan 1984) also means that the results of a study must be reexamined skeptically in light of the context in which they were obtained. Were the data solicited or unsolicited? How representative of the larger group is the person who is the source of the data? What might have been the influence of the observer or the interviewer on the data obtained or of other people present when the data were collected? What assumptions or presuppositions does the interviewer, observer, or analyst bring to the data that might distort the conclusions?

None of these questions will have unequivocal answers. What is important is that each question be raised and considered as the conclusions of a study are being formulated. Evidence in the report that the questions have been seriously considered tends to increase the confidence of the reader in the conclusions drawn and presented.

Summary

In conclusion, it should be clear from this chapter that the analysis of narrative data can be a productive, creative, and yet scientific process. It should also be clear that it is a time-consuming and demanding one. Content analysis involves in overlapping fashion data reduction, data analysis, and data display. Coding, or the organization of the data into conceptually meaningful categories, lies at the heart of the process. Because the nature of the coding is determined by the content of the data themselves, there are few concrete rules to govern or guide coding. There are many guidelines that may be applied, however, to help ensure that the description rendered and conclusions drawn are as trustworthy—or reliable—and valid as possible. These guidelines are based on the importance both of self-examination and a degree of skepticism about the data, attitudes that lie at the heart of scientific method.

17

Descriptive Statistics

The term statistics often evokes powerful negative feelings. Many people, especially those in the helping professions who tend to think of themselves as intuitive, presume they will not be able to understand statistics and so they do not give the field a chance. Other people, again frequently including those in the helping professions, tend to regard the use of numbers as dehumanizing or as oversimplifying the complexity of real life. Finally, some think that statistics may be a helpful tool, but they are sure that learning statistics would be very difficult, especially if they have not studied much mathematics in the past or if they had trouble when they did. However, descriptive statistics are simply techniques for extracting meaning from numerical data.

Statistics really are not difficult. There are a few basic concepts to understand, but once these concepts are learned, knowledge of statistics can be seen for what it really is: a powerful tool for making sense of numerical data and having confidence in the conclusions drawn from them. In fact, the use of statistics depends more on logic and understanding some key concepts in probability than it does on specific knowledge of mathematics.

Learning statistical concepts does include becoming familiar with some technical terminology and certain symbols that are used as shorthand. Like learning a new language, using these terms and symbols may seem awkward at first. However, as with other forms of professional and technical terminology, when learned they can provide a familiar and powerful way to communicate with others who know the language, in this case, with other professionals and researchers. Initially, however, these terms and symbols can contribute to making the topic of statistics seem remote and difficult. The truth is that the concepts themselves are generally not complicated and are not that difficult to understand once the language is understood.

The second objection to statistics is more philosophical. There is some merit to the argument that the availability of statistics as a method for making sense of numerical information has perhaps served to lure researchers into investigating questions that lend themselves to statistical answers. There is also some merit to the argument that, on occasion, researchers have framed their research questions so that they could use statistical methods to answer them, even when more qualitative and nonnumerical approaches to the problem might have been more useful. These problems are examples of what is referred to as the "Drunkard's Search," that is, of looking for answers under the streetlight where it may seem easier to look for them rather than where they are most likely to be found.

Just because statistics have sometimes been misused, they are not always misused. On the contrary, statistical methods are a powerful and useful tool for doing what every researcher must find some way to do: organizing the information that has come out of his or her study, summarizing that information, and drawing conclusions from it in ways that are warranted from the evidence available.

Statistics is a branch of applied mathematics. It, in turn, has two branches, descriptive and inferential statistics. The first branch, *descriptive statistics,* will be the focus of this chapter. The second branch, inferential statistics, will be taken up in chapter 18. Both chapters will deal with statistics conceptually, not computationally. In this age of computers, calculating statistics is best done electronically, and for those with little background in mathematics, dwelling on the mathematical basis of the statistics in common use can make the job of understanding them more difficult, not less. Chapter 19 will cover the use of computers in research, both for statistical aspects of data analysis and for the analysis of narrative data. Additional examples of some of the statistics discussed in this chapter and chapter 18 can be found in chapter 19.

Defining Statistics

Descriptive statistics are true to their name: They are statistics, or numbers, that describe. This description is of the sample itself, of the people (or groups or organizations) that were directly studied in the research. Inferential statistics, on the other hand, are used for making generalizations from samples to populations or for answering questions about how specific variables may relate to each other, in traditional terms, for testing hypotheses.

The average number of cases carried by workers in a community mental health center, for example, is a descriptive statistic because it describes how many cases on average are assigned to each worker. Descriptive statistics are used when there is a large body of numerical information to make sense of. Suppose, for example, there was a list of each worker's caseload in a very large agency, which might look like table 17–1.

In order to make sense of these data, it is necessary to organize and then summarize them in some way: to describe them more efficiently, which is the task of descriptive statistics. Descriptive statistics, then, are a means for summarizing, and therefore condensing and simplifying, the information provided by sets of numbers. Naturally, the larger the set of numbers a study generates, the more pressing the need to find a way to summarize them becomes.

Table 17–1 Hypothetical Data Reporting Number of Cases Carried by Each Worker in an Agency

38	29	41	32	25	28	44
27	32	37	36	31	42	32
33	26	40	35	33	39	

Some research requires the use only of descriptive statistics; other studies require that inferential statistics also be used. Inferential statistics build on descriptive ones, making it essential to know about descriptive statistics for any quantitative study. Because the field of descriptive statistics consists of a set of tools for organizing and summarizing quantitative or numerical information, to understand statistics one must begin with numbers.

The Nature of Numbers

Most of you would probably be surprised at this point in your education if someone were to tell you that the statement $2 = 2$ is not always true. Your surprise would come from the fact that you have come to think of 2 as a symbol that tells you how many of something there are. It turns out, though, that the same symbol, the number 2, can have different meanings, and, in fact, there are four different meanings it can have.

Quantitative information is information about the amount, or quantity, of a measured phenomenon or quality. In fixed method research, the variables to be investigated and the way they will be measured are specified before data collection begins. Sometimes there are ways to quantify a variable, that is, to say how much of a quality or phenomenon is present. At other times, however, all that is possible is to recognize whether a phenomenon or quality is or is not present. In both cases, however, the measurement is likely to be recorded as a number, a numerical code.

What numbers mean, that is, what information a numerical symbol like 2 conveys, differs depending on the measurement method that was used to derive them. If the measurement method involved counting something, then the number symbolizes the amount of what was counted. However, if the measurement method involved only looking to see whether something was or was not there, then the number symbolizes or labels only the presence or absence of that quality or phenomenon.

The psychometrician S. S. Stevens (1946) developed a schema laying out the different meanings a number can have expressed as different levels of measurement. Stevens concluded that what made numbers different from one another was the underlying properties of how they were derived. In research, numbers are obtained by performing some measurement operation. In the most concrete case, as in studying weight, a scale would be used to weigh people and to get numbers, in pounds or kilograms, for each of them. More generally, whenever there is a quantitative variable, some form of measurement, some procedure to assign numbers or quantitative values, to each person (organization, etc.) being studied, has been used.

The scale of measurement used to derive numbers, Stevens reasoned, could itself have different properties, and the different properties of these scales of measurement would dictate what can be done with the numbers obtained by using them. These different properties and the names of the different scales or levels of measurement Stevens developed are presented in table 17–2. This schema holds that there are three fundamental properties on which measurement methods can differ: whether they do or do not measure quantity or magnitude, whether they do or do not have equal intervals between adjacent units, and whether they do or do not have an absolute zero. In all cases, different numbers signify or label differing, discrete categories or values. The more information a number contains, that is, the more of these properties that it expresses, the higher the level of measurement is said to be. Ratio is thus the highest level of measurement in this system.

The qualities of the levels of measurement are cumulative; numbers that represent a higher level of measurement have the qualities of numbers at a lower level of measurement. At the ratio level of measurement, for example, all of the qualities are present, including those of nominal data. This means that a number that represents a higher level of measurement, with more of the qualities present, can always be transformed to a simpler form. However, the reverse is not true: Lower levels of measurement cannot be transformed to higher ones because they lack specific qualities that higher ones have.

As will become clear in considering each of these levels of measurement in turn, the answer to each of the questions in table 17–2 does not just determine the name of the level of measurement of a variable. It dictates what mathematical operations, and therefore what descriptive and inferential statistical procedures, it is and is not appropriate to use with a specific number or piece of numerical data, depending on what that number means based on how it was derived.

Nominal Level

The simplest, least precise level of measurement is the one where the measuring instrument does not get at quantity or magnitude: *nominal*. The term nominal indicates naming. A nominal variable uses numbers or numerals simply to name categories. If the concept or measurement procedure is not about quantity, there can be no particular order or hierarchy among the categories, there are no adjacent numerical units to be equidistant from each other, and there is no way to measure the quantity of zero. In this form of measurement, all the procedure is doing is classifying

Table 17–2 Names and Properties of the Scales of Measurement

	Type of Scale			
Property of the Number	*Nominal*	*Ordinal*	*Interval*	*Ratio*
Does it indicate discrete categories or values?	Yes	Yes	Yes	Yes
Does it measure quantity?	No	Yes	Yes	Yes
Are there equal distances between all the adjacent numbers on the scale?	No	No	Yes	Yes
Is there an absolute zero?	No	No	No	Yes

participants into one of two or more categories on the basis of whether they do or do not display the defining characteristics designating category membership.

Consider ethnic grouping. The federal government's category system for racial and ethnic classification in the 1990 census included these categories based on two questions that were asked of everyone (McKenney & Bennett 1994):

This system for race is often condensed to five categories:

WHITE (1)
BLACK (2)
AMERICAN INDIAN, ESKIMO AND ALEUT (3)
ASIAN AND PACIFIC ISLANDER (4)
OTHER (5)

4. Race Fill ONE circle for the race that the person considers himself/herself to be. If Indian (Amer.), print the name of the enrolled or principal tribe. ⟶	○ White ○ Black or Negro ○ Indian (Amer.) (Print the name of the enrolled or principal tribe.)
	○ Eskimo ○ Aleut
If Other Asian or Pacific Islander (API), print one group, for example: Hmong, Fijian, Laotian, Thai, Tongan, Pakistani, Cambodian, and so on. ⟶	Asian or Pacific Islander (API) ○ Chinese ○ Japanese ○ Filipino ○ Asian Indian ○ Hawaiian ○ Samoan ○ Korean ○ Guamanian ○ Vietnamese ○ Other API
If Other race, print race, ⟶	○ Other race (Print race)

7. Is this person of Spanish/Hispanic origin? Fill ONE circle for each person	○ No (not Spanish/Hispanic)
	○ Yes, Mexican, Mexican-Am., Chicano ○ Yes, Puerto Rican ○ Yes, Cuban ○ Yes, other Spanish/Hispanic (Print one group, for example: Argentinean, Columbian, Dominican, Nicaraguan, Salvadoran, Spaniard, and so on.)
If Yes, other Spanish/Hispanic, print one group. ⟶	

Figure 17–1 U.S. Census Bureaus Questions About Race and Ethnicity from the 1990 Census

Measuring a person's racial and ethnic grouping using this measurement schema, then, involves inviting the participant to designate the categories that best fits his or her self-identification by matching that self-definition to the category definitions given and then assigning the participant a number representing membership in that category. Translating the verbal category label (e.g., Asian and Pacific Islander) into a numerical category label (e.g., 4) is called coding.

The numbers chosen to represent the verbal categories are arbitrary. There is no reason for representing the category "Asian American" with "4" and "Black" with "2." The numbers only represent, label, or name which one of two or more category groupings of the variable best captures the characteristics of the person "measured" or classified. All the number does, then, is substitute for the verbal category label. It, like the verbal label, gives the name of the person's appropriate category. It should be noted that the U.S. Census Bureau has identified many difficulties with these questions based on changing concepts of racial and ethnic identity and the classification of people with mixed-race parents, among other issues (McKenney & Bennett 1994).

Since nominal variables represent only a name, and since the numbers are arbitrary category labels, there is very little that can be done mathematically with nominal level variables. All that can be said is that participants do or do not belong in the same category and therefore do or do not have the same numerical code. As will be seen, this means that it is possible to talk about being the same or being different. It is also possible to talk about the proportion or percentage of a sample that falls into each category. However, it makes no sense to consider computing any statistic that involves adding, subtracting, or any other form of arithmetic besides counting, that is, counting up the number of people in each category, who are like or unlike each other.

Considering another case of nominal measurement may show its implications for the other properties measurement scales can have. Suppose marital status was measured in a group of people using a system with these categories:

SINGLE, MARRIED/COHABITING, DIVORCED/SEPARATED, and **WIDOWED**

which are symbolized respectively with the numbers 1, 2, 3, and 4. Person A, who is married, would have a score of 2 on the variable of marital status; Person B, who is widowed, would have a score of 4. It is easy to see from this example that nominal numbers do not reflect quantity, since although Person B's score is higher than Person A's, it makes no sense to think of Person B as having more marital status than Person A.

Scores derived by using nominal scales of measurement can be best thought of as designating whether participants are the same or different from other participants on the variable being measured, such as gender, marital status, or racial and/or ethnic identity. Such scores give no information about the nature of those differences. Clearly, then, the amount of information conveyed by scores from nominal scales of measurement is very limited. In research, the general rule is that more information is better. So whenever possible, it is preferable to measure variables with scales that yield numbers that do reflect some information about the quantity of what is being measured when that makes conceptual sense.

From a statistical point of view, there is a second reason for preferring more complex numbers. Scores that do not reflect quantity cannot be added or subtracted from one another, much less multiplied or divided. To illustrate, consider Person C who is single, represented by a score of 1. Person A is married, which is represented by a score of 2. Notice that it makes no sense to add their two scores together to get a score of 3, since 3 represents a different category, not a sum of the first two categories.

In general, when using nominal scores, all that is possible is to characterize sample members as in the same or different categories from each other. Mathematically, all that is possible is to determine the number of people in the sample who fall into each category on the scale, that is, to count up people by category. Such a count is termed a *frequency*. It is not possible to perform mathematical operations with the numbers that label the categories since nominal scales do not provide a measurement of quantity.

Ordinal Level

Numbers derived by using *ordinal* scales of measurement do provide some information about quantity although the information is limited. Ordinal measurement scales are ones that assign numbers to the people in a group on the basis of what order or rank the people hold in that group of people. There are two forms of nominal level variables. Some, like social class, present a limited set of ordered categories with many people fitting into each one. Rankings, like those in a horse race, assign each individual in the group a unique number based on how he or she compared to the other individuals in the group.

Rank in class is a well-known example of a score or rank derived using an ordinal scale of measurement. Person A's score on this variable is 2, Person B's score on this variable is 1, and Person C's score on this variable is 3. What information do these three scores provide? It is possible to conclude that Person A's grades were higher than Person C's, and that Person B's grades were higher than Person A's. However, it is impossible to tell how high Person A's grades were although her grades were the best in the class. It is unclear what that "best" was, for instance, a 3.44 or a 3.97.

Ordinal scales measure quantity, then, but relative, not absolute, quantity. Rank in class shows grade point average relative to the grade point averages of the other people in the group, not grade point average on an absolute 0.00 to 4.00 scale. Perhaps it will bring this point home to consider that if one person were ranked 1 in the class of '95 while a second person were ranked number 2 in the class of '96, it would be impossible to determine which of these two people had higher grades, since it's entirely possible that the class of '95 highest grade was lower than the class of '96 second highest grade. Ordinal scores, then, give information only about quantity, or amount, compared against a single reference group. To be comparable to one another, ordinal scores must express rank relative to the same reference group.

There are additional limitations to how much meaning is conveyed by ordinal scores. Just because three scores are next to one another (as 1, 2, and 3 are) does not allow us to conclude that the difference between the grades of Person B and Person A is equal to the difference between the score of Person A and Person C. Although we're used to thinking of the numerical symbols 1 and 2 as being the same distance apart from one another as are the numerical symbols 2 and 3, when those numbers represent ranks instead of quantities there will not be equal differences (i.e., distances) between them. In a horse race, for example, the first place horse may have crossed the finish line many lengths (or several seconds) ahead of the second place finisher, while the second and third place horses may have crossed the finish line almost neck-and-neck, or with very little time difference in how fast they ran the race.

The fact that ordinal scales give us number symbols that represent relative amounts instead of absolute amounts places limitations on what mathematical operations can be performed with them. While it is possible to make quantitative comparisons of "greater than" or "less than" with respect to the reference group or the continuum of categories, it is not possible to add and subtract ordinal scores, since the mathematical operations of addition and subtraction assume that the distance between adjacent units on the scale are equal.

Interval Level

Interval level measurements are in fact quite common in social and psychological research. Scores derived from interval level scales have two key properties associated with numbers as we ordinarily think of them: that they symbolize quantity and that the distances between numbers are equal. This means that 1 is as far from 2 as 2 is from 3. An IQ score of 120 differs as much from an IQ score of 110 as it does from one of 130. A temperature of 40°F differs as much from one of 30°F as a temperature of 90°F differs from 80°F. Examples of interval level scores include temperature, IQ, and scores from many other psychometric instruments, as in Hudson's (1982) Child's Attitude Toward Mother Scale used in the Richey and Hodges (1992) study reprinted in chapter 8.

Interval level scores, however, are not organized around a zero point that indicates the absence of the quality being measured. Using the example of temperature, the zero point is arbitrary; 0°F, for example, is not the same as 0°C, and neither zero point indicates the total absence of heat or of cold as qualities. Thus it is not possible to say that when it is 80°F, it is twice as warm as when it is 40°F. This kind of calculation is only possible when both numbers are based on a common, real zero point.

Scores derived using interval measurement scales are desirable because they convey a lot of information and because it is possible to perform at least some mathematical operations on them. Specifically, it is possible to add and subtract interval scale scores from each other. Again, the advantage of being able to perform mathematical operations is that they extend the flexibility available in working with numbers. Counting how many times a certain score occurred or looking to see whether a certain score is higher or lower than another one is all that is possible with numbers coming from nominal and ordinal measurement scales. With interval scales it is possible to determine how much higher or lower one score is than another. It is also possible to find true averages of sets of interval scores, which is often a very desirable computation to be able to make.

Ratio Level

In measurement, researchers always strive for greater knowledge and precision. Therefore it is not surprising that scores from a scale that shows quantity *and* equal intervals between adjacent units as well as an absolute zero point, would be considered the most desirable—what is known as ratio measurement. A common form of ratio measurement in the helping professions is scores representing counts of repeated acts. The number of cigarettes smoked per day, for example, is an instance of ratio measurement: The number reflects quantity, there is equal distance between adjacent units, and there is an absolute zero point, since a zero score would represent smoking no cigarettes. Other examples of ratio measurement include age, height, weight, household income, number of siblings or number of children, and number of cases carried by each social worker, as in the example given in table 17–1.

Ratio scale numbers have very desirable properties mathematically. The fact that there's an absolute zero means that it is possible not only to add and subtract ratio scale scores, but it is also possible to multiply and divide them. Therefore it is possible to state that someone who is 40 years old has lived twice as long as someone who is 20 or that someone who has 2 children has half as many as someone else who has 4. Being able to perform all four basic arithmetic operations—adding, subtracting, multiplying, and dividing—with these sorts of scores increases considerably the amount of flexibility in the statistics that can be computed using them, which can be very useful.

It should be noted that having a real zero point in the scale does not mean that any person actually has a score of zero on the variable. In the example in table 17–1, no worker had a caseload of zero, although such a score was hypothetically possible. Even when it is not hypothetically possible, as with height or weight, the important fact is that the whole scale of measurement is anchored to a zero point that represents the absence of the quality in question. Thus height, weight, and caseload are all true ratio level variables.

Although there is an important difference between interval and ratio scales, in statistics interval and ratio level variables are often treated similarly. Specifically, because interval level variables reflect quantity in fairly precise ways, the most common and powerful statistical techniques are generally used with both interval and ratio level data. However, understanding the differences between all the different types of numbers is important. Because statistics use mathematics to extract meaning from scores derived in research, it is essential to know what can and cannot be done mathematically as well as to know what any number means. What descriptive statistics do is use mathematics to help organize and describe sets of numerical data in ways that make sense based on the level of measurement used to derive them. The rest of this chapter will consider various ways to do that.

Summarizing Information: Frequency Distributions

The first step in working with a data set is to try to make sense of it by organizing it. This process begins by rearranging the numbers or scores from a specific sample into numerical order, that is, to list them, lowest to highest or highest to lowest. Then the number of people who were assigned each score, the frequency or count, is listed next to each score obtained. The result is called a *frequency distribution*.

The name of this procedure comes from what it does: It lists all the possible scores over which the variable could be distributed, from the lowest to the highest score, and then indicates the frequency, or count, with which each of those scores actually appears in the data set. In this manner, one can literally see the frequency with which the measured scores are distributed across the range of values of the variable. Frequency distributions are used with variables at all levels of measurement, although it should be noted that with nominal level variables arranging the scores in numerical order is an artifact of using numerical symbols as codes to label categories and does not represent quantity or order in any conceptual sense.

To construct a frequency distribution for the caseload data in table 17–1, the first step is to determine the lowest and highest scores on the variable in the data set, which in this case are 29 and 44, arranging the others in a column between them. The top number in the column would be the lowest score on the variable; the second number in the column would be the next lowest number the variable could assume, whether or not it actually appeared in our data set;[1] and so forth. The last number in the column would be the highest number observed in the data set.

After setting up the scores in a column, the number of people who obtained each score would be tallied and listed beside the score. In other words, the procedure counts the number of scores in the data set that fell into each possible value of the variable. If a number is listed that did not appear in the data set, the count listed for it is zero. This count is termed the frequency with which each score appears, forming a frequency distribution (see table 17–3).

What the frequency distribution does is immediately apparent when the frequency distribution and the original raw data are compared. The original data, as in table 17–1, give very little information. It is difficult to tell at a glance what the lowest score is, what the highest score is, or what the pattern is of how the scores are distributed across the values of the variable. The frequency distribution does all of these things. In the example given, the frequency distribution shows at once that the smallest caseload was 25 cases and the largest caseload was 44 cases. And finally, by glancing down the numbers in the frequency column of the frequency distribution, it is easy to see that most of the workers in the sample had caseloads of between 30 and 40 clients. Frequency distributions, then, are enormously useful methods for organizing numerical information, and they are also a useful illustration of how organizing numerical data reveals information that isn't immediately apparent from the data alone.

Relative Frequency Distributions

With large data sets, frequency distributions sometimes are less informative than is desirable because with large numbers it is sometimes difficult to see the pattern of

---

1. In practice, a frequency distribution is often formed using only the numbers or values that actually appear in the distribution. If a graph is to be made from the data, however, it is important to include the values that do not appear as well. These will be represented on a graph as data points with zero cases in them.

Table 17–3 Frequency Distributions Formed from the Hypothetical Data on Worker Caseload

Caseload	Frequency (f)	Relative Frequency (%)	Cumulative Frequency	Cumulative Percentage Distribution
25	1	5	1	5
26	1	5	2	10
27	1	5	3	15
28	1	5	4	20
29	1	5	5	25
30	0	0	5	25
31	1	5	6	30
32	3	15	9	45
33	2	10	11	55
34	0	0	11	55
35	1	5	12	60
36	1	5	13	65
37	1	5	14	70
38	1	5	15	75
39	1	5	16	80
40	1	5	17	85
41	1	5	18	90
42	1	5	19	95
43	0	0	19	95
44	1	5	20	100
	20	100	—	—

where in the distribution the scores in the data set are concentrated. Relative frequency distributions formally compare the number of scores there are for each value of the variable to the total number of scores. What results is a distribution of proportions, or relative frequencies, which shows whether there were many or few scores at each point in the distribution. These are usually expressed as percentages.

The first step in constructing a relative frequency distribution is to start with a simple frequency distribution. To create the relative frequency, the frequency for each possible value of the variable gets converted from a raw, or absolute, frequency to a relative frequency by dividing it by the total number of scores. A frequency says that 3 people had caseload scores of 32. A relative frequency says that 3 of 20 people in the total sample had a caseload of 32. Expressed as a percentage, this translates to a relative frequency score of 15%. Three out of 20 people with a caseload of 32 is quite different from 3 out of 6 people with the same caseload, which is expressed in different relative frequencies of 15% and 50%.

At this point, it is useful to introduce some statistical shorthand. A frequency, which just means a count of how many, is typically symbolized by a lower-case f in statistics. The number of people our scores are based on, the number in a data set, is typically symbolized by N. These two symbols are the ones used to compute relative frequencies. For any given value, then, the relative frequency equals f divided by N: f/N. This proportion can easily be transformed into a percentage.

Consider again what a relative frequency is: It's the number of scores at a given value of the variable relative to (divided by) the total number of scores. This value, a proportion, can easily be converted to a percentage. Saying that 51.2% of the children born in the United States are male babies means that the number of male babies born in a given year is divided by the total number of male and female babies born in that year and then multiplied by 100 to get 51.2%. (For 1991, that would be 2,101,518 divided by 4,110,907 = .511 times 100 = 51.1%.). It follows, then, that a relative frequency distribution can be converted into a percentage distribution by multiplying each entry in it by 100. The result will be a distribution showing the percentage of scores from the data set falling into each of the possible score values.

Cumulative Frequency Distribution

Much of statistics is based on simple concepts and procedures that are then elaborated. A frequency distribution can be elaborated in two ways. However, based on the fundamental concept of the distribution, it is easy to follow and understand the elaborations of it. First, the frequency distribution can be used to develop other types of distributions: a relative frequency distribution and a cumulative percentage distribution. In each case, what is developed is tables, or lists, of numbers that are organized in such a way as to provide easy access to the information contained in the numbers. This is, of course, the same principle as the one underlying even simple frequency distributions: The data are summarized and organized in such a manner as to make information in the numbers understandable.

Cumulative Percentage Distributions

The cumulative percentage distribution builds on the relative frequency distribution. What a cumulative frequency distribution calls for in addition is how these percentages add up, or cumulate, across the score ranges. To generate such a distribution, the percentages are cumulated from the lowest value of the variable to the highest. The cumulative frequency distribution shown in table 17–3, for example, shows that only 25 percent of workers in this hypothetical social agency carried 24 or fewer cases at the time of the hypothetical study.

Grouped Frequency Distributions

When a distribution contains many scores and the scores vary over a wide range of numbers, the types of frequency distributions already discussed do not really help very much. Although one can see at a glance what the lowest and highest scores are, the problem is that the tables themselves remain confusing because there are so many entries in the lefthand column that it is hard to take in all the information about the data set as a whole. Consequently, what is needed is some way of summarizing the information so that it will be manageable, which can be done by constructing a grouped frequency distribution.

Grouped frequency distributions are just like simple frequency distributions except that they have groups (or sets) of scores in the left column instead of single scores. The categories in the left column contain groups or intervals of scores. When creating a grouped frequency distribution, scores in the raw data are tallied into score intervals rather than into single score categories.

Table 17–4 Grouped Frequency Distribution Formed from the Hypothetical Data on Caseload

Caseload	Frequency	Relative Frequency (%)	Cumulative Frequency	Cumulative Percentage Distribution
25–29	5	25	5	25
30–34	6	30	11	55
35–39	5	25	16	80
40–44	4	20	20	100
Total	20	100	—	—

Although the data do not really require it, for purposes of illustration a grouped frequency distribution for the caseload variable has been developed and is presented in table 17–4. Also presented in this figure are the grouped relative frequency distribution and the grouped cumulative distribution. Each of these grouped score distributions is built on the grouped score frequency distribution.

There is an important point about statistics and statistical methods to be gleaned from the grouped score distributions: that some information is inevitably lost in summarizing. Consider for a moment two scores from the hypothetical data set showing caseloads of 27 and 28. These scores symbolize values of a variable that was measured at a ratio level in quantitative units that appear at equal intervals, and on a scale that has an absolute zero point. These two scores, then, are mathematically and conceptually different from one another, and people with those two scores have different caseloads. The raw score frequency distribution preserves this difference because the scores are tallied separately. In contrast, in the grouped score frequency distribution, the two scores are tallied into the same category: the 25 to 29 group. Information about their difference is not preserved. This loss of information occurs fairly often in statistics. In general, when information is summarized rather than just organized, part of the information summarized is lost.

Raw score frequency, relative frequency, and cumulative percentage distributions are each methods to organize data. These distributions are all very useful. They show at a glance what the lowest and highest scores are and how the scores are distributed across the possible values the variable can assume. Each distribution reflects this information a little differently. The raw score distribution gives information about the count of scores at each value. The relative frequency distribution shows what proportion of the total number of scores falls in each interval. And the cumulative percentage distribution shows how the scores are mounting up over the intervals. Grouped score frequency, relative frequency, and cumulative percentage distributions provide the same sort of information but in summarized form. While there is something lost in the process of this summarizing, namely precision about the exact rather than approximate value of some of the data points, there is something gained: clarity that facilitates making sense of the data at hand.

Graphs

Visual or graphical methods for organizing, summarizing, and displaying data, which are built on frequency distributions, are also very useful. Graphs use pictorial images and space on the page to represent visually the kind of information about relative quantity that frequency distributions, especially relative or percentage distributions, provide in table form. Different types of graphs are used for different variables depending on their level or scale of measurement.

Pie Charts

Consider the pie graph or chart familiar since grade school (see figure 17–2). The pie chart shows at a glance the relative sizes of parts of a whole, in this case, the proportion of the federal budget for 1994 that was devoted to national defense, direct benefits payments to individuals, grants to states and localities, interest on the national debt, and other categories.

In measurement terms, pie charts are used for nominal level variables. In the case of federal expenditures, while the number of dollars spent in each category is a ratio number, the categories of spending are nominal. In this case, the count is of dollars, rather than people, per category.

When working with data to create a pie chart, two pieces of information are needed: information about the categories, that is, what they are, and information about the proportion of the whole that falls in to each category. Pie charts are set up so that the total entity or sample under consideration is the whole circle, "the whole pie." First the categories that represent the parts of that whole are identified. Then the circle is divided into as many parts or "slices" as there are categories with the size of each category relative to the whole determining the area of the circle apportioned to represent it. In figure 17–2, for instance, in 1994, the

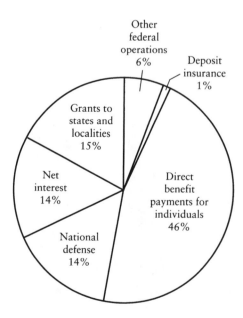

Figure 17–2 A Pie Chart Showing Proposed Federal Spending for 1994

Source: *Budget of the United States Government: Fiscal Year 1994.* (1993) Washington, D.C.: Executive Office of the President of the United States.

President's budget proposed that 14% of federal spending should go to defense, 46% to direct benefit payments to individuals, and 15% to grants to states and localities. The slices of the pie show graphically the relative size of each category of spending.

Bar Graphs

The bar graph is another technique used to summarize nominal data. Like pie charts, bar graphs represent information about the categories and about the relative size of the categories using two dimensions. An example of a bar graph is given in figure 17–3, showing the percentage of males and females in the NASW membership in three different years.

Bar graphs can also be used for ordinal variables when they consist of a finite number of ordered categories. They cannot be used for ranked data because the frequencies of ranked variables do not vary; each person has a unique rank, and the frequency with which each rank occurs is, by definition, 1.

To construct a bar graph, points are arranged on a horizontal line, or axis, to be the center of the bar for each category, or attribute, of the variable. A frequency distribution is used to determine the frequency with which each score or category was observed. The vertical axis is labeled to show the range of frequencies encountered. Above each category's location, a vertical bar (hence the term bar graph) is drawn high enough to represent the frequency, or number of people in this case, in each category or with each score. For example, a bar representing a category with 40 people in it, then, would be twice as high as a bar representing a category with only 20 people in it.

Although the bars in a bar graph are of differing heights, the width of each bar must be the same so that the visual impression of the relative frequencies represented will be accurate. Bars of the same height but different widths would seem to represent categories of different sizes because each would cover a different area

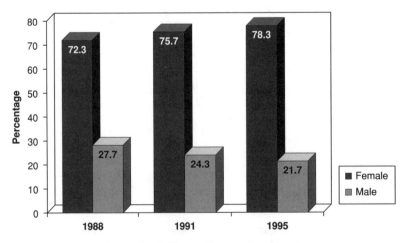

Figure 17–3 Example of a Bar Graph

or amount of space on the page. As in all graphing, it is the area on the page that reflects the relative quantities that the data show.

There is another important point about the bar graph that is related to level of measurement. Nominal numbers, it will be recalled, do not give information about quantity: There is no numerical relationship between the numerical category labels 1 and 2, for instance. In fact, all that can be determined from two nominal numbers is that the people measured on that variable are different from one another but not by how much. Even ordinal numbers show only order among categories, not how far apart or close to each other the categories are. Even when the numbers represented are "next" to one another, as in the case of 1 and 2 and the bars representing them are drawn touching one another, they don't form a continuum mathematically.

Histograms

One graphical summary method used for interval or ratio data is very similar to the bar graph and is called the *histogram*. The difference between bar graphs and histograms reflects the different qualities of the levels of measurement involved. Histograms are constructed by plotting the possible values a variable can assume on a horizontal line or axis, termed by convention the X axis, and then showing the frequency with which each possible value of the variable occurred on the vertical, or Y, axis using bars.

Histograms can be created directly from frequency distributions with either raw or grouped scores. As was true with bar graphs, the height to represent the frequency of score or set of scores must be proportional to the relative frequency of scores in the distribution. As was also true with bar graphs, the width of each bar and, for grouped data, each interval, must be the same.

The *frequency polygon* is a graph much like the histogram that is commonly used to describe the distributions of interval and ratio level variables. Frequency polygons can be created simply by labeling the possible values of an interval or ratio level variable at equal intervals on the X axis, labeling possible frequencies on the Y axis, and then drawing a line connecting the points marking the observed frequency for each value of the variable. This procedure is like connecting the tops of all the bars of a histogram. What results is a line that rises and falls over the X axis, reflecting rising and falling frequencies over the range of values of the variable. This line defines a curve, often irregular in shape. As an example, frequency polygons for the raw and grouped score frequency distributions of caseload data presented earlier are shown in figure 17–4.

The Shapes of Distributions

Histograms and frequency polygons are very handy drawings. Since the curve is higher where there are more scores and lower where there are fewer scores, they come in a variety of shapes. Some sample frequency polygons are shown in figure 17–5. In

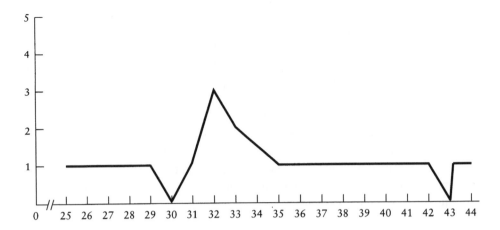

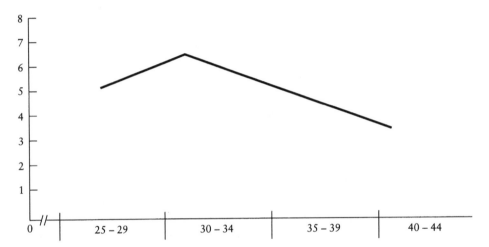

Figure 17–4 Frequency Polygons for the Hypothetical Caseload Data, Ungrouped and Grouped

the first (see figure 17–5a), there were many more low scores than high scores. Distributions shaped like this, where there are many more scores at one end of the variable's range than there are at the other, are called skewed. Distributions skewed in this direction, like income data, are called positively skewed. Distributions with many more high than low scores are called negatively skewed; the hypothetical distribution in figure 17–5b is an example of a negatively skewed distribution.

Histograms and frequency polygons are often named for the way they look. Some are called J-shaped (figure 17–5c), an inverted U (figure 17–5d), or rectangular (figure 17–5e). The histogram in figure 17–5f is called bell-shaped; the bell-shaped curve is also called the normal curve. A distribution that is very narrow or peaked, illustrating kurtosis, is shown in figure 17–5h; one that is very flat is shown in figure 17–5i.

The bell-shaped curve or distribution is a very famous one in statistics. The curve was originally named the "normal curve" because it was believed to capture the shape of human characteristics as they were distributed in nature. It was

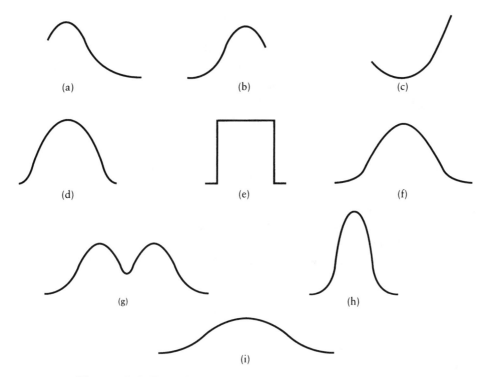

(a)   (b)   (c)

(d)   (e)   (f)

(g)   (h)

(i)

Figure 17–5 Variations in the Shapes of Frequency Polygons

believed that, given any naturally occurring characteristic, such as height, weight, or reaction time, most people would have an "average" amount of it, a few people would have very little of it, and a few people would have a great deal of it. In fact, such distributions *are* found for some characteristics of human groups. However, most population characteristics are not normally distributed in this way (Gould 1996). Some events that occur randomly, such as the distribution of scores obtained over many rolls of the dice or tosses of a coin, do show a bell-shaped or normal distribution. Therefore the concept of the normal or bell-shaped curve, which dates back to the early 1700s (Bernstein 1996), represents a key concept in inferential statistics, as will be shown in the next chapter.

Frequency distributions and graphs are all ways of organizing and summarizing data. They show, in tabular or pictorial form, how different distributions can be from one another. However, descriptive statistics offers additional ways to organize and summarize data, methods that summarize the information contained in a frequency distribution or graph even further and that help express the ways in which distributions differ.

Summary Statistics

Descriptive statistics offer even more condensed ways to convey information about frequency distributions: summary statistics. These summary statistics boil down information about key features of a frequency distribution into a single number. There are two features of a distribution that are most often summarized in this way: its *central tendency,* which describes where the middle of the distribution lies, and its *variability,* sometimes called *dispersion,* which describes the amount of variation there is around its middle. As with any summarizing technique, information and detail are lost when these measures are used, but measures of central tendency and variability are powerful tools for describing data efficiently. In addition, they are building blocks to understanding inferential statistics.

Measures of Central Tendency

One way to summarize a distribution or set of scores is to talk about where its middle, or central tendency, is. There are three methods used to describe the central tendency or midpoint of a distribution depending on the level or scale of measurement of the variable. Because the qualities of measurement are cumulative, all three of the methods can be used with interval and ratio data, and two can be used with ordinal data. Only one of the methods can be used with nominal data. Each of these three methods summarizes a distribution's central tendency in a different way; when they can all be used, each measure conveys something different.

Mode. The first and simplest measure of central tendency is called the *mode.* The mode is simply the typical, most common, or most frequently occurring score in the distribution. It is the only measure of central tendency that can be used with nominal level data for a simple reason: "calculating" the mode requires no calculations, no addition or subtraction. All that's involved in finding the mode is counting scores. Nominal scores, which cannot be added, subtracted, multiplied, or divided because of the basic meaning of nominal numbers, can be counted. So the mode is always used as the measure of central tendency when dealing with nominal scores. With nominal data, central tendency is indicated by naming the category into which the largest number of sample members were classified, that is, the modal category. The symbol for the mode is M_o.

The mode can be identified directly by looking at a frequency distribution and seeing which score has the highest frequency. In a grouped score frequency distribution, the mode is typically considered either the modal interval as a whole or the center point of the modal interval. The mode can also be identified from a bar graph or histogram by looking to see which bar is tallest or, in a histogram or frequency polygon, over what point on the X axis the histogram is tallest.

The mode is the simplest index of central tendency to derive, but it is also the least useful for interval or ratio data. It only provides information about which category, score, value, or interval is the most commonly occurring one, which may be different from where most of the other scores in the distribution are. The mode has another weakness: It can be drastically affected by a shift in one score. Consider these two sets of scores:

1	1	2	3	4	5	6	7	8	9	10
1	2	3	4	5	6	7	8	9	10	10

Only one score differs between these two sets, but the mode of 1 in the first set becomes a mode of 10 in the second. This dramatic shift happens despite the fact that 90% of the scores stay exactly the same. These disadvantages, of ambiguity of meaning and of instability, limit the use of the mode as an index of central tendency except with nominal data.

One more note about the mode: Sometimes frequency ties occur. In other words, sometimes there will be sets of scores or distributions that have equally high frequencies for two (or more) categories or values of the variable. When two values of the variable are tied for the highest frequency, the distribution is termed bimodal and both values are reported as modes. When three scores are tied, the term is trimodal, and all three values are given as modes. A frequency polygon for a bimodal distribution is given in figure 17–5g.

Median. The second statistic used to describe the central tendency of a set or distribution of scores is called the *median*. Determining the median, like the mode, does not involve performing any mathematical operations, but it does involve ranking individual scores. For this reason, the median cannot be used to summarize the central tendency of a set of nominal scores since nominal scores have no meaningful order. The median can be used, however, for ordinal, interval, and ratio scores. The symbol for the median is M_d.

The median is like the median strip on a superhighway, which divides the pavement in half. The median in a set of scores is the score that divides the set of scores in half in such a way that half of the people in a sample or half of the scores in the distribution are above it and half of the people in the sample or scores in the distribution are below it.

The median is derived by listing all the individual scores in rank order from lowest to highest, including ties. The median score is the score that falls in the exact center of this list. If there is an odd number of scores, the median score is the one that has $(N - 1)/2$ of the scores above it and $(N - 1)/2$ of the scores below it. If there is an even number of scores, the median is the score that is numerically half way in between the N/2th score and the n/2th + 1 score on the list. For example, in the data set: 1, 3, 7, 8, 11, the median is 7: it is the exact middle score, since an equal number of scores are above and below it. In the data set 1, 3, 7, 8, 11, 24, 25, 33, the median is 9.5, which is (8 + 11)/2, or the value halfway between the two scores that have an equal number of scores above and below them. Using a cumulative percentage distribution, the median can be found by identifying the score or score interval in which the 50th percentile falls.

With the median, the magnitude of the scores above and below it does not matter. The median is located by counting scores, not by assessing how high or low the scores are. For this reason, the median tends to be a somewhat insensitive measure of central tendency. For example, note that the two score sets below, which are very different, have the same median:

1	2	3	4	5	6	7	7	8	9	10	11	89
7	7	7	7	7	7	7	89	89	89	89	89	89

This insensitivity also means that it is a stable measure of central tendency, one that is not raised or lowered by an extremely high or low score in the distribution that is not typical of the others.

Because the median depends on ordering scores from highest to lowest (or lowest to highest), it is the appropriate index to use whenever summarizing the central tendency of ordinal scores, although it may not have much meaning with ranks. Since interval and ratio scores can be added and subtracted, a more sensitive measure of central tendency is most often used. However, the median can also be used to describe the central tendency of interval and ratio scores. Because it is stable, it is the preferred measure of central tendency to use with interval and ratio data when the distribution is skewed, that is, when one or more atypically high or low scores occur.

Mean. The index of central tendency most often used with interval and ratio level variables is called the mean, or arithmetic average. The mean is found by computation: First the sum of all the scores in the data set is added up, and then the total is divided by the number of scores that have been added. The symbol for the mean is $\overline{X}$ (read **X bar**). The formula describing the computation is: $\overline{X} = \Sigma X/N$. Following convention, the symbol for an individual score is **X**, and the symbol (Σ) indicates that summing up will occur. As always, the total number of scores is symbolized by the letter **N**.

The mean is a very useful index of central tendency, and it has several important properties. First, since the mean is a composite of all the scores in the distribution, it is sensitive to the exact values of each score. If even one score in the distribution changes, the mean will change.

The second property of the mean follows from the first: The mean is very sensitive to extreme scores. Consider these two distributions:

1	2	3	4	5	6	7
1	2	3	4	5	6	700

The mean of the first data set is 4, and the mean of the second data set is 103. There is only one score that is different between these two distributions, and yet this one (extreme) score that is different makes the mean very different.

Distributions that have a small number of very extreme scores, it will be recalled, are called skewed. Because these few extreme scores have such a dramatic effect on the value of the mean, most people regard the median as a better index of central tendency for interval and ratio scores that fall in a skewed distribution. For example, it is for this reason that the median rather than the mean is most often used to describe a community's household income.

There is a third property of the mean, a mathematical one, that should be noted: The sum of the deviations of the individual scores in a data set from the mean will always equal zero. That is because the numerical differences in scores below the mean is the same as the numerical differences in scores above the mean. In other words, the mean is the score that is in the exact middle of the quantitative values of the data set.

Comparing Measures of Central Tendency

These three statistics, the mean (used for nonskewed interval and ratio data), the median (used for skewed interval and ratio data and for ordinal data), and the mode (used for nominal data), are all indices or measures of central tendency. Each of these indices captures one of the two essential, defining features of a set of scores in a different way. The example of the hypothetical data on caseload illustrates the different meanings of each measure of central tendency (see table 17–5).

The modal score for this distribution is 32. The modal score is the most frequently occurring score, the most typical score. If the challenge were to guess the exact caseload of the next social worker to walk through the door from that hypothetical agency, the best guess to use would be the mode. The median score in the distribution is 33. The median caseload is the middle of the distribution defined as the point at which half the social workers would have higher caseloads and half would have lower ones, ignoring how high or how low the caseloads are at the extreme. Note that in this case it is an actually occurring value because the 10th and 11th workers both carry 33 cases. Finally, the *mean* is the average; it is the number of cases, 34, that each worker would carry if all the cases could be redistributed so that each worker would be carrying exactly the same number of cases as every other worker. In this case the mean is a value that doesn't actually occur; no one actually carries 34 cases.

With interval or ratio data, then, it can be useful to consider all the measures of central tendency because each describes the midpoint of the distribution somewhat differently. The best measure of central tendency to use, of course, depends

Table 17–5 Measures of Central Tendency Based on the Hypothetical Caseload Data

Caseload	*f*	ΣX	Cumulative percentages
25	1	25	5
26	1	26	10
27	1	27	15
28	1	28	20
29	1	29	25
31	1	31	30
32	3	96	45
33	2	66	55
35	1	35	60
36	1	36	65
37	1	37	70
38	1	38	75
39	1	39	80
40	1	40	85
41	1	41	90
42	1	42	95
44	1	44	100
	20	680	

Mode = 32
Median = 33
Mean = ΣX/N = 680/20 = 34

on the level of measurement of the variable, how the variable is distributed (for example, whether or not the distribution is skewed), and, most especially, the question that is being asked of the data.

Measures of Variability

The second essential, distinguishing feature of distributions is score variability. There are several methods to describe the variability seen in distributions of scores, and, as with measures of central tendency, the method used depends on the type of score or level of measurement of the variable.

Index of dispersion. The first method considered is the least well known. This method, called the index of dispersion, is appropriate for use with nominal scores. Researchers often do not consider variability when summarizing nominal scores, partially because variability typically involves figuring how much scores vary from, or around, a midpoint. And since nominal scores do not really have a "center" around which to vary, as the mode cannot really be considered central so much as typical—or most frequent—the concept of variability has limited application to nominal scores.

The index of dispersion is one measure that can meaningfully be used. It calculates how much the scores vary from one another relative to the amount they *could* vary from one another. In other words, the index of variability is a ratio of actual to possible or maximum variation. It is derived by subtracting the actual percentage of cases in the modal category from 100%. A category could be the modal one by having a bare plurality of cases or it could be the modal one because a majority of all the cases fall into the modal group. The index of dispersion shows what percentage of cases are *not* in the modal category, that is, the proportion that varies from the modal group.

The concept behind the index of dispersion is an important one: the notion is to quantitatively summarize how much the scores differ from one another. This notion is also at the heart of the second method of measuring variability.

Range. This second measure of variability, appropriate for ordinal, interval, and ratio measurement is called the range. The range, which has two forms, is very simple to determine. The range can be given simply by stating the highest and lowest scores that occur. With interval and ratio data, it can also be expressed by subtracting the smallest from the largest score. The difference is the range expressed as the numerical distance between the extreme scores in the distribution, reflecting how much at least the two extreme scores differ, or vary, from one another.

Because the range depends on the difference between only two scores, and the two most extreme scores at that, there are some objections to relying too heavily on it. Consider the two score sets below:

1   2   3   4   5   6   7

1   2   3   4   5   6   70

Only one score is different between them, and yet the ranges of the two distributions are very different: 6 (7 minus 1) for the first distribution, and 69 (70 – 1) for the second. In one sense, this great difference accurately reflects a real difference in variability: the numerical difference between the lowest and the highest scores extends over a range of only 6 units in the first distribution and over 69 units in the second distribution. But it is also true that this measure of the variability in scores is dominated by the two extreme scores and is less influenced by the scores overall. This index of variability is thus greatly influenced by the shift in one extreme score. The range can be viewed, then, as an index of score spread.

Standard deviation. The index of variability that has been developed to reflect variability between scores most sensitively is called the *standard deviation*. It takes each score in the distribution into account rather than just two of them, as is the case with the range. The standard deviation is the measure of variability used with interval and ratio level data, or whenever the mean is used to measure central tendency. In addition to its use as a descriptive statistic, the standard deviation is very important in inferential statistics as well because much of inferential statistics is based on the idea of variability. It is also the first summary statistic that involves more complicated computations.

The meaning of the standard deviation can be described by contrasting it to the meaning of the range. Recall for a moment how the range was computed: by naming or subtracting the smallest from the largest score in the set. This operation is analogous to standing at one end of the distribution of scores, looking down toward the other end of the distribution of scores, and seeing how far away the score at the other end of the distribution is. In other words, the range involves looking from outside the distribution to see how much spread there is in the scores.

The standard deviation involves looking at variability from another vantage point: Rather than standing outside the distribution and looking end to end, the standard deviation is analogous to standing inside the distribution, at its midpoint, and looking to see how far away every single score is from that middle point. Once each of those distances is identified, the "typical" distance can be calculated as something like an average. This typical, expected, or "standard" difference observed between the midpoint of the distribution and each score in it is what is captured by the standard deviation.

There are many advantages to using the mean as the reference point for measuring variability, but there is a complication as well. The complication arises from the fact that, since the mean is in the exact mathematical center of the distribution of scores, the total distance between the mean and all the scores below it will equal by definition the total distance between the mean and all the scores above it. Since the mathematical differences between the mean and the scores below it are negative, and the mathematical differences between the mean and scores above it are positive, the sum of these distances will always be equal to zero. To illustrate, look at table 17–6 to see what happens when computing the difference (that is, the mathematical distance) between each of the scores in the set below and the mean of the distribution, and then sum these differences. What happened with these of scores will always happen as a by-product of the nature of the mean itself.

Table 17–6 Deviations from the Mean in the Frequency Distribution of the Hypothetical Caseload Data

Caseload	f	$(X-\overline{X})$	$\Sigma(X-\overline{X})$	$(X-\overline{X})^2$	$\Sigma(X-\overline{X})^2$
25	1	−9	−9	81	81
26	1	−8	−8	64	64
27	1	−7	−7	49	49
28	1	−6	−6	36	36
29	1	−5	−5	25	25
31	1	−3	−3	9	9
32	3	−2	−6	4	12
33	2	−1	−2	1	2
35	1	+1	+ 1	1	1
36	1	+2	+ 2	4	4
37	1	+3	+ 3	9	9
38	1	+4	+ 4	16	16
39	1	+5	+ 5	25	25
40	1	+6	+ 6	36	36
41	1	+7	+ 7	49	49
42	1	+8	+ 8	64	64
44	1	+10	+10	100	100
	20		0		582

One way to eliminate negative scores mathematically is to square them, which is the preferred one for dealing with negative deviation scores. Using squaring, then, the standard deviation is derived by taking each score and finding out by how much it deviates from the mean (that is, how far away it is from the mean mathematically), squaring each of those differences or deviations, and then taking the average of the squared deviations by summing them and dividing by the number of scores summed. The number obtained at this point in the calculation is another descriptive statistic called the variance. Finally, the standard deviation is obtained from the variance by taking its square root to return to the unit of measurement of the original distribution. In formula form,

$$s = \sqrt{\frac{\Sigma(X-\overline{X})^2}{N}}$$

To carry forward the calculation for the distribution given in table 17–6, the standard deviation is:

$$\sqrt{\frac{582}{20}} = 5.39$$

Sometimes there is no interest in taking the square root of the average squared deviation from the mean. The average squared deviation from the mean for a set of scores, instead of the square root of the average squared deviation, is a fourth index of variability called the variance. It is symbolized by s^2, and its formula is:

$$s^2 = \frac{\Sigma(X-X)^2}{N}$$

Its value in the example is $582 \div 20 = 29.1$.

The symbols and formulas for the standard deviation and variance, **s** and **s²**, show the difference between these two indices of variability clearly. The variance is the square of the standard deviation; stated in reverse, the standard deviation is the square root of the variance.

The standard deviation is the most widely used measure of variability for two reasons. First, the standard deviation provides a descriptive measure of the amount of variability in a distribution relative to the most common measure of central tendency: the mean. Unlike the variance, which is squared, it is expressed in the units of the original measurement. Comparing two distributions can easily be done by comparing their means and standard deviations. A larger standard deviation shows that there was more variance around the mean; a smaller standard deviation shows that there was less. Second, the standard deviation and its by-product, the variance, are also at the base of many other procedures in inferential and descriptive statistics. Their role in inferential statistics will be covered in chapter 18. In addition, the standard deviation has been used to create a universal unit of measurement in descriptive statistics, a unit of measurement that has a constant meaning distribution to distribution, range to range, and raw score unit to raw score unit. This unit of measure is called the *standardized score*.

Standardized Scores

The wide use of the standard deviation has led to the development of a way to compare distributions and scores directly across distributions even when they describe quite different qualities: the standardized score. Standardized scores are created by translating scores into their standard deviation equivalents, that is, by expressing scores not in raw numbers but in terms of how far above or below the distribution mean they are when that distance is measured in standard deviation units. Pictorially, it's as if we stand on the mean, look to see how far away from the mean a particular score is, and measure that distance in standard deviation units.

When scores are expressed in terms of their distance from the mean measured in standard deviation units, they are translated into what are known as standardized or standard scores. Standard scores are also known as z-scores. The formula for a standard or z-score is:

$$z = \frac{(X - \overline{X})}{s}$$

Distributions of z-scores have certain properties, properties that are apparent from the formula for finding them and that indicate what they mean. Notice the numerator of the formula for the z-score: it reflects the distance between the mean and the score being translated. Given this numerator, it follows that when the score being translated *is* the mean, the z-score will be zero. And in fact, this is always the case: the mean of a set of z-scores will always be equal to zero. Descriptively, then, a z-score that is a small number reflects a raw score that is close to the mean for the distribution as a whole. A z-score that is a large number reflects a score that is many standard deviations away from the mean.

A second property is apparent. When finding the difference between a score that is below the mean and the mean, that difference will always be negative (subtracting a larger number from a smaller one always yields a negative result), and the resulting z score will have a negative sign. Therefore, z-scores for raw scores below the mean will always have negative values. By the same reasoning, z-scores for raw scores above the mean will always have positive values.

There is another property of a distribution of scores translated into z-scores that is apparent from the formula. Since the denominator is **s**, it follows that the raw score that is one standard deviation above the mean will have a z-score of 1. Therefore, the standard deviation of a set of z-scores is always 1.

When a raw score is translated into a z-score, it is easy to tell by inspection where that score stands on that variable relative to the rest of the group, to the total distribution of scores. Is the sign of the z-score positive or negative? The answer to this question tells whether the score falls above or below the mean. Is the z-score small (near 0) or large? The answer will show whether the score is close to or far away from the mean for the group. In fact, the value of the z-score—1, 2, 3, or more—tells how many standard deviations away from the mean the score actually is.

Z-Scores and the Bell-Shaped Curve

One particular distribution that was discussed in the context of histograms is of special interest to statisticians: the bell-shaped distribution, or normal curve. It is without question the most studied of all curves or distributions in statistics, and by virtue of this study a great deal is known about it. This additional information turns out to be very important in probability and inferential statistics, which are the topics taken up in chapter 18. Standardized or z-scores are one of the tools used to describe key properties of the normal curve and of all distributions that conform to that shape.

For instance, it has already been noted that when scores are expressed as z-scores, the mean of the distribution of scores is always zero. Since this is true of all distributions, regardless of shape, it is true of the normal distribution as well. In addition, the standard deviation of a set of normally distributed standardized scores is always 1.

The exact shape of a normal curve, which does not change regardless of the original raw or standardized score unit it is based on, is also known:

The picture and mathematical formula for the normal curve have allowed statisticians to generate information about its shape known as the Empirical Rule. The shape of the normal curve, its characteristics as defined in the Empirical Rule, is defined by its midpoints and in standard deviation units.

One characteristic of the normal curve is that the mean, median, and mode fall at the *same* point in the distribution. Graphically, the mode, the most frequently occurring score, is the highest point above the X, or horizontal, axis. With the bell-shaped curve, this point occurs at the center, at the mean. This center point also represents the median score, with half of the scores falling above it and half below it. This characteristic defines the symmetry of the curve; if it were folded at the midpoint, the two halves would match exactly because the areas on each side, the frequency of scores above and below the mean and how they are distributed, is the same.

This additional information about the normal curve also involves its standard deviation. In fact, the Empirical Rule describes exactly what percentages of the scores in a normal distribution appear in which ranges of scores defined by standard deviations. For instance, it is known that if a curve is normally shaped, then exactly 34.13% of the scores will fall between the mean and the point that is one standard deviation above the mean. And because the normal distribution is perfectly symmetrical, it follows that the exact same percentage of scores, 34.13%, falls between the mean and the point that is exactly one standard deviation below the mean of the distribution. By the same token, it is known that exactly 47.72% of the scores fall between the interval marked off by two standard deviations above (and below) the distribution mean. Thus less than 5% of all scores fall as far as 2 standard deviations away from the mean.

In fact, statisticians have computed the percent of scores in any normally shaped distribution that will fall between the mean and any point in the distribution. This information is expressed in terms of z-scores, and an abbreviated table of z-scores is given in table 17–7. It shows that 40% of scores fall between a z-score of .524 and

Table 17–7 Table of z Values and the Proportions of the Distribution Associated with Them

Value of z	Proportion of the Distribution Between +z and −z	Proportion of the Distribution Higher and Lower Than +z and −z
.126	.10	.90
.253	.20	.80
.385	.30	.70
.524	.40	.60
.674	.50	.50
.842	.60	.40
1.036	.70	.30
1.282	.80	.20
1.645	.90	.10
1.960	.95	.05
2.326	.98	.02
2.576	.99	.01
2.807	.995	.005
3.290	.999	.001
3.480	.9995	.0005
3.890	.9999	.0001
4.420	.99999	.00001
4.900	.999999	.000001

Adapted from Hamilton, L. C. (1990). Modern data analysis: A first course in applied statistics. Pacific Grove, CA: Brooks/Cole Publishing Co, p. 669, Table A2.

–.524, and 60% of scores fall outside that range. Similarly, 90% of scores fall between a z-score of 1.645 and –1.645, and only 10% of scores in the distribution fall outside that range. While the figure shows the proportions for only some values of z, other tables exist that allow these proportions to be worked out for any value of z obtained.

Standardizing scores, that is, expressing them as z-scores or as a number of standard deviation units above or below the mean, locates scores exactly in relation to the whole distribution of scores. In other words, if a phenomenon is normally distributed, transforming a score to a standardized score conveys a lot of additional information about the score, information about its relation to all of the other possible scores in the distribution.

Z-Scores and Multiple Variables

It turns out that being able to express scores in terms of a common metric, that is, in standard deviation units, is useful for another reason: making comparisons between scores on different variables. You're no doubt familiar with the saying "You can't compare apples and oranges." The basis for this truism, of course, is that it makes no sense to compare things that are fundamentally different. It is only possible to compare things that have something in common.

Frequently in research two or more things are measured that, in their raw form, are fundamentally different. Depression and alcohol consumption, for instance, are fundamentally different: While depression is a subjective, internal experience often measured by a self-report scale, alcohol consumption is an observable behavior measured by observation or by a self-report of frequency counts. These two scores, one measuring depression and one measuring alcohol consumption, would be fundamentally different in their raw score forms. However, if measured for every person in a group of people and if expressed not as raw scores but as z-scores, in standard deviation units, then the scores on the two variables can be compared. Each score would then show how far above or below the group's mean an individual's score on each of these variables was, with that distance expressed in standard deviation units, because scores would be expressed as the individual's standing relative to the rest of the sample on that variable. If a person's score is relatively high for depression, is it relatively high for alcohol consumption as well or not? Looking at the two scores in standardized form would answer that question for an individual.

Z-scores provide a way, then, to consider more than one variable at once. This possibility opens a whole new vista, and a very important one, since in fact much of research is designed not just to find out about single variables (age, income, etc.), but to find out whether there are relationships among different variables in general or within a specific group. Descriptive statistics also offers several techniques for doing just that.

Measures of Association

Associations or relationships between variables are described in two ways: with graphs and with summary statistics. These summary scores, termed *measures of association,* quantify the amount of relationship that exists between variables. Because the statistical, or numerical, measures of association are also used in hypothesis testing, in inferential statistics, only one of them, the Pearson **r**, will be discussed here. The rest of them will be discussed in chapter 18 even though, strictly speaking, the measures themselves are descriptive ones. It should also be noted that this discussion is limited to associations between two variables, termed *bivariate* relationships. Some techniques exist for examining relationships among more than two variables, termed *multivariate* relationships, but multivariate statistical techniques are beyond the scope of this text.

Picturing Relationships Between Variables

The most common method of describing a relationship between two interval or ratio variables graphically is the *scattergram.* Because there are two variables, two dimensions are needed to represent them. Scattergrams make use of the Cartesian coordinate system from algebra, using one axis, or dimension, to represent one variable (X), and the other axis or dimension to represent the other variable (Y). By convention, the X axis, the horizontal one, is used to represent the independent variable and the Y axis, the vertical one, is used to represent the dependent variable. Points are plotted or located in this space between the two axes, with each point representing one person's scores on the two variables being considered (see figure 17–6).

The hypothetical data on caseloads can be used to demonstrate what a scattergram, or scatterplot, might look like. The data show both the number of cases workers are carrying and the number of home visits each has made in the last three months. Worker A, for example, carried 25 cases and has made 10 home

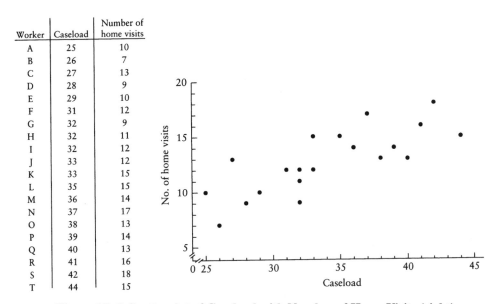

Worker	Caseload	Number of home visits
A	25	10
B	26	7
C	27	13
D	28	9
E	29	10
F	31	12
G	32	9
H	32	11
I	32	12
J	33	12
K	33	15
L	35	15
M	36	14
N	37	17
O	38	13
P	39	14
Q	40	13
R	41	16
S	42	18
T	44	15

Figure 17–6 Scatterplot of Caseload with Number of Home Visits (right)
Data Used to Develop Scatterplot (hypothetical) (left)

visits; Worker B, for example, has carried 26 cases and has made 7 home visits, and so on. The point representing each worker's scores on these two variables is located by going out to the point on the X axis corresponding to the score on the caseload variable and upward or downward on the Y axis corresponding to the score on home visits. For Worker J, for example, a point (33, 12) is entered on the scattergram to represent the scores on these two variables. The scattergram contains one point or dot plotted in this way for each member of the sample. When there is a relationship between the two variables, the points on a scattergram tend to cluster, as in figure 17–7b, c, and e; when there is not, the points tend to spread themselves out evenly across the space (see figure 17–7a).

Two statistical methods are used to summarize the information presented in a scattterplot. One method is based on developing an equation to identify the specific Y score that corresponds to (or is associated with, or related to) a specific X score. This method of summarizing the XY relationship presented in a data set is called linear regression; it rests on finding the formula for the straight line that comes closest to going through all the points in the scatterplot.

The equation for such a line is:

$$Y = a + bX$$

The "a" in the formula gives the intercept, that is, the point where the regression line crosses the Y axis, or the predicted value of Y when X is equal to 0. The "b" in the formula is termed the slope; it defines mathematically the slant the line will take. The slope can have a positive or negative sign denoting increasing or decreasing value of Y as the values of X increase, which changes the direction of the line in space. Figure 17–7b shows a positive slope, or a positive correlation. Figure 17–7c shows a graph of a negative slope or a negative relationship between

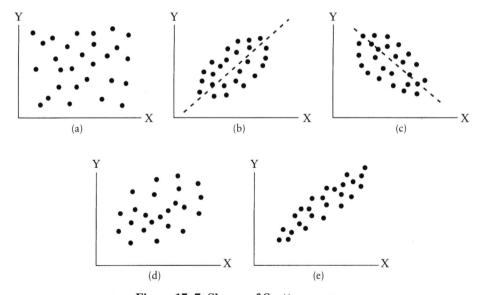

Figure 17–7 Shapes of Scattergrams

two variables. Using this formula for the regression line summarizing the general XY relationship in a data set, predictions can be made about what the specific Y value is likely to be for a given X score.

The Pearson Correlation Coefficient

The second method for summarizing the XY relationship between two variables describes the overall relationship between all the X's and all the Y's in the data set, taken as a group. It answers the question: In general, how closely are scores on variable X related to scores on variable Y? This method of summarizing the overall XY relationship is called *correlation,* and it is also based on the amount of linear relationship there is between two variables.

Earlier it was suggested that z-scores could be used to examine a person's relative position on two variables at the same time. The Pearson correlation coefficient takes advantage of this fact by finding the average relationship between two variables for all the people in a sample or studied group using standardized scores. The formula for the Pearson correlation coefficient, which is symbolized as **r** is:

$$r = \frac{\Sigma z_x z_y}{N}$$

The formula shows how the Pearson correlation coefficient is obtained.[2] It is done by (1) transforming each person's score on each variable, X and Y, to a standardized score, z_x and z_y; (2) finding the crossproducts of the z-scores, that is, multiplying each person's z-score for X by each person's z-score for Y; (3) summing, or adding up, the crossproducts for the whole sample; and (4) dividing the total obtained by **N**, the number of people in the group, to find the average intercorrelation of X and Y for the group as a whole.

Correlation coefficients provide several pieces of information about how two interval or ratio level variables are related to each other. First of all, they show the strength of the relationship. Correlations range between +1.00 and –1.00. Both +1.00 and –1.00 represent perfect correlations or perfect associations between X and Y. When there is absolutely no relationship between X and Y, such that low and high scores on X are equally likely to be associated with low and high scores of Y, there is no correlation between X and Y, and the correlation coefficient will be 0.0. The closer the Pearson **r** obtained is to 0, then, the weaker the correlation is said to be; the closer it is to 1.00, the stronger it is said to be.

Correlation coefficients also show the direction of the relationship between the variables. A positive correlation means that, on average, the more of X there is, the more of Y there will be, and, conversely, the less of X there is, the less of Y there will be. This result can be traced to the formula for **r**. A z-score below the mean will be negative; a z-score above the mean will be positive. If people tend to be high on X and Y at the same time, two positive z-scores will be multiplied to

---

2. The version of the formula given for **r** here (and for all other statistics illustrated) is the one that best shows what the statistic means. There are other versions of these formulas that are easier to use and are used for actually calculating them.

yield a positive crossproduct. If they also tend to be low on both at the same time, multiplying the two negative z-scores will also yield a positive crossproduct. If, on the other hand, being high on one variable is associated with being low on the other, a negative and a positive z-score will be multiplied together, yielding a negative crossproduct and ultimately an **r** with a negative sign. Positive and negative correlations are illustrated in figure 17–7b and 17–7c, respectively.

The coefficient of determination. As noted earlier, the field of statistics often proceeds by taking a simple concept and elaborating on it. Pearson **r** and the regression equation form the basis of many such elaborations. The first elaboration is that the **r** value can be squared to yield what is termed the *coefficient of determination,* or r^2. The r^2 is used because it has a particular meaning and interpretation: It is the proportion of variation in the scores on variable Y that can be attributed to the variation in variable X.

Based in part on coefficients of determination and in part on the statistical literature (Sprinthall 1990), guidelines can be given for interpreting Pearson **r** values (see table 17–8).

Pearson correlation coefficients are decimal numbers; squaring a decimal number makes it smaller. Thus a seemingly large **r**, like .7, yields only a relatively modest r^2, .49. Like any proportion, a coefficient of determination can be transformed to a percentage by multiplying the proportion by 100. Thus an r^2 of .49 means that 49% of the variation in Y can be attributed to variation in X, a result that most in social work or the social sciences would feel quite satisfied with. However, an **r** of .3, which seems much different from 0, yields an r^2 of only .09, or 9%, which is why a correlation of .3 is termed only a weak relationship between variables.

Correlation and Regression

Correlation coefficients and the regression equation are connected with one another. When the regression equation uses z-scores, the slope of the regression line, b, is equal to the correlation coefficient, **r**. Also, the closer the correlation coefficient comes to being plus or minus one, the closer the scatterplot based on it comes to being a perfectly straight line. All of this information—z-scores, correlation coefficients, coefficients of determination, and scatterplots—are descriptive. They show *what is* based on data that are in hand describing a sample or group.

Table 17–8 Interpreting the Strength of Correlations

r Value	Max. r^2 Value	Strength of Relationship
.00–.20	.04 (4%)	Very weak
.21–.40	.16 (16%)	Weak
.41–.60	.36 (36%)	Moderate
.61–.80	.64 (64%)	Strong
.81–1.00	1.00 (100%)	Very strong

However, as the next chapter will show, they also form the basis of some of the techniques that exist for answering more general questions about relationships between and among variables.

Summary

Whenever working with quantitative data describing a group or groups of people, there is a need to organize it and summarize it in order to make sense of it, to extract its meaning. Understanding different kinds of measurement and the types of numbers they yield is an essential first step in statistics because the descriptive and inferential techniques that can be used depends on the properties of the numbers available. Although the terms and symbols used in descriptive statistics might initially seem strange, the concepts that underlie them are generally simple and logical.

All of the material discussed in this chapter addresses alternative methods for extracting meaning from numerical data. Frequency distributions and various graphs can be used to describe a study's findings, variable by variable. For single variables, there are methods to describe two fundamental properties of frequency distributions: their central tendency and their variability. For paired variables, there are similar methods to describe their degree of association or relatedness. In addition, from these descriptive techniques have grown a variety of methods for using quantitative data to go beyond description to answering questions about how generalizable quantitative results might be and for testing specific hypotheses, which are introduced in chapter 18.

18

Principles of Inferential Statistics

T here are two branches of statistics: descriptive and inferential. In descriptive statistics, the intent is to describe and derive meaning from numerical sample data at hand. However, researchers are rarely interested in describing only the individuals studied in a particular sample. For example, Gomez (1990) studied the relationship between biculturalism and mental health among Cuban Americans in one city. He was examining some specific hypotheses or propositions about variations in cultural adaptation in immigrant groups and how these might affect mental health. The information drawn from his study is of value in large part because it sheds light on the larger population the sample was intended to represent and on general concepts and social processes that may apply across populations. The inferential statistics Gomez used provide rules and techniques for drawing inferences about populations based on samples and for sorting out which theoretical propositions or descriptions are most likely to have been supported by the numerical data collected.

As with descriptive statistics, there are special terms and symbols used in inferential statistics that must be learned. This language differentiates samples from the populations that, according to sampling logic, they are intended to represent. Numbers that describe the samples themselves are termed statistics; numbers that describe populations of interest are termed *parameters*. Symbols used to represent population parameters are drawn from the Greek alphabet; symbols used to represent sample statistics are drawn from the English alphabet. By tradition, the Greek alphabet is also used for some other terms and concepts in inferential statistics as well.

The field of inferential statistics involves making inferences or conjectures about samples or about what theoretical propositions are most likely to be supported by the data. Some degree of uncertainty is therefore inherent in all of inferential statistics. *Probability theory* is the tool used to capture and quantify the uncertainties involved in all inferential statistics. In this, inferential statistics are profoundly different from descriptive statistics. There is no uncertainty in descriptive statistics because they are drawn directly from sample data collected. In contrast, *all* results in inferential statistics are presented in terms of probabilities because there is no certainty about the inferences made even though there are guidelines for making them. However, inferential statistics provide a consensual set of standards for drawing conclusions from data.

This chapter differs somewhat from traditional accounts of statistics. From the standpoint of fallibilistic realism, "facts" or data and their associated statistical probabilities cannot be taken as proofs (Manicas & Secord 1983) as they are from the logical positivist or logical empiricist position. However, inferential statistics remain very useful tools for distinguishing descriptions or theoretical propositions that can be demonstrated to exist through observation from those that have not.

There are literally scores of inferential statistical techniques in use in social work and social science research today, and it would take one or more books to adequately describe them all. This chapter instead is designed to present the *principles* of inferential statistics, principles that are much the same no matter what specific test or technique is being employed. These principles will be illustrated using some common techniques and illustrations from the exemplars. Finally, guidelines for choosing among inferential techniques and additional resources to consult will also be provided. This chapter is thus not meant to substitute for a text on statistics but rather to place the use of inferential statistics in context, connecting it to research design. The availability of computers and sophisticated statistical software has both made the use of inferential statistics more accessible and, by automating their use, also reduced the need to dwell on the specific mathematics of each test and technique. Chapter 19 explains concretely how computers are used in the analysis of both narrative and numerical data.

Types of Inference

Inferential statistics give rules for drawing three types of inferences. The first type is called *parameter estimation*. This type of inference involves drawing conclusions about what a population's parameters are likely to be given statistics describing a random sample drawn from that population. Political polling is the most common illustration of this use of statistics. During presidential elections, for instance, polls are often taken of samples of registered voters to ask them which presidential candidate they favor. The percentage of the sample favoring a candidate is a statistic describing the studied sample. The poll extrapolates from that sample statistic and draws an inference about the parameter, the percentage of the American electorate more generally, that is, both the registered voters included in the sample and similar voters not included in the sample, that currently favors that candidate. Reports of poll results will typically state that the observed sample percentage has a certain "margin of error," describing a range in which the population percentage is *most likely* to fall. The sample percentage is known; the population percentage is inferred or estimated as likely, although not certain, to fall within a specific range. While parameter estimation is well understood, probability and likelihood as opposed to certainty are at its core.

The other two types of inferences drawn using inferential statistics both involve using theory and connecting it to description. In fixed method research, general theoretical ideas are examined using specific propositions called hypotheses. For statistical purposes, these hypotheses can be classified as falling into one of two groups based on their form: *hypotheses of association* and *hypotheses of difference* (Sprinthall 1990).

A study using an hypothesis of difference answers a question by comparing two or more subgroups in a study to each other on a set of predefined characteristics. If the scores in the two or more subsamples are different, inferential statistics provide a set of rules for examining whether the degree of difference observed between the subsamples can be reasonably regarded as a description of a real difference between them, not just an artifact of sampling. The El-Bassel et al. (1995) study in chapter 7, for example, answers its questions about the effects of a preventive intervention by comparing a group of women who received the treatment with a group of women who did not. Inferential statistics were employed to determine whether or not the groups were substantially different from each other on the studied variables and how likely any differences were to be real. Hypotheses of difference always involve different sample subgroups compared on the same variables.

The second type of hypothesis, the hypothesis of association, is designed to examine whether, in a studied sample, a certain degree of association or relationship is observed to exist between the two (or more) variables in the group as a whole. This association or relationship is quantified in the sample using a measure of association. An example of this kind of statistic was presented in chapter 17: the Pearson correlation coefficient. Inferential statistics are then used to draw conclusions about whether the two (or more) variables are likely to be meaningfully related rather than only an artifact of sampling. For example, the Gomez (1990) study proceeds in this way: Measures of association are calculated between several mental health variables and the variable biculturalism, and then the "significance" or likely trustworthiness of the observed associations is determined using inferential statistics. Hypotheses of association always involve one group, the total sample, and relationships among two or more variables that describe that group.

Conventions of Hypothesis Testing

In inferential statistics, there are some conventions to be learned that apply both to hypotheses of difference and hypotheses of association. The first is that theoretical propositions or hypotheses are examined for whether or not they can be demonstrated to exist through observation by testing or subjecting them to efforts at disproof. The usual explanation of this method of demonstration is that it is considered easier to disprove or to cast doubt on an idea than to support it.

In designing research studies, hypotheses are stated in positive terms as propositions. The El-Bassel et al. (1995) study stated, "We hypothesized that women in the SS [social support or prevention] group would exhibit higher rates of safer sex practices (consistent condom use or abstinence), perceived vulnerability to HIV/AIDS, improvement in coping skills, perceived emotional support, and sexual self-efficacy at follow-up one month after release than women in the AI [AIDS information] group" (p. 132). The Gomez (1990) study stated: ". . . there would be a positive linear relationship between subjective mental health and one's level of biculturalism" using four variables to measure subjective mental health (p. 377). These are the substantive or research propositions or hypotheses guiding each study. The first is a hypothesis of difference. The second is a hypothesis of association.

Once the data have been collected, however, for purposes of statistical analysis, a specific tool is used: the *null hypothesis*. The null hypothesis states each proposition to be examined in the negative: there will be no difference observed between the groups (El-Bassel et al.), or there will be *no* "positive linear relationship" observed (Gomez). It is the null hypothesis that is subjected to disproof through inferential statistics. If the null hypotheses cannot be disproved, then it is argued that the *research* or *alternative hypothesis* has found support in the study's data. The idea of scientific skepticism is thus built right into the rules and procedures of inferential statistics through considering the opposite of a beloved hypothesis and through efforts at disproof.

However logical it may be, this seemingly backward approach is a little complicated. The biggest challenge it poses may be in getting used to a language that sounds both technical and complex. The language of much inferential statistics is about rejecting or failing to reject a null hypothesis. Inferential statistics provide rules for deciding whether or not to reject a specific null hypothesis. While this language of null hypotheses and of rejection and failure to reject may sound odd, with practice it becomes familiar and understandable. In return for some complexity of language, what inferential statistics offer is an accepted tool for identifying among propositions or hypotheses the ones that have been empirically demonstrated to be reflective of aspects of the real world.

Probability

The field of inferential statistics has its foundation in two other fields: descriptive statistics (for it is not possible to infer from a sample to a population without first describing the characteristics of the sample) and probability. Descriptive statistics have already been covered in the previous chapter. Before proceeding to learn about specific inferential statistical techniques, it is necessary to consider some principles of probability theory.

Probability is a core concept in inferential statistics. The field of probability consists of mathematical rules for figuring out what it is reasonable to expect, given certain assumptions. For instance, it is probability theory that allows a pollster to infer the range of approval a candidate is *most likely* to enjoy in a population of voters given what was observed in a sample. As a field, probability theory did not begin to develop until the end of the seventeenth century (Bernstein 1996).

The probability of an event refers to the chances that the event will happen under a certain set of circumstances if that set of circumstances is repeated over and over and over again. Probability, then, refers to how reasonable it is to expect a certain event to happen over the long run. Since the event or outcome of interest is only one of two or more possible events or outcomes, probabilities are expressed as fractions, decimal numbers, or proportions.

There are two ways to derive the probability for an event: on the basis of what has been observed in the past, and on the basis of a theory. Probabilities based on what has been observed in the past are called *empirical probabilities*. Probabilities based on theory are called *theoretical probabilities*. The methods for finding both kinds of probability derive from the fundamental definition of probability: the chance that an event will happen under a certain set of circumstances, over the long run, if that set of circumstances occurs over and over and over again.

Empirical probability is found by observing and keeping track of what happens under a certain set of circumstances, circumstances that recur again and again over a period of time. The number of times that a certain event of interest occurs, like obtaining "heads" in a coin toss, is kept track of. The probability of the event is then found by dividing the number of times the event of interest was the outcome by the number of times the circumstances recurred. Probability theory was first developed empirically and then derived mathematically (Bernstein 1996).

When there is a theory about what outcomes can be expected to occur under a specified set of circumstances, then there is a basis for determining the theoretical probability of an event. Theoretical probability is determined by first identifying all the possible outcomes that could occur, theoretically, under a given set of circumstances and then classifying those outcomes in terms of whether they are or are not instances of the event of interest. The theoretical probability of an event is found by dividing the number of outcomes classifiable as the event of interest by the total number of possible outcomes.

In the case of a coin, for instance, there are two possible outcomes on a single flip: getting a head and getting a tail. If we are interested in deriving the theoretical probability of getting a head using a fair coin, we simply divide the number of outcomes classifiable as a head (1) by the number of possible outcomes (2). The theoretical probability of getting a head when flipping a coin is, therefore, 1/2, .5, or 50%.

The Law of Large Numbers

The Law of Large Numbers clarifies how empirical and theoretical probability are related to one another. The Law of Large Numbers states that, as the number of trials increases, empirical probability approximates theoretical probability and sample statistics will more closely resemble population parameters. These approximations get closer and closer as the number of trials, events, or instances contributing to the calculation of an empirical probability gets larger and larger. Stated another way, even though any one empirical probability may differ from the theoretical probability for an event, the average of a number of empirical trials will more closely reflect the theoretical probability for an event than any one trial may.

Note that the Law of Large Numbers refers to what happens over the long run. That is, the Law of Large Numbers states that if you flip a fair coin 100 times, on average (about) 50% of the flips will be heads. If you flip the coin only 4 times, however, it is not surprising when the proportion of heads obtained is either higher or lower than 50%. That is why this principle is sometimes called the Law of Averages. This figure of 50% refers to the whole run of flips, not to any single one of them. Believing that the Law of Averages refers to single flips, rather than whole sets of flips, is a mistake referred to as the Gambler's Fallacy. Illustration of the mistake shows why. Consider the stereotype of the gambler, the person who sits at a slot machine where he or she has lost 100 spins in a row and then, when told to give it up and cut the losses, replies, "Not now. I know a win is coming up soon: It's the Law of Averages." In reality, the calculated empirical probability for winning at this machine under the circumstances facing the gambler is constant and very low.

The gambler's error in thinking, the Gambler's Fallacy, is believing that the Law of Large Numbers, or the Law of Averages, has implications for the next, or the next few, spins. On any single spin, with a fair slot machine, the chance of winning stays constant regardless of how many wins or losses have occurred on spins preceding it. The gambler's experience in the first 100 spins of the slot machine are actually evidence that wins will likely not occur very often even in the next 100 spins.

Parameter Estimation

Parameter estimation, or calculating the specific characteristics of a population from sample data, is the first form of inferential statistics. Although not common in social work, it is a common use of statistics in many other social and biological sciences. Because it is conceptually simple, it is described here in large part to show the integral role of probability theory in all inferential statistics. Using hypotheses of association and hypotheses of group difference to examine theory is simply an elaboration of the same principles used in parameter estimation.

Imagine a group of 1,000 people whose ages are distributed exactly evenly. There are 10 one year olds, 10 two year olds, 10 three year olds, all the way through age 100. The average age of such a group of people would be 50.5 years. Using Greek letters, the symbol for a population mean is μ (mu), and $\mu = 50.5$.

Suppose that you are interested in studying the ages of people, and suppose, as is most typically the case in research, you don't have either the time or the money to query all 1,000 people to find out what their average age is. Finally, let us assume that any samples to be drawn from the group of 1,000 will be drawn randomly (see chapter 10). This last condition is often important to the mathematics of inferential statistics, as will be illustrated, which is one reason that random sampling is so often considered desirable in fixed method research.

This scenario would put you in the position of having to work with a sample to find out about the population. This situation calls for inferential statistics, moving from what is seen in a sample to what can be concluded reasonably about the population. What is different is that, in this hypothetical example, there is already knowledge about the population, the 1,000 people. In research, it is much more common to have data about a sample but not about the population and to use the sample data to make estimates about the population.

Sampling Error

In order to determine the mean age of the population, the 1,000 people, then, a sample of 20 people is drawn, and the following distribution of ages is obtained:

9	54	42	1	80	6	6	26	57	79
52	80	45	68	59	48	12	35	91	89

As you will recall from the previous chapter, the mean for this sample group is obtained by adding all the sample ages and dividing by the number of ages added (20). The result is a sample mean, $\overline{X}$, of 46.95. Note that the sample mean is not the same as the mean age in the population, 50.5. This difference between any sample mean and a population mean is the result of what is termed *sampling error.*

Sampling error is the result of chance as it operates in the random selection process. Although it cannot be eliminated, inferential statistics rests on the ability to describe and quantify sampling error, to calculate how great it is and thus to know the kind of influence sampling error may have on a statistical result.

To return to probability theory, the Law of Large Numbers consoled us that empirical probability approximates theoretical or actual probability more and more closely as the number of trials gets larger and larger. In other words, the Law of Large Numbers tells us that sampling error will tend to be smaller as the sample gets larger. To test this out, imagine drawing another sample of ages twice as large:

86	96	3	15	47	50	6	92	48	78
7	32	83	1	69	80	15	14	48	44
86	58	54	40	84	74	53	87	21	37
24	59	54	42	86	41	4	79	46	51

The mean for this sample of 40 is 48.575, somewhat closer to the actual population mean. Note that this result, a sample mean closer to the population mean, was not *certain*, only *more likely* because the sample is larger. The Law of Large Numbers holds that the larger the number of trials or selections made, the closer to theoretical probability or an actual population parameter an empirical probability is *likely* to be.

There are two points to take away from this reminder. First, assuming that a sample is not biased (since nothing can make up for the distortions induced by having a biased sample), the larger the sample is, the more accurately it will reflect its parent population. The second point is a confrontation with reality: Inferential statistics and probability theory remind us that what we see in our sample can be expected to only approximate, not mirror exactly, what's true in the population.

Understanding this point may be made easier by returning to the case of flipping coins. Even with a fair coin, sometimes when it is flipped 10 times, the result will be 5 heads, which is the number of heads expected given a theory of coin fairness. This "theory" makes the probability of getting a head on one flip 1/2, and therefore the number of heads expected in 10 flips 5, or 1/2 of 10. But sometimes in 10 flips 6 heads will result, and sometimes 4 heads will result. And sometimes the result will even be 3 or 2 or 1 or even 0 or 10 heads, just by chance alone, when the coin is flipped 10 times. All of the various outcomes, of getting anywhere from 0 to 10 heads on 10 flips, are possible, just by chance alone, when the coin is fair. The more extreme results, like 0 and 10, are *unlikely* and much less likely than are results closer to the expected one of 5 heads. But the point is that any result from 0 to 10 is possible and in fact will sometimes occur just by chance alone when a fair coin is flipped 10 times.

By the same token, in the example of ages, even though 50.5 is the mean age of the 1,000 people in the population, *it is actually unlikely that any sample mean will be exactly what the population mean is* no matter how carefully the sample is drawn. In the midst of all the effort of conducting research, this point is very difficult to remember when sample data have been gathered and so much effort has gone into making them accurate.

The Standard Error of the Mean

Inferential statistics works by providing ways, using probability theory, to quantify the degree of uncertainty that is inherent in data from samples. In the case of a sample mean, there is a specific statistic used to quantify the amount of sampling error that may affect it called the standard error of the mean. The most exact way to calculate the standard error of the mean is to use the population parameter, the standard deviation around the population mean. In the hypothetical example of the 1,000 people and their ages, this strategy in fact could be used. However, most often in research, there is information about the sample and not about the population from which it is drawn. Therefore statisticians have developed a way to calculate the standard error of the mean from sample data. The formula for this statistic is:

$$s_{\bar{x}} = s/\sqrt{N-1}$$

The formula states that to calculate the standard error of a sample mean, one must first calculate the standard deviation, or the amount of variability, in the sample (s). This number is then divided by the square root of the sample size (**N**) minus 1, to make it a conservative estimate. The reason this adjustment is made is that small samples are less likely to include extreme (very high or very low) scores from the population than larger samples are. Therefore, the **s** from a small sample may underestimate the variability in the population. Subtracting 1 from N in the denominator of the formula will make the resulting standard error slightly larger, more reflective of the variability in the population.

The calculation of the standard error of the mean can be illustrated using our hypothetical example of ages. The standard deviation in the sample of 20 is 28.66. This number is a large one, but that is not surprising because the variability in the population from which it is drawn is large since there are as many one, two, and three year olds as there are 50-, 99-, or 100-year-olds in the group. To calculate the standard error of the mean, the sample standard deviation, 28.66, is divided by the square root of $N - 1$ (19). The resulting estimated value of the standard error of the mean is 6.575.

How is this standard error of the sample mean used? In addition to the Law of Large Numbers or the Law of Averages, there is another mathematical law in probability theory that is used in parameter estimation (and other applications) that must be understood: the *Central Limit Theorem*. This theorem states that, if many random samples of the same size were to be drawn from a single population, the mean of the sample means would be at the population mean and a distribution the sample means themselves would form a bell-shaped or normal curve around that mean. The standard deviation of this usually hypothetical distribution of sample means is (or is equal to) the standard error of the mean.

In the example above, note that, by definition, the standard error of the mean is smaller than the standard deviation in the sample and remember that it is the standard deviation of the distribution of sample means. Sample means do not vary as much from the population mean as single cases in any sample may vary from a sample mean. That is because the means themselves average out the extreme individual scores that may occur in any one sample.

The Central Limit Theorem is an important one because it allows us to bring all the knowledge we have about the normal distribution to bear on the distribution of sample means (also called the sampling distribution of means). That knowledge allows us to state, for example, that roughly 68% of all the possible sample means will fall between plus and minus one standard deviation (now termed standard error) from the mean of the distribution of sample means (which is the population mean). In a similar fashion, that knowledge allows us to state that roughly 95% of all possible sample means will fall between plus and minus two standard error units (1.96 standard error units to be exact) of the mean of the distribution of sample means. The Central Limit Theorem has been shown to hold true whenever the set of population scores is shaped normally or the sample size is at least 30, which is another reason that quantitative researchers favor larger samples.

Parameter estimation thus depends on the Law of Averages, the Central Limit Theorem, and knowledge about the bell-shaped or normal curve. In fact, knowing that the distribution of sample means is always shaped normally allows us to combine what is known about how scores fall in the normal distribution, which is summarized in the discussion of z-scores in the previous chapter, with the values obtained from sample data for the size of the mean and the likely standard error of that mean.

In parameter estimation, this logic and information about probabilities is used to reason from the sample mean to the population parameter. Although the sample mean is but one possible value, it is likely to fall near the center of the distribution of sample means (because most sample means do). Therefore, using what is known about the bell-shaped curve and probabilities, there is a 68% chance that the population mean will fall in the range defined as one standard error of the mean above and below the sample mean ($\overline{X}$ +/– $s_{\overline{x}}$) and a 95% chance that the population mean will fall in the range defined as about two standard errors of the mean above and below the sample mean ($\overline{X}$+/– $1.96s_{\overline{x}}$). Stated another way, when there is a given single $\overline{X}$, chances are about 95 out of 100 that if we go about two standard error units (1.96) to the right and left of it, we will have defined an interval of possible $\overline{X}_s$ that has μ (mu) in it. In other words, we can identify an interval that we are 95% confident captures the true population mean (μ). This interval is called the 95% confidence interval. It is found by using $\overline{X}$ as the anchor point for estimating μ and $s_{\overline{x}}$ as the basis for estimating a likely range for it. This confidence interval around the mean is just like the "margin of error" described by pollsters, which is just a confidence interval calculated for a sample percentage rather than a sample mean. In our example, then, based on the sample of 20, we can have 95% confidence that the population mean falls between 34.06 and 59.84 [46.95 +/– 1.96(6.575)]. As we know, the population mean, 50.5, actually does fall in this range.

Parameter estimation in general (and the way the standard error of the mean is derived in particular) helps to explain why quantitative researchers tend to favor large samples. Having large samples (at least over 30) is good, but not because it largeness can make up for bias. Given a choice between the two, sample size is less important than is bias when engaged in making parameter estimates. However, largeness in sample sizes is important for a different reason when estimating parameters: Large samples are better because they allow for more precision in estimation. This is shown in the formula for the standard error of the mean. The sample size, **N**, is in the denominator of the formula for the standard error of the mean. If **N** is a small number (the sample size is small), the standard error of the mean will be a relatively large number; if **N**, the sample size, is a relatively large number, the standard error of the mean will be a relatively small number. Therefore the range in which the population mean will be estimated to fall will be small. Larger samples thus allow for more precision in parameter estimation than smaller samples do. It's built right into the statistics. When political polling results are published with a "margin of error" for their results, this margin of error is from a similar statistic that gives a range in which the population percentage is expected to fall based largely on the sample size.

To illustrate the difference in precision when using a large sample, it may be helpful to return to our example of the ages of the 1,000 people. Remember that when the mean was calculated for a random sample of 40, its value, 48.575, was closer to the actual population mean (50.5) than the mean of the sample of 20 was (46.95). The standard deviation in the sample of 40 is 28.15, again, as in the sample of 20, illustrating the extreme amount of variance in the population and in the samples drawn from it. Returning to the formula for estimating the standard error of the mean from sample data, the sample standard deviation, 28.15, is divided by the square root of 39 (N – 1), or 6.245; the result is 4.508. The 95% confidence interval for the population mean is thus 39.74 through 57.411. Note that because of the larger sample size, the standard error of the mean is smaller and thus the prediction made for the range in which the population mean will fall narrower or more precise. Again, the predicted range does in fact include the population mean (50.5).

Hypothesis Testing and Test Statistics

Parameter estimation and the development of confidence intervals for sample statistics includes most of the basic elements of inferential statistics: the descriptive statistics that they build on and some basic concepts of probability. However, there is one more tool of inferential statistics that has yet to be introduced: the *test statistic*. All hypothesis testing is done using test statistics.

A test statistic is simply a number calculated to serve as a probability indicator. Each test statistic is used with an associated distribution of possible values of that statistic. These distributions are given different names depending upon their shape. In fact, one such distribution has already been described; the normal distribution, or bell-shaped curve. Test statistics that are based on the normal distribution are called z-tests. Other distributions are called, for example, F, U, and chi square distributions. All of these distributions of test statistics have been mathematically derived and intensively studied and, like the normal curve or z distribution, a great deal is known about them (see figure 18–1). This knowledge is then put to use for estimating how likely or unlikely, that is, probable or improbable, actual sample results are under a null hypothesis. The best way to understand how this system of hypothesis testing works is by example.

As you know, many times research is based on an interest in more than one variable at a time, in the relationship between two (or more) variables. In order to answer such questions, measures of association are used to describe what the relationship is between two variables in a sample, with the real interest of knowing what the relationship is between those two variables in the population the sample represents. One descriptive statistic for examining a relationship between variables in a sample has already been introduced in the last chapter: Pearson's **r**.

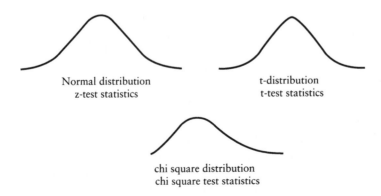

Normal distribution
z-test statistics

t-distribution
t-test statistics

chi square distribution
chi square test statistics

Figure 18–1 Shapes of Some Probability Distribution

This situation presents us with the same situation as in parameter estimation involving single variables: Having in hand information describing a sample and having an interest in what can be demonstrated to exist more generally. What is available is a sample statistic, but the real interest is in a trustworthy general description. In the case of relationships between variables, as was true with single variables, it is possible to make an estimate from what is seen in the sample to what it is reasonable to believe is true about the population the sample came from. Parameter estimation, then, can also be used when the parameter to estimate is a correlation. The standard error of the correlation coefficient is:

$$s_r = s/\sqrt{N-1}$$

Sampling error affects sample correlations exactly the same way that it affects sample means and sample percentages. A correlation coefficient in a sample, then, can never be taken to be an exact reflection of a population or of things in general. Finding out how two variables are related in a population, then, involves two steps. The first step is describing how those variables are related to one another in a random sample drawn so as to represent that population (and this process involves using descriptive statistics to derive correlation coefficients, as was described in chapter 17). The next step is specifying an interval, anchored by the correlation observed in the sample so that it makes sense to have a great deal of confidence that the true correlation (i.e., the one that exists in the population) will be included somewhere in that interval. So far, this is really still parameter estimation from a sample, although using a different sample statistic: a correlation coefficient. Hypothesis testing proceeds a little differently.

As stated early in the chapter, scientific skepticism about beloved theories and hypotheses is built right into inferential statistics. The way this skepticism is demonstrated is to turn a research hypothesis into its opposite, a null hypothesis, and then to subject that hypothesis to efforts at disproof. Sample statistics are then used to calculate a test statistic, a number that can be used to estimate the probability that the null hypothesis is false and therefore should not be rejected.

How does such a system work for a correlation or association between variables? The Gomez (1990) study can provide an example using correlations. The variable biculturalism was correlated with the variable self-esteem with a Pearson r of .87 in Gomez' sample (p. 383). However, Gomez also shows the "significance" of that correlation as less than .001. This result is in fact based on examining an hypothesis, that biculturalism is correlated with self-esteem. To do this, a null hypothesis, that biculturalism is *not* correlated with self-esteem, is tested statistically. Stated statistically, the null hypothesis is that the correlation in the population (ρ or rho) is 0 (zero), representing no correlation. The procedure actually involves calculating a test statistic, in this case a t-test statistic. The formula for this test statistic is given in the section of this chapter devoted to hypotheses of association. The t-test statistic has a probability distribution of a certain and known shape, and values of t based on sample values can be located on this distribution to determine whether the result is a likely or an unlikely one under the null hypothesis. In fact, exact probabilities can be calculated, as with the z distribution or bell-shaped curve, so that decisions can be made about the .05 criterion or any other that is chosen for the test. In fact, it happens that the t distribution is identical in shape to the z distribution under some conditions (but not in others). More details on how the specific test and procedure Gomez used are given in the section of the chapter on hypotheses of association. The point here is to illustrate the processes of hypothesis testing.

The significance figure given by Gomez means that a sample correlation of .87 is likely to occur when the null hypothesis is true less than 1 time out of 1,000. It is thus a highly *un*likely event. This probability was determined by calculating the test statistic, t, based on the actual sample r and the sample size, and then examining where the t value obtained fell on the distribution of all possible t's for samples of this size under the null hypothesis. Gomez then interprets his sample result, an r of .87, as indicating that r (technically rho) is highly unlikely to be 0 in the population, had he interviewed every Cuban American resident of the city. He therefore concludes that some positive relationship between biculturalism and one aspect of self-reported mental health, self-esteem, has been demonstrated to exist based on his observations.

Steps in Hypothesis Testing

There are scores of test statistics used in social science research, each of them calculated in a different way for use with different kinds of sample data. However, the logical steps in hypothesis testing are the same no matter what specific test is used. These steps are:

1. Statement of the research hypothesis in statistical terms.
2. Statement of a null hypothesis that is the opposite of the research hypothesis.
3. Determining which test statistic is best to use based on two factors: (a) the form of the hypothesis, group difference or association, and (b) the levels of measurement of the variable or variables involved.
4. Determining the probability criterion to use when deciding to reject the null hypothesis.
5. Calculating the value of the test statistic based on sample data.
6. Determining the probability of obtaining that specific value of the test statistic under the null hypothesis, which can be done using tables (the distributions of possible values) or exactly by using statistical software on the computer.
7. Based on the probability of obtaining that value of the test statistic and the probability criterion selected in step 4, deciding whether or not to reject the null hypothesis.

The Gomez (1990) example is quite clear about the nature of the research hypothesis, that biculturalism will be correlated with subjective mental health, and the nature of the null hypothesis can be inferred directly from it. The rules for determining which test statistic to use are laid out in this chapter separately for hypotheses of group difference and hypotheses of association. Tradition actually determines the choice of a probability criterion in inferential statistics; this topic is covered in the next section. It is safe to assume that Gomez (1990) used the traditional .05 criterion for the level of risk he was prepared to take in rejecting the null hypothesis.

Gomez does not actually state that a t-test was used, but that, too, can be assumed. Since he gives the probability, or "significance," of obtaining an r of .87 under the null hypothesis as less than .001, it is likely that he obtained his result, his evaluation of probability, from a computer calculation, which can be exact for each statistical test calculated. Tables, by contrast, usually list only the .05 and .01 levels of significance for statistical tests. In rejecting the null hypothesis, Gomez (1990) runs only a 1 in 1,000 chance that a mistake has been made given the sample value of .87 for the correlation coefficient and a sample size of 151 (see table 1 in the article reprinted at the end of chapter 5). Although accounts of data analysis are typically shortened in research reports, again by convention, all of the seven steps listed above are used whenever statistical hypothesis testing is done.

As in all inferential statistics, some degree of risk or uncertainty is always there. There is always the risk that this sample, by chance alone, or sampling error, is atypical as a result of the particular people who were in it. Research designs and statistical decisions are planned to reduce this inevitable uncertainty, but they can never eliminate it. Thus no one demonstration of a proposition using data can ever be taken as an ultimate truth or proof.

Types and Levels of Error in Hypothesis Testing

While some degree of uncertainty exists in all inferential statistics because of sampling error, another source of error must also be considered in hypothesis testing: possible errors made in deciding about the null hypothesis. In hypothesis testing, only two decisions can be made: The null hypothesis may be rejected or it may not be rejected.

If there were perfect knowledge about the population as a whole or about observed reality in general, it would be possible to determine whether the null hypothesis in actuality were true or not. In research, however, studies are only undertaken when knowledge about a population or about reality in general is incomplete or in dispute. Therefore it is not known whether or not the null hypothesis (or the research hypothesis) is or is not true. Statistical decision making takes place, then, in a context of uncertainty.

In hypothesis testing, errors in decision-making can be of two kinds (see figure 18–2). The null hypothesis may be rejected, although if the "truth" about reality were perfectly known, it may be true or false. If it is false and it is rejected, no error has been made. If it is true, however, and it is rejected, an error has been made. Statisticians term this an alpha or Type A error. This possible type of error is the one referred to in Step 4 in hypothesis testing (see above). The alpha level chosen affects the value of the test statistic that will be necessary to "achieve significance." It defines the level of risk of a Type A error that will be considered acceptable when deciding to reject the null hypothesis.

Although the steps in hypothesis testing suggest that the significance or alpha level is chosen, historical tradition has set the criterion or alpha level at .05. This criterion is a stringent one, reflecting the skepticism built into statistical methods.

Decision About Null Hypothesis

Null hypothesis is:	ACCEPT (fail to reject)	REJECT
TRUE	NO ERROR	TYPE A ERROR (alpha)
FALSE	TYPE B ERROR (beta)	NO ERROR

Figure 18–2 Types of Error in Hypothesis Testing

An alpha level of .05 means that a null hypothesis will be rejected only when the mathematics of probability suggest that there is only a 5 in 100, 1 in 20, or 5% chance of being wrong when doing so. Stated another way, a 95% level of confidence in a research hypothesis is necessary; thus a beloved research hypothesis can only be supported when there is a great deal of confidence in doing so.

From time to time, researchers who work in the human services have suggested that the traditional 95% confidence level may not be a good one to use in practice research (Crane 1976). The argument is that interventions that are unlikely to cause any harm but that may do some good may be overlooked because of this stringent, traditional criterion. Especially when samples are small, it is argued, a 10% risk of a Type A error might in fact be acceptable. However, the tradition of using .05 is so strong that the use of any other criterion must be defended.

One reason that the .05 level of Type A error is debated is that there is another type of error that can occur in hypothesis testing: *beta* or *Type B error* (see figure 18–2). If one fails to reject the null hypothesis and if it is true, no mistake has been made. However, if one fails to reject the null hypothesis and it is *not* true, a beta or Type B error has been made. The more stringent the criterion selected for rejecting the null hypothesis, the more likely that the null hypothesis will not be rejected and therefore the more likely that a beta or Type B error will be made. In other words, the risk of a Type A error is inversely related to the risk of making a Type B error. To reduce the risk of making a Type A error is to increase the risk of making a Type B error because the null hypothesis will be rejected less often.

Risk of error may thus seem to be everywhere, and in fact, some degree of uncertainty exists in all inferential statistics. However, it should be noted that in any one actual hypothesis test, only one type of error is risked. Gomez (1990), for example, rejects the null hypothesis that biculturalism and self-esteem are not related to each other. The only type of error he may be making in doing so is a Type A error, which, as has been shown, is only a slight 1 in 1,000 risk. When it is decided *not* to reject the null hypothesis, the only risk is of a Type B error, and there is no possibility of a Type A error.

Specific statistical techniques vary in their capacity to reconcile Type A and Type B errors. The power of a statistical test technique is defined as its capacity to reduce Type A error while also minimizing the chances of making a Type B error.

A more powerful test will involve less of an increase in the chance of a Type B error when the risk of a Type A error is reduced than with a less powerful one. Sometimes there is only one choice of statistical test to use in a given situation based on the form of the hypothesis and the levels of measurement of the variables involved. Sometimes, however, there may be choices about what test to use particularly because levels of measurement may sometimes be converted from one level to another (see chapter 17). The greater power of a test may be a reason to choose it over an alternative (Cohen 1977).

Parametric versus Nonparametric Tests

There is one other important way in which test statistics differ from each other. There are often certain assumptions that must be met in order to use a given statistical technique reliably. For example, the Central Limit Theorem was said to hold true under certain conditions: if the sample size was at least 30 or if the variable was normally distributed in the population. This latter condition is a condition or assumption about a parameter or characteristic of the population. Some test statistics can only be reliably used when certain assumptions are met about population parameters. These are termed *parametric statistics*. Statistical tests that do *not* make such assumptions about population parameters are called *nonparametric statistics* (Pett 1997; Siegel & Castellan 1988).

The assumptions that are involved in parametric statistical tests are similar to those already encountered with the Central Limit Theorem. They typically involve an assumption, for example, that the characteristic in question is distributed approximately normally in the population. Embedded in this assumption, however, is the requirement that the variable in question be in fact a truly quantitative one, that is, interval or ratio in level of measurement. A minimum sample size may be needed as well. When subgroups are compared, an assumption often encountered is that the variability, typically measured using the variance, in the various population subgroups is equal. When learning about or considering using any statistical test, it is essential to determine what assumptions or requirements, if any, must be met for its use.

These assumptions about parameters usually cannot be evaluated by examining the population directly since research is most often done when knowledge about the population is limited. Instead these assumptions are checked by examining characteristics of the sample. If the characteristic is distributed approximately normally in the sample, for example, it is assumed that the same distribution is likely to be seen in the population. Similarly, if the variances in the sample subgroups are essentially equal, it is assumed that the population subgroup variances are also similar.

While this chapter will confine itself largely to discussion of *bivariate* statistical tests, the major bivariate parametric tests are often the basis from which the most common multivariate techniques grow. Multivariate analysis greatly enhances our ability to examine complex phenomena by taking several variables into account at the same time. While the mathematics of multivariate statistics are often difficult, this obstacle to their use has been removed through the development of sophisticated statistical software. The concepts that undergird most forms of multivariate analysis, however, are simply elaborations on common parametric, bivariate tests and techniques.

Nonparametric tests exist that are equivalent to many of the parametric tests in use. Nonparametric techniques are especially useful when dealing with nominal and ordinal level variables, and they are usually the only reliable tests to use when dealing with small samples. The formulas for nonparametric tests are often characterized by including some fixed numbers, or constants, in their equations. However, in general, parametric techniques are more powerful than the equivalent nonparametric ones, which means they are more efficient in keeping the risks of making a beta error as low as possible for a given level of risk of alpha error. The classic text on nonparametric statistics, Siegel and Castellan's *Nonparametric Statistics for the Behavioral Sciences* (1988), compares the power or efficiency of the nonparametric tests to their parametric equivalents when there is one. There are a great number of nonparametric tests used, in part because particular tests have been developed to fit a variety of specific circumstances. Nonparametric tests greatly extend the range of situations in which statistical tests can be used, providing sets of consensual rules for decision-making about hypotheses that can be used with all kinds of numerical data.

Hypotheses of Difference

As already noted, hypotheses can be divided into two groups based on the way that their propositions are stated and in the way their questions get answered. The first type is hypotheses of group difference. Hypotheses of group difference proceed by comparing two or more groups within the sample to each other. Another way of describing this strategy is to state that they proceed by asking whether two (or more) samples do or do not come from the same population with respect to the characteristic of interest. The El-Bassel et al. (1995) study asked whether or not the two sample subgroups defined by whether or not they had received the experimental treatment were or were not from the same population at follow-up with regard to selected outcome measures. This study is a classical example of one using a hypothesis of group difference.

Independent or Correlated Samples

Sample groups or subgroups can be constituted in one of two basic ways. *Independent samples* are formed when in the selection or assignment process each individual is selected or assigned to a group independently of the selection or assignment of each other individual. The El-Bassel et al. (1995) study illustrates independent groups or samples: Drug-using women soon to be released from prison were randomly assigned to the treatment (social skills) or control (standard AIDS education) group. The group to which each individual was assigned was not related in any way to how another individual was assigned; chance in the form of random procedures was the only criterion used. *Correlated,* or related, samples, by contrast, occur when the group membership of individuals or scores is related to or determined by the group membership of others. This kind of sampling can be done in a variety of ways. People can be studied *over time* and their scores at one point in time compared to their scores later on. This kind of pre- and posttest design is a common example of correlated samples. The people included in the second sample are determined entirely by who was in the first: They are the same. Correlated samples occur in other ways as well, as when couples or parent and child are selected. In this situation, once a child is chosen, the parent is by definition included, but no parent of a child not chosen can be in the study. Finally, when matching is used as a sampling strategy, the samples are also said to be correlated (see chapter 10).

This distinction between independent and related samples is an essential one because the mathematics used to make between-group comparisons is quite different in each case. With independent samples, the same sample statistics are calculated for each group and then compared. With related samples, by contrast, statistical comparisons may proceed by examining only the differences between scores without reference to the absolute values of the scores at all. Sometimes similar tests, calculated differently, are used for independent and correlated samples; sometimes entirely different tests and techniques are used.

Degrees of Freedom

Statistical tests for hypotheses of group difference generally have another feature called the *degrees of freedom*. The way the degrees of freedom is calculated for each test is different. The calculation is generally based either on the number of groups being compared, the number of people included in the groups, or both.

What the degrees of freedom really does is designate the exact distribution of possible values for the test statistic to which the results being calculated are to be compared. Distributions such as t, chi square, and F take on very different shapes depending on degrees of freedom. Therefore, each time a test statistic is calculated, the degrees of freedom must be calculated too.

Selecting Tests of Group Difference

As already stated, there are scores of statistical tests in common use in social work and social science research. Each one is calculated differently based on sample values, but the general processes of hypothesis testing are the same no matter what specific test is used. The challenge, then, is to select the right technique to use when analyzing data and to evaluate, when reading the work of others, whether in fact the right statistical test was employed for the situation.

Figure 18–3 provides a flow chart or decision tree to use a as a guide in selecting a statistical test for use with a hypothesis of group difference. The chart is organized by level of measurement. This dimension is based on the level of measurement of the variable on which they the groups are being compared. If the groups are being compared on a nominal level variable, such as marital status, the chart headed "nominal" is used; if they are being compared on a scale score, such as self-esteem, which is an interval level variable, the chart headed "interval-ratio" is used.

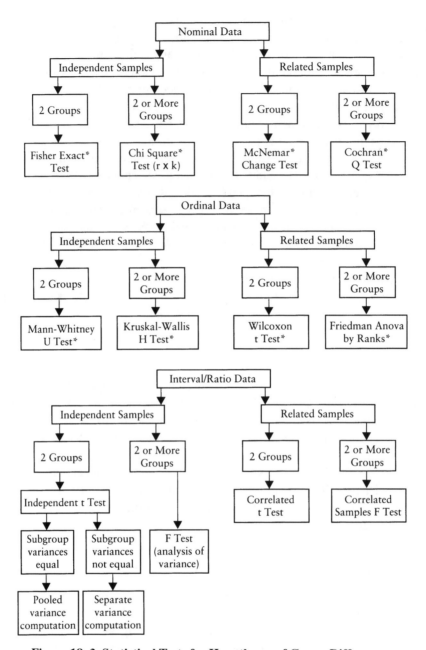

Figure 18–3 Statistical Tests for Hypotheses of Group Differences

* Indicates a nonparametric test.

As expected, the nature of the groups, independent or related, is the next factor used to determine the choice of test. Finally, because two-group comparisons are so common, special techniques exist for making those comparisons. Other tests are used when the comparison includes more than two groups, most of which can be used with two groups as well.

Finally, asterisks (*) are used in the figure to indicate the tests that are nonparametric. While no assumptions about the population parameters are needed to use these tests, most of them have been developed for specific applications, and a text like Siegel and Castellan (1988) or Pett (1997) should be consulted as to which test to use when. The ones listed in the diagram are in fact only the ones most commonly used.

The rest of this section will review some of the most commonly used statistical tests of group difference from the chart. These will focus on independent samples, beginning with tests for interval or ratio level variables.

Finally, both in this section and in the section on hypotheses of association, *defining formulas* are used. The defining formula is the one that shows most clearly what the statistic is and what it does. It is often not the one that is easiest to use for calculations, however. Since the calculation of test statistics is normally done by computer these days, knowledge of the formulas for calculation is not necessary, and defining formulas are emphasized.

A Two-Sample Test for Differences of Means: The t-Test

The most logical way to look for differences between two groups of people who have been measured on the same interval or ratio level variable is to compare their means. However, in the section on parameter estimation, the concept of sampling error was introduced. Sampling error is at work when two means are compared as well; in fact, neither group mean can be taken to be identical with the mean of that subgroup in the population. It is therefore unlikely that two sample means would be exactly the same even if their means in the population were identical. The question for the data analyst working with sample data then becomes: How much of an observed difference between these two sample means is enough to be able to conclude that the population means would indeed be different? The t-test provides a way to answer that question.

In the section on parameter estimation, the concept of the standard error of the mean was introduced. This statistic provided a way to quantify the amount of variance likely to be found around any sample mean, based on the amount of variance in each sample and on the sample size. The t-test depends on being able to quantify the standard error of the differences between two means, that is, the amount of difference that might be expected between two means based on sampling error alone. As with the standard error of the mean, this statistic must be estimated because data are only available on the samples, not on the population(s).

Unfortunately, with the t-test a unique complication arises: This estimate of the standard error of the differences between two means can be made in two different ways. If the variances within each of the two groups can be assumed to be equal (which is in fact determined by a statistical test of its own), the two variances can be pooled for computing the standard error of the differences between two means. If the variances cannot be assumed to be equal, the separate variance estimate method of computing the standard error of the difference between two means must be used. This simply means that the denominator in the formula for the t-test is different in each case, and the degrees of freedom are calculated differently, too. The test itself is otherwise the same.

How is the t-test statistic derived? The defining formula for the t-test is:

$$t = \frac{\overline{X}_1 - \overline{X}_2}{s_{\overline{x}_1 - \overline{x}_2}}$$

The numerator in this formula simply shows the mathematical difference between the two sample means. The denominator is the standard error of the difference between two means, calculated one way or the other depending on whether or not the variances in the two samples are equal. The t statistic is thus a ratio of the actual, observed difference between the two means compared to the expectable variation in differences under the null hypothesis.

The resulting value of t can be either a positive or negative number. If the mean of the first group is larger than the mean of the second group, when the subtraction is made, a positive number will result and t will be a positive number. If the mean of the first group is smaller than the mean of the second group, when the subtraction is made, a negative number will result and t will be a negative number. The sign of t simply indicates the direction of the difference, a feature that can only be present when only two means are compared. What is important is not the sign of t but its value, whether the number, negative or positive, is large or small. The size of the t statistic shows how far out "on the tail" of its distribution it is; the sign shows whether it is to the right (positive, above) or left (negative, below) of the center of the distribution of possible t values.

The t-test statistic has a distribution, just as z statistic has a bell-shaped or "normal" distribution. The t distribution is slightly narrower in its center, more peaked, and slightly wider at its tails than the "normal" distribution is. The mean of this distribution of possible values of t is at zero; under the null hypothesis, the most likely observed difference between sample means would be at or close to zero. If t is a relatively small number, it will fall near the mean of the distribution among the *likely* or common results under the null hypothesis. If the t value that is calculated is a large one, negative or positive in sign, it falls far away from the mean and is thus an *unlikely* event under the null hypothesis. Tables of critical values of t have been made showing the minimum value that t must have at the .05 and .01 levels of significance in order to reject the null hypothesis. To reject the null hypothesis means that the difference observed between the two means is so large that it is unlikely to have occurred as the result of sampling error.[1]

---

1. There is one other variation of the t-test that has not been discussed: whether it is conducted as a *one-tailed* or *two-tailed* test. In a one-tailed test, the research hypothesis specifies which mean is expected to be larger than the other. All the attention is thus to one type of difference and to one tail of the distribution of possible t values. If the actual direction turns out to be different from what was specified, the null hypothesis is not rejected. If the direction was as specified (that is, the sign of the t was as predicted), the probabilities are calculated differently and the test of significance is easier to pass. The 5% of probabilities are located all in one tail of the t distribution rather than being divided at both ends. Tests in which the direction of difference can be specified are only possible (a) when only two groups are involved, and (b) when the level of measurement is such that it makes sense to speak of directionality (greater than or less than). Data that are at least ordinal in nature are required. Additional information on one-tailed tests can be found in Sprinthall (1990) or Hays (1981).

The t distribution, like most distributions of test statistics, is shaped a little differently in mathematical relationship to the size of the samples involved. The mathematical function that describes this difference is called the degrees of freedom. As samples become larger, the t distribution looks just like the z or bell-shaped distribution, so the critical value of t that defines the .05 level of confidence is the same as in the normal distribution: 1.96.

In other words, the t-test, like all test statistics, is based on locating a specific test result for a specific sample among all the possible results for the statistic for samples of this size and deciding if it is a *likely* or *unlikely* event. In the case of t, an additional statistic, the degrees of freedom, is necessary to define the specific distribution of test values based on sample size against which a particular result will be compared. The test statistic is like a reading on a probability thermometer, and the degrees of freedom tells the reader what the scale is, like Celsius or Fahrenheit, when interpreting the specific reading obtained. A 100° reading on a Fahrenheit scale, which is less than half the 212° boiling point of water, and a 100° reading on the Celsius scale, which is the boiling point of water in that system, mean two quite different things. Similarly a t of 1.60 will mean one thing with a certain number of degrees of freedom and something else with another.

Degrees of Freedom for t

The formula for the degrees of freedom associated with the t-test when the variances are equal is a simple function of the number of people in each group: $df = (N_1 - 1) + (N_2 - 1)$, which is the same as $N_1 + N_2 - 2$. When the variances are not equal, the formula is much more complex and gives a smaller number than the first one, equivalent to the degrees of freedom for the other version with a smaller sample. Therefore the situation of equal variances between groups is preferred because it is a more powerful test. When the two subsamples being compared are unequal in size, the variances in the two groups are also likely to be unequal. With equal- or similar-size groups to compare, it is more *likely* (though not certain) that their variances will be equal and therefore that the more powerful version of the t-test can be used. Researchers often plan their designs to achieve equal groups when possible for this reason.

Using the t-Test

Whenever the t-test for independent samples is used, the steps in hypothesis testing are followed. The research hypothesis always takes the form of expecting a significant difference between two sample means ($H_A = \mu_1 \neq \mu_2$). The null hypothesis states that no significant difference will exist. Mathematically, this statement can be represented as one about the two corresponding population means: $H_0 = \mu_1 = \mu_2$ or $\mu_1 - \mu_2 = 0$. The t-test is to be used when two groups are to be compared on an interval or ratio level variable. The level of significance, or the risk of error to be run when deciding to reject the null hypothesis, is then chosen, and the test can begin.

Based on sample values—the actual means in the two subgroups, the variances in each, and the size of each group—the value of the t-test statistic and its associated degrees of freedom is calculated. These calculations are conducted a bit differently depending on whether or not the variances in the two groups are or are not equal. The probability of achieving a specific t value for the specific degrees of freedom under the null hypothesis is then assessed using a table or the more exact results produced by a computer program. Based on whether the probability of the given t is equal to or less than the probability previously specified as necessary, a decision is made to reject (or not) the null hypothesis.

In the end, the steps in hypothesis testing are quite simple, and the process is the same no matter what test statistic is used. What changes is the form of the hypotheses and the specific calculations needed to conduct the test. What results is a standardized way to reason from data, to decide what conclusion to draw from numerical data that others will be likely to agree with.

It has taken a long time to describe the t-test for two reasons. The first is that the t-test in fact has several variations that affect how it is calculated. The other reason is that all the basic principles of statistical testing had to be introduced in order to explain the test. Now that they have been explained, the rest of this section will describe some other commonly used tests of group difference more briefly.

Mann-Whitney U

The Mann-Whitney U test is used to examine differences between two independently selected groups when the variable on which they are to be compared is an ordinal one. When interval or ratio data are used, it is logical to compare means, as in the t-test. When ordinal data are used, it is logical to compare ranks. The Mann-Whitney U test, called by Siegel and Castellan (1990) the Wilcoxon-Mann-Whitney test, or simply the Wilcoxon test, compares the average ranks (as opposed to the average scores) in the two groups. If the two groups are about equal in the population, it would be expected that the ranks would be about equal between the two sample groups. The null hypothesis that is tested is that there is no difference between the ranks of the groups that cannot be attributed to sampling error alone.

To conduct the Mann-Whitney U test, individuals must be ranked, from 1 to N, on the variable in question. Only three characteristics of the sample must be known: the sum of the ranks of individuals in *one* of the groups $\Sigma(R_1)$, the size of that group (n_1), and the size of the other group (n_2). The U test statistic is calculated as follows:

$$U = \frac{n_1 n_2 + n_1(n_1 + 1)}{2 - \Sigma R_1}$$

The resulting number, the U test statistic, is the device used to assess the probability that the null hypothesis is true given the specific sample values observed. If it is rejected, the conclusion is that the ranks of individuals in the two groups are not equal on the variable in question. If it is not rejected, it is concluded that any apparent difference in the ranks is small enough that it is most likely due to sampling error alone.

When the n in each group is 10 or less, tables must be used to determine the probability of obtaining the U value under the null hypothesis (unless a computer is used); these tables are contained in the Siegel and Castellan (1988) text. If the groups are larger than 10, however, the distribution of probabilities is normal. Therefore, a z-test statistic is calculated based on the U value as follows:

$$z_u = \frac{U - n_1 n_2 / 2}{\sqrt{[n_1 n_2 (n_1 + n_2 + 1)]/12}}$$

This z statistic can be evaluated using a z table. For example, a value of +/– 1.96 corresponds to the .05 level of significance; a z_U value that exceeded 1.96 would be significant at the .05 level, meaning that the null hypothesis would be rejected. A statistical software package would evaluate the probability automatically.

Another technique that can be used in this situation—two independent groups compared on an ordinal level variable—is to compare their medians. This comparison is made by determining the median score on the variable for the sample as a whole and then counting up the number of people in each subgroup or subsample with scores above and below the median for the group as a whole. However, this technique actually becomes a version of the Fischer Exact Test (for bivariate nominal data) when the samples are small ($N < 20$) and of the 2×2 chi square test when they are larger ($N > 20$; see Siegel & Castellan: 125). Therefore the median test, unlike the Mann-Whitney U, is not a distinct test within itself but rather an adaptation of others.

F Test and the Analysis of Variance

A major limitation of the t-test and of the Mann-Whitney U test are that they are limited to the comparison of two sample subgroups to each other. Although two-group comparisons are very common, especially in experimental research, there are often times when more than two groups must be compared, when two groups must be compared on more than one interval or ratio variable, or when groups are defined by more than one dimension of difference. All of these situations (and more) can be handled by a general family of statistical techniques termed the *analysis of variance (ANOVA)*.

The best introduction to this family of statistical techniques is through the one-way analysis of variance. The phrase, "one way," refers to the fact that this procedure is the simplest, being based on classification into subgroups based on only one factor, or variable, at a time. Factorial analysis of variance techniques, mentioned in the section on multivariate statistics at the end of this chapter, is based on classifying people into groups based on two or more factors, or variables, at a time. Examples of the use of one-way analysis of variance include comparing sample subgroups based on marital or relationship status (unmarried, married or partnered, and formerly married or partnered, for example), experimental or control group status if more than two intervention groups are being compared, or any other factor or variable that divides people into two or more groups.

The test statistics generated by analysis of variance techniques are called F tests. As their name suggests, although these tests look for differences between sample subgroups, they do it through analyzing variability or variances rather than only by comparing means. The t-test illustrated that even when group means are the focus of comparison, subgroup variances (or standard deviations) are part of the comparison as well.

The analysis of variance proceeds by examining both mean differences between subgroups and the variances in each. The test statistics used in the analysis of variance, F tests, are ratios comparing the amount of variance in the sample explained by subgroup membership to the amount of variance that cannot be explained in this way. The total variance on the variable in question, which must be one of an interval or ratio level, is partitioned into that associated with subgroup membership and that which is not. The F test shows whether subgroup differences are relatively large or relatively small, specifically whether it is likely or unlikely to find variances partitioned in a given way under the null hypothesis.

A picture showing some of the ways that subgroups may relate to a total group may make this process clearer (see figure 18–4). Using a three-group example, at one extreme, sample subgroups may be so different from each other that their means are far apart and the variability within each group is small. In such a case, there is almost no overlap in values of the variable between members of different sample subgroups, and knowing which subgroup a sample member was in would allow one to predict quite accurately the range of values on the variable into which the person would be likely to fall. At the opposite extreme, subgroup means may be very close together and the variances within each subgroup may be large, as in (e) in figure 18–4. In such a case, subgroup membership says very little about where on the continuum of values of the variable in question a sample member is likely to fall. This same logic holds true whether one is talking about two, three, four, or more subgroups in a sample.

The hypotheses in the one-way analysis of variance are based on mean differences between subgroups. In the case of a three-group comparison, the alternative hypothesis states that there is a significant *difference* in the population between subgroup means: $H_A = \mu_1 \neq \mu_2 \neq \mu_3$. The null hypothesis states that there is no

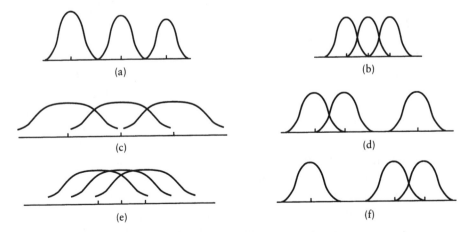

(a)

(b)

(c)

(d)

(e)

(f)

Figure 18–4 Possible Patterns of Differences Between Three Groups

significant difference between the subgroup means: $H_0 = \mu_1 = \mu_2 = \mu_3$. The question becomes whether the observed differences in means between the sample subgroups is large enough to be unlikely under the null hypothesis or whether it is small enough that it is most likely due to sampling error alone.

The calculation of the F statistic involves a statistic called the sums of squares, which measures variance. Recall that when learning about how the standard deviation (and the variance), both descriptive statistics, were derived, each individual score in the sample, X, was subtracted from the overall group mean, $\overline{X}$, to find the deviation. These deviations were then squared (to remove the positive and negative signs) and added together to go into the numerator of the equations. This number is called the sums of squares because it is the sum total of the squared deviations of scores from the mean. In the context of analysis of variance, it is called the total sums of squares (TSS) because it is the total variance of everyone from each of the subgroups together based on the mean for the total sample. This total variability can be divided into two parts: (1) the part that is attributable to subgroup membership, called the between-group sums of squares (BSS), and (2) the part that is due to variability within each group, around each subgroup mean, called the within-group sums of squares (WSS). The between-group sums of squares (BSS) and the within-group sums of squares (WSS) when added together give the total sums of squares (TSS): TSS = BSS + WSS. When the F test statistic is calculated, however, the between sums of squares and the total sums of squares are actually computed; the within sums of squares is derived by subtracting the between sums of squares from the total (WSS = TSS − BSS).

The F test statistic is the ratio of the mean sums of squares between (MS_B) to the mean sums of squares within (MS_W): F = MS_B/MS_W. The mean sums of squares between groups is calculated by subtracting each subgroup mean from the mean for the group as a whole (called the grand mean in this context), squaring that difference, and summing the squared differences. The total sums of squares between groups is then divided by the number of group means used, that is 3 for three groups, 4 for four groups, and so on. The mean sums of squares within groups is calculated by subtracting the total sums of squares between from the total sums of squares and then dividing between-group sums of squares by N − k, the size of the total sample minus the number of subgroups being compared. The F test value is found by dividing the mean sums of squares between groups by the mean sums of squares within groups.

Returning to figure 18–4, when the means of the sample subgroups are close together, the sums of squares between will be small relative to the total, and the F value will be small. Conversely, the amount of variance within the groups will be large compared to the small differences between the group means. When the means of the subgroups are far apart, the sums of squares between will be large relative to the total, leading to a large F value.

Degrees of Freedom for the F test

The distribution of possible F values varies on two dimensions: the number of subgroups being compared and an approximation of the sample size. To identify the correct distribution of possible F values against which to compare an obtained F value, two different degrees of freedom are needed, one for the numerator and one for the denominator of the F ratio. The degrees of freedom for the numerator is a function of the number of groups: $k - 1$. The degrees of freedom for the denominator is a function of the total sample size: $N - k$. Whenever an F value is calculated and reported, then, *two* numbers must be given with it—usually reported in parentheses—as the degrees of freedom.

Post hoc tests. In the one-way analysis of variance, a significant F test means that there is a difference among the groups so large that it is unlikely to be due to sampling error. However, when the F is significant, there is another question to answer: Is this result due to differences among *all* the groups or is it that only one group is quite different from the others? Figures 18–4d and 18–4f illustrates this possibility in the three-group situation.

This question can only be answered by using post hoc tests, or tests that are done only *after* a significant F test has been obtained. Sprinthall (1990) recommends Tukey's HSD test, which is a common and useful test; consult a good book on statistics or the manual for the statistical software being used in order to select a post hoc test when indicated. While this final step in the one-way analysis of variance is often neglected, it is an essential one.

The Kruskal-Wallis Test

There is a nonparametric test similar to the F test for use when ordinal rather than interval or ratio level data are available: the Kruskal-Wallis One-Way Analysis of Variance by Ranks test (Siegel & Castellan 1988). Like the Mann-Whitney U test, this technique proceeds by ranking all the individuals in the total sample on the variable in question and then sorting them into subgroups. The average rank of the people in each subgroup is then computed ($\overline{R}$). The null hypothesis is that the average rank in the sample subgroups is the same; the alternative hypothesis is that the average rank in the subgroups is different.

The formula for the Kruskal-Wallis statistic is:

$$KW = \frac{12}{N(N+1)}\Sigma n_j(\overline{R}_j - \overline{R})^2$$

It shows that the average rank for the sample as a whole ($\overline{R}$) is subtracted from the average rank for each subgroup ($\overline{R}_j$), the difference is squared and then multiplied by the number of people in that subgroup (n_j), and then this product is summed over all the subgroups in the sample. This number is multiplied by the first term in the equation: $12/N(N+1)$. If sample subgroups are very small (equal to or less than 5), a special table must be used to determine the significance of the KW statistic. If the subgroups are larger than 5, the statistic is distributed the same way the chi-square statistic is (see below) with its degrees of freedom based on the number of subgroups ($k - 1$). While there is no nonparametric equivalent to the F test for interval or ratio data, the KW test can be used in that situation as well since interval or ratio data can always be transformed to ordinal, or ranked, data even though some information is lost in the process.

Chi Square Test

The test for group differences using nominal data, the chi square test, is one that is commonly used in social work research. When people are compared on one nominal level variable across groups based on another nominal level variable, they are said to be cross-classified. This cross-classification is usually displayed in a table called a *cross-tabulation*. Calculation of the chi-square test statistic is based on the cells, rows, and columns of the cross-tabulation table.

The null hypothesis for the chi-square test is that there is no difference between the groups in how people are distributed in the categories of the nominal level variable. The alternative hypothesis is that there is a difference between groups, beyond what is expected from sampling error, in how people are distributed in the categories of the nominal variable. This question is answered by comparing the number of people *observed* to fall into each category or cell in the table with the number *expected* to fall in each category under the null hypothesis, that is, if group membership had no effect on what category of the variable people were found in. The number expected in each cell is found by computing the proportion of people in the sample as a whole in the category and then applying that proportion to the number of people in the sample subgroup. The only limitation on the use of the chi-square test is that no fewer than 5 people can be expected in each cell, or square, in the table.

The El-Bassel et al. (1995) study reprinted in chapter 7 can be used to illustrate the use of the chi square test. The study randomly assigned some women prisoners to two groups: an experimental treatment to enhance social support (n = 67) and a traditional AIDS education group (n = 78). As is typical in experiments, even though random assignment was used, the study examined a number of client demographic characteristics to see if they were the same or different in the two groups. If not, any differences observed between the groups at follow-up might be due to differing characteristics at the beginning of the study rather than to the effects of differing treatments. Table 1 in the article gives these findings. These data examine the proportion of women with children under 18 in each since this factor might affect both the capacity to benefit from treatment and or the variables used to assess treatment outcome.

How is the chi square test applied to data like these? The data show that a slightly lower percentage of the women in the experimental group than the other group had children under 18. The chi square test will show whether this variation was large enough to suggest that having children under 18 rather than the type of treatment received could account for any differences between groups at follow-up.

The chi square test itself has the following formula:

$$\chi^2 = \Sigma \frac{(f_o - f_e)^2}{f_e}$$

The symbol, f_o, simply refers to the count, or frequency, in each cell as observed in the data. The symbol, f_e, refers to the frequency, or count, expected in each cell or square of the table under the null hypothesis. For example, if overall 76.6% of the sample had children under 18, one would expect 77.6% of the 67 women in the social support group, or 51.3 women, to have children under 18. This number represents the expected frequency for the table cell for experimental group women with children. In fact, there were 50 women in the experimental group with children under 18.

The chi square statistic is calculated by (a) finding the expected frequency for each cell in the table, (b) subtracting it from the actual count, or the observed frequency, for the cell, (c) squaring that difference, (d) dividing that number by the number expected in the cell, and (e) adding up the resulting numbers for all the cells in the table. The sum is the value of chi square. When, as in this example, the chi square is calculated for a 2×2 table, a Yates correction is applied to make the test more conservative. This correction consists of subtracting .50 from the differences found in step b above for each cell of the table, resulting in a smaller chi square value.

As with every other test statistic, the obtained value of chi square must be compared with the distribution of possible chi square results. The distribution of chi square values differs in shape with table size, that is, with the number of cells in it. The degrees of freedom for the chi square test, then, is based on table size. Its formula is: $df = (r - 1) \times (k - 1)$. The number or rows in the table (r) and the number of columns in the table (k) are used. In the case of a 2×2 table, the degrees of freedom for the chi square statistic is 1. While El-Bassel et al. (1995) do not give the value of the chi square statistic, the probability of getting that value of the chi square statistic under the null hypothesis is given as .512. The observed differences between observed and expected frequencies is therefore not statistically significant. In other words, the small observed differences could easily have been due to sampling error alone. However, there were other preexisting differences between the two groups, and these factors were analyzed together with treatment group status when examining treatment outcomes using multivariate techniques.

Tests for Correlated Samples

Because this chapter is just an overview of hypothesis testing, tests for correlated samples will just be mentioned, not described in detail. For interval or ratio data, the tests used for correlated or related samples are the same as those used for independent samples although calculated differently. Both the t-test and the F test can be calculated for correlated samples, but their formulas and those for their associated degrees of freedom are different when the samples are paired. For ordinal data, the Friedman analysis of variance technique for related samples, like the tests for independent samples, uses ranks instead of average scores. For nominal data, the McNemar test examines changes (from time 1 to time 2) or matches; the Cochran Q test uses a similar method, calling matches "successes." As figure 18–3 shows, most of these techniques are nonparametric ones; Siegel and Castellan (1988) or Pett (1997) should be consulted.

Summary

This section of the chapter has given a rapid overview of the most common statistical tests of group difference used in social work research. It has focussed on the examination of differences between independent samples or sample subgroups. While the specific tests or the specific methods of calculation for tests and their degrees of freedom differ when related samples are examined, the basic principles of statistical hypothesis testing remain the same.

This summary of tests of group difference is not exhaustive of the tests that exist, especially the nonparametric ones. However, the principles of inferential statistics that guide the tests presented here guide them all, namely the application of the mathematics of probability in order to provide a set of agreed upon rules for the evaluation and interpretation of the numerical data found in samples. As the next section will demonstrate, the steps in statistical hypothesis testing and the use of probability for decision-making remain the same even when hypotheses of association are used.

Hypotheses of Association

Hypotheses of association, unlike statistical tests of group difference, build directly on measures of association that describe relationships between variables as observed in the sample. The concept of a measure of association or relationship between variables was introduced in the previous chapter. The example given of a measure of association was the Pearson r. A measure of association simply describes whether or not and to what extent variables vary together rather than independently. Covariation is a core concept in causation but it is not the same as causation. This meaning, covariation as opposed to causation, must be remembered when interpreting any measure of association or test of its statistical significance.

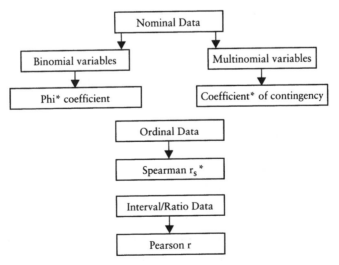

Figure 18–5 Statistical Tests for Hypothesis of Association

*Indicates a nonparametric test.

A measure like the Pearson r taken by itself, however, is purely descriptive; it describes numerically what is in the sample. Just like a sample mean, though, it is subject to sampling error, and there is no reason to assume that what is seen in the sample data is exactly reflective of what exists in the larger population from which the sample was drawn. When statistics are used to test hypotheses of association, the mathematics of probability are applied to assess the likelihood of obtaining a particular, observed value for a measure of association in a sample of a given size under the null hypothesis. Tests of hypotheses of association, then, unlike statistical tests for group difference, build on measures that *do* have descriptive meaning *in addition to* being employed as probability indicators.

A guide to selecting tests for hypotheses of association is given in figure 18–5. As with tests of group difference, the technique to use is guided by the level of measurement of the variables involved. The flowchart is simpler for tests of hypotheses of association because, unlike with groups, there are fewer variations in the kinds of comparisons made.

It should be noted that the flowchart lists only the most commonly used and most flexible measures of association. Others exist that can provide useful alternatives for specific situations (Siegel & Castellan 1988; Hays 1981). In addition, as with tests of group difference, the list is confined to bivariate, or two-variable, techniques.

A final note: The flowchart for selecting a test of a hypothesis of association is based on both variables being at the level of measurement specified. For example, the test for ordinal data can only be used if *both* measures to be related to each other are *at least* ordinal in measurement. If two variables are to be related to each other and one is at a higher or more complex level than the other, it can be converted to a lower level and then the appropriate measure used. For example, if an interval and an ordinal variable are to be correlated, the interval level variable should be converted to ranks and thus treated as ordinal, and the statistics for two ordinal level variables used.

Pearson's r for Interval or Ratio Data

The Pearson r statistic is one of the most commonly used statistics in all of social research. The formula for and descriptive meaning of the Pearson correlation coefficient have already been presented in chapter 17. This discussion will focus on hypothesis testing using the Pearson r statistic.

It happens that the test statistic used to evaluate the statistical significance of an r is a t-test, although one that is calculated based on sample correlations and not on sample means. Its distribution is called the t distribution, which has already been described in the section above on the t-test for differences in sample means. As already noted, when the sample size is large enough, the t distribution is exactly like the z distribution, and under some conditions a z-test statistic can be used (Hays 1981). The formula for the t-test for sample correlations is:

$$t = \frac{r_{xy}\sqrt{N-2}}{\sqrt{1 - r_{xy}^2}}$$

The numerator simply multiplies the sample r by the square root of the sample size minus 2. The denominator looks at the unexplained variance, the total variance (1) minus the coefficient of determination or the explained variance, using its square root. Thus the t value is a function of the size of the r itself and the size of the sample. The larger the observed r and the larger the sample, the larger the t value will be and the more likely it is that the null hypothesis will be rejected.

The degrees of freedom used to test the significance of the correlation is $N-2$, two less than the number of pairs of scores or people in the sample. Although some statistics texts simply offer tables of r values and the associated degrees of freedom for determining the significance of a correlation coefficient, a more precise result can be obtained by calculating the t-test for r and the degrees of freedom for it directly and then using a t table (Sprinthall 1990).

To review the steps in hypothesis testing with an hypothesis of association, the alternative hypothesis in the case of a Pearson r is that the correlation in the population, rho, is *not* 0; the null hypothesis is that rho is 0, that there is no relationship between the two variables in the population. The question is whether an actual, nonzero r in a sample is due to sampling error or whether it can be taken as evidence of a correlation in the larger population from which the sample was drawn.

Whenever there are two interval or ratio level variables, the measure used to describe the degree of their association is the Pearson r. The requirements for this parametric measure to be used are similar to those for the t and F tests; they are that the sample be randomly selected, that the characteristics being correlated are approximately normally distributed in the population (or at least in the sample), and that the variances of the two variables be approximately equal. However, this measure, the Pearson r, is actually a very robust one, meaning that it is quite accurate even when the assumptions have not been fully met. As already stated, a t-test is then used to evaluate the probability of obtaining an observed, sample r value under the null hypothesis and with a given number of degrees of freedom based on sample size. A table of t values can be consulted, or statistical software that provides the exact probability for the r can be utilized. A decision is then made to reject (or not to reject) the null hypothesis of no relationship based on whether this observed r is a likely or unlikely one under the null hypothesis. In the case of the Gomez (1990) example already discussed, for example, based on a sample r of .87, the null hypothesis of no relationship between biculturalism and self-esteem was rejected.

The descriptive features of the correlation coefficient must be emphasized at this point. Returning to the formula for the t-test for r, a large sample size can exert considerable influence on whether a correlation coefficient is found to be significant or not. In fact, with very large samples, very small values of r will be found to be statistically significant. Statistical significance in this case simply means that the r in the population is not likely to be zero. It is fortunate that the sample r can still be interpreted descriptively, that is, as a weak, moderate, or strong correlation in itself (see chapter 17).

Spearman's r_s for Ordinal Variables

The Spearman r_s, sometimes called the Spearman rho, is an alternative to Pearson's r that can be used when ordinal variables are being described or when the assumptions for the use of Pearson's r cannot be met. Spearman's r_s is a nonparametric measure; that is, it does not require that any assumptions about how the variables are distributed in the population be met.

The Spearman r_s is based on ranks, that is, how each of the N people in the sample is ranked, from 1 to N, on each of two variables.[2] In fact, calculating the value of the Spearman r_s requires calculating a d value for each person representing the difference in ranks on the two variables. If scores on the two variables were correlated, someone who was ranked high on one variable would likely be ranked high on the other as well, resulting in a small difference in ranks. If scores were not correlated, a high rank on one would likely be found with a low rank on the other, resulting in a big difference score. These difference scores are squared and then summed for the sample as a whole.

The formula for the Spearman r_s is as follows:

$$r_s = 1 - \frac{(6)\Sigma d^2}{N(N^2 - 1)}$$

The sum of the squared difference scores is multiplied by 6 and then divided by the sample size multiplied by the square of the sample size minus 1. This fraction is then subtracted from another constant, 1. The larger the sum of the difference scores, the bigger the fraction that is subtracted from 1 and the smaller r_s becomes.

Descriptively, the Spearman r_s is interpreted the same way the Pearson r is (see chapter 17). The larger the value of the r_s, the stronger the relationship between the two variables. The sign of the r_s indicates whether the relationship is positive or negative (inverse). In fact, the Spearman r_s was derived directly from the Pearson r.

The null hypothesis for the Spearman r_s is that there is no association between the two variables in the population; the alternative hypothesis is that there is one. When N is small (under 25), tables are generally used to determine the significance of r_s; such a table can be found in Siegel and Castellan (1988). When N is larger than about 20 to 25 people, a z-test statistic is used: $z = r_s\sqrt{N-1}$. This z statistic is normally distributed; thus for a .05 level of significance, a z value of 1.96 or greater would lead to rejection of the null hypothesis.

To summarize, hypotheses of association are tested by developing a descriptive measure of association from sample data and then, most often, by calculating a test statistic based on it. These test statistics function in the same way as test statistics for hypotheses of group difference do: by serving as a probability indicator. This process—calculating a measure of association and then applying a test—is reversed when nominal data are used, as the next section will explain.

---

2. Siegel and Castellan (1988) provide details on how to handle ties in rank when computing the Spearman r_s.

The Contingency Coefficient for Nominal Data

The test statistic used for hypotheses of group difference with nominal level variables is the chi square test. To examine a hypothesis of association for two nominal level variables, first the chi square test statistic is calculated and then one or another measure of association is derived from it. In fact, a number of different measures of association exist for use with nominal level variables, all based on the chi square statistic. Two will be introduced here, one that is quite general and can be used in a range of situations, the contingency coefficient (C), and one that is specialized for use with 2×2 tables, the phi coefficient.

Since nominal variables consist by nature of discrete categories, relating two nominal level variables to each other can only be done using a cross-tabulation, just as was done with hypotheses of group difference. The contingency coefficient (C) can be used with any size cross-tabulation table to provide a descriptive measure of association between the two variables. The C statistic is calculated from the chi square value:

$$C = \sqrt{\frac{\chi^2}{N + \chi^2}}$$

The chi square value is divided by the sum of the chi square value and the number of people on whom there are data; then the square root of this figure is taken to yield C.

The C statistic that results is always a decimal number. Because it is a nonparametric statistic and not as powerful as the Pearson r, its maximum value even with a perfect correlation is less than 1.0 (Sprinthall 1990). Thus, compared to the Pearson r, C gives a conservative measure of the strength of a relationship between two variables. Because the C statistic is based on nominal level variables that themselves have no "less" or "more," the concept of a direction of relationship has no meaning and does not apply.

The fact that C cannot reach 1.0 and thus cannot be compared with an r is a disadvantage. For this reason, some authors recommend the use of Cramer's coefficient instead (Hays 1981; Siegel & Castellan 1988). This statistic is calculated similarly:

$$C = \sqrt{\frac{\chi^2}{N(L-1)}}$$

The L in the equation refers to the minimum number of rows or columns in the table. For a 2×3 table, for example, L would be 2.

The statistical significance of any contingency coefficient is based on the statistical significance of the chi square statistic from which it is calculated. Since chi square must be calculated in order to derive C or the Cramer coefficient, no additional test of significance is needed. The chi square statistic, though, has no descriptive meaning; what C and the other measures of association based on it offer is a way to quantify the strength of the relationship, or the degree of association, between two nominal level variables.

The Phi Coefficient: The Binomial Case

The phi coefficient is used to describe the relationship between nominal level variables when both are *binomial*, that is, both have only two categories. This situation results, of course, in a 2×2 cross-tabulation, or contingency table.

The phi coefficient can be derived directly from the frequencies in the four cells of the table or it can be calculated from the chi square statistic:

$$r_\phi = \sqrt{\frac{\chi^2}{N}}$$

As shown by the formula, this statistic is but a special case of Cramer's coefficient; with a 2×2 table, $L - 1$ is equal to 1 and drops out of the formula entirely.

The phi coefficient (r_ϕ) can be regarded as exactly analogous to the Pearson r for interval level variables and can be interpreted in just the same way. Its significance, as with the other measures derived from the chi square, is based on it.[3]

Common Multivariate Tests and Techniques

This chapter has provided an overview of how inferential statistics are used for parameter estimation and, more commonly in social work and the human services, for hypothesis testing. This discussion, however, has been confined to bivariate techniques, that is, techniques for examining variables only two at a time. When studying complex social and psychological phenomena, however, often it is necessary to examine more than two variables at a time. Multivariate statistical techniques exist that do just that. This section will name some of the most common of them. Excellent works exist that can be used to learn more about them (Afifi & Clark 1984, Grimm & Yarnold 1995, Stevens 1996).

One multivariate technique has already been mentioned in the section on the analysis of variance: the factorial analysis of variance or factorial ANOVA. This technique is employed when people are grouped on more than one dimension, or factor, and then compared on a single interval or ratio level variable. Its logic is the same as in the one-way analysis of variance except for its complexity. F tests of group difference are generated separately for each grouping factor; an analysis using two grouping factors, one with 3 categories and one with four, would be called a 3×4 analysis of variance. In addition to F tests for each of the grouping factors (two of them in the above instance), an F test for interaction effects would also be performed. Such a test would show whether the factors were independent of each other in their effects on the subgroup means or whether they combined in some way so that specific combinations of groups were associated with unique effects on the means.

Another variation on the analysis of variance is the analysis of covariance (ANCOVA). The analysis of covariance corrects mathematically for a preexisting factor, called a covariate, before conducting the test of group difference. Analysis of variance can also be extended to the simultaneous analysis of multiple depen-

---

3. The phi statistic is calculated based on the raw, not the corrected, chi square.

dent variables, called MANOVA. In addition, any of these elaborations can be combined. Factors and covariates can be used at the same time if needed; independent and correlated groups can be included, termed a mixed model. The analysis of variance, then, is actually a whole family of techniques from the simple to the complex.

The other major family of multivariate statistical techniques are extensions of the concept of correlation and regression (see chapter 17). As with factorial analysis of variance, regression techniques can be expanded to examine the relationships of multiple independent variables to one dependent one, termed multiple regression. This technique yields a statistic, the multiple R^2, which describes the amount of variability in the dependent variable that can be explained by the combined effects of all the independent ones in the regression equation. Each of these, in turn, can also be described in terms of a partial correlation, that is, the relationship of one independent variable to a dependent variable while controlling for the effects of one or more others. Gomez (1990) used multiple regression to examine the joint and separate effects of biculturalism and various background variables on each of his measures of subjective mental health. He found that biculturalism was significantly correlated with all of them even when controlling for other factors (see table 3 in his article). The multiple regression technique, in turn, has given rise to a correlational modeling technique called path analysis.

All of these regression techniques, however, are still limited to looking at one dependent variable at a time. There are other correlational techniques, however, which are based on the analysis of whole matrixes of intercorrelations among variables, each to all of the others. These include reliability analysis, or the study of the intercorrelations among component item scores that comprise a scale; factor analysis, which looks for underlying dimensions in a group of variables, or subgroups of variables that vary more closely with each other than with others in the larger set; and cluster analysis, which uses correlation matrixes to identify cases or subgroups of cases in a sample that resemble each other, or cluster, based on their similarities on a variety of variables at the same time. Finally, there is an increasing use of multivariate techniques for the analysis of nominal or discrete (categorical) data (Bishop, Fienberg, & Holland 1975; Knocke & Burke 1980). Many of these have been developed by biostatisticians for epidemiological studies. Logistic regression, one of these techniques, was used in the El-Bassel et al. (1995) study to examine client characteristics and type of treatment received together in relation to outcome at follow-up.

Summary

The field of inferential statistics, which includes parameter estimation and, more commonly, hypothesis testing, applies mathematical laws of probability to sample data in order to generate guidelines for drawing conclusions from them. Statistical hypotheses, in turn, can be divided into two types: hypotheses of group difference and hypotheses of association, based on the ways questions are put and the ways various research designs are used in order to answer research questions. Once the type of hypothesis has been identified, the specific statistical test to be used can be determined by knowing the level of measurement of the variable(s) involved. Logical and mathematical conventions guide how all statistical hypotheses are tested; these logical conventions are the same no matter what specific statistical test is used.

This chapter has emphasized the logic that underlies the field of inferential statistics. It has also been limited to a survey of bivariate statistical techniques even though the use of multivariate techniques is becoming ever more common. Just as inferential statistics build on descriptive statistics, multivariate techniques build on the bivariate ones. For this reason, the fundamental concepts in descriptive statistics and beginning inferential statistics have been emphasized. The next chapter, in turn, will illustrate how data, quantitative and narrative, are prepared for computer analysis and in addition will demonstrate how several of the statistical tests introduced in this chapter are actually carried out.

19

Computer-Assisted Data Analysis

James W. Drisko, DSW

I n recent years, computers have strongly influenced how we communicate, play, and work. Access to computers has grown tremendously, and their use in social service agencies is now common. Computers are everyday equipment in educational institutions and research centers. They have influenced literature search processes, aiding social workers' ability to find articles, chapters, and books on specific topics. Through the Internet, they have added an enormous, though unregulated, body of information and resources with many ties to the human services. In many cases computers make communication with other professionals working on a topic possible and easy through e-mail, list servs, and chat groups. Computers have also changed how we write: word processors make editing, revising, and saving documents much easier. Spelling and grammar checkers can improve the quality of writing as well.

Focusing on data analysis, computers have added to the speed and ease of handling data sets of all types, qualitative and quantitative, and of all sizes, from small to extremely large. Computers help us organize, manage, and review research data sets in preparation for data analysis. The power of recent computers and the sophistication of recent software packages make both quantitative and qualitative data analysis available to a wide range of researchers. Computers can also be used to present both quantitative and qualitative data in a range of complex graphic formats. Used for more than four decades to analyze human service data, the "user friendliness" of these computers has improved dramatically in the past few years. This makes it possible for students and professionals to run sophisticated data analyses on their own. Still, using programs for qualitative and quantitative data analysis involves considerable learning time. Even for veterans, changes in computer hardware and software require continuous new learning. Fortunately, most old knowledge is transferable to later versions of computer programs.

The Strengths and Limitations of Computerization

The human services literature indicates that computerization can have many merits for professionals and clients alike. Liederman, Guzetta, Struminger, and Monnickendam (1993) see the use of computer technology in human services as a way to a better society. They note computers can promote public access to resources and expand knowledge and empowerment. For example, Wimberly and Blazyk (1989) describe a computer-supported follow-up tracking system for elderly clients. Cuvo, Hall, and Milder (1988) note computerized central intake processes can improve accountability. Pirog-Good and Brown (1996) report that expanded computerization could improve the fairness of child support programs. Grasso, Epstein, and Tripodi (1988) state that computerization of residential child care organizations could enhance both accountability and research. Computers generally ease repetitive tasks, allow quick manipulation of data, and allow easy backup and retrieval of important data. These functions can be applied to improving the quality of human services in a variety of ways.

At the level of direct practice, Marks, Shaw, and Parkin (1998) note computer-aided treatments for mental health problems are still in their infancy. Such treatments do only a few tasks in the treatment process, most typically assessment (Greist 1998). All computer treatments require oversight by a human clinician and few are widely available (Marks, Shaw, & Parkin 1998). Computer-aided treatment also has limits: Risdale and Hudd (1997) also found that clients do not want to learn about serious medical or emotional conditions via computer, apart from a human relationship. Training, too, is using more computer technology. Several schools of social work now use computer-based distance education models. Such training also takes careful planning: Hannafin and Land (1997) report that computer-based learning must be carefully organized to highlight cognitive issues. They believe computers can be excellent sources of training in problem-solving, decision-making, interpreting, hypothesizing, and experimenting. They note computer-based learning addresses fundamentally different learning goals than those of more traditional classroom and professional learning. The integration of human- and computer-based instruction must be well planned. Further, in order to realize any of these goals, a good deal of money, time, and effort must be directed to technology.

Nurius and Nicoll (1989) identify ambivalence toward computers, ambiguity about their labor-saving potential, and alienation as three key obstacles to computerization in the human services. Murphy and Pardeck (1992) note computers can have a dehumanizing effect in limiting the kinds of human experiences and knowledge that are viewed as important. They state that computers are supported by particular philosophy that has both strengths and limitations. They state practitioners must identify the knowledge amenable to computerization and remain aware of the importance of other knowledge that does not fit so well. Indeed, as we shall see, differences in philosophy have important implications for the selection and optimal use of qualitative data analysis software. Still, some forms of knowledge may remain fugitive from computer-based analysis.

Learning to use computers and software applications is a costly and time consuming process. Both the purchase of and technical support for computer equipment are expensive. Computer technology evolves very rapidly, requiring new equipment on a steady basis. New equipment typically requires training. Such training is costly and takes time away from other work. Nonetheless, Bloch (1995) reports that very high percentages of social work students and faculty desire computer training.

The growing importance of computer technology in human services is apparent in yet other ways. The journals *Computers in Human Services* and *Social Sciences Computer Review* are now well established. Both offer original articles on computer use, as well as software, book, and even web site reviews. Conferences on Human Service Information Technology Applications and on Information Technology for Social Work Education have been well attended. While books on computers in the human services are still not common, chapters on computer applications are quite frequent. All the major social work professional and educational organizations have had Internet web sites since 1997. Yaffe's (1998) *Quick Guide to the Internet for Social Work* is a useful introduction and list of web sites of interest to social workers and clients.

Since computer technology is a growing influence on human services, it is useful to learn about computers and the main software applications used in social services research. To begin, a brief overview of computer hardware and software will be useful. Computer equipment consists of hardware, the machinery itself, and software, the program code that directs the machinery and the specific tasks that the computer will perform.

Computer Hardware

Computer *hardware* comes in three main forms: free standing personal computers, large and fast mainframe computers, and computer networks that may consist of a few linked computers to thousands of linked computers. Freestanding personal computers are today the most common form of computer hardware. However, they became commonplace only in the early 1980s. They have developed from difficult-to-use and slow devices, to fast, multifunction devices—although they still pose some challenges to the user. Personal computers come as desktop machines or as portables, also known as laptops or notebooks. Desktop computers are fairly large and not intended to be portable. They are generally less expensive than portables and offer more features that do portables. They are also easier to repair and can often be upgraded—have new components installed to improve their performance. Portable computers are lightweight and readily moved. They can offer performance near that of the best desktops, with excellent display screens, CD or DVD drives, and speakers common. They can run for several hours solely on batteries. Their small size and battery power makes it possible to use a portable computer at remote sites, which can be very useful in social services research. Portable computers are considerably more expensive than desktops with similar features. Portables are also more difficult to repair and to upgrade.

Personal computer systems consist of a central processing unit (CPU), which is the heart of the computer. Using random access memory (RAM), the CPU "holds" vast amounts of information for processing via software program code. The CPU is connected to floppy and hard disks on which programs and data are shared and stored over time. Read-only or rewritable compact disk (CD) devices and digital videodisc (DVD) devices also store data and programs. A monitor or visual display presents the operations occurring within the CPU. Speakers offer audio output. Input devices such as a keyboard and a mouse provide ways to enter data into the computer. Other devices called *peripherals* can be installed in or connected to a personal computer. There are several types of peripheral devices. Printers make paper "hard" copies of material from computer programs as text or images. Scanners convert written text or images into digital form for storage and modification. Voice recognition systems convert oral, spoken input into text form for word processing and print use. Modems allow data to be shared from one personal computer to others via telephone lines, direct cable connections, or even satellite links. Modems, connected to the Internet, allow truly worldwide communication and data sharing. All peripheral devices are installed in, or directly connected to, the computer.

Mainframe computers are large and very expensive, high-speed, systems used to analyze very large data sets quickly. From the beginnings of computing in the 1940s through the 1980s, mainframe computers were the mainstays: there were no smaller personal systems or those few available were extremely limited. Mainframe computers consist of one or several interconnected CPUs, large amounts of internal memory, and very large tape or hard disk drives. Data is input via keyboard, electronic file transfer, or tape. Output from mainframes is either printed or displayed on a monitor, just as it is with personal computers. Today, very high-speed mainframes are still used to process large data sets and to model complex multivariate systems. However, for most forms of human service research, the personal computer is equal to most data management and data analysis tasks. Cautions about analyzing large data sets (over 1,500 cases) no longer apply as recent personal computers can handle this volume of data. Notable, software that was common on mainframes, such as SPSS, has largely been replaced by personal computer versions of the same software. Indeed, fewer and fewer social sciences data analysis packages are available for mainframe computers.

Local Area Networks (LANs), also called "Networks," connect many computers through a centralized system of wires or fiber-optic cables. Such networks may join personal computers and mainframes to form a large system with shared capabilities. Some LANs connect very simple computers using the processing power of shared servers to run several workstations. One common example is the computerized catalog of most libraries. A single server runs a large number of workstations that have limited processing units. *Servers* are powerful versions of personal computers with large amounts of RAM and data storage capacity. Servers are designed to serve many users simultaneously. Users at each workstation look at equipment much like a freestanding computer system, except that the programs and data are stored on the server, which is often in another location. Users of LANs log in with their name and a password that allows them to use the system. LANs may be created to offer different users access to specialized resources and programs. For example, a group of researchers may share a data base which each has "privileges" to modify. However, students using the data set may be limited to using the data for a given set of tasks but are not authorized to alter the database. LANs may also be limited to serving a set number of users. For example, a university may hold a license for 25 users on ATLAS•ti qualitative data analysis software. The server will allow up to 25 users at one time, but will be unable to allow a 26th simultaneous user under this contract.

The growing interconnection of personal computers via the Internet creates the sense that even personal computers are part of a worldwide network. While this is true for communication and data sharing, individual personal computer users do not run or control other computers. Instead, Internet browsers allow a user to access only those materials set up for public admittance by the owner of the distant computer. It is now possible to access a personal computer connected to a modem or the Internet from a remote location, but only when the user has installed programs and passwords to make this possible.

Computer Software

Software refers to disks of computer program code or files that direct the computer and all its installed components to work in a specific manner. The manufacturer, user, or technician installs most software on a personal computer's or network's hard drive. The *operating system,* such as Windows, Mac OS, UNIX, DOS, or OS2, joins the program code with the computer's hardware resources. The operating system is the foundation for other software application choices that are specifically designed to run on only one operating system. That is, you need application programs specifically designed for Windows to run on computers using Windows, and for Mac OS to run on Macintosh computers. Applications software, such as word processing programs or programs for statistical analysis, are what we typically think of as computer software. Applications software performs a specific task or set of tasks. The user enters data such as text or numbers or data files, which are "processed" by the software code in the CPU, leading to a specific, chosen result. Output from applications software may be printed, e-mailed, or saved as a new data file.

Our focus will now turn to software applications programs for the analysis of and quantitative and qualitative data for human service research purposes. To begin, we will examine the ethical and legal issues related to software use, and then move to an examination of the similarities of all computer-aided data analysis for either quantitative and qualitative research.

Legal and Ethical Issues in Computer Use

Computer software is licensed to the user rather than sold outright. The fine print reveals that users are legally allowed to install the software they purchase *on only a single computer.* Some companies allow use of a program on both a home computer and a portable computer, so long as they are not both used at the same time. It is worth the time to understand software licensing agreements. Like most intellectual properties (books, videotapes, CDs), the goal of licensure is to fairly compensate the authors of the program for their work. Making copies of software is only permissible to create backup copies for personal use if the originals are damaged. Copying for distribution to others is both illegal and professionally unethical.

Kesar and Rogerson (1998) note an increase of misuse of computers. This encompasses both misuse of software and of computerized data. They suggest human services workers need to be clear about the ethical issues involved in computer use. Issues of confidentiality, informed consent, and other issues of professional conduct all impact the use of computerized data.

Maintaining the Confidentiality of Data

Access to data on computer disks or tapes raises the same ethical issues as does access to any other information about clients and colleagues. Assuming the data were collected under a clear informed consent agreement, the uses of the data set are defined at the time of data collection. That is, when the research participant gives informed consent, the participant should understand how their privacy will be protected and how the data will be used. Access to and use of computerized data sets falls under these restrictions as does data in any other form.

Researchers generally agree that once data is collected with informed consent, the collected data are "owned" by the researcher. However, the use of the data remains restricted by the original informed consent agreement. An ethical issue arises when the researcher wishes to use a data set for later, or secondary, analyses on new topics. For example, if data were collected with informed consent to examine the effects of child abuse, the same data set might be used later to examine community supports for these children and their families. Such use is only ethical if the original informed consent statements made clear that the data might be used later for additional research. The NASW *Code of Ethics* (1996) section 5.02(l) states:

> Social workers engaged in evaluation or research should ensure the anonymity or confidentiality of participants and of the data obtained from them. Social workers should inform participants of any limits of confidentiality, the measures that will be taken to ensure confidentiality, and when any records containing research data will be destroyed (p. 26).

Yet many researchers note the value of secondary analyses of existing data sets. The data are already collected and organized into computer-ready form. The data may be revealing of more than the original researcher imagined. Despite these benefits, such use is ethical only if the participants gave consent for it. Secondary use of data sets may also conflict with the ethical requirement to inform participants when the data set will be destroyed. Unless future use is clearly defined in the consent forms, it is likely to raise ethical challenges.

Specific steps may be taken to protect the privacy of computerized data. To limit access to data sets on computer networks, passwords are often assigned. Only those persons with the correct password can gain access to the data set. Use of passwords to limit access to authorized users is now a common feature in human service agency life, where client information is often kept on computers. Bennenishty and Ben-Zaken (1988) note use of passwords on computer systems may provide better protection of client data than do paper file systems.

The Benefits of Computer-Assisted Research

Researchers are often faced with a large volume of data accumulated during data collection. *Organizing* the data and *managing* it as the project evolves are two key tasks in which computer programs may be of service. This is true for both qualitative and quantitative research. *Data reduction* is the task of focusing on the most important information in a data set. *Analyzing* the data is a vital task in which computers are often a major help. *Interpreting* the results of analyses is still mainly a human role and is pivotal to quality research. These tasks will be reviewed in order.

Data Organization and Management

One aspect of a research design is a plan to organize the data to be collected and analyzed. Such organizational decisions range from deciding how to label each research case (by the person's name? fictional name? random initials? a number?) and how to identify the items of interest (by a number for each answer? by each separate response to a question? by researcher-assigned code?). Making these decisions carefully helps both the researcher and ultimately the reader of the report to organize material in a clear and meaningful manner. Such *data management* helps the researcher stay focused and also may provide a framework for sharing the material with others. Organizing the data set helps the researcher locate key material and may be central to the statistical analysis of quantitative data.

Quantitative researchers typically organize their data in detail before it is collected. That is, they determine the tests and measures they will use as data, and develop a codebook defining the variables of interest. Such a codebook is used to organize data entry—the process of putting the data into the computer. For example, it might be used to inform a typist about the order in which data from questionnaires is to be entered into a computer file. The codebook also serves as a directory of key information about the data, useful for selecting statistical analyses.

Qualitative researchers must also organize their data. Some data organization may precede data collection, such as making decisions about how to label each case. Other data organization issues arise only when data analysis begins. That is, as codes and memos are assigned to texts, these new elements must be organized for clarity and easy retrieval.

Data Reduction

Data analysis involves focusing attention on the topic of interest. From all possible information, the data set is *reduced* to its key elements. For example, the choice to use quantitative tests and measures implicitly includes a choice about data reduction. From the realm of all possible kinds of long, short, and complex, nuanced responses the participant is asked to select a single response from the options provided by the researcher's test or measure. Some forms of information are purposefully ignored or determined to be unimportant to the researcher's purposes. So long as the tests and measures are valid and reliable for the topic and population under study, this from of data reduction is an asset to the researcher. Attention is focused on data collected in a specific form that allows comparison with other studies using the same tests. Irrelevant data are excluded, reducing the size of the data set the researcher must organize and manage.

In contrast, qualitative researchers often collect mountains of data that they must organize and manage immediately. Reducing the size of the data set to key elements is a process, much of which occurs after the data collection is completed. This qualitative data reduction may require a lot of labor. Conversations or observations generate considerable data that may prove ultimately irrelevant to the topic of study. The qualitative researcher must read through all the data and then decide which is meaningful and worthy of further analyses and which data is not. This process of data reduction takes considerable time and judgement. There are rarely preestablished guidelines about what data are important and what are not, so the research must make a series of critical choices about the data during the data analysis. The qualitative researcher must also provide enough information in the final report to make these decisions clear, credible, and trustworthy for the reader.

Quantitative researchers perform one form of data reduction by deciding which tests and measures to use. Other data reduction choices come in the form of variables to analyze and report. Qualitative researchers must first organize a very large pool of data and then perform data reduction through a careful and thoughtful process of coding each case in the data set. Both approaches do data reduction, but its timing and form vary markedly.

Data Analysis

Once the data are organized, quantitative researchers are likely to employ various forms of statistical analysis on it. Statistics are well-developed methods for understanding the nature of quantitative data sets and their distributions. Statistics also allow researchers to make decisions about data on a well-understood mathematical basis. Inferential statistics allow researchers to make decisions about an entire population from a smaller and less costly, probability sample. Thus statistics can save money and time, while allowing studies of entire populations to be undertaken. One everyday example of this is the use of political polls that can quite accurately describe the views of a population while based in a much smaller sample. Computer technology to perform statistics is a mature technology. It is a great time- and work-saver.

Qualitative data analysis may take many forms. Qualitative researchers can employ a range of philosophies and methods: Tesch (1990:58) lists fifty types! However, all will need to mark selected passages of text and then assign a code to them to allow later retrieval. Computer software can be used to speed this process and also to make sure text searches are done thoroughly. Computers can also be used to find specific words or phrases within a set of texts. Some qualitative researchers also use computers to develop theory. This is often done through network maps that lay out key concepts and the relationships among them. Computer software can be applied to this process. While computer-assisted qualitative data analysis is a newer technology than quantitative, it too can save labor and money while improving results.

Computer graphics allow quick and dramatic visual analysis of data sets. Quantitative programs such as SPSS and SAS offer spectacular visual presentation of data in multicolor and multidimensional graphics. Visual inspection of such computer output may suggest new approaches to statistical analysis. Some qualitative data analysis programs can also generate graphical network maps. These maps can quickly convey complex relationships found in qualitative data.

Interpretation

Computers are very limited in their ability to interpret the meaning of the analyses they do so well. The researcher must have enough knowledge and skill to ask good, important questions; to create an appropriate and revealing research design; to ethically collect adequate and appropriate data; to guide computer analysis, and to make sense of the computer output. While using computers may impart the appearance of objectivity to a piece of research, this is solely an appearance (Roid & Gorsuch 1984). Computer analysis implies nothing about the overall quality of a piece of research. "Garbage in, garbage out"—the line of computer programmers—applies in human services research too. Murphy and Pardeck (1988:120) rephrase this maxim as "Garbage in, gospel out" noting that computers may also be used to cover up shortcomings in research designs and data. To avoid such misuse solid knowledge of research has no substitute.

Having described the types of tasks computer software can perform, a detailed look at software for both quantitative and qualitative data analysis will link key issues in the research process to the use of each type of software. Several software packages will be mentioned and two widely used packages will be used for illustration purposes. This use does not imply endorsement of the software used for illustration. There are many fine programs available (see the resource list at the end of the chapter.), and each researcher or institution should make this decision on its own merits. However, the two packages described here—SPSS 9.0 and ATLAS•ti version 4.2—illustrate well how computers can enhance data analysis in human services research.

Computer-Assisted Quantitative Data Analyses

From the abacus of the Chinese to Babbage's "Difference Engine," the origins of computers center around the need to process numerical data rapidly and accurately. This need was apparent early on to quantitative researchers and statisticians, who had conceptualized very complex research designs and the multivariate analytic procedures to match them (Fisher 1935–1971). Simple descriptive and inferential statistics could be calculated by hand successfully. However, the sheer volume of numerical procedures required to complete complex statistical calculations made human calculation time-consuming "drudge work." The vast numbers of calculations required by complex statistical analyses on large data sets also made some mistakes inevitable, although errors could be identified through mathematical checks. Computers have now made possible the widespread, accurate use of complex statistical procedures. They have also opened up new forms of research, such as the meta-analysis of sets of prior studies on a topic. Such meta-analyses are common in psychotherapy outcome research.

Computers have also made quantitative data organization, manipulations, and statistical analysis quicker and more accurate. They can facilitate the calculation of simple descriptive and inferential statistics. They can also help in data organizing and manipulation. For example, computers can be programmed to calculate a scale score from a set of items on a test, or to score an entire test. Data can be recoded to create new variables or alter existing ones. Computers have also made data entry and organization more efficient.

Computerization has led to new standards by which both quantitative studies and analyses are judged. The ease with which statistical analyses can be produced requires that producers and consumers have detailed knowledge to ensure that they are implemented accurately and interpreted correctly. This takes very high levels of knowledge and skill in researchers, reviewers and readers/consumers. Learning to use computers to correctly implement statistical procedures also takes considerable learning. Data entry has shifted over the past twenty years from punched holes in paper cards to writing out the code for job control language in a computer file to using preset menus that write the job control code for you. Software evolves rapidly, sometimes in small steps, but occasionally in major revisions. For example, key statistical analysis programs for personal computers had to evolve to shift from DOS to Windows formats. This takes training but saves effort and time in the long run.

Software Packages for Quantitative Data Analysis

There are many computer software packages for quantitative data analysis. All of the major packages offer an elaborate range of functions for data organization and data analysis. The major statistical software packages currently used in the social sciences are SPSS and SAS. Others include SyStat, WINKS, BMDP, and KWIK-STAT (see Resource List). Differences between these software packages are slight for routine use but are more apparent in large scale data-entry situations or when using advanced data definition and statistical analysis procedures. The major applications were previously available in both mainframe (UNIX) and personal computer (DOS, Windows, or Macintosh) formats, but mainframe choices are now limited. New programs such as SAS, SPSS for Windows, SyStat, and WINKS are geared mainly to personal computers. Even business-oriented spreadsheet programs, such as Excel, can perform a wide range of statistical analyses. Indeed, the differences between the mainframe and personal computer packages are now very slight.

Personal computer programs for quantitative data analysis are increasingly easy to use, although mainframes versions are still faster for very large data sets. Other software packages (such as those included in many statistics textbooks) offer few features and typically handle only small data sets. The quality of their printed output is generally adequate but unappealing. However, some, such as WINKS or KWIK-STAT, offer many of the features of the major software packages. The main differences are in purchase price, the range of complex statistical analyses offered, and the form and quality of graphical display of results available.

Since computers are able to calculate statistics quickly, it is vital to ensure that the data are accurate and the statistics requested appropriate to the research question, sample, and types of data collected. Computers can generate vast amounts of output, so it is important that the researcher select only what is needed and relevant to the study at hand. Most researchers begin with a set, or *run*, of frequency tables. This output allows a check for the accuracy of the data that were entered. It also provides important information about the distribution of key variables. In turn, this information is used to guide the choice of statistical tests that can be run on the data in a valid manner.

It is important to remember that each statistic has limiting assumptions that guide its appropriate use. One such assumption is that the level of measure (LOM) of each variable must fit with the assumptions of the statistic employed. For example, the mode is the only descriptive statistic appropriate to use with nominal level measures. The mode, median, or mean may be used with an interval level measure. Many statistics require interval- or ratio-level measures for dependent (also called test) variables. Another limiting assumption is that the dependent variable must be normally distributed. This assumption may be evaluated using descriptive statistics drawn from a frequency output. Other assumptions, such as the use of the independent or the paired version of the t-test, require knowledge of the nature of the study sample. The researcher must insure these limiting assumptions are met because the computer will merrily provide output for any data set—whether it's appropriate or valid or not.

Another concern is the accuracy of the data set entered into the computer. Errors in the data set can have a cumulative effect on other values. That is, if an extra digit is entered in a row of values for a case, all values from the error on will be incorrect. Errors in defining variables may generate errors for all the cases in a data set. Care in organizing and reviewing the data can help minimize these errors or help identify them when they occur. One valuable tool in this process is the codebook.

Computer-Aided Quantitative Data Entry and Analysis

It is important to bear in mind that the research question, design, and measures selected for a quantitative research project orient all later steps in the project. Let's take as an example a comparative study of female and male social work students on attitudes toward research. We will need to collect, at minimum, data from students of both genders on their attitudes toward research. We might also wonder if their attitudes change from beginning to end of their studies. Computers can aid the data organization and analysis phases of the research to help complete the study. They do not automatically make the question important, nor do they ensure the research design is appropriate and adequate to examining the question. However, computers are very helpful adjuncts to the organization and analysis of the data you collect. While the measures selected by the researcher orient the data collection, these measures can also be used to organize the data analysis. With a little planning, they form a plan to enter them into the computer for analysis. We will use the research attitude study to see how data is organized in quantitative data analysis. But a review of terminology will be needed first.

Cases, Variables, and Values

The *case* is all the data for each person, test, or observation a researcher makes. To create a complete data set, information on each case is entered one case at a time. Working case by case allows you to track what data have been entered as you move along. The data for each case consist of information on all the variables for which you have collected data.

Each piece of information you wish to track is a *variable*. For example, you might want to know the ages of students in the research attitude study. One variable is "Age" and another would be "Research Attitude Scale Score." For the variable Age a participant might give the value of 27. From the answers a participant gives to the Research Attitude Scale her score might be 19.

Researchers often assign shorter labels called *variable names* when the full name of a variable is long. For example, Research Attitude Scale Score might be contracted to the variable name "ResAttSc." By convention, variable names are usually eight characters long and should start with a letter rather than a number. (These conventions are the legacy of the DOS operating system and choices made by the creators of the early statistical packages. They are still useful, but not always necessary with all current software.) When variable names are shortened, it is wise to make the name clear and unique enough so that you can identify each variable later on in the research process. The variable marital status might be given the name "MarStat," or Father's Education might be "PaEduc." Complex data, such as date of birth, can be coded in parts as "BirthDay" = 27, "BirthMon" = 11, "BirthYr" = 1973 for November 27, 1973. Note that this is actually three variables, each with different names.

We might assign *value labels* to each value of a variable. This might not be necessary for a variable like Age, where we know the meaning is age in years since birth. But on our Research Attitude Scale, which is the sum of 25 Yes or No items, we might want to know that a score of 0 is the lowest possible score and represents an extremely negative attitude toward research, while 25 is the highest possible score and represents an extremely positive attitude toward research. We might also know that according to the test's psychometric properties a score of 20 represents a moderately positive attitude.

Variable names and values help us create a codebook that helps organize and check the data set. Variables, by definition, can take on more than one value. A *value* is the score for the variable. For example, the value on the variable Age in the example above is 27 (years). Other participants in the study (cases) will give differing values on the variable age reflecting their ages in years.

Creating a Codebook—Organizing the Data

The bridge between collecting data and entering it into the computer is the coding process. Typically, a good deal of the conceptual work of coding precedes the data collection—to insure the data you will need to complete the study will be collected. Early on in the study, it is wise to create a codebook for all the data needed under study. Assigning numerical values to data is called *coding*. Codes may have everyday meanings (such as those for age and date of birth above) or more complex meanings. The codebook is a map or legend to the nature and interpretation of the coded quantitative data. It is important because the data file the computer reads is simply a long row of numbers.

The codebook helps you track what data is collected or missing. It helps us recall the properties of quantitative data and helps organize the entry of quantitative data into the computer. The codebook also clarifies the interpretation of statistical analyses. The codebook maps out the information on each variable under study.

The typical codebook is a grid of rows and columns. Each answer or item of data collected has a separate entry. In the example above, each participant was given

```
1021271226649546454442552432125253333334525511151515239331225
142134020858666065655465211511265653335351525155252252251332
12622522479447525366654555431134565532555424442242244149231
1071990180784626555475716163611165663656361515154251525533
```

Figure 19–1 Example of a Partial Data File

Line ____							Page ____
Item #	Variable Name	Variable Label	# Digits	LOM	Columns	Value Labels	Missing Values

Figure 19–2 Quantitative Data Cookbook Blank

Item #	Variable Name	Variable Label	# Digits	LOM	Columns	Value Labels	Missing Values
1	ID	----	3	N	1-3	-----	--
2	Gender	----	1	N	4	1 = Female	9
						2 = Male	
3	Age	Age in Years	2	I	5-6		99
4	Year	Year in Program	1	O	7	0 = Entering	9
						1 = End 1st Year	
						2 = End 2nd Year	
5	ResAttSc	Research Attitude Scale Score	2	I	8-9	0 = Lowest Possible Score -Extremely Negative Attitude	99
						15 = Slightly Positive Attitude	
						20 = Positive Attitude	
						25 = Highest Possible - Extremely Positive Attitude	

Figure 19–3 An Example of a Partial Quantitative Data

a unique identification number. This was a three column number (such as 100, 101, 102, etc.). The variable name is ID and no variable label was included since the meaning of the variable name is obvious. The ID value is three digits long, so 3 is entered in the digits column. ID is a nominal, level variable, representing only an identifying number. An N, for nominal, is entered in the LOM column. The value for ID will be the first three columns in our data file. This information helps locate a given variable's value in the long string of numbers that is a quantitative data file. While the numbers are sequential, they only represent each participant, and the numerical values have no mathematical meaning. No value labels are included as each ID number is unique. No missing values are noted since only those participants who provide data will be entered—so none can be missing (see figure 19–3).

For Item 2, the variable Gender, no variable name is entered as it, too, is obvious. The data is a single digit (1 column long). Gender is a nominal level measure representing categories. The value for Gender will be in column number

4 of a data list (after the three digits of the ID number). A value of 1 for the variable Gender represents a female, while a value of 2 represents a male. These labels will be printed along with the values on computer printouts. Finally, if no value is provided by the participant for this variable, a value of 9 will be entered to represent a *missing value*. This means the computer program will interpret the 9 as reflecting that the participant gave no value for this variable. By convention, missing values are represented by nines for clarity. Alternately, any other value that does not reflect a valid response can be used to represent a missing value.

Either way, it is important that the running data set stays in the correct sequential order, otherwise the computer will incorrectly read the value for the next variable Age as representing Gender. *All* later values will be incorrectly located and will be errors unless each variable's values are found in the correct column by the computer. For the third variable Age, the variable label Age in Years will be printed. Values for Age can be two digits long (no one-hundred-year-olds are expected in this study). Age is an interval/ratio level variable, in which values reflect a true hierarchy with each value representing an equal unit of one year. The values for age will be digits 5 and 6 in the running list of data. No value labels are included. If the participant does not provide a response to Age, a missing value of 99 will be entered. Note that a 99 could be a valid, if unlikely, age of a student. By assigning the value 99 to missing data, it cannot be used for a valid age value. It will fill two digits and keep the data set in register and accurate.

Using the codebook, we can now interpret the raw data in figure 19–1. We find that the first row in the data file represents participant number 102 (first three digits), a female (the fourth digit is a 1), who is 27 years old (the fifth and sixth digits are 27), is at the end of her first year in the program (seventh digit is a 1) and has a Research Attitude Score of 22, which is quite positive (eighth and ninth digits are 22).

In this example, there is only one line of data per participant or case. In larger studies, several lines of data may be collected on each case. To track this data, the line numbers (of data) are numbered at the top of the codebook sheet. Lines may be of any length, but should be fully visible on a computer monitor if entered directly to a file (roughly 50 characters in length). Make line breaks between variables, and do not divide data for the same variable across lines for clarity's sake. To keep the codebook organized, each page of the codebook may be numbered. Fortunately, most current computer programs, such as SPSS, have built-in data entry forms that are not limited to any number of cases and that create the data files automatically from the data entry screen. That is, there are no line or page concerns for the researcher. Still, data must be entered accurately and completely.

The SPSS Data Editor allows you to enter variable information directly into the computer. The data editor is formatted much like a codebook and requires all the information described above. It opens automatically unless you identify an existing data set for SPSS to open. A blank spreadsheet appears with vertical columns for each variable and horizontal rows to reflect each case. Right clicking on the heading of a column (Var) opens a variable definition menu. You then type in the variable name, define the length of the variable in digits including decimals, enter value labels, define missing values, and enter the level of measure. Once the

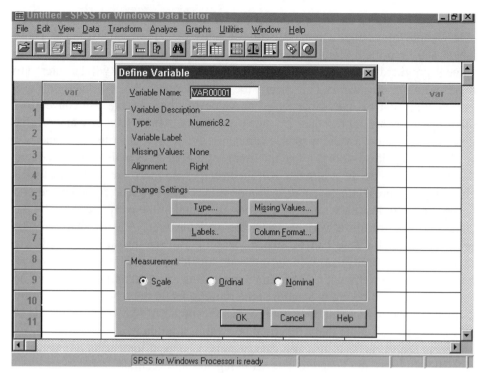

Figure 19–4 The SPSS Data Editor Screen

variable information is entered, the column heading changes to reflect the new variable name (aee figure 19–4). The resulting data set is saved automatically by SPSS in a file format which joins the raw data and the codebook information.

Manipulating Data

There is a wide range of useful and appropriate data manipulations or data transformations that are useful to quantitative researchers. They are quite legitimate and are used for altering data in valid and justifiable ways. These range from computing new variables through arithmetic functions, recoding values of variables, selecting certain segments of the data set, and transforming entire data distributions to better meet the limiting assumptions of statistical tests. Standard statistical packages offer many more of these data manipulation functions than do smaller packages or business-oriented spreadsheets.

It is common in quantitative research to collect data on a number of items that are then combined to compute a single, scaled score. For example, the Research Attitude Scale is the sum of 25 Yes or No items. The participant's responses to the 25 statements are coded "0" for No and "1" for Yes. The 25 coded scores are then added up. The sum of the responses is the Research Attitude Scale Score. While it is possible to do such arithmetic by hand, we can easily direct the computer to add up the scores. Using the Compute command, the computer is instructed to add up Item 1, Item 2—through Item 25. The sum is the value for the variable Research

Attitude Scale Score. The Compute command can be used to define and process simple, or very complex, mathematical formulas.

Data may also be Recoded to reflect new ways of viewing the data. For example, we might decide to compare the research attitudes of older and younger students. One way to do this would be to Recode the Age data into two groups: Younger and Older students. We might define all students whose age was less than or equal to the obtained mean of 29 years as value 1 or as younger students on the new variable Agegroup. Students over the age of 29 would be assigned a value of 2 or older on the variable Agegroup. Current computer programs can recode data using simple menu-driven procedures. Yet it remains up to the researcher to conceptualize the research questions and to insure the necessary raw data is collected.

Other data manipulation features include the ability to Select only those participants with a given characteristic or to Count the number of times a specific participant gives the same response. For example, we might wish to Select only female students for a question in our study. Or we might wish to Count how may times a participant gives a positive response to negatively worded items on the questionnaire.

Data transformations require strong knowledge of statistics. They are most often used to mathematically change the distribution of data on a single variable in order to meet the limiting assumptions of a specific statistic. Most often, the raw data on a variable deviates markedly from a normal distribution. Using a logarithmic transformation, the distribution data—but not the values themselves—are converted in form. In many cases the resulting logarithmic transformation will be normally distributed or nearly so. The transformed distribution may then be included in statistical analysis that require normal distributions for key variables. These data manipulation and data transformation options are easily employed in current quantitative data analysis programs.

Data Processing—Statistical Analyses

Current quantitative data analysis programs use a series of on-screen menus to guide users through the selection of statistical procedures. The software writes the job control code based on menu choices and specifications made by the user. The user need not write the job control code directly, which is a real convenience. For example, mouse clicking on the SPSS option called Analyze starts a drop-down menu of several categories of statistical tests, such as Descriptive Statistics, Correlate, Compare Means, Regression, etc. The user then clicks on a type of analysis, starting another menu listing several statistical tests. The user need not write any computer code as the program does this "behind the scenes" for the user. However, the user must know which statistics are appropriate to use and how to correctly identify the variables to be examined. This decision-making is beyond the capabilities of any computer or computer program.

Descriptive Statistics

The first step in most statistical analyses is to run a set of frequency tables on each variable under study. Current statistical packages offer Frequency tables as an option on a list of many types of statistical analyses. For example, in SPSS, the user mouse clicks on the Analyze option, then Descriptive Statistics, then Frequencies. A menu appears with a list of all the variable names in the data set. From this list of variables, the user selects the variable or set of variables to be analyzed by highlighting them with the mouse. Finally, the desired statistics and graphs are chosen from menu options on the Frequencies window.

A frequency tables give the counts, or frequencies, for each value available for each variable (see figure 19–5). As a start, it is useful to make sure there are no unexpected values present for any variable in the data set. For example, a value of 7 may appear for an item where only 1 and 2 are valid responses. The researcher may then determine if the 7 represents a typographical error—or worse, a series of numbers all entered incorrectly.

Frequencies

Statistics

Race/Ethnicity

N	Valid	48
	Missing	2
Mean		2.96
Std. Error of Mean		.16
Median		3.00
Mode		3
Std. Deviation		1.09
Variance		1.19
Skewness		.496
Std. Error of Skewness		.343
Kurtosis		1.927
Std. Error of Kurtosis		.674
Range		5
Minimum		1
Maximum		6
Sum		142

Race/Ethnicity

		Frequency	Percent	Valid Percent	Cumulative Percent
Valid	African Am/Black	6	12.0	12.5	12.5
	Asian Am/Pacific Is	3	6.0	6.3	18.8
	Non-His White	32	64.0	66.7	85.4
	Latina/Latino	3	6.0	6.3	91.7
	Native Amer	2	4.0	4.2	95.8
	Other	2	4.0	4.2	100.0
	Total	48	96.0	100.0	
Missing	System	2	4.0		
Total		50	100.0		

Figure 19–5 SPSS Frequencies Output with All Descriptive Statistics

Frequency tables can also provide descriptive statistics. Both measures of central tendency (such as the mode, median, and mean) and measures of dispersion (range, variance, and standard deviation) can be generated for one or all variables under study. Most programs allow the user to select which statistics are printed. Most also offer information about the characteristics of the distribution of the chosen variables, including skewness and kurtosis measures.

Inferential Statistics

Current statistical software can quickly generate a wide variety of inferential statistics. In fact, the ease and speed of computer-based statistical analysis makes it imperative that the user understand the purposes and limiting assumptions of the statistical tests they employ. The computer will perform inappropriate and meaningless analyses if the user so commands. The old computer saying "garbage in,

T-Test

Group Statistics

	SEX	N	Mean	Std. Deviation	Std. Error Mean
Gender	Male	14	5.00	1.11	.30
	Female	34	5.18	1.17	.20

Independent Samples Test

		Levene's Test for Equality of Variances	
		F	Sig.
Gender	Equal variances assumed	.065	.800
	Equal variances not assumed		

Independent Samples Test

		t-test for Equality of Means			
		t	df	Sig. (2-tailed)	Mean Difference
Gender	Equal variances assumed	-.483	46	.632	-.18
	Equal variances not assumed	-.493	25.463	.626	-.18

Figure 19–6 SPSS T-Test Output

garbage out!" is an important reminder for researchers. However, if chosen well, computer-based statistical analyses are wonderfully efficient.

SPSS offers a number of tests of difference, ranging from chi square for pairs of nominal measures, through the Mann-Whitney U and Kruskal-Wallis H tests for examining nonparametric differences, to the t-test and several forms of Analysis of Variance (ANOVA). All relevant values are calculated and reported, including the value of the statistics, the associated degrees of freedom, and the probability level. Most of these SPSS analyses of difference include options to evaluate some of the statistic's limiting assumptions. For example, the typical chi-square output not only gives values of the Chi-square statistics, but also reminds the user how many cells have expected cell frequencies of less than five. Figure 19–6 shows output for a t-test.

SPSS also offers a number of tests of association, ranging from the bivariate Spearman's r_s for pairs of ordinal variables, to the Pearson's r for pairs of interval level variables, to several forms of multivariate regression analyses. Figure 19–7 shows SPSS output with Pearson r.

Users may specify the type of regression model to be calculated. Some of these SPSS analyses of association also include options to evaluate some of the statistics' limiting assumptions.

Additional software options for data modeling, data exploration, and data reduction are also available in the advanced and professional modules of SPSS and in SysStat. Analysis such as Path Analyses, Cluster Analysis, and Discriminant Analysis allow the study of complex multivariate relationships. Reliability and Factor Analysis options allow the examination of items in a test or measure. Several forms of Time-Series Analyses, which may be applicable to single-subject research, are also available.

All these statistical tests are selected from drop-down menus. The user mouse clicks on the Statistics option, the desired statistic. Variable lists and menus of options help the user make the necessary choices to complete the test.

Correlations

Correlations

		Current Physical Health	Minutes Exercise in Past 7 Days	Physical Condition
Current Physical Health	Pearson Correlation	1.000	.066	.594**
	Sig. (2-tailed)	.	.655	.000
	N	48	48	48
Minutes Exercise in Past 7 Days	Pearson Correlation	.066	1.000	.170
	Sig. (2-tailed)	.655	.	.247
	N	48	48	48
Physical Condition	Pearson Correlation	.594**	.170	1.000
	Sig. (2-tailed)	.000	.247	.
	N	48	48	48

**. Correlation is significant at the 0.01 level (2-tailed).

Figure 19–7 SPSS Pearson's Correlation Coefficient Output

Interpreting Quantitative Printouts

The output of quantitative data analysis can vary from lengthy to very brief. The software can provide most of the necessary technical data to test the limiting assumptions of an extensive range of statistics. The user, however, must know how to interpret statistical output. Major software packages are accompanied by manuals (such as the SPSS Base 8.0 Applications Guide, 1998), which offer detailed information about the appropriate use and interpretation of the output they generate. There is no easy way around learning and understanding the appropriate, meaningful use of statistics in computer software.

Quantitative data analysis software is a very well developed and quite easy-to-learn technology. The software is geared to users with knowledge of the kinds of statistics they want to employ and the assumptions for correctly using each statistic. Recent versions seek to make data entry and manipulation as quick and undemanding as possible—and succeed quite well. Nonetheless, the software takes hands-on practice to learn. With experience, many additional convenience features are also available.

Computer-Assisted Qualitative Data Analysis

Computer-assisted qualitative data analysis is a relatively new innovation. Although word processors have long been a central application of computers, only recently have capable and easy-to-use software programs been developed (Dey 1993). This may, in part, reflect the great variety of approaches to qualitative research reflected in the social sciences literature. It may also reflect the predominance of quantitative research methods in the social sciences. Widespread interest in qualitative research methods is a relatively new phenomena.

Qualitative research refers to a number of research approaches and methods (Denzin & Lincoln 1994; Drisko 1997; Riessman 1994; Sherman & Reid 1994; Tesch 1990). Qualitative research includes different epistemologies, ideologies, goals, and analytic methods. It is possible, nonetheless, to identify some tasks qualitative researchers must accomplish despite their differences (Drisko 1998; Miles & Huberman 1994). These tasks include organizing often massive data sets, which are typically text documents, identifying meaningful passages within these texts, assigning codes to the text passages, and collating all the texts passages with similar meaning or codes for retrieval and analysis. Most qualitative researchers also need to annotate texts or passages with notes, often called memos. Many but not all qualitative researchers organize and present conceptual networks of texts or passages (Strauss & Corbin 1990; Tesch 1990). Computers now can be applied to all these tasks.

Computers may also help the researcher ensure a complete search of all documents for words and phrases of particular meaning. In this sense, computers can add to the thoroughness of qualitative research. Computers can save many versions of codes and text, creating what Strauss and Corbin (1990) call an audit trail. An audit trail helps both the researchers and later reviewers recall and identify how key decisions were made. This can be used to assess or enhance the rigor of a qualitative study. Finally, simply saving copies of code structures and texts via backups to computer file is a time-saver. It also allows easy storage of what might otherwise be several boxes of printed and coded text.

Appropriate and rigorous use of qualitative data analysis software requires that the user have a clear understanding of qualitative research methods (Kelle 1995). Some features of the software can appear to "automate" the analysis, but such undertakings still require careful, ongoing review by the researcher (Lee & Fielding 1995). Some authors note that use of qualitative data analysis software can undermine attention to the context in which meanings are embedded (Agar 1991; Denzin 1988). Use of a computer may give the appearance of rigor while actually distancing the researcher from the data (Agar 1991). Immersion in the data set and ongoing attention to finding emic (local) meaning is vital to qualitative research and not necessarily improved by use of computer software.

Finally, some researchers find qualitative data analysis software to offer an inflexible approach to the research. This may be viewed as an advantage by newcomers to qualitative research, or a constraint by veterans who are knowledgeable in a given method. Qualitative data analysis programs replace processes and procedures that can be done (and have been for nearly a century) using pencil-and-paper methods. They offer tremendous advantages in managing the data set, but do not (yet) offer capabilities beyond what is possible by hand (Drisko 1998).

Matching Hardware and QDA Software

Each qualitative data analysis (QDA) software package represents the preferences and methodologies of its authors (Drisko 1998). All current QDA software was designed specifically for use on personal computers. However, some software, such as ATLAS•ti (Muhr 1994), is available only for Windows or DOS computers. Others, such as NUD*IST (QSR 1995), come in both Macintosh and Windows versions. QDA software will run on most recent personal computers, though faster processors and more will make them run faster. Demonstration or trial versions of several QDA software packages can be downloaded from the World Wide Web for hands-on exploration (see sources below).

Preparing the Data Set

The initial step in using QDA software is to collect the data and enter it into computer files. Most often, this means typing out the transcripts of interviews, stories, or observations sessions. Spoken words, records of observations, notes, feelings, and contextual issues may all be included. Some qualitative researchers are now using QDA software with images and audio files and even short video clips. Prior to entry into QDA software, the researcher must type or print out and proofread all texts very carefully. Similarly, the quality of all image files must be ascertained. Full knowledge of the data set, often called immersion, is vital to the creative work of qualitative data analysis.

Some additional planning is useful to organizing the data. For example, labels for each speaker or actor must be added to the text transcript to clarify who is speaking or acting. These may be names, abbreviations, of code numbers that identify each interview and each research participant. It is also helpful to include a blank line whenever the speaker or actor changes to make this change more apparent in the transcript. If an ordered interview protocol is followed, adding this structure to the text will both speed data searches and add clarity. Right hand margins for the text are typically set to about 3 1/2 inches. This generates a printed copy with a wide right margin area for making notes and adding codes. Such a format is also used by most paper-and-pencil researchers, and it fits well with most QDA software packages. Finally, each text file should be saved to disk and given a unique file name, such as "Int01" or "Case22." Most qualitative data sets will include several data files representing different cases or occasions of data collection.

Some QDA software packages require that the texts be reformatted into ASCII or ANSI format, while others can do this conversion for the user. Such reformatting removes page breaks and other markers that are specific to a word-processing program such as Word or WordPerfect. This process is simple: it is a file save option on all current word processors. However, the resulting texts must be renamed or given a new file extension (*.asc) to distinguish them from versions that include word-processing formatting. Recent software sets no limit to the length of texts or to the size of text or image files. However, some older QDA software was limited in the file sizes the software could process.

Projects, Texts, and Codes

The first step in using QDA software is to give a name to each research project, such as "Selfawareness Study." This identifies the *project* to which the data is linked. Most QDA programs can manage multiple projects, but some work on only one at a time (Drisko 1998). The project name serves to distinguish it from other different projects loaded on the computer. The software also organizes all the files related to the project under this main label. Next, the user must next assign or introduce each data file into the project. This is done by identifying those files that include the project data. Usually this is a simple process of mouse highlighting the files to be included in the project. Most programs copy the original texts or images and make no changes to the originals. It is important not to change the program's internal working files once the project is begun as QDA software locates text passages using line numbers within each data file. Changing these internal files may render the program unable to find the correct data.

Assigning Codes

A key aspect of QDA is to identify passages of text that convey information or meaning. This process requires the researcher to find meaningful passages of text and identify them. In pencil-and-paper qualitative coding, the researcher typically marks the meaningful text with a line in the margin. Computer software uses one of two ways to identify text passage. Some programs simply require the user to highlight the text with the mouse (as you would to move a passage in a word processor). This is a very quick process. An equally effective, but less convenient, way used by some programs is to require the user to type in the line numbers that include the beginning and end points of the selected text. Line numbers are automatically assigned to the text and available on the screen. Over many texts, efficient coding is an important ease-of-use feature and time-saver.

For illustration, ATLAS•ti offers the user access to a lengthy section of text in the main (or hermeneutic unit) window, a delineation of the text passages and assigned codes in the righthand margin, and a wide range of icons or buttons that start the coding, memo-making and data management tools around the screen. Full lists of text files, all code, all marked texts passages, and all memos are available using drop-down lists. This format is shown in figure 19–8.

In all qualitative data analysis programs, once text passage is identified, a code name is assigned to it. This involves clicking on an icon to open the coding menu and typing in the selected code name. The code name allows the text passage to be identified and retrieved easily for later use. Depending on the researcher's philosophical and methodological orientation, this code may simply be a descriptive label or may also have some conceptual meaning. For example, the code being assigned in figure 19–9 simply identifies where the respondent obtained a degree. Other codes might address component issues of the respondent's apparent self-awareness. These we might treat as reflecting more complex and rich conceptual material that we might interpret or join into a network of relationships.

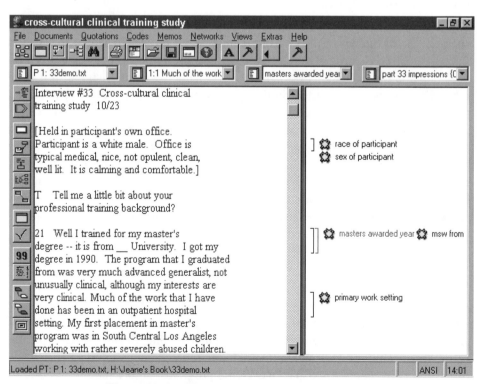

Figure 19–8 ATLAS•ti Hermeneutic Unit Editor

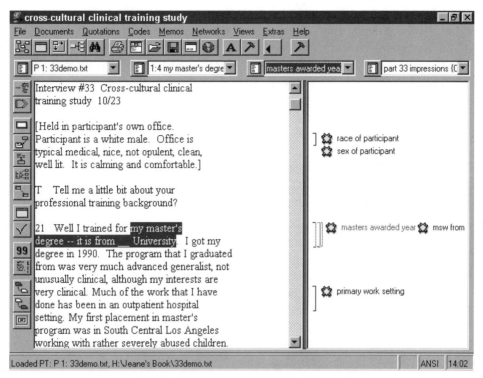

Figure 19–9 ATLAS•ti Coding Screen

Some QDA software, such as ATLAS•ti, offers several approaches to coding. ATLAS•ti uses the coding approach of Glaser and Strauss' (1967) grounded theory model. The program offers options for open coding, or assigning a new code name to a text passage, for in vivo coding, or using the text itself as the code name, and also for coding a passage from a list of codes already assigned to text (via open coding). This range of coding options makes the coding process quick across a large set of cases.

Multiple codes may be assigned to the same passage of text. Codes may also be assigned to overlapping text passages by current QDA programs. Finally, the programs allow all the text passages marked with a given code, or set of codes, to be printed out together. This allows review of all the material coded in the same manner.

Making Memos

Memos or clarifying notes allow researchers to record and recall thoughts about the data (Strauss & Corbin 1990). It is always a good idea to write a memo about your ideas and views at the start of a new research project. Then, as new material changes your views, you can review how your views have evolved. Memos might also be used to clarify the definition of a code, to raise questions about subtle differences between texts passages, or to record new ideas about the data and their meaning. QDA software offers a range of memo-making options. The Ethnograph

(Seidel, Friese, & Leonard 1995) can only assign memos only to specific text passages. NUD*IST links memos to codes and to entire text documents. ATLAS•ti can attach memos to codes, texts, other memos, and entire projects.

A series of memos is an important part of the audit trail of a qualitative project (Strauss & Corbin 1990). It allows the researcher and others to track how decisions and changes were made over the course of the project. In this way memos can enhance the trustworthiness of a qualitative data analysis (Drisko 1997).

Searching for Specific Text Passages and Codes

Some researchers employing phenomenological or microethnographic methods seek only to easily "code and retrieve" selected text passages (Tesch 1990). These researchers view codes solely as markers for the text passage, with no further conceptual meaning. All current QDA software offers strong code and retrieve features. Some programs, such as the Ethnograph, emphasize these functions (Seidel, Friese, & Leonard 1995). Other programs, such as NUD*IST and ATLAS•ti can also create links among the codes researchers generate, known as hypertext links. Hypertext links allow rapid movement among connected text passages. For example, ATLAS•ti allows hypertext links among texts, codes, and memos. Hypertext links allow the user to review all the material related to a specific issue or topic, adding to the contextualization of the data and the completeness of the a search.

All current QDA programs can search for and retrieve all the codes and associated text assigned to a project. Where the programs differ is in the ways they search for codes and passages. One common approach is a *Boolean search.*

Boolean searches employ logical operations such as *And, Not,* and *Or* to create connections among codes and text passages. For example, a researcher might seek all text passages coded for self-awareness *And* cross-cultural training *And* masters degree program but *Not* supervision. Such a Boolean search would find and collate all text passages marked with this set of codes. The Boolean search may be familiar from the search process used by libraries to link several keywords in literature searches. NUD*IST includes several, flexible Boolean search features. ATLAS•ti uses a variation of Boolean search called a GREP search.

Other search types include *proximity searches* to locate co-occurrences of two or more codes within a specified number of lines within the text. *Wildcard searches* locate all the permutations of a specified phrase. For example, a symbol, usually an asterisk, is used to retrieve all the characters (letters or numbers) from a base phase. For example, the code "talk*" will retrieve "talk," "talks," "talked," and "talking." ATLAS•ti also offers a form of *"equivalent term" search* called a "disjunctive category search." Here the researcher identifies different terms that have similar meanings. The equivalent term search will locate text passages with all the different forms at once. Muhr (1994:62) gives the example: *cause* | why | *eforeI since, as elements of a related terms search. This search would retrieve passages including the terms "'cause," "causes," "because," "why," "therefore," and "since." A detailed summary of the search features in QDA software may be found in Weitzman & Miles (1995). Figure 19–10 shows how search commands are entered in ATLAS•ti.

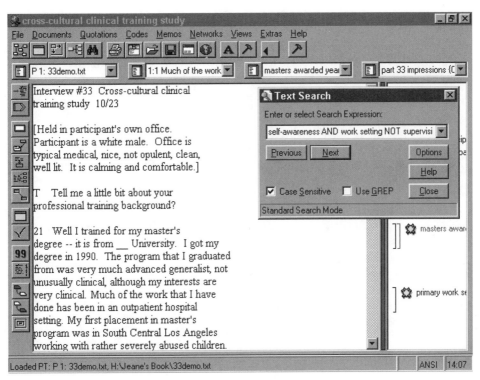

Figure 19–10 ATLAS•ti Search Screen

These search features can help the researcher refine and reduce a list of codes. This can improve the consistency of the assignment of codes across texts and across researchers. Search features can also be used to identify negative cases or disconfirming material, an important aspect of the rigor of qualitative studies (Drisko 1997).

Developing Theory—Creating Network Maps

Many qualitative researchers seek to develop theory from the data they have collected. Typically, theory is developed via induction and created to reflect the "theory in use" of the participants in their local setting or culture. In this process, the codes assigned to text passages are treated as conceptually meaningful. That is, the codes serve as a sort of shorthand for the meaning in the texts. The connections among the codes may then be studied, leading to a set of relationships among the meanings the represent. Glaser and Strauss (1967) and Strauss and Corbin (1990) call the relationships among concepts in the data a grounded theory. A diagram of the relationships among codes is a network map. Network maps, in turn, visually portray the researcher's working theory about concepts and meanings in the data.

Some qualitative data analysis software packages can be used to create network maps. For example, ATLAS•ti can create network maps using codes, entire texts, or memos as nodes. Nodes are concepts or entities on the map, which

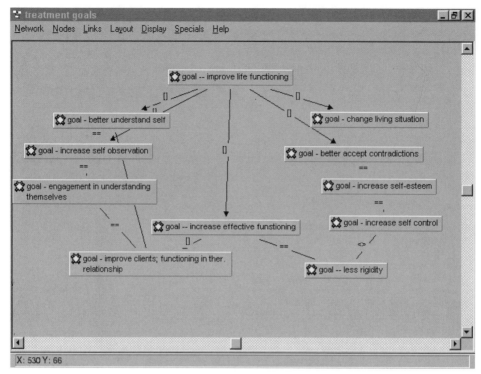

Figure 19–11 ATLAS•ti Network View

are joined by links. Links reflect the relationships among the nodes. Links may be assigned labels to clarify their nature. For example, a link may be labeled to show one code is a part of another, higher-order code. Links may also be assigned directional arrows to show how the nodes are related. ATLAS•ti allows elements to be moved within a network map, or removed from it. Both nodes and relationships may be changed as the researcher desires.

Network maps add a visual dimension to our understanding of the relationships within a data set (Weitzman & Miles 1995). This can be very useful as a complement to our understanding of the relationships within the text per se. The size and quality of network maps is limited in most qualitative data analysis software. The network metaphors of these packages vary considerably (Drisko 1998), so potential buyers should be careful to check how program features fit their desired methods.

Summary—Qualitative Data Analysis Software

QDA can speed many research tasks, from backing up the data set to coding to generating network maps. Expanding on pencil-and-paper methods, the software can perform thorough text searches and quickly generate frequency counts of word or phrase occurrences. Keeping data sets and coding structures on computer files also allows researchers to collaborate over great distances. This process was nearly impossible when it meant shipping boxes full of texts which had been cut apart and pasted back together. Computer data sets also can enhance audit trails to improve the validity of qualitative research. However, maintaining data in context, making judgements about the meaning of texts, and developing networks is solely the work of the human researcher (Drisko 1998). Qualitative research has different purposes, philosophical foundations, and methods. Therefore qualitative researchers should evaluate these software packages carefully to find the one that best fits their goals.

Conclusion

Computers and software applications are important tools for both quantitative and qualitative research. The strengths of computers are equally well suited to work with numbers and texts. Computers can store, manipulate, analyze, and report large amounts of data very quickly and accurately. Increases in computer power have improved the range of features available to qualitative and quantitative researchers. The maturity of most software packages has also led to improved ease of use.

Still it is up to the human researcher to identify worthy and useful topics, to select feasible research questions and methodologies, to collect data ethically with high regard for the gifts participants give to us, to interpret results fairly and accurately, and to report results clearly. Computers cannot make these judgements. They can, however, serve as important tools to the realization of our research goals.

Quantitative Resources

SPSS (originally Statistical Package for the Social Sciences) was developed by a number of authors over many years. SPSS data management, statistical analysis, and data presentation software is available for a wide range of operating systems. Special student and graduate student versions are available at reduced cost through college or university bookstores only. SPSS, Inc., also offers books and training. The Internet address for SPSS is *http://www.spss.com.*

SAS was also developed by a number of authors over many years. SAS Institute offers a system of data management, statistical analysis, and data presentation software modules. The software is available for a wide range of operating systems. The Internet address for SAS is *http://www.sas.com.*

Systat is a personal computer program originally developed for Macintosh computers systems, but now available for Windows-based systems as well. Systat is available through SPSS, Inc. The Internet address is *http://www.spss. com/software/science/SYSTAT/.*

WINKS (the Windows version of KWIKSTAT) was developed by Texasoft. This is an inexpensive but full-featured package for personal computer offering data entry, management, and statistical analysis features. Graphical display is good, but not so polished as the higher-priced packages. Texasoft's Internet address is *http://www.texasoft.com/*. Texasoft also offers an on-line tutorial on statistics at *http://204.215.60.174/tutindex.html*.

BMDP is a widely used set of statistical programs for DOS-based personal computers. BMDP can be run on very old computers, an asset for some users. BMDP is available as a "classic" through SPSS, Inc., at *http://www.spss.com/ software/science/Bmdp/*.

KWIKSTAT is Texasoft's DOS-based data entry, management, and statistical analysis software package. Like BMDP, KWIKSTAT can be run on very old computers and printers as well as more current ones. KWIKSTAT is available at *http://www.texasoft.com/*.

Qualitative Resources

ATLAS•ti was developed by Thomas Muhr of Scientific Software Development, Berlin, Germany. The Internet address is *http://www.atlasti.de* for more information and download of demonstration copies. ATLAS•ti is available from Scolari, 2455 Teller Rd., Thousand Oaks, CA, or *http://www.scolari.com*.

NUD*IST was developed by Thomas and Lyn Richards, Qualitative Solutions and Research Pty., Ltd., Melbourne. Their Internet address is *http//:www.qsr.com/ au* NUD*IST is available through Scolari at *http://www.scolari.com*.

The Ethnograph was developed by John Seidel, Susanne Friese, and D. Christopher Leonard of Qualis Research Associates, Amherst, MA 01004. The Ethnograph is available through Scolari at *http://www.scolari.com*.

HyperRESEARCH concept was developed by Sharlene Hesse-Biber, with user interface and programming by T. Scott Kinder and Paul R. Dupuis of ResearchWare, Inc. Their Internet address is *http://www.researchware.com/*.

20

Writing About Research

Although we live in an information age, social and human service workers continue to complain that the kind of knowledge that they need for practice does not exist in written form. It has long been acknowledged that the helping professions need more practitioners who write about their work, who can generate the needed knowledge, and convey it effectively to other practitioners. Generating and disseminating knowledge about the effectiveness of what social workers and other human service professionals do is increasingly vital for gaining support and recognition in an increasingly cost-conscious public and private human service marketplace. This book as a whole is about generating knowledge through research; this chapter is about how to disseminate that knowledge once a piece of research has been completed.

Social workers and others have many skills that can serve them well in writing professionally. They are usually skilled in the verbal communication of complicated and abstract ideas to clients and other professionals. They often grapple with difficult chronic or emergent social and human problems, which means they have interesting and important issues to talk about. They are often working at the forefront of innovation in delivering human services, which means they have insight to offer about what is and what is not working in our human service system.

On the other hand, the conditions under which most social workers labor and some of the habits of mind developed in practice may present obstacles when attempting to translate this knowledge into professional writing. For example, clinicians doing research may find it somewhat difficult to strike "a balance between noting uncertainties on the one hand and taking findings seriously enough on the other" (Goering & Strauss 1987:421).

Most social and human service workers, even those initially drawn to do so, find the idea of writing for publication intimidating. As this chapter will explain, some of the ways in which writing has traditionally been taught may hinder rather than help in learning to write professionally. In addition, demystifying the process of getting into print or onto the conference circuit can also help, and there really are "tricks of the trade," or strategies that can enable the beginner to write more effectively. This chapter will cover all of these areas as they relate to preparing and presenting research work for journal publication. It will also offer some suggestions for overcoming the obstacles that may prevent even a motivated social and human service worker from achieving the goal of publication with the aim of encouraging and enabling the practitioner or researcher to "get the word out" about what they know.

Focus and Audience: Key Concepts

There are two concepts that are key to any piece of writing: *focus* and *audience*. What is the specific message that a written piece is designed to convey? And for whom is the message intended? Focus means that a given piece of writing is designed to convey a specific message. Since an article is a short piece of work, the message in an article must be a limited one. It may be a message with great significance or far-reaching implications that will stimulate wide-ranging thoughts in the reader, but to be effective the message must to some extent be simple, or at least simply stated and clearly defined.

Clarity about the audience to whom a given piece of writing is addressed is also essential. It is critical in defining the focus and message of the piece and also in selecting the best forum or market for it. Sometimes the audience for a piece of writing is a given, as when producing a research report for the agency that funded it or the degree program that required it. Sometimes defining and selecting an audience is a matter of choice or priority of the author. Whatever the case, keeping the particular audience in mind is essential in both crafting and marketing a piece of writing.

At all of the stages of writing, from developing the idea for a specific piece to revising and editing the work once completed, these two concepts—focus and audience—must be kept in the forefront. Therefore they are terms and concepts that will keep reappearing throughout this chapter in all aspects of the writing and publication process described.

Routes of Dissemination

There are many forms in which research results are disseminated. Oral reports or presentations may be given in agency or conference settings. Writing often enters into oral presentations as well, whether in submitting an abstract that will be read in competition with others in order to get on a conference program or in preparing material to read. In written form, results can be disseminated as mandated reports and technical monographs, as articles in professional journals, or in book form. Because journal publication represents the place where research results are usually first published and most widely disseminated among professionals, the emphasis of this chapter will be on journal publication, although the other written forms will be briefly described as well.

Mandated reports include written and oral presentations prepared for the agencies that sponsor or fund research projects and research reports prepared as part of completing requirements for a degree, such as master's thesis and doctoral dissertation reports. This kind of writing is typically unpublished and unpublishable in the form in which it is first prepared. The audience for reports like these is quite limited and specialized. The agency hosting or funding a piece of research has a particular set of interests and typically an unlimited appetite for detail and technical information. A school or educational program has specific requirements that must be met and a similar appetite for technicalities. Both of these kinds of documents also share to a greater or lesser degree the purpose of evaluating the competence and skills of the author in relation to granting a degree or renewing a funding decision. This purpose shapes the writing of the report but typically interferes in producing the kind of exposition likely to appeal to a wider professional audience. However, the work described in such reports can represent state-of-the-art knowledge and can often be recast later into a form suitable for a professional journal, where it is likely to be much more widely read.

The book market is fundamentally a commercial one, although there are many commercially viable niches within it that are quite specialized and narrow relative to what is termed the mass market. Aspiring book authors are generally advised to seek a contract with a publisher before all the work of writing an entire book is completed. Publishers evaluate proposed book ideas, often with the assistance of paid outside reviewers who are recognized as experts in the field, based on a prospectus. The prospectus gives an overview of the projected contents, a discussion of the potential market for the book, and a sample, perhaps a chapter, of the work. Each publisher has developed unique prospectus requirements that should be followed. When a publisher offers to buy a book based on the review of a prospectus, a contract is negotiated that usually transfers ownership of the completed work to the publisher and specifies the financial arrangements and other mutual obligations between publisher and author.

Books are products that are purchased by publishers largely based on their earnings potential in the targeted market and their utility in relation to the publisher's mission. Journals do not have to make money separately on each piece of work and can often afford to publish more specialized work, and they also can do so more rapidly, at least in brief form. While the scope afforded by a book's length is appealing, few people undertake or are invited to publish a book without at least some prior experience in journal publication. However, the possibility of publishing a book should not be overlooked or assumed to be out of reach even to the novice author.

Conference Presentation

Presenting research results at a professional conference can be both an end in itself and an important "way station" in the development of a paper for publication. Conference presentation may seem a less intimidating way to get started to the professional more familiar with case presentations and speaking before small groups than with publishing. It also may offer immediate rewards in feedback from those who attend, as allowing for audience questions and comments must be part of any effective oral presentation. Presenting will also tend to connect the presenter with others interested in the topic and may lead, in turn, to invitations to make additional presentations or to submit the material for publication. While national conferences offer the largest audiences and the greatest prestige, it is important not to overlook local or regional conferences, which are often much more accessible and often require less advanced planning for participation.

Many experienced authors use conference presentation as a technique for developing their work for publication. Giving a draft paper at a conference is a chance to get immediate feedback from an audience of interested experts and potential consumers. In particular, alternative ways in which results could be interpreted or applied are often evident in audience comments and questions. In addition, the obligation to make a public presentation on a given date can help impose discipline and a time frame on an otherwise potentially endless writing process.

With national conferences, sometimes the link between conference presentation and publication is very explicit, as when conference proceedings are published or when a journal published by the sponsoring organization invites and gives an "inside track" to papers given at the conference. There is always a time limit on such offers and frequently a deadline, pre- or postconference, when the written version of the presentation must be submitted for the use of moderators and discussants or for the opportunity to publish. Thus conference presentation can provide both a timeframe and an early forum for written work as it is developed for eventual publication.

Presentation at national and some regional conferences is usually determined by submitting competing abstracts for review by a panel selected for the purpose, a process similar to journal review. This review is often "blind," that is, conducted at least at the initial stage without knowledge of who has submitted the abstract. A call for proposals is often issued as much as a year or more before the conference is to take place. This "call" gives the date and location of the conference, the conference theme, the types of presentations possible, and the requirements for submission. The deadlines and submission requirements stated must be taken seriously as many proposals are usually received, and the committee that reviews them is usually looking for ways to eliminate rather than include submissions.

The text of the abstract of the proposed presentation is usually the main evidence on which the selection decision is based. Relating the abstract and presentation content to the conference theme is essential, in the first sentence if possible. A catchy title is a plus. The abstract itself must be informative, giving the conceptual content and essential points that the presentation will make. The central research question(s), theories, or concepts employed, methodology in broad terms, and conclusions drawn must all be included. Results should be related to the conference theme and their relevance for the conference audience indicated. It is best to adopt a positive tone and to use direct, simple language, which leaves the impression that the presentation will be clear, accessible, and interesting to the audience. Boiling any presentation down to 150, 250, or even

500 words is difficult, so be prepared to revise the draft abstract repeatedly before submission.

When submitting an abstract to a conference, the question of audience is defined by the nature of the event. The challenge, then, is to focus the abstract and the content of the presentation for that audience. When planning to write an article, however, both focus and audience are defined by the author, which is where planning begins.

Planning to Publish

The first step in planning an article for journal publication is to return to the concepts of focus and audience. What is the main message the article should convey? For whom is this message intended? It should be noted that a single piece of research may give rise to more than one article if there are multiple messages or audiences to reach with the findings. There are many conceptual and technical aspects of successfully writing for publication that must be considered (Beebe 1993).

In working on the focus for an article, it must be remembered that an article is a short piece that attempts to convey a specific message in a condensed form. An article manuscript is on average only 14 to 16 pages long, double-spaced. While the conventions of the research report permit and demand economy of expression, this length is still an important reminder that the scope of any one article must be clear and limited.

In thinking about the intended audience for the article, it is important to think about their knowledge, attitudes, and needs (Flower 1985). One writes for a particular audience because one believes that they need to know about what one has to say. But what do they already know? What assumptions might they bring to the subject being addressed? What terms and concepts will they be familiar (and unfamiliar) with? Why should the topic matter to them? Journals choose to publish articles that will make "a contribution" to the existing knowledge base. What will be new or especially interesting to the intended audience about the content to be presented? By the time the answer to that question is defined, questions both of focus and of audience have been answered.

Because focus and audience are so important in writing, experienced authors do not just write "an article." They write specific articles each targeted to an individual journal based on the kinds of material the journal generally publishes and on the audience or readership it attracts. Therefore it is useful very early in the process of writing a research report to identify the market or journal that the report is being prepared for. Having a target journal in mind will define and maintain both focus and audience throughout the writing process.

Learning About Journals

Before the actual writing begins, then, an appropriate target journal must be identified. The number of journals in every field has grown rapidly in recent years. Because of the many journals that are most likely available in a given field, it is important to be sure that all the options for publishing have been identified and considered. Some journals are sent automatically to organization members; others are available by subscription only. Some reach large and diverse audiences, others small and specialized ones. As computerized data bases and indexing services become ever more widely available to individuals and institutions, the need to be published in a journal with the widest circulation is less compelling than it was in the past. If the journal is indexed or abstracted in the major databases, anyone doing a computerized literature search (see chapter 2) will find the material whatever the journal it was published in.

Aside from the audience a journal reaches, it is important to consider the mission and scope of interest of the journal in question. Some journals publish on a wide range of topics, others quite narrowly. Some publish only research reports or research of a specific type; others publish many kinds of articles. Some publish only articles of limited length; others provide for full-length or discursive pieces and or short reports or works in progress.

Most important is the mission of the journal as stated in the masthead or in the information for authors it provides. Space in its pages is the most valuable resource a journal has, and it is guarded zealously. A journal's mission and purpose is the first standard against which all articles are measured when considered for publication. Editors ask such questions as: Does this article help us meet our goals? Will it interest our readership? Will it contribute something that they need to know?

Guides to journals. Because of the proliferation of options, an aspiring author cannot be sure that he or she knows about all the possible journals that should be considered. Reading done for the research itself may suggest some options. However, it may be useful in addition to consult one of the many published guides to the journals in a specific field. In social work, the most widely known is *An Author's Guide to Social Work Journals* (4th ed.) (Mendelsson 1997). Guides for related fields may also be useful, particularly if one wants to reach an interdisciplinary audience. These include one for psychology and education (Loke 1990), psychology (APA 1997), and the behavioral sciences in general (Wang 1989).

In addition to simply collecting the names of many of the journals in one place, guides to journals focus on the needs of authors. In them can be found information about the mission, circulation, and editorial standards of journals as well as their procedures for submitting articles. Some guides give manuscript acceptance and rejection rates, estimates of turnaround time for manuscript review, or summaries of the topics most often included in recent issues. Some of this information is available from each journal individually, but it is often useful to review and compare it collected all in one place. Journals generally make this information available to authors on an "Information for Authors" page in each issue. This information, especially about focus and submission requirements, is to be taken seriously as it is related directly to the review process (see below). The point being made here is that the chances of successful publication are markedly improved if the author is targeting the piece to a specific journal and working to meet that journal's requirements from the outset.

Parts of the Research Report

While journals are diverse in their specific interests and requirements, there are certain conventions governing the writing of a research report that are quite universal. The space and emphasis given to the various parts of an article may differ, but the basic elements of a report of empirical research remain similar across journals, disciplines, and even many styles of research.

Most reports begin with a brief introduction that defines the purpose and nature of the study and argues for its importance. The scope and urgency of the problem under study should be given, and the theoretical framework guiding the investigation should be set forth. In articles, this section leads rapidly into the review of the literature, which must also of necessity be brief. This review introduces the reader to the prior work bearing on the study issue and presents the writer's analysis of it. Sometimes this analysis suggests ways to build on prior work; sometimes its purpose is to critique what has gone before and to suggest, therefore, that a new approach to the topic is needed. Taken together, the introduction and literature review should build a case for the importance of the study issue and for the particular approach to the topic being taken. They both provide what the reader needs in order to understand and appreciate the study results and demonstrate the writer's knowledge of the subject matter.

The next section of the research report sets forth the study methods. This section usually begins with the statement of the questions or hypotheses that guided the research and with a statement of the general research strategy or design employed—fixed or flexible and any subtype within each. Subsections then address sampling, data collection, and data analysis methods separately. The degree of detail offered in each section depends on the nature of the methods used and the conventions of the journal publishing the work. For example, in fixed designs for relational or experimental research, much more technical information on measurement and data analytic or statistical issues is often needed, while in flexible method research, more description of the writer's experiences in the research process and the incremental design decisions made is typically given.

Unlike in a thesis, dissertation, or book-length or mandated research report, copies of any standardized data gathering instruments used are generally not included in published journal articles. However, anyone who develops and publishes results from an original data collection instrument is obligated by scholarly convention to make a copy of that instrument available to anyone who requests it. Sometimes, though, key sections of data collection instruments may be included in a figure or as part of the text of a table.

The core and typically the longest section of any published research report is the *findings* section. This part of the report sets forth the key results of the research, organized and presented in order to shed light on the research questions as previously stated. While reports of the results of some experiments may be brief and can be encompassed in one table, typically research findings must be sifted through and reorganized ex post facto to give the clearest picture possible of the data obtained. For example, in reports of fixed method, quantitative studies, more space and attention is typically given to hypotheses confirmed and to findings that were statistically significant than to those that were not. Findings addressing relationships among variables are generally presented following descriptive results, and serendipitous or unexpected findings typically follow after planned or expected results.

Statistical results may be given in tables or in the text, with the choice being made based on the method of display that will be easiest for the reader to comprehend. When constructing tables or graphs, it is often possible to combine or compare findings, as when sample demographic characteristics are given together. Text and tables should supplement and not repeat each other. Tables, while often effective devices, should generally be used sparingly to highlight the most important results of the study. Table design—general format, the precise wording of the title, and the labeling of the rows, columns, variables and numerical values entered—must be carefully considered. While a confusing table will not be read, a well-designed and attractive figure or table can be a powerful tool in getting complex information across.

The findings of flexible method studies employing narrative data are often lengthy and difficult to condense. In these studies, the credibility of results rests not on technical demonstrations of reliability, validity, or statistical significance but on the veracity of the author's renditions of the participants' accounts of their experiences. Therefore direct quotations from participants in the study are often extensively used. These quotations should be clearly set off from the text either with quotation marks or by using a block (indented) format.

To protect the confidentiality of participants when such quotations are used, care must be taken that descriptive information about individual people or sites is kept to a minimum and is separated from the quotations given. Even if names are not used, identity can sometimes be inferred by the right reader, and precautions must be taken to prevent this, whether by disguise and/or by keeping identifying information about individual informants out of the text as much as possible.

Once the findings of the study have been described, the report ends with a *discussion* or *conclusion* section. Here the implications and possible meanings of the study results must be set forth, including their implications for practice, policy or program development, theory, and future knowledge development. This section of the report should also help the reader gain a sense of the relationships among the various results reported and between the study's findings and prior knowledge as presented in the literature review. Strengths and weaknesses of the research itself should be discussed in terms of how they bear on the interpretation of results. Obviously, the issues that receive emphasis in this section depend not just on the study results but on the specific audience to which the journal and hence the article is addressed. In sum, this section provides an overview and evaluation of the study findings. At the end of the discussion section, the answer to the question "So what?" should be clear.

The Process of Writing for Publication

So far, this chapter has addressed itself to the "why," the "where," and the "what" of writing for publication. This section is addressed to the "how" of writing. It will suggest that writing at a professional level is a process that is often misunderstood and that knowing more about how most writing is really done will help social workers develop realistic expectations for themselves and thereby succeed in publishing their work (Beebe 1993).

Getting Started: Alternative Approaches

There are two general views about how to write. The first, with which most people are familiar, is that the best way to proceed is to work out the ideas and content of a piece before the writing actually begins, typically developing an outline or other form of written plan in advance. A piece of nonfiction writing is seen as linear and sequential, and the challenge is to set forth a series of ideas logically connected from beginning to end (Zinsser 1988). Writing the text then consists of the process of developing prose to describe the ideas already named and ordered in the plan. Rewriting and revision are then used to achieve the optimal clarity of expression of ideas already formed.

An alternative view is that of writing as an act of discovery. Thoughts and the organization of ideas are developed through the process of writing itself. From this perspective, writing an article can even begin with free-form writing or notes to oneself in which ideas still nascent can be discovered. This process of self-discovery and reflection is carried out through multiple drafts as thoughts are clarified and a more structured article draft is gradually developed. This method can help to break down misapprehensions and unrealistic expectations based on years of writing term papers and aiming for a "perfect" written product from a one-shot attempt (Becker 1986).

Each beginning writer should explore both methods of writing to discover which is the most productive for him or her. Some people always work one way and some the other. Others find that they use different methods for different tasks or projects. Explanatory writing is designed to convey information and ideas; exploratory writing is designed for the writer to discover what the message will be (Zinsser 1988). The outline method may work best in the former situation and a looser approach in the latter. Most writing about research is explanatory writing, but, as Becker (1986) suggests, exploratory writing may be a good way to begin work of that kind as well.

The most important thing to remember is that both views of the writing process are predicated on the fact that the end result must be clarity of thinking and expression. Thus writing at a professional level always involves extensive rewriting and revision. Writing is time-consuming, and for every project sufficient time must be planned to prepare, incubate, execute, and revisit for revision.

Learning by Imitation

There is no better way to learn to write well than by writing. One way of getting started as a beginner is to imitate examples of good writing. All of us can think of books or articles we have read that have been clear, inspiring, elegant in exposition, and full of useful and memorable information. Identifying and analyzing such pieces of writing can help each writer remember what she or he is aiming for. An author should try to offer a reader the same things that he or she enjoys when reading.

On a more concrete level, when writing for a specific journal for the first time, finding a recently published article of the same type in that journal can provide a framework for planning one's own piece. The length of the introduction and literature review sections, the specific terminology to use for methodology sections, and conventions in the presentation of data or discussion can all be gleaned from what is already in print. It may be easier to fit one's own data to an identified plan than to have to invent the presentation of both content and structure at once.

When a dancer first learns a new step or dance, she does so by following the movements of the choreographer. Once the dance is known, however, the execution and interpretation are invariably her own. Imitation of form or method is not plagiarism of content, and the style or voice of each writer will inevitably emerge and grow more distinctive with use.

Writing and Thinking

Whatever the purpose of a piece or the model of writing being used, writing is increasingly being taught and understood as a process rather than a product. This process is about thinking clearly. As Zinsser (1988) has said, "Clear writing is the logical arrangement of thought; a scientist who thinks clearly can write as well as the best writer" (1988:xiii). By extension, a human service professional who can think clearly about practice or about a piece of research has the capacity to write well about it, too.

The words most often used to describe an effective writing style are "simple," "clear," and "direct." However, very few people are able to produce prose that is simple, clear, and direct in a first draft. In fact, it is very important that a writer first get the essential thoughts down on paper without censorship. Too much attention to issues of expression, mechanics, or style in an initial draft can be inhibiting. However, "writer-based prose" (Flower 1985), which is characterized by a focus on the writer or a structure based on the writer's own discovery process, must later be reorganized to meet the reader's needs.

Word processing has proven a wonderful tool for writers. Free-form text can be easily produced, catalogued, and saved for later reference. Text can be built around outlines already stored. However, it is at the stage of editing and revision that word processing is most useful, allowing, as it does, for the instantaneous incorporation of changes into a draft and for the production and reproduction of altered versions of the text. Sentences, paragraphs, and pages can be rearranged with a few mouse clicks. Spelling errors can be identified, and programs are available that include dictionaries of synonyms or that can flag questionable grammar or usage. With these tools, a manuscript can easily be revised as often as needed to produce a polished product.

Problems in writing, however, are rarely just mechanical. Although there are rules of spelling, punctuation, and usage that must be learned and applied to make a work intelligible, problems in writing usually reflect problems in thinking, which can only be solved by clarification and hard work by the author.

Becoming Your Own Editor

The revision of a manuscript must take place at all levels: the organization of the piece as a whole and of its constituent sections, paragraphs, sentences, and words. There are specific techniques that can be useful in editing one's own work at each of these levels.

It should be noted that revision is best undertaken a while after a draft has been completed. Especially when the prose is new, the eye tends to see what was intended, not what is. Therefore it is easier to be effectively self-critical when the material has been allowed to sit a while before the final revision begins.

Overall Structure

The purpose and organization of the article as a whole and of each section in it should be stated for the reader clearly at the beginning. Visual aids such as headings and subheadings should be used to provide additional visual signposts to the direction each section of the report is taking. Headings also contribute to an economy of style when they can substitute for lengthy verbal transitions. However, even when an article has been carefully planned, it is essential to begin the process of revision by reviewing the overall structure of the piece to see what has in fact emerged.

After a draft has been completed, a map of the structure of the manuscript can be quickly developed and analyzed by listing the headings and subheadings used on a sheet of paper. Examining the outline of headings after the fact can suggest alternative or more efficient ways to organize the flow of ideas. It can also identify gaps in the content or argument that need to be filled in.

A more detailed analysis of the overall structure of a piece can be made by making a sentence outline "after the fact," that is, writing a sentence to describe the content of each paragraph in the draft in the order they occur. Paragraphs are key structural units in any piece of writing because each one should contain a set of thoughts all related to one idea, and this main idea of the paragraph should be expressible in a single or topic sentence. These sentences, like headings but with more detail and substance, show the skeleton of the paper as it stands.

Sentence outlining can reveal a number of ways to improve the organization of a draft. For example, if a paragraph cannot easily be summed up in a single sentence, it probably needs to be broken down into more than one. Sometimes the outline will show similar sentences from different places; this suggests that the draft could be condensed or clarified by eliminating redundancies or reorganizing its content. Places where more material is needed to fill in an argument can also be identified from the outline. While sentence outlining is a somewhat time-consuming process, it is an extremely powerful tool for analyzing the overall structure of a piece, a technique that can be especially useful when an article does not have a standard or conventional format.

Once the best possible order of content has been established, it is important to consider the points of transition in the text, both beginnings and endings. Headings and subheadings are the clearest markers of shifts in content. However, the beginnings and endings of individual paragraphs can also be used to ease the reader's progression through the piece.

The first sentence of an article, section, or paragraph is essential; it must "hook" the reader and draw her in for more. Similarly, the last sentence must both sum up and lead on. Sections of text must not just stop; they must end. When material is as condensed and densely packed as it must be in most articles, the reader can only absorb the material effectively when the writer makes it flow smoothly for efficient ingestion.

Some Useful Rhetorical Rules

Good writing at bottom consists of well-chosen and well-ordered words. Revision must of course include close attention to the words that are used and how they are organized into sentences. This is the art of *rhetoric:* "Rhetoric shows you how to put words together so that the reader not simply may but must grasp your meaning" (Barzun 1975:2).

Improving rhetoric means attending to the writing not only at the level of overall structure but also at the levels of the sentence and word. The time to fuss over the fine points of rhetoric is at the stage of revision rather than first draft. However, it is essential that adequate time be given to revision before a paper is sent out for review. Even a paper with terrific ideas will be rejected by a journal if it is not also written well.

Sentences. Once the overall plan of the piece has been considered, the revision process must address the sentences that make up each paragraph. Sentences are the building blocks of prose because each sentence is a unit of meaning, a complete thought.

Each sentence in an article must be able to stand alone, conveying a clear unit of meaning in and of itself. Sentences may be either simple or complex in structure. The parts of the sentence—subject, verb, and all the modifiers of each—must be organized so they stand in the optimal relationship to each other. As the basic rule of rhetoric reminds us, a well-written sentence can be understood in only one way.

To be complete, a sentence must contain both a subject (usually a noun) and a predicate (a verb). These basic elements of a sentence can be constituted and arranged in a variety of ways, and additional modifiers—words, clauses, or phrases—can be added to these basic ingredients. Sentence structures are classified according to the elements that are included and how they are arranged. Basic rules of *usage* govern how the elements in a sentence must be put together, such as that the subject and predicate must agree, that is, both be either singular or plural. There are many sources available that review these rules for writers. Strunk and

White (1979) and Barzun (1975) are among the more readable ones. Even style manuals for publication often contain useful style guidelines (American Psychological Association 1994).

In general, it is better to use short sentences than long ones. Just like in an overly long paragraph, in a long and complex sentence the meaning may be lost. In an overly long sentence, the structure may be lost as well, leaving only a collection of clauses or phrases in a confused relationship to each other. A short declarative sentence in which verb follows noun usually seems strong and forceful. However, varying sentence structures somewhat in each paragraph results in a smoother flow of words.

Words. The first rule of word choice is like the first rule for writing a sentence: Keep it simple. Choose a short word over a longer one. In most instances, choose a common or concrete noun over a technical or abstract one. Eliminate all extra words. Beebe (1993) gives good examples of how to do this.

The greatest temptation for the beginning professional writer is to attempt to sound authoritative by using professional jargon. This tendency most often results in long sentences made up of long words, especially strings of abstract nouns, joined together with passive verbs and lots of qualifying modifiers, like "may," "might," and "probably." Barzun (1975) calls this "the noun plague."

While jargon is used to seek precision, it usually obscures. Examples of writing obscured by jargon are unfortunately easy to find:

> The economic-compulsive explanation for a relationship between cocaine and crime argues that the relationship between expensive drug use and criminal activity is a direct function of physical need (addiction or compulsion) producing economic needs unmet through traditional channels. (Hunt 1991:140)

This proposition might be restated more simply as:

> One theory is that cocaine addiction leads directly to crime because the amount of the drug needed costs more than the addict can pay for through legal means.

Note how much easier it is to understand the second version. [An alternative theory is that both cocaine use and crime are part of a deviant lifestyle chosen by the individual (Hunt 1991).]

Changing to short sentences with simple structures and plain words is hard to do precisely because it means that the thoughts behind the words must be clear. However, simple words will in the end convey a much more authoritative tone than jargon-based, long, and jaw-breaking ones.

Diction, or word choice, is at the heart of good writing. Words come complete with definitions, meanings, connotations, and resonances. They also come with common usages, such as the prepositions that follow and link them to other words. All of these aspects of the word must be considered when deciding which one to use. For example, there could be debate in the jargon example above about whether "crime" or "criminal activity" is the better term to use. The latter, although longer, may be more accurate or inclusive in that it connotes activity whether or not an official crime occurs by virtue of an arrest.

Writing about research generally requires especially precise and careful choice of terms. For example, while "self-esteem" and "self-concept" may seem synonymous in ordinary usage, the terms are often used distinctively in research. "Self-esteem" to a psychologist signifies "positive self-regard," which may or may not be part of what is meant when the term "self-concept" is used. A measure labeled "self-esteem" should not be called "self-concept" in the paper that describes the study. Similar precision must be used with all the concepts identified and described in a research report.

Computerized Aids in Editing

Specialized software packages have been developed to aid the writer in editing her or his own work, and most sophisticated word-processing programs now incorporate such programs within them. Each piece of software varies in its ease of use and in the dimensions of the prose that it deals with. Most incorporate a feature addressing spelling that flags any word not matching a correctly spelled one in its dictionary. They also often check punctuation, usage, as in whether "affect" or "effect" are being employed correctly, and sentence structure, identifying overly long sentences or incomplete ones. Some analyze each piece of writing for level of difficulty according to several common measures of reading complexity and provide a summary description of each piece of text reviewed. Consistent use of such a program, which flags and queries the author at each "mistake," can be a powerful training tool for improving one's writing style.

Advanced editing programs can be customized. That is, different parameters, like sentence length or whether or not passive verb constructions will be permitted, can be set individually. The user can also choose among bundled style options—general readership, business style, or technical writing, for example—which change several parameters or style standards at once.

It should be noted that technical writing is often needed in research reports, and good research writing is unlikely to fit all the parameters for good writing for a general readership. Therefore, if an editing program is to be used, select one that will allow parameters realistic for research writing. This does not excuse research writing that is unnecessarily complex or obscure. It merely recognizes the reality that scientific reporting is generally aimed at a professional rather than a general audience and must fit the conventions of its genre.

Reading Aloud

Once the research report has been edited and revised, a good way to check over one's own work is to read it aloud. Problems with sentence structure or ambiguous phrasing missed by the eye are often detected by the ear. If the reader must hesitate in speaking or change inflection in order to convey the sentence clearly, it is likely that at least some readers will miss the meaning that was intended. Such a sentence or passage should be revised and edited until it flows more smoothly off the page.

Getting Feedback

Once the ideas are as clearly expressed as the author can make them, feedback on the content should be sought prior to submission for publication and scrutiny by an editorial board or other evaluative body. The best way to do this is to ask a colleague to read and comment on the work. Choose someone knowledgeable in the content area and/or someone who reflects the readership anticipated for the piece. Because a careful reading and critique of another person's work takes considerable time and energy, choose someone conscientious and someone for whom you can return the favor at some future point. Aspiring authors who form writing groups with peers often do so in part for the mutual feedback opportunities such groups offer.

Feedback of this kind is generally directed toward content primarily rather than style. It can prove invaluable in identifying problems or gaps in the material presented or in sharpening the focus of the piece by highlighting what is most interesting or most relevant to an informed reader. However, if a reader is willing to offer feedback on style as well, use it. Some writers consult with professional editors for this purpose.

Preparing the Manuscript

Making a manuscript ready for dissemination or review is a part of the writing job that is often overlooked. Each piece of professional writing should go out as "well turned out" as possible. If a specific bibliographic style is required for the report or the journal, be sure to use it. The analogy here is to the job interview: The well-groomed applicant may have the edge. Not only does a good-looking manuscript increase legibility for the reviewer or receiver, it also gives a general impression of investment in and care about the contents.

If professional help is used in typing and manuscript preparation, the author must be clear about the mutual expectations, including time. The *APA Manual* has an excellent section on how to work with a typist (APA 1994). Both parties may be helped by a written or verbal contract between them describing the duties and responsibilities of each. For example, while some experienced typists may informally offer assistance with editing, the only function that should be expected is that of setting forth clearly on the page the text in the form that the author supplied it within the agreed-upon time frame. With documents prepared with a word processor, it is usually cheaper and more efficient to supply a typist with diskettes containing text, paying only for the time required to format and print out the final paper copy. However, attention must be paid, then, to compatibility of software and hardware between writer and typist. Book publishers often want a manuscript in both paper and digital form, and journals are increasingly asking for material in electronic form as well, especially after the decision to publish has been made.

With the advent of computerized word processing, however, more and more professional writers are preparing their own manuscripts for publication. This means that time for the task of formatting and printing out the text must be allowed. Such processes often take longer than one might think, especially for the novice typist or the one with a printer that turns out pages slowly. In addition to spell-checkers and editing programs, there are also computer programs that can take a manuscript prepared under one convention, such as APA style, and convert it to another system, such as MLA style, saving enormous amounts of time. Time spent in presenting a manuscript attractively, however, is generally an excellent investment in the reception the contents will receive.

Understanding the Journal Review Process

So far, this chapter has described principles of writing about research that apply to any research report, regardless of the audience for whom it is intended. This section is addressed specifically to writing for journal publication. Understanding journal review processes will make it easier to deal with the publication process and may lead to a greater chance of success when submitting a research report to a journal (Beebe 1993).

Most scientific and professional journals operate under a system of peer review. Volunteer reviewers serve on editorial boards. These professionals, recognized for their expertise in the content addressed by the journal, have responsibility both for setting policy about the standards for publication in the journal and for reading and evaluating the manuscripts the journal receives. Each journal also has a professional staff that administers the review process and the production of the journal itself. Editorial board membership is always listed in the journal itself. Board members serve without compensation and often devote large amounts of time to the enterprise in return for the prestige of being recognized as an expert arbiter of what is deemed publishable. A journal also may use consulting editors for manuscript review if the volume of submissions is large and/or there is a need for expertise in specific areas to supplement that of board members. Consulting editors are generally listed once annually in the journal. In this way, those who submit articles can learn about the people who may review them.

Usually at least two reviewers rate each manuscript received, more if the first two reviewers disagree. Each manuscript is reviewed "blind," that is, with the identity and affiliation of the author(s) unknown to the reviewers. This system is designed to depersonalize the review process as much as possible. Many of the conventions used in preparing a manuscript—a separate title and authorship page and brief "running" headings at the top of each manuscript page to identify it—are designed to facilitate the blind review process. Reviewers are asked to disqualify themselves if they know or can identify the author of an article from the text. Reviewers are also "blind" to the opinion of any other reviewer at the time of the review.

The blind peer review process is designed both to be as open as possible to new people and ideas and to subject new works to informed scrutiny from recognized professional experts. This system is dependent on large amounts of volunteer labor from reviewers. Hence a major "rule of the game" in seeking journal publication is that a piece may be submitted to *only one journal at a time*. This prevents an editorial board from spending time evaluating a piece that may be accepted somewhere else first. It also prevents journals from devoting space in their pages to materials that their readers may not experience as new or recent content.

Selecting a Journal

A major challenge for the writer who aspires to publish an article is to select the best journal for submission. Because each review takes some time—generally at least three months—and because an article can be under review in only one place at one time, the choice of journal should be made to maximize the odds of success. The number of journals in social work and related fields has been increasing, and the use of computerized databases for literature searching means that material that first appears in small but indexed journals may get fairly wide use, at least by scholars. Thus it may not be necessary to select the largest, most prestigious, or most selective journal as a market.

Each journal has a specific mission, stated on the masthead or in its information for authors. This mission tells the writer what topics and types of articles the publication is likely to be interested in. This interest is of course defined by the journal's readership. After all, a journal's main mission is to sell subscriptions, so each journal tries to give its readers what they want to read. The choice of a journal, then, is really a choice about the audience to whom the article will be addressed. The intended audience, in turn, will shape the nature of the piece as it is being written. As already noted, the target journal for a piece, then, should be chosen before the piece is written, and there are several guides to scholarly journals that may help in identifying possible markets or in selecting among them.

Standards of Review

Every journal defines the standards against which all articles are evaluated by the reviewers. The first is always that the article "make a contribution," adding to what is already known in some significant and potentially useful way. This potential contribution is evaluated in relation to the specific journal and its particular readership; thus what is "old hat" to one audience may be new to another. Content addressing oppressed and underserved populations is especially welcome in many journals because of the relative lack of previous research on these populations in most fields.

Equally important is the fit of the article to the mission and audience of the journal. For example, journals whose readers are primarily practitioners will be eager to publish material about practice. In the review process, each reviewer is asked to consider whether this journal is the best place for this material at this time. Also considered, of course, are the quality of the research methods, the clarity of presentation, evidence of familiarity with the field, relevance to practice, and other dimensions the editors think are important in evaluating work. The precise nature of these standards and how they are interpreted varies from publication to publication. Thus one journal's "reject" is another journal's "accept."

If an article's content is new, important, and suitable for the readership in question, the editorial board may be willing to work with an author on other aspects of the manuscript if possible (see below). However, problems in methodology or exposition can be enough to keep interesting material from publication. If the methodology is not sound, the results lack credibility; if the exposition is poor, the points the author wishes to make will be misunderstood or missed altogether.

Outcomes of a Review

Editorial feedback to authors has two purposes—evaluation and education. While some boards take the educational aspect of their work more seriously than others, reviewers invest considerable energy in developing their comments. It is usually possible to learn a great deal from the comments about how to improve one's work. Even when an article has not been accepted, the comments may still be useful in revising the piece before sending it out to another journal.

Acceptance. The outcomes of a journal review fall into several categories. The first and, of course, most desirable is an "accept." Once an article is accepted for publication, the next step is to schedule it for an actual publication date. The timing of this depends on the backlog of accepted articles at the journal and on other editorial decisions, such as assembling content for a special issue on a particular theme.

Journals differ in the work they put into preparing an accepted manuscript for publication. Some treat the manuscript as accepted as "camera ready," which means that the author alone will bear the responsibility for proofreading and copyediting. Others invest considerable staff resources in copyediting and proofreading the manuscript after acceptance and before print. Some ask authors to review prepublication printings, such as "galley proofs"; others do not. In the end, however, it is the author who is responsible for the accuracy of what appears in print.

All journals will require that copyright to the article be signed over to them before publication. A journal that publishes an article owns the work, which also means that they will defend the work from any copyright infringement or illegal use of it without compensation. There is no financial compensation to authors who publish in scholarly journals as they are not money-making enterprises.

Rejection. At the other extreme, a journal may reject an article. Almost all journals will return copies of the anonymous reviewers' comments on the article. These will explain why the journal editor reached the decision made. Some of these comments may be painful to read or hard to understand. If so, it may be useful to put them aside for a while and return to them later. However, some may reflect a bias of the reviewer or a misapprehension of the author's intent. Such comments, of course, are not so useful unless they suggest features of the article that need further clarification or help in identifying the preferences of the journal for future reference. It is also common for multiple reviewers to disagree or to emphasize different things in their feedback (Fiske & Fogg 1990). It is up to the author to sift through all of the editorial comments, positive and negative, to accept those that will help, find a way to answer those that miss the mark or that ask for changes that cannot be made, and identify those that can be safely ignored.

When a journal rejects an article, it does not necessarily mean that the article is not publishable. It does mean that one should not resubmit it to the same journal again. However, the comments offered should be used to help in revising the article for submission elsewhere. Many published articles were rejected somewhere else before being published. Sometimes the difference is a better fit between the content and the journal that ultimately published it. Sometimes it is the product of the revision process, aided by the feedback from the rejecting journal. Sometimes it is just the "luck of the draw" among reviewers.

Requests for revision. Often journals take some middle ground in evaluating a piece. They may reject an article but suggest resubmission after revision or accept an article provisionally subject to revision. In such situations, extensive editorial commentary describing both the strengths and weaknesses of the work is usually provided. While the negative part of the commentary may initially be wounding, the fact is that if the problems noted can be addressed one way or another, this is a good outcome for a review, and the success rate upon resubmission is usually very high. In some cases, the re-review is expedited by return of the manuscript to one or more of the original reviewers; in others cases, new reviewers are used. A cover letter with the resubmitted article describing how each critique was addressed and why some of them were not will help.

Facing the outcome of the journal review process can be very exciting or very upsetting. When results are not immediately favorable, it should be remembered that there are almost always options, such as revision and resubmission. For the aspiring author, openness to feedback and persistence usually pay off.

Overcoming Obstacles to Writing for Publication

There are many obstacles to writing for publication. Some of them are ignorance of the actual and technical parts of the process of writing and marketing an article, which this chapter has tried to address. Others are both psychological and structural.

Many myths color our feelings about professional writing in general (Becker 1986). The idea that really talented writers create a perfect draft at one sitting is simply untrue. The "term paper" model of the one-time, "give it my best shot" method of writing learned in school is poor preparation for the world of write, rewrite, and revise that characterizes professional writing.

Some also believe that writers rely on a process of "inspiration" that comes magically to some people and not to others. While a few writers may describe their work in this way, many more speak of hard labor and persistence as the main ingredients in what they do. Once inspired, the work must still be spelled out, word by word and line by line. Clearly the drive that propels an author through the periods of hard work involved in any research project and writing it up is often a very personal one. This inspiration must be supplemented, however, by qualities of persistence, self-discipline, and perseverance.

The work lives of most human service professionals (and of most students) are designed to discourage rather than encourage the knowledge development we say that we want. Few jobs allow time for reflection and writing. Many professionals work more than one job, reducing the personal time available for research and writing. Some work settings, however, do try to offer some inducements to scholarly work, like reimbursement for travel to conferences to give a paper, for workshops, or by providing occasions to showcase the work of colleagues.

Peer support groups, formed at work or from among other colleagues, can be a powerful source of mutual support for scholarly work. Such groups are often ideal resources for initial feedback on drafts of articles or works in progress. The stimulation gained from colleagues' ideas as well as the feedback from others about one's own is encouraging. The rewards of participating in such a group are often like those of publication and conference presentation themselves.

Finally, there is no substitute for scheduling and self-discipline once the commitment to a writing project is made. Regular "appointments" for at least two periods of work each week will go a long way toward bringing a project to a successful conclusion. Whatever the specific schedule developed, however, it is necessary to put in the time, and it is this element of the process—sufficient time for the effort—that is more often lacking than any other.

Conclusions

The social work and human service professions are coming of age, and human service professionals have a lot to offer the other helping professions, each other, and their clients by getting what they know into print and into use. The field is open to increasingly diverse models of research and practice. Knowledge of what is required in a research report, review of some basic principles of good writing, and knowledge about the systems and processes involved in journal publication are essential. Armed with this information, social workers and other human service professionals should be better able to "get the word out" about what they know and about the research that they do.

Glossary

Abstract: A brief statement about a paper or a presentation that summarizes its main points succinctly. Sometimes used for competitive review of possible conference presentations; common at the beginning of published articles and used for indexing of them.

Accidental sample: A form of nonrandom sampling that selects research participants primarily based on their availability (given that inclusion and exclusion criteria are met). Equivalent to *convenience sample*.

Alpha coefficient: A statistical measure of the reliability, or internal consistency, of a scale.

Alpha (Type A or 1) error: In statistical hypothesis testing, the mistake that results if the null hypothesis is rejected when it is in fact true. It is also therefore the support of a research or alternative hypothesis that is not true.

Alpha level: The proportional level of risk of error that is the criterion in deciding whether to reject a null hypothesis. By convention, it is generally set at . 05 or 5%, although with the help of statistical software, the exact probability is often reported.

Alternative hypothesis: In statistical hypothesis testing, a null hypothesis is accepted or rejected, which determines whether or not its *alternative,* which contains the research idea, is supported or not.

Analysis of variance: A family of statistical techniques based on comparing the amount of variation within and between sample subgroups.

Anchoring terms: The words used to assign interpretations to a series of preset answer options in interviews and questionnaires, for example, when words such as "agree" or "disagree" are used to correspond to numerical responses.

ANOVA: An acronym for analysis of variance (see above).

Appeal to authority: One of the five ways of knowing identified by Charles Peirce in which belief is based on the reputation of the person who makes the statement.

Attrition: Loss over time, or dropout, from a research sample between data collection points.

Audience: The people for whom a presentation, report, or paper is prepared.

Audit trail: In flexible method or qualitative research, a record of all decision-making about sampling, data collection, and data analysis that others can potentially review.

Baseline: In single-subject research and some longitudinal group designs in which the same people are followed over time, the period during which research participants are assessed to determine their preintervention or pre-follow-up functioning.

Beneficence: One of three major principles underlying research ethics that calls for maximizing the benefits and minimizing the possible harm resulting from a research study.

Beta (Type B or 2) error: In statistical hypothesis testing, the mistake that results if the null hypothesis is *not* rejected when it is in fact *false*. The failure to support an alternative or research hypothesis that is true.

Between-group designs: Relational research designs (fixed method) that answer questions by comparing two or more sample subgroups to each other when the composition of those groups is independent of each other.

Bias: Systematic error in measurement or conclusions that pushes assessments or findings in a particular direction. Bias is sometimes based on status variables, such as race, gender, and the like, but includes other more idiosyncratic distortions as well.

Binomial (variable): A nominal level variable that has only two categories.

Bipolar: A set of answer options in fixed response questions that are on a continuum between two opposites, like "agree" and "disagree. "

Bivariate: Statistical procedures and techniques that involve examining two variables at a time.

Bounded recall: A technique used in writing fixed response questions that specifies the time period or range of situations the respondent is asked to think about when answering a question. This technique is thought to increase the accuracy of answers.

Case/control: In single-system designs, the technique of using data on one individual at an earlier point in time for comparison at a later time, usually following the introduction of an intervention in order to assess its effects.

Case study research: Any research that involves examining a single bounded unit or entity in depth. Traditional case studies generally use a flexible or qualitative approach. See also *single-system design*.

Cause/causal: A specific form of proposition in which it is asserted that a change in one variable creates and always will create a change in another variable. Classically it is based on establishing the contiguity of events, their order in time, and constant conjunction between the events (see chapter 7).

Celeration line: A specific analytic technique used in single-system designs in which change is assessed by demonstrating that the rate of increase or decrease of a phenomenon has changed. Graphically and mathematically, this involves a change in the slope of a trend line.

Central Limit Theorem: This theorem states that, if many random samples of the same size were drawn from a single population, the mean of the sample means would be at the population mean and the distribution of the sample means themselves would form a bell-shaped or normal curve around that mean.

Central tendency: The middle of a frequency distribution, which can potentially be assessed in three ways. The mean, the median, and the mode are all measures of central tendency.

Cluster sample: A form of sample selection in which the sample or population is divided into subgroups, such as blocks of a city, only some of which are then chosen as sites from which study participants are recruited.

Codebook: A scheme for translating raw research data into variables or codes for analysis, especially when used with numerical data to show how particular responses will be represented numerically.

Coding: The process of classifying (qualitative) or scoring (quantitative) data for analysis (see chapters 16, 17, and 19).

Coefficient of determination(r^2): A descriptive statistic based on the Pearson r correlation coefficient that can be interpreted as the proportion of variation in one variable that is shared with another.

Comparison group: A group of sample members included in a research design for purposes of contrast with the primary group being studied. Common in variations on experimental design, a comparison group differs from a control group by not being generated through random assignment.

Computational formula: See *defining formula*.

Conceptual definition: The definition of a phenomenon under study in abstract theoretical terms.

Conclusion: See *discussion*.

Concurrent validity: The examination of the meaning and interpretation of data by examining how well more than one measurement or assessment of the same characteristic at the same time correlate with each other.

Confound: In experimental and single-system designs, factors that could be alternative explanations for changes observed instead of the relationship between intervention and outcome posited.

Constant comparison: A technique for coding narrative data, associated with the grounded theory method of Glaser and Strauss (1967), in which coding categories are developed and their definitions theoretically and empirically refined through an ongoing process of comparing new to existing pieces of text given the same code.

Constructionism/constructivism (also called social constructionism/vism): A line of thinking in the social sciences and epistemology that emphasizes how historical, social, and personal, even perceptual, factors influence what is taken to be knowledge and how people know.

Construct validity: The property of a scale or set of items or questions designed to show that, taken together, they can be taken to reflect the complex concept they are designed to measure and not related but different ones. Construct validity is usually demonstrated in relation to both convergent and divergent criteria.

Content validity: The property of a scale or set of items or questions such that, taken together, they can be taken to reflect the full meaning of the concept they are asserted to measure.

Contingency question: A question in a prestructured interview or questionnaire that is to be answered or not depending on the response to a previous one.

Contingency table: A table formed by tabulating cases in a sample according to their classification on two (or more) nominal level variables.

Control group: A group of sample members included in a research design for purposes of contrast with the primary group being studied when that group has been constituted by random assignment of sample members to it.

Convenience sample: A form of nonrandom sampling that selects research participants primarily based on their availability (given that inclusion and exclusion criteria are met). Equivalent to *accidental sample*.

Convergent validity: An empirical demonstration of the meaning of a set of measurements by showing that the results are similar to those obtained when assessing the same concept in a different way.

Correlated samples: Sample subgroups that are formed based on how their members are related to each other. Also used when the same people are compared to themselves over time. Compare to *independent samples*. Different statistical techniques must be used when comparing correlated and independent sample groups.

Correlation: The degree to which there is shared variation in two (or more) variables.

Correlation coefficient: A statistical measure of the amount of covariance between two (or more) variables.

Criterion-related validity: Examination of the meaning of a measure by comparing results to another measure accepted as an indicator of the same concept.

Cross-sectional research: Research that is conducted at one point in time.

Cross-tabulation: See *contingency table*.

Data: The term used for information gathered in the process of doing research. It can be numerical or narrative.

Data array: The result of organizing and displaying a table of data collected, narrative or numerical, in which each row represents a case or unit of study and each column represents a variable or characteristic assessed. Used in data entry and data analysis.

Data entry: The process of getting data, narrative or numerical, into the computer for later analysis.

Data management: The process of organizing, preserving, and keeping records of data collected, usually in both written and electronic form. It can also include activities undertaken to summarize or otherwise reduce the volume of data in order to make it more usable for analysis.

Data reduction: The process of paring down data, narrative or numerical, to its most essential parts, of compiling and summarizing it in a way that best reveals its essential meaning.

Data set: In using computers, a term that indicates the entire body of information gathered from a particular study or data collection effort, inclusive of all cases and all variables to be analyzed.

Deconstruction: A theory deriving from literary criticism that holds that any statement can be taken apart (deconstructed) to reveal multiple and contradictory meanings, none of which can be considered any more legitimate than any other.

Deduction: The process of reasoning from theory to data or observation.

Defining formula: In statistics, the algebraic symbols that best express what a given statistic means. In contrast, *computational formulas* may be easier to use when actually calculating a value for that statistic from data.

Degrees of freedom: A number associated with many test statistics needed for evaluating statistical significance. It is usually a function of sample or table size.

Dependent variable: When, in relational or experimental research, two variables are posited as being related to each other, the dependent variable is the one that conceptually comes after, "depends on," or is the effect of, the other.

Descriptive research: Fixed method studies with the purpose of generating empirical information about what a phenomenon is and is like.

Descriptive statistics: One of two realms of the field of statistics. The set of techniques used to describe and summarize numerical data.

Dichotomism: A form of bias in which the differences between groups are exaggerated and their similarities and/or overlapping characteristics overlooked.

Differential attrition: When two (or more) groups are being followed over time, the loss of sample members at different rates from the groups.

Direct effect: When one variable or factor is related to another, this relationship is considered a direct one when that relationship does not involve and is not altered by any other variable or factor.

Discriminant validity: An empirical demonstration of the meaning of a set of measurements by showing that the results are different from those obtained when assessing a different though related concept.

Discussion: The final or conclusion section of a research paper or report that summarizes the meaning of a study's findings and describes their potential implications for theory, practice, policy, and/or future research.

Dispersion: The amount of scatter or spread of scores or values of a variable around the midpoint of the distribution scores.

Dissemination: The process of conveying the results of a research study to others, in written or oral form.

Double-blind experiment: A type of experiment, common in research on medications, in which neither participant nor treator knows whether the participant is receiving the experimental treatment or an inert substitute (placebo).

Double standard: A form of bias in which the same characteristics are interpreted or evaluated differently in two groups.

Empirical: Based on observation (sensory experience) in the world.

Empirical probability: An estimate of the likelihood of an event derived through experience or experiment.

Empiricism: The belief, as in the scientific method, that the most trustworthy knowledge is based on empirical investigation.

Epistemology: The branch of philosophy that deals with the nature of human knowledge.

Error: When deciding about hypotheses or analyzing data, a mistaken conclusion. In relation to data collection, specifically traditional measurement theory, that part of any observed score that is inevitable and randomly distributed inaccuracy.

Ethics: Rules or standards of professional conduct.

Ethnographic research: A tradition of flexible method research derived from anthropology, often involving participant observation and other data collection methods and focussed on social and cultural issues.

Experimental research: A fixed method type of study that introduces a systematic intervention or procedure (manipulation) to research participants and then examines the changes, if any, that occur afterward in hopes of showing that the changes can logically be attributed to the intervention.

Expert sample: A form of nonrandom sample selection in which participants are chosen because of special characteristics that they share, in this case some expertise or unique experience that makes them the best informants for a study.

Explanation: A conceptual formulation describing events or phenomena and their relationship(s) to each other. It may or may not involve cause and effect reasoning; it may or may not permit prediction. Fallibilistic realism values all forms of explanation, not just those that involve cause and effect or predictive reasoning.

Ex post facto: Any research design that examines a phenomenon after the fact rather than prospectively.

External validity: The degree to which conclusions drawn from a research study might be expected to hold true in other circumstances. Related to fixed method research designs, the generalizability of the conceptual conclusions drawn. In flexible method or qualitative research, this characteristic is usually called *universality*.

Face validity: An evaluation of the meaning of a scale or other structured data collection by examining the content of its constituent items.

Factorial designs: Experimental research designs that involve multiple independent, or grouping, variables defining sample subgroups.

Factors: With respect to structured data collection tools with many items measuring a complex phenomenon, subscales measuring specific aspects of the phenomenon, especially when derived empirically through a multivariate statistical technique called factor analysis. In experimental designs and data analysis, factors are the categorical independent variables that define the sample subgroups being compared.

Fallibilistic realism: An epistemology based in realism, or the idea that there is a mind-independent reality, tempered by the idea that empirical knowledge of the world is inherently imperfect. This imperfection is based both on social, cultural, and historical influences and on the fact that the theories used to apprehend and label phenomena impose a lens of their own on them. See Manicas and Secord (1983).

Findings: The report of the results of a data analysis process explaining what the data gathered in a study were. A major section of any written report on a research project.

Fixed method research: Types of research design that depend on invariant methods and procedures as a means of bias control. Fixed method research includes descriptive, relational, experimental, and single-system studies.

Flexible method research: Types of research design in which the methods of investigation are allowed to vary in response to emerging findings and which include the researcher within the boundary of what is studied. Flexible method designs include what are elsewhere called qualitative research and traditional case studies.

Focal sample: A type of nonrandom sample in which research participants are selected based on the special characteristics they share, often to an extreme. Also known as a *purposive sample.*

Frequency: A count of cases that share a specific value or score on a variable.

Frequency distribution: A listing, in ascending or descending order, of all of the scores of a specific variable that also shows the number of cases found to have each score.

Frequency polygon: A graphical illustration of a frequency distribution used for interval or ratio level variables comprised of a line that rises and falls based on the number of cases showing each value of the variable.

Funneling: A technique of asking a series of questions that moves from one worded in the most general way to successively more specific ones. This method is designed to avoid leading respondents to certain answers while getting them to elaborate on their opinions, beliefs, or experiences.

Generalizability: The degree to which conclusions drawn from a research study might be expected to hold true in other circumstances. Related to fixed method research designs, the general validity of the conceptual conclusions drawn. In flexible method or qualitative research, this characteristic is usually called *universality.*

Grounded theory methods: A specific set of techniques for doing flexible method research developed by Glaser and Strauss (1967). This methodology, commonly cited in social science and human service research, was developed as a way to generate theory rigorously from qualitative data.

Hardware: The actual machinery that makes up a computer or computer system.

Heuristic: Generally, a formulation that guides further knowledge development iteratively. Specifically, heuristics is a particular view of knowledge development advanced by some in social work as an alternative to positivism, which is actually based in realism.

Histogram: A bar graph prepared using ordinal or interval data.

Hypothesis: A statement of a relationship between (or among) phenomena (or variables) posited as true that is then subjected to empirical investigation and, in the case of statistical testing, disproof.

Hypothesis of association: A hypothesis that is stated in the form of a posited relationship between (or among) variables that is investigated by examining two or more variables within one sample group.

Hypothesis of difference: A hypothesis that is stated in the form of a predicted difference between (or among) two (or more) groups that is investigated by examining the same variable(s) in different sample groups.

Independent samples: Sample subgroups formed in such a way that each participant's group membership is not related to the classification of any other participant. Sample group membership based on inherent individual characteristics, such as gender, is an example of independent samples. Compare to *correlated samples*. Different statistical techniques must be used when comparing correlated and independent sample groups.

Independent variable: In relational or experimental research, when two variables are posited as being related to each other, the independent variable is the one that conceptually comes before, is independent of, or is the cause of the other.

Index of dispersion: A statistical measure of variability that can be used with nominal level variables. The percentage of cases not in the modal category.

Indirect effect: When one variable or factor is related to another, the relationship is considered an indirect one when that relationship involves or is altered by another variable or factor.

Induction: Reasoning from data to theory. Starting with observations, or data, and developing a conceptual scheme to describe them.

Inferential statistics: One of two realms of the field of statistics. The set of techniques used to make inferences, either to describe a population based on sample data or to examine the likelihood that an observed relationship among variables is systematic and not just the product of chance. All inferential statistics involve making probabilistic statements.

Insensitivity: A form of bias that occurs when a status variable like race or gender is included in a study but its salience is not adequately examined.

Interaction effect: Occurs when two or more factors in a factorial design have joint and/or indirect effects on the outcome(s) being studied.

Internal consistency: A form of reliability of a scale in which it is shown that responses to its constituent items are highly intercorrelated with each other. Usually measured statistically with a reliability coefficient.

Internal validity: A characteristic of a research design such that its internal logic is strong, that is, statements made about the relationship of one variable to another are logically defensible and alternative explanations have been ruled out.

Interrater reliability: A measure of the dependability or consistency of a measurement based on assessing the amount of agreement between two or more people making the same observation or assessment. Also called *interobserver* reliability.

Interval: A level of measurement in which numbers indicate quantity based on equal intervals between them but that does not have a zero point that indicates absence of the thing being assessed. Examples are temperature and IQ scores.

Interview: A method of data collection in which researcher and researched have a purposeful conversation (verbal interaction) to gather data that bears on a research question. Interviews can be conducted individually or in groups, in person or by telephone, using fixed response or open-ended questions.

Interview guide: A written description of the specific or general questions that will be asked during the course of a research interview.

Intuition: A method of knowing that involves the experience of sudden insight that "feels" correct.

Invisibility: A form of bias in which a group or the experiences of the group go unrecognized.

In vivo code: A term from grounded theory method indicating a code for narrative data that is named using the actual words of a research participant.

Justice: One of three basic principles driving research ethics addressing both basic fairness in processes involving research participants and that the goals of research at some level should advance social justice aims.

Law of Large Numbers: A key principle of inferential statistics stating that, as the number of trials, events, or instances increases, empirical (observed) probability approximates theoretical probability and sample statistics more closely resemble population parameters.

Likert scale: A common form of response option in interview and survey questions in which respondents select a number to indicate the strength of an opinion. The number options are equally spaced visually and anchoring terms are used to label the number options especially at the extremes. Five- or seven-point scales (numbered choices) are the most common.

Literature review: The process of locating, reading, analyzing and synthesizing previous professional writing on the topic of or topics closely related to a specific study. Also the section of a written research report that describes and synthesizes prior research and theory relevant to the study being described.

Logic: One of the methods of knowing in which abstract conceptual propositions are linked to one another as a way of generating or demonstrating the credibility of new ideas.

Logical positivism: An early-twentieth century epistemology positing that logic and empirical observation combined offer the most reliable way of generating knowledge. It is based on an extreme form of realism that holds that facts are dominant and that the world can be known objectively by a properly trained observer.

Longitudinal research: Research that takes place over time.

Manipulation: The process of introducing a specific situation, treatment, or other intervention to research participants in order to examine its effects. A manipulation can take place either in a laboratory or a real-world setting. Manipulation is a defining characteristic of experimental and single-subject research.

Mean: A statistical measure of central tendency showing the middle of a distribution by summing up all scores and taking the average of them. Used with interval or ratio data.

Measurement theory: The traditional view of data collection in the social sciences positing that every observation reflects the real world but is composed of both some truth and some error.

Measures of association: Summary descriptive statistics that quantify the degree of observed relationship or covariation between two (or more) variables.

Median: A statistical measure of central tendency indicating the mid-point of a distribution defined as the point at which half of the sample falls above and half below. Used with ordinal, interval, or ratio data.

Memos: Clarifying notes made by a researcher engaged in flexible method or qualitative research, used either to record personal reflections on the research process and/or to annotate segments of text data being coded.

Method of tenacity: One of Peirce's ways of knowing in which belief is based on repeated assertion. Can be seen as similar to common sense.

Methodology: Those procedures through which a specific research study is conducted, involving specification of the general type of design used, how the sample is obtained, how data are collected, and how data are analyzed.

Mode: A statistical measure of central tendency denoting the most commonly occurring score or the category of the variable into which the most research participants fall. Used with nominal data; a distribution may have two (bimodal) or more modal scores.

Modernism: A general set of ideas ascendant in the early and middle part of the twentieth century, of which logical positivism was an integral part. Rationality, the inevitability of progress, and the importance of science to human well-being were emphasized.

Multidimensional: A term used to describe a concept or measurement tool that has more than one intrinsic aspect, or dimension.

Multilevel/multistage sampling: Used to describe methods of selecting research participants that involve more than one step, such as choosing an organization to be studied and then choosing who from within that organization will be studied.

Multivariate: Statistical techniques that simultaneously examine more than two variables.

Negative case: A technique first described in grounded theory method for enriching the credibility of conclusions generated in flexible method or qualitative research. It involves seeking out and analyzing cases or instances that do not support or tend to disconfirm initial conclusions, either to demonstrate the limits of their applicability or to refine the emergent theory in a way that makes it more inclusive.

Nominal: The simplest level of measurement in which a number serves only as a category label and does not indicate order among scores or quantity in any way.

Nonparametric statistics: Statistical techniques used either when the assumptions of parametric statistics are not met (such as distributions being approximately normal) and/or when sample sizes are small.

Nonprobability sample: A group of participants selected for study without using probability techniques.

Normed: Refers to a scale or measurement in which certain scores have been designated as reliably representing a certain type or level of functioning (i. e. , "normal," clinically significant).

Null hypothesis: A tool of inferential statistics, a statement positing the reverse of the research idea (i. e. , that there will be no difference between groups or no relationship between variables) that is then subjected to disproof.

Observation: A method of data collection involving direct visual experience of the phenomena under study. Observation can be structured or unstructured.

One-tailed test: In hypothesis testing using inferential statistics, a statement of expectation about the direction of difference between two groups or about the direction of relationship (positive or inverse) between two variables, which affects the way probabilities are assessed.

Operating system: In a computer, the software that performs basic functions like turning it off and on, and that provides the framework or environment within which the other software programs operate.

Operational definition: The definition of a phenomenon under study in concrete terms that describe the activities through which the presence/absence or amount of the phenomenon present will be demonstrated or assessed.

Ordinal: The level of measurement in which numbers can be taken to indicate an order (least to most, lowest to highest) but not the amount of difference between them.

Overgeneralization: A form of bias in which observations of one group, ordinarily the more powerful group, are interpreted as applying to all groups.

Paradigm: In the history of science, used to indicate a major body of theory and set of assumptions about the world that defines both what is worth studying and how it is studied.

Parameter: In statistics, a characteristic of a population (rather than a sample drawn from it).

Parameter estimation: Making a probabilistic statement about a population parameter based on a sample statistic. One major use of inferential statistics.

Parametric statistics: The most common and powerful inferential statistical techniques that rely for accurate use on certain assumptions about the population being studied, assumptions usually about the distribution of phenomena in the population (approximately normal) or the similarity of variances in the groups or variables being examined.

Peer review: The system used by most professional journals and scholarly conferences for selecting articles and presentations competitively by having volunteer professional experts read and rate the quality of submissions without knowing who wrote them.

Peripherals/peripheral devices: Equipment such as printers and scanners external, but attached, to a computer, usually used for getting information into or out of it.

Phenomenology: A philosophy concentrating on the appearances of human experience; a line of thinking that underlies some traditions of flexible method or qualitative research.

Pilot test: A formal trial use of a data collection system and instrument prior to embarking on a study in order to refine the data collection methods before use.

Population: The total group sharing certain characteristics of interest, from which a subgroup, or sample, is usually drawn for study.

Post-hoc tests: In analysis of variance involving more than two groups, tests conducted after a statistically significant overall result to pinpoint which specific groups differ from each other.

Postmodernism: A late twentieth-century set of beliefs, contrasted with modernism, that questions the primacy of science and logic, especially the possibility of objectivity in apprehending the world.

Predictive validity: The examination of the meaning and interpretation of data by examining the ability of an assessment made at one point in time to correlate with an assessment or event taking place subsequently.

Pre-post designs: Forms of longitudinal research in which assessments are made of research participants before and after an event or a manipulation.

Probabilistic: Not held with certainty but with a degree of likelihood.

Probabilistic science: Knowledge and methods of inquiry that are based on likelihood, not certainty. For example, cigarette smokers are more likely, but not certain, to get lung cancer. The social, human, biological, and medical sciences are probabilistic.

Probability sample: A group chosen for study using some form of randomization in the selection process.

Probability theory: A set of logical and mathematical propositions useful for understanding the likelihood of events.

Problem formulation: The process of moving from an area of interest to the statement of a researchable question and to the selection of a research design that can be used to answer it.

Prospective: Describing research that begins in advance of the event of interest.

Purposive sample: A nonrandom sample selected on the basis of the specific characteristics of sample members that qualify them to be the most useful informants for a specific study (rather than because, for instance, they represent the general population).

Qualitative: Refers both to certain forms of data, namely narrative or unstructured, and to flexible method research designs, in which the methodology of the study can vary in response to emerging findings and the experiences of the researcher in the field.

Quantitative: Refers both to certain forms of data, namely those that are expressed in numerical form, and sometimes to fixed method research, in which the methodology of the study is invariant throughout the process and data collection is designed to make the generation of numerical data standardized and efficient.

Quasi-experimental designs: Research that is like an experiment but lacks one or more elements of the usual design, typically random assignment to groups.

Questionnaire: A tool for recording written self-reports, typically consisting of a series of questions with pre-structured answer options that the user fills out.

Quota sample: A nonrandom sampling method in which participants are recruited into pre-defined sample subgroups until a specified number, or quota, of participants has been obtained in each group.

Random: In statistics, a series of events or numbers with no order of any kind, in which the same event or number recurs in a way that is completely unpredictable.

Random assignment: Using random numbers or a random event like the flip of a coin to assign sample members to research subgroups, particularly in experiments when some participants receive an experimental treatment and others do not. This procedure is also called a randomized sample.

Random sample: Any sample selected with the use of random numbers.

Range: A measure of variability used with ordinal level numbers that can be expressed in two ways: by listing the highest and lowest value or score, and by subtracting one from the other and reporting the difference.

Rating scale: A scale used by one person to evaluate another.

Raw (as in frequency or score): A score or count of people with a certain score itself, that is, not transformed to a percentage of the whole.

Realism: In philosophy, the belief that there is a material world that exists independent of the mind that perceives it.

Reflexiveness/reflexivity: The practice and quality of engaging in self-examination. Literally, referring back to the self.

Regression (linear): In statistics, an equation that defines a line describing how two interval or ratio level variables are related to each other based on the average interrelation between them.

Regression to the mean: The tendency of events and the measurements of them to revert from extreme to less extreme (closer to the average).

Relational research: A form of fixed method research that examines the interrelation between two (or more) phenomena but does not involve any manipulation of them.

Reliability: The consistency or replicability with which observations are made.

Replication: Doing a study over again to determine whether or not similar findings will occur.

Replication logic: Credibility or generalizability of research designs and findings based on demonstrating that the same ones will occur again on a different occasion (contrast with *sampling logic*).

Research: The process and product of learning about the natural, social, or psychological world systematically through focussed observation and careful conceptualization from a position of skepticism.

Research design: A coherent set of methods for conducting a research study.

Respect: One of three general principles guiding research ethics that calls for providing research participants with autonomy and the right to self-determination in the process of the research.

Response latitude: The amount of variation in answers that is allowed to participants when framing fixed response questions and their answer options.

Response set: The automatic and therefore less meaningful answer choices that are sometimes made when there is not variation in how questions and answer options are worded in a series of fixed response items.

Retrospective: Research that gathers information about events in the past.

Rhetoric: The art of effective expression in language and the study of it.

Rigor: In research, the degree to which a study meets standards of scientific soundness.

Sample: The subgroup of a population of interest that actually participates in a particular study.

Sampling: The process of selection and recruitment (and perhaps retention) of a sample.

Sampling error: Since no sample ever can be expected to be exactly like the population from which it was drawn, the inevitable degree of difference between sample data and what the data would have shown had the whole population been studied.

Sampling frame: A list of population members from which sample members are selected.

Sampling logic: When the generalizability of research findings is considered to be based on the way in which sample members reflect or represent a larger population, as in political polling and other forms of survey research.

Scale: A series of questions or items that together are taken to measure a single, often complex, characteristic or phenomenon.

Scattergram or scatterplot: A graphical display of the interrelationship between two variables in which each point represents a sample member's scores on two variables at once.

Science: See research. Also any field of study in which research is a prominent part of its knowledge base and its practice.

Scientific method: Accepted ways of doing research that are characterized by careful use of theory, systematic empirical examination, and a spirit of skepticism.

Selection criteria (inclusion/exclusion): In sampling, the specification of the characteristics that potential research participants must have (inclusion) or must not have (exclusion) in order to qualify for a given study.

Selection effects: Characteristics drawing people to volunteer for a study or to volunteer to be in a treatment or control group, often unknown, that may have an influence on study outcomes.

Sensitivity: The capacity of a data collection tool to reflect changes in the phenomenon or characteristic it is designed to measure.

Servers: Computers designed to link other computers together into networks that may share hardware and/or software.

Single-system/single-subject design: Quantitative, prospective, longitudinal case studies that examine the impact of an intervention.

Skepticism: A doubting or questioning stance.

Snowball sample: A method of nonrandom sample selection in which a few qualifying research participants are located and studied, and then they are asked to identify others like themselves for inclusion, often in multiple iterations.

Social constructionism/constructivism: A line of epistemological thinking emphasizing the relativity of people's perceptions of the world and the social, historical, political, and cultural influences on them.

Social desirability: An influence on how research participants may represent themselves based on the desire to seem socially or personally acceptable to the researcher or in the research.

Software: The program code that directs the computer to perform tasks specified by the user.

Split-half reliability: A method for examining the internal consistency of a scale or measure quantitatively by correlating answers given on half of the items with those given on the other half.

Stability: The capacity of a data collection tool to reflect consistency in the phenomenon or characteristic it is designed to measure when the characteristic remains unchanged.

Standard deviation: A statistical measure of variability used with interval or ratio level variables.

Standardized scale: A scale in which its item content, item order, scoring, and interpretation remain constant in use and for which it is therefore considered legitimate to compare results across studies.

Standardized score: A score that is expressed in standard deviation units, that is, in terms of how far it lies above or below the group mean.

Statistic: A number that describes some aspect of a sample.

Statistics: Techniques used to describe, summarize, and draw conclusions from quantified research data.

Strata: In multistage sampling, subgroups within a sample such that sample members are selected from all of them but perhaps in different proportions. This result is termed a *stratified sampling*.

Stratified sampling: Drawing a sample using *strata* (see above).

Subscale: A subset of items from a scale that describe a specific aspect of the phenomenon and that typically correlate more closely with each other than with items from other subscales of the same instrument.

Systematic: Done in a planful manner and focused on a specific question.

Systematic random sampling: An alternative to simple random sampling in which a starting point is randomly chosen and then sample members are picked from a list based on a regular interval from that point.

Test-retest reliability: A method for assessing the repeatability of a measure by administering it on a second occasion to the same people and calculating how closely the scores obtained correlate with each other.

Test statistic: In inferential statistics, a number that is a probability indicator, calculated based on sample data, associated with a specific probability distribution, and used in hypothesis testing.

Theoretical probability: A prediction about the occurrence of an event that is derived from theory (substantive or mathematical) rather than from observation alone.

Theoretical sampling: A technique of sample selection in grounded theory method that calls for the recruitment of sample members based on distinctions between people that the emerging theory suggests are relevant.

Theory: A conceptual system for describing and/or explaining phenomena and their relationships to each other.

Triangulation: The use of multiple data sources or measures in a study to enhance its reliability, validity, or overall credibility.

Trustworthiness: A term used in flexible method or qualitative research to indicate data or findings that are credible and meaningful. Incorporates ideas of reliability and validity.

Two standard deviation band: A technique for examining findings in single-subject design in which a band representing two standard deviations above and below the mean during the baseline period is projected into the treatment period of study. Only if data fall outside that range during the treatment period are changes between baseline and treatment considered significant.

Two-tailed test: In hypothesis testing, when there is no specific hypothesis about a direction of difference or correlation, the evaluation of statistical significance using both ends of the probability distribution.

Type 1 error: See *alpha error.*

Type 2 error: See *beta error.*

Typology: A possible outcome of an analysis of qualitative data in which cases tend to cluster into groups or types sharing variation on several variables at once.

Unidimensional: A scale or set of response options that has only one dimension or part.

Unipolar: In relation to answer options in fixed response questions, a series of choices that goes from most to least (or the reverse).

Universality: The degree to which conclusions drawn from a research study might be expected to hold true in other circumstances. The term used in flexible method or qualitative research that is analogous to the concept of *external validity* or *generalizability.*

Usage: The rules of language governing how words should be used.

Validity: The degree to which the data can be taken to mean what they are said to mean conceptually.

Value: A specific score of a variable.

Value label: In using statistical software for quantitative data analysis, a word used to label a specific value or score of a variable.

Variability: The degree of dispersion of scores on a specific variable.

Variable: An assessed characteristic of a sample that differs among research participants.

Variable label: In using statistical software for quantitative data analysis, a word used to explain the meaning of a specific variable and what it was thought to measure.

Within-group designs: Research designs that examine differences or changes in the same people from one time point to another.

Word processor: A computer program designed to assist in the creation, revision, storage, and production of text documents.

Written self-report: A method of data collection in which research participants are asked to describe themselves in writing, usually by means of answering a series of prestructured questions.

References

Preface

Anastas, J. W. (1998). Reaffirming the real: A philosophy of science for social work. Manuscript under review.

Denzin, N. K. & Y. S. Lincoln, eds. (1994). *Handbook of qualitative research*. Thousand Oaks, CA: Sage.

Drisko, J. W. (1997). Strengthening qualitative studies and reports: Standards to enhance academic integrity. *Journal of Social Work Education* 33: 185–197.

Fraser, M. , M. J. Taylor, R. M. Jackson, & J. O'Jack. (1991). Social work and science: Many ways of knowing? *Social Work* 27(4): 5–15.

Gilgun, J. F. (1994). A case for case studies in social work research. *Social Work* 4: 371–380.

Gilgun, J. F. , K. Daly, & G. Handel, eds. (1992). *Qualitative methods in family research*. Newbury Park, CA: Sage.

Harding, S. (1998). *Is science multicultural? Postcolonialisms, feminisms, and epistemologies*. Bloomington, IN: Indiana University Press.

Heineman Pieper, M. (1985). The future of social work research. *Social Work Research & Abstracts* 21(4): 3–11.

———. (1989). The heuristic paradigm: A unifying and comprehensive approach to social work research. *Smith College Studies in Social Work* 60(1): 8–34.

Hess, O. J. (1995). *Science and technology in a multicultural world*. New York: Columbia University Press.

Kazi, M. A. F. (1998). Practice research in England. Paper presented at the International Conference on Research for Social Work Practice, Society for Social Work and Research, North Miami, FL.

Klee, R. (1997). *Introduction to the philosophy of science: Cutting nature at its seams*. New York: Oxford University Press.

LeVay, S. (1996). *Queer science: The uses and abuses of research into homosexuality*. Cambridge, MA: MIT Press.

Manicas, P. T. & P. F. Secord. (1983). Implications for psychology of the new philosophy of science. *American Psychologist* 38: 399–413.

Morse, J. M. & P. A. Field. (1995). *Qualitative research methods for health professionals* (2nd ed.). Thousand Oaks, CA: Sage.

Orange, D. M. (1995). *Emotional understanding: Studies in psychoanalytic epistemology.* New York: Guilford Press.

Padgett, D. K. (1998). *Qualitative methods in social work research: Challenges and rewards.* Thousand Oaks, CA: Sage.

Papineau, D. (1996). Introduction: The epistemology of science. In D. Papineau, ed. , *The philosophy of science* (pp. 1–20). New York: Oxford University Press.

Pawson, R. & N. Tilley (1997). *Realistic evaluation.* London, England: Sage.

Reissman, C. K. , ed. (1994). *Qualitative studies in social work research.* Thousand Oaks, CA: Sage.

Sherman, E. & W. J. Reid, eds. (1994). *Qualitative research in social work.* New York: Columbia University Press.

Swigonski, M. E. (1994). The logic of feminist standpoint theory for social work research. *Social Work* 39(4): 387–393.

Tyson, K. B. (1992). A new approach to relevant scientific research for practitioners: The heuristic paradigm. *Social Work* 37(6): 541–556.

———. (1995). *New foundations for scientific social and behavioral research.* Boston: Allyn & Bacon.

Chapter 1

Akbar, N. (1991). Paradigms of African American research. In R. L. Jones, ed. , *Black psychology* (3rd ed.). Berkeley, CA: Cobb & Henry.

Anastas, J. W. (1998). Reaffirming the real: A philosophy of science for social work. Paper under review.

Bernstein, P. L. (1996). *Against the gods: A remarkable story of risk.* New York: John Wiley & Sons.

Bhaskar, R. (1989). *Reclaiming reality: A critical introduction to contemporary philosophy.* London : Verso.

Bowman, P. J. (1991). Race, class and ethics in research: Belmont principles to functional relevance. In R. L. Jones, ed. , *Black psychology* (3rd ed.). Berkeley, CA: Cobb and Henry.

Collins, P. H. (1991). *Black feminist thought: Knowledge, consciousness and the politics of empowerment.* New York: Routledge.

Davis, L. (1986). A feminist approach to social work research. *Affilia* 1(1): 32–47.

Denzin, N. K. & Y. S. Lincoln, eds. (1994). *Handbook of qualitative research.* Thousand Oaks, CA: Sage.

Eichler, M. (1988). *Nonsexist research methods.* Boston: Unwin Hyman.

Fine, M. (1994). Working the hyphens: Reinventing self and other in qualitative research. In N. K. Denzin & Y. S. Lincoln, eds. *Handbook of qualitative research* (pp. 70–82). Thousand Oaks, CA: Sage.

Fischer, J. (1973). Is casework effective? A review. *Social Work* 18(1): 5–20.

Fraser, M. W. , J. M. Jenson, & R. E. Lewis. (1991). Training for research scholarship in social work doctoral programs. *Social Service Review* 65(4): 597–613.

Fraser, M. , M. J. Taylor, R. M. Jackson, & J. O'Jack. (1991). Social work and science: Many ways of knowing? *Social Work* 27(4): 5–15.

Gergen, K. J. (1985). The social constructionist movement in modern psychology. *American Psychologist* 40(3): 266–275.

Gilgun, J. F. (1994). A case for case studies in social work research. *Social Work* 39: 371–380.

Gilovich, T. (1991). *How we know what isn't so: The fallibility of human reason in everyday life.* New York: Free Press.

Gingerich, W. J. (1990). Rethinking single-case evaluation. In L. Videka-Sherman & W. J. Reid, eds. *Advances in clinical social work research.* Washington, DC: NASW Press.

Glaser, B. G. & A. L. Strauss. (1967). *The discovery of grounded theory: Strategies for qualitative research.* New York: Aldine deGruyter.

Goldstein, E. G. (1983). Issues in developing systematic research and theory. In A. Rosenblatt & D. Waldfogel eds. *Handbook of clinical social work* (pp. 5–25). San Francisco: Jossey-Bass.

Guba, E. , ed. (1991). *The paradigm dialog.* Newbury Park, CA: Sage.

Harding, S. (1991). *Whose science? Whose knowledge?* Ithaca, NY: Cornell University Press.

Harré, R. (1986). *Varieties of realism.* New York: Basil Blackwell.

———. (1972). *The philosophies of science: An introductory survey.* London: Oxford University Press.

Hartman, A. (1990). Many ways of knowing. *Social Work* 35: 3–4.

Heineman, M. B. (1981). The obsolete imperative in social work research. *Social Service Review* 55: 371–397.

Heineman Pieper, M. (1985). The future of social work research. *Social Work Research & Abstracts* 21(4): 3–11.

———. (1989). The heuristic paradigm: A unifying and comprehensive approach to social work research. *Smith College Studies in Social Work* 60(1): 8–34.

Hess, D. J. (1995). *Science and technology in a multicultural world.* New York: Columbia University Press.

Hill, R. B. (1980). Social work research in minorities: Impediments and opportunities. In D. Fanshel, ed. , *The future of social work research.* Washington, DC: NASW Press.

Hudson, W. W. (1978). First axioms of treatment. *Social Work* 24: 65–66.

Imre, R. W. (1984). The nature of knowledge in social work. *Social Work* 29: 41–45.

Jacobs, C. & D. D. Bowles, eds. (1988). *Ethnicity and race: Critical concepts in social work.* Washington, DC: NASW Press.

Klee, R. (1997). *Introduction to the philosophy of science: Cutting nature at its seams.* New York: Oxford University Press.

Kuhn, T. (1970). *The structure of scientific revolutions* (2nd ed.). Chicago: University of Chicago Press.

Manicas, P. T. (1987). *A history and philosophy of the social sciences.* London: Basil Blackwell.

Manicas, P. T. & P. F. Secord. (1983). Implications for psychology of the new philosophy of science. *American Psychologist* 38: 399–413,

McMahon, A. & P. Allen-Meares. (1992). Is social work racist? A content analysis of recent literature. *Social Work* 37(6): 533–540.

Mullen, E. S. et al. eds. (1972). *Evaluation of social intervention.* San Francisco: Jossey-Bass.

Paulos, J. A. (1988). *Innumeracy: Mathematical illiteracy and its consequences.* New York: Hill and Wang.

Peirce, C. (1934). *The collected papers of Charles Sanders Peirce* (Vol. V). Cambridge, MA: Harvard University Press.

Piele, C. (1988). Research paradigms in social work: From stalemate to creative synthesis. *Social Service Review* 62: 1–19.

Pinto-Correia, C. (1997). *The ovary of Eve: Egg and sperm and preformation.* Chicago, IL: University of Chicago Press.

Popper, K. R. (1959). *The logic of scientific discovery.* London: Hutchinson.

Reamer, F. G. (1993). *The philosophical foundation of social work*. New York: Columbia University Press.

Reid, W. J. (1994). Reframing the epistemological debate. In E. Sherman & W. J. Reid, eds. *Qualitative research in social work* (pp. 464–481). New York: Columbia University Press.

Riessman, C. K. , ed. (1994). *Qualitative studies in social work research*. Thousand Oaks, CA: Sage.

Ruckdeschel, R. A. (1985). Qualitative research as a perspective. *Social Work Research & Abstracts* 21(2): 17–21

Swigonski, M. (1994). The logic of feminist standpoint theory for social work research. *Social Work* 39(4): 387–393.

Thyer, B. A. (1993). Social work theory and practice research: The approach of logical positivism. *Social Work and Social Sciences Review* 4(1): 5–26.

Tyson, K. B. (1992). A new approach to relevant scientific research for practitioners: The heuristic paradigm. *Social Work* 37(6): 541–556.

———. (1995). *New foundations for scientific social and behavioral research*. Boston: Allyn & Bacon.

Uchitelle, L. (May 14, 1992). Pay of college graduates is outpaced by inflation. *New York Times*.

Zimbalist, S. W. (1977). *Historic themes and landmarks in social welfare research*. New York: Harper & Row.

Chapter 2

Akbar, N. (1991). Paradigms of African American research. In R. L. Jones, ed. , *Black psychology* (3rd ed.). Berkeley, CA: Cobb and Henry.

American Psychological Association (1994). *Publication manual of the American Psychological Association* (4th ed.). Washington, DC: Author.

Anastas, J. W. , J. L. Gibeau, & P. J. Larson. (1990). Working families and eldercare: A national perspective in an aging America. *Social Work* 35(5): 405–451.

Becerra, R. M. & R. E. Zambrana. (1985). Ethnological approaches to research on Hispanics. *Social Work Research & Abstracts* 2(2): 42–49.

Bloom, M. (1986). *The experience of research*. New York: Macmillan.

Brody, E. M. (1986). Filial care of the elderly and changing roles of women (and men). *Journal of Geriatric Psychiatry* 19(2): 175–201.

Brody, E. M. , P. T. Johnson, M. C. Fulcomer, & A. M. Lang. (1983). Women's changing roles and help to elderly parents: Attitudes of three generations of women. *Journal of Gerontology* 38(5): 597–607.

Brody, E. M. , M. H. Kleban, C. Hoffman, & C. B. Schoonover. (1988). Adult daughters and parent-care: A comparison of one-, two- and three-generation households. *Home Health Care Services Quarterly* 1(4): 19–45.

Brody, E. M. , M. H. Kleban, P. T. Johnson, C. Hoffman, et al. (1987). Work status and parent care: A comparison of four groups of women. *Gerontologist* 27(2): 201–208.

Brody, E. M. & E. B. Schoonover. (1986). Patterns of parent-care when adult daughters work and when they do not. *Gerontologist* 26(4): 372–381.

Broverman, I. K. , S. R. Vogel, S. M. Broverman, F. E. Clarkson, & P. S. Rosenkrantz. (1972). Sex role stereotypes: A current appraisal. *Journal of Social Issues* 28(2): 59–78.

Collins, P. H. (1991). *Black feminist thought: Knowledge, consciousness and the politics of empowerment*. New York: Routledge.

Eichler, M. (1988). *Nonsexist research methods: A practical guide*. Boston: Unwin Hyman.

Feagin, J. R. (1991). The continuing significance of race: Antiblack discrimination in public places. *American Sociological Review* 56(1): 101–116.

Fine, M. (1994). Working the hyphens: Reinventing self and other in qualitative research. In N. K. Denzin & Y. S. Lincoln, eds. *Handbook of qualtitative research* (pp.)Thousand Oaks, CA: Sage.

Fraiberg, S. (1970). The muse in the kitchen: A case study in clinical research. *Smith College Studies in Social Work* 40(2): 101–134.

Gibeau, J. L. & J. W. Anastas. (1989). Breadwinners and caregivers: Interviews with working women. *Journal of Geronotological Social Work* 14: 1–2.

Gilligan, C. (1982). *In a different voice: Psychological theory and women's development.* Cambridge, MA: Harvard University Press.

Golden, M. P. (1976). *The research experience.* Itasca, IL: F. E. Peacock.

Gomez, M. R. (1990). Biculturalism and subjective mental health among Cuban Americans. *Social Service Review* 64(3): 375–389.

Harding, S. (1991). *Whose science? Whose knowledge?* Ithaca, NY: Cornell University Press.

———. (1993). Introduction: Eurocentric scientific illiteracies—A challenge for the world community. In S. Harding (Ed.), *The "racial" economy of science* (pp. 1–22). Bloomington and Indianapolis, IN: Indiana University Press.

Hartman, A. (1990). Many ways of knowing. *Social Work* 35: 3–4.

Heineman Pieper, M. (1989). The heuristic paradigm: A unifying comprehensive approach to social work research. *Smith College Studies in Social Work* 60(1): 8–34.

Herek, G. M. , D. C. Kimmel, H. Amaro, & G. B. Melton. (1991). Avoiding heterosexist bias in psychological research. *American Psychologist* 46(9): 957–963.

Hess, D. J. (1995). *Science and technology in a multicultural world.* New York: Columbia University Press.

Hooker, E. (1957). The adjustment of the male overt homosexual. *Journal of Projective Techniques* 21: 18–31.

Hyde, C. (1994). Reflections on a journey: A research story. In C. K. Riessman, ed. , *Qualitative Studies in Social Work* (pp. 169–189). Thousand Oaks, CA: Sage.

Kelley, P. , V. Kelley, & B. Williams. (1989). Treatment of adolescents: A comparison of individual and family therapy. *Social Casework* 70(8): 461–468.

Kuhn, T. S. (1970). *The structure of scientific revolutions* (2nd ed.). Chicago: University of Chicago Press.

Lang, A. M. & E. M. Brody. (1983). Characteristics of middle-aged daughters and help to their elderly mothers. *Journal of Marriage and the Family* 45(1): 193–202.

LeVay, S. (1996). *Queer science: The use and abuse of research into homosexuality.* Cambridge, MA: MIT Press.

Marshall, C. & G. B. Rossman. (1989). *Designing qualitative research.* Newbury Park, CA: Sage,

McMahon, A. & P. Allen-Meares. (1992). Is social work racist? A content analysis of recent literature. *Social Work* 37(6): 533–540.

Miller, C. & K. Swift. (1980), *The handbook on nonsexist writing.* New York: Barnes and Noble.

National Academy of Science. (1993). Methods and values in science. In S. Harding (Ed.), *The "racial" economy of science* (pp. 341–343). Bloomington and Indianapolis, IN: Indiana University Press.

Olesen, V. (1994). Feminisms and models of qualitative research. In N. K. Denzin & Y. S. Lincoln eds. *Handbook of qualitative research.* (pp. 33–44). Thousand Oaks, CA: Sage.

Outhwaite, W. (1987). *New philosophies of social science: Realism, hermeneutics and critical theory.* New York: St. Martin's Press.

Piele, C. (1988). Research paradigms in social work: From statement to creative synthesis. *Social Service Review* 62: 1–19.

Reinharz, S. (1985). Feminist distrust: Problems of context and content in sociological work. In D. N. Berg & K. K. Smith, eds. *Exploring clinical methods for social research.* Beverly Hills, CA: Sage.

Rogler, L. H. (1999). Methodological sources of cultural insensitivity in mental health research. *American Psychologist* 54(6): 424–433.

Ruckdeschel, R. A. (1985). Qualitative research as a perspective. *Social Work Research & Abstracts* 21(2): 17–21.

Schoonover, C. B. , E. M. Brody, C. Hoffman, & M. H. Kleban. (1988). Parent care and geographically distant children. *Research on Aging* 10(4): 472–492.

Smith, A. W. (1993). Survey research on African Americans: Methodological innovations. In J. H. Stanfield (Ed.), *Race and ethnicity in research methods* (pp. 217–229). Newbury Park, CA: Sage.

Stanfield, J. H. (1993). *Race and ethnicity in research methods.* Newbury Park, CA: Sage.
———. (1994). Ethnic modeling in qualitative research. In N. K. Denzin & Y. S. Lincoln, eds. *Handbook of qualitative research* (pp. 175–188). Thousand Oaks, CA: Sage.

Swigonski, M. (1994). The logic of feminist standpoint theory for social work research. *Social Work* 39(4): 387–393.

U. S. Census Bureau. (1998). *Household and family characteristics: March 1998 (Update).* (P20-515). Washington, DC: Author.

Wechsler, H. , H. Z. Reinharz, & D. D. Dobbin. (1976). *Social work research in the human services.* New York: Human Sciences Press.

Wilson, W. J. (1978). *The declining significance of race.* Chicago: University of Chicago Press.
———. (1987). *The truly disadvantaged: The inner city, the underclass, and public policy.* Chicago: University of Chicago Press.

Chapter 3

Akbar, N. (1991). Paradigms of African American Research. In R. L. Jones, ed. , *Black psychology* (3rd ed.). Berkeley, CA: Cobb and Henry.

Allen, K. R. & K. M. Baber. (1992). Ethical and epistemological tensions in applying a postmodern perspective to feminist research. *Psychology of Women Quarterly* 16: 1–15.

Bunin, A. , J. Einzig, D. Judd, & N. Staver. (1983). Inside the interview: Clinical considerations in the research interview. *Clinical Social Work Journal* 10(1): 22–32.

Brun, C. (1997). The process and implications of doing qualitative research: An analysis of 54 doctoral dissertations. *Journal of Sociology and Social Welfare* 24(4): 95–112.

Campbell, D. T. & J. C. Stanley. (1963). *Experimental and quasi-experimental designs for research.* Chicago: Rand McNally.

Davis, L. V. (1986). A feminist approach to social work research. *Affilia* 1(1): 32–47.

Dean, R. G. & B. L. Fenby. (1989). Exploring epistemologies: Social work action as a reflection of philosophical assumptions. *Journal of Social Work Education* 25(1): 46–54.

Denzin, N. K. & Y. S. Lincoln, eds. (1994). *Handbook of qualitative research.* Thousand Oaks, CA: Sage

Drisko, J. W. (1997). Strengthening qualitative studies and reports: Standards to enhance academic integrity. *Journal of Social Work Education* 33: 1–13.

Dudley, J. R. (1989). The role of residential program staff in facilitating positive relations with the neighborhood: What should it be? *Administration in Social Work* 13(1): 95–111.

Edgerton, R. B. (1967). *The cloak of competence: Stigma in the lives of the mentally retarded.* Berkeley and Los Angeles: University of California Press.

Eisner, E. W. (1991). *The enlightened eye: Qualitative inquiry and the enhancement of educational practice.* New York: Macmillan.

Feagin, J. R. (1991). The continuing significance of race: Antiblack discrimination in public places. *American Sociological Review* 56: 101–116.

Fraiberg, S. (1970). The muse in the kitchen: A case study in clinical research. *Smith College Studies in Social Work* 40(2): 101–134.

Glaser, B. G. & A. L. Strauss. (1967). *The discovery of grounded theory: Strategies for qualitative research.* New York: Aldine de Gruyter.

Gilgun, J. F. (1994). Hand into glove: The grounded theory approach and social work practice. In E. Sherman & W. J. Reid, eds. *Qualitative research in social work* (pp. 115–125). New York: Columbia University Press.

Goetz, J. P. & M. D. LeCompte. (1984). *Ethnography and qualitative designs in educational research.* San Diego, CA: Academic Press.

Guba, E. G. & Y. S. Lincoln. (1994). Competing paradigms in qualitative research. In N. K. Denzin & Y. S. Lincoln, eds. *Handbook of qualitative research* (pp. 105–117). Thousand Oaks, CA: Sage.

Hartman, A. (1990). Education for direct practice. *Families in Society* 71(1): 44–50.

Heineman, M. B. (1981). The obsolete imperative in social work research. *Social Work Research & Abstracts* 1(4): 3–11.

———. (1985). The future of social work research. *Social Work Research & Abstracts* 21(4): 3–11.

Heineman Pieper, M. B. (1989). The heuristic paradigm: A unifying and comprehensive approach to social work research. *Smith College Studies in Social Work* 60(1): 8–34.

Kuhn, T. (1970). *The structure of scientific revolutions* (2nd ed.). Chicago: University of Chicago Press.

LeComte, M. D. & J. Preissle. (1993). *Ethnography and qualitative design in educational research* (2nd ed.). San Diego, CA: Academic Press.

Liebow, E. (1993). *Tell them who I am: The lives of homeless women.* Boston, MA: Little, Brown.

Luborsky, M. R. & R. L. Rubinstein. (1995). Sampling in qualitative research: Rationale, issues, and methods. *Research on Aging* 17(1): 89–113.

Manicas, P. T. (1987). *A history and philosophy of the social sciences.* London: Basil Blackwell.

Manicas, P. T. & P. F. Secord. (1983). Implications for psychology of the new philosophy of science. *American Psychologist* 38: 399–413.

Marshall, C. & G. B. Rossman. (1989). *Designing qualitative research.* Newbury Park, CA: Sage.

Millman, M. (1977). *The unkindest cut: Life in the backrooms of medicine.* William Morrow.

Morse, J. M. & P. A. Field. (1995). *Qualitative research methods for health professionals* (2nd ed.). Thousand Oaks, CA: Sage.

Myerhoff, B. (1978). *Number our days.* New York: Simon and Schuster.

Olesen, V. (1994). Feminisms and models of qualitative research. In N. K. Denzin & Y. S. Lincoln, eds. *Handbook of qualitative research* (pp. 158-174). Thousand Oaks, CA: Sage.

Orange, D. (1995). *Emotional understanding.* New York: Guilford Press.

Padgett, D. K. (1998a). Does the glove really fit? Qualitative research and clinical social work practice. *Social Work* 43(4): 373–381.

———. (1998b). *Qualitative methods in social work research: Challenges and rewards.* Thousand Oaks, CA: Sage.

Patton, M. Q. (1990). *Utilization-focused evaluation.* Newbury Park, CA: Sage.

Piele, C. (1989). Research paradigms in social work: From stalemate to creative synthesis. *Social Service Review* 62(1): 1–19.

Poland, B. D. (1995). Transcription quality as an aspect of rigor in qualitative research. *Qualitative Inquiry* 1(3): 290–310.

Reamer, F. G. (1993). *The philosophical foundations of social work*. New York: Columbia University Press.

Riessman, C. K. , ed. (1994). *Qualitative studies in social work research*. Thousand Oaks, CA: Sage.

Ruckdeschel, R. (1985). Qualitative research as a perspective. *Social Work Research & Abstracts* 21(2): 17–21.

Sherman, E. & W. J. Reid, eds. (1994). *Qualitative research in social work*. New York: Columbia University Press.

Siegel, S. J. & N. J. Castellan. (1988). *Nonparametric statistics* (2nd ed.). New York: McGraw-Hill.

Social Work Research. (1995). Book forum on qualitative methods 19(1): pp. 5–47.

Stack, C. B. (1974). *All our kin: Strategies for survival in a black community*. New York: Harper & Row.

Strauss, A. & J. Corbin. (1990). *Basics of qualitative research*. (2nd ed.). Newbury Park, CA: Sage.

Taylor, S. J. & R. Bogdan. (1984). *Introduction to qualitative research methods: The search for meanings* (2nd ed.). New York: John Wiley & Sons.

Thyer, B. A. (1993), Social work theory and practice research: The approach to logical positivism. *Social Work and Social Science Review* 4(1): 5–26.

Tyson, K. B. (1992). A new approach to relevant scientific research for practitioners: The heuristic paradigm. *Social Work* 37(6): 541–556.

———. (1995). New foundations for scientific social and behavioral research. Boston: Allyn & Bacon.

Williams, L. W. & J. G. Hopps. (1988). On the nature of professional communication: Publication for practitioners. *Social Work* 33(5): 453–459.

Chapter 4

Fonagy, P. & G. Moran. (1993). Selecting single case research designs for clinicians. In N. E. Miller, L. Luborsky, J. P. Barber, & J. P. Dockerty, eds. *Psychodynamic treatment research* (pp. 62–95).

Fraiberg, S. (1970). The muse in the kitchen: A case study in clinical research. *Smith College Studies in Social Work* 40(2): 101–134.

Gilgun, J. F. (1994). A case study for case studies in social work research. *Social Work* 39(4): 371–380.

Jarrett, R. L. (1992). A family case study: An examination of the underclass debate. In J. F. Gilgun, K. Daly & G. Handel, eds. *Qualitative methods in family research* (pp. 172–197). Newbury Park, CA: Sage.

———. (1994). Living poor: Family life among single African-American women. *Social Problems* 41(1): 30–49.

Kuhn, T. S. (1970). *The structure of scientific revolutions* (2nd ed.). Chicago: University of Chicago Press.

Manicas, P. T. & P. F. Secord. (1983). Implications for psychology of the new philosophy of science. *American Psychologist* 38: 399–413.

Martin, R. R. (1995). *Oral history in social work: Research, assessment and intervention.* Thousand Oaks, CA: Sage.

Padgett, D. K. (1998). *Qualitative methods in social work research: Challenges and rewards.* Thousand Oaks, CA: Sage.

Patton, M. Q. (1990). *Utilization-focused evaluation.* Newbury Park, CA: Sage.

Ruckdeschel, R. , P. Earnshaw, & A. Firrek. (1994). The qualitative case study in evaluation: Issues, methods and examples. In E. Sherman & W. J. Reid, eds. *Qualitative Research in Social Work* (pp. 251–264). New York: Columbia University Press.

Stake, R. E. (1994). Case studies. In N. K. Denzin & Y. S. Lincoln, eds. *Handbook of qualitative research* (pp. 236–247). Thousand Oaks, CA: Sage.

Strauss, A. & J. Corbin. (1990). *Basics of qualitative research* (2nd ed.). Newbury Park, CA: Sage.

Wilson, W. J. (1987). *The truly disadvantaged: The innercity, the underclass, and public policy.* Chicago: University of Chicago Press.

Yin, R. K. (1994). *Case study research: Design and methods* (2nd ed.). Thousand Oaks, CA: Sage.

Chapter 5

Anderson, S. C. & D. L. Mandell. (1989). The use of self-disclosure by professional social workers. *Social Casework* 70(5): 259–267.

Comrey, A. L. (1979). J. P. Guilford. In D. L. Sills, ed. , *International encyclopedia of the social sciences: Biographical supplement* (vol. 18, pp. 358–259). New York: Free Press.

Fraiberg, S. (1970). The muse in the kitchen: A case study in clinical research. *Smith College Studies in Social Work* 49(2): 101–134.

Gould, S. J. (1981). *The mismeasure of man.* New York: W. W. Norton.

Guilford, J. P. (1967). *The nature of human intelligence.* New York: McGraw-Hill.

———. (1977). *Way beyond the IQ.* Buffalo: Creative Education Foundation.

Harré, R. (1972). *The philosophies of science: An introductory survey.* London: Oxford University Press.

Hernnstein, R. J. & C. M. Murray. (1994). *The bell curve: Intelligence and class structure in American life.* New York: Free Press.

Jensen, A. R. (1969). How much can we boost IQ and scholastic achievement? *Harvard Educational Review* 33: 1–123.

Kuhn, T. S. (1970). *The structure of scientific revolutions* (2nd ed.). Chicago: University of Chicago Press.

Manicas, P. T. & P. F. Secord. (1983). Implications for psychology of the new philosophy of science. *American Psychologist* 38: 399–413.

Matarazzo, J. D. & D. R. Denver. (1984). Intelligence measures. In R. J. Corsini, ed. , *Encyclopedia of psychology* (vol. 2, pp. 231–234). New York: John Wiley & Sons.

Chapter 6

Afifi, A. A. & V. Clark. (1984). *Computer-aided multivariate analysis.* Belmont, CA: Lifetime Learning Publications.

Anastas, J. W. & H. Z. Reinherz. (1984). Gender differences in learning and adjustment problems in school. *American Journal of Orthopsychiatry* 54(1): 110–122.

Brigham, T. A. (1989). On the importance of recognizing the differences between experiments and correlational studies. *American Psychologist* 44(7): 1077–1078.

Brody, E. M. , M. H. Kleban, P. T. Johnson, C. Hoffman, et al. (1987). Work status and parent care: A comparison of four groups of women. *Gerontologist* 27(2): 201–208.

Cook, T. D. & D. T. Campbell. (1979). *Quasi-experimentation: Design and analysis issues of field settings*. Boston, Houghton-Mifflin.

Daniels, A. (1993). Reminiscence, object relations and depression in the elderly. Unpublished dissertation: Smith College School for Social Work, Northampton, MA.

Ell, K. O. & R. H. Nishimoto. (1989). Coping resources in adaptation to cancer: Socioeconomic and racial differences. *Social Service Review* 63(3): 433-446.

Epstein, S. (1996). *Impure science: AIDS, activism, and the politics of knowledge*. Berkeley, CA: University of California Press.

Garrison, W. & F. Earls. (1981). Preschool behavior problems and the multigenerational family: An island community study. *International Journal of Family Psychiatry* 2(1–2): 125–137.

Gomez, M. R. (1990). Biculturalism and subjective mental health among Cuban Americans. *Social Service Review* 64(3): 375–389.

Grimm, L. G. & P. R. Yarnold, eds. (1995). *Reading and understanding multivariate statistics*. Washington, DC: American Psychological Association.

Manicas, P. T. & P. F. Secord. (1983). Implications for psychology of the new philosophy of science. *American Psychologist* 38: 399–413.

Sechrest, L. & M. Hannah. (1990). The critical importance of nonexperimental data. In L. Schrest, E. Perrin, & J. Bunker, eds. *Research methodology: Strengthening causal interpretations of nonexperimental data*. Washington, DC: U. S. Dept. Of Health and Human Services, Public Health Service, Agency for Health Care Policy and Research.

Smith, C. (1996). The link between childhood maltreatment and teenage pregnancy. *Social Work Research* 20(3): 131–141.

Springer, C. & J. S. Wallerstein. (1983). Young adolescents' responses to their parents' divorce. *New Directions for Child Development* 19: 15–27.

Stevens, J. P. (1996). *Applied multivariate statistics for the social sciences* (3rd ed.) Mahwah, NJ: Laurence Erlbaum Associates.

Wallerstein, J. S. (1984). Children of divorce: Preliminary report of a ten-year follow-up of older children and adolescents. *Journal of the American Academy of Child Psychiatry* 24(5): 545–553.

Werner, E. E. , J. M. Bierman, & F. E. French. (1971). *The children of Kauai*. Honolulu: University of Hawaii Press.

Werner, E. E. & R. S. Smith. (1977). *Kauai's children come of age*. Honolulu: University of Hawaii.

———. (1982). *Vulnerable but invincible: A longitudinal study*. New York: McGraw-Hill

———. (1992), *Overcoming the odds: High risk children from birth to adulthood*. Ithaca, NY: Cornell University Press.

Chapter 7

Applegate, J. S. (1992) The impact of subjective measures on nonbehavioral practice research: Outcome versus process. *Families in Society* 73: 100–108

Bryman, A. & D. Cramer. (1990). *Quantitative data analysis for social scientists*. New York: Routledge.

Campbell, D. T. & J. C. Stanley. (1963). *Experimental and quasi-experimental designs for research*. Boston: Houghton Mifflin.

Cook, T. D. & D. T. Campbell. (1979). *Quasi-experimentation: Design and analysis issue for field setting*. Boston: Houghton Mifflin.

El-Bassel, N. , A. Ivanoff, R. F. Schilling, L. Gilbert, D. Borne, & D. R. Chen. (1995). Preventing HIV-AIDS in drug-abusing incarcerated women through skills building and social support enhancement: Preliminary outcomes. *Social Work Research, 19*(3), 131–141.

Gorey, K. M. (1996). Effectiveness of social work intervention research: Internal versus external evaluations. *Social Work Research* 20(2): 119–128.

Hawking, S. W. (1988). *A brief history of time.* New York: Bantam Books,

Hays, W. L. (1981). *Statistics* (3rd ed.). New York: Holt, Rinehart and Winston.

Hume, D. (1988). *An enquiry concerning human understanding.* LaSalle, IL: Open Court (originally published in 1748).

Jarrett, R. L. (1992). A family case study: An examination of the underclass debate. In J. F. Gilgun, K. Daly & G. Handel, eds. *Qualitative methods in family research* (pp. 172–197). Newbury Park, CA: Sage.

Kuhn, T. S. (1970) *The structure of scientific revolutions* (2nd ed.). Chicago: University of Chicago Press,

Manicas, P. T. & P. F. Secord. (1983). Implications for psychology of the new philosophy of science. *American Psychologist* 38: 399–413.

Nagel, E. , ed. (1950). *John Stuart Mill's philosophy of scientific method.* New York: Hafner Publishing Company.

Paviour, R. (1988). The influence of class and race on clinical assessments by MSW students. *Social Service Review* 62(4): 684–693.

Popper, K. L. (1959). *The logic of scientific discovery.* London: Hutchinson.

Rosnow, R. L. & R. Rosenthal. (1982). The volunteer subject revisited. *Australian Journal of Psychology* 28(2): 97–108.

Thyer, B. A. (1993). Social work theory and practice research: The approach of logical positivism. *Social Work and Social Sciences Review* 4(1): 5–26.

Williams, J. B. W. & K. Ell. (1998). *Mental health research: Implication for practice.* Washington, DC: NASW Press.

Chapter 8

Applegate, J. S. (1992). The impact of subjective measure on nonbehavioral practice research: Outcome vs. Process. *Families in Society* 73(2): 100–108.

Barlow, D. H. , S. C. Hayes, & R. O. Nelson. (1984). *The scientist-practitioner.* New York: Pergamon Press.

Bloom, M. , J. Fischer, & J. Orme. (1995). *Evaluating practice: Guidelines for the accountable professional* (2nd ed.). Englewood Cliffs, NJ: Prentice-Hall.

Bloom, M. & J. Orme. (1993). Ethics and the single-system design. *Journal of Social Service Research* 18(1–2): 161–180.

Blythe, B. J. & A. Y. Rodgers. (1993). Evaluating our own practice: Past, present, and future trends. *Journal of Social Service Research* 18(1–2): 101–119.

Blythe, B. J. , T. Tripodi, & S. Briar. (1994). *Direct practice research in human service agencies.* New York: Columbia University Press.

Corcoran, K. (1993). Practice evaluation: Problems and promises of single-system designs in clinical practice. *Journal of Social Service Research* 18(1–2): 147–159.

Dean, R. & H. Z. Reinherz. (1986). Psychodynamic practice and single-system design: The odd couple. *Journal of Social Work Education* 22: 71–81.

Edelson, J. L. , D. M. Miller, G. W. Stone, & D. G. Chapman. (1985). Group treatment for men who batter. *Social Work Research & Abstracts* 21(3): 18–21.

Fischer, J. & K. Corcoran. (1994). *Measures for clinical practice: A sourcebook* (2nd ed. , vols. 1 & 2). New York: Free Press.

Heineman Pieper, M. (1989). The heuristic paradigm: A unifying and comprehensive approach to social work research. *Smith College Studies in Social Work* 60(1): 8–34.

Hollis, F. & M. E. Wood. (1981). *Casework: A psychosocial therapy* (3d ed.). New York: Random House.

Hudson, W. W. (1982). *The clinical measurement package: A field manual.* Homewood, IL: Dorsey Press.

Jarrett, R. L. (1992). A family case study: An examination of the underclass debate. In J. F. Gilgun, K. Daly, & G. Handel, eds. *Qualitative methods in family research* (pp. 172–197). Newbury Park, CA: Sage.

Jayaratne, S. (1978). Analytic procedures for single-subject designs. *Social Work Research & Abstracts* 14(3): 30–40.

Kirk, S. A. & J. Fischer. (1976). Do social workers understand research? *Journal of Education for Social Work* 12(1): 63–70.

Manicas, P. T. & P. F. Secord. (1983). Implications for psychology of the new philosophy of science. *American Psychologist* 38: 399–413.

Nelson, J. C. (1981). Issues in single-subject research for non-behaviorists. *Social Work Research & Abstracts* 17(2): 31–37.

———. (1985). Verifying the independent variable in single-subject research. *Social Work Research & Abstracts* 21(2): 3–8.

———. (1993). Testing practice wisdom: Another use for single-system design. *Journal of Social Service Research* 18(1–2): 65–82.

———. (1994). Ethics, gender and ethnicity in single-case research and evaluation. *Journal of Social Service Research* 18(3–4): 139–152.

Nugent, W. R. (1991). An experimental and qualitative analysis of a cognitive-behavioral interventions for anger. *Social Work Research & Abstracts* 27(3): 3–8.

Penka, C. E. & S. A. Kirk. (1991). Practitioner involvement in clinical evaluation. *Social Work* 36: 513–518.

Rabin, C. (1981). The single-case design in family therapy evaluation research. *Social Process* 20: 351–366.

Reid, W. J. (1993). Fitting the single-system design to family treatment. *Journal of Social Service Research* 18(1–2): 83–99.

Richey, C. A. & V. G. Hodges. (1992). Empirical support for the effectiveness of respite care in reducing caregiver burden: A single-case analysis. *Research on Social Work Practice* 2(2): 143–160.

Rosen, A. (1996). The scientific practitioner revisited: Some obstacles and prerequisites for fuller implementation in practice. *Social Work Research* 20(2): 105–111.

Stocks, J. T. & M. Williams. (1995). Evaluation of single-subject data using statistical hypothesis tests versus visual inspection of charts with and without celeration lines. *Journal of Social Service Research* 20(3–4): 105–126.

Thomas, E. J. (1978). Research and service in single-case experimentation. *Social Work Research & Abstract* 14(4): 20–31.

Thyer, B. A. (1996). Forty years of progress toward empirical clinical practice? *Social Work Research* 20(2): 77–81.

Tyson, K. B. (1992). A new approach to relevant scientific research for practitioners: The heuristic paradigm. *Social Work* 37(6): 541–556.

Wakefield, J. C. & S. A. Kirk. (1996). Unscientific thinking about scientific practice: Evaluating the scientist-practitioner model. *Social Work Research* 20(2): 83–95.

Chapter 9

American Psychological Association (1992). Ethical principles of psychologists and code of conduct. *American Psychologist* 47: 1597–1611.

Bloom, M. & J. Orme. (1993). Ethics and single-system design. *Journal of Social Service Research* 18(1–2): 161–180.

Bowman, D. J. (1991). Race, class and ethics in research: Belmont principles to functional relevance. In R. L. Jones, ed. , *Black psychology* (3rd ed.). Berkeley, CA: Cobb & Henry.

Burgess, R. G. (1989). Grey areas: Ethical dilemmas in educational ethography. In R. G. Burgess, ed. , *The ethics of educational research*. Philadelphia: Falmer Press.

Campbell, D. T. & J. C. Stanley. (1963). *Experimental and quasi-experimental designs for research*. Boston: Houghton Mifflin.

Ceci, S. J. , D. Peter, & J. Plotkin. (1985). Human subjects review, personal values, and the regulation of social science research. *American Psychologist* 40: 994–1002.

Crane, J. A. (1976). The power of social experimentation to discriminate differences between experimental and control groups. *Social Service Review* 50(2): 224–242.

Cronbach, L. J. (1957). The two disciplines of scientific psychology. *American Psychologist* 12: 671–684.

Engram, E. (1982). *Science, myth, reality: The black family in one-half century of research*. Westport, CT: Greenwood Press.

Feinberg, L. (October 22, 1988). Social researcher's ethics challenged. *Washington Post,* p. A12.

Fine, G. A. (1993). Ten lies of ethnography: Moral dilemmas of field research. *Journal of Contemporary Ethnography* 22(3): 267–294.

Goleman, D. (September 27, 1988). Researcher is criticized for test of journal bias. *New York Times,* Section III, p. 9.

Herek, G. H. , D. S. Kimmel, H. Amaro, & G. B. Melton. (1991). Avoiding heterosexist bias in psychological research. *American Psychologist* 46(9): 957–963.

Jones, J. H. (1993). *Bad blood: The Tuskegee syphilis experiment* (rev. ed.). New York: The Free Press.

Milgram, S. (1963). Behavioral study of obedience. *Journal of Abnormal and Social Psychology* 67(4): 71–78.

Myers, L. L. & B. A. Thyer. (1997). Should social work clients have the right to effective treatment? *Social Work* 42(3): 288–298.

National Association of Social Workers (1997). *Code of ethics*. Silver Spring, MD: Author.

Nelson, J. C. (1994). Ethics, gender, and ethnicity in single-case research and evaluation. *Journal of Social Service Research* 18(3–4): 139–152.

Nugent, W. R. (1991) An experimental and qualitative analysis of cognitive-behavioral intervention for anger. *Social Work Research & Abstracts* 27(3): 3–8.

Rollins, J. (1992). *Between women: Domestics and their employers*. Philadelphia: Temple University Press.

Sieber, J. E. (1992). *Planning ethically responsible research: A guide for students and internal review boards*. Newbury Park, CA: Sage.

Sieber, J. E. & B. Stanley. (1988). Ethical and professional dimensions of socially sensitive research. *American Psychologist* 43(1): 49–55.

Williams, T. (1992). *Crack house: Notes from the end of the line*. Reading, MA: Addison-Wesley.

Chapter 10

Anastas, J. W. , J. L. Gibeau, & P. J. Larson. (1990). Working families and eldercare: A national perspective in an aging American. *Social Work* 35(5): 405–411.

Becerra, R. M. & R. E. Zambrana. (1985). Methodological approaches to research on Hispanics. *Social Work Research & Abstracts* 21(2): 42–49.

Bloom, B. L. (1976). Definitional aspects of the crisis concept. In H. Wechsler, H. Z. Reinherz, & D. D. Dobbins, eds. *Social work research in the human services.* New York: Human Sciences Press. (Originally published in the *Journal of Consulting Psychology* (1963) 27(6): 498–502).

Bloom, B. & J. Fischer. (1982). *Evaluating practice: Guidelines for the accountable professional.* Englewood Cliffs, NJ: Prentice-Hall.

Bodgan, R. & S. J. Taylor. (1975). *Introduction to qualitative research methods.* New York: John Wiley & Sons.

Bureau of Census (1978). *1976 Survey of Institutional Persons (SIP): A study of persons receiving long-term care.* Washington, DC: United States Government Printing Office.

Cochran, W. C. (1977). *Sampling techniques* (3rd ed.). New York: John Wiley & Sons.

Drisko, J. W. (1997). Strengthening qualitative studies and reports: Standards to promote academic integrity. *Journal of Social Work Education* 33(1): 185–197.

Feagin, J. R. (1991). The continuing significance of race: Antiblack discrimination in public places. *American Sociological Review* 56(1): 101–116.

Glaser, B. G. & A. L. Strauss. (1967). *The discovery of grounded theory: Strategies for qualitative research.* New York: Aldine de Gruyter.

Gibeau, J. L. & J. W. Anastas. (1989). Breadwinners and caregivers: Interviews with working women. *Journal of Gerontological Social Work* 14(1–2): 19–40.

Gibelman, M. & P. H. Schervish. (1997). *Who we are: A second look.* Washington, DC: NASW Press.

Gilgun, J. F. (1994). A case for case studies in social work research. *Social Work* 39(4): 371–380.

Gilligan, C. (1972). *In a different voice: Psychological theory and women's development.* Cambridge, MA: Harvard University Press.

Gomez, M. R. (1990). Biculturalism and subjective mental health among Cuban Americans. *Social Service Review* 64(3): 375–389.

Kalton, C. (1983). *Introduction to survey sampling.* Beverly Hills, CA: Sage.

Padgett, D. K. (1998). *Qualitative methods in social work research: Challenges and rewards.* Thousand Oaks, CA: Sage.

Smith, A. W. (1993). Survey research on African Americans: Methodological innovations. In J. H. Stanfield, ed. , *Race and ethnicity in research methods* (pp. 217–229). Newbury Park, CA: Sage.

Strauss, A. & J. Corbin. (1990). *Basics of qualitative research.* Newbury Park, CA: Sage.

Waldorf, D. , C. Reinarman, & S. Murphy. (1991). *Cocaine changes: The experience of using and quitting.* Philadelphia: Temple University Press.

Williams, T. M. (1989). *Cocaine kids: The inside story of a teenage drug ring.* Reading, MA: Addison-Wesley.

Williams, T. M. (1992). *Crack house: Notes from the end of the line.* Reading, MA: Addison-Wesley.

Yin, R. K. (1994). *Case study research: Design and methods.* (2nd ed.). Thousand Oaks, CA: Sage.

Chapter 11

Ainsworth, M. D. S. , M. D. Slater, M. C. Blehar, E. Waters, & S. Wall. (1978). *Patterns of attachment: A psychological study of the strange situation.* Hillsdale, NJ: Lawrence Erlbaum Associates.

American heritage dictionary of the English language (3rd ed.). Boston, MA: Houghton Mifflin Co.

Aronson, P. J. , P. C. Ellsworth, J. M. Carlsmith, & M. H. Gonzales. (1990). *Methods of research in social psychology* (2d ed.). New York: McGraw-Hill.

Beck, A. T. & R. A. Steer. (1987). *The Beck depression inventory* (rev. ed.). New York: The Psychological Corporation.

Bowman, P. J. (1991). Race, class and ethic research: Belmont principles to functional relevance. In R. L. Jones, ed. , *Black psychology* (3rd. ed.). Berkeley, CA: Cobb & Henry.

Bradburn, N. M. & D. Caplovitz. (1965). *Report on happiness: A pilot study of behavior related to mental health.* Chicago: Aldine.

Bunin, A. , J. Einzig, D. Judd, & N. Staver. (1983). Inside the interview: Clinical considerations in the research interview. *Clinical Social Work Journal* 10(1): 22–32.

Derogatis, L. R. (1983). *SCL-90-R.* Towson, MD: Leonard R. Derogatis.

Drisko, J. W. (1997). Strengthening qualitative studies and reports: Standards to promote academic integrity. *Journal of Social Work Education* 33(1): 185–197.

El-Bassel et al. (1995). Preventing HIV-AIDS in drug-abusing incarcerated women through skills building and social support enhancement: Preliminary outcomes. *Social Work Research* 19(3): 131–141.

Epstein, S. (1996). *Impure science: AIDS, activism, and the politics of knowledge.* Berkeley, CA: University of California Press.

Foddy, W. (1993). *Constructing questions for interviews and questionnaires: Theory and practice in social research.* Cambridge, UK: Cambridge University Press.

Gomez, M. R. . (1990). Biculturalism and subjective mental health. *Social Service Review* 64(3): 375–389.

Kirk, J. & M. L. Miller. (1986). *Reliability and validity in qualitative research.* Beverly Hills, CA: Sage.

Lincoln, Y. S. & E. G. Guba. (1985). *Naturalistic Inquiry.* Beverly Hills, CA: Sage.

Landrine, H. , E. A. Klonoff, & A. Brown-Collins. (1992). Cultural diversity and methodology in feminist psychology. *Psychology of Women Quarterly* 16: 145–163.

Manicas, P. T. & P. F. Secord. (1983). Implications for psychology of the new philosophy of science. *American Psychologist* 38: 399–413.

Padgett, D. K. (1998). *Qualitative methods in social work research: Challenges and rewards.* Thousand Oaks, CA: Sage.

Strauss, A. L. (1987). *Qualitative analysis for social scientists.* Cambridge, England: Cambridge University Press.

Strauss, A. & Corbin, J. (1990). *Basics of qualitative research.* Newbury Park, CA: Sage.

Williams, T. M. (1992). *Crackhouse: Notes from the end of the line.* Reading, MA: Addison-Wesley.

Chapter 12

Adler, P. A. & P. Adler. (1994). Observational techniques. In N. K. Denzin & Y. S. Lincoln eds. *Handbook of qualitative research* (pp. 377–392). Thousand Oaks, CA: Sage.

Ainsworth, M. D. S. , M. D. Slater, M. C. Blehar, E. Waters, & S. Wall. (1978). *Patterns of attachment: A psychological study of the strange situation.* Hillsdale, NJ: Lawrence Erlbaum Associates.

Atkinson, P. & M. Hammersley. (1994). Ethnography and participant observation. In N. K. Denzin & Y. S. Lincoln eds. *Handbook of qualitative research* (pp. 248–261). Thousand Oaks, CA: Sage.

Fetterman, D. M. (1989). *Ethnography: Step by step.* Newbury Park, CA: Sage.

Fraiberg, S. (1970). The muse in the kitchen: A case study in clinical research. *Smith College Studies in Social Work* 40(2): 101–134.

Golden, M. P. , ed. (1970). *The research experience.* Itasca, IL: F. E. Peacock.

Hochschild, A. (1989). *The second shift: Working parents and the revolution of the home.* New York: Viking.

Humphreys, L. (1970). *Tearoom trade: Impersonal sex in public places.* Chicago: Aldine,

Jarrett, R. L. (1992). A family case study: An examination of the underclass debate. In J. F. Gilgun, K. Daly & G. Handel, eds. *Qualitative methods in family research* (pp. 172–197). Newbury Park, CA: Sage.

Jorgensen, D. L. (1989). *Participant observation: A methodology for human studies.* Beverly Hills, CA: Sage.

Kent, R. N. & S. L. Foster. (1977). Direct observational procedures: Methodological issues in naturalistic settings. In A. R, Ciminero, K. S. Calhoun, & H. E. Adams eds. *Handbook of behavioral assessment* (pp. 217–328). New York: Wiley.

Landrine, H. , E. A. Klonoff, & A. Brown-Collins. (1992). Cultural diversity and methodology in feminist psychology. *Psychology of Women Quarterly* 16: 145–163.

Padgett, D. K. (1998). *Qualitative methods in social work research: Challenges and rewards.* Thousand Oaks, CA: Sage.

Rollins, J. (1985). *Between women: Domestics and their employers.* Philadelphia: Temple University Press.

Stern, D. N. (1985). *The interpersonal world of the infant.* New York: Basic Books.

Taylor, S. J. & R. Bogdan. (1984). *Introduction to qualitative research methods: The search for meaning. (*2nd ed.). New York: John Wiley & Sons.

Williams, T. M. (1989). *Cocaine kids: The inside story of a teenage drug ring.* Reading, MA: Addison-Wesley.

———. (1992). *Crack house: Notes from the end of the line.* Reading, MA: Addison-Wesley.

Williamson, J. B. , D. A. Karp, J. R. Dalphin, & P. S. Gray. (1982). *The research craft* (2nd ed.). Boston: Little, Brown.

Chapter 13

Anastas, J. W. (1997). *Daybreak Project final evaluation report.* Prepared for the Center of Substane Abuse Prevention, U. S. Department of Health and Human Services.

Briggs, C. L. (1986). *Learning how to ask: A sociolinguistic appraisal of the role of the interview in social science research.* New York: Cambridge University Press,

Bunin, A. , J. Einzig, D. Judd, & N. Staver. (1983). Inside the interview: Clinical considerations in the research interview. *Clinical Social Work Journal* 10(1): 22–32.

Feagin, J. R. (1991). The continuing significance of race: Antiblack discrimination in public places. *American Sociological Review* 56(1): 101–116.

Fine, S. E. (1990), Comment: Interactional troubles in face-to-face surveys. *Journal of the American Statistical Association* 85(409): 241–244.

Foddy, W. (1993). *Constructing questions for interviews and questionnaires: Theory and practice in social research.* Cambridge, UK: Cambridge University Press.

Fontana, A. & J. A. Frey. (1994). Interviewing: The art of science. In N. K. Denzin & Y. S. Lincoln eds. *Handbook of qualitative research* (pp. 361–376). Thousand Oaks, CA. Sage.

Fraiberg, S. A. (1970). The muse in the kitchen: A case study in clinical social work. *Smith College Studies in Social Work* 40(2): 101–134.

Gomez, M. R. . (1990). Biculturalism and subjective mental health. *Social Service Review* 64(3): 375–389.

Herek, G. M. , D. C. Kimmel, H. Amaro, & G. B. Melton. (1991). Avoiding heterosexist bias in psychological research. *American Psychologist* 46(9): 957–963.

Landrine, H. , E. A. Klonoff, & A. Brown-Collins. (1992). Cultural diversity and methodology in feminist psychology. *Psychology of Women Quarterly* 16: 145–163.

Merton, R. K. (1987). The focused interview and focus groups: Continuities and discontinuities. *Public Opinion Quarterly* 5: 550–566.

Merton, R. K. , M. Fiske, & P. L. Kendall. (1956). *The focussed interview.* New York: Free Press,

Miller, R. (1990). A method of quantifying unstructured data. *Social Work Research & Abstracts* 26(3): 31–34.

Oakley, A. (1981). Interviewing women: A contradiction in terms. In H. Roberts (Ed.), *Doing feminist research* (pp. 30–61). London: Routledge & Kegan Paul.

Padgett, D. K. (1998). *Qualitative methods in social work research: Challenges and rewards.* Thousand Oaks, CA: Sage.

Patton, M. Q. (1980), *Qualitative evaluation methods.* Beverly Hills, CA: Sage.

Rogler, L. H. (1999). Methodological sources of cultural insensitivity in mental health research. *American Psychologist* 54(6): 17–21.

Salant, P. & D. Dillman. (1994). *How to conduct your own survey.* New York: John Wiley & Sons.

Strauss, A. & J. Corbin. (1990). *Basics of qualitative research.* Newbury Park, CA: Sage.

Suchman, L. & B. Jordan. (1990). Interactional troubles in the face-to-face survey interviews. *Journal of the American Statistical Association* 85(409): 232–241.

Tausig, J. E. & E. W. Freeman. (1988). The next best thing to being there: Conducting the clinical research interview by telephone. *American Journal of Orthopsychiatry* 58(3): 418–427.

Weiss, R. S. (1994). *Learning from strangers: The art and method of qualitative interview studies.* New York: Free Press.

Chapter 14

Aday, L. A. (1989). *Designing and conducting health surveys.* San Francisco: Jossey-Bass.

Anderson, S. C. & D. L. Mandell. (1989). The use of self-disclosure by professional social workers. *Social Casework* 70(5): 259–267.

Dillman, D. A. (1978). *Mail and telephone surveys: The total design method.* New York: John Wiley & Sons.

Foddy, W. (1993). *Constructing questions for interviews and questionnaires: Theory and practice in social research.* Cambridge, UK: Cambridge University Press.

Hartley, D. & H. Strupp. (1983). The therapeutic alliance: Its relationship to outcome in brief psychotherapy. In J. Masling, ed. , *Empirical studies of psychoanalytic theories* (Vol. 1, pp. 1–38). Hillsdale, NJ: Analytical Press.

Horvath, A. O. & L. S. Greenberg. (1989). Development and validation of the Working Alliance Inventory. *Journal of Counseling Psychology* 36(2): 223–233.

Kagay, M. R. (July 8, 1994). Poll on doubt of Holocaust corrected. *New York Times,* A10.

Luborsky, L. , P. Crits-Christoph, L. Alexander, M. Margolis, & M. Cohen. (1983). Two helping alliance methods for predicting outcome of psychotherapy. *Journal of Nervous and Mental Disease* 171: 480–491.

Patton, M. Q. (1980). *Qualitative evaluation methods.* Beverly Hills, CA: Sage.

Poulin, J. & T. Young. (1997). The development of a Helping Relationship Inventory for social work practice. *Research on Social Work Practice* 7(4): 463–489.

Rodriguez, R. G. (1992). *Self-devaluation processes among gay-identified men.* Unpublished master's thesis, University of Massachusetts at Amherst.

Salant, P. & D. Dillman. (1994). *How to conduct your own survey.* New York: John Wiley & Sons.

Sudman, S. & N. M. Bradburn. (1982). *Asking questions.* San Francisco: Jossey-Bass.

Woodworth, R. S. (1917). *Personal Data Sheet.* Chicago, IL: Stoelting.

Chapter 15

Achenbach, T. M. & C. Edelbrock. (1983). *Manual for the Child Behavior Check List and Revised Child Behavior Profile.* Burlington: University of Vermont Department of Psychiatry.

———. (1987). *Manual for the Youth Self-Report Profile.* Burlington: University of Vermont Department of Psychiatry.

Anastasi, A. (1988). *Psychological testing* (6th ed.). New York: Macmillan.

Anderson, S. C. & D. L. Mandell. (1989). The use of self-disclosure by professional social workers. *Social Casework* 70(5): 259–267.

Beck, A. T. & R. A. Steer. (1987). *The Beck Depression Inventory* (rev. ed.). New York: The Psychological Corporation.

Beere, C. A. (1990a). *Gender roles: A handbook of tests and measures.* Westport, CT: Greenwood Press.

———. (1990b). *Sex and gender issues: A handbook of tests and measures.* Westport, CT: Greenwood Press.

Blatt, S. J., J. P. D'Afflitti, & D. M. Quinlan. (1979). *Depressive Experiences Questionnaire (DEQ).* New Haven: Yale University.

Endicott, J. & R. Spitzer. (1978). A diagnostic interview: the schedule for affective disorders and schizophrenia. *Archives of General Psychiatry* 35: 837–844.

Fischer, J. & K. Corcoran. (1994). *Measures for clinical practice: A sourcebook* (2 vols.). New York: Free Press.

Gomez, M. R. (1990). Biculturalism and subjective mental health among Cuban Americans. *Social Service Review* 64(3): 375–389.

Gould, S. J. (1981). *The mismeasure of man.* New York: W. W. Norton.

Hase, M. D. & L. R. Goldberg. (1967). The comparative validity of different strategies of deriving personality inventory scales. *Psychological Bulletin* 67: 231–248.

Hathaway, S. R., J. C. McKinley, & J. N. Butcher. (1990). *The Minnesota Multiphasic Personality Inventory.* Minneapolis, MN: University of Minnesota Press.

Herek, G. M., D. C. Kimmel, H. Amaro, & G. B. Melton. (1991). Avoiding heterosexist bias in psychological research. *American Psychologist,* 96(9), 957–963.

Honacker, L. M., T. H. Harrell, & A. M. Ciminero. (1986). *The Chemical Dependency Assessment Profile.*

Horvath, A. O. (1984). Working Alliance Inventory. Unpublished manuscript.

Horvath, A. O. & L. S. Greenberg. (1989). Development and validation of the Working Alliance Inventory. *Journal of Counseling Psychology* 36(2): 223–233.

Hudson, W. W. (1982). *The clinical measurement package.* Homewood, IL: Dorsey Press.

Jones, R. L. (1996). *Handbook of test and measurements for black populations* (2 vols.). Hampton, VA: Cobb and Henry.

Lake, G., M. B. Niles, & R. B. Earle. (1973). *Measuring human behavior: Tools for the assessment of social functioning.* New York: Teachers College Press.

Lyerly, S. B. & P. S. Abbott. (1970). *Handbooks of psychiatric rating scales.* Washington, DC: The National Institute of Mental Health (PHS Publication No, 1495).

Marsella. A. J. , R. Hirschfeld, & M. M. Katz. (1987). *The measurement of depression.* New York: Guilford Press.

McLellan, A. T. , H. Kushner, D. Metzger, R. Peters, I. Smith, G. Grissom, H. Pettinati, & M. Argeriou. (1992). The fifth edition of the Addiction Severity Index. *Journal of Substance Abuse Treatment* 9: 199–213.

Mitchell, J. V. , ed. (1983). *Tests in print III: An index to tests, reviews, and the literature on specific tests.* Lincoln: University of Nebraska Press.

Poulin, J. & T. Young. (1997). The development of a Helping Relationship Inventory for social work practice. *Research on Social Work Practice* 7(4): 463–489.

Robinson, J. P. & P. R. Shaver. (1973). *Measures of social psychological attitudes* (Rev. ed.). Ann Arbor, MI: Institute for Social Research.

Rogler, L. H. (1999). Methodological sources of cultural insensitivity in mental health research. *American Psychologist* 54(6): 424–433.

Selzer, M. L. (1971). The Michigan Alcoholism Screening Test: The quest for a new diagnostic instrument. *American Journal of Psychiatry* 127: 89–94.

Waskow, I. W. & M. B. Parloff, eds. (1975). *Psychotherapy change measures.* Washington, DC: National Institute of Mental Health.

Woodworth, R. S. (1917) *Personal Data Sheet.* Chicago, IL: Stoelting.

Zung, W. W. K. (1975). *Self-Rating Depression Scales (SDS).* Cincinnati, OH: Merrell-National Laboratories.

Chapter 16

Beeman, S. (1995). Maximazing credibility and accountability in qualitative data collection and data analysis: A social work case example. *Journal of Sociology and Social Welfare* 22: 99–114.

Boyatzis, R. E. (1998). *Transforming qualitative information: Thematic analysis and code development.* Thousand Oaks, CA: Sage.

Drisko, J. W. (1997). Strengthening qualitative studies and reports: Standards to promote academic integrity. *Journal of Social Work Education* 33(1): 185–197.

Dudley, J. R. (1989). The role of residential program staff in facilitating positive relations with the neighborhood: What should it be? *Administration in Social Work* 13(1): 95–111.

Feagin, J. R. (1991), The continuing significance of race: Antiblack discrimination in public places. *American Sociological Review* 56(1): 101–116.

Geis, S. & R. L. Fuller. (1985). The impact of the first gay AIDS patient on hospice staff. *Hospice Journal* 1(3): 17–36.

Glaser, B. J. & A. L. Strauss. (1967). *The discovery of grounded theory: Strategies for qualitative research.* Chicago: Aldine de Gruyter.

Hollis, F. & M. E. Woods. (1981). *Casework: A psychosocial approach. (*3d. ed.). New York: Random House.

Kirk, J. & M. L. Miller. (1986). *Reliability and validity in qualitative research.* Beverly Hills, CA: Sage.

Krippendorf, L. (1980). *Content analysis: An introduction to its methodology.* Beverly Hills, CA: Sage.

Lincoln, Y. S. & E. G. Guba. (1985). *Naturalistic inquiry.* Beverly Hills, CA: Sage.

Marshall, C. & G. B. Rossman. (1989). *Designing qualitative research.* Newbury Park, CA: Sage.

Miles, M. B. & A. M. Huberman. (1984). *Qualitative data analysis.* Beverly Hills, CA: Sage.

Miller, R. (1990). A method for quantifying unstructured data. *Social Work Research and Abstracts* 26(3): 31–34.

Padgett, D. K. (1998). *Qualitative methods in social work research: Challenges and rewards.* Thousand Oaks, CA: Sage.

Reissman, C. K. , ed. (1994). *Qualitative studies in social work research.* Thousand Oaks, CA: Sage.

Ruckdeschel, R. A. (1985), Qualitative research as a perspective. *Social Work Research & Abstracts* 21(2): 17–21.

Strauss, A. L. (1987). *Qualitative analysis for social scientists.* New York: Cambridge University Press.

Strauss, A. & J. Corbin. (1990). *Basics of qualitative research.* Newbury Park, CA: Sage.

Taylor, S. J. & R. Bogdan. (1984). *Introduction to qualitative research methods* (2nd ed.). New York: John Wiley & Sons.

Chapter 17

Bernstein, R. L. (1996). *Against the gods: The remarkable story of risk.* New York: John Wiley & Sons, Inc.

Gould, S. J. (1996). *Full house: The spread of excellence from Plato to Darwin.* New York: Harmony Books.

Hudson, W. W. (1982). *The clinical measurement package: A field manual.* Homewood, IL: Dorsey Press.

McKenney, N. R. & C. E. Bennett. (1994). Issues regarding data on race and ethnicity: The Census Bureau experience. *Public Health Reports* 109(1): 16–25.

Richey, C. A. & V. G. Hodges. (1992). Empirical support for the effectiveness of respite care in reducing caregiver burden: A single-case analysis. *Research on Social Work Practice* 2(2): 143–160.

Sprinthall, R. C. (1990). *Basic statistical analysis* (3rd ed.). Englewood Cliffs, NJ: Prentice-Hall.

Stevens, S. S. (1946). On the theory of scales of measurement. *Science* 103: 677–680.

Chapter 18

Afifi, A. A. & J. Clark. (1984). *Computer-aided multivariate analysis.* Belmont, CA: Lifetime Learning Publications.

Bernstein, P. L. (1996). *Against the gods: The remarkable story of risk.* New York: John Wiley & Sons.

Bishop, Y. M. M. , S. E. Feinberg, & P. W. Holland. (1975). *Discrete multivariate analysis: Theory and practice.* Cambridge, MA: MIT Press.

Cohen, J. (1977). *Statistical power analysis for the behavioral sciences* (rev. ed.). Orlando, FL: Academic Press.

Crane, J. A. (1976). The power of social experimentation to discriminate differences between experimental and control groups. *Social Service Review* 50(2): 224–242.

El-Bassel, N. , A. Ivanoff, R. F. Schilling, L. Gilbert, D. Borne, & D. R. Chen. (1995). Preventing HIV/AIDS in drug-abusing incarcerated women through skills building and social support enhancement: Preliminary outcomes. *Social Work Research* 19(3): 131–141.

Gomez, M. R. (1990). Biculturalism and subjective mental health among Cuban Americans. *Social Service Review* 64(3): 375–389.

Grimm, L. G. & P. R. Yarnold, eds. (1995). *Reading and understanding multivariate statistics.* Washington, DC: American Psychological Association.

Hays, W. L. (1981). *Statistics* (3d ed.). New York: Reinhart and Winston.

Knoke, D. & P. J. Burke. (1980). *Log-linear models.* Newbury Park, CA: Sage.

Manicas, P. T. & P. F. Secord. (1983). Implications for psychology of the new philosophy of science. *American Psychologist* 38: 399–413.

Pett, M. A. (1997). *Nonparametric statistics for health care research: Statistics for small samples and unusual distributions.* Thousand Oaks, CA: Sage.

Siegel, S. & J. Castellan. (1988). *Nonparametric statistics for the behavioral sciences* (2d ed.). New York: McGraw-Hill.

Sprinthall, R. C. (1990). *Basic statistical analysis.* (3d ed.). Englewood Cliffs, NJ: Prentice-Hall.

Stevens, J. P. (1996). *Applied multivariate statistics for the social sciences* (3rd ed.) Mahwah, NJ: Laurence Erlbaum Associates.

Chapter 19

Agar, M. (1991). The right brain strikes back. In N. Fielding & R. Lee, eds. *Using computers in qualitative research* (pp. 181–194). Newbury Park, CA: Sage.

Bennenishty, R. & A. Ben-Zaken. (1988). Computer-aided process of monitoring task-centered family interventions, *Social Work Research and Abstracts* 24: 7–9.

Bloch, J. (1995). A strategic planning model for meeting the information technology needs in a school of social work. Unpublished doctoral dissertation, Hunter College School of Social Work, New York, NY.

Cuvo, D. , F. Hall, & G. Milder. (1988). Computerized central intake: A means towards accountability. *Social Casework* 69(4): 214–223.

Denzin, N. (1988). Qualitative analysis for social scientists [Review of the book *Qualitative analysis for social scientists*]. *Contemporary Sociologist* 17(3): 430–432.

Denzin, N. & Y. Lincoln, eds. (1994). *Handbook of qualitative research.* Thousand Oaks, CA: Sage.

Dey, I. (1993). *Qualitative data analysis: A user-friendly guide for social scientists.* New York: Routledge.

Drisko, J. (1997). Strengthening qualitative studies and reports: Standards to enhance academic integrity. *Journal of Social Work Education* 33: 185–197.

———. (1998). Using qualitative data analysis software. *Computers in Human Services* 15(1): 1–19.

Fisher, R. A. (1935–1971). *The design of experiments.* New York: Hafner Press.

Glaser, B. & A. Strauss. (1967). *The discovery of grounded theory.* Chicago: Aldine.

Grasso, A. , I. Epstein, & T. Tripodi. (1988). Agency-based research utilization in a residential child care setting. *Administration in Social Work* 12(4): 61–80.

Greist, J. (1998). The computer as clinician assistant: Assessment made simple. *Psychiatric Services* 49(4): 467–472.

Hannafin, M. & S. Land. (1997) . The foundations and assumptions of technology-enhanced student-centered environments. *Instructional Science* 25(3): 167–202.

Kelle, U. , ed. (1995). *Computer-aided qualitative data analysis: Theory, methods and practice.* Thousand Oaks, CA: Sage.

Kesar, S. & S. Rogerson. (1998). Developing ethical practices to minimize computer misuse. *Social Sciences Computer Review* 16(3): 240–251.

Lee, R. & N. Fielding. (1995). User's experiences of qualitative data analysis software. In U. Kelle, ed. , *Computer-aided qualitative data analysis: Theory, methods and practice* (pp. 29–40). Thousand Oaks, CA: Sage.

Liederman, M. , C. Guzetta, L. Struminger, & M. Monnickendam, eds. (1993). Technology in people services: Research, theory, and applications. *Computers in Human Services* 9(1–2): entire issue.

Marks, I. , S. Shaw, & R. Parkin. (1998). Computer-aided treatments of mental health problems. *Clinical Psychology—Science and Practice* 5(2): 151–170.

Miles, M. A. & A. Huberman. (1994). Data management and analysis methods. In N. Denzin & Y. Lincoln, eds. *Handbook of qualitative research* (pp. 428–444). Thousand Oaks, CA: Sage.

Muhr, T. (1994). *ATLAS • ti [manual]: Computer aided text interpretation and theory building* (2nd ed.). Berlin: Author.

Murphy, J. & J. Pardeck. (1988). Technology in clinical practice and the "technological ethic. " *Journal of Sociology and Social Welfare* 15: 119–128.

———. (1992). Computerization and the dehumanization of social services. *Administration in Social Work* 16(2): 61–72.

National Association of Social Workers [NASW]. (1996). *Code of Ethics*. Washington, DC: Author.

Nurius, P. & A. Nicoll. (1989). Computer literacy preparation: Conundrums and opportunities for the social work educator. *Journal of Teaching in Social Work* 3(2): 65–81.

Pirog-Good, M. & P. Brown. (1996). Accuracy and ambiguity in the application of state child support guidelines. *Family Relations* 45(10): 3–10.

Qualitative Solutions and Research [QSR]. (1995). *User's guide for QSR NUD*IST*. Distributed by Sage-Scolari.

Riessman, C. K. , ed. (1994). *Qualitative studies in social work*. Thousand Oaks, CA: Sage.

Richards, T. & L. Richards,(1994). Using computers in qualitative research. In N. Denzin & Y. Lincoln, eds. *Handbook of qualitative research* (pp. 445–462). Thousand Oaks, CA: Sage.

Risdale, L. & S. Hudd. (1997). What do patients want and not want to see about themselves on the computer screen. *Scandinavian Journal of Primary Health Care* 15(4): 180-183.

Roid, G. & R. Gorsuch. (1984). Development and clinical use of test-interpretive programs on microcomputers, In M. Schwartz, ed. , *Using computers in clinical practice*. New York: Haworth Press.

Seidel, J. , S. Friese, & D. C. Leonard. (1995). *The Ethnograph v4. 0 [manual]: A program for the analysis of text based data*. Amherst, MA: Qualis Research Associates.

Sherman, E. & W. Reid, eds. (1994). *Qualitative research in social work*. New York, NY: Columbia.

SPSS Inc. (1998). *SPSS Base 8. 0 Applications Guide*. Chicago, IL: Author.

Strauss, A. & J. Corbin. (1990). *Basics of qualitative research: Grounded theory procedures and techniques*. Newbury Park, CA: Sage.

Tesch, R. (1990). *Qualitative analysis: Analysis types and software tools*. Philadelphia: Falmer Press.

Weitzman, E. & M. Miles. (1995). *Computer programs for qualitative data analysis: a software sourcebook*. Thousand Oaks, CA: Sage.

Wimberly, E. & S. Blazyk. (1989). Monitoring patient outcome following discharge: A computerized geriatric case-management system. *Health and Social Work* 14(4): 269–76.

Yaffe, J. (1998). *Quick guide to the Internet for social work*, Boston: Allyn & Bacon.

Chapter 20

American Psychological Association (1994). *Publication manual of the American Psychological Association* (3d ed.). Washington, DC: Author.

————. (1997). *Journals in psychology: A resource for listing for authors* (5th ed.). Washington, DC: Author.

Barzun, J. (1975). *Simple and direct: A rhetoric for writers*. New York: Harper & Row.

Becker, H. (1986). *Writing for social scientists*. Chicago, IL: University of Chicago Press.

Beebe, L. (1993). Basic writing techniques. In L. Beebe, ed., *Professional writing for human services*. pp. 9–29. Washington, DC: NASW Press.

Beebe, L. , ed. (1993). *Professional writing for human services*. Washington, DC: NASW Press.

Fiske, D. W. & L. Fogg. (1990). But the reviewers are making different criticisms of my paper! Diversity and uniqueness in reviewer comments. *American Psychologist* 45(5): 591–598.

Flower, L. (1985). *Problem-solving strategies for writing* (2d ed.). San Diego: Harcourt Brace Jovanovich, Publishers.

Goering, P. & J. S. Strauss. (1987). Teaching clinical research: What clinicians need to know. *American Journal of Orthopsychiatry* 57: 418–423.

Hunt, D. (1991). Stealing and dealing: Cocaine and property crimes. In S. Schober & C. Schade eds. *The epidemiology of cocaine use and abuse*. Washington, DC: U. S. Dept. of Health and Human Services; Alcohol, Drug Abuse, and Mental Health Administration (NIDA Research Monograph 110).

Loke, W. (1990). *A guide to journals in psychology and education*. Metuchen, NJ: The Scarecrow Press, Inc.

Mendelson, H. N. (1997). *An author's guide to social work journals*. (4th ed.). Washington, DC: NASW Press.

Strunk, W. & E. B. White. (1979). *The elements of style* (3d ed.). New York: Macmillan.

Wang, A. (1989). *Author's guide to journals in the behavioral sciences*. Hillsdale, NJ: L. Erlbaum, Associates.

Zinsser, W. K. (1988). *Writing to learn*. New York: Harper & Row.

Index